THE CLASSICAL PSYCHOLOGISTS

THE CLASSICAL PSYCHOLOGISTS

SELECTIONS
ILLUSTRATING PSYCHOLOGY
FROM ANAXAGORAS TO WUNDT

COMPILED BY

BENJAMIN RAND, Ph.D.

HARVARD UNIVERSITY

University Press of the Pacific
Honolulu, Hawaii

The Classical Psychologists:
Selections Illustrating Psychology from
Anaxagoras to Wundt

Compiled by
Benjamin Rand

ISBN: 1-4102-1361-7

Reprinted from the 1912 edition

University Press of the Pacific
Honolulu, Hawaii
http://www.universitypressofthepacific.com

In order to make original editions of historical works
available to scholars at an economical price, this
facsimile of the original edition of 1912 is
reproduced from the best available copy and has
been digitally enhanced to improve legibility, but the
text remains unaltered to retain historical
authenticity.

PREFACE

"THE CLASSICAL PSYCHOLOGISTS" is a companion volume in the field of psychology to the author's "The Classical Moralists" in the sphere of ethics, and also to his "Modern Classical Philosophers" in the domain of philosophy. Its aim is to present in a series of selections some of the most essential features of the psychological doctrines which have appeared from Anaxagoras to Wundt. The book is thus virtually a history of psychology, not derived from an ordinary description of systems, but based upon extracts from original sources and upon translations of the authors themselves. Such a work, it is hoped, may prove adapted for colleges and universities as a text-book of reading accompanying courses of lectures in general psychology, and may become a necessary requirement of study made of all students before entering upon the study of the special divisions of existing psychology. The general reader, moreover, will find it an interesting volume of original material of the great psychologists from the earliest to the most recent times.

From Aristotle's "De Anima" there is reproduced at the outset the first extant history of psychological theories. With the name of Anaxagoras, who emphasizes the Nous as present in all things, but with insight as to its different forms in mind and matter, it was thought the work might fittingly begin. Empedocles is mentioned, who maintains that like is known by like, and that perception is due to elements in us coming in contact with similar elements outside. Democritus is also included, who believes the soul to consist of atoms, the peculiar fineness, smoothness, and mobility of which cause perception and thought. The second selection is taken from the Theaetetus of Plato, which Professor Jowett describes as the oldest work in psychology that has come down to us, and which here contains the contending Sophistic and Socratic views on the nature of perception. In it Protagoras affirms that the individual man is the measure of all things, whereas Socrates seeks to conduct Theaetetus by means of the dialogue to the acceptance of a universally valid knowledge. Although Plato's psychological views are scattered through various dialogues, the Republic best contains his treatment of the fundamental problem of the relation of soul and body. There is consequently printed from it, his presentation of the three faculties of the soul, of the correlation of the faculties, and of the soul's immortality. In Aristotle we have the greatest psychologist of the ancient world, and the one who first treated psychology as a separate science. To the introductory account of earlier theories by him, with which this work began, is here added a description from the " De Anima" of his own doctrines. His conceptions of the essence of the soul, and its relation to the body as form to matter, of the various activities of the five senses and the common sense, and of the functions of sensation, imagination, and thought, are given in full, as their importance demands. From Diogenes Laertius' " Lives and Opinions of Eminent Philosophers" is drawn the psychology of the Stoics, in which the animating principle of the soul is described as a warm breath within us, with a resultant trichotomy of body, soul and spirit. From Diogenes Laertius is likewise taken the Epicurean psychology, in which the soul is conceived to be a bodily substance composed of exceedingly fine atoms, which are allied in nature to air and fire, and are diffused throughout the whole body. Lucretius in the didactic poem on "The Nature of Things," whereby Hellenistic thought was transferred to Rome, follows next with a description, like that of Epicurus, of sensation as everywhere occurring in the body; but he regards the mind as the directing principle "holding the fastnesses of life." From the "Enneades" of Plotinus, who was the most eminent of the Neoplatonists, is reproduced the theory of emanation, in which the soul is deemed the image and product of the Nous, just as the Nous is of the One.

In the mediæval period, Tertullian, one of the greatest of the early Christian fathers, sets forth in the extracts presented from his "Treatise on the Soul," the corporeal nature of the soul, its simplicity, its source in the breath of God, its rationality, and its immortality. Gregory of Nyssa, who wrote in the latter part of the fourth century, here argues in the "Endowment of Man," that the intellect pervades all parts of the body alike, but has in itself a divine beauty, since it is created in the image of the most beautiful. Augustine, in whom the Patristic period reached its culmination, emphasizes in his work "On the Trinity," self-consciousness as the distinguishing characteristic of the mind arising from its immateriality, and regards memory, understanding, and particularly will, as its most important faculties. Thomas Aquinas, who represents scholasticism in its full development, returns in the "Summa Theologica" to the Aristotelian doctrine of the rational soul as the essential form of the body, and contends as against Augustine for the superiority of reason to will.

The modern period is introduced with chapters from Thomas Hobbes' "Human Nature," in which the founder of empirical psychology reduces all mental processes to motions. An ample presentation is given of Descartes' "The Passions of the Soul," of which Professor David Irons says that "it would be difficult indeed to find any treatment of the emotions much superior to it in originality, thoroughness, and suggestiveness." Spinoza, who teaches in "The Ethics" that the soul and body are not two distinct substances, but that thought and extension are two of the many attributes of the one real being, seeks to prove by the mathematical method in the part reproduced, that the order and connection of ideas are identical with the order and connection of things. From Leibnitz' "Philosophical Works" selections have been made in which he presents his theory of monads, and likewise illustrates the interaction of soul and body after the manner of two clocks so constructed as to run in perfect harmony. Christian Wolff, whose name is chiefly associated with the faculty psychology, designates in those sections of the "Rational Psychology" here chosen, the *vis repraesentiva* as the fundamental force and sufficient ground for everything that takes place in the soul.

English empirical psychology is next traced through Locke, Berkeley, and Hume. From Locke's "Essay on the Human Understanding" there is given, as Locke believes, "the true history of the beginning of human knowledge," wherein all our ideas are derived from sensation and reflection. Berkeley's "Essay towards a new Theory of Vision" is reproduced with desirable fullness, as it contains his noted research into the difference between the ideas of sight and touch, wherein he draws the striking inference that the visible world is a visible language, which we learn to translate into the tactual experience that the visible phenomena naturally signify. Hume in the chapters from the "Treatise of Human Nature" would resolve all perceptions of the human mind into "impressions" and "ideas," differing only in force and liveliness, and also would derive our conception of necessary connection solely from the experience of the constant association of certain objects. Hartley was the chief precursor of English associational psychology, although preceded as he confesses by the modest Gay, and from the "Observations on Man" are reprinted his two principal doctrines of *vibrations*, and of *association*.

Charles Bonnet, the Swiss, and an early founder of physiological psychology, in the "Analytical Essay upon the Faculties of the Soul" of which his own "Abstract" has been in part translated, lays stress throughout on the dependence of psychical phenomena upon physical conditions, and considers the diversity of mental perceptions as really due to the different structures of the various sensory fibres. The French psychologist Condillac, in the chapters from the "Treatise of Sensations," views all psychical functions as transformations of sensations, and graphically illustrates his theory by the endowment of a marble statue with the different senses of man in succession. From Reid, founder of the Scotch School of common sense, those portions of the "Essays on the Intellectual Powers of Man" are given in which he analyzes the fundamental acts of sensation and perception, contending that the former is confined to the soul, but that the latter implies a belief in the existence of an external world. Brown's eloquent "Lectures on the Philo-

sophy of the Human Mind," published after his death, contains
a most subtle and brilliant analysis of muscular sensations,
the inclusion of which, it is believed, must add substantial
value to the pages of this work.

With Herbart's " Textbook of Psychology" begins scientific
psychological research, in which from the intensive relations of
ideas and the laws of their change it is sought to derive the possibility and necessity of applying mathematics to psychology.
In Beneke's " Textbook of Psychology as Natural Science" a
profound German psychologist seeks to reduce all psychical
phenomena to four "fundamental processes." Drobisch, who
may be regarded as one of the distinguished representatives of
mathematical psychology, presents in his "Empirical Psychology," the dynamics of ideas as the fundamental principle of explanation of psychical phenomena. Maine de Biran, whom
Cousin thought the first metaphysician of the nineteenth century, has written some most instructive chapters in his "Essay
upon the Foundations of Psychology," wherein he treats of
voluntary effort as the primordial fact of our psychical life,
analyzing it into the two distinct but inseparable elements of
will and resistance of our own body, from which he derives the
beginning of personality.

The revival of English associational psychology is to be
found in the chapters taken from James Mill's "Analysis of the
Phenomena of the Human Mind "; but its fullest fruition appears in the laws of association reproduced at considerable
length from Bain's " The Senses and the Intellect." The cardinal feature of Spencer's "Principles of Psychology" is here presented in the evolution of mind "from an indefinite incoherent
homogeneity to a definite coherent heterogeneity." The selection from Johannes Mueller's "Elements of Physiology" will
render more accessible his very important account of the general laws of sensation. A fitting place is naturally given also to
Lotze's theory of "local signs" as embodied in his "Outlines of
Psychology."

In more recent psychology, translations from Weber's "The
Sense of Touch and the Common Feeling" of his well known

Law, and from Fechner's "Elements of Psychophysics" of his "Measurement of Sensation," are indispensable contributions in the domain of psychophysics, being the experiments of the former, well described by Professor E. B. Titchener, as "the foundation stone of experimental psychology," and the interpretation of the latter as the erection in large measure of "a whole building." The Young-Helmholtz theory of color vision has been translated from Helmholtz's "Manual of Physiological Optics," which is regarded as the most important work that has yet appeared on the physiology and physics of vision. "The Fundamental Principles of a Theory of Light Sensation" by Hering will serve also to supplement those of Helmholtz, as a necessary foundation for the study of the more recent valuable contributions which have been made to this subject. From Mach's "Analysis of Sensations" is reproduced his theory of space perception, preceded by an account of the self intuition of the ego, which "every student of psychology should know." Stumpf's "Tone Psychology" contains a theory of tonal fusion, written by a recognised authority in this domain. The remarkable chapter of William James entitled "The Stream of Consciousness" is taken from his introductory "Psychology." Then follows the James-Lange theory of emotions, in which a novel doctrine is set forth by both writers with unusual brilliancy of style. Most characteristic and authoritative chapters from Wundt's "Principles of Physiological Psychology" on the problem of physiological psychology, and from his "Outlines of Psychology" on volition and apperception, conclude the work.

The outline of the selections in the preceding paragraphs traces the attempt, here made for the first time, to present historically in a single volume original texts containing fundamental theories of the classical psychologists, alike in ancient, mediaeval, and modern times. The study of psychology as pursued to-day in several important divisions might suggest the desirability of a work of recent material from these various domains. An historical volume of the character of this book was, however, deemed not only more in harmony with the other works of the author's series, but also as much more necessary for the use of students before entering upon investigations in special fields. Whilst a chronological order has been followed in general, slight variations have made it possible to group psychologists somewhat according to their schools, and the emphasis, moreover, in the most recent period, has been placed on the selection of those important laws and theories which have already taken on a classical importance. The selections have been given with sufficient fullness, it is hoped, always to reproduce the author and subject in an intelligible and connected way. Authorities will differ concerning the choice of authors and subjects. In this matter important advice has been received from the psychologists alike of Harvard University and also of other large American Universities. Although such valuable opinion always has been carefully considered, the responsibility for the final decision naturally rests upon the editor.

Thirteen authors appear in this work in selections translated for the first time into English. To my colleague Professor Edward Kennard Rand, of the classical department of Harvard University, I am indebted for the translation from the Latin of "The essence and nature of the soul" contained in Christian Wolff's "Rational Psychology"; and to Dr. Herbert Sidney Langfeld of the Harvard Psychological Department for the translation from the German of "The measurement of sensation" in Gustav Fechner's "Elements of Psychophysics." The translations from the Greek of Gregory of Nyssa, from the Latin of Thomas Aquinas, from the French of Charles Bonnet and Maine de Biran, and from the German of Friedrich Eduard Beneke, Moritz Wilhelm Drobisch, Ernst Heinrich Weber, Heinrich von Helmholtz, Ewald Hering, Carl Stumpf, and Carl Lange in the text of H. Kurella, have been made by the author of this work. In French Professor Irving Babbitt and Dr. C. J. Ducasse, and in German Prof. W. G. Howard and Dr. J. Loewenberg of Harvard have made valuable suggestions. My thanks for permission to reprint selections of various psychologists are also due to the publishers and translators whose names will be found at the beginning of the respective chapters accompanying the titles of the works thus utilized. The book will best attain its desired aims if its representative selections shall serve to inspire the perusal of the complete works of the classical psychologists, and if it shall aid in any measure to maintain the importance and prestige of classical psychology.

BENJAMIN RAND.

EMERSON HALL, HARVARD UNIVERSITY.

CONTENTS

CONTENTS

XXVI. JOHANN FRIEDRICH HERBART (1776–1841)

XXVII. FRIEDRICH EDUARD BENEKE (1798–1854)

XXVIII. MORITZ WILHELM DROBISCH (1802–1896)

CONTENTS

CONTENTS

THE
CLASSICAL PSYCHOLOGISTS

ANAXAGORAS   EMPEDOCLES
(500–428 B.C.)   (490–430)
DEMOCRITUS
(460–370)

FROM ARISTOTLE'S *DE ANIMA*

Translated from the Greek* by

R. D. HICKS

BOOK I

CHAPTER I—INTRODUCTION OF ARISTOTLE

COGNITION is in our eyes a thing of beauty and worth, and this
is true of one cognition more than another, either because it is
exact or because it relates to more important and remarkable
objects. On both these grounds we may with good reason claim
a high place for the enquiry concerning the soul. It would seem,
too, that an acquaintance with the subject contributes greatly
to the whole domain of truth and, more particularly, to the
study of nature, the soul being virtually the principle of all
animal life. Our aim is to discover and ascertain the nature and
essence of soul and, in the next place, all the accidents belonging
to it; of which some are thought to be attributes peculiar to the
soul itself, while others, it is held, belong to the animal also, but
owe their existence to the soul. But everywhere and in every
way it is extremely difficult to arrive at any trustworthy con-

---

* From Ἀριστοτέλους Περὶ Ψυχῆς. Reprinted from Aristotle's *De Anima*,
translated by R. D. Hicks. Cambridge, University Press, 1907.

clusion on the subject. It is the same here as in many other enquiries. What we have to investigate is the essential nature of things and the What. It might therefore be thought that there is a single procedure applicable to all the objects whose essential nature we wish to discover, as demonstration is applicable to the properties which go along with them: in that case we should have to enquire what this procedure is. If, however, there is no single procedure common to all sciences for defining the What, our task becomes still more difficult, as it will then be necessary to settle in each particular case the method to be pursued. Further, even if it be evident that it consists in demonstration of some sort or division or some other procedure, there is still room for much perplexity and error, when we ask from what premisses our enquiry should start, for there are different premisses for different sciences; for the science of numbers, for example, and plane geometry.

The first thing necessary is no doubt to determine under which of the summa genera soul comes and what it is; I mean, whether it is a particular thing, i.e. substance, or is quality or is quantity, or falls under any other of the categories already determined. We must further ask whether it is amongst things potentially existent or is rather a sort of actuality, the distinction being all-important. Again, we must consider whether it is divisible or indivisible; whether, again, all and every soul is homogeneous or not; and, if not, whether the difference between the various souls is a difference of species or a difference of genus: for at present discussions and investigations about soul would appear to be restricted to the human soul. We must take care not to overlook the question whether there is a single definition of soul answering to a single definition of animal; or whether there is a different definition for each separate soul, as for horse and dog, man and god: animal, as the universal, being regarded either as non-existent or, if existent, as logically posterior. This is a question which might equally be raised in regard to any other common predicate. Further, on the assumption that there are not several souls, but merely several different parts in the same soul, it is a question whether we should begin by investigating soul as a whole or its several parts. And here again it is difficult to determine which of these parts are really distinct from one another and whether the several parts, or their functions, should be investigated first. Thus, e.g., should the process of thinking come first or the mind that thinks, the process of sensation or the sensitive faculty? And so everywhere else. But, if the functions should come first, again will arise the question whether we should first investigate the correlative objects. Shall we take, e.g., the sensible object before the faculty of sense and the intelligible object before the intellect?

It would seem that not only is the knowledge of a thing's essential nature useful for discovering the causes of its attributes, as, e.g., in mathematics the knowledge of what is meant by the terms straight or curved, line or surface, aids us in discovering to how many right angles the angles of a triangle are equal: but also, conversely, a knowledge of the attributes is a considerable aid to the knowledge of what a thing is. For when we are able to give an account of all, or at any rate most, of the attributes as they are presented to us, then we shall be in a position to define most exactly the essential nature of the thing. In fact, the starting point of every demonstration is a definition of what something is. Hence the definitions which lead to no information about attributes and do not facilitate even conjecture respecting them have clearly been framed for dialectic and are void of content, one and all.

A further difficulty arises as to whether all attributes of the soul are also shared by that which contains the soul or whether any of them are peculiar to the soul itself: a question which it is indispensable, and yet by no means easy, to decide. It would appear that in most cases soul neither acts nor is acted upon apart from the body: as, e.g., in anger, confidence, desire and sensation in general. Thought, if anything, would seem to be peculiar to the soul. Yet, if thought is a sort of imagination, or not independent of imagination, it will follow that even thought cannot be independent of the body. If, then, there be any of the functions or affections of the soul peculiar to it, it will be possible for the soul to be separated from the body: if, on the

other hand, there is nothing of the sort peculiar to it, the soul
will not be capable of separate existence. As with the straight
line, so with it. The line, *quâ* straight, has many properties; for
instance, it touches the brazen sphere at a point; but it by no
means follows that it will so touch it if separated. In fact it is
inseparable, since it is always conjoined with body of some sort.
So, too, the attributes of the soul appear to be all conjoined with
body: such attributes, viz., as anger, mildness, fear, pity, courage; also joy, love and hate; all of which are attended by some
particular affection of the body. This indeed is shown by the
fact that sometimes violent and palpable incentives occur without producing in us exasperation or fear, while at other times
we are moved by slight and scarcely perceptible causes, when
the blood is up and the bodily condition that of anger. Still
more is this evident from the fact that sometimes even without
the occurrence of anything terrible men exhibit all the symptoms of terror. If this be so, the attributes are evidently forms
or notions realised in matter. Hence they must be defined accordingly: anger, for instance, as a certain movement in a body
of a given kind, or some part or faculty of it, produced by such
and such a cause and for such and such an end. These facts at
once bring the investigation of soul, whether in its entirety or
in the particular aspect described, within the province of the
natural philosopher. But every such attribute would be differently defined by the physicist and the dialectician or philosopher. Anger, for instance, would be defined by the dialectician
as desire for retaliation or the like, by the physicist as a ferment
of the blood or heat which is about the heart: the one of them
gives the matter, the other the form or notion. For the notion
is the form of the thing, but this notion, if it is to be, must be
realised in matter of a particular kind; just as in the case of a
house. The notion or definition of a house would be as follows:
a shelter to protect us from harm by wind or rain or scorching
heat; while another will describe it as stones, bricks and timber; and again another as the form realised in these materials
and subserving given ends. Which then of these is the true physicist? Is it he who confines himself to the matter, while ignor-

ing the form? Or he who treats of the form exclusively? I answer, it is rather he who in his definition takes account of both. What then of each of the other two? Or shall we rather say that there is no one who deals with properties which are not separable nor yet treated as separable, but the physicist deals with all the active properties or passive affections belonging to body of a given sort and the corresponding matter? All attributes not regarded as so belonging he leaves to someone else: who in certain cases is an expert, a carpenter, for instance, or a physician. The attributes which, though inseparable, are not regarded as properties of body of a given sort, but are reached by abstraction, fall within the province of the mathematician: while attributes which are regarded as having separate existence fall to the first philosopher or metaphysician. But to return to the point of digression. We were saying that the attributes of the soul are as such, — I mean, as anger and fear, inseparable from the physical matter of the animals to which they belong, and not, like line and surface, separable in thought.

CHAPTER II — EARLY PSYCHOLOGICAL THEORIES

IN our enquiry concerning soul it is necessary to state the problems which must be solved as we proceed, and at the same time to collect the views of our predecessors * who had anything to say on the subject, in order that we may adopt what is right in their conclusions and guard against their mistakes. Our enquiry will begin by presenting what are commonly held to be in a special degree the natural attributes of soul. Now there are two points especially wherein that which is animate is held to differ from the inanimate, namely, motion and the act of sensation: and these are approximately the two characteristics of soul handed down to us by our predecessors. There are some who

---

* Aristotle introduces here the first extant history of psychological theories.

maintain that soul is preëminently and primarily the cause of movement. But they imagined that that which is not itself in motion cannot move anything else, and thus they regarded the soul as a thing which is in motion. Hence Democritus affirms the soul to be a sort of fire or heat. For the "shapes" or atoms are infinite and those which are spherical he declares to be fire and soul: they may be compared with the so-called motes in the air, which are seen in the sunbeams that enter through our windows. The aggregate of such seeds, he tells us, forms the constituent elements of the whole of nature (and herein he agrees with Leucippus), while those of them which are spherical form the soul, because such figures most easily find their way through everything and, being themselves in motion, set other things in motion. The atomists assume that it is the soul which imparts motion to animals. It is for this reason that they make life depend upon respiration. For, when the surrounding air presses upon bodies and tends to extrude those atomic shapes which, because they are never at rest themselves, impart motion to animals, then they are reinforced from outside by the entry of other like atoms in respiration, which in fact, by helping to check compression and solidification, prevent the escape of the atoms already contained in the animals; and life, so they hold, continues so long as there is strength to do this. The doctrine of the Pythagoreans seems also to contain the same thought. Some of them identified soul with the motes in the air, others with that which sets these motes in motion: and as to these motes it has been stated that they are seen to be in incessant motion, even though there be a perfect calm. The view of others who describe the soul as that which moves itself tends in the same direction. For it would seem that all these thinkers regard motion as the most distinctive characteristic of the soul. Everything else, they think, is moved by the soul, but the soul is moved by itself: and this because they never see anything cause motion without itself being in motion. Similarly the soul is said to be the moving principle by Anaxagoras and all others who have held that mind sets the universe in motion; but not altogether in the same sense as by Democritus. The latter, indeed, absolutely identified soul and mind, holding that the presentation to the senses is the truth: hence, he observed, Homer had well sung of Hector in his swoon that he lay 'with other thoughts.' Democritus, then, does not use the term mind to denote a faculty conversant with truth, but regards mind as identical with soul. Anaxagoras, however, is less exact in his use of the terms. In many places he speaks of mind as the cause of goodness and order, but elsewhere he identifies it with the soul: as where he attributes it to all animals, both great and small, high and low. As a matter of fact, however, mind in the sense of intelligence would not seem to be present in all animals alike, nor even in all men.

Those, then, who have directed their attention to the motion of the animate being, conceived the soul as that which is most capable of causing motion: while those who laid stress on its knowledge and perception of all that exists identified the soul with the ultimate principles, whether they recognised a plurality of these or only one. Thus Empedocles compounded soul out of all the elements, while at the same time regarding each one of them as a soul. His words are "With earth we see earth, with water water, with air bright air, but ravaging fire by fire, love by love, and strife by gruesome strife." In the same manner Plato in the *Timaeus* constructs the soul out of the elements. Like, he there maintains, is known by like, and the things we know are composed of the ultimate principles. In like manner it was explained in the lectures on philosophy, that the self-animal or universe is made up of the idea of One, and of the idea-numbers Two, or primary length, Three, primary breadth, and Four, primary depth, and similarly with all the rest of the ideas. And again this has been put in another way as follows: reason is the One, knowledge is the Two, because it proceeds by a single road to one conclusion, opinion is the number of a surface, Three, and sensation the number of a solid, Four. In fact, according to them the numbers, though they are the ideas themselves, or the ultimate principles, are nevertheless derived from elements. And things are judged, some by reason, others by knowledge, others again by opinion and others by sensation: while these idea-numbers are forms of things. And since the soul was held to be thus cognitive as well as capable of causing motion, some thinkers have combined the two and defined the soul as a self-moving number.

But there are differences of opinion as to the nature and number of the ultimate principles, especially between those thinkers who make the principles corporeal and those who make them incorporeal; and again between both of these and others who combine the two and take their principles from both. But, further, they differ also as to their number: some assuming a single principle, some a plurality. And, when they come to give an account of the soul, they do so in strict accordance with their several views. For they have assumed, not unnaturally, that the soul is that primary cause which in its own nature is capable of producing motion. And this is why some identified soul with fire, this being the element which is made up of the finest particles and is most nearly incorporeal, while further it is preëminently an element which both moves and sets other things in motion. Democritus has expressed more neatly the reason for each of these facts. Soul he regards as identical with mind, and this he makes to consist of the primary indivisible bodies and considers it to be a cause of motion from the fineness of its particles and their shape. Now the shape which is most susceptible of motion is the spherical; and of atoms of this shape mind, like fire, consists. Anaxagoras, while apparently understanding by mind something different from soul, as we remarked above, really treats both as a single nature, except that it is preëminently mind which he takes as his first principle; he says at any rate that mind alone of things that exist is simple, unmixed, pure. But he refers both knowledge and motion to the same principle, when he says that mind sets the universe in motion. Thales, too, apparently, judging from the anecdotes related of him, conceived soul as a cause of motion, if it be true that he affirmed the loadstone to possess soul, because it attracts iron. Diogenes, however, as also some others, identified soul with air. Air, they thought, is made up of the finest particles and is the first principle: and this explains the fact that the soul knows and is a cause of motion, knowing by virtue of being the primary element from which all else is derived, and causing motion by the extreme fineness of its parts. Heraclitus takes soul for his first principle, as he identifies it with the vapour from which he derives all other things, and further says that it is the least corporeal of things and in ceaseless flux; and that it is by something in motion that what is in motion is known; for he, like most philosophers, conceived all that exists to be in motion. Alcmaeon, too, seems to have had a similar conception. For soul, he maintains, is immortal because it is like the beings which are immortal; and it has this attribute in virtue of being ever in motion: for he attributes continuous and unending motion to everything which is divine, moon, sun, stars and the whole heaven. Among cruder thinkers there have been some, like Hippon, who have even asserted the soul to be water. The reason for this view seems to have been the fact that in all animals the seed is moist: in fact, Hippon refutes those who make the soul to be blood by pointing out that the seed is not blood, and that this seed is the rudimentary soul. Others, again, like Critias, maintain the soul to be blood, holding that it is sentience which is most distinctive of soul and that this is due to the nature of blood. Thus each of the four elements except earth has found its supporter. Earth, however, has not been put forward by anyone, except by those who have explained the soul to be derived from, or identical with, all the elements.

Thus practically all define the soul by three characteristics, motion, perception and incorporeality; and each of these characteristics is referred to the ultimate principles. Hence all who define soul by its capacity for knowledge either make it an element or derive it from the elements, being on this point, with one exception, in general agreement. Like, they tell us, is known by like; and therefore, since the soul knows all things, they say it consists of all the ultimate principles. Thus those thinkers who admit only one cause and one element, as fire or air, assume the soul also to be one element; while those who admit a plurality of principles assume plurality also in the soul. Anaxagoras alone says that mind cannot be acted upon and has nothing in common with any other thing. How, if such be its nature, it will know anything and how its knowledge is to be explained, he has omitted to state; nor do his utterances afford a clue. All those who introduce pairs of opposites among their principles make the soul also to consist of opposites; while those who take one or other of the two opposites, either hot or cold or something else of the sort, reduce the soul also to one or other of these elements. Hence, too, they etymologise according to their theories; some identify soul with heat, deriving ζῆν from ζεῖν, and contend that this identity accounts for the word for life; others say that what is cold is called soul from the respiratory process and consequent "cooling down," deriving ψυχή from ψύχειν. Such, then, are the views regarding soul which have come down to us and the grounds on which they are held.

PROTAGORAS   SOCRATES
(480–411)   (469–399)

From PLATO'S *THEAETETUS*

Translated from the Greek* by
SAMUEL WALTERS DYDE

THE NATURE OF PERCEPTION
Socrates   Theaetetus

Steph. 152.

Soc. . . . Knowledge is perception, you say?

Theaet. Yes.

Soc. This is surely no trifling matter, for you have likely given, though in other words, the definition of Protagoras. He says that man is the measure of all things (πάντων χρημάτων μέτρον ἄνθρωπον), both of the existence of things which exist, and the non-existence of things which exist not (τῶν μὲν ὄντων, ὡς ἔστι, τῶν δὲ μὴ ὄντων, ὡς οὐκ ἔστιν). Have you never read that?

Theaet. Yes, many a time.

Soc. Does he not mean that things exist for me as they appear (φαίνηται) to me, and for you as they appear to you, since you and I are men?

Theaet. So he says, at any rate.

Soc. As it is highly probable that a wise man does not talk nonsense, let us look for his meaning. Sometimes when the wind is blowing on all alike is not one of us cold and another not, or one slightly and another exceedingly cold?

Theaet. No doubt.

Soc. In that case shall we say that the wind in itself (αὐτὸ ἐφ' ἑαυτό) is cold or not cold? Or shall we agree with Protagoras that it is cold to him who is cold and not to him who is not?

Theaet. Protagoras seems to be right.

---

* From Πλάτωνας Θεαίτητος. Reprinted from *The Theaetetus of Plato*, translated by S. W. Dyde. Glasgow, 1899.

Soc. Then it is to each as it appears to him?

Theaet. Yes.

Soc. And what appears is perceived?

Theaet. Truly.

Soc. Then in the case of such things as heat and cold appearance (φαντασία) and perception are one and the same. Every such thing, I daresay, exists as it is perceived?

Theaet. That would seem to be so.

Soc. And perception of reality (τοῦ ὄντος), since it is knowledge, can never be false?

Theaet. So it appears.

Soc. Then charmingly keen-witted was it of Protagoras to hint darkly at these things to us of the common crowd, while telling the truth to his disciples in secret.

Theaet. What do you mean by that, Socrates?

Soc. I shall tell you of a by no means contemptible theory to the effect that nothing exists purely by itself (αὐτὸ καθ' αὐτό), nor can you rightly give anything an exclusive name. If you speak of the large, you suggest the small, if of the heavy, you suggest the light, and so on. Nothing, be it either an attribute (τινός), or a kind of thing (ὁποιουοῦν), exists alone (ἑνός). Moreover, it is inaccurate to speak of existence as the result of motion, collision and combination, since nothing really exists, but everything is always in process of change (γίγνεται). On this point the whole array of wise men, except Parmenides, are agreed, Protagoras, Heraclitus, Empedocles, also the most famous names in both kinds of poetry, in comedy Epicharmus, and in tragedy Homer. When Homer says: Ocean and mother Tethys are the parents of the gods, he means that all the gods have sprung from ceaseless movement (ῥοῆς τε καὶ κινήσεως). Do you not think that this was his view?

Theaet. Yes.

Soc. Could we contend with this mighty host, whose captain is Homer, without laying ourselves open to ridicule?

Theaet. It would be a risk, Socrates.

Soc. Yes indeed, Theaetetus, since there are good proofs that what appears to be and comes into existence is produced by motion, and what does not exist and perishes is produced by rest. For example, heat and fire, which produce and nourish everything else, are themselves produced by friction, which is motion. Is not that the source of fire?

Theaet. Yes.

Soc. And has not the race (γένος) of animals sprung from the same source?

Theaet. It has surely.

Soc. Why, what else? Is not the fashion (ἕξις) of the body destroyed by rest and inaction and preserved largely by exercise and movement?

Theaet. Certainly.

Soc. And the soul, is it not taught and preserved and improved by study and practice, which are motions, while through idleness, neglect and inattention it fails to learn, or what it learns it forgets?

Theaet. That is true.

Soc. Is motion not a good, then, for soul and body, and rest the reverse of good?

Theaet. Evidently.

Soc. May I not say further that storms preserve, while stillness and calm and all such states of rest corrupt and destroy? And I am constrained to give this crowning illustration, that so long as the universe and the golden chain, as Homer calls the sun, move onward in their course, all things divine and human manifestly contrive to exist and are preserved; but, if they should stand still, everything would be destroyed, and then would come to pass the saying that the whole world is turned upside down.

Theaet. Your explanation, I think, is clear, Socrates.

Soc. Consider this, my friend, with regard first of all to the sense of sight. What you call whiteness does not exist in your eyes nor as an object outside of them, nor could you assign to it any particular place, for it would then be something fixed and stationary and not continuously generated.

Theaet. How is that?

Soc. Let us apply our former argument, in which we decided that nothing exists as one thing and utterly by itself, and it will appear that white, black, or any other colour is produced when the glance of the eye comes into contact with the proper motion. What we call a colour is neither the eye nor the object, but something which arises between them, and is different with different individuals. Or, would you contend that a colour appears to you as it does to an animal, a dog for instance?

Theaet. No indeed, I would not.

Soc. Then would you hold that two human beings might have the same perceptions? Are you not sure, rather, that not even to yourself does a thing twice appear the same, since both you and it are continually changing?

Theaet. Yes, I feel sure of that.

Soc. Yet if the object, which we touch and compare in size with ourselves, be large or white or hot, it would not, when contrasted with one thing, be different from what it is when contrasted with another, provided that it itself had suffered no change. Or, if it is the faculty, whether of measuring or touch, which is large or white or hot, then, if it were itself unmodified, it would not be changed merely by experiencing and coming into contact with different objects. So, you see, our want of thought leads us into amazing absurdities, as Protagoras and his school would say.

Theaet. What do you mean by that?

Soc. You will understand what I mean, if I use a simple illustration. If you take six dice, you would say that they, when compared with four, were more by half as many again, and when compared with twelve they were less and only one-half. Could you deny the truth of that?

Theaet. No indeed.

Soc. Well then, if Protagoras or somebody else says to you, O Theaetetus, can a thing possibly become more or greater, unless it be increased? What will you answer?

Theaet. If I answer the simple question as I really think, I must say No, but in view of what you have just said and to avoid a contradiction, I must say Yes.

Soc. Well and divinely spoken, friend! And yet it strikes me that if you say Yes, it will be with you according to the saying of Euripides: 'The tongue will be unrefuted, but the mind not unrefuted.'

Theaet. True.

Soc. If we had been veteran sophists (δεινοὶ καὶ σοφοί), you and I, and had carefully scrutinized all the things of the mind, we would at the very outset have made an abundant trial of our opponents, as they of us; we would have come up to the contest warily (σοφιστικῶς), and there would have been a clashing of words with words. But, as it is, we are only private folks whose foremost wish is to behold things as they are (αὐτὰ πρὸς αὐτά), and to see if our thoughts are consistent or not.

Theaet. That is certainly my desire.

Soc. And mine. Shall we not, then, as we have lots of time, retrace our steps a little, and examine ourselves calmly and earnestly, in order to see what these images in us are? The first of them we shall, I think, decide to be that nothing ever becomes more or less either in size or number, while it is equal to itself. Is not that so?

Theaet. Yes.

Soc. And the second is that that, to which nothing is added and from which nothing is taken away, is neither increased nor diminished, but is always equal to itself.

Theaet. Assuredly.

Soc. Is there not a third, that nothing, which did not exist before, can now exist, without becoming and having become?

Theaet. Agreed.

Soc. These three postulates, I think, were striving together in our soul when we spoke of the dice, and are present again in the following instance: Suppose that you were shorter than I at the beginning of the year, but taller at the end, not because I had diminished in size, for men of my age do not change, but because you, who are young, had meanwhile grown. It is manifest that I was once what I was not afterwards, although I had not become. For, as to have become is plainly impossible without becoming, I could not have become smaller without losing in size. And there are thousands of similar instances, if indeed we choose to admit them. I see that you follow me, Theaetetus, for you are likely not unacquainted with such puzzles.

Theaet. By the gods, Socrates, when I look into them I am smitten with wonder, and truly sometimes my brain reels.

Soc. So Theodorus made not a bad guess at your disposition, my friend, since the very state of a philosopher is wonder. Indeed the man seems to have been a wise genealogist who said that Iris was the daughter of Thaumas, for wonder is the only beginning of philosophy. Do you begin to understand what is the solution of your difficulty on the views which we are ascribing to Protagoras?

Theaet. Not yet.

Soc. Will you count it a favour if I examine with you into the secret reasoning, which is held as the truth by him and other celebrated men ?

Theaet. I will count it a very great favour.

Soc. Look over the company, so that no profane person may overhear. For there are people who believe in nothing but what they can fasten upon with both hands, contending that action and generation and all the things, which are not seen, do not exist at all.

Theaet. They must be hardened and repulsive creatures.

Soc. That they are, my boy, utterly illiterate. But it is another much more subtle sect, of whose mysteries I mean to inform you. Their first principle, that upon which our statement depends, is that all is motion (τὸ πᾶν κίνησις) or that nothing exists except motion. There are two kinds (εἴδη) of motion, each unlimited in its range, to act and to suffer or be acted upon. From the strife and union of these two powers (δυνάμεις) is produced an innumerable brood twofold in its nature, namely the object of sense, and sense, which is always connate and coincident with it, object. The sensible perceptions are called sight, hearing, smell, the sense of hot and cold, and also pleasures, pains, desires and fears. These and many others have names, and there are numberless others without names. Correlative with sight are colours of all kinds, sounds with hearing, and with each of the other senses its kindred objects. Has this tale anything to do, Theaetetus, with what has gone before? Do you know?

Theaet. Socrates, I do not.

Soc. Give heed, then, and you shall see the connection. All these things, as we have said, are in movement. Now in the movement of them there are swiftness and slowness. That which is slow moves in one place, and is affected by things close at hand, and so produces, but the things produced by it are swifter, since their movement is a change of place. Let us suppose that the eye and its corresponding visible object approach and produce whiteness and the concomitant sensation, a result which would not take place if either the eye or the object came into contact with anything else. When the union of these two occurs, sight moving from the eye and meeting whiteness moving from the object, which helps to produce the colour, the eye becomes filled with vision, and now sees, and becomes not vision but seeing eye. The object, in turn, having aided in making the colour, is filled with whiteness, and becomes not whiteness but white, be it wood or stone or any object, which chanced to be of this colour. All other sensations, hard, warm and the rest, must be treated in the same way. Not one of them, as we have said already, can be understood as having any existence of itself (αὐτὸ καθ' αὑτό), but all are produced by movement through union each with its proper counterpart. There can be no solid cognition (νοῆσαι), as they say, of either the active element or the passive element taken separately (ἐπὶ ἑνός); for there is an active element only as it is found in union with the passive, and a passive element only as it is found in union with the active. The uniting and active element, when it comes into contact with another thing, is to be regarded as passive. Accordingly on all these counts, nothing, as we said at the outset, exists as one thing by itself (ἓν αὐτὸ καθ' αὑτό), but everything always becomes for some other thing (τινι γίγνεσθαι). Being or existence (τὸ εἶναι) must be thoroughly eradicated, though we are often, as just now, compelled, it would seem, through custom and ignorance to make use of the term. And yet, according to the wise (οἱ σοφοί), we must not permit anyone to use such expressions as 'it' or 'of it' or 'mine' or 'this' or 'that' or any other name which gives fixity, but only to conform to nature and say that things become, are in process of creation, and are being destroyed and changed. Thus, if anyone in an argument establishes anything, he is easy to refute. Besides, we must speak in this way not only of separate things but of any collection, such as man, stone, any species of animal or any genus (εἶδος). Do these things seem pleasant to you, Theaetetus, and have they a grateful flavour?

Theaet. I am sure I do not know, Socrates, for I cannot decide whether you believe what you say or are only making trial of me.

Soc. You really forget, my friend, that I know nothing and produce nothing of my own, for I am childless. But I wait on you, and therefore seek to charm you by giving you to taste of every philosopher (σοφός), until at last I may have aided in bringing your theory out into the light. When this is done, I shall see whether it is an empty thing or a genuine reality. So, be bold, and persevere, and answer sturdily to what I ask you.

Theaet. Well then, put your questions.

Soc. Tell me again if you are satisfied that nothing is, but all is ever becoming, the good and beautiful as well as all the things which we have just enumerated.

Theaet. To speak frankly, when I hear your argument in detail, I think it very reasonable and must accept it.

Soc. Let us, then, see the theory completed. It remains to speak of dreams and diseases, especially madness with its illusions of sight and hearing and other senses. In all these cases, as you must admit, the position which we have just taken seems to be refuted, since manifestly there arise in ourselves perceptions which are false. Consequently what appears to each person is far from being real; on the exact contrary not a single appearance is real.

Theaet. You speak truly, Socrates.

Soc. What argument (λόγος), my boy, is left to him who holds that sensible perception is knowledge, and that each one's appearances (τὰ φαινόμενα) are for him real?

Theaet. I hesitate to tell you, Socrates, that I do not know what to say, because you reproved me a moment ago for giving this answer. Yet I cannot, indeed, argue that madmen and dreamers think truly, some in supposing that they are gods, and others in dreaming that they have wings and are flying.

Soc. Do you not perceive that in these cases, especially in dreams and madness, a rejoinder may be made of this nature?

Theaet. Of what nature?

Soc. You have doubtless often heard it asked: What proof would you give, if you were questioned at this moment whether we are sleeping and dreaming all this discussion, or awake and conversing about a waking thought?

Theaet. Truly, Socrates, it would be hard to prove it, for sleep and waking are equally real, and one is the counterpart of the other. There is nothing to prevent our supposing that we are now talking together in our sleep. And when in dreams we seem to be telling our dreams, such a state strangely resembles our waking life.

Soc. It is not hard, you see, to carry on the dispute, when it may be doubted even whether we are asleep or awake. If we divide time about equally between sleep and waking, in each period our souls are maintaining that their present opinions (δόγματα) are true. Thus for one half of our days we say that some opinions are true, and for the other half that different opinions are true. Yet we hold fast by both.

Theaet. Clearly.

Soc. Does not the same argument apply to diseases and madness, except only that the time is not divided equally?

Theaet. True.

Soc. And is the truth to be determined by length or shortness of time?

Theaet. That would be absurd.

Soc. Can you by any other way clearly show on which side the truth is?

Theaet. I think not.

Soc. You shall hear, then, what is said about this by those who determine that what seems (τὰ δοκοῦντα) to anyone to be true is true for him. They would put some such question as this to you, "O Theaetetus, can two things entirely different have the same quality (δύναμις)?" Their question, let us understand, is of things not partially but wholly different.

Theaet. Things utterly different cannot possibly have a quality or anything else the same.

Soc. Must we confess that these things are therefore unlike?

Theaet. I should say so.

Soc. Suppose that a thing happened to become like or unlike itself or another thing, shall we say that what is made like becomes the same, and what unlike different?

Theaet. We must.

Soc. We said before, did we not, that the active elements were many and infinite, and likewise the passive elements?

Theaet. Yes.

Soc. And if a thing combines with different things, the products will be different?

Theaet. Surely.

Soc. Let us apply this to you or me or anything, Socrates sick and Socrates well, for example. Shall we say that these are like or unlike?

Theaet. Am I to take Socrates sick as one separate whole, and Socrates well as another?

Soc. You understand exactly; that is what I mean.

Theaet. They are unlike doubtless.

Soc. And different because unlike?

Theaet. Necessarily.

Soc. And will you say the same of Socrates asleep or in the other states we mentioned?

Theaet. I would.

Soc. Then would I not be affected by any active element in nature differently in sickness and in health?

Theaet. How could it be otherwise?

Soc. Would not the active element and I, the patient, produce a different result in each case?

Theact. Certainly.

Soc. The wine I drink when I am in health appears to me sweet and pleasant?

Theaet. Yes.

Soc. It follows from our previous admissions that the active and passive elements, when they unite, produce sweetness and the sensation of sweetness. The sensation arising from the patient renders the tongue percipient, and sweetness moving in the wine and arising from it meets the healthy tongue, and causes the wine both to be and to appear sweet.

Theaet. That is the consequence of what we formerly admitted.

Soc. But when I am sick, does not the object affect a person who, because unlike, is really different?

Theaet. Yes.

Soc. In that case Socrates and the drinking of the wine produce a different result, the sensation of bitterness in the tongue and bitterness moving in the wine. The wine becomes not bitterness but bitter, and I become not perception but perceiving.

Theaet. Certainly.

Soc. There is no other thing, from which I shall ever receive the same perception. The perception of different things is different, and makes him, who perceives, of another nature and another man. Nor does the object, which affects me, produce the same result and become the same object, when it comes into contact with another person. When objects produce different results in contact with different subjects, they become of another nature.

Theaet. It is true.

Soc. The object and I will not become what we are independently of each other.

Theaet. By no means.

Soc. I must become percipient of something when I perceive, for it is impossible in perceiving to perceive nothing. And when the object becomes sweet or bitter or something else, it must do so for some one, since to become sweet and yet sweet for nobody is not possible.

Theaet. Assuredly not.

Soc. We must conclude that the object and I are or become only one for the other. Necessity couples us to each other, but does not couple our joint existence to any other thing or even to ourselves. Each is bound simply to the other. Accordingly when a thing is said to be or become, it must be spoken of as for or of or in regard to something. The argument, which we have traversed, points out that no one must say, or permit anyone else to say, that anything is or becomes wholly of itself (αὐτὸ ἐφ' αὑτοῦ).

Theaet. No, by no means, Socrates.

Soc. When anything, which affects me, exists for me and no other person, is it not perceived by me and no other?

Theaet. That is evident.

Soc. Then my sensation is true for me since it is inseparable from my existence. As Protagoras says, I am judge both of the existence of what is for me and the non-existence of what is not.

Theaet. That seems to be the case.

Soc. If I am infallible and sure-footed in my judgments concerning being (τὰ ὄντα) and becoming (τὰ γιγνόμενα), how can I fail to know that of which I am the percipient (αἰσθητής)?

Theaet. Not in any way.

Soc. Right noble, then, was your decision that knowledge was nothing else than perception. Homer and Heraclitus with their crew, who say that all things flow and are in a state of motion, and the all-wise Protagoras with his view that man is the measure of all things, and Theaetetus, who concludes from these theories that knowledge is sensation, are all of one accord. Is that not true, O Theaetetus? Shall we call this result the young child at whose birth I have assisted? Or what do you say?

Theaet. It must be so, Socrates.

. . . .

Steph. 184b.

Soc. Once again, Theaetetus, address yourself to our former inquiry. You answered that knowledge was sensible perception, did you not?

Theaet. Yes.

Soc. If some one were to put this question to you, With what does a man see white and black colours and with what does he hear high and low tones? you would say, I think, with his eyes and ears.

Theaet. I should.

Soc. To handle names and terms freely and without critical minuteness is often a mark of wide culture, and though the opposite is as a rule churlish, it is sometimes, as in the present instance, a necessity. For I must indicate a want of exactness in this very answer. Reflect, is it more correct to say that it is with the eyes (ὀφθαλμοῖς) that we see or through them (δι' ὀφθαλμῶν), and that it is with the ears or through them that we hear?

Theaet. I think 'through' is better, Socrates.

Soc. Surely, for it would be a singular thing, my lad, if each of us was, as it were, a wooden horse, and within us were seated many separate senses, since manifestly these senses unite into one nature (ἰδέα), call it the soul or what you will; and it is with this central form through the organs of sense that we perceive sensible objects.

Theaet. I agree with your view; the contrary would indeed be singular.

Soc. I am precise with you, in order to find out if it is with one and the same part of ourselves that we have various impressions, although at the same time through different faculties. Would you, if you were asked, refer all our impressions to the body? But perhaps you would answer better without my interference. Tell me, then, do you assign the faculties, through which you perceive hot and hard and light and sweet, to the body or to something else?

Theaet. To the body.

Soc. And would you be willing to allow that what you perceive through one faculty (δύναμις) you cannot perceive through another? You cannot, that is, hear through the eye or see through the ear?

Theaet. I grant that readily.

Soc. If you make a judgment common to the two organs (ὄργανα), you cannot perceive it through either of them.

Theaet. Certainly not.

Soc. In the case of sound and colour you may surely decide that they both are.

Theaet. Surely.

Soc. Is not each different (ἕτερον) from the other and the same (ταὐτόν) with itself?

Theaet. No doubt.

Soc. They are two and each is one?

Theaet. I grant that also.

Soc. You would be able to observe whether they are like or unlike each other?

Theaet. Probably.

Soc. Through what do you make these several judgments? For it is not possible either through hearing or sight to get anything common to the two (τὸ κοινόν). Let us take an illustration. Suppose it to be a sensible question to ask whether you judge colours and sounds to be saline or not, you would be able to say what faculty you would use in order to decide, and this faculty would be not sight or hearing but some other.

Theaet. Another of course, the faculty of taste.

Soc. That is well said. And what faculty will reveal to you the common elements not only of sensible qualities, but of all things, those elements, I mean, which you call being (τὸ ἔστιν) and not being (τὸ οὐκ ἔστιν) and the others, about which we were speaking a moment ago? To what organ will you attribute our perception of each of these?

Theaet. You allude to being (οὐσία) and not being (τὸ μὴ εἶναι), likeness (ὁμοιότης) and unlikeness, the same (τὸ ταὐτόν) and the other (τὸ ἕτερον), and unity (ἕν) also, and other numbers applicable to things, and you evidently wish to know through what bodily instrument the soul perceives odd (περιττόν) and even (ἄρτιον) and all that is akin to them.

Soc. You follow me surpassingly well, Theaetetus; that is just what I want.

Theaet. Verily, Socrates, I cannot tell what to say, if not that these things unlike sensible objects seem to need no special organ, but that the soul contemplates the common elements (τὰ κοινά) of all things through itself (δι᾽ αὑτῆς).

Soc. You are beautiful, Theaetetus, and not ill-favoured, as Theodorus said, for he who says beautiful things, is beautiful and good. And not only are you beautiful but you have done well in delivering me from a long harangue, if you are satisfied that some things the soul contemplates through itself and others through the bodily faculties. For that was my opinion too, and I was anxious for you to agree with me.

Theaet. I am convinced of the truth of that.

Soc. On which side would you place being, which is in a unique way associated with all things?

Theaet. I would place it amongst those things, which the soul strives to grasp of itself (καθ᾽ αὑτήν).

Soc. And would you place there the like and unlike, the same and the other?

Theaet. Yes.

Soc. And what of the noble and base, good and evil?

Theaet. In this case quite specially the soul views the essence (οὐσία) of each in relation to its opposite, contrasting within itself the past and present with the future.

Soc. Stay a moment. Does the soul not perceive the hardness of a hard object through the touch, and in the same way the softness of a soft object?

Theaet. Yes.

Soc. But the essence and existence of these, and the opposition of each to the other, and the essence of this opposition, the soul itself judges, bringing them all together and passing them in review.

Theaet. Certainly.

Soc. Men and animals from their very birth perceive by nature those feelings (παθήματα) which reach the soul through the body; but reflections (ἀναλογίσματα) on the essence of these and on their use come to those who have them only after effort and with the lapse of years through education and a wide experience.

Theaet. That is very true.

Soc. Is it possible to gain truth, if we have no hold of being?

Theaet. Impossible.

Soc. If we fall short of the truth of anything, can we be said to know it?

Theaet. By no means, Socrates.

Soc. Then in feelings there is no knowledge but only in reasonings (συλλογισμοί) upon them, for in reasonings it is possible to touch being and truth, but in feelings it is impossible.

Theaet. That is evident.

Soc. Do you call reasonings and feelings, the same, when they differ so widely?

Theaet. That would hardly be just.

Soc. What name do you give to seeing, hearing, smelling, being cold and being warm?

Theaet. Perceiving, I would call them. I have no other name.

Soc. Perception then, you say, covers them all?

Theaet. It must.

Soc. And this has no share in truth, because it lays not hold on being.

Theaet. None.

Soc. Then it has no share in knowledge.

Theaet. No.

Soc. Then, Theaetetus, sensible perception and knowledge will never be the same.

Theaet. Clearly not, Socrates; indeed it is now quite evident that knowledge and sensation are different.

PLATO

(427–347)

THE REPUBLIC

Translated from the Greek * *by*

JOHN LLEWELYN DAVIES AND
DAVID JAMES VAUGHAN

BOOK IV. THE THREE FACULTIES OF THE SOUL

SOCRATES   *GLAUCON*

Steph. 435.

I PROCEEDED to ask: When two things, a greater and a less, are called by a common name, are they, in so far as the common name applies, unlike or like?

Like.

Then a just man will not differ from a just state, so far as the idea of justice is involved, but the two will be like.

They will.

Well, but we resolved that a state was just, when the three classes of characters present in it were severally occupied in doing their proper work: and that it was temperate, and brave, and wise, in consequence of certain affections and conditions of these same classes.

True.

Then, my friend, we shall also adjudge, in the case of the individual man, that, supposing him to possess in his soul the same generic parts, he is rightly entitled to the same names as the state, in virtue of affections of these parts identical with those of the classes in the state.

It must inevitably be so.

* From Πλάτωνος Πολιτεία. Reprinted from *The Republic of Plato*, translated by J. L Davies and D. J. Vaughan, Cambridge, 1852, etc.

Once more then, my excellent friend, we have stumbled on an easy question concerning the nature of the soul, namely, whether it contains these three generic parts or not.

Not so very easy a question, I think: but perhaps, Socrates, the common saying is true, that the beautiful is difficult.

It would appear so; and I tell you plainly, Glaucon, that in my opinion we shall never attain to exact truth on this subject, by such methods as we are employing in our present discussion. However, the path that leads to that goal is too long and toilsome; and I dare say we may arrive at the truth by our present methods, in a manner not unworthy of our former arguments and speculations.

Shall we not be content with that? For my part it would satisfy me for the present.

Well, certainly it will be quite enough for me.

Do not flag then, but proceed with the inquiry.

Tell me then, I continued, can we possibly refuse to admit that there exist in each of us the same generic parts and characteristics as are found in the state? For I presume the state has not received them from any other source. It would be ridiculous to imagine that the presence of the spirited element in cities is not to be traced to individuals, wherever this character is imputed to the people, as it is to the natives of Thrace, and Scythia, and generally speaking, of the northern countries; or the love of knowledge, which would be chiefly attributed to our own country; or the love of riches, which people would especially connect with the Phœnicians and the Egyptians.

Certainly.

This then is a fact so far, and one which it is not difficult to apprehend.

No, it is not.

But here begins a difficulty. Are all our actions alike performed by the one predominant faculty, or are there three faculties operating severally in our different actions? Do we learn with one internal faculty, and become angry with another, and with a third feel desire for all the pleasures connected with eating and drinking, and the propagation of the species; or upon every impulse to action, do we perform these several operations with the whole soul? The difficulty will consist in settling these points in a satisfactory manner.

I think so too.

Let us try therefore the following plan, in order to ascertain whether the faculties engaged are distinct or identical.

What is your plan?

It is manifest that the same thing cannot do two opposite things, or be in two opposite states, in the same part of it, and with reference to the same object; so that where we find these phenomena occurring, we shall know that the subjects of them are not identical, but more than one.

Very well.

Now consider what I say.

Speak on.

Is it possible for the same thing to be at the same time, and in the same part of it, at rest and in motion?

Certainly not.

Let us come to a still more exact understanding, lest we should chance to differ as we proceed. If it were said of a man who is standing still, but moving his hands and his head, that the same individual is at the same time at rest and in motion, we should not, I imagine, allow this to be a correct way of speaking, but should say, that part of the man is at rest, and part in motion: should we not?

We should.

And if the objector should indulge in yet further pleasantries, so far refining as to say, that at any rate a top is wholly at rest and in motion at the same time, when it spins with its peg fixed on a given spot, or that anything else revolving in the same place, is an instance of the same thing, we should reject his illustration, because in such cases the things are not both stationary and in motion in respect of the same parts of them; and we should reply, that they contain an axis and a circumference, and that in respect of the axis they are stationary, inasmuch as they do not lean to any side; but in respect of the circumference they are moving round and round: but if, while the rotatory motion continues, the axis at the same time inclines to the right or to the left, forwards or backwards, then they cannot be said in any sense to be at rest.

That is true.

Then no objection of that kind will alarm us, or tend at all to convince us that it is ever possible for one and the same thing, at the same time, in the same part of it, and relatively to the same object, to be acted upon in two opposite ways, or to be two opposite things, or to produce two opposite effects.

I can answer for myself.

However, that we may not be compelled to spend time in discussing all such objections, and convincing ourselves that they are unsound, let us assume this to be the fact, and proceed forwards, with the understanding that, if ever we take a different view of this matter, all the conclusions founded on this assumption will fall to the ground.

Yes, that will be the best way.

Well then, I continued, would you place assent and dissent, the seeking after an object and the refusal of it, attraction and repulsion, and the like, in the class of mutual opposites? Whether they be active or passive processes will not affect the question.

Yes, I should.

Well, would you not, without exception, include hunger and thirst, and the desires generally, and likewise willing and wishing, somewhere under the former of those general terms just mentioned? For instance, would you not say that the mind of a man under the influence of desire always either seeks after the object of desire, or attracts to itself that which it wishes to have; or again, so far as it wills the possession of anything, it assents inwardly thereto, as though it were asked a question, longing for the accomplishment of its wish?

I should.

Again: shall we not class disinclination, unwillingness, and dislike, under the head of mental rejection and repulsion, and of general terms wholly opposed to the former?

Unquestionably.

This being the case, shall we say that desires form a class, the most marked of which are what we call thirst and hunger?

We shall.

The one being a desire of drink, and the other of food?

Yes.

Can thirst then, so far as it is thirst, be an internal desire of anything more than drink? That is to say, is thirst, as such, a thirst for hot drink or cold, for much or little, or, in one word, for any particular kind of drink? Or, will it not rather be true that, if there be heat combined with the thirst, the desire of cold drink will be superadded to it, and if there be cold, of hot drink; and if owing to the presence of muchness, the thirst be great, the desire of much will be added, and if little, the desire of little: but that thirst in itself cannot be a desire of anything else than its natural object, which is simple drink, or again, hunger, of anything but food?

You are right, he replied; every desire in itself has to do with its natural object in its simply abstract form, but the accessories of the desire determine the quality of the object.

Let not any one, I proceeded, for want of consideration on our part, disturb us by the objection, that no one desires *drink* simply, but good drink, nor food simply, but good food; because, since all desire good things, if thirst is a desire, it must be a desire of something good, whether that something, which is its object, be drink or anything else; — an argument which applies to all the desires.

True, there might seem to be something in the objection.

Recollect, however, that in the case of all essentially correlative terms, when the first member of the relation is qualified, the second is also qualified, if I am not mistaken; — when the first is abstract, the second is also abstract.

I do not understand you.

Do you not understand that 'greater' is a relative term, implying another term?

Certainly.

It implies a 'less,' does it not?

Yes.

And a much greater implies a much less, does it not?

Yes.

Does a once greater also imply a once less, and a future greater a future less?

Inevitably.

Does not the same reasoning apply to the correlative terms, 'more' and 'fewer,' 'double' and 'half,' and all relations of quantity; also to the terms, 'heavier' and 'lighter,' 'quicker' and 'slower;' and likewise to 'cold' and 'hot,' and all similar epithets?

Certainly it does.

But how is it with the various branches of scientific knowledge? Does not the same principle hold? That is, knowledge in the abstract is knowledge simply of the knowable, or of whatever that be called which is the object of knowledge; but a particular science, of a particular kind, has a particular object of a particular kind. To explain my meaning:—as soon as a science of the construction of houses arose, was it not distinguished from other sciences, and therefore called the science of building?

Undoubtedly.

And is it not because it is of a particular character, which no other science possesses?

Yes.

And is not its particular character derived from the particular character of its object? and may we not say the same of all the other arts and sciences?

We may.

This then you are to regard as having been my meaning before; provided, that is, you now understand that in the case of all correlative terms, if the first member of the relation is abstract, the second is also abstract; if the second is qualified, the first is also qualified. I do not mean to say that the qualities of the two are identical, as for instance, that the science of health is healthy, and the science of disease diseased; or that the science of evil things is evil, and of good things good: but as soon as science, instead of limiting itself to the abstract object of science, became related to a particular kind of object, namely, in the present case, the conditions of health and disease, the result was that the science also came to be qualified in a certain manner, so that it was no longer called simply science, but, by the addition of a qualifying epithet, medical science.

I understand, and I think what you say is true.

To recur to the case of thirst, I continued, do you not consider this to be one of the things whose nature it is to have an object correlative with themselves, assuming that there is such a thing as thirst?

I do, and its object is drink.

Then, for any particular kind of drink there is a particular kind of thirst; but thirst in the abstract is neither for much drink, nor for little, neither for good drink nor for bad, nor, in one word, for any kind of drink, but simply and absolutely thirst for drink, is it not?

Most decidedly so.

Then the soul of a thirsty man, in so far as he is thirsty, has no other wish than to drink; but this it desires, and towards this it is impelled.

Clearly so.

Therefore, whenever anything pulls back a soul that is under the influence of thirst, it will be something in the soul distinct from the principle which thirsts, and which drives it like a beast to drink: for we hold it to be impossible that the same thing should, at the same time, with the same part of itself, in reference to the same object, be doing two opposite things.

Certainly it is.

Just as, I imagine, it would not be right to say of the bowman, that his hands are at the same time drawing the bow towards him, and pushing it from him; the fact being, that one of his hands pushes it from him, and the other pulls it to him.

Precisely so.

Now, can we say that people sometimes are thirsty, and yet do not wish to drink?

Yes, certainly; it often happens to many people.

What then can one say of them, except that their soul contains one principle which commands, and another which forbids them to drink, the latter being distinct from and stronger than the former?

That is my opinion.

Whenever the authority which forbids such indulgences grows up in the soul, is it not engendered there by reasoning; while the powers which lead and draw the mind towards them, owe their presence to passive and morbid states?

It would appear so.

Then we shall have reasonable grounds for assuming that these are two principles distinct one from the other, and for giving to that part of the soul with which it reasons the title of the rational principle, and to that part with which it loves and hungers and thirsts, and experiences the flutter of the other desires, the title of the irrational and concupiscent principle, the ally of sundry indulgences and pleasures.

Yes, he replied: it will not be unreasonable to think so.

Let us consider it settled, then, that these two specific parts exist in the soul. But now, will spirit, or that by which we feel indignant, constitute a third distinct part? If not, with which of the two former has it a natural affinity?

Perhaps with the concupiscent principle.

But I was once told a story, which I can quite believe, to the effect, that Leontius, the son of Aglaion, as he was walking up from the Piræus, and approaching the northern wall from the outside, observed some dead bodies on the ground, and the executioner standing by them. He immediately felt a desire to look at them, but at the same time loathing the thought he tried to divert himself from it. For some time he struggled with himself, and covered his eyes, till at length, over-mastered by the desire, he opened his eyes wide with his fingers, and running up to the bodies, exclaimed, 'There! you wretches! gaze your fill at the beautiful spectacle!'

I have heard the anecdote too.

This story, however, indicates that anger sometimes fights against the desires, which implies that they are two distinct principles.

True, it does indicate that.

And do we not often observe in other cases that when a man is overpowered by his desires against the dictates of his reason, he reviles himself, and resents the violence thus exerted within him, and that, in this struggle of contending parties, the spirit sides with the reason? But that it should make common cause with the desires, when the reason pronounces that they ought not to act against itself, is a thing which I suppose you will not profess to have experienced yourself, nor yet, I imagine, have you ever noticed it in any one else.

No, I am sure I have not.

Well, and when any one thinks he is in the wrong, is he not, in proportion to the nobleness of his character, so much the less able to be angry at being made to suffer hunger or cold or any similar pain at the hands of him whom he thinks justified in so treating him; his spirit, as I describe it, refusing to be roused against his punisher?

True.

On the other hand, when any one thinks he is wronged, does he not instantly boil and chafe, and enlist himself on the side of what he thinks to be justice; and whatever extremities of hunger and cold and the like he may have to suffer, does he not endure till he conquers, never ceasing from his noble efforts, till he has either gained his point, or perished in the attempt, or been recalled and calmed by the voice of reason within, as a dog is called off by a shepherd?

Yes, he replied, the case answers very closely to your description; and in fact, in our city we made the auxiliaries, like sheep-dogs, subject to the rulers, who are as it were the shepherds of the state.

You rightly understand my meaning. But try whether you also apprehend my next observation.

What is it?

That our recent view of the spirited principle is exactly reversed. Then we thought it had something of the concupiscent character, but now we say that, far from this being the case, it much more readily takes arms on the side of the rational principle in the party conflict of the soul.

Decidedly it does.

Is it then distinct from this principle also; or is it only a modification of it, thus making two instead of three distinct principles in the soul, namely, the rational and the concupiscent?
Or ought we to say that, as the state was held together by three
great classes, the producing class, the auxiliary, and the deliberative, so also in the soul the spirited principle constitutes a
third element, the natural ally of the rational principle, if it be
not corrupted by evil training?

It must be a third, he replied.

Yes, I continued; if it shall appear to be distinct from the rational principle, as we found it different from the concupiscent.

Nay, that will easily appear. For even in little children any
one may see this, that from their very birth they have plenty
of spirit, whereas reason is a principle to which most men only
attain after many years, and some, in my opinion, never.

Upon my word you have well said. In brute beasts also one
may see what you describe exemplified. And besides, that passage in Homer, which we quoted on a former occasion, will support our view:

'Smiting his breast, to his heart thus spake he in accents of chiding.'

For in this line Homer has distinctly made a difference between
the two principles, representing that which had considered the
good or the evil of the action as rebuking that which was in-
dulging in unreflecting resentment.

You are perfectly right.

Here then, I proceeded, after a hard struggle, we have, though
with difficulty, reached the land; and we are pretty well satisfied that there are corresponding divisions, equal in number,
in a state, and in the soul of every individual.

. . . .

BOOK VI. THE CORRELATION OF THE FACULTIES

Steph. 508 D.

JUST in the same way understand the condition of the soul
to be as follows. Whenever it has fastened upon an object, over
which truth and real existence are shining, it seizes that object

by an act of reason, and knows it, and thus proves itself to be possessed of reason: but whenever it has fixed upon objects that are blent with darkness, — the world of birth and death, — then it rests in *opinion*, and its sight grows dim, as its opinions shift backwards and forwards, and it has the appearance of being destitute of reason.

True it has.

Now, this power, which supplies the objects of real knowledge with the truth that is in them, and which renders to him who knows the faculty of knowing them, you must consider to be the essential form of good, and you must regard it as the origin of science, and of truth, so far as the latter comes within the range of knowledge; and though knowledge and truth are both very beautiful things, you will be right in looking upon good as something distinct from them, and even more beautiful. And just so, in the analogous case, it is right to regard light and vision so resembling the sun, but wrong to identify them with the sun; so, in the case of science and truth, it is right to regard both of them as resembling good, but wrong to identify either of them with good; because, on the contrary, the quality of good ought to have a still higher value set upon it.

That implies an irrepressible beauty, if it not only is the source of science and truth, but also surpasses them in beauty; for, I presume, you do not mean by it pleasure.

Hush! I exclaimed, not a word of that. But you had better examine the illustration further, as follows.

Shew me how.

I think you will admit that the sun ministers to visible objects, not only the faculty of being seen, but also their vitality, growth, and nutriment, though it is not itself equivalent to vitality.

Of course it is not.

Then admit that, in like manner, the objects of knowledge not only derive from the good the gift of being known, but are further endowed by it with a real and essential existence; though the good, far from being identical with real existence, actually transcends it in dignity and power.

Hereupon Glaucon exclaimed with a very amusing air, Good heavens! what a miraculous superiority!

Well, I said, you are a person to blame, because you compel me to state my opinions on the subject.

Nay, let me entreat you not to stop, till you have at all events gone over again your similitude of the sun, if you are leaving anything out.

Well, to say the truth, I am leaving out a great deal.

Then pray do not omit even a trifle.

I fancy I shall leave much unsaid; however, if I can help it under the circumstances, I will not intentionally make any omission.

Pray do not.

Now understand that, according to us, there are two powers reigning, one over an intellectual, and the other over a visible region and class of objects; — if I were to use the term 'firmament,' you might think I was playing on the word. Well then, are you in possession of these as two kinds, — one visible, the other intellectual?

Yes, I am.

Suppose you take a line divided into two unequal parts, — one to represent the visible class of objects, the other the intellectual, — and divide each part again into two segments on the same scale. Then, if you make the lengths of the segments represent degrees of distinctness or indistinctness, one of the two segments of the part which stands for the visible world will represent all images: — meaning by images, first of all, shadows; and, in the next place, reflections in water, and in closegrained, smooth, bright substances, and everything of the kind, if you understand me.

Yes, I do understand.

Let the other segment stand for the real objects corresponding to these images, — namely, the animals about us, and the whole world of nature and of art.

Very good.

Would you also consent to say that, with reference to this class, there is, in point of truth and untruthfulness, the same distinction between the copy and the original, that there is between what is matter of opinion and what is matter of knowledge?

Certainly I should.

Then let us proceed to consider how we must divide that part of the whole line which represents the intellectual world.

How must we do it?

Thus: one segment of it will represent what the soul is compelled to investigate by the aid of the segments of the other part, which it employs as images, starting from hypotheses, and travelling not to a first principle, but to a conclusion. The other segment will represent the objects of the soul, as it makes its way from an hypothesis to a first principle which is not hypothetical, unaided by those images which the former division employs, and shaping its journey by the sole help of real essential forms.

I have not understood your description so well as I could wish.

Then we will try again. You will understand me more easily when I have made some previous observations. I think you know that the students of subjects like geometry and calculation, assume by way of materials, in each investigation, all odd and even numbers, figures, three kinds of angles, and other similar data. These things they are supposed to know, and having adopted them as hypotheses, they decline to give any account of them, either to themselves or to others, on the assumption that they are self-evident; and, making these their starting point, they proceed to travel through the remainder of the subject, and arrive at last, with perfect unanimity, at that which they have proposed as the object of investigation.

I am perfectly aware of the fact, he replied.

Then you also know that they summon to their aid visible forms, and discourse about them, though their thoughts are busy not with these forms, but with their originals, and though they discourse not with a view to the particular square and diameter which they draw, but with a view to the absolute square and the absolute diameter, and so on. For while they employ by way of images those figures and diagrams aforesaid, which again have their shadows and images in water, they are really endeavoring to behold those abstractions which a person can only see with the eye of thought.

True.

This, then, was the class of things which I called intellectual; but I said that the soul is constrained to employ hypotheses while engaged in the investigation of them, — not travelling to a first principle, (because it is unable to step out of, and mount above, its hypotheses,) but using, as images, just the copies that are presented by things below, — which copies, as compared with the originals, are vulgarly esteemed distinct and valued accordingly.

I understand you to be speaking of the subject-matter of the various branches of geometry and the kindred arts.

Again, by the second segment of the intellectual world understand me to mean all that the mere reasoning process apprehends by the force of dialectic, when it avails itself of hypotheses not as first principles, but as genuine hypotheses, that is to say, as stepping-stones and impulses, whereby it may force its way up to something that is not hypothetical, and arrive at the first principle of everything, and seize it in its grasp; which done, it turns round, and takes hold of that which takes hold of this first principle, till at last it comes down to a conclusion, calling in the aid of no sensible object whatever, but simply employing abstract, self-subsisting forms, and terminating in the same.

I do not understand you so well as I could wish, for I believe you to be describing an arduous task; but at any rate I understand that you wish to declare distinctly, that the field of real existence and pure intellect, as contemplated by the science of dialectic, is more certain than the field investigated by what are called the arts, in which hypotheses constitute first principles, which the students are compelled, it is true, to contemplate with the mind and not with the senses; but, at the same time, as they do not come back, in the course of inquiry, to a first principle, but push on from hypothetical premises, you think that they do not exercise pure reason on the questions that engage them, although taken in connexion with a first principle these questions come within the domain of the pure reason. And I believe you apply the term understanding, not pure reason, to the mental habit of such people as geometricians, — regarding understanding as something intermediate between opinion and pure reason.

You have taken in my meaning most satisfactorily; and I beg you will accept these four mental states, as corresponding to the four segments, — namely pure reason corresponding to the highest, understanding to the second, belief to the third, and conjecture to the last; and pray arrange them in gradation, and believe them to partake of distinctness in a degree corresponding to the truth of their respective objects.

I understand you, said he. I quite agree with you, and will arrange them as you desire.

BOOK X. THE SOUL'S IMMORTALITY

Steph. 609.

AGAIN: do you maintain that everything has its evil, and its good? Do you say, for example, that the eyes are liable to the evil of ophthalmia, the entire body to disease, corn to mildew, timber to rot, copper and iron to rust, or, in other words, that almost everything is liable to some connatural evil and malady?

I do.

And is it not the case that, whenever an object is attacked by one of these maladies, it is impaired, and, in the end, completely broken up and destroyed by it?

Doubtless it is so.

Hence everything is destroyed by its own connatural evil and vice; otherwise, if it be not destroyed by this, there is nothing else that can corrupt it. For that which is good will never destroy anything, nor yet that which is neither good nor evil.

Of course not.

If then we can find among existing things one which is liable to a particular evil, which can indeed mar it, but cannot break it up or destroy it, shall we not be at once certain that a thing so constituted can never perish?

That would be a reasonable conclusion.

Well, then, is not the soul liable to a malady which renders it evil?

Certainly it is; all those things which we were lately discussing, — injustice, intemperance, cowardice, and ignorance, — produce that result.

That being the case, does any one of these things bring about the dissolution and destruction of the soul? Turn it over well in your mind, that we may not be misled by supposing that, when the crimes of the unjust and foolish man are found out, he is destroyed by his injustice, which is a depraved state of the soul. No, consider the case thus. The depravity of the body, that is to say, disease, wastes and destroys the body, and reduces it to a state in which it ceases to be a body; and all the things, which we named just now, are brought by their own proper vice, which corrupts them by its adhesion or indwelling, to a state in which they cease to exist. I am right, am I not?

Yes.

Then proceed to examine the soul on the same method. Is it true that, when injustice and other vices reside in the soul, they corrupt and wither it by contact or indwelling, until they have brought it to death, and severed it from the body?

Certainly, they do not produce that effect.

Well but, on the other hand, it is irrational to suppose that a thing can be destroyed by the depravity of another thing, though it cannot be destroyed by its own.

True, it is irrational.

Yes it is, Glaucon; for you must remember that we do not imagine that a body is to be destroyed by the proper depravity of its food, whatever that may be, whether mouldiness or rottenness or anything else. But if the depravity of the food itself produces in the body a disorder proper to the body, we shall assert that the body has been destroyed by its food remotely, but by its own proper vice, or disease, immediately: and we shall always disclaim the notion that the body can be corrupted by the depravity of its food, which is a different thing from the body, — that is to say, the notion that the body can be corrupted by an alien evil, without the introduction of its own native evil.

You are perfectly correct.

Then according to the same reasoning, I continued, unless depravity of body introduces into the soul depravity of soul, let us never suppose that the soul can be destroyed by an alien evil without the presence of its own peculiar disease; for that would be to suppose that one thing can be destroyed by the evil of another thing.

That is a reasonable statement.

Well then, let us either refute this doctrine and point out our mistake, or else, so long as it remains unrefuted, let us never assert that a fever, or any other disease, or fatal violence, or even the act of cutting up the entire body into the smallest possible pieces, can have any tendency to destroy the soul, until it has been demonstrated, that, in consequence of this treatment of the body, the soul itself becomes more unjust and more unholy. For, so long as a thing is exempt from its own proper evil, while an evil foreign to it appears in another subject, let us not allow it to be said that this thing, whether it be a soul or anything else, is in danger of being destroyed.

Well, certainly no one will ever prove that the souls of the dying become more unjust in consequence of death.

But in case any one should venture to encounter the argument, and to assert that the dying man becomes more depraved and unjust, in order to save himself from being compelled to admit that the soul is immortal, I suppose we shall infer that, if the objector is right, injustice is as fatal as a disease to its possessor; and we shall expect those who catch this essentially deadly disorder to die by its agency, quickly or slowly, according to the violence of the attack; instead of finding, as we do at present, that the unjust are put to death in consequence of their injustice, by the agency of other people who punish them for their crimes.

Then really, said he, injustice cannot be thought such a very dreadful thing, if it is to be fatal to its owner; because in that case it will be a release from evils. But I am inclined to think that, on the contrary, we shall find that it kills other people if it can, while it endows its possessor with peculiar vitality, and with sleeplessness as well as vitality. So widely and permanently is it removed, to all appearance, from any tendency to destroy its owner.

You say well, I replied. For surely when the soul cannot be killed and destroyed by its own depravity and its own evil, hardly will the evil, which is charged with the destruction of another thing, destroy a soul or anything else, beyond its own appropriate object.

Yes, hardly; at least that is the natural inference.

Hence, as it is destroyed by no evil at all, whether foreign to it or its own, it is clear that the soul must be always existing, and therefore immortal.

It must.

Well then, I continued, let us consider this proved. And, if so, you understand that the souls that exist must be always the same. For, if none be destroyed, they cannot become fewer. Nor yet can they become more numerous; because if any class of things immortal became more numerous, you know that something mortal must have contributed to swell its numbers; in which case, everything would finally be immortal.

True.

But reason will forbid our entertaining this opinion, which we must therefore disavow. On the other hand, do not let us imagine that the soul in its essential nature, and viewed by itself, can possibly be fraught with abundance of variety, unlikeness, and disagreement.

What do you mean?

A thing cannot easily be eternal, as we have just proved the soul to be, if it is compounded of many parts, and if the mode of composition employed is not the very best.

Probably it cannot.

ARISTOTLE

(384–322)

PSYCHOLOGY

Translated from the * Greek by

WILLIAM ALEXANDER HAMMOND

BOOK II. THE FACULTIES OF THE SOUL

CHAPTER I. DEFINITION OF THE SOUL

412a

LET the foregoing † suffice as a discussion of the traditional theories of the soul; and now let us resume our subject from the start, and attempt to determine the nature of the soul and its most general definition. One class of realities we call 'substance.' This 'substance' may be regarded on the one hand as matter, which in itself is no definite thing; on the other hand, as form and idea, in terms of which definite individuality is ascribed to a thing. A third meaning of substance is the composite of matter and form. Matter is potentiality; form is actuality or realization. The latter may be looked at in two ways, either as complete realization, — comparable with perfected knowledge, or as realization in process, — comparable with the activity of contemplation. The notion of substance appears to be most generally employed in the sense of body, and particularly of physical body; for this is the source of all other bodies. Some physical bodies have, and others have not, life. By life we understand an inherent principle of nutrition, growth, and decay. So that every natural body endowed with life would be substance, and substance in this composite sense.

---

* From Ἀριστέλους περὶ ψυχῆς. Reprinted from Aristotle's *Psychology, A Treatise on the Principle of Life*, translated by W. A. Hammond, London, Swan Sonnenschein & Co. Ltd. 1902.

† Supra, pp. 5-11.

The body, therefore, would not be soul, since body is of such nature that life is an attribute of it. For body is not predicated of something else, but is rather itself substrate and matter. The soul must, then, be substance in this sense: it is the form of a natural body endowed with the capacity of life. In this meaning substance is the completed realization. Soul, therefore, will be the completed realization of a body such as described. Complete realization is employed in two senses. In the one sense it is comparable with perfected knowledge; in another, it is comparable with the active process of contemplation. It is evident that we mean by it here that realization which corresponds to perfected knowledge. Now, both waking and sleeping are included in the soul's existence: waking corresponds to active contemplation; sleep to attained and inactive knowledge. In a given case science is earlier in origin than observation. Soul, then, is the first entelechy of a natural body endowed with the capacity of life. Such a body one would describe as organic. The parts of plants are also organs, although quite simple in character, *e.g.* the leaf is the covering of the pericarp, and the pericarp is covering of the fruit; the roots are analogous to mouths, both being channels of nutrition. If then we were obliged to give a general description applicable to all soul or life, we should say that it is the first entelechy of a natural organic body. It is therefore unnecessary to ask whether body and soul are one, as one should not ask whether the wax and the figure are one, or, in general, whether the matter of a particular thing and the thing composed of it are one. For although unity and being are predicated in several senses, their proper sense is that of perfect realization.

We have now given a general definition of the soul. We have defined it as an entity which realizes an idea. It is the essential notion which we ascribe to a body of a given kind. As an illustration, suppose that an instrument, *e.g.* an axe, were a natural body. Here the notion of axe constitutes its essential nature or reality, and this would be its soul. Were this taken away it would no longer be an axe, except in the sense of a homonym. It is in reality, however, merely an axe, and of a body of this sort soul is not the notional essence and the idea, but soul applies only to a natural body of a given kind, viz. a body whose principle of movement and rest is in itself. The principle expressed here should be observed in its application to particular parts of the body. For if the eye were an animal, vision would be its soul, *i.e.* vision is the notional essence of the eye. The eye, however, is the matter of vision, and if the vision be wanting the eye is no longer an eye, save in the meaning of a homonym, as a stone eye or a painted eye. What applies here to a particular member, must also apply to the entire living body; for as the particular sensation is related to the particular organ of sense, so is the whole of sensation related to the entire sensitive organism, in so far as it has sensation. 'Potentiality of life' does not refer to a thing which has become dispossessed of soul, but to that which possesses it. Seed and fruit are potentially living bodies. As cutting is the realization of the axe, and vision is the realization of the eye, so is the waking state the realization of the living body; and as vision and capacity are related to the organ, so is the soul related to the body. Body is the potential substrate. But as vision and pupil on the one hand constitute the eye, so soul and body in the other case constitute the living animal. It is, therefore, clear that the soul is not separable from the body; and the same holds good of particular parts of the soul, if its nature admits of division, for in some cases the soul is the realization of these very parts; not but that there are certain other parts where nothing forbids their possible separation, because they are not realizations of any bodily nature. And yet it is uncertain whether the soul as realization of the body is separable from it in a sense analogous to the separability of sailor and boat. Let this suffice as a definition and outline sketch of the soul.

CHAPTER II. THE PRINCIPLE OF LIFE

INASMUCH as the certain and the conceptually more knowable is derived from what is uncertain, but sensibly more apparent, we must resume the investigation of the soul from this standpoint. For it is necessary that the definition show not merely what a thing is, as most definitions do, but it must also contain and exhibit the cause of its being what it is. In reality, the terms of definitions are ordinarily stated in the form of conclusions. What, *e.g.*, is the definition of squaring? The reply is that squaring is the conversion of a figure of unequal sides into a right-angled equilateral figure equal to the former. Such a definition is the expression of a conclusion. But to define squaring as the discovery of a mean proportional line is to define the thing in terms of its cause. Resuming our inquiry, we say, therefore, that the animate is distinguished from the inanimate by the principle of life. But inasmuch as life is predicated in several senses, *e.g.* in the sense of reason, sensation, local movement and rest, and furthermore movement in the sense of nutrition, decay, and growth; if any one of these is discerned in a thing we say that it has life. All plants, therefore, are supposed to have life; for evidently they have within them a potency and principle whereby they experience growth and decay in opposite processes. For their growth is not merely upwards or downwards, but in both these directions alike and in every point where nutrition takes place, and they continue to live as long as they are capable of nutrition. Now this faculty of nutrition is separable from the other forms of life, but the other forms cannot exist in perishable creatures apart from this principle of nutrition. This is made clear in the instance of plants; for they have no other capacity of soul (or life) than this nutritive one. Owing to this fundamental principle of nourishment, therefore, life is found in all animated living things, but the primary mark which distinguishes an animal from other forms of life is the possession of sensation. For even those creatures which are incapable of locomotion or change of place, but which possess sensation, are called animals and are not merely said to live. Touch is the primary form of sensation and is found in all animals. But as the nutritive faculty is separable from touch and sensation in general, so touch can exist apart from the other forms of sensation. By the nutritive power we understand that part of the soul in which plants share; and by the sensation of touch we mean that capacity which all animals possess. We shall later on give the explanation of these phenomena.

For the present let it suffice that the soul is the causal principle of the aforesaid phenomena, and is defined in terms of them, I mean, in terms of nutrition, sensation, reason, motion. To the question whether each of these forms of life is a soul or a part of the soul; and, if a part, whether in the sense that the part is only notionally separable or really separable in space, — the reply is in some respects easy and in others difficult. For in the case of plants, some of them appear to live when they are divided up and the parts are separated from each other, indicating that there is in each of these plants in actuality an unitary soul, but in potentiality several souls. And we observe the same thing taking place in different varieties of soul, as *e.g.* in the case of insects which have been dismembered. Here each part is capable of sensation and locomotion, but if it is capable of sensation it is also capable of imagination and impulse. For where there is sensation, there is also pleasure and pain, and where there is pleasure and pain there is necessarily also desire. Now in regard to reason and the speculative faculty, we have as yet no certain evidence, but it seems to be a generically distinct type of soul and it alone is capable of existing in a state of separation from the body, as the eternal is separable from the mortal. The remaining parts of the soul, however, are from the foregoing considerations evidently not separable, as some assert. But that they are notionally separable, is clear; for if perceiving is distinct from opining, the faculty of sensation or perception is distinct from that whereby we opine, and each of these is in turn distinct from the faculties above mentioned. Furthermore, all of these are found in some animals, while only certain of them are found in others, and in still others only a single one (and this is the cause of distinctions amongst animals). The reason for this must be investigated hereafter. A parallel instance is found in regard to sensation; some animals possess all the faculties of sense, others only certain of them, and still others only the single most fundamental one, viz. touch.

The principle by which we live and have sensation, then, is employed in a twofold sense. Similarly, we employ the principle by which we know in a twofold sense, viz. science and the knowing mind (for we say we know by means of each of these), and in a like manner the principle by virtue of which we are healthy is in one sense health itself, and in another sense a part of the body or the whole of it. In these cases knowledge and health constitute the form, notion, idea, and, as it were, the realization of a potential subject, — the one of a knowing subject and the other of a healthy one, (realization is supposed to attach to that which has power to effect changes and is found in a passive and recipient subject). The soul is that principle by which in an ultimate sense we live and feel and think; so that it is a sort of idea and form, not matter and substrate. Now, substance is employed, as we have said, in a threefold meaning, viz. as form, as matter, and as a composite of these two. Amongst these meanings of substance matter signifies potentiality; form signifies actuality or complete realization. Inasmuch as it is the composite which is the animate creature, body cannot be regarded as the complete realization of the soul, but the soul is the realization of a given body. The conjecture, therefore, appears well founded that the soul does not exist apart from a body nor is it a particular body. The soul is not itself body, but it is a certain aspect of body, and is consequently found in a body, and furthermore in a body of such and such a kind. It is not to be regarded as it was amongst our predecessors who thought that it is introduced into body without prior determination of the particular sort of body, although no casual subject appears capable of undergoing any casual or haphazard effect.[1] This same result is also reached by an analysis of the notion itself; for complete realization in every instance is naturally found in a definite potentiality and in an appropriate matter. From this it is evident that the soul is a kind of realization and expressed idea of a determinate potentiality.

[1] Trendelenburg thinks the Pythagoreans are meant here, owing to their doctrine of transmigration of souls. Cf. *De anima*, 407 b 22.

*CHAPTER III. THE VARIOUS MEANINGS OF
THE SOUL*

In some creatures, as we have said, all of the above mentioned psychic powers are found, in others certain of them, and in still others only one. By powers we mean here the power of nutrition, of appetite, of sensation, of movement in space, and of rational thought. In plants, only the nutritive power is found; in other creatures the power of sensation is added. If sensation is added, impulse or appetite is also implied. For appetite includes desire and impulse and wish. All animals have at least one sense — touch; and to whatever creature sensation is given, to it are also given pleasure and pain, and objects appear to be pleasant or painful. Creatures which distinguish these, possess also desire; for desire is an impulse towards what is pleasant. Further, animals possess a sense for food, and this is the sense of touch; for all animals are nourished by means of the dry and moist, the warm and cold, and it is touch which apprehends these. It is only incidentally that animals discern food through other sensible qualities; neither sound nor colour nor smell contributes at all to food. Flavour, however, is one of the haptic qualities. Hunger and thirst are desires; hunger is a desire of the dry and warm; thirst a desire of the cool and moist, and flavour is a sort of seasoning in these objects. We must explain these subjects minutely hereafter; for the present let the statement suffice, that amongst animals where we find touch we find appetite also. The subject of imagination in animals is uncertain and must be investigated later. In addition to these attributes we find amongst some animals the power of local movement and in others we find the power of understanding and reason, as in man and in other creatures that are, if there be such, similar or superior to man. It is evident that a single definition can be applied to soul in the same way as a single definition can be applied to figure. As in the latter case, there is no figure beyond that of the triangle and its derivations, so in the former case there is no soul beyond those enumerated. A common definition might also be applied to figures which would fit them all and be peculiar to no particular figure. The same holds good in the case of the above mentioned types of soul. It is, therefore, absurd, both in these instances and in others, to search for a common definition which shall not apply to any individual real thing nor to any peculiar and irreducible species, thereby neglecting the particular meaning in the general. The facts touching the soul are parallel to this case of figure; for both in figures and in animate creatures, the prior always exists potentially in the later, *e.g.* the triangle is contained potentially in the square and the nutritive power in that of sensation. We must, therefore, investigate the nature of the soul in particular things, *e.g.* in a plant, a man, or a lower animal. And we must consider the cause of their order of succession. The sensitive soul, for example, presupposes the nutritive, but in the case of plants the nutritive exists apart from the sensitive. Again, the sense of touch is presupposed by all the other senses, but touch exists apart from them and does not presuppose them. Many animals have no sense of sight, hearing, or smell. Some that are capable of sensation have also power of local movement, others have not; finally the smallest number possess the power of reason and understanding. Mortal creatures who possess the power of reason, possess all the other psychic faculties, but those which have each of these others do not all have the power of reason, and certain of them do not even possess imagination, while still others live by this alone. At another time we shall give an account of the speculative reason. It is evident, however, that this account touching each particular form of soul is also the most fitting description of the soul in general.

CHAPTER IV. THE SOUL AND FINAL CAUSE

IF one intends to make an investigation of the faculties of the soul, it is necessary first to inquire into their several natures, and then by the same method to inquire further into other related problems. If, then, one is obliged to describe the nature of each several faculty, *e.g.* the nature of the faculty of reason, of sense-perception, or of nutrition, one must first be able to say what thinking and sense-perception mean. For the activities and processes are notionally prior to the faculties to which they belong. If this is true, we must further observe the objects of the activities before the activities themselves, and we should for the same reason first determine our position regarding these objects, *e.g.* regarding food, the sensible, and the intelligible. First, then, we must speak of food and generation. For the nutritive power is found in all living things, and is the primary and most universal faculty of soul, by virtue of which all creatures possess life. Its functions are to procreate, and to assimilate food. In all animals that are perfect and not abnormal, or that are not spontaneously generated, it is the most natural function to beget another being similar to itself, an animal to beget another animal, a plant another plant, in order that they attain, as far as possible, the immortal and divine; for this is what every creature aims at, and this is the final cause of every creature's natural life. We understand by final cause two things: the purpose aimed at, and the person who is served by the purpose. Since it is impossible for an individual to partake of the immortal and divine in its own continuous life, because no perishable creature continues self-identical and numerically one, it partakes therefore of the immortal in that way in which it is able to share it, one thing in a higher degree and another in a lower; it does not itself abide, but only a similar self abides; in its continuity it is not numerically, but only specifically, one.

The soul is the cause and principle of a living body. These terms are used in several senses. Corresponding to these differences, the soul is referred to as cause in three distinct meanings; for it is cause in the sense of the source of movement, of final cause, and as the real substance of animate bodies. That it is a cause in the sense of real substance is evident, for real substance is in every case the cause of being, and the being of animals is their life, and soul is the cause and principle of life. Furthermore, it is the complete realization that gives us the real significance of a potential being. Soul is also evidently cause in the sense of final cause. For nature, like reason, acts with purpose, and this purpose is its end. In animals the soul is, by virtue of its nature, a principle similar to this. For the soul uses all natural bodies as its instruments, the bodies of animals and the bodies of plants alike, which exist for the soul as their end. End is used in two senses: the purpose, and the person or thing which the purpose serves. Soul also means the primary source of local movement. This power of local movement is not possessed by all living creatures. Transformation and growth are also due to the soul. For sense-perception is supposed to be a kind of transformation, and nothing is capable of sense-perception unless it has a soul. The case is similar with growth and decay. For nothing grows or decays by natural processes unless it admit of nutrition, and nothing is capable of nutrition unless it has a soul. Empedocles ascribes downward growth to plants where they are rooted, because the earth naturally tends downward, and upward growth, because fire tends in that direction, and in these respects is not right. For Empedocles does not employ the terms 'up' and 'down' correctly. 'Up' and 'down' are not the same for all things nor in all parts of the universe, for roots are to plants what the head is to animals, if one is to describe organs as identical or different in terms of their functions. In addition, what principle is it that holds together these two elements of fire and earth, tending, as they do, in opposite directions? For they will scatter asunder, if there be no hindering principle. And if there is such a principle, it is the soul and the cause of growth and nourishment. Some regard fire as the real cause of nutrition and growth. For this seems to be the only body or element that feeds and increases itself. One might, therefore, conjecture that this is the element that causes growth and nutrition in animals and plants. In a certain sense, it is true, fire is a co-ordinate cause, but not the absolute cause, of growth; this is rather the soul. For the growth of fire is indeterminate so long as there is material to burn; on the other hand, in all bodies developed in nature there is a limit and significance to size and growth. These attributes ([of limit and significance]) belong to soul, not to fire, to reason rather than to matter.

Since the same power of the soul is both nutritive and generative, we must first investigate nutrition; for it is by this function of nutrition that the faculty in question is distinguished from other faculties. Nutrition is supposed to take place by the law of opposites, although not every opposite is nourished by every other, but such opposites only as derive both their origin and their growth from each other. Many things are derived from one another, but they are not all quantitative changes, as *e.g.* healthy from sickly. Nutrition is not applied to these cases in the same sense, for while water is nutriment for fire, fire does not nourish water. The opposites of food and nourishment appear to apply particularly to simple bodies. There is, however, a difficulty here. For there are some who maintain that like is nourished by like, as like is also increased by like, while others, as we said, affirm the converse of this, viz., that opposites are nourished by opposites, on the ground that like is incapable of being affected by like. Food, however, undergoes transformation and is digested, and transformation is in every case toward the opposite or the intermediate. Further, food is affected by the body which assimilates it; the latter, however, is not affected by the food, just as the builder is not affected by his material, although the material undergoes change through him. The builder merely passes from a state of inactivity into one of activity. The question whether nourishment is to be understood to apply to the final condition in which it is taken up by the body, or to its original condition, creates a difficulty. If both are meant, only in the one case the food is indigested and in the other digested, it would be possible to speak of nourishment conformably to both of the above theories; for in so far as it is indigested, we should have opposite nourished by opposite; in so far as it is digested, we should have like nourished by like; so that in a certain sense, it is evident they are both right and both wrong. Since nothing is nourished which does not share life, the object of nutrition would be an animate body as animate; so that food is determined by its relation to an animate object and is not accidental. There is a difference between the nourishment and the principle of growth; in so far as the animate thing is quantitative, the notion of growth applies; in so far as it is a particular substance, the notion of nourishment. For food preserves a being as a substantial thing, and it continues to exist so long as it is nourished. Nourishment is productive of generation, not the generation of the nourished thing, but of a being similar to it. For the former exists already as a reality, and nothing generates, but merely preserves, itself. So then, such a principle of the soul as we have described is a power capable of preserving that in which this principle is found, in so far as it is found; nourishment equips it for action. When, therefore, it is deprived of nourishment, it can no longer exist. Since there are three distinct things here: the object nourished, the means of nourishment, and the power that causes nutrition, we shall say that it is the elemental soul that causes nutrition, the object nourished is the body which possesses this soul, and the means of nourishment is the food. And since it is fair to give everything a name in terms of its end, and since here the end of the soul is to generate a creature like to itself, the elemental soul might be called generative of that which is like to itself. The means of nourishment is used in two senses, as is also the means of steering a ship; for one may refer to the hand, or to the rudder, the one being both actively moving and moved; the other only passively moved. All nutriment must be capable of being digested; heat is the element which accomplishes digestion. Everything animate, therefore, possesses heat. We have explained now, in outline, what nutriment is. The subject must be more minutely treated later on in its proper place.

CHAPTER V. SENSATION AND THOUGHT

Now that we have arrived at the foregoing conclusions, let us discuss in general the entire question of sense-perception. It consists, as we have said, in being moved and affected; for it is supposed to be a sort of internal transformation. Some maintain that like is affected by like. In what sense this is possible and in what sense impossible, I have explained in a general treatise *On Activity and Passivity*. A difficulty is raised by the question why it is that perceptions do not arise from the senses themselves, and why it is that without external stimuli they produce no sensation, although fire and earth, and the other elements of which we have sense-perception, are, either in their essential nature or in their attributes, found in the senses. It is, therefore, evident that the organ of sense-perception is not a thing in actuality but only in potentiality. It is consequently analogous to the combustible which does not itself ignite without something to set it ablaze. Otherwise it would have burned itself and had no need of an active fire. Inasmuch as we say that perceiving is used in two meanings (*e.g.* we call the capacity to hear and see, hearing and sight, although they may chance to be dormant, and we apply the same terms where the senses are actively exercised), so sense-perception also would be used in two senses, the one potential and the other actual. First of all let us understand that the terms affection, motion, and activity, are used in the same meaning. For motion is a sort of activity, although incomplete, as we have said elsewhere. Everything is affected and set in motion by an active agent and by something that exists in activity. Therefore in one sense a thing is affected by like, in another by unlike, as we have said; for it is the unlike that is affected, but after being affected it is like.

We must, further, make a distinction touching potentiality and actuality, for we are now using these terms in a general sense. There is a sense in which we speak of a thing as knowing, as when we call man knowing, because man belongs to the class of creatures that know and are endowed with knowledge. There is another sense in which we speak of a man as possessing the particular knowledge of grammar. In each of these cases a man possesses knowledge potentially, but not in the same sense; the former is knowing as belonging to a certain genus and as having a native endowment; the latter is knowing in the sense of being able to exercise his knowledge at will, when nothing external prevents. In a still different sense there is the man who is actually exercising his knowledge, and is in a condition of complete realization, having in the strict sense knowledge of a particular thing, as *e.g.* A. The first two know in a potential sense; the one of them, however, knows when he is transformed through a discipline of knowledge, and has passed repeatedly out of an opposite condition; the other knows in the sense of possessing arithmetical or grammatical science; and their passing from non-actual to actual knowledge is different. Again, neither is the term 'passivity' used in an absolute meaning: in one meaning, it is destruction by an opposite principle; in another meaning, it is the preservation of the potentially existent by means of the actual and similar, just as potentiality is related to actuality. That which possesses potential knowledge, for instance, comes to the actual use of it — a transition that we must either not call transformation (for the added element belongs to its own nature and tends to its own realization), or else we must call it a special kind of transformation. It is, therefore, incorrect to speak of thinking as a transformation when one thinks, just as the builder is not transformed when he is building a house. That which conduces to actualization out of a potential state in the matter of reasoning and thinking is not fairly called teaching, but must be given another name. Again, that which passes out of a potential state by learning or by acquiring knowledge at the hands of what actually knows and can teach, must either not be said to be affected as a passive subject, or we must admit two meanings of transformation, the one a change into a negative condition and the other into a positive condition and the thing's natural state.

The first change in the sentient subject is wrought by the generating parent, but after birth the creature comes into the possession of sense-perception as a species of knowledge. Active sensation is used in a way similar to active thinking. There is, however, this difference, that the objects which produce sensation are external, *e.g.* the visible and the audible, and similarly other sensible qualities. The reason for this is that active sense-perception refers to particular things, while scientific knowledge refers to the universal. These universals, however, are, in a certain sense, in the mind itself. Therefore it is in one's power to think when one wills, but to experience sense-perception is not thus in one's power; for a sensible object must first be present. This also holds good of those sciences which deal with sensible realities, and for the same reason, viz. because these sensible realities belong to the world of particular and external phenomena.

To go into the details of these questions would be more suitable at another time. For the present so much may be regarded as fixed, viz. that the term 'potential' is not used in any absolute sense, but in one case its meaning is similar to our saying that a boy has in him the potentiality of a general, and in another case to our saying that a man in his prime has that potentiality — a distinction which also applies to the capacity for sense-perception. Inasmuch as this distinction has no particular name in our language, although we have remarked that the things are different and how they differ, we must simply employ the terms affection and transformation as applicable here. That which is capable of sense-perception is, as we have said, potentially what the sensible is actually. It is, therefore, affected at a moment when it is unlike, but when it has been affected it becomes like and is as its object.

CHAPTER VI. SENSE QUALITIES

IN discussing any form of sense-perception we must begin with the sensible object. The 'object of sense' is used in three meanings, two of which touch the essential nature of sensation and one its accidents. Of the two first-named, one applies specially to each particular sense, the other is common to them all. By 'peculiar object of sense' I mean a sense-quality which cannot be apprehended by a sense different from that to which it belongs, and concerning which that sense cannot be deceived, e.g. colour is the peculiar object of vision, sound of hearing, flavour of taste. Touch, however, discriminates several sense-qualities. The other particular senses, on the contrary, distinguish only their peculiar objects, and the senses are not deceived in the fact that a quality is colour or sound, although they may be deceived as to what or where the coloured or sonorous object may be. Such qualities are called the peculiar objects of particular senses, whereas common objects are motion, rest, number, form, magnitude. Properties of the latter kind are not the peculiar objects of any sense, but are common to them all. Motion is apprehended by touch and by sight. A thing is an object of sense accidentally, *e.g.* when a white object proves to be the son of Diares. The latter is perceived accidentally, for the person whom one perceives is an accident of the white object. Therefore, the sense as such is not affected by the sensible object ([as a person]). To the objects of sense, strictly regarded, belong such properties as are peculiarly and properly sense-qualities, and it is with these that the essential nature of each sense is naturally concerned.

BOOK III.   SENSATION, IMAGINATION AND THOUGHT

CHAPTER I.   THE 'COMMON SENSIBLES'

THAT there is no additional sense beyond the five we have enumerated (I mean sight, hearing, smell, taste, and touch), one may believe from the following considerations. Granted that we really have perception of everything for which touch is the appropriate sense (for all the qualities of the tangible as such are apprehended by touch), it is necessary that if any sensation is lacking, some organ must also be lacking in us. Whatever we perceive by contact is perceived by the sense of touch, with which we are endowed. On the other hand, whatever we perceive through media and not by direct contact, is perceived by simple elements, such as air and water. The conditions here are such that if several sensible objects which differ from each other generically are perceived by a single medium, then anyone who has a sense-organ analogous to this medium must be capable of perceiving these several sense-objects. For example, if the sense-organ is composed of air and the air is the medium of both sound and colour, the organ would perceive both these sense-qualities. If, on the other hand, several elements are mediators of the same sense-qualities, as *e.g.* colour is mediated both by air and water (for both are diaphanous), then the organ which contains one of these elements alone will perceive that which is mediated by both of them. The sense-organs are composed exclusively of these two simple elements, air and water (for the pupil of the eye is composed of water, the hearing of air, smell of one or the other of these). Fire, however, belongs to no organ or it is common to them all (for nothing is sentient without heat). Earth belongs either to no organ or it is chiefly and in a special manner combined with touch. Nothing would remain, therefore, excepting air and water, to constitute a sense-organ. Some animals have, in actual fact, these organs as described. Animals which are perfect and not defective have all these senses. For even the mole, as one may observe, has eyes underneath its skin. Consequently, unless there are bodies other than those known to us, or qualities other than those which belong to earthly bodies, we may conclude there is no sense lacking in us.

Neither is it possible that there should be any peculiar organ for the perception of common properties such as we perceive accidentally by means of the individual senses, *e.g.* common properties like motion, rest, form, magnitude, number, unity. For all these properties we perceive by means of motion, *e.g.* magnitude is perceived by motion. So also is form, for form is a sort of magnitude, and rest we perceive from the absence of motion. We perceive numbers by the negation of continuity and by the special senses, for each sensation is experienced as a unit. So, then, it is clearly impossible that any particular sense should apply to these common properties, such as motion. For this would be like one now perceiving the sweet by means of sight. This is because we happen to have senses for both qualities ([*i.e.* for the sweet and for colour]), whereby when the given qualities coincide in one object, we recognize the object as sweet. Otherwise we do not perceive the sweet, excepting in the sense of accident, as *e.g.* when we recognize the son of Cleon not because he is Cleon's son, but because he is a fair object, which for the son of Cleon is an accident.

We have indeed a 'common sense' for the perception of common qualities. I do not mean accidentally. It is therefore not a particular sense, for in that case we should perceive in no other way than as just now described in the illustration of Cleon. A sense, however, perceives accidentally the qualities that are peculiar to a different sense, not in their own nature but because of the unity of these qualities, as when two sense-qualities apply to the same object, *e.g.* in the case of bile that it is both bitter and yellow. Now, it is not the function of either particular sense to say that both these qualities inhere in one thing and it is owing to this fact that error arises, when in the case of a yellow substance one opines it to be bile. One might ask why we are endowed with several senses and not with one only. Is it not that facts of sequence and coincidence, such as motion, magnitude, and number, might the less escape us? For if we possessed sight only, and this were limited to the perception of whiteness, then all other distinctions would the more easily escape our knowledge, and because colour and magnitude are always coincident, they would appear to be identical. In point of fact, however, since these common qualities are found in different sense-objects, it is evident that the several qualities themselves are different.

CHAPTER II. THE 'COMMON SENSE'

But inasmuch as we perceive that we see and hear, we must have this consciousness of vision either by the instrument of sight or by some other faculty.[1] The same faculty will then apply both to sight and to colour, the object of sight. In this case, either we shall have two senses for the same thing, or a sense will be conscious of itself. Further, if there is another sense for the perception of sight, either we shall have an infinite regressus, or a given sense must finally be cognizant of itself, in which case one would better admit this in the instance of the

[1] This function of consciousness is performed by the ' sensus communis.'

original sense itself, *i.e.* sight. Here, however, is a difficulty. For, if sensation by means of sight is vision, and colour or that which possesses colour is what we see, then the seeing faculty itself must first of all have colour in order to be seen. It is plain, therefore, that sensation by means of sight is not employed in a single meaning. For even when we do not see, it is by means of sight that we judge both of darkness and light, although not in the same way. Furthermore, the seeing subject is in a certain sense saturated with colour, since each sentient organ receives into itself the sensible object without its matter. This explains the fact that when objects of sense have been removed, the sensations and images still persist in the sense-organ.

The actualization of the object of sense and of the sense itself is one and the same process; they are not, however, identical with each other in their essential nature. I mean, for instance, actual sound and actual hearing are not the same. For it is possible for one who has hearing not to hear, and for a sonorous body not to emit sound at every instant. When, however, that which has the potentiality of hearing and that which has the potentiality of sounding, actually hear and actually emit sound, at that moment the realized hearing and the realized sound are simultaneously complete, and one would call them respectively the sensation of hearing and the act of sounding. If, then, movement, activity, and passivity are implied in the produced object, it must be that actual sound and hearing exist in a potential state. For creative and motive activity is given in antecedent passivity. It is, therefore, not necessary for the moving principle to be itself in actual motion. For as action and passion find their expression in the object acted upon and not in the producing agent, so too the actualization of the sensible object and the sense-organ is expressed in the latter. The actualization of a sonorous body is sound or sounding; the actualization of the hearing organ is audition or hearing. For hearing is twofold and sound is twofold, and the same statement applies to other senses and sense-objects. In some instances the two have a distinct name, as *e.g.* hearing and sounding; in other instances one of the two is nameless. For the actualization of sight is called seeing, but the actualization of colour has no name; the actualization of the organ of taste is called tasting, while the actualization of flavour is nameless. Inasmuch as the actualization of the sense-object and the sense-organ is one and the same process, although the two things differ in their essential nature, it is necessary that hearing and sound, in this sense, should be both either destroyed together or preserved together; and the same applies to flavour and taste, and to the other sense-correlates. This necessity does not, however, apply to the sense-correlates in their potential signification. On the contrary, the old naturalists were wrong here, supposing, as they did, that neither white nor black has existence apart from sight, nor flavour apart from taste. In one way they were right and in another wrong. For owing to the fact that sense and sense-object have a twofold signification, namely that of potentiality and that of actuality, their dictum was applicable to the one meaning, but not to the other. They applied it, however, to things absolutely which are not predicated absolutely.

If harmony is voice of a certain kind, and if voice and hearing are in a sense one and the same, and in another sense not one and the same, and if, further, harmony is a relation of parts, hearing must likewise be a relation of parts. It is for this reason ([*i.e.* because sensation is a kind of proportion]) that every excessive stimulus, whether acute or grave, disturbs hearing. In like manner the sense of taste is disturbed by excessive flavours, the sense of sight by extremely glaring or extremely faint colours, smell by excessive odours, whether cloying or acrid. Consequently, qualities are agreeable when, pure and unmixed, they are reduced to proportion, as *e.g.* the pungent, sweet, or saline, or in the domain of touch, the warm and cool. It is then that properties are pleasant. In general, the mixed, rather than the acute or grave alone, is harmony. And sensation is proportion. Excessive stimuli either produce pain or pervert the organ.

Every sense is directed to its own peculiar sense-object; it is given in the sense-organ as such, and it distinguishes the different qualities in its appointed sense-object, as *e.g.* white and black in the case of sight, sweet and bitter in the case of taste. And the same can be said of other senses. Now inasmuch as we distinguish white, sweet, and every sense-quality by its relation to a particular sense, by what instrument do we perceive that these qualities differ from one another? We must do so by means of sensation, for they are sense-qualities. Is it not plain that the flesh is not the final organ of sense? For the judging subject would then necessarily distinguish an object by contact. Neither is it possible by means of the distinct senses to judge that sweet is different from white, but it is necessary that both these qualities be cognized by some one faculty; otherwise it would be like my perceiving one thing and you another, and so proving that they are different. A single faculty must, therefore, say that they are different. For the sweet is actually different from the white. One and the same faculty, then, must affirm this. And as this faculty affirms, so do thought and perception agree. It is clear that we cannot judge of distinct qualities by different senses, and we can conclude from this that we cannot judge of them at distinct intervals of time. For it is one and the same principle in us which says that the good is different from the bad. Further, it says that they are different and distinct at the moment when this affirmation is made. And *when* is not used here in an accidental sense, by which I mean: *when* does not apply merely to the time of the affirmation, *e.g.* I *say now* that it is different, but it applies also to the thing affirmed, I say that it is *different now, i.e.* the time applies to the assertion and thing coincidently. So the two elements here are inseparable, and are given in an indivisible moment of time. It is impossible for the same thing or an indivisible entity to undergo opposite processes simultaneously and in an indivisible moment of time. For if sweetness stimulates sensation or thought in one way, then bitter stimulates it in an opposite way and whiteness in some other way. Is, then, the judging principle[1] something at once numerically indivisible and inseparable, yet separable in the mode of its existence? There is a sense,

---

[1] The judging principle is the 'common sense.'

then, in which as divisible it perceives the divisible, and a sense in which as indivisible it perceives the indivisible. For in its significant being it is divisible, but spatially and numerically it is indivisible. Or is this not possible? Potentially, indeed, one and the same indivisible thing may contain opposite properties, but not in actuality; in its realized self it is separate, and it is impossible for a thing to be at the same moment both black and white. So that it is not possible for even the forms of experience to undergo these opposites, if sensation and thought be such forms. Rather the case here is similar to what some call a point, which is divisible or indivisible, as one regards it in its single or dual nature. In so far as it is indivisible, the judging principle is one and coincident with perception; in so far as it is divisible, it is not one, for it employs twice and simultaneously the same mark. In so far as it employs a terminal mark as two, it distinguishes two things, and these are separable for it as a separable faculty. In so far as it regards the point as one, it judges singly and coincidently with perception.

In this way, then, let us state our definition of the principle by virtue of which we say that animals are sentient beings.

CHAPTER III. IMAGINATION

INASMUCH as the soul is defined mainly by means of two attributes, namely by locomotion on the one hand and by thought, judgment, and sensation on the other, it is supposed that thought and reflexion are a kind of sensation (for in both instances the soul discriminates and cognizes some reality), and even the old writers tell us that reflexion and sensation are identical, as e.g. Empedocles, who said: "Wisdom groweth in man in the face of a present object"; and in another verse: "Hence is given unto them the power of reflecting ever and anon on diverse things"; and the words of Homer have the same meaning: "Such is the mind." For all of these ancient writers regard thought as something somatic, like sensation, and believe that both in sensation and thought like is apprehended by like, as we said in the beginning of this treatise. They should at the same time have spoken of error, for to animals this is more natural than truth, and their souls pass most of their existence in error. According to this theory, as some hold, either all phenomena must be true or else error consists in the contact of the unlike, for this is the opinion that is opposed to the cognition of like by like. Further, in this case error and knowledge of opposites seem to be identical. That sensation and reflexion, therefore, are not identical is evident. For all animals share in the one, but few only in the other. Neither is thought, in which right and wrong are determined, *i.e.* right in the sense of practical judgment, scientific knowledge, and true opinion, and wrong in the sense of the opposite of these, — thought in this signification is not identical with sensation. For sensation when applied to its own peculiar objects is always true, and is inherent in all animals; but it is possible for discursive thought to be false, and it is found in no animal which is not also endowed with reason. Imagination, too, is different from sensation and discursive thought. At the same time, it is true that imagination is impossible without sensation, and conceptual thought, in turn, is impossible without imagination. That thought and conception, however, are not one and the same is evident. For imagination is under our control, and can be stimulated when we wish (for it is possible to call up before our eyes an imaginary object, as one employs images in the art of mnemonics). Conception, on the other hand, is not under our control. For it must be either false or true. Furthermore, when we conceive that something is terrible or fearful, we have at once a corresponding feeling, and the same may be said of what inspires courage. But in the case of imagination we are in the same condition as if we were to place a terrible or a courage-inspiring object before us in a picture. In conception itself there are distinct forms, such as knowledge, opinion, reflexion, and their opposites, concerning whose different meanings we shall speak later.

Since thinking differs from sense-perception, and in one signification appears to be imagination and in another signification conception, we must proceed to the treatment of the latter, after we have defined imagination. If imagination means the power whereby what we call a phantasm is awakened in us, and if our use of language here is not merely metaphorical, then imagination is one of those faculties or mental forces in us by virtue of which we judge and are capable of truth and error. And these faculties include sensation, opinion, scientific knowledge, and reasoning. That imagination is not to be confounded with sense-perception is plain from the following considerations. Sensation is either a mere power or a distinct act, like sight and seeing, but imagination is present when neither of these conditions is realized, viz. in the phantasms of dreams. Again, sensation is always present, but this is not true of imagination. If in reality it were identical with sensation, then all animals would have imagination. This does not seem to be the fact, as we find in the case of the ant, the bee, and the worm. Again, sensations are always true, while imaginations are for the most part false. In the next place, we do not say when we are accurately observing a sense-object, that we imagine it to be a man. We say this rather when we do not clearly perceive [and when the perception may be true or false], and as we said above, we see imaginary pictures even when our eyes are closed. But neither is imagination one of those faculties whose deliverances are always true, as *e.g.* scientific knowledge and reason. For imagination can also be false. It remains to be considered whether it is opinion, for opinion can be either true or false. Opinion, however, is followed by belief (for no man can have an opinion and not believe what he opines), and none of the lower animals possesses belief, although imagination is found in many of them. [Again, every opinion is followed by belief, as belief is followed by persuasion, and persuasion by reason. Now, some of the lower animals have imagination, but none of them have reason.] It is plain, then, that imagination is not opinion combined with sensation, nor mediated by sensation, nor a complex of opinion and sensation, and, for the same reason, it is clear that opinion has for its object nothing else than what sensation has for its object. I mean *e.g.* that imagination is the complex of an opinion of whiteness and a sensation of whiteness, and not the complex of an opinion of goodness and a sensation of white-ness. To imagine, therefore, is to opine what, strictly regarded, is a sense-object. Again, there are false appearances when we have correct conceptions, as *e.g.* in the case of the sun which appears to be a foot in diameter, whereas we believe it to be larger than the inhabited earth. The consequence is that we must either have thrown aside our true opinion which we held, without the thing having changed and without any forgetful-ness or change of conviction on our part; or if one still holds it, it is necessary that the same opinion be both true and false. But an opinion has become false in a case where an object, with-out our knowing it, has changed. Imagination, then, is not one of these faculties nor a derivative of them.

Since one thing when moved can communicate motion to another, and since imagination is held to be a form of motion which does not come into existence without sense-perception, but only in sentient creatures or in reference to objects to which sensation applies, and since motion is produced by the action of sense-perception, and this motion must be equal to the strength of the sensation, one can affirm that the motion of imagination would never be possible without sensation nor could it take place in non-sentient creatures. Further, the one who experiences it can act and be acted upon in many ways, and one's experiences may be true or false. This truth or falsehood is due to the following causes. Sense-perception is true when it concerns its own peculiar objects; at any rate, there is involved in this case, the least possible amount of error. In the second place, sense-perception may concern the accidental, and here error begins to be possible. One is not mistaken in saying that a thing is white, but if one says the white object is this or that particular thing, error arises. In the third place, error applies to common properties and concomitants of the accidental, in which peculiar properties are involved. I mean *e.g.* motion and magnitude, which are accidental properties of sensible objects, and concerning which we are especially liable to error in sense-perception. The motion set up by the activity of sensation will differ in terms of the three following forms of sense-percep-

tion. The first movement is when the sense-perception continues present, and this is true; the other two may be false
whether the object is present or withdrawn, but are especially
liable to error when the sense-object is removed.

If imagination contains nothing but the elements named and
is what we have described it to be, it would be a movement
stimulated by actualized sense-perception. Since sight is our
principal sense, imagination has derived its name from light,
because sight is impossible without light. Because images persist and resemble sense-perceptions, animals regulate their
actions to a large degree by imagination, some of them because
they are incapable of reason, as the lower brutes, others because
reason is sometimes veiled by passion, disease, or sleep, as is the
case amongst men. Concerning imagination, what its nature
is and what end it subserves, let the foregoing suffice.

CHAPTER IV. THE THEORY OF REASON

REGARDING that part of the soul by virtue of which one
knows and reflects, whether it be a distinct part or whether it
be distinct only notionally and not really, we have now to consider what its differential mark is, and by what process thinking
is exercised. If thinking is like sense-perception, it would be
either a kind of impression made by the object of cognition or
some analogous process. It must, then, be impassive and yet
receptive of the form, and in its nature potentially like to the
object of thought without being this object; and as the sense-
organ is related to the object of sense, in a similar way thought
must be related to the object of thought. Reason must, therefore, be unmixed, as Anaxagoras says, since it thinks everything, in order that it may rule, *i.e.* in order that it may know.
It is the nature of thought to preclude and restrain the element
that is foreign and adjacently seen. Its nature is, therefore,
exclusively potentiality. What we call reason in the soul (by
reason I mean the instrument by which the soul thinks and
forms conceptions) is, prior to the exercise of thought, no reality
at all. It is, therefore, wrong to suppose that reason itself is

mixed with the body. For in that case it would have certain qualitative distinctions such as warm or cold, or it would be a sort of instrument, like a sense-organ. But in point of fact it is nothing of the kind. Certain writers[1] have happily called the soul the place of ideas, only this description does not apply to the soul as a whole, but merely to the power of thought, and it applies to ideas only in the sense of potentiality, and not of actuality. It is evident from the sense-organ and from the nature of sensation, that the term impassivity is employed in a different meaning in sensation and in thinking. For sense-perception cannot take place when the sense-stimulus is excessive, as one does not hear sound in the midst of loud noises, neither can one see nor smell in the midst of excessively bright colours and strong odours. On the other hand, when the mind thinks a very profound thought, it thinks not in a lesser but in a deeper degree minor details. For the power of sensation is not independent of the body, while the mind is separable. When reason becomes its several objects in the sense in which an actually learned man is said to be learned (and this takes place when he can exercise knowledge through his own agency), even then reason is in a certain sense potential, although this potentiality differs from that which preceded learning and discovery. In the latter case, potentiality signifies the capacity of thinking itself.

There is a difference between concrete magnitude and the ultimate nature of magnitude, between water and the ultimate nature of water (the same distinction can be applied to other instances, though not to all, for in some cases they are identical). Concrete flesh and the ultimate nature of flesh one judges either by a different and distinct faculty or by the same faculty under differing conditions. Flesh is not separate from matter, but like a snub-nose, it is a particular thing in a given something. By means of a sense-organ one discriminates heat and cold and those qualities of which flesh is a sort of register. On the other hand, reason judges of the essential nature of flesh either by a different and distinct faculty, or in the way in which

[1] Plato and the Academy.

a bent line is related to itself when straightened. We refer the straight line as we do the snub-nose to abstract entities, for they are both associated with the continuous. But the essential notion of a thing, if straightness and the straight line are different (and they are two things), is apprehended by a different power. The mind, then, judges in the two cases by means of a different power or by means of a power differently conditioned. In a word, therefore, as there are things abstracted from matter, so there are things that concern the reason. If the mind is simple and impassive, and has nothing in common with anything else, as Anaxagoras[1] says, and if thinking means to be somehow impressed, one might ask, How will thought be possible? For it is only in so far as there is something common to two things that the one appears to act and the other to be acted upon. A further question might be raised, viz. whether the mind itself is the object of thought. If it is, mind will then either be found in other things, unless it is the object of thought in some way different from other objects, and unless the object of thought is a specific and single thing; else it will have a mixed composition which makes it like other things, the object of thought. According to our former definition, 'to be affected in reference to a common element,' means that the mind is potentially the object of thought, though perhaps not actually so until thought takes place. It must be that the case here is similar to that of the tablet on which nothing has been actually written. This is what takes place in the case of mind, and it is the object of thought as other things are. Where entities are without matter, the subject and object of thought are identical. Speculative thought and the thing speculatively known are one and the same. The reason why thought is not continuous must be investigated. On the other hand, when entities are material they are severally the object of thought only potentially; mind is not an element in them (for reason is the potentiality of such objects in abstraction from their matter), whereas it is in the reason itself that the object of thought will be found.

[1] In his theory of sensation Anaxagoras says we do not apprehend like by like (Empedocles), but unlike by unlike, e.g. heat by cold.

CHAPTER V. ACTIVE AND PASSIVE REASON

In the whole of nature there is on the one hand a material factor for every kind of thing (and this is what all things are in their potentiality), and another factor which is causative and productive of things, by virtue of its making all objects, as art stands related to the matter it employs. These distinctions must also hold good when applied to the soul. Reason is of such character that on the one hand it becomes all things, and on the other creates all things, in this respect resembling a property like light. For light in a certain sense converts potential into actual colours, and reason, in the present meaning, is separate, impassive, and unmixed, being in its essential nature an energizing force. Now, action is always higher than passion and causal force higher than matter. Actual knowledge is identical with its object. Potential knowledge, on the other hand, pre-exists in the individual; regarded absolutely it does not so pre-exist. For mind does not at one moment think and at another not. In its separated state alone reason is what it is, immortal and eternal. We have no memory of it, because this part of reason is impassive. The passive reason, on the other hand, is perishable, and without it there can be no thought.

CHAPTER VI. THOUGHT AND TRUTH

When thought is applied to indivisible terms, error does not arise. Where error and truth are both found is just in the combination of thoughts into a sort of unity. Empedocles *e.g.* says: "Wherefore the heads of many creatures sprang into life without necks," and later on by the attraction of Friendship they were joined together. So, too, these disjoined ideas are combined together by the reason, as *e.g.* the ideas of the incommensurable and the diagonal. If the ideas refer to the past or to the future, the element of time is added in the mind and combined with the ideas. Error is always due to the combination. For even in the case where one might think the white not to be white, one has made the combination of the 'not-white.' It is further possible to apply disjunction to everything. It is not only possible for the statement 'Cleon is fair' to be true or false, but this may be applied to the past or to the future. The unifying principle is in every case the reason. Since the simple or indivisible may be looked at from two standpoints, viz. either as potentiality or as actuality, there is nothing to prevent the mind from thinking the indivisible when it thinks of extension (which in its actual state is indivisible), and when it thinks it in an indivisible moment of time. For divisibility and indivisibility apply to time just as they do to length. It is, therefore, impossible to say what the mind thinks in each half of a time-division. For the half does not exist, except in potentiality, if the division has not been made. But in the act of thinking each half separately, the mind divides the time also, and then the time corresponds in its division to the two lengths. If, however, the mind thinks the object as a whole composed of two halves, it does this also with regard to time in its relation to the two halves.

That which is not quantitatively but only notionally indivisible, the mind thinks in an indivisible time and by an indivisible power of the soul. It does this, however, accidentally and not in so far as the factors of thought and time are divisible, but in so far as they are indivisible. And there is also in these cases an objective factor which is indivisible, although perhaps not a separate entity, that gives a unity to time and extension. And this is likewise true of everything that is continuous, whether in time or space. The point and everything obtained by division, and whatever (like a point) is no longer divisible, are explicable in terms of privation. Similar reasoning may be applied to other cases, as *e.g.* the way in which we know evil or black. For we know them somehow or other by means of their contraries. But the knowing mind must be these things potentially, and they must be reduced to unity in the mind itself. If, however, in the case of any causal principle there is no opposite, then it knows itself, and is in actuality and is separate. A predication, as *e.g.* an affirmation, asserts something of something else, and is in every instance either true or false. This does not apply to the mind always, but when the mind asserts what a thing is in its essential nature and not what attaches to something as a predicate, then it is true. And just as sight is true when it concerns its own proper object, and on the other hand the opinion that a visible white object is or is not a man may not always be true, so it is with all immaterial entities.

CHAPTER VII. THOUGHT AND ITS OBJECT

ACTUAL knowledge is identical with its object. Potential knowledge is earlier in time in the individual, but taken absolutely it is not earlier in time. For all becoming proceeds from actual being. The sensible object appears to convert the potentially sensitive organ into an actually sensitive organ. For the sense-organ itself is not affected, and undergoes no change. That is the reason why we have here to do with a form of motion different from motion in the ordinary sense. Motion was defined as a realization of the incomplete, but motion, absolutely regarded, is a different kind of activity, viz. the activity of the perfected thing. Mere sense-perception, then, is like a simple expression or a simple thought; when, however, the sensation is pleasant or painful, and thus corresponds to affirmation or negation, the thing is pursued or avoided. To feel pleasure or pain signifies to experience an activity in a mean function of the sense-organ relative to good or bad as such. Avoidance and pursuit in their actual natures are identical, and the appetitive power whereby we desire or pursue a thing is not different from the power whereby we avoid a thing. They do not differ from each other or from the sensitive faculty. Only the expression of their being is different. Images are employed by the conceptual reason as sense-presentations are by the sentient faculty. When the mind makes an affirmation or negation touching the good or bad, it avoids the one and pursues the other. The soul, therefore, never thinks without the use of images. As the air produces such or such an effect on the pupil of the eye, and the pupil in turn produces another effect (the same illustration may be applied to hearing), and yet the ultimate interpreter or medium of sensation is a single power whose being is expressed in several ways, ([so it is with images in reference to thought.]) As to the faculty by which we discriminate sweet and warm, although the problem has been mentioned above, it must be again discussed as follows. There is some unitary principle, and this unitary principle has the character of an ultimate term. Its deliverances are reduced to unity by means of comparison and numerical statement, and related to each other as the outward things are related to each other. The question as to how the mind judges like qualities, does not differ from the question as to how it judges opposite qualities such as white and black. Let A, the objectively white, be related to B; the objectively black, as the idea C is related to the idea D, or it may be stated conversely. Now, if the ideas CD attach to a certain thing, they will be related to each other ([in the concept]) just as AB are related to each other, — they will form one and the same thing, though not identical in mode of being; and the former combination (CD) is analogous to the latter (AB). The same reasoning holds in case one were to apply A to a sweet object, and B to a white object.

The reasoning mind thinks its ideas in the form of images; and as the mind determines the objects it should pursue or avoid in terms of these images, even in the absence of sensation, so it is stimulated to action when occupied with them. For example, when one sees that a beacon is lighted, and observes by means of the 'common sense' that it is in motion, one comprehends that an enemy is near. Sometimes by means of the images or ideas in the soul the mind reasons as a seeing person, and takes thought for the future in terms of things before one's eyes. When the mind there in its world of images says that a thing is pleasant or painful, here in the world of things it pursues or avoids, — in a word, it acts. Apart from action the true and false belong to the same category as the good and bad. They differ, however, in the absolute character of the one and the relative character of the other.

The mind thinks abstractions, as *e.g.* when it thinks the snub-nosed. which in one sense is a snub-nose, and in another sense, if one thinks it actually, one would think it as a curvature without the flesh in which the curvature is found. So too with mathematical figures, though in actuality not separate from bodies, the mind thinks them as separated, when it thinks them. In a word the mind *is* the thing when actually thinking it. Whether or not it is possible to think any abstraction when the mind itself is not separate from magnitude, must be investigated later.

CHAPTER VIII. IDEAS AND IMAGES

LOOKING at the main features of what has been said of the soul, let us reiterate the statement that it is in a sense all reality. For everything, whether sensible or intelligible, is psychical; intelligible objects are in a sense knowledge, and sensible realities are sensations. How this is possible remains to be investigated. Conceptual knowledge and sense-perception are each divided into two minds, corresponding to their objects; potential knowledge corresponding to potential objects, and actual to actual. The sensitive and conceptual powers of the soul are, potentially regarded, the objective things, viz. the intelligible and the sensible. The soul, then, must be either the things themselves or their form. It cannot, of course, be the things themselves. For a stone is not in the soul, but the form or idea of the stone. Consequently, the soul is to be thought of as a hand; for a hand is the instrument of all instruments, and the reason is the form of all forms and sensation in the form of all sensible realities. Since, however, there is no object, as is supposed, apart from sensible magnitudes, it follows that intelligible objects, — I mean abstractions, as we call them, on the one hand, and the qualities and conditions of the sensibles, on the other, — must be sought in the sense-forms. For this reason, also, it would be impossible for one to learn anything or understand anything without sense-perception, and when one contemplates a thing, one is forced to contemplate it in conjunction with an internal image. These images are like sense-presentations, with the exception that they are without matter. Imagination is different from affirmation and negation; for the true and the false are the combination of ideas into a judgment. In what way are the primary ideas to be distinguished from imagination? Or is it true that these ideas are not themselves images, yet they cannot be produced independently of images?

CHAPTER IX. REASON AND DESIRE

SINCE the soul of living beings is defined in terms of two powers, viz. the power of judgment (which is the function of thought) and the power of sensation on the one hand, and the power of locomotion on the other, let the above suffice for our treatment of sensation and thought, and let us now consider the moving principle and ask what part of the soul it may be. The further question arises whether it is an individual part of the soul and separate, either concretely or notionally, or whether it is the entire soul. If it is only a part, we must ask whether it is a peculiar part and distinct from those usually described and already mentioned here, or whether it is one of these. There is a difficulty at the start concerning the sense in which we are to employ the term 'parts' of the soul, and concerning their number. For in a certain way they seem to be innumerable, and not merely confined to those which certain writers distinguish, viz. reason, will, and desire,[1] and others classify as rational and irrational elements. For according to the differences by which they distinguish these parts, there seem to be other parts that are even more distinct from each other than these, concerning which we have just now spoken, viz. the nutritive part, which is found even in plants as well as in all animals, and the sensitive part, which one could not easily classify either as irrational or as rational. Again, the power of imagination, which is different in its mode of being from the others, appears to be a distinct part, but in what particular it is identical with or different from the others, is very difficult to say, if one is to regard the parts of the soul as existing independently of one another. In addition to these, there is the desiderative part, which both notion-

---

[1] Plato, *Republic* 441 A (λογιστικόν, θυμοειδές, ἐπιθυμητικόν).

ally and functionally might be supposed to differ from all the other parts. And yet it would be absurd to sever this from the others. For it is in the thinking element that volition arises, and in the irrational element we have desire and passion. But if the soul has three distinct parts, then the desiderative element must be in all of them. Moreover, the question again comes up which we raised just now, viz. what is the principle in animals that produces locomotion? One might suppose that it is the generative and nutritive powers, found in all living things, that produce the motion involved in growth and decay common to them all. The subjects of inspiration and expiration, sleeping and waking, must be investigated later, for all of them present great difficulties. But regarding locomotion, we must inquire what it is that gives animals the power of progressive movement. It is evidently not the nutritive power, for progressive movement is always towards some end and accompanied either by some image or desire. For where there is no desire or revulsion, there is no motion, excepting where external force is used. Further, if motion were due to the nutritive power, plants would be capable of locomotion and would have some organic member adapted to this motion. So, too, it cannot be the sensitive power that is the source of motion; for there are many animals which have sensation and yet, throughout their existence, are stationary and motionless. If, then, nature creates nothing in vain, neither does she omit anything that is necessary, save in cases of deformed or imperfect beings. And such animals as we have in mind are normal and not deformed. A test of perfection is the capacity to reproduce, to reach the prime of growth, and then decline. Consequently, such animals should also have organs of movement.

But neither is the thinking power nor what we call reason the cause of animal motion. For the contemplative power does not think upon what is to be carried into execution, neither has it anything to say touching what is to be avoided or pursued, whereas motion always belongs to that which pursues or avoids an object. On the contrary, when one contemplates anything, the mind does not bid one pursue or avoid; e.g. the fearful or pleasant is often the subject of thought, but the feeling of fear is not suggested; the heart, however, is agitated, or if the feeling is pleasure, some other organ is stirred. More than this, even when the reason commands and intelligence tells us to avoid or to pursue a thing, motion does not follow, but one acts according to one's desire, like an intemperate man. We observe, in general, that the man versed in medicine does not heal, because it is something other than science that has the power of acting according to the principles of science. Neither, again, is desire the dominating principle in this motion; for continent men, though filled with desire and appetite, do not do the things for which they lust; on the contrary, they follow reason.

CHAPTER X. PSYCHOLOGY AND CONDUCT

THERE are two powers in the soul which appear to be moving forces — desire and reason, if one classifies imagination as a kind of reason. For many creatures follow their imaginations contrary to rational knowledge, and in animals other than man it is not thought nor rational procedure that determines action, but imagination. Consequently, both of these, reason and desire, can produce locomotion — I mean here the reason that considers ends and is concerned with conduct. It differs from the theoretical reason in having a moral end. Every desire aims at something. It is the final end that is the initial cause in conduct. So that it is reasonable to regard these two principles, viz. desire and practical reason, as motor forces. For the object of desire stimulates us, and through it reason stimulates us, because the object of desire is the main thing in the practical reason. Imagination, too, when it stimulates us to action, does not do so independently of desire. The one single moving force is the object of desire. For even if there were two moving powers, reason and desire, still they would produce movement in accordance with some common idea. As a matter of fact, however, reason does not appear to produce movement independently of desire. For volition is a form of desire, and when one is prompted to action in accordance with reason, the action follows also in accordance with volition. But desire prompts actions in violation of reason. For appetite is a sort of desire. Reason, then, is in every case right, but desire and imagination may be right or wrong. It is, therefore, always the object of desire that excites action, and this is either the good or the apparent good — yet not every good, but only the good in conduct, and this practical good admits of variation.

Evidently the psychical power which excites to action has the nature of desire, as we call it. In analysing the elements of the soul, if one analyses and distinguishes them in terms of powers, they become very numerous, as *e.g.* the nutritive, sensitive, rational, deliberative, and desiderative. For these differ from each other more than do the desiderative and spirited elements. Although desires arise which are opposed to each other, as is the case when reason and appetite are opposed, it happens only in creatures endowed with a sense of time. (For reason, on account of the future, bids us resist, while desire regards the present; the momentarily pleasant appears to it as the absolutely pleasant and the absolutely good, because it does not see the future.) The moving principle, which is the desiderative faculty as such, is specifically one, though numerically several motive forces may be included in it. The main element here is the object of desire (for this by being the object of thought or imagination excites movement, while it is itself unmoved). There are, then, three terms to consider here: first the motor power, secondly the instrument of motion, and thirdly the object set in motion. The motor power is twofold: on the one hand, it is an unmoved element, and on the other, a moving and moved element. The unmoved element is the good to be done; the moving and moved element is the desiderative faculty (for the desiderative faculty in so far as it desires is moved, and desire in process of realization is a form of motion); the object which is set in motion is the animal. The instrument by which desire effects motion, is of course the body, and consequently it must be investigated where we have to do with functions which are common to the body and the soul. One may, however, say summarily here that motion is organic in those cases where beginning and end are one, as *e.g.* in a joint. For here the convex and concave are beginning and end. Therefore the one is at rest and the other in motion, and while they are notionally distinct, they are concretely inseparable. Everything is set in motion by push or pull, and there must be, consequently, a fixed point, as the centre in a circle, and this is the initial point of motion. In a word, then, as we said before, an animal in so far as it is capable of desire is capable of self-movement. Desire, however, is not found apart from imagination, and all imagination is either rational or sensitive in origin, and the lower animals share in it.

CHAPTER XI. THE MOVING PRINCIPLE

WE must inquire also into the nature of the moving principle in those imperfect animals which possess only the sense of touch. Is it possible for them to have imagination or desire? They appear to feel pleasure and pain, and if these are felt they must necessarily have desire also. But how could they have imagination? Or are we to say that just as their movements are indefinite, so too this power is possessed by them, only it is infinitely developed. Imagination derived from sensation is, as we said before, found in the lower animals, but deliberative imagination is found only in those animals which are endowed with reason. For whether one shall do this or that is, of course, a matter of deliberation, and there must be some single instrument of measurement at hand (for it is the greater good that is to be pursued), and so the mind is able to make a single representation out of several images. The ground for supposing that animals do not have opinion is that they do not have the faculty for drawing rational conclusions, and opinion involves this. Consequently, their desire lacks the deliberative quality. Sometimes the desire overpowers the deliberative element in man and excites to action. At other times the will overpowers the desire, and again, like a ball tossed to and fro, one desire overpowers another, as in the case of intemperance. In the workings of nature the higher element always has the greater authority and is the moving power. There are, then, three forms of movement. The faculty of conceptual thought is not moved, but remains at rest. Since we have two principles in conduct, on the one hand the general conception and notion, and on the other hand the particular notion (of which the one says a man of such and such a kind shall act in such a way, and the other that this particular man — and I am that particular man — shall act in a given way), it is the latter notion that incites to action, but the general one does not. Or both of them combined may lead to action, although the general notion is quiescent, and the particular one active.

ZENO

(356-264)

From DIOGENES LAERTIUS' *LIVES AND OPINIONS OF EMINENT PHILOSOPHERS*

Translated from the Greek* by
CHARLES D. YONGE

BOOK VII. THE PSYCHOLOGY OF THE STOICS

THE Stoics have chosen to treat, in the first place, of perception and sensation, because the criterion by which the truth of facts is ascertained is a kind of perception, and because the judgment which expresses the belief, and the comprehension, and the understanding of a thing, a judgment which precedes all others, cannot exist without perception. For perception leads the way; and then thought, finding vent in expressions, explains in words the feelings which it derives from perception. But there is a difference between φαντασία and φάντασμα. For φάντασμα is a conception of the intellect, such as takes place in sleep; but φαντασία is an impression, τύπωσις, produced on the mind, that is to say, an alteration, ἀλλοίωσις, as Chrysippus states in the twelfth book of his treatise on the Soul. For we must not take this impression to resemble that made by a seal, since it is impossible to conceive that there should be many impressions made at the same time on the same thing. But φαντασία is understood to be that which is impressed, and formed, and imprinted by a real object, according to a real object, in such a way as it could not be by any other than a real object; and, according to their ideas of the φαντασίαι, some are

* From Διογένους Λαερτίου περὶ βίου δογμάτων καὶ ἀποφθεγμάτων τῶν ἐν φιλοσοφίᾳ εὐδοκιμησάντων βιβλία δέκα Reprinted from Diogenes Laertius's *Lives and Opinions of Eminent Philosophers*, translated by C. D. Yonge. Lond., 1853.

sensible, and some are not. Those they call sensible, which are derived by us from some one or more senses; and those they call not sensible, which emanate directly from the thought, as for instance, those which relate to incorporeal objects, or any others which are embraced by reason. Again, those which are sensible, are produced by a real object, which imposes itself on the intelligence, and compels its acquiescence; and there are also some others, which are simply apparent, mere shadows, which resemble those which are produced by real objects.

Again, these φαντάσιαι are divided into rational and irrational; those which are rational belong to animals capable of reason; those which are irrational to animals destitute of reason. Those which are rational are thoughts; those which are irrational have no name; but are again subdivided into artificial and not artificial. At all events, an image is contemplated in a different light by a man skilful in art, from that in which it is viewed by a man ignorant of art.

By sensation, the Stoics understand a species of breath which proceeds from the dominant portion of the soul to the senses, whether it be a sensible perception, or an organic disposition, which, according to the notions of some of them, is crippled and vicious. They also call sensation the energy, or active exercise, of the sense. According to them, it is to sensation that we owe our comprehension of white and black, and rough and smooth: from reason, that we derive the notions which result from a demonstration, those for instance which have for their object the existence of Gods, and of Divine Providence. For all our thoughts are formed either by indirect perception, or by similarity, or analogy, or transposition, or combination, or opposition. By a direct perception, we perceive those things which are the objects of sense; by similarity, those which start from some point present to our senses; as, for instance, we form an idea of Socrates from his likeness. We draw our conclusions by analogy, adopting either an increased idea of the thing, as of Tityus, or the Cyclops; or a diminished idea, as of a pigmy. So, too, the idea of the centre of the world was one derived by analogy from what we perceived to be the case of the smaller spheres. We use transposition when we fancy eyes in a man's breast; combination, when we take in the idea of a Centaur; opposition, when we turn our thoughts to death. Some ideas we also derive from comparison, for instance, from a comparison of words and places.

There is also nature; as by nature we comprehend what is just and good. And privation, when for instance, we form a notion of a man without hands. Such are the doctrines of the Stoics, on the subject of phantasia, and sensation, and thought.

XXXVII. They say that the proper criterion of truth is the comprehension, φαντασία; that is to say, one which is derived from a real object, as Chrysippus asserts in the twelfth book of his Physics; and he is followed by Antipater and Apollodorus. For Boethius leaves a great many criteria, such as intellect, sensation, appetite, and knowledge; but Chrysippus dissents from his view, and in the first book of his treatise on Reason, says, that sensation and preconception are the only criteria. And preconception is, according to him, a comprehensive physical notion of general principles. But others of the earlier Stoics admit right reason as one criterion of the truth; for instance, this is the opinion of Posidonius, and is advanced by him in his essay on Criteria.

LXIII. The Stoics also say that the mind is divisible into eight parts; for that the five organs of sensation, and the vocal power, and the intellectual power, which is the mind itself, and the generative power, are all parts of the mind. But by error, there is produced a perversion which operates on the intellect, from which many perturbations arise, and many causes of inconstancy. And all perturbation is itself, according to Zeno, a movement of the mind, or superfluous inclination, which is irrational, and contrary to nature. Moreover, of the superior class of perturbations, as Hecaton says, in the second book of his treatise on the Passions, and as Zeno also says in his work on the Passions, there are four kinds, grief, fear, desire, and pleasure. And they consider that these perturbations are judgments, as Chrysippus contends in his work on the Passions; for covetousness is an opinion that money is a beautiful object, and in like manner drunkenness and intemperance, and other things of the sort, are judgments. And grief they define to be an irrational contraction of the mind, and it is divided into the following species, pity, envy, emulation, jealousy, pain, perturbation, sorrow, anguish, confusion. Pity is a grief over some one, on the ground of his being in undeserved distress. Envy is a grief, at the good fortune of another. Emulation is a grief at that belonging to some one else, which one desires one's self. Jealousy is a grief at another also having what one has one's self. Pain is a grief which weighs one down. Perturbation is grief which narrows one, and causes one to feel in a strait. Sorrow is a grief arising from deliberate thought, which endures for some time, and gradually increases. Anguish is a grief with acute pain. Confusion is an irrational grief, which frets one, and prevents one from clearly discerning present circumstances. But fear is the expectation of evil; and the following feelings are all classed under the head of fear: apprehension, hesitation, shame, perplexity, trepidation, and anxiety. Apprehension is a fear which produces alarm. Shame is a fear of discredit. Hesitation is a fear of coming activity. Perplexity is a fear, from the imagination of some unusual thing. Trepidation is a fear accompanied with an oppression of the voice. Anxiety is a fear of some uncertain event.

Again, desire is an irrational appetite; to which head, the following feelings are referrible: want, hatred, contentiousness, anger, love, enmity, rage. Want is a desire arising from our not having something or other, and is, as it were, separated from the thing, but is still stretching, and attracted towards it in vain. And hatred is a desire that it should be ill with some one, accompanied with a certain continual increase and extension. Contentiousness is a certain desire accompanied with deliberate choice. Anger is a desire of revenge, on a person who appears to have injured one in an unbecoming way. Love is a desire not conversant about a virtuous object, for it is an attempt to conciliate affection, because of some beauty which is seen. Enmity is a certain anger of long duration, and full of hatred, and it is a watchful passion, as is shown in the following lines: —

For though we deem the short-liv'd fury past,
'T is sure the mighty will revenge at last.*

But rage is anger at its commencement.

Again, pleasure is an irrational elation of the mind over something which appears to be desirable; and its different species are enjoyment, rejoicing at evil, delight, and extravagant joy. Enjoyment, now, is a pleasure which charms the mind through the ears. Rejoicing at evil (ἐπιχαιρεκακιά), is a pleasure which arises at the misfortunes of others. Delight (τέρψις) that is to say turning (τρέψις), is a certain turning of the soul (προτροπή τις ψυχῆς), to softness. Extravagant joy is the dissolution of virtue. And as there are said to be some sicknesses (ἀῤῥωστήματα) in the body, as, for instance, gout and arthritic disorders; so too are those diseases of the soul, such as a fondness for glory, or for pleasure, and other feelings of that sort. For an ἀῤῥώστημα is a disease accompanied with weakness; and a disease is an opinion of something which appears exceedingly desirable. And, as in the case of the body, there are illnesses to which people are especially liable, such as colds or diarrhœa; so also are there propensities which the mind is under the influence of, such as enviousness, pitifulness, quarrelsomeness, and so on.

There are also three good dispositions of the mind; joy, caution, and will. And joy they say is the opposite of pleasure, since it is a rational elation of the mind; so caution is the opposite of fear, being a rational avoidance of anything, for the wise man will never be afraid, but he will act with caution; and will, they define as the opposite of desire, since it is a rational wish. As therefore some things fall under the class of the first perturbations, in the same manner do some things fall under the class of the first good dispositions. And accordingly, under the head of will, are classed goodwill, placidity, salutation, affection; and under the head of caution are ranged reverence and modesty; under the head of joy, we speak of delight, mirth, and good spirits.

* Hom. Il. I. 81. Pope's Version, l. 105.

EPICURUS
(341–270)

From DIOGENES LAERTIUS' *LIVES AND OPINIONS OF EMINENT PHILOSOPHERS*

Translated from the Greek by
CHARLES D. YONGE

BOOK X. THE EPICUREAN PSYCHOLOGY

XX. Now, in the Canon, Epicurus says that the criteria of truth are the senses, the preconceptions, and the passions. But the Epicureans, in general, add also the perceptive impressions of the intellect. And he says the same thing in his Abridgment, which he addresses to Herodotus, and also in his Fundamental Principles. For, says he, the senses are devoid of reason, nor are they capable of receiving any impressions of memory. For they are not by themselves the cause of any motion, and when they have received any impression from any external cause, then they can add nothing to it, nor can they subtract anything from it. Moreover, they are out of the reach of any control; for one sensation cannot judge of another which resembles itself; for they have all an equal value. Nor can one judge of another which is different from itself; since their objects are not identical. In a word, one sensation cannot control another, since the effects of all of them influence us equally. Again, the reason cannot pronounce on the senses; for we have already said that all reasoning has the senses for its foundation. Reality and the evidence of sensation establish the certainty of the senses; for the impressions of sight and hearing are just as real, just as evident, as pain.

It follows from these considerations that we ought to judge of things which are obscure by their analogy to those which we perceive directly. In fact, every notion proceeds from the senses, either directly, or in consequence of some analogy, or proportion, or combination. Reasoning having always a share in these last operations. The visions of insanity and of sleep have a real object, for they act upon us; and that which has no reality can produce no action.

XXI. By preconception, the Epicureans mean a sort of comprehension as it were, or right opinion, or notion, or general idea which exists in us; or, in other words, the recollection of an external object often perceived anteriorly. Such for instance, is this idea: "Man is a being of such and such a nature." At the same moment that we utter the word man, we conceive the figure of a man, in virtue of a preconception which we owe to the preceding operations of the senses. Therefore, the first notion which each word awakens in us is a correct one; in fact, we could not seek for anything if we had not previously some notion of it. To enable us to affirm that what we see at a distance is a horse or an ox, we must have some preconception in our minds which makes us acquainted with the form of a horse and an ox. We could not give names to things, if we had not a preliminary notion of what the things were.

XXII. These preconceptions then furnish us with certainty. And with respect to judgments, their certainty depends on our referring them to some previous notion, of itself certain, in virtue of which we affirm such and such a judgment; for instance, " How do we know whether this thing is a man?"

The Epicureans call opinion (δόξα) also supposition (ὑπό-ληψις). And say that it is at times true, and at times false; for that, if it is supported by testimony, and not contradicted by testimony, then it is true; but if it is not supported by testimony, and is contradicted by testimony, then it is false. On which account they have introduced the expression of " waiting," as if, before pronouncing that a thing seen is a tower, we must wait till we come near, and learn what it looks like when we are near it.

XXIII. They say that there are two passions, pleasure and pain, which affect everything alive. And that the one is natural, and the other foreign to our nature; with reference to which all objects of choice and avoidance are judged of. They say also, that there are two kinds of investigation; the one about facts, the other about mere words. And this is as far as an elementary sketch can go — their doctrine about division, and about the criterion.

XXIV. Let us now go to the letter: —

EPICURUS TO HERODOTUS, WISHING HE MAY DO WELL

.   .   .   .

"MOREOVER, there are images resembling, as far as their form goes, the solid bodies which we see, but which differ materially from them in the thinness of their substance. In fact it is not impossible but that there may be in space some secretions of this kind, and an aptitude to form surfaces without depth, and of an extreme thinness; or else that from the solids there may emanate some particles which preserve the connection, the disposition, and the motion which they had in the body. I give the name of images to these representations; and, indeed, their movement through the vacuum taking place, without meeting any obstacle or hindrance, perfects all imaginable extent in an inconceivable moment of time; for it is the meeting of obstacles, or the absence of obstacles, which produces the rapidity or the slowness of their motion. At all events, a body in motion does not find itself, at any moment imaginable, in two places at the same time; that is quite inconceivable. From whatever point of infinity it arrives at some appreciable moment, and whatever may be the spot in its course in which we perceive its motion, it has evidently quitted that spot at the moment of our thought; for this motion which, as we have admitted up to this point, encounters no obstacle to its rapidity, is wholly in the same condition as that the rapidity of which is diminished by the shock of some resistance.

"It is useful, also, to retain this principle, and to know that the images have an incomparable thinness; which fact indeed is in no respect contradicted by sensible appearances. From which it follows that their rapidity also is incomparable; for they find everywhere an easy passage, and besides, their infinite smallness causes them to experience no shock, or at all events to experience but a very slight one, while an infinite multitude of elements very soon encounter some resistance.

"One must not forget that the production of images is simultaneous with the thought; for from the surface of the bodies images of this kind are continually flowing off in an insensible manner indeed, because they are immediately replaced. They preserve for a long time the same disposition, and the same arrangement that the atoms do in the solid body, although, notwithstanding, their form may be sometimes altered. The direct production of images in space is equally instantaneous, because these images are only light substances destitute of depth.

"But there are other manners in which natures of this kind are produced; for there is nothing in all this which at all contradicts the senses, if one only considers in what way the senses are exercised, and if one is inclined to explain the relation which is established between external objects and ourselves. Also, one must admit that something passes from external objects into us in order to produce in us sight and the knowledge of forms; for it is difficult to conceive that external objects can affect us through the medium of the air which is between us and them, or by means of rays, whatever emissions proceed from us to them, so as to give us an impression of their form and colour. This phenomenon, on the contrary, is perfectly explained, if we admit that certain images of the same colour, of the same shape, and of a proportionate magnitude pass from these objects to us, and so arrive at being seen and comprehended. These images are animated by an exceeding rapidity, and, as on the other side, the solid object forming a compact mass, and comprising a vast quantity of atoms, emits always the same quantity of particles, the vision is continued, and only produces in us one single perception which preserves always the same relation to the object. Every conception, every sensible perception which bears upon the form or the other attributes of these images, is only the same form of the solid perceived directly, either in virtue of a sort of actual and continued condensation of the image, or in consequence of the traces which it has left in us.

"Error and false judgments always depend upon the supposition that a preconceived idea will be confirmed, or at all events will not be overturned, by evidence. Then, when it is not confirmed, we form our judgment in virtue of a sort of initiation of the thoughts connected, it is true with the perception, and with a direct representation; but still connected also with a conception peculiar to ourselves, which is the parent of error. In fact the representations which intelligence reflects like a mirror, whether one perceives them in a dream, or by any other conceptions of the intellect, or of any other of the criteria, can never resemble the objects that one calls real and true, unless there were objects of this kind perceived directly. And, on the other side, error could not be possible, if we did not receive some other motion also, a sort of initiative of intelligence connected; it is true with direct representation, but going beyond that representative. These conceptions being connected with the direct perception which produces the representation, but going beyond it, in consequence of a motion peculiar to the individual thought, produces error when it is not confirmed by evidence, or when it is contradicted by evidence; but when it is confirmed, or when it is not contradicted by evidence, then it produces truth.

"We must carefully preserve these principles in order not to reject the authority of the faculties which perceive truth directly; and not, on the other hand, to allow what is false to be established with equal firmness, so as to throw everything into confusion.

.   .   .   .

"Let us now return to the study of the affections, and of the sensations; for this will be the best method of proving that the soul is a bodily substance composed of slight particles, diffused over all the members of the body, and presenting a great analogy to a sort of spirit, having an admixture of heat, resembling at one time one, and at another time the other of those two principles. There exists in it a special part, endowed with an extreme mobility, in consequence of the exceeding slightness of the elements which compose it, and also in reference to its more immediate sympathy with the rest of the body. That it is which the faculties of the soul sufficiently prove, and the passions, and the mobility of its nature, and the thoughts, and, in a word, everything, the privation of which is death. We must admit that it is in the soul most especially that the principle of sensation resides. At the same time, it would not possess this power if it were not enveloped by the rest of the body which communicates it to it, and in its turn receives it from it; but only in a certain measure; for there are certain affections of the soul of which it is not capable.

"It is on that account that, when the soul departs, the body is no longer possessed of sensation; for it has not this power, (that of sensation namely) in itself; but, on the other hand, this power can only manifest itself in the soul through the medium of the body. The soul, reflecting the manifestations which are accomplished in the substance which environs it, realises in itself, in a virtue or power which belongs to it, the sensible affections, and immediately communicates them to the body in virtue of the reciprocal bonds of sympathy which unite it to the body; that is the reason why the destruction of a part of the body does not draw after it a cessation of all feeling in the soul while it resides in the body, provided that the senses still preserve some energy; although, nevertheless, the dissolution of the corporeal covering, or even of any one of its portions, may sometimes bring on with it the destruction of the soul.

"The rest of the body, on the other hand, even when it remains, either as a whole, or in any part, loses all feeling by the dispersion of that aggregate of atoms, whatever it may be, that forms the soul. When the entire combination of the body is dissolved, then the soul too is dissolved, and ceases to retain those faculties which were previously inherent in it, and especially the power of motion; so that sensation perishes equally as far as the soul is concerned; for it is impossible to imagine that it still feels, from the moment when it is no longer in the same conditions of existence, and no longer possesses the same movements of existence in reference to the same organic system; from the moment, in short, when the things which cover and surround it are no longer such, that it retains in them the same movements as before.

(Epicurus expresses the same ideas in other works, and adds that the soul is composed of atoms of the most perfect lightness and roundness; atoms wholly different from those of fire. He distinguishes in it the irrational part which is diffused over the whole body, from the rational part which has its seat in the chest, as is proved by the emotions of fear and joy. He adds that sleep is produced when the parts of the soul diffused over the whole of the body concentre themselves, or when they disperse and escape by the pores of the body; for particles emanate from all bodies.)

"It must also be observed, that I use the word incorporeal (ἀσώματος) in the usual acceptation of the word, to express that which is in itself conceived as such. Now, nothing can be conceived in itself as incorporeal except the vacuum; but the vacuum cannot be either passive or active; it is only the condition and the place of movement. Accordingly, they who pretend that the soul is incorporeal, utter words destitute of sense; for, if it had this character, it would not be able either to do or to suffer anything; but, as it is, we see plainly enough that it is liable to both these circumstances.

"Let us then apply all these reasonings to the affections and sensations, recollecting the ideas which we laid down at the beginning, and then we shall see clearly that these general principles contain an exact solution of all the particular cases.

"As to forms, and hues, and magnitudes, and weight, and the other qualities which one looks upon as attributes, whether it be of every body, or of those bodies only which are visible and perceived by the senses, this is the point of view under which they ought to be considered: they are not particular substances, having a peculiar existence of their own, for that cannot be conceived; nor can one say any more that they have no reality at all. They are not incorporeal substances inherent in the body, nor are they parts of the body. But they constitute by their union the eternal substance and the essence of the entire body. We must not fancy, however, that the body is composed of them, as an aggregate is formed of particles of the smallest dimensions of atoms or magnitudes, whatever they may be, smaller than the compound body itself; they only constitute by their union, I repeat, the eternal substance of the body. Each of these attributes has ideas and particular perceptions which correspond to it; but they cannot be perceived independently of the whole subject taken entirely; the union of all these perceptions forms the idea of the body. Bodies often possess other attributes which are not eternally inherent in them, but which, nevertheless, cannot be ranged among the incorporeal and invisible things. Accordingly, it is sufficient to express the general idea of the movement of transference to enable us to conceive in a moment certain distinct qualities, and those combined beings, which, being taken in their totality, receive the name of bodies; and the necessary and eternal attributes without which the body cannot be conceived.

"There are certain conceptions corresponding to these attributes; but, nevertheless, they cannot be known abstractedly, and independently of some subjects; and further, inasmuch as they are not attributes necessarily inherent in the idea of a body, one can only conceive them in the moment in which they are visible; they are realities nevertheless; and one must not refuse to them an existence merely because they have neither the characteristic of the compound beings to which we give the name of bodies, nor that of the eternal attributes. We should be equally deceived if we were to suppose that they have a separate and independent existence; for that is true neither of them nor of the eternal attributes. They are, as one sees plainly, accidents of the body; accidents which do not of necessity make any part of its nature; which cannot be considered as independent substances, but still to each of which sensation gives the peculiar character under which it appears to us."

TITUS LUCRETIUS CARUS
(95–51)

ON THE NATURE OF THINGS

Translated from the Latin * *by*
H. A. J. MUNRO

BOOK III. THE MIND

. . . .

FIRST then I say that the mind which we often call the understanding, in which dwells the directing and governing principle of life, is no less part of the man, than hand and foot and
eyes are parts of the whole living creature. [Some however
affirm] that the sense of the mind does not dwell in a distinct
part, but is a certain vital state of the body, which the Greeks
call harmonia, because by it, they say, we live with sense, though
the understanding is in no one part; just as when good health
is said to belong to the body, though yet it is not any one part
of the man in health. In this way they do not assign a distinct
part to the sense of the mind; in all which they appear to me
to be grievously at fault in more ways than one. Oftentimes the
body which is visible to sight, is sick, while yet we have pleasure
in another hidden part; and oftentimes the case is the very
reverse, the man who is unhappy in mind feeling pleasure in his
whole body; just as if, while a sick man's foot is pained, the
head meanwhile should be in no pain at all. Moreover when
the limbs are consigned to soft sleep and the burdened body lies
diffused without sense, there is yet a something else in us which
during that time is moved in many ways and admits into it all

* From *T. Lucretii Cari De Rerum Natura libri sex.* Reprinted from Lucretius' *On the Nature of Things,* translated by H. A. J. Munro, London,
1864; '86.

the motions of joy and unreal cares of the heart. Now that you may know that the soul as well is in the limbs and that the body is not wont to have sense by any harmony, this is a main proof: when much of the body has been taken away, still life often stays in the limbs; and yet the same life, when a few bodies of heat have been dispersed abroad and some air has been forced out through the mouth, abandons at once the veins and quits the bones: by this you may perceive that all bodies have not functions of like importance nor alike uphold existence, but rather that those seeds which constitute wind and heat, cause life to stay in the limbs. Therefore vital heat and wind are within the body and abandon our frame at death. Since then the nature of the mind and that of the soul have been proved to be a part as it were of the man, surrender the name of harmony, whether brought down to musicians from high Helicon, or whether rather they have themselves taken it from something else and transferred it to that thing which then was in need of a distinctive name; whatever it be, let them keep it: do you take in the rest of my precepts.

Now I assert that the mind and the soul are kept together in close union and make up a single nature, but that the directing principle which we call mind and understanding, is the head so to speak and reigns paramount in the whole body. It has a fixed seat in the middle region of the breast: here throb fear and apprehension, about these spots dwell soothing joys; therefore here is the understanding or mind. All the rest of the soul disseminated through the whole body obeys and moves at the will and inclination of the mind. It by itself alone knows for itself, rejoices for itself, at times when the impression does not move either soul or body together with it. And as when some part of us, the head or the eye, suffers from an attack of pain, we do not feel the anguish at the same time over the whole body, thus the mind sometimes suffers pain by itself or is inspirited with joy, when all the rest of the soul throughout the limbs and frame is stirred by no novel sensation. But when the mind is excited by some more vehement apprehension, we see the whole soul feel in unison through all the limbs, sweats and paleness spread over the whole body, the tongue falter, the voice die away, a mist cover the eyes, the ears ring, the limbs sink under one; in short we often see men drop down from terror of mind; so that anybody may easily perceive from this that the soul is closely united with the mind, and, when it has been smitten by the influence of the mind, forthwith pushes and strikes the body.

This same principle teaches that the nature of the mind and soul is bodily; for when it is seen to push the limbs, rouse the body from sleep, and alter the countenance and guide and turn about the whole man, and when we see that none of these effects can take place without touch nor touch without body, must we not admit that the mind and the soul are of a bodily nature? Again you perceive that our mind in our body suffers together with the body and feels in unison with it. When a weapon with a shudder-causing force has been driven in and has laid bare bones and sinews within the body, if it does not take life, yet there ensues a faintness and a lazy sinking to the ground and on the ground the turmoil of mind which arises, and sometimes a kind of undecided inclination to get up. Therefore the nature of the mind must be bodily, since it suffers from bodily weapons and blows.

I will now go on to explain in my verses of what kind of body the mind consists and out of what it is formed. First of all I say that it is extremely fine and formed of exceedingly minute bodies. That this is so you may, if you please to attend, clearly perceive from what follows: nothing that is seen takes place with a velocity equal to that of the mind when it starts some suggestion and actually sets it agoing; the mind therefore is stirred with greater rapidity than any of the things whose nature stands out visible to sight. But that which is so passing nimble, must consist of seeds exceedingly round and exceedingly minute, in order to be stirred and set in motion by a small moving power. Thus water is moved and heaves by ever so small a force, formed as it is of small particles apt to roll. But on the other hand the nature of honey is more sticky, its liquid more sluggish and its movement more dilatory; for the whole

mass of matter coheres more closely, because sure enough it is
made of bodies not so smooth, fine and round. A breeze however gentle and light can force, as you may see, a high heap of
poppy seed to be blown away from the top downwards; but on
the other hand eurus itself cannot move a heap of stones.
Therefore bodies possess a power of moving in proportion to
their smallness and smoothness; and on the other hand the
greater weight and roughness bodies prove to have, the more
stable they are. Since then the nature of the mind has been
found to be eminently easy to move, it must consist of bodies
exceedingly small, smooth and round. The knowledge of which
fact, my good friend, will on many accounts prove useful and
be serviceable to you. The following fact too likewise demonstrates how fine the texture is of which its nature is composed,
and how small the room is in which it can be contained, could it
only be collected into one mass: soon as the untroubled sleep of
death has gotten hold of a man and the nature of the mind and
soul has withdrawn, you can perceive then no diminution of the
entire body either in appearance or weight: death makes all
good save the vital sense and heat. Therefore the whole soul
must consist of very small seeds and be inwoven through veins
and flesh and sinews; inasmuch as, after it has all withdrawn
from the whole body, the exterior contour of the limbs preserves
itself entire and not a tittle of the weight is lost. Just in the
same way when the flavour of wine is gone or when the delicious
aroma of a perfume has been dispersed into the air or when the
savour has left some body, yet the thing itself does not therefore look smaller to the eye, nor does aught seem to have been
taken from the weight, because sure enough many minute seeds
make up the savours and the odour in the whole body of the
several things. Therefore, again and again I say, you are to
know that the nature of the mind and the soul has been formed
of exceedingly minute seeds, since at its departure it takes away
none of the weight.

We are not however to suppose that this nature is single.
For a certain subtle spirit mixed with heat quits men at death,
and then the heat draws air along with it; there being no heat

which has not air too mixed with it: for since its nature is rare, many first-beginnings of air must move about through it. Thus the nature of the mind is proved to be threefold; and yet these things all together are not sufficient to produce sense; since the fact of the case does not admit that any of these can produce sense-giving motions and the thoughts which a man turns over in mind. Thus some fourth nature too must be added to these: it is altogether without name; than it nothing exists more nimble or more fine, or of smaller or smoother elements: it first transmits the sense-giving motions through the frame; for it is first stirred, made up as it is of small particles; next the heat and the unseen force of the spirit receive the motions, then the air; then all things are set in action, the blood is stirred, every part of the flesh is filled with sensation; last of all the feeling is transmitted to the bones and marrow, whether it be one of pleasure or an opposite excitement. No pain however can lightly pierce thus far nor any sharp malady make its way in, without all things being so thoroughly disordered that no room is left for life and the parts of the soul fly abroad through all the pores of the body. But commonly a stop is put to these motions on the surface as it were of the body: for this reason we are able to retain life.

Now though I would fain explain in what way these are mixed up together, by what means united, when they exert their powers, the poverty of my native speech deters me sorely against my will: yet will I touch upon them and in summary fashion to the best of my ability: the first-beginnings by their mutual motions are interlaced in such a way that none of them can be separated by itself, nor can the function of any go on divided from the rest by any interval; but they are so to say the several powers of one body. Even so in any flesh of living creature you please without exception there is smell and some colour and a savour, and yet out of all these is made up one single bulk of body. Thus the heat and the air and the unseen power of the spirit mixed together produce a single nature, together with that nimble force which transmits to them from itself the origin of motion; by which means sense-giving motion first takes its rise through the fleshly frame. For this nature lurks secreted in its inmost depths, and nothing in our body is farther beneath all ken than it, and more than this it is the very soul of the whole soul. Just in the same way as the power of the mind and the function of the soul are latent in our limbs and throughout our body, because they are each formed of small and few bodies: even so, you are to know, this nameless power made of minute bodies is concealed and is moreover the very soul so to say of the whole soul, and reigns supreme in the whole body. On a like principle the spirit and air and heat must, as they exert their powers, be mixed up together through the frame, and one must ever be more out of view or more prominent than another, that a single substance may be seen to be formed from the union of all, lest the heat and spirit apart by themselves and the power of the air apart by itself should destroy sense and dissipate it by their disunion. Thus the mind possesses that heat which it displays when it boils up in anger and fire flashes from the keen eyes; there is too much cold spirit comrade of fear, which spreads a shivering over the limbs and stirs the whole frame; yes and there is also that condition of still air which has place when the breast is calm and the looks cheerful. But they have more of the hot whose keen heart and passionate mind lightly boil up in anger. Foremost in this class comes the fierce violence of lions who often as they chafe break their hearts with their roaring and cannot contain within their breast the billows of their rage. Then the chilly mind of stags is fuller of the spirit and more quickly rouses through all the flesh its icy currents which cause a shivering motion to pass over the limbs. But the nature of oxen has its life rather from the still air, and never does the smoky torch of anger applied to it stimulate it too much, shedding over it the shadow of murky gloom, nor is it transfixed and stiffened by the icy shafts of fear: it lies between the other two, stags and cruel lions. And thus it is with mankind: however much teaching renders some equally refined, it yet leaves behind those earliest traces of the nature of each mind; and we are not to suppose that evil habits can be so thoroughly plucked up by the roots, that one man shall not be more

prone than another to keen anger, a second shall not be somewhat more quickly assailed by fear, a third shall not take some
things more meekly than is right. In many other points there
must be differences between the varied natures of men and the
tempers which follow upon these; though at present I am unable
to set forth the hidden causes of these or to find names enough
for the different shapes which belong to the first-beginnings,
from which shapes arises this diversity of things. What herein
I think I may affirm is this: traces of the different natures left
behind, which reason is unable to expel from us, are so exceedingly slight that there is nothing to hinder us from living a life
worthy of gods.

Well this nature is contained by the whole body and is in
turn the body's guardian and the cause of its existence; for the
two adhere together with common roots and cannot it is plain
be riven asunder without destruction. Even as it is not easy to
pluck the perfume out of lumps of frankincense without quite
destroying its nature as well; so it is not easy to withdraw from
the whole body the nature of the mind and soul without dis-
solving all alike. With first-beginnings so interlaced from their
earliest birth are they formed and gifted with a life of joint
partnership, and it is plain that the faculty of the body and of
the mind cannot feel separately, each alone without the other's
power, but sense is kindled throughout our flesh and blown into
flame between the two by the joint motions on the part of both.
Moreover the body by itself is never either begotten or grows
or, it is plain, continues to exist after death. For not in the way
that the liquid of water often loses the heat which has been
given to it, yet is not for that reason itself riven in pieces, but
remains unimpaired, — not in this way, I say, can the abandoned frame endure the separation of the soul, but riven in
pieces it utterly perishes and rots away. Thus the mutual connexions of body and soul from the first moment of their existence learn the vital motions even while hid in the body and
womb of the mother, so that no separation can take place without mischief and ruin. Thus you may see that, since the cause
of existence lies in their joint action, their nature too must be
a joint nature.

Furthermore if any one tries to disprove that the body feels and believes that the soul mixed through the whole body takes upon it this motion which we name sense, he combats even manifest and undoubted facts. For who will ever bring forward any explanation of what the body's feeling is, except that which the plain fact of the case has itself given and taught to us? But when the soul it is said has departed, the body throughout is without sense; yes, for it loses what was not its own peculiar property in life; ay and much else it loses, before that soul is driven out of it.

Again to say that the eyes can see no object, but that the soul discerns through them as through an open door, is far from easy, since their sense contradicts this; for this sense e'en draws it and forces it out to the pupil: nay often we are unable to perceive shining things, because our eyes are embarrassed by the lights. But this is not the case with doors; for, because we ourselves see, the open doors do not therefore undergo any fatigue. Again if our eyes are in the place of doors, in that case when the eyes are removed the mind ought it would seem to have more power of seeing things, after doors, jambs and all, have been taken out of the way.

And herein you must by no means adopt the opinion which the revered judgment of the worthy man Democritus lays down, that the first-beginnings of body and mind placed together in successive layers come in alternate order and so weave the tissue of our limbs. For not only are the elements of the soul much smaller than those of which our body and flesh are formed, but they are also much fewer in number and are disseminated merely in scanty number through the frame, so that you can warrant no more than this: the first-beginnings of the soul keep spaces between them at least as great as are the smallest bodies which, if thrown upon it, are first able to excite in our body the sense-giving motions. Thus at times we do not feel the adhesion of dust when it settles on our body, nor the impact of chalk when it rests on our limbs, nor do we feel a mist at night nor a spider's slender threads as they come against us, when we are caught in its meshes in moving along, nor the same insect's flimsy web when it has fallen on our head, nor the feathers of birds and down of plants as it flies about, which commonly from exceeding lightness does not lightly fall, nor do we feel the tread of every creeping creature whatsoever nor each particular foot-print which gnats and the like stamp on our body. So very many first-beginnings must be stirred in us, before the seeds of the soul mixed up in our bodies feel that these have been disturbed, and by thumping with such spaces between can clash unite and in turn recoil.

The mind has more to do with holding the fastnesses of life and has more sovereign sway over it than the power of the soul. For without the understanding and the mind no part of the soul can maintain itself in the frame the smallest fraction of time, but follows at once in the other's train and passes away into the air and leaves the cold limbs in the chill of death. But he abides in life whose mind and understanding continue to stay with him: though the trunk is mangled with its limbs shorn all round about it, after the soul has been taken away on all sides and been severed from the limbs the trunk yet lives and inhales the ethereal airs of life. When robbed, if not of the whole, yet of a large portion of the soul, it still lingers in and cleaves to life; just as, after the eye has been lacerated all round if the pupil has continued uninjured, the living power of sight remains, provided always you do not destroy the whole ball of the eye and pare close round the pupil and leave only it; for that will not be done even to the ball without the entire destruction of the eye. But if that middle portion of the eye, small as it is, is eaten into, the sight is gone at once and darkness ensues, though a man have the bright ball quite unimpaired. On such terms of union soul and mind are ever bound to each other.

PLOTINUS

(205 A.D.–270)

ENNEADES

Translated from the Greek * *by*
THOMAS TAYLOR

VII. THE SOUL
(IV. VII)

I. WHETHER each [part] of us is immortal, or the whole perishes, or one part of us is dissipated and corrupted, but another part perpetually remains, which part is the man himself, may be learned by considering conformably to nature as follows: Man, indeed, is not something simple, but there is in him a soul, and he has also a body, whether it is annexed to us as an instrument, or after some other manner. However this may be, it must be admitted, that the nature and essence of each of these must be thus divided. Since the body, therefore, is itself a composite, reason shows that it cannot remain [perpetually the same]. The senses likewise perceive that it is dissolved and wastes away, and receives destructions of every sort; since each of the things inherent in it tends to its own proper nature, and one thing belonging to it corrupts another, and changes and perishes into something else. This, too, is especially the case when the soul, which causes the parts to be in friendly union with each other, is not present with the corporeal mass. If each body, likewise, is left by itself, it will not be one, since it is capable of being dissolved into form and matter, from which it is also necessary that simple bodies should have their composition. Moreover, as bodies they have magnitude, and consequently may be cut and broken into the smallest parts, and

* From Πλωτίνου Ἐννεάδες. Reprinted with verbal changes from *Select Works of Plotinus*, translated by Thomas Taylor, London, 1817; *ib.*, 1895.

for this reason are subject to corruption. Hence, if body is a part of us, we are not wholly immortal. But if it is an instrument [of the soul] it is necessary that being given for a certain time, it should be naturally a thing of this kind. That, however, which is the most principal thing, and the man himself, will be that with reference to the body which form is with reference to matter, since this according to form is as body to matter, or according to that which uses, the body has the relation to it of an instrument. But in either case the soul is the man himself.

II. What, therefore, is the nature of the soul? If indeed it is a body, it is in every respect capable of being analyzed. For every body is a composite. But if it is not a body, but of another nature, that also must be considered, either after the same, or after another manner. In the first place, [if the soul be corporeal], it must be considered into what this body which they call soul ought to be analyzed. For since life is necessarily present with soul, it is also necessary that this body which is supposed to be soul, if it consists of two or more bodies, should have life innate in both, or in each of them; or that one of these should have life, but the other not, or that neither should be vital. If, therefore, life is present with one of them only, this very thing will be soul. Hence, what body will this be which has life from itself? For fire, air, water and earth, are of themselves inanimate; and with whichever of these soul is present, the life which it uses is adventitious. There are not, however, any other bodies besides these. And those to whom it appears that there are other bodies which are the elements of these, do not assert that they are souls, or that they have life.

But if it should be said, that though no one of these bodies possesses life, yet the conjunction of them produces life, one would speak absurdly. And if each of them has life, one will be sufficient. Or rather, it is impossible that a combination of bodies should produce life, and things void of intellect generate intellect. Moreover, neither will these, in whatever manner they may say they are mixed, generate either intellect or soul. Hence, it is necessary there should be that which arranges, and which is the cause of the mixture; so that this will have the order of soul. For that which is compounded cannot be that which arranges and produces the mixture. But neither can there be a simple body in the series of things, without the existence of soul in the universe; if reason [or a productive principle] entering into matter, produces body. For reason cannot proceed from any thing else than from soul.

III. . . . Indeed, neither will there be any body, if there is no psychical power. For body [perpetually] flows, and its nature is in [continual] motion. The universe would rapidly perish if all things were bodies; though some one of them should be denominated "soul." For it would suffer the same things as other bodies, since there would be one matter in all of them. Or rather, nothing would be generated, but all things would remain mere matter, as there would not be any thing to invest it with form. Perhaps, too, neither would matter have any subsistence whatever. This universe also would be dissolved, if it is committed to the connexion of body, and the order of soul is given to body, as far as the name went, ascribing it to air and dissoluble spirits, which have not of themselves any unity. For how is it possible, since all bodies are divisible, that this universe if it is committed to any one of them, should not be borne along in a foolish and casual manner? What order is there, or reason or intellect, in a pneumatic substance, which is in want of order from soul? But if soul, indeed, has a subsistence, all these will be subservient to it in the composition of the world, and in the existence of every animal, in that one power arising from another contributes to [the perfection of] the whole. If soul, however, is not present to the whole of things, these will neither have a subsistence, nor any arrangement.

VI. But that if soul is body, there would be no sensation, nor thought, nor undertaking, nor virtue, nor any thing beautiful [in human conduct,] will be manifest from the following considerations. Whatever is able to have a sensible perception of any thing, ought itself to be one, and to apprehend every thing by one and the same power. This will also be the case, if many things enter through many organs of sense, or there are many qualities about one thing, and likewise when there is a variegated appearance such as that of the face, through one thing. For one thing does not perceive the nose, and another the eyes, but the same thing perceives at once all the parts of the face. And though one sensation proceeds through the eyes, but another through the ears, yet it is necessary there should be some one thing at which both arrive. Or how could the soul say that these are different, unless the perceptions of sense at once terminated in the same thing? It is necessary, therefore, that this should be as it were a centre, that the senses should on all sides be extended to this, like lines from the circumference of a circle, and that a thing of this kind which apprehends the perceptions of sense should be truly one. . . .

VII. The same thing also may be seen from pain and the sensation of pain; when a man is said to have a pain in or about his finger. For then it is manifest that the sensation of pain is produced in the principal or ruling part. A portion of the spirit being pained, the ruling part has a perception of the pain, and the whole soul in consequence of this suffers the same pain. How, therefore, does this happen? They will say by transmission, the psychical spirit about the finger suffering in the first place, but imparting the passion to that which is next to it, and afterwards to something else, until the passion arrives at the ruling part. Hence, it is necessary if that which is primarily pained perceives, that there should be another sensation of that which is second, provided sensation is produced by transmission. Likewise, it is necessary that there should be another sensation of that which is the third in order; that there should be many and infinite sensible perceptions of one and the same pain; and that afterwards all these should be perceived by the ruling part, and besides these, that it should have a perception of its own passion. In reality, however, each of these does not perceive the pain that is in the finger; but one sensation perceives that the part of the palm of the hand which is next to the finger is pained, and another more remote sensation perceives the pain which is in a more remote part.

There will also be many pains, the ruling faculty not perceiving the passion which is in the finger, but that which is present with itself. And this it will alone know, but will bid farewell to the others, not perceiving that the finger is pained. It, therefore, is not possible that sensible perception of a thing of this kind should subsist according to transmission. Nor can any one part of the body—which is an extended mass—be aware of another's suffering, since in every magnitude the parts are distinct. If this be the case, it is necessary that the perceiving faculty should be of such a nature, as to be every where identical with itself. But this pertains to any thing else rather than to body.

VIII. Moreover, that it would be impossible to perceive intellectually if the soul is body, may be demonstrated as follows. For if to perceive sensibly is, for the soul using the body to apprehend sensible objects, intellectual perception will not be an apprehension of the objects of such perception, through body. For unless this is admitted, intellectual will be the same with sensible perception. Hence, if to perceive intellectually is to apprehend without body, by a much greater priority it is necessary that the nature which thus perceives should not be body. Farther still, if sense indeed is the perception of sensible objects, intellection is the perception of intelligible objects. If, however, they are not willing to admit this, yet there must be in us thoughts of certain intelligible objects, and apprehensions of things without magnitude. How, therefore, will intellect if it is magnitude, understand that which is not magnitude, and with its divisible nature, think that which is indivisible? Shall we say it will understand it by a certain indivisible part of itself? But if this be the case, that which understands will not be body. For there is no need of the whole in order to come into contact with the object of its thought; since contact of a single part is sufficient.

If, therefore, they admit that the most abstract thoughts are entirely liberated from body, it is necessary that the nature which intellectually perceives the form separate from body of each thing, should know either real being, or that which is becoming pure. But if they say that thoughts are of forms inherent in matter, yet they are then only apprehended when by intellect they are separated from body. For the separation [i.e.

abstraction] of a circle and triangle, of a line and a point, is not effected in conjunction with flesh, or in short, with matter. Hence it is necessary that the soul also, in a separation of this kind, should separate itself from the body. And therefore it is necessary that it should not be itself body. I think, likewise, that the beautiful and the just are without magnitude, and consequently the thought of these is unattended with magnitude. Hence, these approaching to us are apprehended by that which is indivisible in the soul, and in the soul they reside in the indivisible. How also, if the soul is body, can temperance and justice be the virtues of it, which are its saviours, so far as they are received by it?

IX. There must, therefore, be another nature which possesses existence from itself, and such is every thing which is truly being, and which is neither generated, nor destroyed. For without the subsistence of this, all things would vanish into non-entity, and this perishing, would not afterwards be generated; since this imparts safety to all other things, and also to the universe which through soul is preserved and adorned. For soul is the principle of motion, with which it supplies other things, itself moving itself, and imparting life to the animated body. But it possesses life from itself, which it will never lose, because it is derived from itself. For all things do not use an adventitious life, or there would be a progression of life to infinity. But it is necessary there should be a certain nature primarily vital, which is also necessarily indestructible and immortal, as being the principle of life to other things. . . .

X. That the soul, however, is allied to a more divine and eternal nature, is evident from its not being body as we have demonstrated, and also because it has neither figure nor colour. Moreover, this likewise may be shown from the following considerations. It is acknowledged by all of us, that every divine nature, and one which is truly being, enjoys an excellent and wise life. This, therefore, being admitted, it is necessary to consider in the next place, what is the nature of our soul. We must assume the soul, however, not as receiving in the body irrational desires and angers, and other passions, but as abolishing all these, and as much as possible having no communication with the body. For such a soul as this will clearly show that evils are an addition to the soul, and are externally derived; and that the most excellent things are inherent in it when it is purified, viz. wisdom and every other virtue, which are its proper possessions.

If, therefore, the soul is such when it returns to itself, how is it possible it should not belong to that nature which we say is possessed by every thing eternal and divine? For wisdom and true virtue being divine, cannot be inherent in any vile and mortal thing; but that which is of this kind is necessarily divine, as being full of divine goods, through an alliance and similitude of essence to a divine nature. Hence, whoever of us resembles a soul of this description, will in soul itself differ but little from superior beings; in this alone being inferior to them, that he is in body. On which account, also, if every man was such, or if the multitude employed souls of this kind, no one would be so incredulous as not to believe that our soul is entirely immortal.

XII. Farther still, if they say that every soul is corruptible, it would be requisite that all things should have long since perished. But if they assert that one soul is corruptible, and another not, as for instance, that the soul of the universe is immortal, but ours not, it is necessary that they should assign the cause of this difference. For each is the cause of motion, and each lives from itself. Each, likewise, comes into contact with the same things by the same power, intellectually perceiving the natures in the heavens, and also those that are beyond the heavens, investigating everything which has an essential subsistence, and ascending as far as to the first principle of things. To which may be added, that it is evident the soul gave being to itself prior to the body, from its ability of apprehending what each thing is, by itself, from its own inherent spectacles, and from reminiscence. And from its employing eternal sciences, it is manifest that it is itself perpetual.

Besides, since everything which can be dissolved receives composition, hence, so far as a thing is a composite, it is naturally adapted to be dissolved. But soul being one simple energy, and a nature characterized by life, cannot be corrupted as a composite. Will it, therefore, through being divided and distributed into minute parts, perish? Soul, however, is not, as we have demonstrated, a certain bulk or quantity. May it not, therefore, through being changed in quality, be corrupted? Change in quality however which corrupts takes away form, but leaves the subject matter. But this is the nature of a composite. Hence, if it is not possible for the soul to be corrupted according to any of these modes, it is necessarily incorruptible.

VIII. THE INTELLECT
(v. 1.)

III. Hence, as the soul is so honourable and divine a thing, now confiding in a cause of this kind, ascend with it to divinity. For you will not be very distant from him; nor are the intermediate natures many. In this, therefore, which is divine, receive that part which is more divine, viz. the vicinity of the soul to that which is supernal, to which the soul is posterior, and from which it proceeds. For though it is so great a thing as we have demonstrated it to be, yet it is a certain image of intellect. And, just as external discourse is an image of the discursive energy within the soul, after the same manner, soul, and the whole of its energy, are the thought of intellect, and a life which it emits in order to the hypostasis of another thing. It is just as in fire, where the inherent heat of it is one·thing, and the heat which it imparts another. It is necessary, however, to assume there, not a life flowing forth, but partly abiding in intellect, and partly giving subsistence to another life. Hence, since soul is derived from intellect, it is intellectual, and the intellect of soul is conversant with discursive energies.

Again, the perfection of soul is from intellect, as from a father that nourishes it, who generated soul, as with reference to himself, not perfect. This hypostasis, therefore, is from intellect, and is also reason in energy when it perceives intellect. For when it looks to intellect, it possesses internally, and appropriately, the things which it understands, and the energies which it performs. And it is necessary to call those energies alone the energies of the soul, which are intellectual and dwell with it. But its subordinate energies have an external source, and are the passions of a soul of this kind.

Intellect, therefore, causes the soul to be more divine, both because it is the father of it, and because it is present with it. For there is nothing between them, except the difference of one with reference to the other; soul being successive to, and the recipient of intellect, but intellect subsisting as form. The matter also of intellect is beautiful, since it has the form of intellect, and is simple. The great excellence, however, of intellect, is manifest from this, that though soul is such as we have described it to be, yet it is surpassed by intellect.

IX.
(V. XI.)

IV. Why, therefore, is it necessary to ascend to soul, and yet not admit that it is the first of things? Is it not because in the first place, indeed, intellect is different from, and more excellent than soul? But that which is more excellent is prior by nature. For soul when perfect, does not, as some fancy it does, generate intellect. For whence will that which is in capacity become in energy, unless there is a cause which leads into energy? Since if it becomes in energy casually, it is possible that it may not proceed into energy. Hence, it is necessary that first natures should be established in energy, and that they should be wanting nothing and perfect. But imperfect natures are posterior to them. The progeny also of imperfect, are perfected by first natures, who after the manner of fathers give perfection to what posterior natures generated imperfect from the beginning. That, likewise, which is generated, has at first the relation of matter to the maker of it, but is afterwards rendered perfect by the participation of form. But if it is necessary that soul should be connected with passion, and if it is likewise necessary that there should be something impassive, or all things would perish in time; it is necessary that there should be something prior to soul. And, if soul is in the world, but it is necessary there should be something beyond the world, on this account also it is necessary that there should be something prior to soul. For if that which is in the world, is in body and matter, nothing would remain the same [if that which is mundane only existed]. So that man, and all productive principles, would not be perpetual, nor always the same. Hence, that it is necessary intellect should be prior to soul, may be seen from these and many other arguments.

V. It is necessary, however, to consider intellect truly so called neither as intellect in capacity, nor as proceeding from the privation to the possession of intellect. For if we do not, we must again investigate another intellect prior to this. But we must assume intellect in energy, and eternally. If such an intellect, however, has not adventitious thought, whatever it intellectually perceives, it perceives from itself. And whatever it possesses, it possesses from itself. But if it perceives intellectually by and from itself, it is itself that which it perceives. For if the essence of it were one thing, and the object of its perception another, its very essence would not be an intelligible object; and again, it would be intellect in capacity, but not in energy. Neither of these, therefore, must be separated from the other. With us, however, it is usual, from the things with which we are conversant, to separate in our conceptions intellect, and the objects of its perception. . . .

VI. Let, therefore, intellect be [real] beings, and possess all things in itself, not as in place but as itself, and as being one with them. But all things there subsist together, and nevertheless are separated from one another. For the soul also which has many notions in itself simultaneously, possesses them without any confusion. Each also, when it is requisite, performs what pertains to it, without the co-operation of the rest. And each conception energizes with a purity unmingled with the other inward conceptions. Thus, therefore, and in a still greater degree, intellect is at once all things; and yet, not together, because each real existence is a peculiar power. Every intellect, however, includes all things, in the same manner as genus comprehends species, and as a whole comprehends its parts.

QUINTUS SEPTIMIUS FLORENS TERTULLIANUS
(160–220)

A TREATISE ON THE SOUL

Translated from the Latin * *by*
PETER HOLMES

CHAPTER IV. THE SOUL CREATED

AFTER settling the origin of the soul, its condition or state comes up next. For when we acknowledge that the soul originates in the breath of God, it follows that we attribute a beginning to it. This Plato, indeed, refuses to assign to it, for he will have the soul to be unborn and unmade.[1] We, however, from the very fact of its having had a beginning, as well as from the nature thereof, teach that it had both birth and creation. And when we ascribe both birth and creation to it, we have made no mistake: for being *born*, indeed, is one thing, and being *made* is another, — the former being the term which is best suited to living beings. When distinctions, however, have places and times of their own, they occasionally possess also reciprocity of application among themselves. Thus, the being made admits of being taken in the sense of being brought forth;[2] inasmuch as everything which receives *being* or *existence*, in any way whatever, is in fact generated. For the maker may really be called the parent of the thing that is made: in this sense Plato also uses the phraseology. So far, therefore, as con-

---

* From *De Anima* (about 210). Reprinted from the ANTE-NICENE CHRISTIAN LIBRARY, vol. XV, *The Writings of Tertullian*, translated by Peter Holmes, Edinburgh, 1870, vol. II.

[1] See his *Phædrus*, c. xxiv.

[2] Capit itaque et facturam provenisse poni.

cerns our belief in the souls being made or born, the opinion of the philosopher is overthrown by the authority of prophecy [1] even.

CHAPTER V. THE SOUL'S CORPOREAL NATURE

SUPPOSE one summons a Eubulus to his assistance, and a Critolaus, and a Zenocrates, and on this occasion Plato's friend Aristotle. They may very possibly hold themselves ready for stripping the soul of its corporeity, unless they happen to see other philosophers opposed to them in their purpose — and this, too, in greater numbers — asserting for the soul a corporeal nature. Now I am not referring merely to those who mould the soul out of manifest bodily substances, as Hipparchus and Heraclitus [do] out of fire; as Hippon and Thales [do] out of water; as Empedocles and Critias [do] out of blood; as Epicurus [does] out of atoms, since even atoms by their coherence form corporeal masses; as Critolaus and his Peripatetics [do] out of a certain indescribable *quintessence*,[2] if that may be called a body which rather includes and embraces bodily substances; — but I call on the Stoics also to help me, who, while declaring almost in our own terms that the soul is a spiritual essence (inasmuch as breath and spirit are in their nature very near akin to each other), will yet have no difficulty in persuading [us] that the soul is a corporeal substance. Indeed, Zeno, defining the soul to be a spirit generated with [the body], constructs his argument in this way: That substance which by its departure causes the living being to die is a corporeal one. Now it is by the departure of the spirit, which is generated with [the body], that the living being dies; therefore the spirit which is generated with [the body] is a corporeal substance. But this spirit which is generated with [the body] is the soul: it follows, then, that the soul is a corporeal substance. Cleanthes, too, will have it that family likeness passes from parents to their children not merely in bodily features, but in characteristics of the soul; as

[1] Or, "inspiration."
[2] Ex quinta nescio qua substantia. Comp. Cicero's *Tuscul.* i. 10.

if it were out of a mirror of [a man's] manners, and faculties, and affections, that bodily likeness and unlikeness are caught and reflected by the soul also. It is therefore as being corporeal that it is susceptible of likeness and unlikeness. Again, there is nothing in common between things corporeal and things incorporeal as to their susceptibility. But the soul certainly sympathizes with the body, and shares in its pain, whenever it is injured by bruises, and wounds, and sores: the body, too, suffers with the soul, and is united with it (whenever it is afflicted with anxiety, distress, or love) in the loss of vigour which its companion sustains, whose shame and fear it testifies by its own blushes and paleness. The soul, therefore, is [proved to be] corporeal from this intercommunion of susceptibility. Chrysippus also joins hands in fellowship with Cleanthes, when he lays it down that it is not at all possible for things which are endued with body to be separated from things which have not body; because they have no such relation as mutual contact or coherence. Accordingly Lucretius says:[1]

"Tangere enim et tangi nisi corpus nulla potest res."
"For nothing but body is capable of touching or of being touched."

[Such severance, however, is quite natural between the soul and the body]; for when the body is deserted by the soul, it is overcome by death. The soul, therefore, is endued with a body; for if it were not corporeal, it could not desert the body.

CHAPTER X. THE SOUL'S SIMPLICITY

IT is essential to a firm faith, to declare with Plato[2] that the soul is simple; in other words, uniform and uncompounded; simply, that is to say, in respect of its substance. Never mind men's artificial views and theories, and away with the fabrications of heresy! Some maintain that there is within the soul a natural substance — the spirit — which is different from it: as if to have life — the function of the soul — were one thing; and

---

[1] *De Nat. Rer.* i. 305.
[2] See his *Phædo*, p. 80; *Timæus*, § 12, p. 35 (Bekker, pp. 264, 265).

to emit breath — the alleged function of the spirit — were another thing. Now it is not in all animals that these two functions are found; for there are many which only live, but do not breathe, in that they do not possess the organs of respiration — lungs and windpipes. But of what use is it, in an examination of the soul of man, to borrow proofs from a gnat or an ant, when the great Creator in His divine arrangement has allotted to every animal organs of vitality suited to its own disposition and nature, so that we ought not to catch at any conjectures from comparisons of this sort? Man, indeed, although organically furnished with lungs and windpipes, will not on that account be proved to *breathe* by one process, and to *live* by another;[1] nor can the ant, although defective in these organs, be on that account said to be without respiration, as if it lived and that was all. . . .

You think it possible for a thing to live without breath; then why not suppose that a thing might breathe without lungs? Pray, tell me, what is it to breathe? I suppose it means to emit breath from yourself. What is it not to live? I suppose it means not to emit breath from yourself. This is the answer which I should have to make, if "to breathe" is not the same thing as "to live." It must, however, be characteristic of a dead man not to respire: to respire, therefore, is the characteristic of a living man. But to respire is likewise the characteristic of a breathing man: therefore also to breathe is the characteristic of a living man. Now, if both one and the other could possibly have been accomplished without the soul, to breathe might not be a function of the soul, but merely to live. But indeed to live is to breathe, and to breathe is to live. Therefore this entire process, both of breathing and living, belongs to that to which living belongs — that is, to the soul. Well, then, since you separate the spirit (or breath) and the soul, separate their operations also. Let both of them accomplish some act apart from one another — the soul apart, the spirit apart. Let the soul live without the spirit; let the spirit breathe without the

---

[1] Aliunde spirabit, aliunde vivet. "In the nature of man, life and breath are inseparable" (Bp. Kaye).

soul. Let one of them quit men's bodies, let the other remain; let death and life meet and agree.

If indeed the soul and the spirit are two, they may be divided; and thus, by the separation of the one which departs from the one which remains, there would accrue the union and meeting together of life and of death. But such a union never will accrue: therefore they are not two, and they cannot be divided; but divided they might have been, if they had been [two]. Still two things may surely coalesce in growth. But the two in question never will coalesce, since to live is one thing, and to breathe is another. Substances are distinguished by their operations. How much firmer ground have you for believing that the soul and the spirit are but one, since you assign to them no difference; so that the soul is itself the spirit, respiration being the function of that of which life also is! But what if you insist on supposing that the day is one thing, and the light, which is incidental to the day, is another thing, whereas day is only the light itself? There must, of course, be also different kinds of light, as [appears] from the ministry of fires. So likewise will there be different sorts of spirits, according as they emanate from God or from the devil. Whenever, indeed, the question is about soul and spirit, the soul will be [understood to be] itself the spirit, just as the day is the light itself. For a thing is itself identical with that by means of which itself exists.

CHAPTER XII. THE MIND AND SOUL

IN like manner the mind also, or *animus*, which the Greeks designate NOYΣ, is taken by us in no other sense than as indicating that faculty or apparatus which is inherent and implanted in the soul, and naturally proper to it, whereby it acts, whereby it acquires knowledge, and by the possession of which it is capable of a spontaneity of motion within itself, and of thus appearing to be impelled by the mind, as if it were another substance, as is maintained by those who determine the soul to be the moving principle of the universe [1] — the god

[1] Comp. *The Apology*, c. xlviii ; August. *De Civ. Dei*, xiii. 17.

of Socrates, Valentinus' "only-begotten" of his father[1] *Bythus*, and his mother *Sige*. How confused is the opinion of Anaxagoras! For, having imagined the mind to be the initiating principle of all things, and suspending on its axis the balance of the universe; affirming, moreover, that the mind is a simple principle, unmixed, and incapable of admixture, he mainly on this very consideration separates it from all amalgamation with the soul; and yet in another passage he actually incorporates it with the soul. This [inconsistency] Aristotle has also observed; but whether he meant his criticism to be constructive, and to fill up a system of his own, rather than destructive of the principles of others, I am hardly able to decide. As for himself, indeed, although he postpones his definition of the mind, yet he begins by mentioning, as one of the two natural constituents of the mind, that divine principle which he conjectures to be impassible, or incapable of emotion, and thereby removes from all association with the soul. For whereas it is evident that the soul is susceptible of those emotions which it falls to it naturally to suffer, it must needs suffer either by the mind or with the mind. Now if the soul is by nature associated with the mind, it is impossible to draw the conclusion that the mind is impassible; or again, if the soul suffers not either by the mind or with the mind, it cannot possibly have a natural association with the mind, with which it suffers nothing, and which suffers nothing itself. Moreover, if the soul suffers nothing by the mind and with the mind, it will experience no sensation, nor will it acquire any knowledge, nor will it undergo any emotion through the agency of the mind, as they maintain it will. For Aristotle makes even the senses passions, or states of emotion. And rightly too. For to exercise the senses is to suffer emotion, because to suffer is to feel. In like manner, to acquire knowledge is to exercise the senses, and to undergo emotion is to exercise the senses; and the whole of this is a state of suffering. But we see that the soul experiences nothing of these things, in such a manner as that the mind also is not affected by the emotion, by which, indeed, and with which, all is effected. It fol-

---

[1] Comp. *Adv. Valentin.* vii.

lows, therefore, that the mind is capable of admixture, in opposition to Anaxagoras; and passible or susceptible of emotion, contrary to the opinion of Aristotle.

Besides, if a separate condition between the soul and mind is to be admitted, so that they be two things in substance, then of one of them, emotion and sensation, and every sort of taste, and all action and motion, will be the characteristics; whilst of the other the natural condition will be calm, and repose, and stupor. There is therefore no alternative: either the mind must be useless and void, or the soul. But if these affections may certainly be all of them ascribed to both, then in that case the two will be one and the same, and Democritus will carry his point when he suppresses all distinction between the two. The question will arise how two can be one — whether by the confusion of two substances, or by the disposition of one? We, however, affirm that the mind coalesces with the soul, — not indeed as being distinct from it in substance, but as being its natural function and agent.

CHAPTER XVI. THE SOUL'S RATIONAL AND IRRATIONAL PARTS

THAT position of Plato's is also quite in keeping with the faith, in which he divides the soul into two parts — the rational and the irrational. To this definition we take no exception, except that we would not ascribe this twofold distinction to the nature [of the soul]. It is the rational element which we must believe to be its natural condition, impressed upon it from its very first creation by its Author, who is Himself essentially rational. For how should that be other than rational, which God produced on His own prompting; nay more, which He expressly sent forth by His own *afflatus* or breath? The irrational element, however, we must understand to have accrued later, as having proceeded from the instigation of the serpent — the very achievement of [the first] transgression — which thenceforward became inherent in the soul, and grew with its growth, assuming the manner by this time of a natural development, happening as it did immediately at the beginning of nature. But, inasmuch as the same Plato speaks of the rational element only as existing in the soul of God Himself, if we were to ascribe the irrational element likewise to the nature which our soul has received from God, then the irrational element will be equally derived from God, as being a natural production, because God is the author of nature. Now from the devil proceeds the incentive to sin. All sin, however, is irrational: therefore the irrational proceeds from the devil, from whom sin proceeds; and it is extraneous to God, to whom also the irrational is an alien principle. The diversity, then, between these two elements arises from the difference of their authors. When, therefore, Plato reserves the rational element [of the soul] to God alone, and subdivides it into two departments — the *irascible*, which they call θυμικόν, and the *concupiscible*, which they designate by the term ἐπιθυμητικόν (in such a way as to make the first common to us and lions, and the second shared between ourselves and flies, whilst the rational element is confined to us and God). . . .

CHAPTER XXII. RECAPITULATION

HERMOGENES has already heard from us what are the other natural faculties of the soul, as well as their vindication and proof; whence it may be seen that the soul is rather the offspring of God than of matter. The names of these faculties shall here be simply repeated, that they may not seem to be forgotten and passed out of sight. We have assigned, then, to the soul both that freedom of the will which we just now mentioned, and its dominion over the works of nature, and its occasional gift of divination, independently of that endowment of prophecy which accrues to it expressly from the grace of God. We shall therefore now quit this subject of the soul's disposition, in order to set out fully in order its various qualities. The soul, then, we define to be sprung from the breath of God, immortal, possessing body, having form, simple in its substance, intelligent in its own nature, developing its powers in various ways, free in its determinations, subject to the changes of accident, in its faculties mutable, rational, supreme, endued with an instinct of presentiment, evolved out of one [archetypal soul]. It remains for us now to consider how it is developed out of this one original source; in other words, whence, and when, and how it is produced.

GREGORY OF NYSSA

(331–394)

THE ENDOWMENT OF MAN

Translated from the Greek * *by*
BENJAMIN RAND

CHAPTER XII. THE LOCATION OF THE INTELLECT

DISMISS therefore every idle fancy and foolish conjecture of those who confine the intellectual activity to particular locations in the body. Some of them think the heart is the seat of the guiding principle of the soul; others of them say the mind dwells in the brain. And these views they seek to maintain upon certain superficial grounds of probability. Those who give precedence to the heart regard its location as a proof of their affirmation, inasmuch as it occupies to all appearance the central place of the entire body. For this reason any exercise of the will can easily be transmitted from the centre throughout the whole body, and can thus proceed into action. As additional evidence they cite the emotions of pain and of anger in men, since these passions appear in a manner to bring every part into sympathy. The others, who attribute to the brain the faculty of thought, say that nature has constructed the brain as a citadel for the entire body, and the mind reigns therein like a king, with the organs of sense like messengers and armour-bearers standing guard about it. They assert as a convincing proof of their contention that with those who have suffered any lesion of the membrane of the brain an unbalancing and derangement of the faculty of thought commonly occurs, and

---

* From Gregory of Nyssa's Περὶ κατασκευῆς ἀνθρώπου in his *Opera, Gr. et Lat* Paris, 1615; 2 ed. 1638.

that those whose brains are clogged by drunkenness lose all consciousness of what is fitting.

Both parties who accept these views supplement their presumptions concerning the ruling faculty of the soul by reasons more closely derived from nature. One party says that the activity of the intellect has a kinship with the igneous, because both fire and the intellect are in constant motion. Since now they allow that heat has its source in the organ of the heart, they affirm that the activity of the mind is blended with the mobility of the heat, and as a consequence that the heart, which contains the heat, is the repository of the intellectual nature. The other party contend, on the contrary, that the membrane of the brain (as the skin-like cover enveloping the brain is called) is, as it were, the foundation and root of the organs of sense. Their warrant for the truth of this affirmation is because the activity of the perceptive faculty can never be located otherwise, than in this part where both the ear is attached and receives the sounds that fall upon it; where also the sight, inseparably connected with the base of the eyes, transmits the images that strike the pupils and makes an impression of them within; where also the different kinds of scent are discriminated through the sniffing of the organs of smell; and where also the sensation of taste is determined by the testing power of the membrane of the brain, which sends out certain fibrous runners bearing sensation, and proceeding through the vertebræ of the neck into the filterlike passage to the muscles there.

I concede that the intellectual processes of the soul are often disturbed by overpowering diseases, that the natural activity of the understanding is blunted by a bodily cause, and that the heart is a source of bodily fire and becomes aroused to emotional impulses. I admit further also that the membrane of the brain serves as a foundation of the organs of sense, as those affirm who make such investigations, since it envelops the brain and is moistened there by the discharging vapour. I have learned this from those who have made anatomical studies, and have no reason to doubt the truth of what is alleged. Nevertheless I derive therefrom no proof whatever, that the incorporeal nature is confined by certain local barriers. We know, however, that disturbances of the intellect do not originate from the mere clogging of the brain by drunkenness, but rather, as the physicians affirm, if the skin enveloping the sides becomes diseased, the intellect likewise assumes a disordered condition. This disease they call phrenitis, since the name of that skin is phrenes. The theory of joint-sensation occasioned by a pain in the heart is also mistaken. When not the heart indeed but the orifice of the stomach is painfully irritated they ignorantly attribute the suffering to the heart. Those who have made a careful study of diseases explain this as due to the fact that in a painful condition of the whole body there occurs a closing of the ducts, and as a result everything hindered in evaporation is driven back into the depths of the hollow parts of the body. In consequence, therefore, of the compression of the organs of respiration occasioned by the environment, a more powerful respiration takes place through the nature (i.e. of the body), as it seeks to remove the pressure for the purpose of the expansion of the contracted parts. This distress in breathing we regard as a symptom of pain, and call it sighing and groaning. But the pressure also that we imagine is felt in the region of the heart, is occasioned by unpleasant sensations not of the heart, but of the orifice of the stomach, and is due to the same cause, usually the contraction of the ducts, since indeed the gall-bladder as a result of the compression sends forth its sharp and smarting bile into the orifice of the stomach. An evidence of this is the yellow appearance of persons suffering from such disease as jaundice, due to the powerful contraction of the gall, which causes its juice to flow into the veins.

But the opposite emotion also, that of joy or laughter, affords our position still stronger support. If one is gladdened by a pleasant communication the ducts of the body will also be enlarged owing to the pleasure. Now in the case of pain the fine and invisible evaporations of the ducts are checked, and as the viscera within is bound in tighter position, the moist vapour is forced to the head, and to the membrane of the brain.

This vapour being accumulated in the hollows of the brain is then pressed out through the ducts lying beneath to the eyes, where the contraction of the eyelashes segregates the moisture in the form of drops called tears. Likewise, on the other hand, it must be observed that if the ducts are enlarged beyond their accustomed size in consequence of the opposite affections, a quantity of air is drawn through them toward the depths, and is there again naturally expelled through the mouth, since the entire viscera, and especially it is said the liver, forcefully ejects this air by a convulsive and violent movement. Nature therefore provides for the passage of this air through an enlargement of the aperture of the mouth by means of the pushing apart of the cheeks enclosing the air. This condition is termed laughter. Thus neither on account of the alleged reason can the intellectual faculty be attributed preferably to the liver; nor on account of the agitation of the blood of the heart in agreeable emotion can the location of the faculty of thought be supposed in the heart. These phenomena must therefore be referred to some special organization of the body, and it must be believed that the mind through some inexplicable plan of blending is distributed in all parts of the body, relatively to their importance.

If on the other hand one should oppose to us, that Holy Writ (Psalm VII, 6) attributes to the heart most important psychical activities, we cannot consent to such affirmation without a closer examination. For he who makes mention of the heart includes therewith the reins, saying God "who trieth the heart and reins," so that one must apply the seat of thought to both, or to neither of the two. But though one proves to me that the powers of the intellect are blunted in certain conditions of the body, or are even forced completely into inaction, I do not consider this fact sufficient evidence, that the power of thought is limited to any one locality in such wise that it would be driven from its accustomed place of sojourn owing to inflammation befalling the parts. For it is a truth applicable to all bodily things, that if a vessel is already occupied by anything which fills it, nothing else can find therein a place.

For the intellectual nature neither takes possession of the empty parts of the body, nor permits itself to be expelled by any superabundant flesh; but the entire body is similar in its organisation to a wind instrument, which a musician oftentimes knows how to play, but cannot show his knowledge because the uselessness of the instrument prevents the display of his art. Either it is unfit owing to age, or cracked from a fall, or unusable on account of rust or mould. As a result it is mute and ineffective, even if played upon by the most expert master of the pipes. Even so the mind pervades the entire organism, and acting in harmony with the powers of thought, as it naturally can, operates upon each one of the individual parts. In the case of those that are in their natural condition it produces the customary effect, but in bodies which are too weak to receive the operation of its art, it remains inactive and inefficacious. For it is the peculiar quality of the mind that it maintains friendly relationship with that which is in its natural conditions, but is alienated from whatever has receded from nature.

At this stage a principle suggests itself to me, which is based even more upon the natural inner consideration of things, and from which we can derive still higher precepts. For the divine nature is itself the most beautiful of all things that is pre-eminently good; and the essence towards which anything which possesses the desire for the beautiful is drawn. We, therefore, affirm that the mind, precisely because it is created after the image of the most beautiful, can itself abide in the beautiful so long as it possesses the amount of similarity with its prototype that it receives; and that on the contrary if it recedes in any measure from this resemblance, it is deprived of that beauty in which it was resident. But just as we said the mind possesses in itself beauty from similarity with its prototype, and like a mirror profits by the image of the form appearing in it; so in a similar manner we reason that nature also stands subject to the guidance and ruling of reason, and profits by its beauty and perfection. It is, as it were, a mirror of a mirror, and the material of our personality in which our nature is observed, is governed, and held together by reason. So long as the one cleaves to the other the community also of true beauty and perfection pervades in right relation all the parts, and transfers the lustre of divine grandeur to that connected with it. On the other hand, if a sundering of this incorporation with the good occurs, or if the higher appears in a subordinate relation to the lower, then also the unloveliness of the material abundance by nature reveals itself, (for matter is in itself something unformed and crude). Thus owing to this formlessness, that beauty of nature which adorns it through reason is also destroyed. Hence the unloveliness of matter passes over through nature to the mind itself, in such a manner that the image of God is seen no longer in the impression on the features. For the mind now receives the picture of the (divine) perfections as upon the back of the mirror, and although it reflects the rays of the splendour reflected from the good, it also rubs off the form-lessness of matter upon itself. Thus evil originates, the ex-istence of which commences with the deprivation of the good. But the beautiful is everything that stands in harmonious rela-tions with the original good; but everything that stands out-side of this relation, and of similarity with it, has no part in the beautiful. If now according to the reasoning we have observed there is only one original good, and if the mind in virtue of its creation in the image of the beautiful has itself beauty, and if the nature comprised by the mind is as it were an image of an image, then it is thereby proved that our material principle has persistence and continued support just as long as it is guided and kept in order by nature, but that it is committed to dissolution and decay if it forsakes that which gives it support and persistence, and is torn from its incorpora-tion with the beautiful. But this does take place precisely when there has been a reversion from nature towards the opposite. For there is every necessity that matter robbed of its own form must likewise suffer an alteration corresponding to this shape-lessness and unloveliness.

This is nevertheless an incidental explanation which has developed from our discussion upon the principal topic at issue. The chief question was, whether the intellect has its location in one special part of us, or whether it pervades all parts alike. For the reasoning of those who circumscribe the mind with local parts, and cite as a proof of their assumption the fact that if the membrane of the brain is in an unnatural condition thought is impaired, has disclosed that the power of the soul is in every part of the human organism that is in a condition to receive its activity, and similarly becomes inactive so soon as any part loses its natural condition. For that reason there was necessarily involved in the argument, the proposal by which we learn that in the human organism the mind is regulated by God, and through that in turn the material life is guided so long as it remains in the service of nature, but that if it turns aside from nature it also loses the power of activity, derived from the mind. Thus we return again to our point of departure, to wit, that the mind exercises power in such parts of the body as have not lost their natural constitution as a result of disease, and remains effective if they continue in conformity to nature, but on the contrary is powerless in those parts which are incapable of maintaining its activity.

SAINT AUGUSTINE
(354–430)

ON THE TRINITY

Translated from the Latin * by
ARTHUR WEST HADDAN

BOOK X. CHAPTER X. THE NATURE OF MIND

13. LET it not then add anything to that which it knows itself to be, when it is bidden to know itself. For it knows, at any rate, that this is said to itself; namely, to itself, that is, and that lives, and that understands. But a dead body also is, and cattle live; but neither a dead body nor cattle understand. Therefore it so knows that it so is, and that it so lives, as an understanding is and lives. When, therefore, for example's sake, the mind thinks itself air, it thinks that air understands; it knows, however, that itself understands, but it does not know itself to be air, but only thinks so. Let it separate that which it thinks itself; let it discern that which it knows; let this remain to it, about which not even have they doubted who have thought the mind to be this corporeal thing or that. For certainly every mind does not consider itself to be air; but some think themselves fire, others the brain, and some one kind of corporeal thing, others another, as I have mentioned before; yet all know that they themselves understand, and are, and live; but they refer understanding to that which they understand, but to be, and to live, to themselves. And no one doubts, either that no one understands who does not live, or that no one lives of whom it is not true that he is; and that therefore by consequence that which understands both is and lives; not as a

* From *De Trinitate*, Strasburg, 1477. Reprinted from Augustine's *On the Trinity*, translated by Arthur West Haddan, Edinburgh, 1873.

dead body is which does not live, nor as a soul lives which does not understand, but in some proper and more excellent manner. Further, they know that they will, and they equally know that no one can will who is not and who does not live; and they also refer that will itself to something which they will with that will. They know also that they remember; and they know at the same time that nobody could remember, unless he both was and lived; but we refer memory itself also to something, in that we remember those things. Therefore the knowledge and science of many things are contained in two of these three, memory and understanding; but will must be present, that we may enjoy or use them. For we enjoy things known, in which things themselves the will finds delight for their own sake, and so reposes; but we use those things, which we refer to some other thing which we are to enjoy. Neither is the life of man vicious and culpable in any other way, than as wrongly using and wrongly enjoying. But it is no place here to discuss this.

14. But since we treat of the nature of the mind, let us remove from our consideration all knowledge which is received from without, through the senses of the body; and attend more carefully to the position which we have laid down, that all minds know and are certain concerning themselves. For men certainly have doubted whether the power of living, of remembering, of understanding, of willing, of thinking, of knowing, of judging, be of air, or of fire, or of the brain, or of the blood, or of atoms, or besides the usual four elements of a fifth kind of body, I know not what; or whether the combining or tempering together of this our flesh itself has power to accomplish these things. And one has attempted to establish this, and another to establish that. Yet who ever doubts that he himself lives, and remembers, and understands, and wills, and thinks, and knows, and judges? Seeing that even if he doubts, he lives; if he doubts, he remembers why he doubts; if he doubts, he understands that he doubts; if he doubts, he wishes to be certain; if he doubts, he thinks; if he doubts, he knows that he does not know; if he doubts, he judges that he ought not to assent rashly. Whosoever therefore doubts about anything

else, ought not to doubt of all these things; which if they were
not, he would not be able to doubt of anything.

15. They who think the mind to be either a body or the
combination or tempering of the body, will have all these things
to seem to be in a subject, so that the substance is air, or fire, or
some other corporeal thing, which they think to be the mind;
but that the understanding is in this corporeal thing as its
quality, so that this coporeal thing is the subject, but the
understanding is in the subject, viz. that the mind is the subject, which they rule to be a corporeal thing, but the understanding, or any other of those things which we have mentioned
as certain to us, is in that subject. They also hold nearly the
same opinion who deny the mind itself to be body, but think it
to be the combination or tempering together of the body; for
there is this difference, that the former say that the mind itself
is the substance, in which the understanding is, as in a subject;
but the latter say that the mind itself is in a subject, viz. in the
body, of which it is the combination or tempering together.
And hence, by consequence, what else can they think, except
that the understanding also is in the same body as in a subject?

16. And all these do not perceive that the mind knows itself,
even when it seeks for itself, as we have already shown. But
nothing is at all rightly said to be known while its substance is
not known. And therefore, when the mind knows itself, it
knows its own substance; and when it is certain about itself,
it is certain about its own substance. But it is certain about
itself, as those things which are said above prove convincingly;
although it is not at all certain whether itself is air, or fire, or
some body, or some function of body. Therefore it is not any
of these. And that whole which is bidden to know itself, belongs
to this, that it is certain that it is not any of those things of
which it is uncertain, and is certain that it is that only, which
only it is certain that it is. For it thinks in this way of fire,
or air, and whatever else of the body it thinks of. Neither
can it in any way be brought to pass that it should so think
that which itself is, as it thinks that which itself is not. Since
it thinks all these things through an imaginary phantasy,

whether fire, or air, or this or that body, or that part or combination and tempering together of the body: nor assuredly is it said to be all those things, but some one of them. But if it were any one of them, it would think this one in a different manner from the rest, viz. not through an imaginary phantasy, as absent things are thought, which either themselves or some of like kind have been touched by the bodily sense; but by some inward, not feigned, but true presence (for nothing is more present to it than itself); just as it thinks that itself lives, and remembers, and understands, and wills. For it knows these things in itself, and does not imagine them as though it had touched them by the sense outside itself, as corporeal things are touched. And if it attaches nothing to itself from the thought of these things, so as to think itself to be something of the kind, then whatsoever remains to it from itself, that alone is itself.

CHAPTER XI. MEMORY, UNDERSTANDING, AND WILL

17. Putting aside, then, for a little while all other things, of which the mind is certain concerning itself, let us especially consider and discuss these three — memory, understanding, will. For we may commonly discern in these three the character of the abilities of the young also; since the more tenaciously and easily a boy remembers, and the more acutely he understands, and the more ardently he studies, the more praiseworthy is he in point of ability. But when the question is about any one's learning, then we ask not how solidly and easily he remembers, or how shrewdly he understands; but what it is that he remembers, and what it is that he understands. And because the mind is regarded as praiseworthy, not only as being learned, but also as being good, one gives heed not only to what he remembers and what he understands, but also to what he wishes; not how ardently he wishes, but first what it is he wishes, and then how greatly he wishes it. For the mind that loves eagerly is then to be praised, when it loves that which ought to be loved eagerly. Since, then, we speak of these three

— ability, knowledge, use — the first of these is to be considered under the three heads, of what a man can do in memory, and understanding, and will. The second of them is to be considered in regard to that which any one has in his memory and in his understanding, whither he has attained by a studious will. But the third, viz. use, lies in the will, which handles those things that are contained in the memory and understanding, whether it refer them to anything further, or rest satisfied with them as an end. For to use, is to take up something into the power of the will; and to enjoy, is to use with joy, not any longer of hope, but of the actual thing. Accordingly, every one who enjoys, uses; for he takes up something into the power of the will, wherein he also is satisfied as with an end. But not every one who uses, enjoys, if he has sought after that, which he takes up into the power of the will, not on account of the thing itself, but on account of something else.

18. Since, then, these three, memory, understanding, will, are not three lives, but one life; nor three minds, but one mind; it follows certainly that neither are they three substances, but one substance. Since memory, which is called life, and mind, and substance, is so called in respect to itself; but it is called memory, relatively to something. And I should say the same also of understanding and of will, since they are called understanding and will relatively to something; but each in respect to itself is life, and mind, and essence. And hence these three are one, in that they are one life, one mind, one essence; and whatever else they are severally called in respect to themselves, they are called also together, not plurally, but in the singular number. But they are three, in that wherein they are mutually referred to each other; and if they were not equal, and this not only each to each, but also each to all, they certainly could not mutually contain each other; for not only is each contained by each, but also all by each. For I remember that I have memory, and understanding, and will; and I understand that I understand, and will, and remember; and I will that I will, and remember, and understand; and I remember together my whole memory, and understanding, and will. For that of my memory

which I do not remember, is not in my memory; and nothing is so much in the memory as memory itself. Therefore I remember the whole memory. Also, whatever I understand I know that I understand, and I know that I will whatever I will; but whatever I know I remember. Therefore I remember the whole of my understanding, and the whole of my will. Likewise, when I understand these three things, I understand them together as whole. For there is none of things intelligible which I do not understand, except what I do not know; but what I do not know, I neither remember, nor will. Therefore, whatever of things intelligible I do not understand, it follows also that I neither remember nor will. And whatever of things intelligible I remember and will, it follows that I understand. My will also embraces my whole understanding and my whole memory, whilst I use the whole that I understand and remember. And, therefore, while all are mutually comprehended by each, and as wholes, each as a whole is equal to each as a whole, and each as a whole at the same time to all as wholes; and these three are one, one life, one mind, one essence.

THOMAS AQUINAS

(1225-1274)

SUMMA THEOLOGICA

Translated from the Latin* by
BENJAMIN RAND

QUESTION LXXVI. RATIONALITY THE ESSENTIAL FORM IN MAN

Article 3. Are there besides the Rational Soul in Man, other Souls different in Essence?

(*a*) It would appear that beside the rational soul in man other souls essentially different exist, to wit, the sensitive and nutritive.

I. For what is perishable does not belong to the same substance as what is imperishable. But the rational soul is imperishable, whereas the other souls, that is, the nutritive and the sensitive, are perishable. It is not possible, therefore, that there is in man a single essence of a rational, sensitive, and nutritive soul.

II. If it be said that the sensitive soul of man is imperishable there is opposed to such a view, the declaration of Aristotle (10 *Metaph.*), that what is perishable differs in kind from that which is imperishable. But the sensitive soul in the horse, lion, and other animals is perishable. If therefore it were imperishable in man, then the sensitive soul in man and brute would not be of the same kind. Nevertheless that is called animal which has a sensitive soul. Animal would therefore not be the common genus for man and the other animals. But this is incongruous.

* Freely translated from Thomas Aquinas' *Summa Theologica*, Basil, 1485; in his *Opera Omnia*, Romae, 1889, vol. v.

III. Aristotle says "the embryo is first animal. and then man" (2 *de Gener*, c. 3). But this would not be possible if the sensitive soul had the same essence as the rational. For the animal is thus designated because of its sensitive soul; and man is so called because of his rational soul. Consequently there is in man no single essence composed of a sensitive and a rational soul.

IV. Aristotle says (8 *Metaph*.) "the genus of being is derived from the matter, but the difference from the essential form." Now *rationality* which is the specific difference in man is derived from the rational soul; but the *animal* is so called because it has a body animated by a sensitive soul. The rational soul, therefore, is related to the body animated by the sensitive soul, as form is to matter. The rational soul is not, therefore, identical in essence with the sensitive soul in man, but presupposes the latter as its substrate matter.

But on the other hand it should be said: we do not admit two souls in one and the same man, as Jacobus and the other Syrians affirm, to wit, an animal soul which animates the body, and is mixed with the blood, and a rational soul which ministers to the reason; but there is a single soul in man which animates the body by its presence, and orders by its own principle of reason" (*lib. de eccl. dogm.* c. 15).

(*b*) I reply that Plato postulated (*Timæus*) in one body different souls, distinguished likewise by their organs, to which he attributed diverse vital functions, declaring that there is a nutritive faculty in the liver, an appetitive faculty in the heart, and a rational faculty in the brain.

Aristotle refutes (2 *de Anima*, c. 2) this view so far as it concerns those powers of the soul which in their activities employ bodily organs. His reason is that in case of those animals which though cut in two still live, the different operations of the soul in any one part are still found, such as feeling and desire. But this would not be the case if diverse principles of psychical activities, differing essentially from one another, were ascribed to the different parts of the body. But with regard to the rational soul he appears to have left it an open question, whether it is separated from the other powers of the soul only by virtue of reason, or also in location.

The opinion of Plato would indeed be justified, if one supposed the soul were united to the body not as form, but as moving principle, as Plato assumed. For in that case nothing incongruous results, if the same mobile object be moved by different moving forces, especially in its different subordinate parts.

But if we assume that the soul is united to the body as its form, it is then wholly impossible that several souls, differing essentially from one another, should have existence in a single body. This can be clearly shown in three ways.

1. The animal would not have unity of being in which there were several souls. Nothing has simple unity, save through form alone, by which a thing has its being. For from the same form that a thing derives entity, it derives unity; and therefore what are designated by different forms are not singly one, as for instance a white man. If therefore man were a living being by virtue of some one form, that is the vegetative soul; animal by virtue of another form, the sensitive soul; and were a thinking being by virtue of another form, the rational soul, he would not then be singly one. Thus Aristotle also argues (8 *Metaph.*), as against Plato, that if there were one idea of an animal, and another of a biped, there would be no single entity of a biped animal. Accordingly he asks (1 *de Anima*), in answer to those who assume different souls in the same body, what then holds together these diverse souls, that is, what makes a unity of them. It is not possible to say that they are made indeed into a unity through the body; for the soul contains the body and makes it to be one, rather than the reverse.

2. This appears impossible by the mode of predication. For the attributes which embody different forms in the same thing are predicable of one another, either accidentally, or reciprocally. If these forms have no relation to one another, as if one were to say that what is white may also be sweet, then the attribute does not depend on the substance itself, but arises from other causes, since it is not in the essence of white to be sweet. Or, if

the attributes are naturally related they will be predicated *per se*, according to the second definition of *per se*, because the subject then appears in the definition of the predicate. Thus I can say, the surface must precede the colour, if the surface of the body is coloured, for the existence of a surface must precede the concept of colour. Man is therefore owing to certain forms said to be an *animal*, and to other forms a *man*. The affirmation 'man is an animal,' therefore, must be either purely 'accidental,' or, one of the souls must precede the other. But the former statement is manifestly false, because *animal* is predicated of man *per se*, and not *per accidens;* and the latter is untrue, because *man* is not contained in the definition of animal, but the reverse. It therefore follows, that there can only be one and the same form from which it results, both that man is animal, and that he is also man. If it were otherwise man would not be what is designated by *animal*, since the necessary attribute for animal would be predicated only accidentally of man.

3. Again this appears impossible because of the fact, that one activity of the soul inhibits another, if it be very intense. This would by no means happen unless the principle of action in man were in essence one. It follows, therefore, that there is only one soul as to number in man, which must be deemed at the same time nutritive, sensitive, and rational.

How this can happen may easily be understood by anyone who pays heed to the differences of species and of forms. For the forms and species of things differ from one another, in that one is more or less perfect than another. Thus plants are more perfect than inanimate objects; animals again rank above plants; and man in turn rises above the beasts. And among the individuals of the same class there are also varying degrees of perfection. For this reason Aristotle compares (8 *Metaph.*) the forms of species to numbers, which differ in type according as a unit is added or subtracted. And he compares (2 *de Anima*) the different souls to figures in which one contains another, and yet exceeds it. In like manner the rational soul contains within its powers, both what belongs to the sensitive soul of the brutes, and likewise to the nutritive soul of the plant. The surface, therefore, which has the figure of a pentagon, also is not by one figure in it a square, and by another a pentagon; for in that case the square would be superfluous, since it is contained in the pentagon. Thus Socrates also is not by virtue of one soul a man, and by virtue of another an animal; but he is both, through one and the same soul.

(c) I. The sensitive soul is imperishable, not because of its sensitive nature, but because it possesses rationality. If the soul be thus capable only of being sensitive, it is perishable; but if it has with the sensitive nature also rationality, it is imperishable. For though the sensitive does not impart incorruptibility, nevertheless it is impossible to dissociate incorruptibility from the rational.

II. Forms do not belong to species and to genus, but the composites. Man however is mortal, as are all other animals. The difference therefore between the perishable and imperishable, which proceeds from the forms, does not cause man to differ in genus from the other animals.

III. The embryo has at first only a sensitive soul. If this be superseded, it receives a more perfect one, which is both sensitive and rational.[1]

IV. One should not apply different kinds of reasoning or logical deduction, which are involved in methods of cognition, to determine diversity in natural object. For in reasoning it is possible to apprehend one and the same thing in different ways. Hence, since the rational soul contains in its powers everything that belongs to the sensitive soul, and also something more; the reason too can distinguish from itself, what pertains to the powers of the sensitive soul, and regard it as something incomplete and material. Moreover, because it finds this incompleteness to be something common to man and to other animals, it formulates therefrom the nature of the genus. But that in which the rational soul exceeds and surpasses the sensitive soul, it regards as the forming and perfecting principle which differentiates the being of man.

[1] This is more fully developed by Thomas Aquinas in Question cxviii, Art. 2 of the *Summa Theolo:ica.*

QUESTION LXXVI. THE RELATION OF SOUL AND BODY

Article VI. Is the Soul united to the Body without any further Intermediation?

(*a*) IT would appear that the rational soul is united to the body by the intermediation of certain special properties. For:

I. Every form exists in matter suited and adjusted to it. But such preadjustment to the form is effected by certain accidents. Hence some accidental properties must be thought present in matter before the entrance of the soul as substantial form.

II. Different forms of one and the same species are adapted to different parts of matter. But different parts presuppose the apportioning of measurable quantities. Therefore one cannot assume such apportioning of matter before the entrance of substantial forms, of which many unite in one species.

III. The spiritual effects the body through its operating activity. But the activity of the soul is its intellectual power. Therefore the soul is united to the body by means of its intellectual power, which is so to speak an accidental property.

But on the other hand it should be said: Every such property exists posterior to substance, and thus presupposes both time and reason (7 *Metaph.*). Therefore the accidental form cannot be thought as existing in the matter before the soul is there as substantial form.

(*b*) I answer: if the soul were only the mover of the body, nothing need be said against this view. On the contrary, it would be necessary to assume that particular properties intermediate between soul and body; namely, upon the part of the soul the ability to move the body, and upon the part of the body, its moveability.

But since the rational soul is the substantial form of the body, it is impossible that there should be any accidental intermediation between the soul and body, or between any substantial form and its matter. Since matter is potentially disposed in a certain order for all actualities, that which in point of simplicity is first in actualities is first in matter. But the first of all actualities is being. It is impossible, therefore, to conceive a substance as either cold, or to have size, before it has actual existence. But everything has actual existence in virtue of its substantial form. Therefore, it is impossible that there should be any preparatory accidental quality in the matter before the substantial form; and consequently nothing in the body before the soul.

(c) To the first position we must say, as is clear from the previous discussion, that a form of more perfect powers comprises whatever inferior forms there are. Therefore one and the same existing form perfects its matter in different grades of perfection. It is one and the same essential form by which man has being, possesses body, is living, is animal, and is man. It is now apparent, that certain peculiar properties correspond to every one of these different kinds of actuality. Hence as matter is conceived as perfected in being before it can be apprehended as corporeal, so the properties which accompany being are conceived before their incorporation. So too adjustments of matter are conceived before the form, not as if these were present in actual being, but because they accompany its activities.

II. The kinds of magnitude which are the necessary properties of materiality, correspond to those which belong in general to matter. Matter, therefore, can be viewed as already corporeal, and of various magnitudes, and yet be regarded as different in its various parts; and therefore as capable of receiving a further degree of perfection in its diverse forms. For though it is always one and the same form in its essence, through which the different degrees of perfection are attributed to matter, still reason makes distinctions in these perfections.

III. The spiritual substance that is united to the body merely as its motive force, is united to it by its potential and actual powers. But the intellective soul is united to the body, as form in its absolute essence. It however regulates the body by its potential and actual powers.

QUESTION LXXXII. THE SUPERIORITY OF REASON TO WILL

Article III. Is the Nature of Reason superior to that of Will?

(*a*) This appears not to be the case. For:

I. The final cause or the good is the object of the will. But the final cause is the first and highest of causes. The will, therefore, is the first and highest of the faculties.

II. Natural objects ascend from the imperfect to the perfect. Thus also in the faculties of the soul, the order of progress is from the senses to the reason, which is superior. But the natural process is from an act of mind to an act of will. The will is therefore superior to and more perfect than the intellect.

III. States of mind correspond to their potencies. But love which is a state of mind achieved by the will stands as the highest virtue. For it is written: "Though I know all mysteries and have all faith but have not love I am nothing." 1 Cor. 13, v. 2. The will is therefore a higher potency than the intellect.

On the other hand, Aristotle gives (10 *Ethics*, 7) the first place among the faculties to reason.

1. I answer, the rank of a faculty in relation to others can be viewed: (1) in accordance to the nature possessed by each *absolutely;* and (2) in accordance to a certain aspect only *relatively.*

If the first view be considered, it is self-evident that the reason is superior to the will. For the nature of a faculty is judged according to its objects. Now the object of the reason is more simple, absolute, and less conditioned, than that of the will. For the object of the reason is the very idea of desirable good. The will however is directed towards a desirable good, the idea of which is in the reason. Now the more simple, the less conditioned, and the more detached from particulars, anything is, so much the higher does it stand in the rank and the value of its being. The faculty of reason is, therefore, in its nature more noble, and more sublime, than that of the will.

Relatively, however, and in comparison with something else,

it may chance at times that the will stands higher than the intellect. This is true because the object of the will may belong to a higher type of being than the object of the reason. Thus I could say that hearing is superior to sight, because the object from which the object proceeds is more noble than that which has the color, although color in itself may stand higher and be purer than sound. In a similar manner, the action of the intellect consists in this, that the nature of the thing known is comprehended by the knower; but the action of the will is consummated in the will's inclining to the object as it is in itself, whatever its nature may be. For this reason, Aristotle says, "good and evil which are the objects of the will belong to things; true and false which are objects of the intellect belong to the mind" (6 *Metaph*.). When, therefore, the actual being in which the good exists as object of reason, is superior to the soul itself in which its nature is comprehended, then in comparison to such an object, the will is superior to the reason. But if the desired object is lower than the soul, then the reason in comparison to such an object is superior to the will. It is, therefore, better to love God, than merely to know God; and, conversely, it is better only to know corporeal things, than to love them. Nevertheless absolutely, reason is superior to will.

(*c*) II. Whatever is earlier in time or origin is the more imperfect. For in one and the same thing, the potency precedes activity. At first there is the imperfect, later the perfected. But that which is before absolutely, and according to the order of nature, is the more perfect. Thus the activity is earlier than the potency. And in like manner, the reason precedes the will, as the moving force precedes that which is moved, and as activity precedes the affected. For in so far as the good is conceived by the reason, it moves the will.

III. Through love we cleave to God, who is transcendently raised above the soul. For that reason, the will is in this instance superior to the reason.

THOMAS HOBBES
(1588–1679)

HUMAN NATURE*

CHAPTER I.   INTRODUCTION

1. THE true and perspicuous explication of the elements of *laws natural and politic (which is my present scope)* dependeth upon the knowledge of what is *human nature*, what is *body politic*, and what it is we call a *law;* concerning which points, as the *writings* of men from antiquity downwards have still increased, so also have the *doubts* and *controversies* concerning the same: and seeing that true knowledge begetteth not doubt nor controversy, but knowledge, it is manifest from the present controversies, that they, which have *heretofore* written thereof, have not well understood their own subject.

2. *Harm* I can do none, though I err no less than they; for I shall leave men but as they are, in doubt and dispute: but, intending not to take any principle upon *trust*, but only to put men in mind of what they *know already*, or *may know* by their own experience, I hope to err the less; and when I do, it must proceed from too *hasty concluding*, which I will endeavour as much as I can to avoid.

3. On the other side, if *reasoning aright* win not *consent*, which may very easily happen, from them that being confident of their own knowledge weigh not what is said, the *fault* is not mine, but theirs; for as it is my part to *shew* my reasons, so it is theirs to bring *attention*.

4. Man's *nature* is the *sum of his natural faculties and powers*, as the faculties of *nutrition, motion, generation, sense, reason,*

* *Humane Nature, or the fundamental elements of policie.* London, 1651. Reprinted here from Hobbes' *English Works*, collected and edited by Sir William Molesworth, London, 1839, vol. iv.

&c. These powers we do unanimously call *natural*, and are contained in the definition of man, under these words, *animal* and *rational*.

5. According to the two principal parts of man, I divide his faculties into two sorts, faculties of the *body*, and faculties of the *mind*.

6. Since the minute and distinct anatomy of the powers of the *body* is nothing necessary to the present purpose, I will only sum them up in these three heads, power *nutritive*, power *motive*, and power *generative*.

7. Of the powers of the *mind* there be two sorts, *cognitive*, *imaginative*, or *conceptive*, and *motive;* and first of *cognitive*.

For the understanding of what I mean by the power *cognitive*, we must remember and acknowledge that there be in our minds continually certain *images* or conceptions of the things without us, insomuch that if a man could be alive, and all the rest of the world annihilated, he should nevertheless retain the *image* thereof, and all those things which he had before seen or perceived in it; every one by his own experience knowing, that the *absence* or *destruction* of things once imagined doth not cause the *absence* or *destruction* of the *imagination* itself. This *imagery* and *representations* of the qualities of the thing without, is that we call our *conception, imagination, ideas, notice* or *knowledge* of them; and the *faculty* or power by which we are capable of such knowledge, is that I here call cognitive *power*, or *conceptive*, thͬ power of knowing or conceiving.

CHAPTER II. THE SENSE AND ITS MAIN DECEPTION

1. HAVING declared what I mean by the word *conception*, and other words equivalent thereunto, I come to the *conceptions* themselves, to shew their *differences*, their *causes*, and the *manner of the production*, so far as is necessary for this place.

2. Originally all *conceptions* proceed from the *action* of the thing itself, whereof it is the conception: now when the action is

present, the conception it produceth is also called *sense;* and the thing by whose action the same is produced, is called the *object of the sense*.

3. By our several *organs* we have several *conceptions* of several qualities in the objects; for by *sight* we have a conception or image composed of *colour* and *figure*, which is all the notice and knowledge the object imparteth to us of its nature by the eye. By *hearing* we have a conception called *sound*, which is all the knowledge we have of the quality of the object from the ear. And so the rest of the senses are also conceptions of several qualities, or natures of their objects.

4. Because the *image* in vision consisting of *colour* and *shape* is the knowledge we have of the qualities of the object of that sense; it is no hard matter for a man to fall into this opinion, that the same *colour* and *shape* are the *very qualities themselves;* and for the same cause, that *sound* and *noise* are the *qualities of the bell*, or of the air. And this opinion hath been so long received, that the *contrary* must needs appear a great paradox; and yet the introduction of *species visible* and *intelligible* (which is necessary for the maintenance of that opinion) passing to and fro from the *object*, is *worse* than any paradox, as being a plain *impossibility*. I shall therefore endeavour to make plain these points:

That the subject wherein colour and image are inherent, is *not* the *object* or thing seen.

That there is nothing *without us* (really) which we call an *image* or colour.

That the said image or colour is but an *apparition* unto us of the *motion*, agitation, or alteration, which the *object* worketh in the *brain*, or spirits, or some internal substance of the head.

That as in *vision*, so also in conceptions that arise from the *other senses*, the subject of their *inherence* is not the *object*, but the *sentient*.

5. Every man hath so much experience as to have seen the *sun* and the other visible objects by reflection in the *water* and *glasses;* and this alone is sufficient for this conclusion, that *col-*

our and *image* may be there where the *thing seen* is *not*. But because it may be said that notwithstanding the *image* in the water be not in the object, but a thing merely *phantastical*, yet there may be *colour* really in the thing itself: I will urge further this experience, that divers times men see directly the *same* object *double*, as *two candles* for *one*, which may happen from distemper, or otherwise without distemper if a man will, the organs being either in their right temper, or equally distempered; the *colours* and *figures* in two such images of the same thing *cannot be inherent* therein, because the thing seen cannot be in *two places*.

One of these images therefore is *not inherent* in the object: but seeing the organs of the sight are then in equal temper or distemper, the *one* of them is no more inherent than the *other;* and consequently *neither* of them both are in the object; which is the first proposition, mentioned in the precedent number.

6. Secondly, that the image of any thing by *reflection* in a *glass* or *water* or the like, is *not* any thing *in* or *behind* the glass, or *in* or *under* the water, every man may grant to himself; which is the second proposition.

7. For the third, we are to consider, first that upon every *great agitation* or *concussion* of the *brain* (as it happeneth from a stroke, especially if the stroke be upon the eye) whereby the optic nerve suffereth any great violence, there *appeareth* before the *eyes* a certain light, which light is *nothing without*, but an apparition only, all that is real being the concussion or motion of the parts of that nerve; from which experience we may conclude, that *apparition of light is really nothing but motion* within. If therefore from *lucid bodies* there can be derived *motion*, so as to affect the optic nerve in such manner as is proper thereunto, there will follow an *image* of light somewhere in that line by which the motion was last derived to the eye; that is to say, in the object, if we look directly on it, and in the glass or water, when we look upon it in the line of reflection, which in effect is the third proposition; namely, that image and colour is but an apparition to us of that motion, agitation, or alteration

which the object worketh in the brain or spirits, or some *internal* substance in the head.

8. But that *from all lucid*, shining and illuminate bodies there is a *motion produced* to the eye, and, through the eye, to the *optic* nerve, and so into the *brain*, by which that apparition of *light* or *colour* is affected, is not hard to prove. And first, it is evident that the *fire*, the only lucid body here upon earth, worketh by *motion* equally every way; insomuch as the motion thereof *stopped* or inclosed, it is presently *extinguished*, and no more fire. And further, that that motion, whereby the fire worketh, is *dilation*, and *contraction* of itself *alternately*, commonly called *scintillation* or glowing, is manifest also by experience. From such *motion* in the fire must needs arise a *rejection* or casting from itself of that part of the *medium* which is *contiguous* to it, whereby that part also rejecteth the *next*, and so successively one part beateth back another to the very *eye;* and in the same manner the *exterior* part of the eye presseth the *interior*, (the laws of refraction still observed). Now the interior coat of the eye is nothing else but a piece of the *optic* nerve; and therefore the motion is still continued thereby into the *brain*, and by *resistance* or reaction of the brain, is also a *rebound* into the optic nerve again; which we *not conceiving* as motion or rebound from *within*, do think it is *without*, and call it *light;* as hath been already shewed by the experience of a stroke. We have no reason to doubt, that the fountain of light, the *sun*, worketh by any other ways than the *fire*, at least in this matter. And thus all *vision* hath its original from such *motion* as is here described: for where there is no light, there is no sight; and therefore *colour* also must be the same thing with *light*, as being the effect of the lucid bodies: their *difference* being only this, that when the light cometh *directly* from the fountain to the eye, or *indirectly* by reflection from *clean* and *polite* bodies, and such as have *not* any particular motion internal to alter it, we call it *light;* but when it cometh to the eye by reflection from *uneven, rough*, and coarse bodies, or such as are affected with internal motion of their own that may alter it, then we call it *colour;* colour and light differing only in this, that the one is *pure*, and the other *perturbed*

light. By that which hath been said, not only the truth of the third proposition, but also the whole manner of producing light and colour, is apparent.

9. As colour is not inherent in the object, but an effect thereof upon us, caused by such motion in the object, as hath been described: so neither is *sound* in the thing we hear, but in ourselves. One manifest sign thereof is, that as a man may *see*, so also he may *hear double* or *treble*, by multiplication of *echoes*, which echoes are sounds as well as the original; and *not* being in one and the *same place*, cannot be *inherent* in the body that maketh them. Nothing can make any thing which is not in itself: the *clapper* hath no *sound* in it, but *motion*, and maketh motion in the internal parts of the bell; so the *bell* hath motion, and not sound, that imparteth *motion* to the *air;* and the *air* hath motion, but not sound; the *air* imparteth motion by the *ear* and *nerve* unto the *brain;* and the brain hath motion but not sound; from the *brain*, it reboundeth back into the nerves *outward*, and thence it becometh an *apparition without*, which we call *sound*. And to proceed to the *rest* of the *senses*, it is apparent enough, that the *smell* and *taste* of the *same thing*, are *not* the *same* to *every man;* and therefore are not in the thing *smelt* or *tasted*, but in the men. So likewise the *heat* we feel from the fire is manifestly in *us*, and is quite *different* from the heat which is in the *fire:* for *our* heat is *pleasure* or *pain*, according as it is *great* or *moderate;* but in the *coal* there is no such thing. By this the fourth and last proposition is proved, *viz.* that as in vision, so also in conceptions that arise from *other* senses, the subject of their inherence is not in the object, but in the sentient.

10. And from hence also it followeth, that *whatsoever accidents* or qualities our senses make us think there be in the *world*, they be *not* there, but are *seeming* and *apparitions* only: the things that really *are* in the world without us, are those *motions* by which these seemings are caused. And this is the *great deception of sense*, which also is to be by sense *corrected:* for as sense telleth me, when I see *directly*, that the colour seemeth to *be* in the object; so also sense telleth me, when I see by *reflection*, what colour is not in the object.

CHAPTER III. IMAGINATION AND DREAMS

1. As standing water put into motion by the stroke of a *stone*, or blast of wind, doth *not presently* give over moving as soon as the wind ceaseth, or the stone settleth: so *neither* doth the *effect* cease which the *object* hath wrought upon the *brain*, so soon as ever by turning aside of the organs the *object ceaseth* to work; that is to say, though the *sense* be *past*, the *image* or *conception* remaineth; but more *obscure* while we are *awake*, because some *object* or other continually *plieth* and soliciteth our eyes, and ears, *keeping* the mind in a *stronger* motion, whereby the *weaker* doth not easily *appear*. And this obscure conception is that we call *phantasy*, or *imagination: imagination* being, to define it, *conception remaining, and by little and little decaying from after and the act of sense.*

2. But when present sense is *not*, as in *sleep*, there the *images* remaining after sense, when there be many, as in dreams, are *not obscure*, but *strong* and *clear*, as in sense itself. The reason is, that which obscured and made the conceptions weak, namely sense, and present *operation* of the object, is *removed:* for *sleep* is the *privation of the act of sense*, (the power remaining) and *dreams* are the *imagination* of them that *sleep*.

3. The *causes* of dreams, if they be natural, are the *actions* or violence of the *inward* parts of a man upon his *brain*, by which the *passages* of sense by sleep *benumbed*, are *restored* to their motion. The signs by which this appeareth to be so, are the *differences* of dreams (old men commonly dream oftener, and have their dreams more painful than young) proceeding from the *different* accidents of man's body, as dreams of *lust*, as dreams of *anger*, according as the heart, or other parts within, work more or less upon the brain, by more or less *heat;* so also the descents of different *sorts of phlegm* maketh us a dream of different tastes of meats and drinks; and I believe there is a *reciprocation* of motion from the brain to the vital parts, and back from the vital parts to the brain; whereby not only *imagination* begetteth *motion* in those parts; but also motion in those parts begetteth imagination like to that by which it was begot-

ten. If this be true, and that *sad* imaginations nourish the *spleen*, then we see also a cause, why a strong *spleen* reciprocally causeth *fearful dreams*, and why the effects of *lasciviousness* may in a dream produce the image of some person that had *caused* them. Another sign that dreams are caused by the action of the inward parts, is the *disorder* and casual consequence of one conception or image to another: for when we are *waking*, the *antecedent* thought or conception introduceth, and is cause of the *consequent*, as the water followeth a man's finger upon a dry and level table; but in *dreams* there is commonly *no coherence*, and when there is, it is by chance, which must needs proceed from this, that the *brain* in dreams is *not restored* to its motion in every part alike; whereby it cometh to pass, that our thoughts appear like the stars between the flying clouds, not in the order which a man would choose to observe them, but as the uncertain flight of broken clouds permits.

4. As when the *water*, or any liquid thing moved at once by *divers* movements, receiveth *one* motion compounded of them all; so also the *brain* or spirit therein, having been stirred by *divers* objects, composeth an imagination of *divers* conceptions that appeared single to the sense. As for example, the sense sheweth at one time the figure of a *mountain*, and at another time the colour of *gold;* but the imagination afterwards hath them both at once in a *golden mountain.* From the same cause it is, there appear unto us *castles* in the *air*, *chimeras*, and other monsters which are *not* in *rerum natura,* but have been conceived by the sense in pieces at several times. And this composition is that which we commonly call *fiction* of the mind.

5. There is yet another kind of imagination, which for *clearness contendeth* with *sense*, as well as a *dream;* and that is, when the *action* of sense hath been *long* or *vehement:* and the experience thereof is more frequent in the sense of seeing, than the rest. An example whereof is, the *image* remaining before the *eye* after looking upon the *sun.* Also, those little images that appear before the eyes in the *dark* (whereof I think every man hath experience, but they most of all, who are *timorous* or superstitious) are examples of the same. And these, for distinction-sake, may be called *phantasms.*

6. By the *senses*, which are numbered according to the *organs* to be *five*, we take notice (as hath been said already) of the objects *without* us; and that *notice* is our *conception* thereof: but we take *notice* also some way or other *of our conceptions:* for when the conception of the same thing cometh *again*, we take notice that it is *again;* that is to say, that we have had the same conception *before;* which is as much as to imagine a thing *past;* which is impossible to the *sense*, which is only of things *present.* This therefore may be accounted a *sixth sense*, but *internal*, (not *external*, as the rest) and is commonly called *remembrance.*

7. For the *manner* by which we take notice of a conception *past*, we are to remember, that in the *definition* of *imagination*, it is said to be a conception by *little* and *little decaying*, or growing more *obscure.* An *obscure* conception is that which representeth the *whole object* together, but *none* of the *smaller parts* by themselves; and as *more* or *fewer* parts be represented, so is the conception or representation said to be *more* or *less clear.* Seeing then the *conception*, which when it was *first* produced by sense, was *clear*, and represented the *parts* of the object *distinctly;* and when it cometh *again* is *obscure*, we find *missing* somewhat that we expected; by which we judge it *past* and *decayed.* For example, a man that is present in a foreign *city*, seeth not only *whole* streets, but can also distinguish particular *houses*, and *parts* of houses; but departed thence, he cannot distinguish them so particularly in his mind as he did, some *house* or turning escaping him; yet is this to *remember;* when *afterwards* there escape him *more* particulars, this is also to *remember*, but *not* so well. In process of time, the image of the city *returneth* but as a *mass* of building *only*, which is *almost* to have *forgotten* it. Seeing then remembrance is *more* or *less*, as we find more or less *obscurity*, why may not we well think *remembrance* to be nothing else but the *missing of parts*, which every man expecteth should succeed after they have a conception of the whole? To see at a great distance of place, and to remember at a great distance of time, is to have like conceptions of the thing: for there wanteth distinction of parts in both; the one conception being weak by operation at distance, the other by decay.

8. And from this that hath been said, there followeth, that a man can *never know* he *dreameth;* he *may* dream he *doubteth,* whether it be a dream or no: but the clearness of the imagination representeth every thing with as many parts as doth sense itself, and consequently, he can take notice of nothing but as present; whereas to think he dreameth, is to think those his conceptions, that is to say dreams, obscurer than they were in the sense; so that he must think them both as clear, and not as clear as sense; which is impossible.

9. From the same ground it proceedeth, that men *wonder not* in their dreams at place and persons, as they would do waking: for waking, a man would think it strange to be in a place where he never was before, and remember nothing of how he came there; but in a dream, there cometh little of that kind into consideration. The *clearness* of conception in a dream, taketh away *distrust,* unless the *strangeness* be *excessive,* as to think himself fallen from on high without hurt, and then most commonly he *waketh.*

10. Nor is it *impossible* for a man to be so far deceived, as when his dream is *past,* to think it real: for if he dream of such things as are ordinarily in his mind, and in such order as he useth to do waking, and withal that he laid him down to sleep in the place where he findeth himself when he awaketh; all which may happen: I know no κριτήριον or mark by which he can discern whether it were a dream or not, and therefore do the less wonder to hear a man sometimes to tell his dream for a truth, or to take it for a vision.

CHAPTER IV. THOUGHT

1. THE *succession* of conceptions in the mind, series or consequence of one after another, may be *casual* and incoherent, as in dreams for the most part; and it may be *orderly,* as when the former thought introduceth the latter; and this is *discourse* of the mind. But because the word discourse is commonly taken for the *coherence* and consequence of words, I will, to avoid equivocation, call it *discursion.*

2. The *cause* of the *coherence* or consequence of one conception to another, is their first *coherence* or consequence at that *time* when they are produced by sense: as for example, from St. Andrew the mind runneth to St. Peter, because their names are read together; from St. Peter to a *stone*, for the same cause; from *stone* to *foundation*, because we see them together; and for the same cause, from foundation to *church*, and from church to *people*, and from people to *tumult*: and according to this example, the mind may run almost from anything to anything. But as in the *sense* the conception of cause and effect may succeed one another; so may they after sense in the *imagination:* and for the most part they do so; the *cause* whereof is the *appetite* of them, who, having a conception of the *end*, have next unto it a conception of the next *means* to that end: as, when a man, from a thought of *honour* to which he hath an appetite, cometh to the thought of *wisdom*, which is the next means thereunto; and from thence to the thought of *study*, which is the next means to wisdom.

3. To omit that kind of discursion by which we proceed from anything to anything, there are of the *other* kind *divers* sorts: as first, in the *senses* there are certain coherences of conceptions, which we may call *ranging;* examples whereof are; a man casteth his *eye* upon the *ground*, to look about for some *small* thing lost; the *hounds* casting about at a fault in hunting; and the *ranging* of spaniels: and herein we take a beginning arbitrary.

4. Another sort of discursion is, when the *appetite* giveth a man his beginning, as in the example before, where honour to which a man hath appetite, maketh him think upon the next means of attaining it, and that again of the next, &c. And this the Latins call *sagacitas*, and we may call *hunting* or *tracing*, as dogs trace beasts by the smell, and men hunt them by their footsteps; or as men hunt after riches, place, or knowledge.

5. There is yet another kind of discursion beginning with the appetite to *recover* something lost, proceeding from the *present backward*, from thought of the place where we *miss* at, to the thought of the place from whence we came *last;* and from the

thought of that, to the thought of a place *before*, till we have in our mind some place, wherein we had the thing we miss: and this is called *reminiscence*.

6. The *remembrance* of succession of one thing to another, that is, of what was *antecedent*, and what *consequent*, and what *concomitant*, is called an *experiment;* whether the same be made by us *voluntarily*, as when a man putteth any thing into the fire, to see what effect the fire will produce upon it: or *not* made by us, as when we remember a fair morning after a red evening. To have had many *experiments*, is that we call *experience*, which is nothing else but *remembrance* of what antecedents have been followed by what consequents.

7. No man can have in his mind a conception of the *future*, for the future is *not yet:* but of our conceptions of the *past*, we make a *future;* or rather, call *past, future* relatively. Thus after a man hath been accustomed to see like antecedents followed by like consequents, whensoever he seeth the like come to pass to any thing he had seen before, he looks there should follow it the same that followed then: as for example, because a man hath often seen offences followed by punishment, when he seeth an offence in present, he thinketh punishment to be consequent thereunto; but consequent unto that which is present, men call future; and thus we make *remembrance* to be the *prevision* of things to come, or *expectation* or presumption of the future.

8. In the same manner, if a man seeth in present that which he hath seen before, he thinks that that which was antecedent to that which he saw before, is also antecedent to that he presently seeth: as for example, he that hath seen the ashes remain after the fire, and now again seeth ashes, concludeth again there hath been fire: and this is called again *conjecture* of the past, or presumption of the fact.

9. When a man hath *so often* observed like antecedents to be followed by like consequents, that *whensoever* he seeth the antecedent, he looketh again for the consequent; or when he seeth the consequent, maketh account there hath been the like antecedent; then he calleth both the antecedent and the consequent,

signs one of another, as clouds are signs of rain to come, and rain of clouds past.

10. This taking of signs by *experience*, is that wherein men do ordinarily think, the difference stands between man and man in *wisdom*, by which they commonly understand a man's whole ability or *power cognitive;* but this is an *error:* for the signs are but *conjectural;* and according as they have often or seldom failed, so their *assurance* is more or less; but *never full* and *evident:* for though a man have always seen the day and night to follow one another hitherto; yet can he not thence conclude they shall do so, or that they have done so eternally: *experience concludeth nothing universally.* If the signs hit twenty times for one missing, a man may lay a wager of twenty to one of the event; but may not conclude it for a truth. But by this it is plain, that they shall *conjecture best,* that have *most experience,* because they have most signs to conjecture by: which is the reason *old men* are *more prudent,* that is, conjecture better, *cæteris paribus,* than young: for, being old, they remember more; and experience is but remembrance. And *men* of *quick* imagination, *cæteris paribus,* are more *prudent* than those whose imaginations are slow: for they observe *more* in *less* time. Prudence is nothing but conjecture from experience, or taking of signs from experience warily, that is, that the experiments from which he taketh such signs be all remembered; for else the cases are not alike that seem so.

11. As in conjecture concerning things past and future, it is prudence to conclude from experience, what is like to come to pass, or to have passed already; so it is an error to conclude from it, that *it is* so or so *called;* that is to say, we cannot from experience conclude, that any thing is to be called *just* or *unjust,* *true* or *false,* or any proposition *universal* whatsoever, except it be from remembrance of the use of names imposed arbitrarily by men: for example, to have heard a sentence given in the like case, the like sentence a thousand times is not enough to conclude that the sentence is just; though most men have no other means to conclude by: but it is *necessary,* for the drawing of such conclusion, to *trace* and *find out,* by many experiences, what men

do mean by calling things just and unjust. Further, there is another *caveat* to be taken in concluding by experience, from the tenth section of the second chapter; that is, that we conclude such things to be without, that are within us.

CHAPTER VI. KNOWLEDGE AND BELIEF

1. THERE is a story somewhere, of one that pretends to have been miraculously cured of blindness, wherewith he was born, by St. Alban or other Saints, at the town of St. Alban's; and that the Duke of Gloucester being there, to be satisfied of the truth of the miracle, asked the man, What colour is this? who, by answering, it was green, discovered himself, and was punished for a counterfeit: for though by his sight newly received he might distinguish between green, and red, and all other colours, as well as any that should interrogate him, yet he could not possibly know at first sight which of them was called green, or red, or by any other name. By this we may understand, there be *two kinds* of knowledge, whereof the *one* is nothing else but *sense*, or knowledge *original*, as I have said in the beginning of the second chapter, and *remembrance* of the same; the *other* is called *science* or knowledge of the *truth of propositions*, and how things are called, and is derived from *understanding*. Both of these sorts are but *experience;* the former being the experience of the effects of things that work upon us from *without;* and the latter experience men have from the proper use of *names* in language: and all experience being, as I have said, but remembrance, all knowledge is remembrance: and of the *former*, the register we keep in books, is called *history;* but the registers of the latter are called the *sciences.*

2. There are *two things* necessarily implied in this word *knowledge;* the one is *truth*, the other *evidence;* for what is not truth, can never be known. For, let a man say he knoweth a thing never so well, if the same shall afterwards appear false, he is driven to confession, that it was not knowledge, but opinion. Likewise, if the truth be not evident, though a man holdeth it, yet is his knowledge thereof no more than theirs who hold

the contrary: for if truth were enough to make it knowledge, all truth were known; which is not so.

3. What *truth* is, hath been defined in the precedent chapter; what *evidence* is, I *now* set down: and it is the concomitance of a man's *conception* with the *words* that signify such conception in the act of ratiocination: for when a man reasoneth with his lips only, to which the mind suggesteth only the beginning, and followeth not the words of his mouth with the conceptions of his mind, out of custom of so speakirg; though he begin his ratiocination with true propositions, and proceed with certain syllogisms, and thereby make always true conclusions; yet are not his conclusions *evident* to him, for want of the *concomitance of conception* with his words: for if the words alone were sufficient, a *parrot* might be taught as well to know truth, as to speak it. Evidence is to truth, as the sap to the tree, which, so far as it creepeth along with the body and branches, keepeth them alive; where it forsaketh them, they die: for this evidence, which is meaning with our words, is the life of truth.

4. Knowledge thereof, which we call *science*, I define to be *evidence of truth*, from some beginning or principle of *sense:* for the truth of a proposition is never evident, until we conceive the meaning of the words or terms whereof it consisteth, which are always conceptions of the mind: nor can we remember those conceptions, without the thing that produced the same by our senses. The *first* principle of knowledge is, that we have such and such *conceptions;* the *second*, that we have thus and thus *named* the things whereof they are conceptions; the *third* is, that we have *joined* those *names* in such manner as to make true propositions; the *fourth* and last is, that we have *joined* those *propositions* in such manner as they be concluding, and the truth of the conclusion said to be known. And of these two kinds of knowledge, whereof the former is *experience of fact,* and the latter *evidence of truth;* as the *former,* if it be great, is called *prudence;* so the *latter,* if it be much, hath usually been called, both by ancient and modern writers, *sapience* or wisdom and of this *latter, man* only is capable; of the *former, brute beasts* also participate.

5. A proposition is said to be *supposed*, when, being *not evident*, it is nevertheless *admitted for a time*, to the end, that, joining to it other propositions, we may *conclude* something; and to *proceed* from conclusion to conclusion, for a *trial* whether the same will lead us into any *absurd* or impossible conclusion; which if it *do*, then we know such supposition to have been false.

6. But if running through *many* conclusions, we come to *none* that are *absurd*, then we think the proposition *probable;* likewise we think probable whatsoever proposition we *admit* for truth by error of reasoning, or from trusting to other men: and all such propositions as are admitted by *trust* or error, we are not said to *know*, but to *think* them to be true; and the admittance of them is called *opinion*.

7. And particularly, when the opinion is admitted out of *trust* to *other* men, they are said to *believe* it; and their admittance of it is called *belief*, and sometimes *faith*.

8. It is either *science* or *opinion* which we commonly mean by the word *conscience:* for men say that such and such a thing is true in or upon their conscience; which they *never* do, when they think it *doubtful;* and therefore they *know*, or *think* they know it to be true. But men, when they say things upon their conscience, are not therefore presumed certainly to know the truth of what they say; it remaineth then, that that word is used by them that have an *opinion, not* only of the *truth* of the thing, *but* also of their *knowledge* of it, to which the *truth* of the proposition is consequent. *Conscience* I therefore define to be *opinion of evidence.*

9. *Belief*, which is the admitting of propositions upon *trust*, in many cases is no less free from *doubt*, than perfect and manifest *knowledge:* for as there is nothing whereof there is not some cause; so, when there is doubt, there must be some cause thereof conceived. Now there be many things which we receive from *report of others*, of which it is impossible to imagine any cause of *doubt* for what can be opposed against the consent of all men, in things they can know, and have no cause to report otherwise than they are, such as is a great part of our *histories*, unless a man would say that all the world had *conspired* to deceive him.

And thus much of *sense, imagination, discursion, ratiocination*, and *knowledge*, which are the acts of our *power cognitive*, or *conceptive*. That power of the *mind* which we call *motive*, differeth from the power *motive* of the *body;* for the power *motive* of the *body* is that by which it *moveth other* bodies, and we call *strength :* but the power motive of the *mind*, is that by which the mind giveth *animal motion* to that *body* wherein it existeth; the acts hereof are our *affections* and *passions*, of which I am to speak in general.

CHAPTER VII. THE PASSIONS

1. IN the eighth section of the second chapter is shewed, *that conceptions* and *apparitions* are nothing *really*, but *motion* in some internal substance of the *head;* which motion *not stopping* there, but proceeding to the *heart*, of necessity must there either *help* or *hinder* the motion which is called *vital;* when it *helpeth*, it is called *delight, contentment*, or *pleasure*, which is nothing really but motion about the heart, as conception is nothing but motion in the head: and the *objects* that cause it are called *pleasant* or *delightful*, or by some name equivalent; the Latins have *jucundum, a juvando*, from helping; and the same delight, with reference to the object, is called *love :* but when such motion *weakeneth* or hindereth the vital motion, then it is called *pain;* and in relation to that which causeth it, hatred, which the Latins express sometimes by *odium*, and sometimes by *tædium*.

2. This motion, in which consisteth *pleasure* or *pain*, is also a *solicitation* or provocation either to draw *near* to the thing that pleaseth, or to *retire* from the thing that displeaseth; and this solicitation is the *endeavour* or internal beginning of *animal* motion, which when the object *delighteth*, is called *appetite;* when it *displeaseth*, it is called *aversion*, in respect of the displeasure *present;* but in respect of the displeasure *expected, fear.* So that, *pleasure, love*, and *appetite*, which is also called desire, are *divers names* for divers considerations of the *same thing*.

3. Every man, for his own part, calleth that which *pleaseth*, and is delightful to himself, *good;* and that *evil* which *displeas-*

eth him: insomuch that while every man *differeth* from another in *constitution*, they differ also from one another concerning the common distinction of good and evil. Nor is there any such thing as absolute goodness, considered without relation: for even the goodness which we apprehend in God Almighty, is *his goodness to us*. And as we call *good* and *evil* the *things* that please and displease; so call we *goodness* and *badness*, the *qualities* or powers whereby they do it: and the signs of that goodness are called by the Latins in one word *pulchritudo*, and the signs of evil, *turpitudo;* to which we have no words precisely answerable.

As all conceptions we have immediately by the *sense*, are, *delight*, or *pain*, or *appetite*, or *fear;* so are all the *imaginations* after sense. But as they are weaker imaginations, so are they also weaker pleasures, or weaker pain.

4. As *appetite* is the beginning of *animal* motion towards something that pleaseth us; so is the *attaining* thereof, the *end* of that motion, which we also call the *scope*, and aim, and final cause of the same: and when we attain that end, the delight we have thereby is called the *fruition:* so that *bonum* and *finis* are different names, but for different considerations of the same thing.

5. And of *ends*, some of them are called *propinqui*, that is, near at hand; others *remoti*, far off: but when the ends that be nearer attaining, be compared with those that be further off, they are called not ends, but *means*, and the *way* to those. But for an *utmost* end, in which the ancient *philosophers* have placed *felicity*, and disputed much concerning the way thereto, there is no such thing in this world, nor way to it, more than to Utopia: for while we live, we have desires, and desire presupposeth a further end. Those things which please us, as the way or *means* to a further end, we call *profitable;* and the *fruition* of them, *use;* and those things that profit not, *vain*.

6. Seeing all *delight* is *appetite*, and presupposeth a *further* end, there can be *no contentment* but in *proceeding:* and therefore we are not to marvel, when we see, that as men attain to more riches, honour, or other power; so their appetite continually groweth more and more; and when they are come to the

utmost degree of some kind of power, they pursue some other, as long as in any kind they think themselves behind any other: of those therefore that have attained to the highest degree of honour and riches, some have affected mastery in some art; as Nero in music and poetry, Commodus in the art of a gladiator; and such as affect not some such thing, must find diversion and recreation of their thoughts in the contention either of play or business: and men justly complain of a great grief, that they know not what to do. *Felicity*, therefore, by which we mean continual delight, consisteth *not* in *having* prospered, but in *prospering*.

7. There are few things in this world, but *either* have *mixture* of good and evil, *or* there is a chain of them so necessarily linked together, that the one cannot be taken without the other: as for example, the pleasures of sin, and the bitterness of punishment, are inseparable; as is also labour and honour, for the most part. Now when in the *whole chain*, the *greater part* is good, the *whole* is called *good;* and when the *evil* over-weigheth, the *whole* is called *evil*.

8. There are two sorts of pleasure, whereof the *one* seemeth to affect the *corporeal* organ of the sense, and that I call *sensual;* the *greatest* part whereof, is that by which we are invited to give continuance to our *species;* and the *next*, by which a man is invited to meat, for the preservation of his *individual* person: the *other sort* of delight is not particular to any part of the body, and is called the delight of the *mind*, and is that which we call *joy*. Likewise of *pains*, some affect the *body*, and are therefore called the *pains* of the body; and some *not*, and those are called *grief*.

CHAPTER XII. THE WILL

1. It hath been declared already, how *eternal* objects cause *conceptions*, and conceptions, *appetite* and *fear*, which are the *first unperceived beginnings of our actions;* for *either* the actions immediately follow the first appetite, as when we do anything upon a sudden; *or else* to our first appetite there succeedeth some conception of evil to happen to us by such actions, which

is fear, and which holdeth us from proceeding. And to that fear may succeed a new appetite, and to that appetite another fear alternately, till the action be either done, or some accident come between, to make it impossible; and so this alternate appetite and fear ceaseth. This *alternate succession of appetite and fear* during all the time the action is in our power to do or not to do, is that we call *deliberation;* which name hath been given it for that part of the definition wherein it is said that it lasteth so long as the action, whereof we deliberate, is in our power: for, so long we have liberty to do or not to do; and deliberation signifieth a taking away of our own liberty.

2. *Deliberation* therefore requireth in the action deliberated *two conditions;* one, that it be *future;* the other, that there be *hope* of doing it, or possibility of not doing it; for, *appetite* and *fear* are *expectations* of the future; and there is no expectation of good, without hope; or of evil, without possibility: of *necessaries* therefore there is *no deliberation*. In deliberation, the last appetite, as also the last fear, is called *will*, viz. the last appetite, will to do, or will to omit. It is all one therefore to say *will* and *last will;* for, though a man express his present inclination and appetite concerning the disposing of his goods, by words or writings; yet shall it not be counted his will, because he hath still liberty to dispose of them other ways: but when death taketh away that liberty, then it is his will.

3. *Voluntary* actions and omissions are such as have beginning in the *will;* all other are *involuntary*, or *mixed voluntary; involuntary*, such as he doth by necessity of nature, as when he is pushed, or falleth, and thereby doth good or hurt to another: *mixed*, such as participate of both; as when a man is carried to prison, going is voluntary, to the prison, is involuntary: the example of him that throweth his goods out of a ship into the sea, to save his person, is of an action altogether voluntary: for, there is nothing therein involuntary, but the hardness of the choice, which is not his action, but the action of the winds: what he himself doth, is no more against his will, than to flee from danger is against the will of him that seeth no other means to preserve himself.

4. *Voluntary* also are the actions that proceed from sudden *anger*, or *other* sudden *appetite* in such men as can discern good or evil: for, in them the time precedent *is* to be judged deliberation: for then also he deliberateth in what cases it is good to strike, deride, or do any other action proceeding from anger or other such sudden passion.

5. *Appetite, fear, hope,* and the rest of the passions are *not* called *voluntary;* for they proceed *not from, but are the will;* and the will is not voluntary: for, a man can no more say he will will, then he will will will, and so make an infinite repetition of the word [*will*]; which is absurd, and insignificant.

6. Forasmuch as *will to do* is *appetite,* and *will to omit, fear;* the *cause* of *appetite* and *fear* is the *cause* also of our *will:* but the propounding of the benefits and of harms, that is to say, of reward and punishment, is the cause of our appetite, and of our fears, and therefore also of our wills, so far forth as we believe that such rewards and benefits as are propounded, shall arrive unto us; and consequently, our *wills* follow our *opinions*, as our *actions* follow our *wills;* in which sense they say truly, and properly, that say the world is governed by opinion.

7. When the wills of many concur to one and the same action and effect, this *concourse* of their *wills* is called *consent;* by which we must not understand one will of many men, for every man hath his several will, but many wills to the producing of one effect: but when the *wills* of two divers men *produce* such actions as are reciprocally *resistant* one to the other, this is called *contention;* and, being upon the persons one of another, *battle:* whereas actions proceeding from *consent*, are mutual *aid.*

8. When many wills are involved or included in the will of one or more consenting, (which how it may be, shall be hereafter declared) then is that involving of many wills in one or more, called *union.*

9. In *deliberations* interrupted, as they may be by *diversion* of other business, or by *sleep*, the last *appetite* of such part of the deliberation is called *intention*, or *purpose.*

RENÉ DESCARTES
(1596–1650)

THE PASSIONS OF THE SOUL

Translated from the French * by
HENRY A. P. TORREY

PART I

ARTICLE I

Passion, as respects the subject, is always action in some other respect.

THERE is nothing which better shows how defective the sciences are which we have received from the ancients than what they have written upon the passions; for, although it is a subject the knowledge of which has always been much sought after, and which does not appear to be one of the more difficult sciences, because everyone, feeling the passions in himself, stands in no need whatever of borrowing any observation elsewhere to discover their nature, nevertheless, what the ancients have taught on this subject is of such slight intent, and for the most part so untrustworthy, that I cannot have any hope of reaching the truth, except by abandoning the paths which they have followed. That is the reason why I shall be obliged to write now in the same way as I should if I were treating a topic which no one before me had ever touched upon; and, to begin with, I take into consideration the fact that an event is generally spoken of by philosophers as a passion as regards the subject to which it happens, and an action in respect to that which causes it; so that, although the agent and the patient may often

* From *Les passions de l'âme*, Amst. 1650. In *Œuvres*, t. iv. Reprinted from *The Philosophy of Descartes, in Extracts from his Writings*, selected and translated by Henry A. P. Torrey. New York, Henry Holt and Company, 1892.

be very different, action and passion are always one and the same thing, which has these two names because of the two different subjects to which it can be referred.

ARTICLE II

In order to understand the passions of the soul, it is necessary to distinguish its functions from those of the body.

Next I take into consideration that we know of no subject which acts more immediately upon our soul than the body to which it is joined, and that consequently we must think that what in the one is a passion is commonly in the other an action; so that there is no better path to the knowledge of our passions than to examine into the difference between the soul and the body, in order to know to which of them is to be attributed each of our functions.[1]

ARTICLE III

The rule to be observed to this end.

No great difficulty will be found in this, if it be borne in mind that all that which we experience in ourselves which we see can also take place in bodies entirely inanimate is to be attributed only to our body; and, on the contrary, all that which is in us and which we cannot conceive in any manner possible to pertain to a body is to be attributed to our soul.

ARTICLE IV

That heat and the movement of the limbs proceed from the body, thoughts from the mind.

Thus, because we cannot conceive that the body thinks in any manner whatever, we have no reason but to think that all forms of thought which are in us belong to the mind; and because we cannot doubt that there are inanimate bodies which can move in as many or more different ways than ours, and

[1] Cf. Meditation vi, in *The Method, Meditations and Selections from the Principles.* Translated by John Veitch. Edin., 1850, etc.

which have as much or more heat (as experience teaches us in the case of flame, which alone has more heat and motion than any of our members), we must believe that all the heat and all the motions which are in us, in so far as they do not depend at all on thought, belong only to the body.

ARTICLE V

That it is an error to think that the soul imparts motion and heat to the body.

By this means we shall avoid a very great error, into which many have fallen, an error which I consider to be the principal hindrance, up to the present time, to a correct explanation of the passions and other properties of the soul. It consists in this, that, seeing that all dead bodies are deprived of heat and, consequently, of motion, it is imagined that the absence of the soul causes these movements and this heat to cease; and thus it has been thought, without reason, that our natural heat and all the motions of our body depend upon the soul; instead of which it should be thought, on the contrary, that soul departs, when death occurs, only because this heat fails and the organs which serve to move the body decay.

ARTICLE VI

The difference between a living and a dead body.

In order, then, that we may avoid this error, let us consider that death never takes place through the absence of a soul, but solely because some one of the principal parts of the body has fallen into decay; and let us conclude that the body of a living man differs as much from that of a dead man as does a watch or other automaton (that is to say, or other machine which moves of itself), when it is wound up, and has within itself the material principle of the movements for which it is constructed, with all that is necessary for its action, from the same watch or other machine, when it has been broken, and the principle of its movement ceases to act.

ARTICLE VII

Brief explanation of the parts of the body and of some of its functions.[1]

In order to render this more intelligible, I will explain here in a few words how the entire mechanism of our body is composed. There is no one who does not already know that there is in us a heart, a brain, a stomach, muscles, nerves, arteries, veins, and such things; it is known also that the food we eat descends into the stomach and the bowels, where their juices flowing through the liver and through all the veins, mix themselves with the blood they contain, and by this means increase its quantity. Those who have heard the least talk in medicine know, further, how the heart is constructed, and how all the blood of the veins can easily flow through the *vena cava* on its right side, and thence pass into the lung, by the vessel which is called the arterial vein, then return from the lung on the left side of the heart, by the vessel called the venous artery, and finally pass thence into the great artery, the branches of which are diffused through the whole body. Also, all those whom the authority of the ancients has not entirely blinded, and who are willing to open their eyes to examine the opinion of Hervæus[2] in regard to the circulation of the blood, have no doubt whatever that all the veins and arteries of the body are merely channels through which the blood flows without cessation and very rapidly, starting from the right cavity of the heart by the arterial vein, the branches of which are dispersed throughout the lungs and joined to that of the venous artery, by which it passes from the lungs into the left side of the heart; next, from thence it passes into the great artery, the branches of which, scattered throughout all the rest of the body, are joined to the branches of the vein, which carry once more the same blood into the right cavity of the heart; so that these two cavities are like sluices, through each of which all the blood passes every time it makes the circuit of the body. Still further, it is known that all the

[1] Cf. Discourse on Method, pt. v.; Veitch, p. 46; (*Œuvres*, t. i, p. 173).
[2] Harvey. See tribute to Harvey (*Œuvres*, t. ix, p. 361).

movements of the limbs depend upon the muscles, and that these muscles are opposed to one another in such a way that, when one of them contracts, it draws toward itself the part of the body to which it is attached, which at the same time stretches out the muscle which is opposed to it; then, if it happens, at another time, that this last contracts, it causes the first to lengthen, and draws toward itself the part to which they are attached. Finally, it is known that all these movements of the muscles, as also all the senses, depend upon the nerves, which are like minute threads, or small tubes, all of which come from the brain, and contain, like that, a certain subtle air or breath, which is called the animal spirits.

ARTICLE VIII

The principle of all these functions.

But it is not commonly known in what manner these animal spirits and these nerves contribute to the movements of the limbs and to the senses, nor what is the corporeal principle which makes them act; it is for this reason, although I have already touched upon this matter in other writings,[1] I shall not omit to say here briefly, that, as long as we live, there is a continual heat in our heart, which is a kind of fire kept up there by the blood of the veins, and that this fire is the corporeal principle of the movements of our limbs. . . .

ARTICLE XVI

How all the limbs can be moved by the objects of the senses and by the spirits without the aid of the soul.

Finally, it is to be observed that the machine of our body is so constructed that all the changes which occur in the motion of the spirits may cause them to open certain pores of the brain rather than others, and, reciprocally, that when any one of these pores is opened in the least degree more or less than is usual by the action of the nerves which serve the senses, this changes somewhat the motion of the spirits, and causes them

[1] On Man; also Discourse on Method, etc.; trans. by Veitch, p. 52.

to be conducted into the muscles which serve to move the body in the way in which it is commonly moved on occasion of such action; so that all the movements which we make without our will contributing thereto (as frequently happens when we breathe, or walk, or eat, and, in fine, perform all those actions which are common to us and the brutes) depend only on the conformation of our limbs and the course which the spirits, excited by the heat of the heart, naturally follow in the brain, in the nerves, and in the muscles, in the same way that the movement of a watch is produced by the force solely of its mainspring and the form of its wheels. . . .

ARTICLE XXX

That the soul is united to all parts of the body conjointly.

But, in order to understand all these things more perfectly, it is necessary to know that the soul is truly joined to the entire body, and that it cannot properly be said to be in any one of its parts to the exclusion of the rest, because the body is one, and in a manner indivisible, on account of the arrangement of its organs, which are so related to one another, that when any one of them is taken away, that makes the whole body defective: and because the soul is of a nature which has no relation to extension, or to dimensions, or other properties of the matter of which the body is composed, but solely to the whole collection of its organs, as appears from the fact that we cannot at all conceive of the half or the third of a soul, nor what space it occupies, and that it does not become any smaller when any part of the body is cut off, but that it separates itself entirely from it when the combination of its organs is broken up.

ARTICLE XXXI

That there is a small gland in the brain in which the soul exercises its functions more particularly than in the other parts.

It is, also, necessary to know that, although the soul is joined to the entire body, there is, nevertheless, a certain part of the body in which it exercises its functions more particularly than in all the rest; and it is commonly thought that this part is the brain, or, perhaps, the heart: the brain, because to it the organs of sense are related; and the heart, because it is as if there the passions are felt. But, after careful examination, it seems to me quite evident that the part of the body in which the soul immediately exercises its functions is neither the heart, nor even the brain as a whole, but solely the most interior part of it, which is a certain very small gland, situated in the middle of its substance, and so suspended above the passage by which the spirits of its anterior cavities communicate with those of the posterior, that the slightest motions in it may greatly affect the course of these spirits, and, reciprocally, that the slightest changes which take place in the course of the spirits may greatly affect the motions of this gland.

Article XXXII

How this gland is known to be the principal seat of the soul.

The reason which convinces me that the soul cannot have in the whole body any other place than this gland where it exercises its functions immediately, is the consideration that the other parts of our brain are all double, just as also we have two eyes, two hands, two ears, and, in fine, all the organs of our external senses are double; and inasmuch as we have but one single and simple thought of the same thing at the same time, there must necessarily be some place where the two images which by means of the two eyes, or the two other impressions which come from a single object by means of the double organs of the other senses, may unite in one before they reach the mind, in order that they may not present to it two objects in place of one; and it may easily be conceived that these images or other impressions unite in this gland, through the medium of the spirits which fill the cavities of the brain; but there is no other place whatever in the whole body, where they can thus be united, except as they have first been united in this gland.

Letter to Mersenne, July 30, 1640 [1]

As for the letter of the physician De Sens, it contains no argument to impugn what I have written upon the gland called *conarium*, except that he says that it can be changed like all the brain, which does not at all prevent its being the principal seat of the soul; for it is certain that the soul must be joined to some part of the body, and there is no point which is not as much or more liable to alteration than this gland, which, although it is very small and very soft, nevertheless, on account of its situation, is so well protected, that it can be almost as little subject to any disease as the crystalline humor of the eye; and it happens more frequently indeed that persons become troubled in mind, without any known cause, in which case it may be assigned to some disorder of this gland, than it happens that sight fails by any defect of this crystalline humor, besides that all the other changes which happen to the mind, as when one falls asleep after drinking, etc., may be ascribed to some changes occurring in this gland.

As for what he says about the mind's being able to make use of double organs, I agree with him, and that it makes use also of the spirits, all of which cannot reside in this gland; but I do not at all conceive that the mind is so restricted to it that it cannot extend its activity beyond it; but it is one thing to make use of, and another thing to be immediately joined and united to it; and our mind not being double, but one and indivisible, it seems to me that the part of the body to which it is most immediately united must also be one and not divided into two similar parts, and I find nothing of that kind in the whole brain except this gland.

Article XXXIII

That the seat of the passions is not in the heart.

As for the opinion of those who think that the soul experiences its passions in the heart, it is of no great account, because it is founded only on the fact that the passions cause some stir

---

[1] *Œuvres*, t. viii, p. 301.

to be felt there; and it is easy to see that this change is felt, as if
in the heart, only through the medium of a small nerve, which
descends to it from the brain, just as pain is felt as if in the foot
through the medium of the nerves of the foot, and the stars are
perceived as in the heavens by the medium of their light and the
optic nerves; so that it is no more necessary that our soul exercise its functions immediately in the heart in order to feel there
its passions, than it is necessary that it should be in the heavens
in order to see the stars there.

ARTICLE XXXIV

How the soul and the body act one upon the other.

Let us conceive, then, that the soul has its principal seat in
this little gland in the middle of the brain, whence it radiates
to all the rest of the body by means of the spirits, the nerves,
and even of the blood, which, participating in the impressions
of the mind, can carry them by means of the arteries into all the
members; and, bearing in mind what has been said above concerning the machine of our body, to wit, that the minute filaments of our nerves are so distributed throughout all its parts
that, on occasion of the different motions which are excited there
by means of sensible objects, they open in divers manners the
pores of the brain, which causes the animal spirits contained in
these cavities to enter in various ways into the muscles, by
means of which they can move the limbs in all the different ways
of which they are capable, and, also, that all the other causes,
which in other ways can set the spirits in motion, have the effect
to turn them upon various muscles [keeping all this in mind],
let us add here that the little gland which is the principal seat
of the soul is so suspended between the cavities which contain
the spirits, that it can be affected by them in all the different
ways that there are sensible differences in objects; but that it
can also be variously affected by the soul, which is of such a
nature that it receives as many different impressions — that is
to say, that it has as many different perceptions — as there
occur different motions in this gland; as also, reciprocally, the

machine of the body is so composed that from the simple fact that this gland is variously affected by the soul, or by whatever other cause, it impels the spirits which surround it toward the pores of the brain, which discharge them by means of the nerves upon the muscles, whereby it causes them to move the limbs. . . .

Article XL

The principal effect of the passions.

It is to be noted that the principal effect of all the passions in man is that they incite and dispose the mind to will the things to which they prepare the body, so that the sentiment of fear incites it to will to fly; that of courage, to will to fight; and so of the rest.

Article XLI

The power of the mind over the body.

But the will is so free in its nature that it can never be constrained; and of the two kinds of thoughts which I have distinguished in the mind — of which one is its actions, that is, its volitions; the other its passions, taking this word in its most general signification, comprehending all sort of perceptions — the first of these are absolutely in its power, and can be changed only indirectly by the body, while, on the contrary, the last depend absolutely on the movements which give rise to them, and they can be affected only indirectly by the mind, except when it is itself the cause of them. And the whole action of the mind consists in this, that by the simple fact of its willing anything it causes the little gland, to which it is closely joined, to produce the result appropriate to the volition.

Article XLII

How the things we wish to recall are found in the memory.

Thus, when the mind wills to recall anything, this volition causes the gland, by inclining successively to different sides, to impel the spirits toward different parts of the brain until they come upon that where the traces are left of the thing it wills to remember; for these traces are due to nothing else than the circumstance that the pores of the brain, through which the spirits have already taken their course, on presentation of that object, have thereby acquired a greater facility than the rest to be opened again in the same way by the spirits which come to them; so that these spirits coming upon these pores, enter therein more readily than into the others, by which means they excite a particular motion in the gland, which represents to the mind the same object, and causes it to recognize that it is that which it willed to remember.

ARTICLE XLIII

How the mind can imagine, attend, and move the body.

Thus, when it is desired to imagine something which has never been seen, the will has the power to cause the gland to move in the manner requisite to impel the spirits toward the pores of the brain by the opening of which that thing can be represented; so, when one wills to keep his attention fixed for some time upon the same object, this volition keeps the gland inclined during that time in the same direction; so, finally, when one wills to walk or to move his body in any way, this volition causes the gland to impel the spirits toward the muscles which serve that purpose.

ARTICLE XLIV

That each volition is naturally connected with some motion of the gland, but that, by intention or by habit, the will may be connected with others.

Nevertheless, it is not always the volition to excite within us a certain motion, or other effect, which is the cause of its being excited; but this varies according as nature or habit has variously united each motion of the gland to each thought. Thus, for example, if one desires to adjust his eyes to look at a very distant object, this volition causes the pupil of the eye to expand, and if he desires to adjust them so as to see an object very near, this volition makes it contract; but if he simply thinks of expanding the pupil, he wills in vain — the pupil will not expand for that, inasmuch as nature had not connected the motion of the gland, which serves to impel the spirits toward the optic nerve in the manner requisite for expanding or contracting the pupil, with the volition to expand or contract, but with that of looking at objects distant or near. And when, in talking, we think only of the meaning of what we wish to say, that makes us move the tongue and lips much more rapidly and better than if we thought to move them in all ways requisite for the utterance of the same words, inasmuch as the habit we have acquired in learning to talk has made us join the action of the mind — which, through the medium of the gland, can move the tongue and the lips — with the meaning of the words which follow these motions rather than with the motions themselves. . . .

ARTICLE XLVII

Wherein consist the conflicts which are imagined to exist between the inferior and the superior parts of the soul.

It is only in the opposition between the motions that the body through the spirits, and the soul through the will, tend to excite at the same time in the gland, that all the conflicts consist which are commonly imagined to arise between the inferior part of the soul, which is called sensitive, and the superior part, which is rational, or rather between the natural appetites and the will; for there is but one soul within us, and that soul has in it no diversity of parts whatever; the same which is sensitive is rational, and all its appetites are volitions. The error which is committed in making it play the parts of different persons commonly opposed to each other arises only from the want of a right distinction of its functions from those of the body, to which is to be attributed all that which may be observed within us to be hostile to our reason, so that there is in this no other conflict whatever, except that the little gland which is in the middle of the brain may be pushed on the one side by the soul and on the other by the animal spirits, which are only corporeal, as I have said above, and it often happens that these two impulses are contrary, and the stronger hinders the effect of the other. Now there may be distinguished two kinds of motion excited by the spirits in the gland; the one represents to the soul the objects which move the senses, or the impressions which meet in the brain, and produce no effect upon the will; the other kind is those which produce some effect upon it, namely, those which cause the passions or the movements of the body which accompany them; and as for the first, although they often hinder the actions of the soul, or perhaps may be hindered by them, nevertheless, because they are not directly opposed, no conflict is observed. . . .

PART II

ARTICLE LI

The primary causes of the passions.

IT is understood, from what has been said above, that the last and proximate cause of the passions of the soul is nothing but the motion imparted by the spirits to the little gland in the middle of the brain. But this is not enough to enable us to distinguish them from one another; it is necessary to trace them to their sources and to inquire into their primary causes; now, although they may sometimes be caused by the action of the mind, which determines to think upon such or such objects, and also by the mere bodily temperament or by the impressions which happen to present themselves in the brain, as occurs when one feels sad or joyous without being able to assign any reason for it, it should appear, nevertheless, according to what has been said, that the same passions may all be excited by objects which move the senses, and that these objects are their most ordinary and principal causes; whence it follows that, to discover them all, it is sufficient to consider all the effects of these objects.

ARTICLE LII

What service they render, and how their number may be determined.

I observe, further, that the objects which move the senses do not excite in us different passions by reason of all the diversities which are in them, but solely on account of the different ways in which they can injure or profit us, or, in general, be important to us; and that the service which all the passions render consists in this alone, that they dispose the mind to choose the things which nature teaches us are useful, and to persist in this choice, while also the same motion of the spirits which commonly causes them disposes the body to the movements which serve to the performance of those things; this is why, in order to determine the number of the passions, it is necessary merely to inquire, in due order, how many different ways important to us there are in which our senses can be moved by their objects; and I shall here make the enumeration of all the principal passions in the order in which they may thus be found.

ARTICLE LIII

Wonder.

When on first meeting an object we are surprised, and judge it to be novel, or very different from what we knew it before, or from what we supposed it should be, this causes us to wonder at it and be astonished; and since this may happen before we could know whether this object was beneficial to us or not, it seems to me that wonder is the first of all the passions; and it has no contrary, because, if the object which presents itself has nothing in it which surprises us, we are not at all moved by it, and we regard it without emotion.

ARTICLE LXVIII

Why this enumeration of the passions differs from that commonly received.

Such is the order which seems to me the best in enumerating the passions. I know very well that in this my position is different from that of all who have hitherto written upon them, but it is so not without important reason. For they derive their enumeration from their distinction in the sensitive part of the soul of two appetites, one of which they call *concupiscible*, the other *irascible*.[1] And, inasmuch as I recognize in the soul no distinction of parts, as I have said above, this seems to me to signify nothing else but that it has two faculties: one of desiring, the other of being angry; and because it has in the same way the faculties of admiring, of loving, of hoping, of fearing, and of entertaining each of the other passions, or of performing the actions to which these passions incline it, I do not see why they have chosen to refer all to desire or to anger. Moreover, their enumeration does not include all the principal passions, as I believe this does. I speak only of the principal ones, because there may still be distinguished many other more special ones, and their number is indefinite.

Article LXIX

That there are only six primary passions.

But the number of those which are simple and primary is not very great. For, on reviewing all those which I have enumerated, it is readily observed that there are only six of this sort; to wit, wonder, love, hate, desire, joy, and sadness, and that all the rest are made up of some of these six, or at least are species of them. This is why, in order that their number may not embarrass my readers, I shall here treat separately of the six primaries; and afterward I shall show how all the rest derive their origin from these.

Article LXXIV

In what respect the passions are of service and in what they are harmful.

Now it is easy to see, from what has been said above, that the usefulness of all the passions consists only in this, that they strengthen and make enduring in the mind the thoughts which

---

[1] Plato, *Republic*, bk. iv.

it is well for it to keep, and which but for that might easily be effaced from it. As, also, all the evil they can cause consists in their strengthening and preserving those thoughts in the mind more than there is any need of, or else that they strengthen and preserve others which it is not well for the mind to attend to.

Article LXXIX

Definitions of love and hatred.

Love is an emotion of the soul, caused by the motion of the spirits, which incites it to unite itself voluntarily to those objects which appear to it to be agreeable. And hatred is an emotion, caused by the spirits, which incites the mind to will to be separated from objects which present themselves to it as harmful. I say that these emotions are caused by the spirits, in order to distinguish love and hatred, which are passions, and depend upon the body, as well as the judgments which also incline the mind to unite itself voluntarily with the things which it regards as good, and to separate itself from those which it regards as evil, as the emotions which these judgments excite in the soul.

Article LXXX

What is meant by voluntary union and separation.

For the rest, by the word *voluntarily*, I do not here intend desire, which is a passion by itself, and relates to the future, but the consent wherein one considers himself for the moment as united with the beloved object, conceiving as it were of one whole of which he thinks himself but one part, and the object beloved the other. While on the contrary, in the case of hatred, one considers himself alone as a whole, entirely separated from the object for which he has aversion.

Article LXXXVI

Definition of desire.

The passion of desire is an agitation of the soul, caused by the spirits, which disposes it to wish for the future the objects which it represents to itself to be agreeable. Thus one desires not only the presence of absent good, but also the preservation of the present good, and, in addition, the absence of evil, as well that which is already experienced as that which it is feared the future may bring.

ARTICLE XCI

Definition of joy.

Joy is an agreeable emotion of the soul in which consists the enjoyment that it has in any good which the impressions of the brain represent to it as its own. I say that it is in this emotion that the enjoyment of good consists, for in reality the soul receives no other fruit of all the goods it possesses; and so long as it has no joy in them, it may be said that it has no more fruition of them than if it did not possess them at all. I add, also, that it is of good which the impressions of the brain represent to it as its own, in order not to confound this joy, which is a passion, with the purely intellectual joy, which arises in the mind by the simple activity of the mind, and which may be said to be an agreeable emotion excited within itself, in which consists the enjoyment which it has of the good which its understanding represents to it as it own. It is true that, so long as the mind is joined to the body, this intellectual joy can scarcely fail to be accompanied with that joy which is passion; for, as soon as our understanding perceives that we possess any good, although that good may be as different as imaginable from all that pertains to the body, the imagination does not fail on the instant to make an impression on the brain, upon which follows the motion of the spirits which excites the passion of joy.

ARTICLE XCII

Definition of sadness.

Sadness is a disagreeable languor, in which consists the distress which the mind experiences from the evil or the defect which the impressions of the brain represent as pertaining to it. And there is also an intellectual sadness, which is not the passion, but which seldom fails to be accompanied by it.

Article XCVI

The motions of the blood and the spirits which cause these five passions.

The five passions which I have here begun to explain are so joined or opposed to one another, that it is easier to consider them all together than to treat of each separately (as wonder has been treated); and the cause of them is not as is the case with wonder, in the brain alone, but also in the heart, the spleen, the liver, and in all other parts of the body, in so far as they serve in the production of the blood, and thereby of the spirits; for although all the veins conduct the blood they contain toward the heart, it happens, nevertheless, that sometimes the blood in some of them is impelled thither with more force than that in others; it happens, also, that the openings by which it enters into the heart, or else those by which it passes out, are more enlarged or more contracted at one time than at another. . . .

Article CXXXVII

Of the utility of these five passions here explained, in so far as they relate to the body.

Having given the definitions of love, of hatred, of desire, of joy, of sadness (and treated of all the corporeal movements which cause or accompany them[1]) we have only to consider here their utility. In regard to which it is to be noted that, according to the appointment of nature, they all relate to the body, and are bestowed upon the mind only in so far as it is connected with it; so that their natural use is to incite the mind to consent and contribute to the actions which may aid in the preservation of the body, or render it in any way more perfect; and, in this sense, sadness and joy are the first two which are employed. For the mind is immediately warned of the things which harm the body only through the sensation of pain, which produces in it first the passion of sadness; next, hatred of that which causes this pain; and thirdly, the desire to be delivered

---

[1] In the intervening Articles.

from it; likewise the mind is made aware immediately of things useful to the body only by some sort of pleasure, which excites in it joy, then gives birth to love of that which is believed to be the cause of it, and, finally, the desire to acquire that which can make the joy continue, or else that the like may be enjoyed again. Whence it is apparent that these five passions are all very useful as regards the body, and also that sadness is, in a certain way, first and more necessary than joy, and hatred than love, because it is more important to repel things which harm and may destroy us, than to acquire those which add a perfection without which we can still subsist. . . .

ARTICLE CXLIV

Of desires where the issue depends only on ourselves.

But because the passions can impel us to action only through the medium of the desire which we must take pains to regulate — and in this consists the principal use of morality; now, as I have just said, as it is always good when it follows a true knowledge, so it cannot fail to be bad when it is based on error. And it seems to me that the error most commonly committed in regard to desires is the failure to distinguish sufficiently the things which depend entirely upon ourselves and those which do not; for, as for those which depend only upon ourselves, that is to say, upon our free will, it is sufficient to know that they are good to make it impossible for us to desire them with too great ardor, since to do the good things which depend upon ourselves is to follow virtue, and it is certain that one cannot have too ardent a desire for virtue, and moreover, it being impossible for us to fail of success in what we desire in this way, since it depends on ourselves alone, we shall always attain all the satisfaction that we have expected. But the most common fault in this matter is not that too much, but too little, is desired; and the sovereign remedy against that is to deliver the mind as much as possible from all other less useful desires, then to try to understand very clearly, and to consider attentively, the excellence of that which is to be desired.

Article CXLV

Of those which depend only on other things.

As for the things which depend in no wise upon ourselves, however good they may be, they should never be desired with passion; not only because they may not come to pass, and in that case we should be so much the more cast down, as we have the more desired them, but principally because by occupying our thoughts they divert our interest from other things the acquisition of which depends upon ourselves. And there are two general remedies for these vain desires; the first is high-mindedness (*la générosité*), of which I shall speak presently; the second is frequent meditation on Divine Providence, with the reflection that it is impossible that anything should happen in any other manner than has been determined from all eternity by this Providence; so that it is like a destiny or an immutable necessity, which is to be contrasted with chance in order to destroy it as a chimera arising only from an error of our understanding. For we can desire only those things which we regard as being in some way possible, and we do not regard as possible things which do not at all depend upon ourselves, except in so far as we think that they depend on chance, that is to say, as we judge that they can happen, and that similar things have happened before. Now this opinion is based only on the fact that we do not know all the causes which have contributed to each effect; for when anything which we have thought depended upon chance has not taken place, this shows that some one of the causes necessary to produce it was wanting, and, consequently, that it was absolutely impossible, and the like of it never took place; that is to say, to the production of the like a similar cause was also wanting, so that, had we not been ignorant of that beforehand, we never should have thought it possible, and consequently should not have desired it.

Article CXLVI

Of those things which depend upon ourselves and others.

It is necessary then utterly to reject the common opinion

that there is externally to ourselves a chance which causes
things to happen or not to happen, at its pleasure, and to know,
on the other hand, that everything is guided by Divine Providence, whose eternal decree is so infallible and immutable, that,
excepting the things which the same decree has willed to depend
upon our free choice, we must think that in regard to us nothing
happens which is not necessary, and, as it were, destined, so that
we cannot, without folly, wish it to happen otherwise. But
because most of our desires extend to things, all of which do not
depend upon ourselves, nor all of them upon others, we should
distinguish precisely that in them which depends only on ourselves in order to confine our desires to that; and, moreover,
although we should consider success therein to be altogether a
matter of immutable destiny, in order that our desires may not
be taken up with it, we ought not to fail to consider the reasons
which make it more or less to be hoped for, to the end that they
may serve to regulate our conduct; as, for example, if we had
business in a certain place to which we might go by two different
roads, one of which was ordinarily much safer than the other,
although perhaps the decree of Providence was such that if
we went by the road considered safest we should certainly be
robbed, and that, on the contrary, we might travel the other
with no danger at all, we ought not on that account to be indifferent in choosing between them, nor rest on the immutable
destiny of that decree; but reason would have it that we should
choose the road which was ordinarily considered the safer, and
our desire should be satisfied regarding that when we have followed it, whatever be the evil that happens to us, because that
evil, being as regards ourselves inevitable, we have had no reason to desire to be exempt from it, but simply to do the very
best that our understanding is able to discover, as I assume we
have done. And it is certain that when one thus makes a practice of distinguishing destiny from chance, he easily accustoms
himself so to regulate his desires that, in so far as their accomplishment depends only upon himself, they may always afford
him entire satisfaction.

ARTICLE CXLVII

Of the interior emotions of the mind.

I will simply add a consideration which appears to me of much service in averting from us the disturbance of the passions: it is that our good and our evil principally depend upon the interior emotions, which are excited in the mind only by the mind itself, in which respect they differ from its passions, which always depend upon some motion of the spirits; and although these emotions of the mind are often united with the passions which resemble them, they may often also agree with others, and even arise from those which are contrary to them. . . . And when we read of strange adventures in a book, or see them represented on the stage, this excites in us sometimes sadness, sometimes joy, or love, or hatred, and, in general, all the passions, according to the diversity of the objects which present themselves to our imagination; but along with that we have the pleasure of feeling them excited within us, and this pleasure is an intellectual joy, which can arise from sadness as well as from any other passion.[1]

ARTICLE CXLVIII

That the practice of virtue is a sovereign remedy for all the passions.

Now, inasmuch as these interior emotions touch us more nearly, and in consequence have much greater power over us than the passions from which they differ, which occur with them, it is certain that, provided the mind have that within wherewith it may be content, all the troubles which come from elsewhere have no power whatever to disturb it, but rather serve to augment its joy, in that, seeing that it cannot be troubled by them, it is thereby made aware of its own superiority. And to the end that the mind may have that wherewith to be content, it needs but to follow virtue perfectly. For whoever has lived in such a manner that his conscience cannot reproach him with ever

---

[1] Cf. Aristotle. *Poetics*. 6.

having failed to do any of those things which he has judged to be the best (which is what I call here following virtue), he enjoys a satisfaction so potent in ministering to his happiness, that the most violent efforts of the passions never have power enough to disturb the tranquillity of his mind.

BARUCH DE SPINOZA
(1632–1677)

THE ETHICS

Translated from the Latin * *by*
GEORGE STUART FULLERTON

PART II. OF THE NATURE AND ORIGIN OF THE MIND

I NOW proceed to set forth those things that necessarily had to follow from the essence of God, a Being eternal and infinite. I shall not, indeed, treat of all of them, for I have shown (I, 16) that there must follow from this essence an infinity of things in infinite ways, but I shall treat only of those which may lead us, as it were, by the hand, to a knowledge of the human mind and its highest blessedness.

Definitions

1. By *body* I mean a mode which expresses, in a definite and determinate manner, the essence of God, in so far as he is considered as an extended thing. (*See* I, 25, *cor.*)

2. I regard as belonging to the *essence* of a thing that which, being given, the thing is necessarily given, and which being taken away, the thing is necessarily taken away; in other words, that without which the thing, and, conversely, which without the thing, can neither be nor be conceived.

3. By *idea* I mean a conception of the mind, which the mind forms because it is a thinking thing.

* *Opera posthuma*, Amsterdam, 1677; *Opera*, rec. J. Van Vloten et J. P. Land. Hagae Comitum, 1882–83; ed. altera, *ib.*, 1895–6, tom. i. Reprinted here from *The Philosophy of Spinoza*, translated and edited by George Stuart Fullerton, 2 enl. ed. New York, Henry Holt and Company, 1894.

Explanation. — I say rather conception than perception, because the word perception seems to indicate that the mind is acted upon by the object; but conception seems to express an action of the mind.

4. By *adequate* idea I mean an idea which, in so far as it is considered in itself and without reference to an object, possesses all the properties or intrinsic marks of a true idea.

Explanation. — I say intrinsic, to exclude the extrinsic mark, namely, the agreement of the idea with its object.

5. *Duration* is indefinite continuance in existence.

Explanation. — I say indefinite, because it can in no wise be limited by the nature itself of the existing thing, nor yet by the efficient cause, which, to be sure, necessarily brings about the existence of the thing, but does not sublate it.

6. By *reality* and *perfection* I mean the same thing.

7. By *individual things* I mean things that are finite and have a determinate existence. If, however, several individuals so unite in one action that all are conjointly the cause of the one effect, I consider all these, in so far, as one individual thing.

Axioms

1. Man's essence does not involve necessary existence; in other words, in the order of nature, it equally well may or may not come to pass that this or that man exists.

2. Man thinks.

3. Such modes of thinking as love, desire, or whatever else comes under the head of emotion, do not arise unless there be present in the same individual the idea of the thing loved, desired, etc. But the idea may be present without any other mode of thinking being present.

4. We perceive by sense that a certain body is affected in many ways.

5. We do not feel or perceive any individual things except bodies and modes of thinking.

PROP. 1. *Thought is an attribute of God, that is, God is a thinking thing.*

Proof. — Individual thoughts, or this and that thought, are modes which express in a definite and determinate manner God's nature (I, 25, *cor.*). God therefore possesses (I, *def.* 5) the attribute, the conception of which is involved in all individual thoughts, and through which they are conceived. Hence, thought is one of the infinite attributes of God, and it expresses God's eternal and infinite essence (I, *def.* 6): that is, God is a thinking thing. Q. E. D.

Scholium. — This proposition may also be proved from the fact that we can conceive an infinite thinking being. For the more thoughts a thinking being is capable of having, the more reality or perfection do we regard it as containing; a being, then, that can think an infinity of things in an infinity of ways is necessarily, by virtue of its thinking, infinite. Since, therefore, we conceive an infinite being by fixing attention upon thought alone, thought is necessarily (I, *defs.* 4 *and* 6) one of the infinite attributes of God, as I asserted.

PROP. 2. *Extension is an attribute of God, that is, God is an extended thing.*

Proof. — This is proved like the preceding proposition.

PROP. 3. *There is necessarily in God an idea, both of his own essence, and of all those things which necessarily follow from his essence.*

Proof. — God can (1) think an infinity of things in an infinity of ways, or (*which is the same thing*, I, 16) can form an idea of his own essence, and of all those things which necessarily follow from it. But everything that is within God's power necessarily is (I, 35). Therefore such an idea necessarily is, and (I, 15) it is in God and nowhere else. Q. E. D.

PROP. 6. *The modes of any attribute have God as their cause, only in so far as he is considered under the attribute of which they are modes, not in so far as he is considered under any other attribute.*

Proof. — Each attribute is conceived through itself independently of anything else (I, 10). The modes, then, of each attribute involve the concept of their own attribute, but of no other; therefore (I, *axiom* 4), they have as their cause God, only in so far as he is considered under the attribute of which they are modes, and not in so far as he is considered under any other attribute. Q. E. D.

Corollary. — Hence it follows that the formal being of things, which are not modes of thinking, does not follow from the divine nature because this first knew things; but the objects of ideas follow and are inferred from their attributes in the same manner, and by the same necessity, as we have shown ideas to follow from the attribute of thought.

PROP. 7. — *The order and connection of ideas is the same as the order and connection of things.*

Proof. — The proof is evident from axiom 4, of Part I, for the idea of anything that is caused depends upon a knowledge of the cause whose effect it is.

Corollary. — Hence it follows that God's power of thinking is equal to his realized power of acting. That is, whatever follows formally from God's infinite nature follows also objectively in God in the same order and with the same connection from the idea of God.

Scholium. — Before going further we should recall to mind this truth, which has been proved above, namely, that whatever can be perceived by infinite intellect as constituting the essence of substance belongs exclusively to the one substance, and consequently that thinking substance and extended substance are one and the same substance, apprehended now under this, now under that attribute. So, also, a mode of extension and the idea of that mode are one and the same thing, but expressed in two ways; a truth which certain of the Hebrews appear to have seen as if through a mist, in that they assert that God, the intellect of God, and the things known by it, are one and the same. For example, a circle existing in nature, and the idea, which also is in God, of this existing circle, are one and the same thing, manifested through different attributes; for this reason, whether we conceive nature under the attribute of extension, or under that of thought, or under any other attribute whatever, we shall find there follows one and the same order, or one and the same concatenation of causes, that is, the same thing. I have said that

God is the cause of an idea; for instance, the idea of a circle, merely in so far as he is a thinking thing, and of the circle, merely in so far as he is an extended thing, just for the reason that the formal being of the idea of a circle can only be perceived through another mode of thinking, as its proximate cause, that one in its turn through another, and so to infinity. Thus, whenever we consider things as modes of thinking, we must explain the whole order of nature, or concatenation of causes, through the attribute of thought alone; and in so far as we consider them as modes of extension, we must likewise explain the whole order of nature solely through the attribute of extension. So also in the case of the other attributes. Hence God, since he consists of an infinity of attributes, is really the cause of things as they are in themselves. I cannot explain this more clearly at present.

PROP. 8. *The ideas of individual things or modes which do not exist must be comprehended in the infinite idea of God, in the same way as the formal essences of individual things or modes are contained in the attributes of God.*

Proof. — This proposition is evident from the one preceding, but it may be more clearly understood from the preceding scholium.

Corollary. — Hence it follows that so long as individual things do not exist, except in so far as they are comprehended in the attributes of God, their objective being, that is, their ideas, do not exist, except in so far as the infinite idea of God exists; and when particular things are said to exist, not merely in so far as they are comprehended in the attributes of God, but also in so far as they are said to have a being in time, their ideas, too, involve an existence, through which they are said to have a being in time.

PROP. 10. *Substantive being does not belong to the essence of man, that is, substance does not constitute the essence of man.*

Proof. — Substantive being involves necessary existence (I, 7). If, then, substantive being belongs to the essence of man, granted substance, man would necessarily be granted (*def.* 2):

hence man would necessarily exist, which (*axiom* 1) is absurd. Therefore, etc. Q. E. D.

Scholium. — This proposition is proved also by I, 5, which maintains that there are not two substances of the same nature. As, however, a number of men may exist, that which constitutes the essence of man is not substantive being. This proposition is evident, moreover, from the other properties of substance, to wit, that substance is in its nature infinite, immutable, indivisible, etc.; as anyone may readily see.

Corollary. — Hence it follows that the essence of man consists of certain modifications of God's attributes. Substantive being (*by the preceding proposition*) does not belong to the essence of man. It is, therefore (I, 15), something which is in God, and which without God can neither be nor be conceived, that is (I, 25, *cor.*), a modification, or mode, which expresses God's nature in a definite and determinate manner.

PROP. 11. *The first thing that constitutes the actual being of the human mind is nothing else than the idea of some individual thing actually existing.*

Proof. — Man's essence (*by the corollary to the preceding proposition*) consists of certain modes of the attributes of God; namely (*axiom* 2) of modes of thinking, in all of which (*axiom* 3) an idea is prior by nature, and when this is present the other modes (those, that is, to which the idea is prior by nature) must be present in the same individual (*by the same axiom*). Thus an idea is the first thing that constitutes the being of the human mind. But it is not the idea of a non-existent thing, for in that case (8, *cor.*) the idea itself could not be said to exist; it is, then, the idea of a thing actually existing. Not, however, of an infinite thing. For an infinite thing (I, 21 *and* 22) must always necessarily exist; but this is (*axiom* 1) absurd; therefore the first thing that constitutes the actual being of the human mind is the idea of an individual thing actually existing. Q. E. D.

Corollary. — Hence it follows that the human mind is a part of the infinite intellect of God. When, therefore, we say that the human mind perceives this or that, we say merely that God, not in so far as he is infinite, but in so far as he is manifested by the nature of the human mind, that is, in so far as he constitutes the essence of the human mind, has this or that idea; and when we say that God has this or that idea, not merely in so far as he constitutes the nature of the human mind, but in so far as besides the human mind he has also the idea of another thing, we say the human mind perceives the thing partially or inadequately.

Scholium. — Here, doubtless, my readers will stick, and will contrive to find many objections which will cause delay. For this reason I beg them to proceed with me slowly, and not to pass judgment on these matters until they have read over the whole.

PROP. 12. *Whatever takes place in the object of the idea that constitutes the human mind must be perceived by the human mind; that is, an idea of that thing is necessarily in the mind. In other words, if the object of the idea that constitutes the human mind be a body, nothing can take place in that body without being perceived by the mind.*

Proof. — Whatever takes place in the object of any idea, the knowledge of it is necessarily in God (9, *cor.*), in so far as he is considered as affected by the idea of that object; that is (11), in so far as he constitutes the mind of anything. Whatever, then, takes place in the object of the idea that constitutes the human mind, the knowledge of it is necessarily in God, in so far as he constitutes the nature of the human mind, that is (11, *cor.*), the knowledge of it is necessarily in the mind, or the mind perceives it. Q. E. D.

Scholium. — This proposition is evident also, and more clearly understood, from 7, schol., which see.

PROP. 13. *The object of the idea that constitutes the human mind is the body, that is, a definite mode of extension actually existing, and nothing else.*

Proof. — If the body were not the object of the human mind, the ideas of the modifications of the body would not be in God (9, *cor.*), in so far as he constituted our mind, but in so far as he constituted the mind of something else; that is (11, *cor.*), the ideas of the modifications of the body would not be in our mind. But (*axiom* 4) we have ideas of the modifications of the body. Therefore the object of the idea that constitutes the human mind is the body, and that (11) is a body actually existing. Again, if, besides the body, there was still another object of the mind, then, since nothing (I, 36) exists from which some effect does not follow, there would (11) necessarily have to be in our mind the idea of some effect of this object. But (*axiom* 5) there is no such idea. Therefore the object of our mind is the existing body and nothing else. Q. E. D.

Corollary. — Hence it follows that man consists of mind and body, and that the human body exists, just as we perceive it.

Scholium. — From this we comprehend, not merely that the human mind is united to the body, but also what is meant by the union of mind and body. No one, however, can comprehend this adequately or distinctly, unless he first gain an adequate knowledge of the nature of our body. What I have proved so far have been very general truths, which do not apply more to men than to all other individual things, which are all, though in different degrees, animated. For of everything there is necessarily an idea in God, of which God is the cause, just as there is an idea of the human body; hence, whatever I have said of the idea of the human body must necessarily be said of the idea of everything. Yet we cannot deny that ideas differ among themselves as do their objects, and that one is more excellent than another, and contains more reality, just as the object of the one is more excellent than the object of the other, and contains more reality. Therefore, in order to determine in what the human mind differs from other ideas, and in what it excels the others, we must gain a knowledge, as I have said, of the nature of its object, that is, of the human body. This, however, I cannot here treat of, nor is it necessary for what I wish to prove. I will only make the general statement that, in proportion as any body is more capable than the rest of acting or being acted upon in many ways at the same time, its mind is more capable than the rest of having many perceptions at the same time; and the more the actions of a body depend upon itself alone, and the less other bodies contribute to its action, the more capable is its mind of distinct comprehension. We may thus discern the superiority of one mind over others, and we may see the reason why we have only a very confused knowledge of our body. . . .

Postulates

1. The human body is composed of very many individuals of different natures, each one of which is highly composite.

2. Of the individuals which compose the human body, some are fluid, some soft, and some hard.

3. The individuals which compose the human body, and, consequently, the human body itself, are affected in very many ways by external bodies.

4. The human body needs, for its conservation, very many other bodies, by which it is continually, as it were, born anew.

5. When a fluid part of the human body is determined by an external body to impinge often upon a soft part, it changes the plane of the latter, and imprints upon it certain traces, as it were, of the impelling external body.

6. The human body can move external bodies in very many ways, and arrange them in very many ways.

PROP. 14. *The human mind is capable of having very many perceptions, and the more capable, the greater the number of way in which its body can be disposed.*

Proof. — The human body (*postulates* 3 and 6) is affected in very many ways by external bodies, and is adapted to affect external bodies in very many ways. But (12) the human mind must perceive whatever takes place in the human body. Therefore, the human mind is capable of having very many perceptions, and the more capable, etc. Q. E. D.

PROP. 15. *The idea, which constitutes the essential being of the human mind, is not simple, but composed of very many ideas.*

Proof. — The idea, which constitutes the essential being of the human mind, is the idea of the body (13), and this (*postulate* 1) is composed of many highly composite individuals. But there is necessarily in God (8, *cor.*) an idea of each of the indi-viduals which compose the body. Therefore (7) the idea of the human body is composed of these many ideas of the component parts. Q. E. D.

PROP. 16. *The idea of any mode, in which the human body is affected by external bodies, must involve both the nature of the human body and the nature of the external body.*

Proof. — All the modes, in which any body is affected, are a consequence both of the nature of the body affected, and the nature of the body affecting it (*axiom* 1, *after the cor. to lemma* 3). Hence their idea (I, *axiom* 4) necessarily involves the nature of both bodies. Consequently, the idea of any mode, in which the human body is affected by an external body, involves the nature of the human body and of the external body. Q. E. D.

Corollary 1. — Hence it follows, in the first place, that the human mind perceives the nature of very many bodies along with the nature of its own body.

Corollary 2. — And it follows, in the second place, that the ideas which we have of external bodies indicate rather the con-stitution of our own body than the nature of external bodies; as I have explained with many illustrations in the Appendix to Part I.

PROP. 17. *If the human body is affected in a manner which involves the nature of any external body, the human mind will re-gard this external body as actually existing, or as present to it, until the body is affected with some modification which excludes the exist-ence or presence of this body.*

Proof. — This is evident. For as long as the human body is thus affected, the human mind (12) will contemplate this modi-fication of the body; in other words (*by the preceding proposi-tion*), will have the idea of a mode actually existing, which in-volves the nature of an external body; that is, an idea that does not exclude the existence or presence of the nature of the external body, but affirms it. Therefore the mind (*cor.* 1 *to the preceding proposition*) will regard an external body as actually existing, or as present, until it is affected, etc. Q. E. D.

Corollary. — The mind can contemplate, as if they were

present, external bodies by which the human body has once been affected, although they do not exist and are not present.

Scholium. — Thus we see how it can be that we regard as present things that do not exist, as often happens. It is possible that this is brought about by other causes, but it is here sufficient that I have shown one by which I can explain the thing as well as if I had explained it by its true cause. Nevertheless I do not think I am far wrong, since all the postulates I have assumed contain scarcely anything not in harmony with experience, and experience we may not doubt, after we have shown that the human body exists just as we perceive it (13, *cor.*). Besides (*from the preceding cor., and* 16, *cor.* 2) we clearly comprehend the difference between the idea, for instance, of Peter, which constitutes the essence of the mind of Peter, and the idea of the same Peter, which is in another man, say in Paul. The former directly expresses the essence of Peter's body, nor does it involve existence, except so long as Peter exists; the latter, on the other hand, indicates rather the condition of Paul's body than the nature of Peter; and, therefore, while that condition of Paul's body endures, Paul's mind will regard Peter as present, even if he does not exist. Further, to keep to the usual phraseology, we will call the modifications of the human body, the ideas of which represent external bodies as present to us, images of things, although they do not reproduce the shapes of things. When the mind contemplates bodies in this way, we will speak of it as imagining. And here, that I may begin to show what error is, I would have you note that acts of imagination, in themselves considered, contain no error; that is, that the mind does not err from the mere fact that it imagines, but only in so far as it is considered as lacking the idea, which excludes the existence of the things it imagines as present. For if the mind, when imagining things non-existent as present, knew that these things did not really exist, surely it would ascribe this power of imagination to a virtue in its nature, and not to a defect, especially if this faculty of imagining depended solely upon its nature, that is (I, *def.* 7), if this mental faculty were free.

PROP. 18. *If the human body has once been affected simulta-*

neously by two or more bodies, when the mind after that imagines any one of them it will forthwith call to remembrance also the others.

Proof. — The cause of the mind's imagining any body is (*by the preceding corollary*), that the human body is affected and disposed by the traces of an external body in the same way as it was affected when certain of its parts were impelled by that external body; but (*by hypothesis*) the body was then so disposed that the mind imagined two bodies at the same time; it will therefore now, also, imagine two at the same time; and when the mind imagines either, it will forthwith recollect the other. Q. E. D.

Scholium. — From this we clearly comprehend what *memory* is. It is nothing but a certain concatenation of ideas, involving the nature of things outside of the human body, which arises in the mind according to the order and concatenation of the modifications of the human body. I say, in the first place, that it is a concatenation of those ideas only that involve the nature of things outside of the human body, not of the ideas that express the nature of those things; for these ideas are really (16) ideas of the modifications of the human body, which involve both its nature and that of external bodies. I say, in the second place, that this concatenation follows the order and concatenation of the modifications of the human body, to distinguish it from the concatenation of ideas which follows the order of the understanding, whereby the mind perceives things through their first causes, and which is the same in all men. From this, furthermore, we clearly understand why the mind from the thought of one thing immediately passes to the thought of another which bears no resemblance to the former. For example, from the thought of the word *pomum* (apple) a Roman passes straightway to the thought of the fruit, which bears no resemblance to that articulate sound, and has nothing in common with it, except that the body of the same man has often been affected by these two; that is, the man has often heard the word *pomum* while he saw this fruit. Thus each one passes from one thought to another, according as custom has ordered the images of things in his body. A soldier, for instance, who sees in the sand the tracks of a horse, passes at once from the thought of the horse to the thought of its rider, and from that to the thought of war, etc.; while a rustic passes from the thought of a horse to the thought of a plow, a field, etc. Thus each one, according as he has been accustomed to join and connect the images of things in this or that way, passes from a given thought to this thought or to that.

PROP. 19. *The human mind does not come to a knowledge of the human body itself, or know that it exists, except through the ideas of the modifications by which the body is affected.*

Proof. — The human mind is the idea or knowledge of the human body (13), which (9) is in God, in so far as he is considered as affected by the idea of another individual thing. Or rather, since (*postulate* 4) the human body needs many bodies, by which it is continually born anew, as it were; and since the order and connection of ideas is (7) the same as the order and connection of causes; this idea is in God, in so far as he is considered as affected by the ideas of many individual things. Therefore God has an idea of the human body, or knows the human body, in so far as he is affected by many other ideas; and not in so far as he constitutes the nature of the human mind; that is (11, *cor.*), the human mind does not know the human body. But the ideas of the modifications of the body are in God, in so far as he constitutes the nature of the human mind; that is, the human mind perceives these same modifications (12), and consequently (16) perceives the human body itself, and that (17) as really existing. Therefore, only in so far does the human mind perceive the human body. Q. E. D.

PROP. 20. *There is in God also an idea or knowledge of the human mind, which follows in God in the same way, and is referred to God in the same way, as the idea or knowledge of the human body.*

Proof. — Thought is an attribute of God (1); therefore (3) there must necessarily be in God an idea of it and of all its modifications, and consequently (11) of the human mind also. In the second place, it does not follow that this idea or knowledge of the mind is in God in so far as he is infinite, but in so far as he is affected by another idea of an individual thing (9). But the order and connection of ideas is the same as the order and connection of causes (7). Therefore this idea or knowledge of the mind follows in God, and is referred to God, in the same way as the idea or knowledge of the body. Q. E. D.

PROP. 21. *This idea of the mind is united to the mind in the same way as the mind itself is united to the body.*

Proof. — We have proved that the mind is united to the body, from the fact that the body is the object of the mind (12 *and* 13); hence, for the same reason, the idea of the mind must be united with its object, that is, with the mind itself, in the same way as the mind is united with the body. Q. E. D.

Scholium. — This proposition is much more clearly comprehended from what was said in the scholium to prop. 7 of this Part. I there showed that the idea of the body and the body, that is (13), the mind and the body, are one and the same individual, conceived now under the attribute of thought, now under that of extension. Hence the idea of the mind and the mind itself are one and the same thing, conceived under one and the same attribute, namely, that of thought. The idea of the mind, I say, and the mind itself follow in God, by the same necessity, from the same power of thinking. For, in truth, the idea of the mind — that is, the idea of an idea — is nothing else than the essence of an idea, in so far as this is considered as a mode of thinking, and without relation to its object. For when any one knows a thing, from that very fact he knows that he knows it, and at the same time knows that he knows that he knows it, and so to infinity. But of this more hereafter.

PROP. 22. *The human mind perceives, not merely the modifications of the body, but also the ideas of these modifications.*

Proof. — The ideas of the ideas of modifications follow in God in the same way, and are referred to God in the same way, as the ideas of the modifications. This is proved as is prop. 20. But the ideas of the modifications of the body are in the human mind (12), that is (11, *cor.*), they are in God, in so far as he constitutes the essence of the human mind. Hence, the ideas of these ideas are in God, in so far as he has a knowledge, or idea, of the human mind; that is (21), they are in the human mind itself, which, consequently, perceives not merely the modifications of the body, but also the ideas of these. Q. E. D.

PROP. 23. *The mind only knows itself in so far as it perceives the ideas of the modifications of the body.*

Proof. — The idea or knowledge of the mind (20) follows in God in the same way, and is referred to God in the same way, as the idea or knowledge of the body. But since (19) the human mind does not know the body itself; that is (11, *cor.*), since the knowledge of the human body is not referred to God, in so far as he constitutes the nature of the human mind; neither is the knowledge of the mind referred to God, in so far as he constitutes the essence of the human mind; and hence (11, *cor.*), in so far the human mind does not know itself. In the second place, the ideas of the modifications which the human body receives involve the nature of the human body itself (16), that is (13), they agree with the nature of the mind; hence the knowledge of these ideas necessarily involves the knowledge of the mind. But (*by the preceding proposition*) the knowledge of these ideas is in the human mind itself. Therefore only in so far does the human mind know itself. Q. E. D.

PROP. 48. *There is in the mind no absolute or free will; but the mind is determined to this or that volition by a cause, which has itself been determined by another cause, this again by another, and so to infinity.*

Proof. — The mind is a definite and determinate mode of thinking (11), therefore (I, 17, *cor.* 2) it cannot be a free cause of its own actions, that is, it cannot have an absolute power to will or not to will. It must be determined to this or that volition (I, 28) by a cause, which has itself been determined by another cause, this again by another, etc. Q. E. D.

Scholium. — In the same way it is proved that there is in the mind no absolute power of knowing, desiring, loving, etc. Whence it follows, these and similar faculties are either absolutely fictitious, or only metaphysical entities — universals — that we are accustomed to form from individuals. Thus, understanding and will are related to this or that idea and to this or that volition, as lapidity is related to this or that stone, or man to Peter or Paul. Why men think themselves free I have explained in the Appendix to Part I. Before I go further, it should be noted that I mean by will, not desire, but the faculty of affirming and denying; I mean, I say, the faculty by which the mind affirms or denies what is true or false, and not the desire through which the mind seeks or avoids things. But having proved these faculties to be universal notions, which are not distinguished from the individuals of which we form them, it remains to inquire whether the volitions themselves are anything but just the ideas of things. It remains, I say, to inquire whether there is in the mind any other affirmation or negation than that involved in an idea, in that it is an idea. On this point see the following proposition, and, to avoid confounding ideas with pictures, see, also, def. 3 of this Part. For by ideas I do not mean such images as are formed at the back of the eye, or, if you please, in the middle of the brain, but the conceptions of thought.

PROP. 49. *There is in the mind no volition, that is, no affirmation or negation, except that involved in an idea in that it is an idea.*

Proof. — There is in the mind (*by the preceding proposition*) no absolute power to will or not to will, but only particular volitions, namely, this or that affirmation, and this or that negation. Let us conceive, therefore, some particular volition — for instance, the mode of thinking by which the mind affirms the three angles of a triangle to be equal to two right angles. This affirmation involves the conception or idea of a triangle, that is, it cannot be conceived without the idea of a triangle; for it is the same thing whether I say, A must involve the conception B, or A cannot be conceived without B. In the second place, this affirmation (*axiom 3*), without the idea of a triangle, cannot be. Therefore this affirmation cannot, without the idea of a triangle, either be or be conceived. Moreover, this idea of a triangle must involve this same affirmation of the equality of its three angles to two right angles. Therefore, conversely, this idea of a triangle can neither be nor be conceived without this affirmation. Hence (*def. 2*) this affirmation belongs to the essence of the idea of a triangle, and is nothing but that idea. What I have said of this volition is (since I took it at random) to be said also of every volition, namely, that it is nothing else than an idea. Q. E. D.

Corollary. — Will and understanding are one and the same thing.

Proof.— Will and understanding are nothing but particular volitions and ideas (48 *and schol.*). But a particular volition and a particular idea are (*by the preceding proposition*) one and the same thing. Therefore will and understanding are one and the same thing. Q. E. D.

GOTTFRIED WILHELM VON LEIBNITZ
(1646–1716)

PHILOSOPHICAL WORKS

Translated from the French * by
GEORGE MARTIN DUNCAN

XI. A NEW SYSTEM OF NATURE, AND OF THE INTERACTION OF SUBSTANCES, AS WELL AS OF THE UNION WHICH EXISTS BETWEEN THE SOUL AND THE BODY. 1695

1. I CONCEIVED this system many years ago and communicated it to some learned men, and in particular to one of the greatest theologians and philosophers of our time, who, having been informed of some of my opinions by a very distinguished person, had found them highly paradoxical. When, however, he had received my explanations, he withdrew his condemnation in the most generous and edifying manner; and, having approved a part of my propositions, he ceased censuring the others with which he was not yet in accord. Since that time I have continued my meditations as far as opportunity has permitted, in order to give to the public only thoroughly examined views, and I have also tried to answer the objections made against my essays in dynamics, which are related to the former. Finally, as a number of persons have desired to see my opinions more clearly explained, I have ventured to publish these meditations although they are not at all popular nor fit to be enjoyed by every sort of mind. I have been led to do this principally in order that I might profit by the judgments of those who are learned in these matters, inasmuch as it would be too inconvenient to seek and challenge separately those who

* From *The Philosophical Works of Leibnitz*, translated by G. M. Duncan, New Haven, 1890.

would be disposed to give the instructions which I shall always be glad to receive, provided the love of truth appears in them rather than passion for opinions already held.

2. Although I am one of those who have worked very hard at mathematics I have not since my youth ceased to meditate on philosophy, for it always seemed to me that there was a way to establish in it, by clear demonstrations, something stable. I had penetrated well into the territory of the scholastics when mathematics and modern authors induced me while yet young to withdraw from it. Their fine ways of explaining nature mechanically charmed me; and, with reason, I scorned the method of those who employ only forms or faculties, by which nothing is learned. But afterwards, when I tried to search into the principles of mechanics to find proof of the laws of nature which experience made known, I perceived that the mere consideration of an *extended mass* did not suffice and that it was necessary to employ in addition the notion of *force*, which is very easily understood although it belongs to the province of metaphysics. It seemed to me also that the opinion of those who transform or degrade animals into simple machines, not withstanding its seeming possibility, is contrary to appearances and even opposed to the order of things.

3. In the beginning, when I had freed myself from the yoke of Aristotle, I occupied myself with the consideration of the void and atoms, for this is what best fills the imagination; but after many meditations I perceived that it is impossible to find the principles of *true unity* in mere matter, or in that which is only passive, because there everything is but a collection or mass of parts *ad infinitum*. Now, multiplicity cannot have its reality except from *real unities*, which originate otherwise and are entirely different things from the points of which it is certain the *continuum* could not be composed. Therefore, in order to find these real unities I was compelled to resort to a formal atom, since a material being could not be at the same time material and perfectly indivisible, or in other words, endowed with true unity. It became necessary, therefore, to recall and, as it were, reinstate the *substantial forms*, so descried now-a-days,

but in a way to render them intelligible, and distinguish the use which ought to be made of them from the abuse which had befallen them. I found then that their nature is force and that from this something analogous to sensation and desire results, and that therefore it was necessary to conceive them similarly to the idea which we have of *souls*. But as the soul ought not to be employed to explain the details of the economy of the animal body, likewise I judged that it was not necessary to employ these forms to explain particular problems in nature although they are necessary in order to establish true general principles. Aristotle calls them the *first entelechies*. I call them, perhaps more intelligibly, *primitive forces* which contain in themselves not only the *act* or complement of possibility, but also an original *activity*.

4. I saw that these forms and these souls ought to be indivisible, just as much as our mind, as in truth I remembered was the opinion of St. Thomas in regard to the souls of brutes. But this innovation renewed the great difficulties in respect to the origin and duration of souls and of forms. For every *simple substance* which has true unity cannot begin or end except by miracle; it follows, therefore, that it cannot begin except by creation, nor end except by annihilation. Therefore, with the exception of the souls which God might still be pleased to create expressly, I was obliged to recognize that the constitutive forms of substances must have been created with the world, and that they must exist always. Certain scholastics, like Albertus Magnus and John Bacon, had also foreseen a part of the truth as to their origin. And the matter ought not to appear at all extraordinary for only the same duration which the Gassendists accord their atoms is given to these forms.

5. I was of the opinion, nevertheless, that neither *spirits* nor the rational soul, which belong to a superior order and have incomparably more perfection than these forms implanted in matter which in my opinion are found everywhere — being in comparison with them, like little gods made in the image of God and having within them some rays of the light of divinity, ought to be mixed up indifferently or confounded with other forms or

souls. This is why God governs spirits as a prince governs his subjects, and even as a father cares for his children; while he disposes of the other substances as an engineer manipulates his machines. Thus spirits have peculiar laws which place them above the changes which matter undergoes, and indeed it may be said that all other things are made only for them, the changes even being adapted to the felicity of the good and the punishment of the bad.

6. However, to return to ordinary forms or to *material souls* [*âmes brutes*], the duration which must be attributed to them in place of that which has been attributed to atoms, might raise the question as to whether they pass from body to body, which would be *metempsychosis* — very like the belief of certain philosophers in the transmission of motion and of the species. But this fancy is very far removed from the nature of things. There is no such passage; and here it is that the *transformations* of Swammerdam, Malpighi and Leewenhoeck, who are the best observers of our time, have come to my aid and have made me admit more easily that the animal and every other organized substance does not at all begin when we think it does, and that its apparent generation is only a development and a sort of augmentation. Also I have noticed that the author of the *Search after Truth* [i.e., Malebranche], Rigis, Hartsoeker and other able men, have not been far removed from this opinion.

7. But the most important question of all still remained: What do these souls or these forms become after the death of the animal or after the destruction of the individual of the organized substance? It is this question which is most embarrassing, all the more so as it seems unreasonable that souls should remain uselessly in a chaos of confused matter. This obliged me finally to believe that there was only one reasonable opinion to hold, namely, that not only the soul but also the animal itself and its organic machine were preserved, although the destruction of its gross parts had rendered it so small as to escape our senses now just as much as it did before it was born. Also there is no person who can accurately note the true time of death, which can be considered for a long time solely as a suspension of vis-

ible actions, and indeed is never anything else in mere animals; witness the *resuscitation* of drowned flies after being buried under pulverized chalk, and other similar examples, which make it sufficiently clear that there would be many more resuscitations and of far more intricacy if men were in condition to set the machine going again. And apparently it was of something of this sort that the great Democritus, atomist as he was, spoke, although Pliny makes sport of the idea. It is then natural that the animal having, as people of great penetration begin to recognize, been always living and organized, should so remain always. And since, therefore, there is no first birth nor entirely new generation of the animal, it follows that there will be no final extinction nor complete death taken in its metaphysical rigor, and that in consequence instead of the *transmigration* of souls there is only a *transformation* of one and the same animal, according as its organs are folded differently and more or less developed.

8. Nevertheless, rational souls follow very much higher laws and are exempt from all that could make them lose the quality of being citizens in the society of spirits, God having planned for them so well, that all the changes in matter cannot make them lose the moral qualities of their personality. And it can be said that everything tends to the perfection not only of the universe in general but also of those creatures in particular who are destined to such a measure of happiness that the universe finds itself interested therein, by virtue of the divine goodness which communicates itself to each one, according as sovereign wisdom permits.

9. As regards the ordinary body of animals and of other corporeal substances, the complete extinction of which has up to this time been believed in, and the changes of which depend rather upon mechanical rules than upon moral laws, I remarked with pleasure that the author of the book *On Diet*, which is attributed to Hippocrates, had foreseen something of the truth when he said in express terms that animals are not born and do not die, and that the things which are supposed to begin and to perish only appear and disappear. This was also the opinion of

Parmenides and of Melissus, according to Aristotle, for these ancients were more profound than is thought.

10. I am the best disposed in the world to do justice to the moderns; nevertheless I think they have carried reform too far, for instance, in confounding natural things with artificial, for the reason that they have not had sufficiently high ideas of the majesty of nature. They conceive that the difference between its machines and ours is only that of large to small. This caused a very able man, author of *Conversations on the Plurality of Worlds*, to say recently that in regarding nature close at hand it is found less admirable than had been believed, being only like the workshop of an artisan. I believe that this does not give a worthy idea of it and that only our system can finally make men realize the true and immense distance which there is between the most trifling productions and mechanisms of the divine wisdom and the greatest masterpieces of the art of a finite mind, this difference consisting not merely in degree but also in kind. It must then be known that the machines of nature have a truly infinite number of organs and that they are so well protected and so proof against all accidents that it is not possible to destroy them. A natural machine remains a machine even to its least parts and, what is more, it remains always the same machine it has been, being only transformed by the different folds it receives, and sometimes expanded, sometimes compressed and, as it were, concentrated when believed to be lost.

11. Farther, by means of the soul or of form there arises a true unity which answers to what we call the *I* in us, that which could take place neither in the machines of art nor in the simple mass of matter however well organized it might be, which can only be considered as an army, or as a herd of cattle, or as a pond full of fish, or as a watch composed of springs and wheels. Nevertheless, if there were not real *substantial unities* there would be nothing substantial or real in the mass. It was this which forced Cordemoi to abandon Descartes, and to embrace Democritus' doctrine of the Atoms, in order to find a true unity. But *atoms of matter* are contrary to reason, leaving out

of account the proof that they are made up of parts, for the invincible attachment of one part to another (if such a thing could be conceived or with reason supposed) would not at all destroy their diversity. Only *atoms of substance*, i.e., unities which are real and absolutely destitute of parts, are sources of actions and the absolute first principles of the composition of things, and, as it were, the last elements of the analysis of substances. They might be called *metaphysical points;* they possess a certain *vitality* and a kind of *perception*, and *mathematical points* are their *points of view* to express the universe. But when corporeal substances are compressed all their organs together form only *physical point* to our sight. Thus physical points are only indivisible in appearance; mathematical points are so in reality but they are merely modalities; only metaphysical points or those of substance (constituted by forms or souls) are exact and real, and without them there would be nothing real, for without true unities there could not be multiplicity.

12. After having established these proportions I thought myself entering into port, but when I came to meditate on the union of the soul with the body I was as if cast back into the open sea. For I found no way of explaining how the body can cause anything to pass into the soul, or *vice versa;* nor how one substance can communicate with another created substance. Descartes gave up the attempt on that point, as far as can be learned from his writings, but his disciples seeing that the common view was inconceivable, were of the opinion that we perceive the qualities of bodies because God causes thoughts to arise in the soul on the occasion of movements of matter; and when the soul wished to move the body in its turn they judged that it was God who moved it for the soul. And as the communication of motions again seemed to them inconceivable, they believed that God gave motion to a body on the occasion of the motion of another body. This is what they call the system of *Occasional Causes* which has been much in vogue on account of the beautiful remarks of the author of the *Search after Truth.*

13. It must be confessed that the difficulty has been well

penetrated when the not-possible is stated, but it does not appear that it is done away with by explaining what actually takes place. It is indeed true that there is no real influence of one created substance upon another, speaking in metaphysical strictness, and that all things with all their realities are continually produced by the power of God; but in resolving problems it is not enough to employ a general cause and to call in what is called the *Deus ex Machina*. For when this is done and there is no other explanation which can be drawn from secondary causes, it is, properly, having recourse to miracle. In philosophy it is necessary to try to give reasons by making known in what way things are done by divine wisdom, in conformity to the idea of the subject concerned.

14. Being then obliged to admit that it is not possible for the soul or any true substance to receive any influence from without, if it be not by the divine omnipotence I was led insensibly to an opinion which surprised me but which appears inevitable and which has in truth great advantages and many beauties. It is this: it must then be said that God created the soul, or every other real unity, in the first place in such a way that everything with it comes into existence from its own substance through perfect *spontaneity* as regards itself and in *perfect harmony* with objects outside itself. And that thus our internal feelings (i.e., those within the soul itself and not in the brain or finer parts of the body), being only phenomena consequent upon external objects or true appearances, and like well-ordered dreams, it is necessary that these internal perceptions within the soul itself come to it by its own proper original constitution, i.e., by the representative nature (capable of expressing beings outside itself by relation to its organs), which has been given it at its creation and which constitutes its individual character. This brings it about that each of these substances in its own way and according to a certain point of view, represents exactly the entire universe, and perceptions or impressions of external things reach the soul at the proper point in virtue of its *own laws*, as if it were in a world apart, and as if there existed nothing but God and itself (to make use of the manner of speaking

of a certain person of great elevation of mind, whose piety is well known); there is also perfect harmony among all these substances, producing the same effects as if they communicated with each other by a transmission of kinds or of qualities, as philosophers generally suppose.

Farther, the organized mass, within which is the point of view of the soul, being expressed more nearly by it, finds itself reciprocally ready to act *of itself*, following the laws of corporeal machines, at the moment when the soul *wills* it, without either one troubling the laws of the other, the nerves and the blood having just at that time received the impulse which is necessary in order to make them respond to the passions and perceptions of the soul; it is this mutual relationship, regulated beforehand in every substance of the universe, which produces what we call their *inter-communication* and alone constitutes the *union between the soul and body*. And we may understand from this how the soul has its seat in the body by an immediate presence which could not be greater, for it is there as the unit is in the complex of units, which is the multitude.

15. This hypothesis is very possible. For why could not God give to a substance in the beginning a nature or internal force which could produce in it to order (as in a *spiritual or formal automaton, but free* here since it has reason to its share), all that which should happen to it; that is to say all the appearances or expressions it should have, and that without the aid of any creature? All the more as the nature of the substance necessarily demands and essentially includes a progress or change, without which it would not have power to act. And this nature of the soul, being representative, in a very exact (although more or less distinct) manner, of the universe, the series of representations which the soul will produce for itself will naturally correspond to the series of changes in the universe itself; as, in turn, the body has also been accommodated to the soul, for the encounters where it is conceived as acting from without. This is the more reasonable as bodies are only made for those spirits which are capable of entering into communion with God and of celebrating His glory. Thus from the moment the possibility of

this *hypothesis of harmonies* is perceived, we perceive also that it is the most reasonable and that it gives a marvellous idea of the harmony of the universe and of the perfection of the works of God.

16. This great advantage is also found in it, that instead of saying that we are FREE only in appearance and in a way practically sufficient, as many persons of ability have believed, it must rather be said that we are only enchained in appearance, and that according to the strictness of metaphysical expressions we are in a state of perfect independence as respects the influence of all other creatures. This again places in a marvellous light the *immortality* of the soul and the always uniform preservation of our individuality, regulated perfectly by its own nature beyond the risk of all accidents from without, whatever appearance there may be to the contrary. Never has a system so clearly proved our high standing. Every spirit, being like a separate world sufficient to itself, independent of every other creature, enclosing the infinite, expressing the universe, is as durable, as stable and as absolute as the universe of creatures itself. Therefore we ought always to appear in it in the way best fitted to contribute to the perfection of the society of all spirits, which makes their moral union in the city of God. Here is found also a new *proof of the existence of God*, which is one of surprising clearness. For this perfect harmony of so many substances which have no communication with each other, can only come from a common cause.

17. Besides all these advantages which render this system commendable, it can also be said that this is more than an hypothesis, since it hardly seems possible to explain the facts in any other intelligible manner, and since several great difficulties which have exercised the mind up to this time, seem to disappear of themselves as soon as this system is well understood. The customary ways of speaking can still be retained. For we can say that the substance, the disposition of which explains the changes in others in an intelligible manner (in this respect, that it may be supposed that the others have been in this point adapted to it since the beginning, according to the order of the

decrees of God), is the one which must be conceived of as *acting* upon the others. Also the action of one substance upon another is not the emission or transfer of an entity as is commonly believed, and cannot be understood reasonably except in the way which I have just mentioned. It is true that we can easily conceive in matter both emissions and receptions of parts, by means of which we are right in explaining mechanically all the phenomena of physics; but as the material mass is not a substance it is apparent that action as regards substance itself can only be what I have just said.

18. These considerations, however metaphysical they may appear, have yet a marvellous use in physics in establishing the laws of motion, as our *Dynamics* can make clear. For it can be said that in the collision of bodies, each one suffers only by reason of its own elasticity, because of the motion which is already in it. And as to absolute motion, it can in no way be determined mathematically, since everything terminates in relations; therefore there is always a perfect equality of hypotheses, as in astronomy, so that whatever number of bodies may be taken it is arbitrary to assign repose or a certain degree of velocity to any one that may be chosen, without being refuted by the phenomena of straight, circular and composite motion. Nevertheless it is reasonable to attribute to bodies real movements, according to the supposition which explains phenomena in the most intelligible manner, since this description is in conformity to the idea of action which I have just established.

XIV. Second Explanation of the System of the Communication between Substances. 1696

By your [S. Foucher] reflections, sir, I see clearly that the thought which one of my friends has published in the *Journal de Paris* has need of explanation.

You do not understand, you say, how I could prove that which I advanced concerning the communication or harmony of two substances so different as the soul and the body. It is true that I believe that I have found the means of doing so, and this is how I propose to satisfy you. Imagine two clocks or watches which agree perfectly. Now, this may take place in *three ways*. The *first* consists in a mutual influence; the *second* is to have a skillful workman attached to them who regulates them and keeps them always in accord; the *third* is to construct these two clocks with so much art and accuracy as to assure their future harmony. Put now the soul and the body in place of these two clocks; their accordance may be brought about by one of these three ways. The way of influence is that of common philosophy, but as we cannot conceive of material particles which may pass from one of these substances into the other, this view must be abandoned. The way of the continual assistance of the creator is that of the system of occasional causes; but I hold that this is to make a *Deus ex Machina* intervene in a natural and ordinary matter, in which, according to reason, he ought not to coöperate except in the way in which he does in all other natural things. Thus there remains only my hypothesis; that is, the way of harmony. From the beginning God has made each of these two substances of such a nature that merely by following its own peculiar laws, received with its being, it nevertheless accords with the other, just as if there were a mutual influence or as if God always put his hand thereto in addition to his general coöperation. After this I have no need of proving anything, unless you wish to require me to prove that God is sufficiently skillful to make use of this prevenient contrivance, examples of which we see even among men. Now, taking for granted that he can do it, you easily see that this is the way most beautiful and most worthy of him. You suspected that my explanation would be opposed to the very different idea which we have of the mind and of the body; but you will presently clearly see that no one has better established their independence. For while it has been necessary to explain their communication by a kind of miracle, occasion has always been given to many people to fear that the distinction between the body and the soul was not as real as was believed, since in order to maintain it it was necessary to go so far. I shall not be at all sorry to sound enlightened persons concerning the thoughts which I have just explained to you.

XXXII. The Principles of Nature and of Grace. 1714

1. *Substance* is being, capable of action. It is simple or compound. *Simple substance* is that which has no parts. *Compound* substance is a collection of simple substances or *monads*. *Monas* is a Greek word which signifies unity, or that which is one.

Compounds, or bodies, are multitudes; and simple substances, lives, souls, spirits are unities. And there must be simple substances everywhere, because without simple substances there would be no compounds; and consequently all nature is full of life.

2. Monads, having no parts, cannot be formed or decomposed. They cannot begin or end naturally; and consequently last as long as the universe, which will indeed be changed but will not be destroyed. They cannot have shapes; otherwise they would have parts. And consequently a monad, in itself and at a given moment, could not be distinguished from another except by its internal qualities and actions, which can be nothing else than its *perceptions* (that is, representations of the compound, or of what is external, in the simple), and its *appetitions* (that is, its tendencies from one perception to another), which are the principles of change. For the simplicity of substance does not prevent multiplicity of modifications, which must be found together in this same simple substance, and must consist in the variety of relations to things which are external. Just as in a centre or point, altogether simple as it is, there is found an infinity of angles formed by lines which there meet.

3. Everything in nature is full. There are everywhere simple substances, separated in reality from each other by activities of their own which continually change their relations; and each simple substance, or monad, which forms the centre of a compound substance (as, for example, of an animal) and the principle of its unity, is surrounded by a mass composed of an infinity of other monads, which constitute the body proper of this central monad; and in accordance with the affections of this it represents, as a *centre*, the things which are outside of itself. And this *body* is *organic*, when it forms a sort of automa-

ton or natural machine; which is a machine not only in its entirety, but also in its smallest perceptible parts. And as, because of the plenitude of the world, everything is connected and each body acts upon every other body, more or less according to the distance, and by reaction is itself affected thereby; it follows that each monad is a mirror, living or endowed with internal activity, representative according to its point of view of the universe, and as regulated as the universe itself. And perceptions in the monad spring one from the other, by the law of appetites or by the *final causes of good and evil*, which consist in visible, regulated or unregulated perceptions; just as the changes of bodies and external phenomena spring one from another, by the laws of *efficient causes*, that is, of movements. Thus there is perfect *harmony* between the perceptions of the monad and the movements of bodies, established at the beginning between the system of efficient causes and that of final causes. And in this consists the accord and physical union of the soul and body, although neither one can change the laws of the other.

4. Each monad, with a particular body, makes a living substance. Thus there is not only life everywhere, provided with members or organs, but also there is an infinity of degrees in monads, some dominating more or less over the others. But when the monad has organs so adjusted that by means of them there is clearness and distinctness in the impressions which it receives and consequently in the perceptions which represent them (as, for example, when by means of the shape of the humors of the eyes, the rays of light are concentrated and act with more force); this can extend even to *feeling* [*sentiment*], that is, even to a perception accompanied by *memory*, that is, one a certain echo of which remains a long time to make itself heard upon occasion; and such a living being is called an *animal*, as its monad is called a soul. And when this soul is elevated to *reason* it is something more sublime and is reckoned among spirits, as will soon be explained.

It is true that animals are sometimes in the condition of simple living beings, and their souls in the condition of simple monads, namely, when their perceptions are not sufficiently distinct to be remembered, as happens in a profound, dreamless sleep, or in a swoon. But perceptions which have become entirely confused must be re-developed in animals, for reasons which I shall shortly (§ 12) enumerate. Therefore it is well to make a distinction between the *perception*, which is the internal condition of the monad representing external things, and *apperception*, which is *consciousness* or the reflective knowledge of this internal state; the latter not being given to all souls, nor at all times to the same soul. And it is for want of this distinction that the Cartesians have failed, taking no account of the perceptions of which we are not conscious as people take no account of imperceptible bodies. It is this also which made the same Cartesians believe that only spirits are monads, that there is no soul of brutes, and still less other *principles of life*.

And as they shocked too much the common opinion of men by refusing feeling to brutes, they have, on the other hand, accommodated themselves too much to the prejudices of the multitude, by confounding a *long swoon*, caused by a great confusion of perceptions, with *death strictly speaking*, where all perception would cease. This confirmed the ill-founded belief in the destruction of some souls, and the bad opinion of some so-called strong minds, who have contended against the immortality of our soul.

5. There is a continuity in the perceptions of animals which bears some resemblance to reason; but it is only founded in the memory of *facts*, and not at all in the knowledge of *causes*. Thus a dog shuns the stick with which it has been beaten, because memory represents to it the pain which the stick has caused it. And men in so far as they are empirics, that is to say, in three-fourths of their actions, act simply as brutes. For example, we expect that there will be daylight to-morrow, because we have always had the experience; only an astronomer foresees it by reason, and even this prediction will finally fail when the cause of day, which is not eternal, shall cease. But *true reasoning* depends upon necessary or eternal truths, such as those of logic, numbers, geometry, which establish an indubitable connection

of ideas and unfailing consequences. The animals in which these consequences are not noticed, are called *brutes;* but those which know these necessary truths are properly those which are called *rational animals*, and their souls are called *spirits*. These souls are capable of performing acts of reflection, and of considering that which is called the *ego, substance, monad, soul, spirit*, in a word, immaterial things and truths. It is this which renders us capable of the sciences and of demonstrative knowledge.

6. Modern researches have taught us, and reason approves of it, that living beings whose organs are known to us, that is to say, plants and animals, do not come from putrefaction or from chaos, as the ancients believed, but from *pre-formed* seeds, and consequently by the transformation of pre-existing living beings. There are animalcules in the seeds of large animals, which by means of conception assume a new dress which they make their own and by means of which they can nourish themselves and increase their size, in order to pass to a larger theatre and to accomplish the propagation of the large animal. It is true that the souls of spermatic human animals are not rational and do not become so until conception determines these animals to the human nature. And as generally animals are not born altogether in conception or *generation*, neither do they perish altogether in what we call *death;* for it is reasonable that what does not begin naturally, should not end either in the order of nature. Therefore, quitting their mask or their rags, they merely return to a more subtile theatre where they can, nevertheless, be just as sensitive and just as well regulated as in the larger. And what we have just said of large animals, takes place also in the generation and death of smaller spermatic animals, in comparison with which the former may pass for large; for everything extends *ad infinitum* in nature.

Thus not only souls, but also animals, are ingenerable and imperishable: they are only developed, unfolded, reclothed, unclothed, transformed: souls never quit their entire body and do not pass from one body into another which is entirely new to them.

There is therefore no *metempsychosis*, but there is *metamorphosis;* animals change, take and leave only parts: the same thing which happens little by little and by small invisible particles but continually in nutrition, and suddenly, visibly but rarely in conception or death, which cause a gain or loss of everything at one time.

7. Up to this time we have spoken as simple *physicists:* now we must advance to *metaphysics* by making use of the *great principle*, little employed in general, which teaches that *nothing happens without a sufficient reason;* that is to say, that nothing happens without its being possible for him who should sufficiently understand things, to give a reason sufficient to determine why it is so and not otherwise. This principle laid down, the first question which should rightly be asked, would be *Why is there something rather than nothing?* For nothing is simpler and easier than something. Further, suppose that things must exist, we must be able to give a reason *why they must exist so* and not otherwise.

8. Now this sufficient reason for the existence of the universe could not be found *in the series of contingent things*, that is, of bodies and of their representations in souls; for matter being indifferent in itself to motion and to rest and to this or another motion, we could not find the reason of motion in it, and still less of a certain motion. And although the present motion which is in matter, comes from the preceding motion, and that from still another preceding, yet in this way we should never make any progress, go as far as we might; for the same question would always remain.

Therefore it must be that the sufficient reason which has no need of another reason, be outside this series of contingent things and be found in a substance which is its cause, or which is a necessary being, carrying the reason of its existence within itself; otherwise we should still not have a sufficient reason in which we could rest. And this final reason of things is called *God*.

9. This simple primitive substance must contain in itself eminently the perfections contained in the derivative sub-

stances which are its effects; thus it will have perfect power, knowledge and will: that is, it will have omnipotence and sovereign goodness. And as *justice*, taken generally, is only goodness conformed to wisdom, there must too be sovereign justice in God. The reason which has caused things to exist by him, makes them still dependent upon him in existing and in working: and they are continually receiving from him that which gives them some perfection; but the imperfection which remains in them, comes from the essentia! and original limitation of the creature.

10. It follows from the supreme perfection of God, that in creating the universe he has chosen the best possible plan, in which there is the greatest variety together with the greatest order; the best arranged ground, place, time; the most results produced in the most simple ways; the most of power, knowledge, happiness and goodness in the creatures that the universe could permit. For since all the possibles in the understanding of God laid claim to existence in proportion to their perfections, the actual world, as the resultant of all these claims, must be the most perfect possible. And without this it would not be possible to give a reason why things have turned out so rather than otherwise.

11. The supreme wisdom of God compelled him to choose the *laws of movement* best adjusted and most suited to abstract or metaphysical reasons. He preserves there the same quantity of total and absolute force, or of actions; the same quantity of respective force or of reaction; lastly the same quantity of directive force. Farther, action is always equal to reaction, and the whole effect is always equivalent to the full cause. And it is not surprising that we could not by the mere consideration of the *efficient causes* or of matter, account for those laws of movement which have been discovered in our time, and a part of which have been discovered by myself. For I have found that it was necessary to have recourse to *final causes*, and that these laws do not depend upon the *principle of necessity*, like logical, arithmetical and geometrical truths, but upon the *principle of fitness*, that is, upon the choice of wisdom. And this is one of the

most efficacious and evident proofs of the existence of God, to those who can examine these matters thoroughly.

12. It follows, farther, from the perfection of the supreme author, that not only is the order of the entire universe the most perfect possible, but also that each living mirror representing the universe in accordance with its point of view, that is to say, that each *monad*, each *substantial centre*, must have its perceptions and its desires as well regulated as is compatible with all the rest. Whence it follows, still farther, that *souls*, that is, the most dominating monads, or rather, animals, cannot fail to awaken from the state of stupor in which death or some other accident may put them.

13. For everything in things is regulated once for all with as much order and harmony as is possible, supreme wisdom and goodness not being able to act except with perfect harmony. The present is big with the future, the future could be read in the past, the distant is expressed in the near. One could become acquainted with the beauty of the universe in each soul, if one could unfold all its folds, which only develop visibly in time. But as each distinct perception of the soul includes innumerable confused perceptions which comprise the whole universe, the soul itself knows the things of which it has perception only so far as it has distinct and clear perceptions of them.

Each soul knows the infinite, knows all, but confusedly. As in walking on the sea-shore and hearing the great noise which it makes, I hear the individual sounds of each wave, of which the total sound is composed, but without distinguishing them; so our confused perceptions are the result of the impressions which the whole universe makes upon us. It is the same with each monad. God alone has a distinct consciousness of everything, for he is the source of all. It has been well said that he is as centre everywhere, but that his circumference is nowhere, since without any withdrawal from this centre, everything is immediately present to him.

14. As regards the rational soul, or *spirit*, there is something in it more than in the monads, or even in simple souls. It is not only a mirror of the universe of creatures, but also an image of

the Divinity. The *spirit* has not only a perception of the works of God, but it is even capable of producing something which resembles them, although in miniature. For, to say nothing of the marvels of dreams where we invent without trouble, and even involuntarily, things which when awake we should have to think a long time in order to hit upon, our soul is architectonic in its voluntary actions also, and, discovering the sciences according to which God has regulated things (*pondere, mensura, numero*, etc.), it imitates, in its department and in the little world where it is permitted to exercise itself, what God does in the large world.

15. This is why all spirits, whether of men or of genii, entering by virtue of reason and of the eternal truths into a sort of society with God, are members of the City of God, that is to say, of the most perfect state, formed and governed by the greatest and best of monarchs; where there is no crime without punishment, no good actions without proportionate recompense; and finally as much virtue and happiness as is possible; and this is not by a derangement of nature, as if what God prepares for souls disturbed the laws of bodies, but by the very order of natural things, in virtue of the harmony pre-established for all time between the *realms of nature and of grace*, between God as Architect and God as Monarch; so that *nature* leads to grace and *grace*, while making use of nature, perfects it.

16. Thus although reason cannot teach us the details, reserved to Revelation, of the great future, we can be assured by this same reason that things are made in a manner surpassing our desires. God also being the most perfect and most happy, and consequently, the most lovable of substances, and *truly pure love* consisting in the state which finds pleasure in the perfections and happiness of the loved object, this love ought to give us the greatest pleasure of which we are capable, when God is its object.

17. And it is easy to love him as we ought, if we know him as I have just described. For although God is not visible to our external senses, he does not cease to be very lovable and to give very great pleasure. We see how much pleasure honors give

men, although they do not at all consist in the qualities of the external senses.

Martyrs and fanatics (although the affection of the latter is ill-regulated), show what pleasure of the spirit can accomplish; and what is more, even sensuous pleasures are reduced to confusedly known intellectual pleasures.

Music charms us, although its beauty only consists in the harmony of numbers and in the reckoning of the beats or vibrations of sounding bodies, which meet at certain intervals, of which we are not conscious and which the soul does not cease to make. The pleasures which sight finds in proportions are of the same nature; and those caused by the other senses amount to almost the same thing, although we cannot explain it so clearly.

18. It may be said that even from the present time on, the *love of God* makes us enjoy a foretaste of future felicity. And although it is disinterested, it itself constitutes our greatest good and interest even if we should not seek it therein and should consider only the pleasure which it gives, without regard to the utility it produces; for it gives us perfect confidence in the goodness of our author and master, producing a true tranquillity of mind; not like the Stoics who force themselves to patience, but by a present content which assures us of future happiness. And besides the present pleasure, nothing can be more useful for the future; for the love of God fulfills our hopes, too, and leads us in the road of supreme happiness, because by virtue of the perfect order established in the universe, everything is done in the best possible way, as much for the general good as for the greatest individual good of those who are convinced of this and are content with the divine government; this conviction cannot be wanting to those who know how to love the source of all good. It is true that supreme felicity, by whatever *beatific vision* or knowledge of God it be accompanied, can never be full; because, since God is infinite, he cannot be wholly known. Therefore our happiness will never, and ought not to, consist in full joy, where there would be nothing farther to desire, rendering our mind stupid; but in a perpetual progress to new pleasures and to new perfections.

CHRISTIAN VON WOLFF
(1679–1754)

RATIONAL PSYCHOLOGY

Translated from the Latin * *by*
EDWARD KENNARD RAND

THE ESSENCE AND NATURE OF THE SOUL

§ 48. *The soul is a simple substance.* For the soul is not body
(§ 47) nor an attribute communicated to the body (§ 46), and
further, neither is it a composite entity nor does it inhere in a
composite entity (§ 119, *Cosmol.*[1]). Wherefore since every entity
is either composite or simple (§ 532, 673, *Ontol.*[2]) the soul must
be a simple entity.

Now since acts of thought continually change and succeed
one another in turn, they are to be classed with *modes* (§ 151,
Ontol.) The soul, therefore, to which these modes apply, is subject to modification (§ 764, *Ontol.*), and since it is obvious that
the soul lasts for some time in conjunction with the body (for
whether it can exist apart from the body or not need not be
established here) it is *per durable* (§ 766, *Ontol.*). Certainly a
per durable and modifiable object is a substance. Therefore
the soul is a substance.

But the soul is a simple entity by the foregoing proof. Therefore it is a simple substance.

§ 53. *The soul is endowed with a certain power.* The soul is
a substance (§ 48), and since perceptions succeed one another in
the same, and desires spring from perceptions, and perceptions

---

* From Christian von Wolff's *Psychologia rationalis*. Francof. et Lips. 1734.

[1] Wolff's *Cosmologia generalis*. Francof. et Lips. 1731.

[2] Wolff's *Philosophia prima sive Ontologia*. Francof. et Lips. 1730.

again from desires, as is generally admitted in Empiric Psychology, its condition changes (§ 709, *Ontol.*). It therefore is endowed with a certain power. (§ 776, *Ontol.*).

§ 54. *A power and a faculty of the soul are different from one another.* For power consists in the continual endeavor to act (§ 724, *Ontol.*). Faculties are merely potencies of action on the part of the soul (§ 29, *Psych. Empir.*[1]), and thus have possibilities of action (§ 716, *Ontol.*). Therefore a power of the soul and a faculty differ from one another (§ 183, *Ontol.*).

§ 56. *The soul continually tends to change its conditions.* For it is endowed with a certain power. Wherefore, since a power continually tends to change the condition of the subject in which it is (§ 725, *Ontol.*), the soul, too, through the mediation of its own power, is bound to tend continually to change its condition.

§ 57. *The power of the soul is absolutely simple.* For the soul is simple and thus lacks parts (§ 673, *Ontol.*). Let us now suppose that the soul has more than one power distinct from one another; since each one of them consists in the continued endeavor to act (§ 724, *Ontol.*), each one requires a particular subject in which it is. And so we must conceive of several actual entities distinct from one another (§ 142, 183, *Ontol.*), which when taken together with the soul will be the parts of the same (§ 341, *Ontol.*). But this is altogether absurd by the proof above given.

§ 62. *The soul re-presents to itself this universe in accordance with the location of its organic body in the universe, conformably to the mutations which affect the organs of sensation.* For this law of sensations is constant and inviolable: if a certain mutation is produced in some organ of sensation by some sensible object there coexists in the soul a sensation which may be explained to it in an intelligible way, or which recognises in it a sufficient reason why it should be, and why it should be such as it is. (§ 85, *Psychol. Empir.*) Now sensations are perceptions of external objects, which produce a change in the organs of sensation (§ 67, *Psychol. Empir.*), and hence while the soul feels, it

---

[1] Wolff's *Psychologia Empirica.* Francof. et Lips. 1732.

re-presents those objects to itself (§ 24, *Psychol. Empir.*). And since our body is constantly in this visible world, bodies also which compose the same (§ 119, *Cosmol.*) act constantly upon our body in accordance with its location in the world, or the universe. It is clear, therefore, that the soul re-presents to itself this universe, or this visible world, in accordance with the location of our organic body in the universe, and conformably to the mutations which the bodies of which it is composed produce in the same. When we sleep we perceive nothing clearly and distinctly (§ 15). However since the soul is still in a condition of preception, although all its conceptions are confused or obscure, there is nothing to prevent it from still perceiving obscurely its own body, and the things that impress it, and hence from continuing this re-presentation of the world, so that therefore it may be said without reservation that it re-presents to itself this universe.

§ 66. *The essence of the soul consists in its power of re-presenting (vis repræsentiva) the universe, which power is materially limited by its location in an organic body in the universe, and formally limited by the constitution of the sensory organs.* For this power is the first principle which is conceived with regard to the soul, and on which depend the other attributes which are inherent in it (§ 65). Therefore the essence of the soul consists in the same (§ 168, *Ontol.*).

§ 67. *The nature of the soul consists in the same re-presenting power (vis repræsentiva).* For by this power of the soul everything is activated that is possible through the faculties of the soul. Wherefore since we understand by the nature of the soul that principle of mutations in the soul which is intrinsic in the same, just as by the nature of the universe we understand that principle of mutations in the world which is intrinsic in the same (§ 503, *Cosmol.*); and since this principle of mutations is power (§ 807, *Ontol.*), and since the power with which the soul is endowed (§ 53) is only the power of re-presenting (*vis repræsentiva*) the universe (§ 62), that power of re-presenting (*vis repræsentiva*) the universe is likewise the nature of the soul.

JOHN LOCKE

(1632–1704)

AN ESSAY CONCERNING HUMAN UNDER-STANDING*

BOOK I

CHAPTER I. INTRODUCTION

1. *An inquiry into the understanding, pleasant and useful.* — Since it is the *understanding* that sets man above the rest of sensible beings, and gives him all the advantage and dominion which he has over them, it is certainly a subject, even for its nobleness, worth our labour to inquire into. The understanding, like the eye, whilst it makes us see and perceive all other things, takes no notice of itself; and it requires art and pains to set it at a distance, and make it its own object. But whatever be the difficulties that lie in the way of this inquiry, whatever it be that keeps us so much in the dark to ourselves, sure I am that all the light we can let in upon our own minds, all the acquaintance we can make with our own understandings, will not only be very pleasant, but bring us great advantage in directing our thoughts in the search of other things.

2. *Design.* — This therefore being my purpose, to inquire into the original, certainty, and extent of human knowledge, together with the grounds and degrees of belief, opinion, and assent, I shall not at present meddle with the physical consideration of the mind, or trouble myself to examine wherein its essence consists or by what motions of our spirits, or alterations of our bodies, we come to have any *sensation* by our organs, or any *ideas* in our understandings; and whether those ideas do, in their formation, any or all of them, depend on matter or not:

* London, 1690 ; 2d col. ed. 1694 ; 3d ed. 1697 ; 4th col. ed. 1700 ; ed. A. C. Fraser, 2 vols. Oxford, 1894.

these are speculations which, however curious and entertaining, I shall decline, as lying out of my way in the design I am now upon. It shall suffice to my present purpose, to consider the discerning faculties of a man, as they are employed about the objects which they have to do with; and I shall imagine I have not wholly misemployed myself in the thoughts I shall have on this occasion, if, in this historical, plain method, I can give any account of the ways whereby our understandings come to attain those notions of things we have, and can set down any measures of the certainty of our knowledge, or the grounds of those persuasions which are to be found amongst men, so various, different, and wholly contradictory; and yet asserted somewhere or other with such assurance and confidence, that he that shall take a view of the opinions of mankind, observe their opposition, and at the same time consider the fondness and devotion wherewith they are embraced, the resolution and eagerness wherewith they are maintained, may perhaps have reason to suspect that either there is no such thing as truth at all, or that mankind hath no sufficient means to attain a certain knowledge of it.

3. *Method.* — It is therefore worth while to search out the bounds between opinion and knowledge, and examine by what measures, in things whereof we have no certain knowledge, we ought to regulate our assent, and moderate our persuasions. In order whereunto, I shall pursue this following method: —

First. I shall inquire into the original of those ideas, notions, or whatever else you please to call them, which a man observes, and is conscious to himself he has in his mind; and the ways whereby the understanding comes to be furnished with them.

Secondly. I shall endeavour to show what knowledge the understanding hath by those ideas, and the certainty, evidence, and extent of it.

Thirdly. I shall make some inquiry into the nature and grounds of faith or opinion; whereby I mean, that assent which we give to any proposition as true, of whose truth yet we have no certain knowledge: and here we shall have occasion to examine the reasons and degrees of assent.

BOOK II

CHAPTER I. OF IDEAS IN GENERAL, AND THEIR ORIGINAL

1. *Idea is the object of thinking.* — Every man being conscious of himself, that he thinks, and that which his mind is applied about, whilst thinking, being the ideas that are there, it is past doubt that men have in their mind several ideas, such as are those expressed by the words, whiteness, hardness, sweetness, thinking, motion, man, elephant, army, drunkenness, and others: it is in the first place then to be inquired, How he comes by them? I know it is a received doctrine, that men have native ideas and original characters stamped upon their minds in their very first being. This opinion I have at large examined already; and, I suppose, what I have said in the foregoing book will be much more easily admitted, when I have shown whence the understanding may get all the ideas it has, and by what ways and degrees they may come into the mind; for which I shall appeal to every one's own observation and experience.

2. *All ideas come from sensation or reflection.* — Let us then suppose the mind to be, as we say, white paper, void of all characters, without any ideas: How comes it to be furnished? Whence comes it by that vast store, which the busy and boundless fancy of man has painted on it with an almost endless variety? Whence has it all the materials of reason and knowledge? To this I answer, in one word, From *experience.* In that all our knowledge is founded, and from that it ultimately derives itself. Our observation, employed either about external sensible objects, or about the internal operations of our mind, perceived and reflected on by ourselves, is that which supplies our understandings with all the materials of thinking. These two are the fountains of knowledge, from whence all the ideas we have, or can naturally have, do spring.

3. *The object of sensation one source of ideas.* — First. Our senses, conversant about particular sensible objects, do convey into the mind several distinct perceptions of things, according

to those various ways wherein those objects do affect them; and thus we come by those ideas we have of yellow, white, heat, cold, soft, hard, bitter, sweet, and all those which we call sensible qualities; which when I say the senses convey into the mind, I mean, they from external objects convey into the mind what produces there those perceptions. This great source of most of the ideas we have, depending wholly upon our senses, and derived by them to the understanding, I call, SENSATION.

4. *The operations of our minds the other source of them.* — Secondly. The other fountain, from which experience furnisheth the understanding with ideas, is the perception of the operations of our own minds within us, as it is employed about the ideas it has got; which operations when the soul comes to reflect on and consider, do furnish the understanding with another set of ideas which could not be had from things without; and such are perception, thinking, doubting, believing, reasoning, knowing, willing, and all the different actings of our own minds; which we, being conscious of, and observing in ourselves, do from these receive into our understandings as distinct ideas, as we do from bodies affecting our senses. This source of ideas every man has wholly in himself; and though it be not sense as having nothing to do with external objects, yet it is very like it, and might properly enough be called *internal sense.* But as I call the other *sensation,* so I call this REFLECTION, the ideas it affords being such only as the mind gets by reflecting on its own operations within itself. By reflection, then, in the following part of this discourse, I would be understood to mean that notice which the mind takes of its own operations, and the manner of them, by reason whereof there come to be ideas of these operations in the understanding. These two, I say, viz., external material things as the objects of sensation, and the operations of our own minds within as the objects of reflection, are, to me, the only originals from whence all our ideas take their beginnings. The term *operations* here, I use in a large sense, as comprehending not barely the actions of the mind about its ideas, but some sort of passions arising sometimes

from them, such as is the satisfaction or uneasiness arising from any thought.

5. *All our ideas are of the one or the other of these.* — The understanding seems to me not to have the least glimmering of any ideas which it doth not receive from one of these two. External objects furnish the mind with the ideas of sensible qualities, which are all those different perceptions they produce in us; and the mind furnishes the understanding with ideas of its own operations.

These, when we have taken a full survey of them, and their several modes [combinations, and relations], we shall find to contain all our whole stock of ideas; and that we have nothing in our minds which did not come in one of these two ways. Let any one examine his own thoughts, and thoroughly search into his understanding, and then let him tell me, whether all the original ideas he has there, are any other than of the objects of his senses, or of the operations of his mind considered as objects of his reflection; and how great a mass of knowledge soever he imagines to be lodged there, he will, upon taking a strict view, see that he has not any idea in his mind but what one of these two have imprinted, though perhaps with infinite variety compounded and enlarged by the understanding, as we shall see hereafter.

. . . .

CHAPTER II. OF SIMPLE IDEAS

1. *Uncompounded appearances.* — The better to understand the nature, manner, and extent of our knowledge, one thing is carefully to be observed concerning the ideas we have; and that is, that some of them are *simple*, and some *complex.*

Though the qualities that affect our senses are, in the things themselves, so united and blended that there is no separation, no distance between them; yet it is plain the ideas they produce in the mind enter by the senses simple and unmixed. For though the sight and touch often take in from the same object, at the same time, different ideas — as a man sees at once motion and colour, the hand feels softness and warmth in the same piece of wax — yet the simple ideas thus united in the same subject are as perfectly distinct as those that come in by different senses; the coldness and hardness which a man feels in a piece of ice being as distinct ideas in the mind as the smell and whiteness of a lily, or as the taste of sugar and smell of a rose: and there is nothing can be plainer to a man than the clear and distinct perception he has of those simple ideas; which, being each in itself uncompounded, contains in it nothing but one uniform appearance or conception in the mind, and is not distinguishable into different ideas.

2. *The mind can neither make nor destroy them.* — These simple ideas, the materials of all our knowledge, are suggested and furnished to the mind only by those two ways above mentioned, viz., sensation and reflection. When the understanding is once stored with these simple ideas, it has the power to repeat, compare, and unite them, even to an almost infinite variety, and so can make at pleasure new complex ideas. But it is not in the power of the most exalted wit or enlarged understanding, by any quickness or variety of thought, to invent or frame one new simple idea in the mind, not taken in by the ways before mentioned; nor can any force of the understanding destroy those that are there: the dominion of man in this little world of his own understanding, being much-what the same as it is in the great world of visible things, wherein his power, however managed by art and skill, reaches no farther than to compound and divide the materials that are made to his hand but can do nothing towards the making the least particle of new matter, or destroying one atom of what is already in being. . . .

CHAPTER III. OF SIMPLE IDEAS OF SENSE

1. *Division of simple ideas.* — The better to conceive the ideas we receive from sensation, it may not be amiss for us to consider them in reference to the different ways whereby they make their approaches to our minds, and make themselves perceivable by us.

First, then, there are some which come into our minds by one sense only.

Secondly. There are others that convey themselves into the mind by more senses than one.

Thirdly. Others that are had from reflection only.

Fourthly. There are some that make themselves way, and are suggested to the mind, by all the ways of sensation and reflection.

We shall consider them apart under these several heads.

1. There are some ideas which have admittance only through one sense, which is peculiarly adapted to receive them. Thus light and colours, as white, red, yellow, blue, with their several degrees or shades and mixtures, as green, scarlet, purple, sea-green, and the rest, come in only by the eyes; all kinds of noises, sounds, and tones, only by the ears; the several tastes and smells, by the nose and palate. And if these organs, or the nerves which are the conduits to convey them from without to their audience in the brain, the mind's presence-room (as I may so call it), are, any of them, so disordered as not to perform their functions, they have no postern to be admitted by, no other way to bring themselves into view, and be received by the understanding.

The most considerable of those belonging to the touch are heat, and cold, and solidity; all the rest — consisting almost wholly in the sensible configuration, as smooth and rough; or else more or less firm adhesion of the parts, as hard and soft, tough and brittle — are obvious enough.

2. I think it will be needless to enumerate all the particular simple ideas belonging to each sense. Nor indeed is it possible if we would, there being a great many more of them belonging to most of the senses than we have names for. . . . I shall therefore, in the account of simple ideas I am here giving, content myself to set down only such as are most material to our present purpose, or are in themselves less apt to be taken notice of, though they are very frequently the ingredients of our complex ideas; amongst which I think I may well account "solidity," which therefore I shall treat of in the next chapter.

CHAPTER IV. IDEA OF SOLIDITY

1. *We receive this idea from touch.* — The idea of *solidity* we receive by our touch; and it arises from the resistance which we find in body to the entrance of any other body into the place it possesses, till it has left it. There is no idea which we receive more constantly from sensation than solidity. Whether we move or rest, in what posture soever we are, we always feel something under us that supports us, and hinders our farther sinking downwards; and the bodies which we daily handle make us perceive that whilst they remain between them, they do, by an insurmountable force, hinder the approach of the parts of our hands that press them. That which thus hinders the approach of two bodies, when they are moving one towards another, I call *solidity*. I will not dispute whether this acceptation of the word "solid" be nearer to its original signification than that which mathematicians use it in; it suffices that, I think, the common notion of "solidity," will allow, if not justify, this use of it; but if any one think it better to call it *impenetrability*, he has my consent. Only I have thought the term *solidity* the more proper to express this idea, not only because of its vulgar use in that sense, but also because it carries something more of positive in it than *impenetrability*, which is negative, and is, perhaps, more a consequence of solidity than solidity itself. This, of all other, seems the idea most intimately connected with and essential to body, so as nowhere else to be found or imagined but only in matter; and though our senses take no notice of it but in masses of matter, of a bulk sufficient to cause a sensation in us; yet the mind, having once got this idea from such grosser sensible bodies, traces it farther and considers it, as well as figure, in the minutest particle of matter that can exist, and finds it inseparably inherent in body, wherever or however modified.

2. *Solidity fills space.* — This is the idea which belongs to body, whereby we conceive it to fill space. The idea of which filling of space is, that where we imagine any space taken up by

a solid substance, we conceive it so to possess it that it excludes all other solid substances, and will for ever hinder any two other bodies, that move towards one another in a straight line, from coming to touch one another, unless it removes from between them in a line not parallel to that which they move in. This idea of it, the bodies which we ordinarily handle sufficiently furnish us with.

6. *What it is.* — If any one asks me, *What this solidity is,* I send him to his senses to inform him: let him put a flint or a football between his hands, and then endeavour to join them, and he will know. If he thinks this not a sufficient explication of solidity, what it is, and wherein it consists, I promise to tell him what it is, and wherein it consists, when he tells me what thinking is, or wherein it consists; or explains to me what extension or motion is, which perhaps seems much easier. The simple ideas we have are such as experience teaches them us; but if, beyond that, we endeavour by words to make them clearer in the mind, we shall succeed no better than if we went about to clear up the darkness of a blind man's mind by talking, and to discourse into him the ideas of light and colours. The reason of this I shall show in another place.

CHAPTER VI. OF SIMPLE IDEAS OF REFLECTION

1. *Simple ideas of reflection are the operations of the mind about its other ideas.* — The mind, receiving the ideas mentioned in the foregoing chapters from without, when it turns its view inward upon itself, and observes its own actions about those ideas it has, takes from thence other ideas, which are as capable to be the objects of its contemplation as any of those it received from foreign things.

2. *The idea of perception, and idea of willing, we have from reflection.* — The two great and principal actions of the mind, which are most frequently considered, and which are so frequent that every one that pleases may take notice of them in himself, are these two: *Perception* or *Thinking;* and *Volition* or *Willing.* [The power of thinking is called the *Understanding,*

and the power of volition is called the *Will;* and these two powers or abilities in the mind are denominated "faculties."] . . .

CHAPTER VII. OF SIMPLE IDEAS OF BOTH SENSA-TION AND REFLECTION

1. *Pleasure and pain.* — There be other simple ideas which convey themselves into the mind by all the ways of sensation and reflection; viz., *pleasure* or *delight.* and its opposite, *pain* or *uneasiness; power, existence, unity.*

2. Delight or uneasiness, one or other of them, join themselves to almost all our ideas both of sensation and reflection; and there is scarce any affection of our senses from without, any retired thought of our mind within, which is not able to produce in us pleasure or pain. By "pleasure" and "pain," I would be understood to signify whatsoever delights or molests us; whether it arises from the thoughts of our minds, or any thing operating on our bodies. For whether we call it "satisfaction, delight, pleasure, happiness," &c., on the one side; or "uneasiness, trouble, pain, torment, anguish, misery," &c., on the other; they are still but different degrees of the same thing, and belong to the ideas of pleasure and pain, delight or uneasiness; which are the names I shall most commonly use for those two sorts of ideas.

6. *Pleasure and pain.* — Though what I have here said may not perhaps make the ideas of pleasure and pain clearer to us than our own experience does, which is the only way that we are capable of having them; yet the consideration of the reason why they are annexed to so many other ideas, serving to give us due sentiments of the wisdom and goodness of the Sovereign Disposer of all things, may not be unsuitable to the main end of these inquiries: the knowledge and veneration of Him being the chief end of all our thoughts, and the proper business of all our understandings.

7. *Existence and unity.* — Existence and unity are two other ideas that are suggested to the understanding by every object without, and every idea within. When ideas are in our minds,

we consider them as being actually there, as well as we consider things to be actually without us: which is, that they exist, or have existence: and whatever we can consider as one thing, whether a real being or idea, suggests to the understanding the idea of unity.

8. *Power.* — Power also is another of those simple ideas which we receive from sensation and reflection. For, observing in ourselves that we do and can think, and that we can at pleasure move several parts of our bodies which were at rest; the effects also that natural bodies are able to produce in one another occurring every moment to our senses, we both these ways get the idea of power.

9. *Succession.* — Besides these there is another idea, which though suggested by our senses, yet is more constantly offered us by what passes in our minds; and that is the idea of succession. For if we look immediately into ourselves, and reflect on what is observable there, we shall find our ideas always, whilst we are awake or have any thought, passing in train, one going and another coming without intermission.

10. *Simple ideas the materials of all our knowledge.* — These, if they are not all, are at least (as I think) the most considerable of those simple ideas which the mind has, and out of which is made all its other knowledge: all of which it receives only by the two forementioned ways of sensation and reflection.

· · · · · · · · · · · ·

CHAPTER VIII. SOME FURTHER CONSIDERA-
TIONS CONCERNING OUR SIMPLE
IDEAS OF SENSATION

7. *Ideas in the mind, qualities in bodies.* — To discover the nature of our *ideas* the better, and to discourse of them intelligibly, it will be convenient to distinguish them, as they are ideas or perceptions in our minds: and as they are modifications of matter in the bodies that cause such perceptions in us; that so we may not think (as perhaps usually is done) that they are exactly the images and resemblances of something inherent

in the subject; most of those of sensation being in the mind no more the likeness of something existing without us than the names that stand for them are the likeness of our ideas, which yet upon hearing they are apt to excite in us.

8. Whatsoever the mind perceives in itself, or is the immediate object of perception, thought, or understanding, that I call *idea;* and the power to produce any idea in our mind, I call *quality* of the subject wherein that power is. Thus a snowball having the power to produce in us the ideas of white, cold, and round, the powers to produce those ideas in us as they are in the snowball, I call *qualities;* and as they are sensations or perceptions in our understandings, I call them "ideas"; which *ideas,* if I speak of them sometimes as in the things themselves, I would be understood to mean those qualities in the objects which produce them in us.

9. *Primary qualities.* — [Qualities thus considered in bodies are, First, such as are utterly inseparable from the body, in what estate soever it be;] and such as, in all the alterations and changes it suffers, all the force can be used upon it, it constantly keeps; and such as sense constantly finds in every particle of matter which has bulk enough to be perceived, and the mind finds inseparable from every particle of matter, though less than to make itself singly be perceived by our senses; *e.g.,* take a grain of wheat, divide it into two parts, each part has still solidity, extension, figure, and mobility; divide it again, and it retains still the same qualities: and so divide it on till the parts become insensible, they must retain still each of them all those qualities. For, division (which is all that a mill or pestle or any other body does upon another, in reducing it to insensible parts) can never take away either solidity, extension, figure, or mobility from any body, but only makes two or more distinct separate masses of matter of that which was but one before; all which distinct masses, reckoned as so many distinct bodies, after division, make a certain number. [These I call *original* or *primary* qualities of body, which I think we may observe to produce simple ideas in us, viz., solidity, extension, figure, motion or rest. and number.

10. *Secondary qualities.* — Secondly. Such qualities, which in truth are nothing in the objects themselves, but powers to produce various sensations in us by their primary qualities, *i.e.*, by the bulk, figure, texture, and motion of their insensible parts, as colours, sounds, tastes, &c., these I call *secondary* qualities. To these might be added a third sort, which are allowed to be barely powers, though they are as much real qualities in the subject as those which I, to comply with the common way of speaking, call qualities, but, for distinction, *secondary* qualities. For, the power in fire to produce a new colour or consistency in wax or clay, — by its primary qualities, is as much a quality in fire as the power it has to produce in me a new idea or sensation of warmth or burning, which I felt not before, — by the same primary qualities, viz., the bulk, texture, and motion of its insensible parts.]

11. [*How primary qualities produce their ideas.* — The next thing to be considered is, how bodies produce ideas in us; and that is manifestly by impulse, the only way which we can conceive bodies to operate in.]

12. If, then, external objects be not united to our minds when they produce ideas therein; and yet we perceive these *original* qualities in such of them as singly fall under our senses, it is evident that some motion must be thence continued by our nerves, or animal spirits, by some parts of our bodies, to the brains or the seat of sensation, there to produce in our minds the particular ideas we have of them. And since the extension, figure, number, and motion of bodies of an observable bigness, may be perceived at a distance by the sight, it is evident some singly imperceptible bodies must come from them to the eyes, and thereby convey to the brain some motion which produces these ideas which we have of them in us.

13. *How secondary.* — After the same manner that the ideas of these original qualities are produced in us, we may conceive that the ideas of *secondary* qualities are also produced, viz., by the operation of insensible particles on our senses. For it being manifest that there are bodies, and good store of bodies, each whereof are so small that we cannot by any of our senses dis-

cover either their bulk, figure, or motion (as is evident in the particles of the air and water, and other extremely smaller than those, perhaps as much smaller than the particles of air or water as the particles of air or water are smaller than peas or hailstones): let us suppose at present that the different motions and figures, bulk and number, of such particles, effecting the several organs of our senses, produce in us those different sensations which we have from the colours and smells of bodies; *e.g.*, that a violet, by the impulse of such insensible particles of matter of peculiar figures and bulks, and in different degrees and modifications of their motions, causes the ideas of the blue colour and sweet scent of that flower to be produced in our minds; it being no more impossible to conceive that God should annex such ideas to such motions, with which they have no similitude, than that he should annex the idea of pain to the motion of a piece of steel dividing our flesh, with which the idea hath no resemblance.

14. What I have said concerning colours and smells may be understood also of tastes and sounds, and other the like sensible qualities; which, whatever reality we by mistake attribute to them, are in truth nothing in the objects themselves, but powers to produce various sensations in us, and depend on those primary qualities, viz., bulk, figure, texture, and motion of parts [as I have said].

15. *Ideas of primary qualities are resemblances; of secondary, not.* — From whence I think it is easy to draw this observation, that the ideas of primary qualities of bodies are resemblances of them, and their patterns do really exist in the bodies themselves; but the ideas produced in us by these secondary qualities have no resemblance of them at all. There is nothing like our ideas existing in the bodies themselves. They are, in the bodies we denominate from them, only a power to produce those sensations in us; and what is sweet, blue, or warm in idea, is but the certain bulk, figure, and motion of the insensible parts in the bodies themselves, which we call so.

23. *Three sorts of qualities in bodies.* — The qualities then that are in bodies, rightly considered, are of three sorts: —

First. The bulk, figure, number, situation, and motion or rest of their solid parts; those are in them, whether we perceive them or not; and when they are of that size that we can discover them, we have by these ideas of the thing as it is in itself, as is plain in artificial things. These I call *primary* qualities.

Secondly. The power that is in any body, by reason of its insensible primary qualities, to operate after a peculiar manner on any of our senses, and thereby produce in us the different ideas of several colours, sounds, smells, tastes, &c. These are usually called *sensible* qualities.

Thirdly. The power that is in any body, by reason of the particular constitution of its primary qualities, to make such a change in the bulk, figure, texture, and motion of another body, as to make it operate on our senses differently from what it did before. Thus the sun has a power to make wax white, and fire, to make lead fluid. [These are usually called *powers*.]

The first of these, as has been said, I think may be properly called real, original, or primary qualities, because they are in the things themselves, whether they are perceived or no; and upon their different modifications it is that the secondary qualities depend.

The other two are only powers to act differently upon other things, which powers result from the different modifications of those primary qualities.

· · · · · · · · · · · ·

CHAPTER IX. OF PERCEPTION

1. *Perception the first simple idea of reflection.* — Perception, as it is the first faculty of the mind exercised about our ideas, so it is the first and simplest idea we have from reflection, and is by some called "thinking" in general. Though thinking, in the propriety of the English tongue, signifies that sort of operation of the mind about its ideas wherein the mind is active; where it, with some degree of voluntary attention, considers any thing: for in bare, naked perception, the mind is, for the most part, only passive, and what it perceives it cannot avoid perceiving.

2. *Is only when the mind receives the impression.* — What perception is, every one will know better by reflecting on what he does himself, when he sees, hears, feels, &c., or thinks, than by any discourse of mine. Whoever reflects on what passes in his own mind, cannot miss it; and if he does not reflect, all the words in the world cannot make him have any notion of it.

3. This is certain, that whatever alterations are made in the body, if they reach not the mind; whatever impressions are made on the outward parts, if they are not taken notice of within; there is no perception. Fire may burn our bodies with no other effect than it does a billet, unless the motion be continued to the brain, and there the sense of heat or idea of pain be produced in the mind, wherein consists actual perception.

8. *Ideas of sensation often changed by the judgment.* — We are farther to consider concerning perception, that the ideas we receive by sensation are often in grown people altered by the judgment without our taking notice of it. When we set before our eyes a round globe of any uniform colour, *e.g.*, gold, alabaster, or jet, it is certain that the idea thereby imprinted in our mind is of a flat circle variously shadowed, with several degrees of light and brightness coming to our eyes. But we having, by use, been accustomed to perceive what kind of appearance convex bodies are wont to make in us; what alterations are made in the reflections of light by the difference of the sensible figures of bodies; the judgment presently, by an habitual custom, alters the appearances into their causes; so that, from that which truly is variety of shadow or colour collecting the figure, it makes it pass for a mark of figure, and frames to itself the perception of a convex figure and an uniform colour; when the idea we receive from thence is only a plane variously coloured, as is evident in painting. [To which purpose I shall here insert a problem of that very ingenious and studious promoter of real knowledge, the learned and worthy Mr. Molineaux, which he was pleased to send me in a letter some months since: and it is this: "Suppose a man *born* blind, and now adult, and taught by his *touch* to distinguish between a cube and a sphere of the same metal, and nighly of the same bigness, so as

to tell, when he felt one and the other, which is the cube, which the sphere. Suppose then the cube and sphere placed on a table, and the blind man to be made to see; quære, Whether *by his sight, before he touched them,* he could now distinguish and tell which is the globe, which the cube?" To which the acute and judicious proposer answers: "Not. For though he has obtained the experience of how a globe, how a cube, affects his touch; yet he has not yet obtained the experience, that what affects his touch so or so, must affect his sight so or so; or that a protuberant angle in the cube, that pressed his hand unequally, shall appear to his eye as it does in the cube." I agree with this thinking gentleman whom I am proud to call my friend, in his answer to this his problem; and am of opinion, that the blind man, at first sight, would not be able with certainty to say which was the globe, which the cube, whilst he only saw them; though he could unerringly name them by his touch, and certainly distinguish them by the difference of their figures felt. This I have set down, and leave with my reader, as an occasion for him to consider how much he may be beholden to experience, improvement, and acquired notions, where he thinks he has not the least use of, or help from them. And the rather, because this observing gentleman farther adds, that having upon the occasion of my book proposed this to divers very ingenious men, he hardly ever met with one that at first gave the answer to it which he thinks true, till by hearing his reasons they were convinced.]

9. But this is not, I think, usual in any of our ideas but those received by sight; because sight, the most comprehensive of all our senses, conveying to our minds the ideas of light and colours, which are peculiar only to that sense; and also the far different ideas of space, figure and motion, the several varieties whereof change the appearances of its proper objects, viz., light and colours; we bring ourselves by use to judge of the one by the other. This, in many cases, by a settled habit in things whereof we have frequent experience, is performed so constantly and so quick, that we take that for the perception of our sensation which is an idea formed by our judgment; so that one, viz.,

that of sensation, serves only to excite the other, and is scarce taken notice of itself; as a man who reads or hears with attention and understanding, takes little notice of the characters or sounds, but of the ideas that are excited in him by them.

15. *Perception the inlet of knowledge.* — Perception, then, being the *first* step and degree towards knowledge, and the inlet of all the materials of it, the fewer senses any man as well as any other creature hath; and the fewer and duller the impressions are that are made by them; and the duller the faculties are that are employed about them, — the more remote are they from that knowledge which is to be found in some men. But this, being in great variety of degrees (as may be perceived amongst men), cannot certainly be discovered in the several species of animals, much less in their particular individuals. It suffices me only to have remarked here, that perception is the first operation* of all our intellectual faculties, and the inlet of all knowledge into our minds. . . .

CHAPTER XII. OF COMPLEX IDEAS

1. *Made by the mind out of simple ones.* — We have hitherto considered those ideas, in the reception whereof the mind is only passive, which are those simple ones received from sensation and reflection before mentioned, whereof the mind cannot make one to itself, nor have any idea which does not wholly consist of them. [But as the mind is wholly passive in the reception of all its simple ideas, so it exerts several acts of its own, whereby out of its simple ideas, as the materials and foundations of the rest, the other are framed. The acts of the mind

---

* The other operations of the mind discussed by Locke under simple ideas are retention or memory, discerning, comparing, compounding, and abstraction. He then concludes in part as follows: chap. xi, § 15. *These are the beginnings of human knowledge.* — And thus I have given a short and, I think, true history of the first beginnings of human knowledge, whence the mind has its first objects, and by what steps it makes its progress to the laying in and storing up those ideas out of which is to be framed all the knowledge it is capable of; wherein I must appeal to experience and observation whether I am in the right: the best way to come to truth being to examine things as really they are, and not to conclude they are as we fancy of ourselves, or have been taught by others to imagine.

wherein it exerts its power over its simple ideas are chiefly these three: (1) Combining several simple ideas into one compound one; and thus all *complex ideas* are made. (2) The second is bringing two ideas, whether simple or complex, together, and setting them by one another, so as to take a view of them at once, without uniting them into one; by which way it gets all its *ideas of relations.* (3) The third is separating them from all other ideas that accompany them in their real existence; this is called "abstraction": and thus all its *general ideas* are made. This shows man's power and its way of operation to be much the same in the material and intellectual world. For, the materials in both being such as he has no power over, either to make or destroy, all that man can do is either to unite them together, or to set them by one another, or wholly separate them. I shall here begin with the first of these in the consideration of complex ideas, and come to the other two in their due places.] * As simple ideas are observed to exist in several combinations united together, so the mind has a power to consider several of them united together as one idea; and that not only as they are united in external objects, but as itself has joined them. Ideas thus made up of several simple ones put together I call *complex;* such as are beauty, gratitude, a man, an army, the universe; which, though complicated of various simple ideas or complex ideas made up of simple ones, yet are, when the mind pleases, considered each by itself as one entire thing, and signified by one name.

2. *Made voluntarily.* — In this faculty of repeating and joining together its ideas, the mind has great power in varying and multiplying the objects of its thoughts infinitely beyond what sensation or reflection furnished it with; but all this still confined to those simple ideas which it received from those two sources, and which are the ultimate materials of all its compositions. For, simple ideas are all from things themselves; and of these the mind can have no more nor other than what are suggested to it. It can have no other ideas of sensible qualities

---

* Brackets indicate deviations from the first edition of the *Essay* found by A. C. Fraser in the three other editions of Locke's lifetime.

than what come from without by the senses, nor any ideas of other kind of operations of a thinking substance than what it finds in itself: but when it has once got these simple ideas, it is not confined barely to observation, and what offers itself from without; it can, by its own power, put together those ideas it has, and make new complex ones which it never received so united.

3. *Are either modes, substances, or relations.* — Complex ideas, however compounded and decompounded, though their number be infinite, and the variety endless wherewith they fill and entertain the thoughts of men, yet I think they may be all reduced under these three heads: 1. Modes. 2. Substances. 3. Relations.

4. *Modes.* — First. *Modes* I call such complex ideas which, however compounded, contain not in them the supposition of subsisting by themselves, but are considered as dependences on, or affections of, substances; such are the ideas signified by the words, "triangle, gratitude, murder," &c. And if in this I use the word "mode" in somewhat a different sense from its ordinary signification, I beg pardon; it being unavoidable in discourses differing from the ordinary received notions, either to make new words or to use old words in somewhat a new signification: the latter whereof, in our present case, is perhaps the more tolerable of the two.

5. *Simple and mixed modes.* — Of these *modes* there are two sorts which deserve distinct consideration. First. There are some which are only variations or different combinations of the same simple idea, without the mixture of any other, as a dozen, or score; which are nothing but the ideas of so many distinct units added together: and these I call *simple modes*, as being contained within the bounds of one simple idea. Secondly. There are others compounded of simple ideas, of several kinds, put together to make one complex one, *e.g.*, beauty, consisting of a certain composition of colour and figure, causing delight in the beholder; theft, which, being the concealed change of the possession of any thing, without the consent of the proprietor, contains, as is visible, a combination of several ideas of several kinds: and these I call *mixed modes*.

6. *Substances single or collective.* — Secondly. The ideas of *substances* are such combinations of simple ideas as are taken to represent distinct particular things subsisting by themselves, in which the supposed or confused idea of substance, such as it is, is always the first and chief. Thus, if to substance be joined the simple idea of a certain dull, whitish colour, with certain degrees of weight, hardness, ductility, and fusibility, we have the idea of lead; and a combination of the ideas of a certain sort of figure, with the powers of motion, thought, and reasoning, joined to substance, make the ordinary idea of a man. Now of substances also there are two sorts of ideas:—one of *single* substances, as they exist separately, as of a man or a sheep; the other of several of those put together, as an army of men or flock of sheep — which *collective* ideas of several substances thus put together, are as much each of them one single idea as that of a man or an unit.

7. *Relation.* — Thirdly. The last sort of complex ideas is that we call *Relation*, which consists in the consideration and comparing one idea with another. Of these several kinds we shall treat in their order.

8. *The abstrusest ideas from the two sources.* — If we trace the progress of our minds, and with attention observe how it repeats, adds together, and unites its simple ideas received from sensation or reflection, it will lead us farther than at first perhaps we should have imagined. And I believe we shall find, if we warily observe the originals of our notions, that even *the most abstruse* ideas, how remote soever they may seem from sense, or from any operation of our own minds, are yet only such as the understanding frames to itself, by repeating and joining together ideas that it had either from objects of sense, or from its own operations about them; so that those even large and abstract ideas are derived from sensation or reflection, being no other than what the mind, by the ordinary use of its own faculties, employed about ideas received from objects of sense, or from the operations it observes in itself about them, may and does attain unto.

BOOK IV

CHAPTER I. OF KNOWLEDGE IN GENERAL

1. *Our Knowledge conversant about our Ideas.* — Since the mind, in all its thoughts and reasonings, hath no other immediate object but its own ideas, which it alone does or can contemplate, it is evident that our knowledge is only conversant about them.

2. *Knowledge is the Perception of the Agreement or Disagreement of two Ideas.* — Knowledge, then, seems to me to be nothing but the perception of the connexion and agreement, or disagreement and repugnancy of any of our ideas. In this alone it consists. Where this perception is, there is knowledge; and where it is not, there, though we may fancy, guess, or believe, yet we always come short of knowledge. For when we know that white is not black, what do we else but perceive that these two ideas do not agree? When we possess ourselves with the utmost security of the demonstration, that the three angles of a triangle are equal to two right ones, what do we more but perceive, that equality to two right ones does necessarily agree to, and is inseparable from the three angles of a triangle?

3. *This Agreement fourfold.* — But to understand a little more distinctly wherein this agreement or disagreement consists, I think we may reduce it all to these four sorts:

I. Identity, or diversity.
II. Relation.
III. Co-existence, or necessary connexion.
IV. Real existence.

4. *First, Of Identity, or Diversity.* — First, As to the first sort of agreement or disagreement, viz., identity or diversity. It is the first act of the mind, when it has any sentiments or ideas at all, to perceive its ideas; and so far as it perceives them, to know each what it is, and thereby also to perceive their difference, and that one is not another. This is so absolutely necessary, that, without it, there could be no knowledge, no

reasoning, no imagination, no distinct thoughts at all. By this the mind clearly and infallibly perceives each idea to agree with itself, and to be what it is; and all distinct ideas to disagree, i.e., the one not to be the other; and this it does without pains, labour, or deduction; but at first view, by its natural power of perception and distinction. And though men of art have reduced this into those general rules, "what is, is," and "it is impossible for the same thing to be and not to be," for ready application in all cases, wherein there may be occasion to reflect it on: yet it is certain, that the first exercise of this faculty is about particular ideas. A man infallibly knows, as soon as ever he has them in his mind, that the ideas he calls white and round are the very ideas they are, and that they are not other ideas which he calls red or square. Nor can any maxim or proposition in the world make him know it clearer or surer than he did before, and without any such general rule. This, then, is the first agreement or disagreement which the mind perceives in its ideas, which it always perceives at first sight: and if there ever happen any doubt about it, it will always be found to be about the names, and not the ideas themselves, whose identity and diversity will always be perceived as soon and clearly as the ideas themselves are; nor can it possibly be otherwise.

5. *Secondly, Relative.* — Secondly, The next sort of agreement or disagreement the mind perceives in any of its ideas may, I think, be called relative, and is nothing but the perception of the relation between any two ideas, of what kind soever, whether substances, modes, or any other. For, since all distinct ideas must eternally be known not to be the same, and so be universally and constantly denied one of another, there could be no room for any positive knowledge at all, if we could not perceive any relation between our ideas, and find out the agreement or disagreement they have one with another, in several ways the mind takes of comparing them.

6. *Thirdly, Of Co-existence.* — Thirdly, The third sort of agreement or disagreement to be found in our ideas, which the perception of the mind is employed about, is co-existence

or non-co-existence in the same subject; and this belongs particularly to substances. Thus, when we pronounce concerning gold, that it is fixed, our knowledge of this truth amounts to no more but this, that fixedness, or a power to remain in the fire unconsumed, is an idea that always accompanies and is joined with that particular sort of yellowness, weight, fusibility, malleableness, and solubility in aq. regia, which make our complex idea, signified by the word gold.

7. *Fourthly. Of real Existence.* — Fourthly, The fourth and last sort is that of actual and real existence agreeing to any idea. Within these four sorts of agreement or disagreement is, I suppose, contained all the knowledge we have, or are capable of: for all the inquiries we can make concerning any of our ideas, all that we know or can affirm concerning any of them is, that it is, or is not, the same with some other; that it does or does not always co-exist with some other idea in the same subject; that it has this or that relation with some other idea; or that it has a real existence without the mind. Thus, blue is not yellow, is of identity: two triangles upon equal bases between two parallels are equal, is of relation: iron is susceptible of magnetical impressions, is of co-existence: God is, is of real existence. Though identity and co-existence are truly nothing but relations, yet they are such peculiar ways of agreement or disagreement of our ideas, that they deserve well to be considered as distinct heads, and not under relation in general; since they are so different grounds of affirmation and negation, as will easily appear to any one, who will but reflect on what is said in several places of this essay. . . .

GEORGE BERKELEY

(1685–1753)

AN ESSAY TOWARDS A NEW THEORY OF VISION *

1. MY *design* is (a) to shew the manner wherein we perceive by sight the Distance, Magnitude, and Situation of objects; also (b) to consider the difference there is betwixt the ideas of Sight and Touch, and whether there be any idea common to both senses.

2. It is, I think, agreed by all that Distance of itself, and immediately, cannot be seen. For distance being a line directed endwise to the eye, it projects only one point in the fund of the eye — which point remains invariably the same, whether the distance be longer or shorter.

3. I find it also acknowledged that the estimate we make of the distance of objects *considerably remote* is rather an act of judgment grounded on experience than of sense. For example, when I perceive a great number of intermediate objects, such as houses, fields, rivers, and the like, which I have experienced to take up a considerable space, I thence form a judgment or conclusion, that the object I see beyond them is at a great distance. Again, when an object appears faint and small which at a near distance I have experienced to make a vigorous and large appearance, I instantly conclude it to be far off. — And this, it is evident, is the result of experience; without which, from the faintness and littleness, I should not have inferred anything concerning the distance of objects.

4. But, when an object is placed at so near a distance as that the interval between the eyes bears any sensible proportion to it, the opinion of speculative men is, that the two optic

* Dublin, 1709; Lond., 1711; ib., 1732, etc.

axes (the fancy that we see only with one eye at once being exploded), concurring at the object, do there make an angle, by means of which, according as it is greater or lesser, the object is perceived to be nearer or farther off.

5. Betwixt which and the foregoing manner of estimating distance there is this remarkable difference: — that, whereas there was no apparent *necessary* connexion between small distance and a large and strong appearance, or between great distance and a little and faint appearance, there appears a very necessary connexion between an obtuse angle and near distance, and an acute angle and farther distance. It does not in the least depend upon experience, but may be evidently known by any one before he had experienced it, that the nearer the concurrence of the optic axes the greater the angle, and the remoter their concurrence is the lesser will be the angle comprehended by them.

6. There is another way, mentioned by optic writers, whereby they will have us judge of those distances in respect of which the breadth of the pupil hath any sensible bigness. And that is the greater or lesser divergency of the rays, which, issuing from the visible point, do fall on the pupil — that point being judged nearest which is seen by most diverging rays, and that remoter which is seen by less diverging rays; and so on, the apparent distance still increasing, as the divergency of the rays decreases, till at length it becomes infinite when the rays that fall on the pupil are to sense parallel. And after this manner it is said we perceive distance when we look only with one eye.

7. In this case also it is plain we are not beholden to experience: it being a certain, necessary truth that, the nearer the direct rays falling on the eye approach to a parallelism, the farther off is the point of their intersection, or the visible point from whence they flow.

8. Now, though the accounts here given of perceiving near distance by sight are received for true, and accordingly made use of in determining the apparent places of objects, they do

nevertheless seem to me very unsatisfactory, and that for these following reasons: —

9. *First*, It is evident that, when the mind perceives any idea, not immediately and of itself, it must be by the means of some other idea. Thus, for instance, the passions which are in the mind of another are of themselves to me invisible. I may nevertheless perceive them by sight, though not immediately, yet by means of the colours they produce in the countenance. We often see shame or fear in the looks of a man, by perceiving the changes of his countenance to red or pale.

10. Moreover, it is evident that no idea which is not itself perceived can be to me the means of perceiving any other idea. If I do not perceive the redness or paleness of a man's face themselves, it is impossible I should perceive by them the passions which are in his mind.

11. Now, from sect. ii., it is plain that distance is in its own nature imperceptible, and yet it is perceived by sight. It remains, therefore, that it be brought into view by means of some other idea, that is itself immediately perceived in the act of vision.

12. But those lines and angles by means whereof some men pretend to explain the perception of distance, are themselves not at all perceived, nor are they in truth ever thought of by those unskilful in optics. I appeal to any one's experience, whether, upon sight of an object, he computes its distance by the bigness of the angle made by the meeting of the two optic axes? or whether he ever thinks of the greater or lesser divergency of the rays which arrive from any point to his pupil? nay, whether it be not perfectly impossible for him to perceive by sense the various angles wherewith the rays, according to their greater or lesser divergence, do fall on the eye? Every one is himself the best judge of what he perceives, and what not. In vain shall any man tell me, that I perceive certain lines and angles which introduce into my mind the various ideas of distance, so long as I myself am conscious of no such thing.

13. Since therefore those angles and lines are not themselves

perceived by sight, it follows, from sect. x., that the mind does not by them judge of the distance of objects.

14. *Secondly*, The truth of this assertion will be yet farther evident to any one that considers those lines and angles have no real existence in nature, being only an hypothesis framed by the mathematicians, and by them introduced into optics that they might treat of that science in a geometrical way.

15. The *third* and last reason I shall give for rejecting that doctrine is, that though we should grant the real existence of those optic angles, &c., and that it was possible for the mind to perceive them, yet these principles would not be found sufficient to explain the phenomena of distance, as shall be shewn hereafter.

16. Now, it being already shewn that distance is *suggested* to the mind, by the mediation of some other idea which is itself perceived in the act of seeing, it remains that we inquire what ideas or sensations there be that attend vision unto which we may suppose the ideas of distance are connected, and by which they are introduced into the mind.

And, *first*, it is certain by experience, that when we look at a near object with both eyes, according as it approaches or recedes from us, we alter the disposition of our eyes, by lessening or widening the interval between the pupils. This disposition or turn of the eyes is attended with a sensation, which seems to me to be that which in this case brings the idea of greater or lesser distance into the mind.

17. Not that there is any natural or necessary connexion between the sensation we perceive by the turn of the eyes and greater or lesser distance. But — because the mind has, by constant experience, found the different sensations corresponding to the different dispositions of the eyes to be attended each with a different degree of distance in the object — there has grown an habitual or customary connexion between those two sorts of ideas; so that the mind no sooner perceives the sensation arising from the different turn it gives the eyes, in order to bring the pupils nearer or farther asunder, but it

withal perceives the different idea of distance which was wont
to be connected with that sensation. Just as, upon hearing
a certain sound, the idea is immediately suggested to the
understanding which custom had united with it.

18. Nor do I see how I can easily be mistaken in this matter.
I know evidently that distance is not perceived of itself — that,
by consequence, it must be perceived by means of some other
idea, which is immediately perceived, and varies with the different degrees of distance. I know also that the sensation
arising from the turn of the eyes is of itself immediately perceived, and various degrees thereof are connected with different distances, which never fail to accompany them into my
mind, when I view an object distinctly with both eyes whose
distance is so small that in respect of it the interval between
the eyes has any considerable magnitude.

19. I know it is a received opinion that, by altering the
disposition of the eyes, the mind perceives whether the angle
of the optic axes, or the lateral angles comprehended between
the interval of the eyes or the optic axes, are made greater
or lesser; and that, accordingly, by a kind of natural geometry,
it judges the point of their intersection to be nearer or farther
off. But that this is not true I am convinced by my own experience, since I am not conscious that I make any such use of the
perception I have by the turn of my eyes. And for me to make
those judgments, and draw those conclusions from it, without
knowing that I do so, seems altogether incomprehensible.

20. From all which it follows, that the judgment we make
of the distance of an object viewed with both eyes is entirely
the result of experience. If we had not constantly found certain sensations, arising from the various dispositions of the
eyes, attended with certain degrees of distance, we should never
make those sudden judgments from them concerning the distance of objects; no more than we would pretend to judge of a
man's thoughts by his pronouncing words we had never heard
before.

21. *Secondly*, an object placed at a certain distance from the
eye, to which the breadth of the pupil bears a considerable

proportion, being made to approach, is seen more confusedly. And the nearer it is brought the more confused appearance it makes. And, this being found constantly to be so, there arises in the mind an habitual connexion between the several degrees of confusion and distance; the greater confusion still implying the lesser distance, and the lesser confusion the greater distance of the object.

22. This confused appearance of the object doth therefore seem to be the medium whereby the mind judges of distance, in those cases wherein the most approved writers of optics will have it judge by the different divergency with which the rays flowing from the radiating point fall on the pupil. No man, I believe, will pretend to see or feel those imaginary angles that the rays are supposed to form according to their various inclinations on his eye. But he cannot choose seeing whether the object appear more or less confused. It is therefore a manifest consequence from what has been demonstrated that, instead of the greater or lesser divergency of the rays, the mind makes use of the greater or lesser confusedness of the appearance, thereby to determine the apparent place of an object.

23. Nor doth it avail to say there is not any necessary connexion between confused vision and distance great or small. For I ask any man what necessary connexion he sees between the redness of a blush and shame? And yet no sooner shall he behold that colour to arise in the face of another but it brings into his mind the idea of that passion which hath been observed to accompany it.

24. What seems to have misled the writers of optics in this matter is, that they imagine men judge of distance as they do of a conclusion in mathematics; betwixt which and the premises it is indeed absolutely requisite there be an apparent, necessary connexion. But it is far otherwise in the sudden judgments men make of distance. We are not to think that brutes and children, or even grown reasonable men, whenever they perceive an object to approach or depart from them, do it by virtue of geometry and demonstration.

25. That one idea may suggest another to the mind, it will

suffice that they have been observed to go together, without any demonstration of the necessity of their coexistence, or without so much as knowing what it is that makes them so to coexist. Of this there are innumerable instances, of which no one can be ignorant.

26. Thus, greater confusion having been constantly attended with nearer distance, no sooner is the former idea perceived but it suggests the latter to our thoughts. And, if it had been the ordinary course of nature that the farther off an object were placed the more confused it should appear, it is certain the very same perception that now makes us think an object approaches would then have made us to imagine it went farther off — that perception, abstracting from custom and experience, being equally fitted to produce the idea of great distance, or small distance, or no distance at all.

27. *Thirdly,* an object being placed at the distance above specified, and brought nearer to the eye, we may nevertheless prevent, at least for some time, the appearance's growing more confused, by straining the eye. In which case that sensation supplies the place of confused vision, in aiding the mind to judge of the distance of the object; it being esteemed so much the nearer by how much the effort or straining of the eye in order to distinct vision is greater.

28. I have here set down those sensations of ideas that seem to be the constant and general occasions of introducing into the mind the different ideas of near distance. It is true, in most cases, that divers other circumstances contribute to frame our idea of distance, viz. the particular number, size, kind, &c. of the things seen. Concerning which, as well as all other the fore-mentioned occasions which suggest distance, I shall only observe, they have none of them, in their own nature, any relation or connexion with it: nor is it possible they should ever signify the various degrees thereof, otherwise than as by experience they have been found to be connected with them.

41. From what has been premised, it is a manifest consequence, that a man born blind, being made to see, would at

first have no idea of Distance by sight: the sun and stars, the remotest objects as well as the nearer, would all seem to be in his eye, or rather in his mind. The objects intromitted by sight would seem to him (as in truth they are) no other than a new set of thoughts or sensations, each whereof is as near to him as the perceptions of pain or pleasure, or the most inward passions of his soul. For, our judging objects perceived by sight to be at any distance, or without the mind, is (vid. sect. 28) entirely the effect of experience. which one in those circumstances could not yet have attained to.

42. It is indeed otherwise upon the common supposition — that men judge of distance by the angle of the optic axes, just as one in the dark, or a blind man by the angle comprehended by two sticks, one whereof he held in his hand. For, if this were true, it would follow that one blind from his birth, being made to see, should stand in need of no new experience, in order to perceive distance by sight. But that this is false has, I think, been sufficiently demonstrated.

43. And perhaps, upon a strict inquiry, we shall not find that even those who from their birth have grown up in a continued habit of seeing are irrecoverably prejudiced on the other side, to wit, in thinking what they see to be at a distance from them. For, at this time it seems agreed on all hands, by those who have had any thoughts of that matter, that *colours, which are the proper and immediate object of sight, are not without the mind.* — But then, it will be said, by *sight* we have also the ideas of *extension*, and *figure*, and *motion;* all which may well be thought without and at some distance from the mind, though colour should not. In answer to this, I appeal to any man's experience, whether the visible extension of any object do not appear as near to him as the colour of that object; nay, whether they do not both seem to be in the very same place. Is not the extension we see coloured, and is it possible for us, so much as in thought, to separate and abstract colour from extension? Now, where the extension is, there surely is the figure, and there the motion too. I speak of those which are perceived by sight.

44. But, for a fuller explication of this point, and to shew that the immediate objects of sight are not so much as the ideas or resemblances of things placed at a distance, it is requisite that we look nearer into the matter, and carefully observe what is meant in common discourse when one says, that which he sees is at a distance from him. Suppose, for example, that looking at the moon I should say it were fifty or sixty semidiameters of the earth distant from me. Let us see what moon this is spoken of. It is plain it cannot be the visible moon, or anything like the visible moon, or that which I see — which is only a round luminous plain, of about thirty visible points in diameter. For, in case I am carried from the place where I stand directly towards the moon, it is manifest the object varies still as I go on; and, by the time that I am advanced fifty or sixty semidiameters of the earth, I shall be so far from being near a small, round, luminous flat that I shall perceive nothing like it — this object having long since disappeared, and, if I would recover it, it must be by going back to the earth from whence I set out. Again, suppose I perceive by sight the faint and obscure idea of something, which I doubt whether it be a man, or a tree, or a tower, but judge it to be at the distance of about a mile. It is plain I cannot mean that what I see is a mile off, or that it is the image or likeness of anything which is a mile off; since that every step I take towards it the appearance alters, and from being obscure, small, and faint, grows clear, large, and vigorous. And when I come to the mile's end, that which I saw first is quite lost, neither do I find anything in the likeness of it.

45. In these and the like instances, the truth of the matter, I find, stands thus: — Having of a long time experienced certain ideas perceivable by *touch* — as distance, tangible figure, and solidity — to have been connected with certain ideas of sight, I do, upon perceiving these ideas of sight, forthwith conclude what tangible ideas are, by the wonted ordinary course of nature, like to follow. Looking at an object, I perceive a certain visible figure and colour, with some degree of faintness and other circumstances, which, from what I have formerly

observed, determine me to think that if I advance forward so many paces, miles, &c., I shall be affected with such and such ideas of touch. So that, in truth and strictness of speech, I neither see distance itself, nor anything that I take to be at a distance. I say, neither distance nor things placed at a distance are themselves, or their ideas, truly perceived by sight. This I am persuaded of, as to what concerns myself. And I believe whoever will look narrowly into his own thoughts, and examine what he means by saying he sees this or that thing at a distance, will agree with me, that what he sees only *suggests* to his understanding that, after having passed a certain distance, *to be measured by the motion of his body, which is perceivable by touch*, he shall come to perceive such and such tangible ideas, which have been usually connected with such and such visible ideas. But, that one might be deceived by these suggestions of sense, and that there is no necessary connexion between visible and tangible ideas suggested by them, we need go no farther than the next looking-glass or picture to be convinced. — Note that, when I speak of tangible ideas, I take the word *idea* for any immediate object of sense or understanding — in which large signification it is commonly used by the moderns.

46. From what we have shewn, it is a manifest consequence that the ideas of Space, Outness, and things placed at a distance are not, strictly speaking, the object of sight; they are not otherwise perceived by the eye than by the ear. Sitting in my study I hear a coach drive along the street; I look through the casement and see it; I walk out and enter into it. Thus, common speech would incline one to think I heard, saw, and touched the same thing, to wit, the coach. It is nevertheless certain the ideas intromitted by each sense are widely different, and distinct from each other; but, having been observed constantly to go together, they are spoken of as one and the same thing. By the variation of the noise, I perceive the different distances of the coach, and know that it approaches before I look out. Thus, by the ear I perceive distance just after the same manner as I do by the eye.

47. I do not nevertheless say I hear distance, in like manner

as I say that I see it — the ideas perceived by hearing not
being so apt to be confounded with the ideas of touch as those
of sight are. So likewise a man is easily convinced that bodies
and external things are not properly the object of hearing, but
only sounds, by the mediation whereof the idea of this or that
body, or distance, is suggested to his thoughts. But then one
is with more difficulty brought to discern the difference there is
betwixt the ideas of sight and touch: though it be certain, a
man no more sees and feels the same thing, than he hears and
feels the same thing.

48. One reason of which seems to be this. It is thought a
great absurdity to imagine that one and the same thing should
have any more than one extension and one figure. But, the
extension and figure of a body being let into the mind two ways,
and that indifferently, either by sight or touch, it seems to follow that we see the same extension and the same figure which
we feel.

49. But, if we take a close and accurate view of the matter,
it must be acknowledged that *we never see and feel one and the
same object.* That which is seen is one thing, and that which is
felt is another. If the visible figure and extension be not the
same with the tangible figure and extension, we are not to infer
that one and the same thing has divers extensions. The true
consequence is that the objects of sight and touch are two distinct things. It may perhaps require some thought rightly to
conceive this distinction. And the difficulty seems not a little
increased, because the combination of visible ideas hath constantly the same name as the combination of tangible ideas
wherewith it is connected — which doth of necessity arise from
the use and end of language.

50. In order, therefore, to treat accurately and unconfusedly
of vision, we must bear in mind that there are two sorts of
objects apprehended by the eye — the one primarily and
immediately, the other secondarily and by intervention of the
former. Those of the first sort neither are nor appear to be
without the mind, or at any distance off. They may, indeed,
grow greater or smaller, more confused, or more clear, or more

faint. But they do not, cannot approach or recede from us. Whenever we say an object is at a distance, whenever we say it draws near, or goes farther off, we must always mean it of the latter sort, which properly belong to the touch, and are not so truly perceived as *suggested* by the eye, in like manner as thoughts by the ear.

51. No sooner do we hear the words of a familiar language pronounced in our ears but the ideas corresponding thereto present themselves to our minds: in the very same instant the sound and the meaning enter the understanding: so closely are they united that it is not in our power to keep out the one except we exclude the other also. We even act in all respects as if we heard the very thoughts themselves. So likewise the secondary objects, or those which are only suggested by sight, do often more strongly affect us, and are more regarded, than the proper objects of that sense; along with which they enter into the mind, and with which they have a far more strict connexion than ideas have with words. Hence it is we find it so difficult to discriminate between the immediate and mediate objects of sight, and are so prone to attribute to the former what belongs only to the latter. They are, as it were, most closely twisted, blended, and incorporated together. And the prejudice is confirmed and riveted in our thoughts by a long tract of time, by the use of language, and want of reflection. However, I doubt not but any one that shall attentively consider what we have already said, and shall say upon this subject before we have done (especially if he pursue it in his own thoughts), may be able to deliver himself from that prejudice. Sure I am, it is worth some attention to whoever would understand the true nature of vision.

52. I have now done with distance, and proceed to shew how it is that we perceive by sight the Magnitude of objects. It is the opinion of some that we do it by angles, or by angles in conjunction with distance. But, neither angles nor distance being perceivable by sight, and the things we see being in truth at no distance from us, it follows that, as we have shewn lines

and angles not to be the medium the mind makes use of in apprehending the apparent place, so neither are they the medium whereby it apprehends the apparent magnitude of objects.

53. It is well known that the same extension at a near distance shall subtend a greater angle, and at a farther distance a lesser angle. And by this principle (we are told) the mind estimates the magnitude of an object, comparing the angle under which it is seen with its distance, and thence inferring the magnitude thereof. What inclines men to this mistake (beside the humour of making one see by geometry) is, that the same perceptions or ideas which suggest distance do also suggest magnitude. But, if we examine it, we shall find they suggest the latter as immediately as the former. I say, they do not first suggest distance and then leave it to the judgment to use that as a medium whereby to collect the magnitude; but they have as close and immediate a connexion with the magnitude as with the distance; and suggest magnitude as independently of distance, as they do distance independently of magnitude. All which will be evident to whoever considers what has been already said and what follows.

54. It has been shown there are two sorts of objects apprehended by sight, each whereof has its distinct magnitude, or extension — the one, properly tangible, *i.e.* to be perceived and measured by touch, and not immediately falling under the sense of seeing; the other, properly and immediately visible, by mediation of which the former is brought in view. Each of these magnitudes are greater or lesser, according as they contain in them more or fewer points, they being made up of points or minimums. For, whatever may be said of extension in abstract, it is certain sensible extension is not infinitely divisible. There is a *minimum tangibile*, and a *minimum visibile*, beyond which sense cannot perceive. This every one's experience will inform him.

55. The magnitude of the object which exists without the mind, and is at a distance, continues always invariably the same: but, the visible object still changing as you approach

to or recede from the tangible object, it hath no fixed and determinate greatness. Whenever therefore we speak of the magnitude of any thing, for instance a tree or a house, we must mean
the tangible magnitude; otherwise there can be nothing steady
and free from ambiguity spoken of it. Now, though the tangible and visible magnitude do in truth belong to two distinct
objects, I shall nevertheless (especially since those objects are
called by the same name, and are observed to coexist), to avoid
tediousness and singularity of speech, sometimes speak of them
as belonging to one and the same thing.

56. Now, in order to discover by what means the magnitude of tangible objects is perceived by sight, I need only reflect
on what passes in my own mind, and observe what those things
be which introduce the ideas of greater or lesser into my
thoughts when I look on any object. And these I find to be,
first, the magnitude or extension of the visible object, which,
being immediately perceived by sight, is connected with that
other which is tangible and placed at a distance: *secondly*, the
confusion or distinctness: and *thirdly*, the vigorousness or faintness of the aforesaid visible appearance. *Cæteris paribus*, by
how much the greater or lesser the visible object is, by so much
the greater or lesser do I conclude the tangible object to be.
But, be the idea immediately perceived by sight never so large,
yet, if it be withal confused, I judge the magnitude of the thing
to be but small. If it be distinct and clear, I judge it greater.
And, if it be faint, I apprehend it to be yet greater. . . .

57. Moreover, the judgments we make of greatness do, in
like manner as those of distance, depend on the disposition of
the eye; also on the figure, number, and situation of intermediate objects, and other circumstances that have been observed to attend great or small tangible magnitudes. Thus,
for instance, the very same quantity of visible extension which
in the figure of a tower doth suggest the idea of great magnitude shall in the figure of a man suggest the idea of much smaller
magnitude. That this is owing to the experience we have had
of the usual bigness of a tower and a man, no one, I suppose,
need be told.

58. It is also evident that confusion or faintness have no more a necessary connexion with little or great magnitude than they have with little or great distance. As they suggest the latter, so they suggest the former to our minds. And, by consequence, if it were not for experience, we should no more judge a faint or confused appearance to be connected with great or little magnitude than we should that it was connected with great or little distance.

63. Moreover, it is not only certain that any idea of sight might not have been connected with this or that idea of touch we now observe to accompany it, but also that the greater visible magnitudes might have been connected with and introduced into our minds lesser tangible magnitudes, and the lesser visible magnitudes greater tangible magnitudes. Nay, that it actually is so, we have daily experience — that object which makes a strong and large appearance not seeming near so great as another the visible magnitude whereof is much less, but more faint, and the appearance upper, or which is the same thing, painted lower on the retina, which faintness and situation suggest both greater magnitude and greater distance.

64. From which, and from sect. 57 and 58, it is manifest that, as we do not perceive the magnitude of objects immediately by sight, so neither do we perceive them by the mediation of anything which has a necessary connexion with them. Those ideas that now suggest unto us the various magnitudes of external objects before we touch them might possibly have suggested no such thing; or they might have signified them in a direct contrary manner, so that the very same ideas on the perception whereof we judge an object to be small might as well have served to make us conclude it great; — those ideas being in their own nature equally fitted to bring into our minds the idea of small or great, or no size at all, of outward objects, just as the words of any language are in their own nature indifferent to signify this or that thing, or nothing at all.

65. As we see distance so we see magnitude. And we see both in the same way that we see shame or anger in the looks

of a man. Those passions are themselves invisible; they are nevertheless let in by the eye along with colours and alterations of countenance which are the immediate object of vision, and which signify them for no other reason than barely because they have been observed to accompany them. Without which experience we should no more have taken blushing for a sign of shame than of gladness.

66. We are nevertheless exceedingly prone to imagine those things which are perceived only by the mediation of others to be themselves the immediate objects of sight, or at least to have in their own nature a fitness to be suggested by them before ever they had been experienced to coexist with them. From which prejudice every one perhaps will not find it easy to emancipate himself, by any the clearest convictions of reason. And there are some grounds to think that, if there was one only invariable and universal language in the world, and that men were born with the faculty of speaking it, it would be the opinion of some, that the ideas in other men's minds were properly perceived by the ear, or had at least a necessary and inseparable tie with the sounds which were affixed to them. All which seems to arise from want of a due application of our discerning faculty, thereby to discriminate between the ideas that are in our understandings, and consider them apart from each other; which would preserve us from confounding those that are different, and make us see what ideas do, and what do not, include or imply this or that other idea.

77. [¹ For the further clearing up of this point, it is to be observed, that what we immediately and properly see are only lights and colours in sundry situations and shades, and degrees of faintness and clearness, confusion and distinctness. All which visible objects are only in the mind; nor do they suggest aught external, whether distance or magnitude, otherwise than by habitual connexion, as words do things. We are also to remark, that beside the straining of the eyes, and beside the

---

¹ What follows in this section is not in the first edition.

vivid and faint, the instinct and confused appearances (which, bearing some proportion to lines and angles, have been substituted instead of them in the foregoing part of this Treatise), there are other means which suggest both distance and magnitude — particularly the situation of visible points or objects, as upper or lower; the former suggesting a farther distance and greater magnitude, the latter a nearer distance and lesser magnitude — all which is an effect only of custom and experience, there being really nothing intermediate in the line of distance between the uppermost and the lowermost, which are both equidistant, or rather at no distance from the eye; as there is also nothing in upper or lower which by necessary connexion should suggest greater or lesser magnitude. Now, as these customary experimental means of suggesting distance do likewise suggest magnitude, so they suggest the one as immediately as the other. I say, they do not (Vid. sect. 53) first suggest distance, and then leave the mind from thence to infer or compute magnitude, but suggest magnitude as immediately and directly as they suggest distance.]

78. This phenomenon of the horizontal moon is a clear instance of the insufficiency of lines and angles for explaining the way wherein the mind perceives and estimates the magnitude of outward objects. There is, nevertheless, a use of computation by them — in order to determine the apparent magnitude of things, so far as they have a connexion with and are proportional to those other ideas or perceptions which are the true and immediate occasions that suggest to the mind the apparent magnitude of things. But this in general may, I think, be observed concerning mathematical computation in optics — that it can never be very precise and exact, since the judgments we make of the magnitude of external things do often depend on several circumstances which are not proportional to or capable of being defined by lines and angles.

79. From what has been said, we may safely deduce this consequence, to wit, that a man born blind, and made to see, would, at first opening of his eyes, make a very different judgment of the magnitude of objects intromitted by them from

what others do. He would not consider the ideas of sight with reference to, or as having any connexion with the idea of touch. His view of them being entirely terminated within themselves, he can no otherwise judge them great or small than as they contain a greater or lesser number of visible points. Now, it being certain that any visible point can cover or exclude from view only one other visible point, it follows that whatever object intercepts the view of another hath an equal number of visible points with it; and, consequently, they shall both be thought by him to have the same magnitude. Hence, it is evident one in those circumstances would judge his thumb, with which he might hide a tower, or hinder its being seen, equal to that tower; or his hand, the interposition whereof might conceal the firmament from his view, equal to the firmament: how great an inequality soever there may, in our apprehensions, seem to be betwixt those two things, because of the customary and close connexion that has grown up in our minds between the objects of sight and touch, whereby the very different and distinct ideas of those two senses are so blended and confounded together as to be mistaken for one and the same thing — out of which prejudice we cannot easily extricate ourselves.

127. It having been shewn that there are no abstract ideas of figure, and that it is impossible for us, by any *precision* of thought, to frame an idea of extension separate from all other visible and tangible qualities, which shall be common both to sight and touch — the question now remaining is, Whether the *particular* extensions, figures, and motions perceived by sight, be of the same *kind* with the *particular* extensions, figures, and motions perceived by touch? In answer to which I shall venture to lay down the following proposition: — *The extension, figures, and motions perceived by sight are specifically distinct from the ideas of touch, called by the same names; nor is there any such thing as one idea, or kind of idea, common to both senses.* This proposition may, without much difficulty, be collected from what hath been said in several places of this Essay. But, because it seems so remote from, and contrary to the

received notions and settled opinion of mankind, I shall attempt to demonstrate it more particularly and at large by the following arguments: —

128. *First,* When, upon perception of an idea, I range it under this or that sort, it is because it is perceived after the same manner, or because it has likeness or conformity with, or affects me in the same way as the ideas of the sort I rank it under. In short, it must not be entirely new, but have something in it old and already perceived by me. It must, I say, have so much, at least, in common with the ideas I have before known and named, as to make me give it the same name with them. But, it has been, if I mistake not, clearly made out that a man *born* blind would not, *at first reception of his sight,* think the things he saw were of the same nature with the objects of touch, or had anything in common with them; but that they were a new set of ideas, perceived in a new manner, and entirely different from all he had ever perceived before. So that he would not call them by the same name, nor repute them to be of the same sort, with anything he had hitherto known.

129. *Secondly,* Light and colours are allowed by all to constitute a sort or species entirely different from the ideas of touch; nor will any man, I presume, say they can make themselves perceived by that sense. But there is no other immediate object of sight besides light and colours. It is therefore a direct consequence, that there is no idea common to both senses.

130. It is a prevailing opinion, even amongst those who have thought and writ most accurately concerning our ideas, and the ways whereby they enter into the understanding, that something *more* is perceived by sight than barely light and colours with their variations. Mr. Locke termeth sight 'the most comprehensive of all our senses, conveying to our minds the ideas of light and colours, which are peculiar only to that sense; and also the far different ideas of space, figure, and motion.' (*Essay on Human Understanding,* b. II. ch. 9. s. 9.) Space or distance, we have shewn, is no otherwise the object of sight than of hearing. (Vid. sect. 46.) And, as for figure and extension, I leave it to any one that shall calmly attend

to his own clear and distinct ideas to decide whether he had any idea intromitted immediately and properly by sight save only light and colours: or, whether it be possible for him to frame in his mind a distinct abstract idea of visible extension, or figure, exclusive of all colour; and, on the other hand, whether he can conceive colour without visible extension? For my own part, I must confess, I am not able to attain so great a nicety of abstraction. I know very well that, in a strict sense, I see nothing but light and colours. with their several shades and variations. He who beside these doth also perceive by sight ideas far different and distinct from them, hath that faculty in a degree more perfect and comprehensive than I can pretend to. It must be owned, indeed, that, by the mediation of light and colours, other far different ideas are *suggested* to my mind. But then, upon this score, I see no reason why sight should be thought more 'comprehensive' than the hearing, which, beside sounds which are peculiar to that sense, doth, by their mediation, suggest not only space, figure, and motion, but also all other ideas whatsoever that can be signified by words.

131. *Thirdly*, It is, I think, an axiom universally received, that 'quantities of the same kind may be added together and make one entire sum.' Mathematicians add lines together; but they do not add a line to a solid, or conceive it as making one sum with a surface. These three kinds of quantity being thought incapable of any such mutual addition, and consequently of being compared together in the several ways of proportion, are by them for that reason esteemed entirely disparate and heterogeneous. Now let any one try in his thoughts to add a *visible* line or surface to a *tangible* line or surface, so as to conceive them making one continued sum or whole. He that can do this may think them homogeneous; but he that cannot must, by the foregoing axiom, think them heterogeneous. A blue and a red line I can conceive added together into one sum and making one continued line; but, to make, in my thoughts, one continued line of a visible and tangible line added together, is, I find. a task far more difficult, and even insurmountable — and I leave it to the reflec-

tion and experience of every particular person to determine for himself.

132. A farther confirmation of our tenet may be drawn from the solution of Mr. Molyneux's problem, published by Mr. Locke in his *Essay:* which I shall set down as it there lies, together with Mr. Locke's opinion of it: — 'Suppose a man born blind, and now adult, and taught by his touch to distinguish between a cube and a sphere of the same metal, and nighly of the same bigness, so as to tell when he felt one and the other, which is the cube, and which the sphere. Suppose then the cube and sphere placed on a table, and the blind man made to see: Quære, Whether by his sight, before he touched them, he could now distinguish, and tell, which is the globe, which the cube. To which the acute and judicious proposer answers: Not. For, though he has obtained the experience of how a globe, how a cube affects his touch; yet he has not yet attained the experience, that what affects his touch so or so must affect his sight so or so: or that a protuberant angle in the cube, that pressed his hand unequally, shall appear to his eye as it doth in the cube. I agree with this thinking gentleman, whom I am proud to call my friend, in his answer to this his problem; and am of opinion that the blind man, at first sight, would not be able with certainty to say, which was the globe, which the cube, whilst he only saw them.' (Locke's *Essay on Human Understanding*, b. II. ch. 9. s. 8.[1])

133. Now, if a square surface perceived by touch be of the *same sort* with a square surface perceived by sight, it is certain the blind man here mentioned might know a square surface as soon as he saw it. It is no more but introducing into his mind, by a new inlet, an idea he has been already well acquainted with. Since therefore he is supposed to have known by his touch that a cube is a body terminated by square surfaces; and that a sphere is not terminated by square surfaces — upon the supposition that a visible and tangible square differ only *in numero*, it follows that he might know, by the unerring

---

[1] See Leibnitz (*Nouveaux Essais*, liv. II. ch. 9), who disputes the alleged heterogeneity.

mark of the square surfaces, which was the cube, and which not, while he only saw them. We must therefore allow, either that visible extension and figures are specifically distinct from tangible extension and figures, or else, that the solution of this problem, given by those two thoughtful and ingenious men, is wrong.

134. Much more might be laid together in proof of the proposition I have advanced. But, what has been said is, if I mistake not, sufficient to convince any one that shall yield a reasonable attention. And, as for those that will not be at the pains of a little thought, no multiplication of words will ever suffice to make them understand the truth, or rightly conceive my meaning.

135. I cannot let go the above-mentioned problem without some reflection on it. It hath been made evident that a man blind from his birth would not, at first sight, denominate anything he saw, by the names he had been used to appropriate to ideas of touch. (Vid. sect. 106.) Cube, sphere, table are words he has known applied to things perceivable by touch, but to things perfectly intangible he never knew them applied. Those words, in their wonted application, always marked out to his mind bodies or solid things which were perceived by the resistance they gave. But there is no solidity, no resistance or protrusion, perceived by sight. In short, the ideas of sight are all new perceptions, to which there be no names annexed in his mind; he cannot therefore understand what is said to him concerning them. And, to ask of the two bodies he saw placed on the table, which was the sphere, which the cube, were to him a question downright bantering and unintelligible; nothing he sees being able to suggest to his thoughts the idea of body, distance, or, in general, of anything he had already known.

136. It is a mistake to think the *same* thing affects both sight and touch. If the same angle or square which is the object of touch be also the object of vision, what should hinder the blind man, at first sight, from knowing it? For, though the manner wherein it affects the sight be different from that wherein it affected his touch, yet, there being, beside this man-

ner of circumstance, which is new and unknown, the angle or figure, which is old and known, he cannot choose but discern it.

147. Upon the whole, I think we may fairly conclude that the proper objects of vision constitute the Universal Language of Nature, whereby we are instructed how to regulate our actions, in order to attain those things that are necessary to the preservation and well-being of our bodies, as also to avoid whatever may be hurtful and destructive of them. It is by their information that we are principally guided in all the transactions and concerns of life. And the manner wherein they signify and mark out unto us the objects which are at a distance is the same with that of languages and signs of human appointment; which do not suggest the things signified by any likeness or identity of nature, but only by an habitual connexion that experience has made us to observe between them.

148. Suppose one who had always continued blind be told by his guide that after he has advanced so many steps he shall come to the brink of a precipice, or be stopped by a wall; must not this to him seem very admirable and surprising? He cannot conceive how it is possible for mortals to frame such predictions as these, which to him would seem as strange and unaccountable as prophecy does to others. Even they who are blessed with the visive faculty may (though familiarity make it less observed) find therein sufficient cause of admiration. The wonderful art and contrivance wherewith it is adjusted to those ends and purposes for which it was apparently designed; the vast extent, number, and variety of objects that are at once, with so much ease, and quickness, and pleasure, suggested by it — all these afford subject for much and pleasing speculation, and may, if anything, give us some glimmering analogous prænotion of things, that are placed beyond the certain discovery and comprehension of our present state.

DAVID HUME

(1711–1776)

A TREATISE OF HUMAN NATURE*

BOOK I. OF THE UNDERSTANDING

PART I. OF IDEAS, THEIR ORIGIN, COMPOSITION, CONNEXION, &C.

SECTION I. OF THE ORIGIN OF OUR IDEAS

ALL the perceptions of the human mind resolve themselves into two distinct kinds, which I shall call IMPRESSIONS and IDEAS. The difference betwixt these consists in the degrees of force and liveliness with which they strike upon the mind, and make their way into our thought or consciousness. Those perceptions, which enter with most force and violence, we may name *impressions;* and under this name I comprehend all our sensations, passions and emotions, as they make their first appearance in the soul. By *ideas* I mean the faint images of these in thinking and reasoning; such as, for instance, are all the perceptions excited by the present discourse, excepting only those which arise from the sight and touch, and excepting the immediate pleasure or uneasiness it may occasion. I believe it will not be very necessary to employ many words in explaining this distinction. Every one of himself will readily perceive the difference betwixt feeling and thinking. The common degrees of these are easily distinguished; tho' it is not impossible but in particular instances they may very nearly approach to each other. Thus in sleep, in a fever, in madness, or in any very

---

* London, 1739–40; *ib.*, 1817; edit. with analytical index by T. Selby-Bigge, Oxford, 1888; edit. with preliminary dissertations and notes by T. H. Green and T. H. Grose, 2 vols., Lond., 1874; new ed. *ib.*, 1888.

violent emotions of soul, our ideas may approach to our impressions: As on the other hand it sometimes happens, that our impressions are so faint and low, that we cannot distinguish them from our ideas. But notwithstanding this near resemblance in a few instances, they are in general so very different, that no-one can make a scruple to rank them under distinct heads, and assign to each a peculiar name to mark the difference.[1]

There is another division of our perceptions, which it will be convenient to observe, and which extends itself both to our impressions and ideas. This division is into SIMPLE and COMPLEX. Simple perceptions or impressions and ideas are such as admit of no distinction or separation. The complex are the contrary to these, and may be distinguished into parts. Tho' a particular colour, taste, and smell are qualities all united together in this apple, 't is easy to perceive they are not the same, but are at least distinguishable from each other.

Having by these divisions given an order and arrangement to our objects, we may now apply ourselves to consider with the more accuracy their qualities and relations. The first circumstance, that strikes my eye, is the great resemblance betwixt our impressions and ideas in every other particular, except their degree of force and vivacity. The one seem to be in a manner the reflexion of the other; so that all the perceptions of the mind are double, and appear both as impressions and ideas. When I shut my eyes and think of my chamber, the ideas I form are exact representations of the impressions I felt; nor is there any circumstance of the one, which is not to be found in the other. In running over my other perceptions, I find still the same resemblance and representation. Ideas and impressions appear always to correspond to each other. This circum-

---

[1] I here make use of these terms, *impression* and *idea*, in a sense different from what is usual, and I hope this liberty will be allowed me. Perhaps I rather restore the word, idea, to its original sense, from which Mr. *Locke* had perverted it, in making it stand for all our perceptions. By the term of impression I would not be understood to express the manner, in which our lively perceptions are produced in the soul, but merely the perceptions themselves; for which there is no particular name either in the *English* or any other language, that I know of.

stance seems to me remarkable, and engages my attention for a moment.

Upon a more accurate survey I find I have been carried away too far by the first appearance, and that I must make use of the distinction of perceptions into *simple and complex*, to limit this general decision, *that all our ideas and impressions are resembling*. I observe, that many of our complex ideas never had impressions, that corresponded to them, and that many of our complex impressions never are exactly copied in ideas. I can imagine to myself such a city as the *New Jerusalem*, whose pavement is gold and walls are rubies, tho' I never saw any such. I have seen *Paris;* but shall I affirm I can form such an idea of that city, as will perfectly represent all its streets and houses in their real and just proportions?

I perceive, therefore, that tho' there is in general a great resemblance betwixt our *complex* impressions and ideas, yet the rule is not universally true, that they are exact copies of each other. We may next consider how the case stands with our *simple* perceptions. After the most accurate examination, of which I am capable, I venture to affirm, that the rule here holds without any exception, and that every simple idea has a simple impression, which resembles it; and every simple impression a correspondent idea. That idea of red, which we form in the dark, and that impression, which strikes our eyes in sunshine, differ only in degree, not in nature. That the case is the same with all our simple impressions and ideas, 't is impossible to prove by a particular enumeration of them. Every one may satisfy himself in this point by running over as many as he pleases. But if any one should deny this universal resemblance, I know no way of convincing him, but by desiring him to shew a simple impression, that has not a correspondent idea, or a simple idea, that has not a correspondent impression. If he does not answer this challenge, as 't is certain he cannot, we may from his silence and our own observation establish our conclusion.

Thus we find, that all simple ideas and impressions resemble each other; and as the complex are formed from them, we may affirm in general, that these two species of perception are exactly correspondent. Having discover'd this relation, which requires no farther examination, I am curious to find some other of their qualities. Let us consider how they stand with regard to their existence, and which of the impressions and ideas are causes, and which effects.

The *full* examination of this question is the subject of the present treatise; and therefore we shall here content ourselves with establishing one general proposition, *That all our simple ideas in their first appearance are deriv'd from simple impressions, which are correspondent to them, and which they exactly represent.*

In seeking for phænomena to prove this proposition, I find only those of two kinds; but in each kind the phænomena are obvious, numerous, and conclusive. I first make myself certain, by a new review, of what I have already asserted, that every simple impression is attended with a correspondent idea, and every simple idea with a correspondent impression. From this constant conjunction of resembling perceptions I immediately conclude, that there is a great connexion betwixt our correspondent impressions and ideas, and that the existence of the one has a considerable influence upon that of the other. Such a constant conjunction, in such an infinite number of instances, can never arise from chance; but clearly proves a dependence of the impressions on the ideas, or of the ideas on the impressions. That I may know on which side this dependence lies, I consider the order of their *first appearance;* and find by constant experience, that the simple impressions always take the precedence of their correspondent ideas, but never appear in the contrary order. To give a child an idea of scarlet or orange, of sweet or bitter, I present the objects, or in other words, convey to him these impressions; but proceed not so absurdly, as to endeavour to produce the impressions by exciting the ideas. Our ideas upon their appearance produce not their correspondent impressions, nor do we perceive any colour, or feel any sensation merely upon thinking of them. On the other hand we find that any impression either of the mind or body is constantly followed by an idea, which resembles it, and is only different in the degrees of force and liveliness. The constant conjunction of our resembling perceptions, is a convincing proof, that the one are the causes of the other; and this priority of the impressions is an equal proof, that our impressions are the causes of our ideas, not our ideas of our impressions.

To confirm this I consider another plain and convincing phænomenon; which is, that where-ever by any accident the faculties, which give rise to any impressions, are obstructed in their operations, as when one is born blind or deaf; not only the impressions are lost, but also their correspondent ideas; so that there never appear in the mind the least traces of either of them. Nor is this only true, where the organs of sensation are entirely destroy'd, but likewise where they have never been put in action to produce a particular impression. We cannot form to ourselves a just idea of the taste of a pine-apple, without having actually tasted it.

There is however one contradictory phænomenon, which may prove, that 't is not absolutely impossible for ideas to go before their correspondent impressions. I believe it will readily be allow'd, that the several distinct ideas of colours, which enter by the eyes, or those of sounds, which are convey'd by the hearing, are really different from each other, tho' at the same time resembling. Now if this be true of different colours, it must be no less so of the different shades of the same colour, that each of them produces a distinct idea, independent of the rest. For if this shou'd be deny'd, 't is possible, by the continual gradation of shades, to run a colour insensibly into what is most remote from it; and if you will not allow any of the means to be different, you cannot without absurdity deny the extremes to be the same. Suppose therefore a person to have enjoyed his sight for thirty years, and to have become perfectly well acquainted with colours of all kinds, excepting one particular shade of blue, for instance, which it never has been his fortune to meet with. Let all the different shades of that colour, except that single one, be plac'd before him, descending gradually from the deepest to the lightest; 't is plain, that he will perceive a blank, where that shade is wanting, and will be sensible, that there is a greater distance in that place betwixt the contiguous colours, than in any other. Now I ask, whether 't is possible for him, from his own imagination, to supply this deficiency, and raise up to himself the idea of that particular shade, tho' it had never been conveyed to him by his senses? I believe there are few but will be of opinion that he can; and this may serve as a proof, that the simple ideas are not always derived from the correspondent impressions; tho' the instance is so particular and singular, that 't is scarce worth our observing, and does not merit that for it alone we should alter our general maxim.

But besides this exception, it may not be amiss to remark on this head, that the principle of the priority of impressions to ideas must be understood with another limitation, *viz.* that as our ideas are images of our impressions, so we can form secondary ideas, which are images of the primary; as appears from this very reasoning concerning them. This is not, properly speaking, an exception to the rule so much as an explanation of it. Ideas produce the images of themselves in new ideas; but as the first ideas are supposed to be derived from impressions, it still remains true, that all our simple ideas proceed either mediately or immediately from their correspondent impressions.

This then is the first principle I establish in the science of human nature; nor ought we to despise it because of the simplicity of its appearance. For 't is remarkable, that the present question concerning the precedency of our impressions or ideas, is the same with what has made so much noise in other terms, when it has been disputed whether there be any *innate ideas,* or whether all ideas be derived from sensation and reflexion. We may observe, that in order to prove the ideas of extension and colour not to be innate, philosophers do nothing but shew, that they are conveyed by our senses. To prove the ideas of passion and desire not to be innate, they observe that we have a preceding experience of these emotions in ourselves. Now if we carefully examine these arguments, we shall find that they prove nothing but that ideas are preceded by other more lively perceptions, from which they are derived, and which they represent. I hope this clear stating of the question will remove all disputes concerning it, and will render this principle of more use in our reasonings, than it seems hitherto to have been.

SECTION II. DIVISION OF THE SUBJECT

SINCE it appears, that our simple impressions are prior to their correspondent ideas, and that the exceptions are very rare, method seems to require we should examine our impressions, before we consider our ideas. Impressions may be divided into two kinds, those of SENSATION and those of REFLEXION. The first kind arises in the soul originally, from unknown causes. The second is derived in a great measure from our ideas, and that in the following order. An impression first strikes upon the senses, and makes us perceive heat or cold, thirst or hunger, pleasure or pain of some kind or other. Of this impression there is a copy taken by the mind, which remains after the impression ceases; and this we call an idea. This idea of pleasure or pain, when it returns upon the soul, produces the new impressions of desire and aversion, hope and fear, which may properly be called impressions of reflection, because derived from it. These again are copied by the memory and imagination, and become ideas; which perhaps in their turn give rise to other impressions and ideas. So that the impressions of reflection are only antecedent to their correspondent ideas; but posterior to those of sensation, and deriv'd from them. The examination of our sensations belongs more to anatomists and natural philosophers than to moral; and therefore shall not at present be enter'd upon. And as the impressions of reflection, *viz.* passions, desires, and emotions, which principally deserve our attention, arise mostly from ideas, 't will be necessary to reverse that method, which at first sight seems most natural; and in order to explain the nature and principles of the human mind, give a particular account of ideas, before we proceed to impressions. For this reason I have here chosen to begin with ideas.

SECTION III. OF THE IDEAS OF THE MEMORY AND IMAGINATION

WE find by experience, that when any impression has been present with the mind, it again makes its appearance there as an idea; and this it may do after two different ways; either when in its new appearance it retains a considerable degree of its first vivacity, and is somewhat intermediate betwixt an impression and an idea; or when it entirely loses that vivacity, and is a perfect idea. The faculty, by which we repeat our impressions in the first manner, is called the MEMORY, and the other the IMAGINATION. 'T is evident at first sight, that the ideas of the memory are much more lively and strong than those of the imagination, and that the former faculty paints its objects in more distinct colours, than any which are employ'd by the latter. When we remember any past event, the idea of it flows in upon the mind in a forcible manner; whereas in the imagination the perception is faint and languid, and cannot without difficulty be preserv'd by the mind steady and uniform for any considerable time. Here then is a sensible difference betwixt one species of ideas and another. But of this more fully hereafter.[1]

There is another difference betwixt these two kinds of ideas, which is no less evident, namely that tho' neither the ideas of the memory nor imagination, neither the lively nor faint ideas can make their appearance in the mind, unless their correspondent impressions have gone before to prepare the way for them, yet the imagination is not restrain'd to the same order and form with the original impressions; while the memory is in a manner ty'd down in that respect, without any power of variation.

'T is evident, that the memory preserves the original form, in which its objects were presented, and that where-ever we depart from it in recollecting any thing, it proceeds from some defect or imperfection in that faculty. An historian may, perhaps, for the more convenient carrying on of his narration,

---

[1] Part III. sect. 5.

relate an event before another, to which it was in fact posterior;
but then he takes notice of this disorder, if he be exact; and by
that means replaces the idea in its due position. 'T is the same
case in our recollection of those places and persons, with which
we were formerly acquainted. The chief exercise of the memory
is not to preserve the simple ideas, but their order and position. In short, this principle is supported by such a number of
common and vulgar phænomena, that we may spare ourselves
the trouble of insisting on it any farther.

The same evidence follows us in our second principle, *of the
liberty of the imagination to transpose and change its ideas.* The
fables we meet with in poems and romances put this entirely
out of question. Nature there is totally confounded, and nothing mentioned but winged horses, fiery dragons, and monstrous giants. Nor will this liberty of the fancy appear strange,
when we consider, that all our ideas are copy'd from our impressions, and that there are not any two impressions which are
perfectly inseparable. Not to mention, that this is an evident
consequence of the division of ideas into simple and complex.
Where-ever the imagination perceives a difference among ideas,
it can easily produce a separation.

SECTION **IV**. OF THE CONNEXION OR ASSOCIATION OF IDEAS

As all simple ideas may be separated by the imagination,
and may be united again in what form it pleases, nothing wou'd
be more unaccountable than the operations of that faculty,
were it not guided by some universal principles, which render
it, in some measure, uniform with itself in all times and places.
Were ideas entirely loose and unconnected, chance alone wou'd
join them; and 't is impossible the same simple ideas should
fall regularly into complex ones (as they commonly do) without some bond of union among them, some associating quality,
by which one idea naturally introduces another. This uniting
principle among ideas is not to be consider'd as an inseparable
connexion; for that has been already excluded from the imagination: Nor yet are we to conclude, that without it the mind

cannot join two ideas; for nothing is more free than that faculty: but we are only to regard it as a gentle force, which commonly prevails, and is the cause why, among other things, languages so nearly correspond to each other; nature in a manner pointing out to every one those simple ideas, which are most proper to be united into a complex one. The qualities, from which this association arises, and by which the mind is after this manner convey'd from one idea to another, are three, viz. RESEMBLANCE, CONTIGUITY in time or place, and CAUSE and EFFECT.

I believe it will not be very necessary to prove, that these qualities produce an association among ideas, and upon the appearance of one idea naturally introduce another. 'T is plain, that in the course of our thinking, and in the constant revolution of our ideas, our imagination runs easily from one idea to any other that *resembles* it, and that this quality alone is to the fancy a sufficient bond and association. 'T is likewise evident, that as the senses, in changing their objects, are necessitated to change them regularly, and take them as they lie *contiguous* to each other, the imagination must by long custom acquire the same method of thinking, and run along the parts of space and time in conceiving its objects. As to the connexion, that is made by the relation of *cause and effect*, we shall have occasion afterwards to examine it to the bottom, and therefore shall not at present insist upon it. 'T is sufficient to observe, that there is no relation, which produces a stronger connexion in the fancy, and makes one idea more readily recall another, than the relation of cause and effect betwixt their objects.

That we may understand the full extent of these relations, we must consider, that two objects are connected together in the imagination, not only when the one is immediately resembling, contiguous to, or the cause of the other, but also when there is interposed betwixt them a third object, which bears to both of them any of these relations. This may be carried on to a great length; tho' at the same time we may observe, that each remove considerably weakens the relation.

Cousins in the fourth degree are connected by *causation*, if I may be allowed to use that term; but not so closely as brothers, much less as child and parent. In general we may observe, that all the relations of blood depend upon cause and effect, and are esteemed near or remote, according to the number of connecting causes interpos'd betwixt the persons.

Of the three relations above-mention'd this of causation is the most extensive. Two objects may be consider'd as plac'd in this relation, as well when one is the cause of any of the actions or motions of the other, as when the former is the cause of the existence of the latter. For as that action or motion is nothing but the object itself, consider'd in a certain light, and as the object continues the same in all its different situations, 't is easy to imagine how such an influence of objects upon one another may connect them in the imagination.

We may carry this farther, and remark, not only that two objects are connected by the relation of cause and effect, when the one produces a motion or any action in the other, but also when it has a power of producing it. And this we may observe to be the source of all the relations of interest and duty, by which men influence each other in society, and are plac'd in the ties of government and subordination. A master is such-a-one as by his situation, arising either from force or agreement, has a power of directing in certain particulars the actions of another, whom we call servant. A judge is one, who in all disputed cases can fix by his opinion the possession or property of any thing betwixt any members of the society. When a person is possess'd of any power, there is no more required to convert it into action, but the exertion of the will; and *that* in every case is consider'd as possible, and in many as probable; especially in the case of authority, where the obedience of the subject is a pleasure and advantage to the superior.

These are therefore the principles of union or cohesion among our simple ideas, and in the imagination supply the place of that inseparable connexion, by which they are united in our memory. Here is a kind of ATTRACTION, which in the mental world will be found to have as extraordinary effects as in the natural, and to shew itself in as many and as various forms. Its effects are every where conspicuous; but as to its causes, they are mostly unknown, and must be resolv'd into *original* qualities of human nature, which I pretend not to explain. Nothing is more requisite for a true philosopher, than to restrain the intemperate desire of searching into causes, and having establish'd any doctrine upon a sufficient number of experiments, rest contented with that, when he sees a farther examination would lead him into obscure and uncertain speculations. In that case his enquiry wou'd be much better employ'd in examining the effects than the causes of his principle.

Amongst the effects of this union or association of ideas, there are none more remarkable, than those complex ideas, which are the common subjects of our thoughts and reasoning, and generally arise from some principle of union among our simple ideas. These complex ideas may be divided into *Relations*, *Modes*, and *Substances*. We shall briefly examine each of these in order, and shall subjoin some considerations concerning our *general* and *particular* ideas, before we leave the present subject, which may be consider'd as the elements of this philosophy.

Section V. Of Relations

The word Relation is commonly used in two senses considerably different from each other. Either for that quality, by which two ideas are connected together in the imagination, and the one naturally introduces the other, after the manner above-explained; or for that particular circumstance, in which, even upon the arbitrary union of two ideas in the fancy, we may think proper to compare them. In common language the former is always the sense, in which we use the word, relation; and 't is only in philosophy, that we extend it to mean any particular subject of comparison, without a connecting principle. Thus distance will be allowed by philosophers to be a true relation, because we acquire an idea of it by the comparing of objects: But in a common way we say, *that nothing can be more distant than such or such things from each other, nothing can have less relation;* as if distance and relation were incompatible.

It may perhaps be esteemed an endless task to enumerate all those qualities, which make objects admit of comparison, and by which the ideas of *philosophical* relation are produced. But if we diligently consider them, we shall find that without difficulty they may be compriz'd under seven general heads, which may be considered as the source of all *philosophical* relation.

1. The first is *resemblance:* And this is a relation, without which no philosophical relation can exist; since no objects will admit of comparison, but what have some degree of resemblance. But tho' resemblance be necessary to all philosophical relation, it does not follow, that it always produces a connexion or association of ideas. When a quality becomes very general, and is common to a great many individuals, it leads not the mind directly to any one of them; but by presenting at once too great a choice, does thereby prevent the imagination from fixing on any single object.

2. *Identity* may be esteem'd a second species of relation. This relation I here consider as apply'd in its strictest sense to constant and unchangeable objects; without examining the nature and foundation of personal identity, which shall find its place afterwards. Of all relations the most universal is that of identity, being common to every being, whose existence has any duration.

3. After identity the most universal and comprehensive relations are those of *Space* and *Time*, which are the sources of an infinite number of comparisons, such as *distant, contiguous, above, below, before, after,* &c.

4. All those objects, which admit of *quantity*, or *number*, may be compar'd in that particular; which is another very fertile source of relation.

5. When any two objects possess the same *quality* in common, the *degrees*, in which they possess it, form a fifth species of relation. Thus of two objects, which are both heavy, the one may be either of greater, or less weight than with the

other. Two colours, that are of the same kind, may yet be of different shades, and in that respect admit of comparison.

6. The relation of *contrariety* may at first sight be regarded as an exception to the rule, *that no relation of any kind can subsist without some degree of resemblance*. But let us consider, that no two ideas are in themselves contrary, except those of existence and non-existence, which are plainly resembling, as implying both of them an idea of the object; tho' the latter excludes the object from all times and places, in which it is supposed not to exist.

7. All other objects, such as fire and water, heat and cold, are only found to be contrary from experience, and from the contrariety of their *causes* or *effects*; which relation of cause and effect is a seventh philosophical relation, as well as a natural one. The resemblance implied in this relation, shall be explain'd afterwards.

It might naturally be expected, that I should join *difference* to the other relations. But that I consider rather as a negation of relation, than as any thing real or positive. Difference is of two kinds as oppos'd either to identity or resemblance. The first is called a difference of *number;* the other of *kind.*

SECTION VI. OF MODES AND SUBSTANCES

I WOU'D fain ask those philosophers, who found so much of their reasonings on the distinction of substance and accident, and imagine we have clear ideas of each, whether the idea of *substance* be deriv'd from the impressions of sensation or reflection? If it be convey'd to us by our senses, I ask, which of them; and after what manner? If it be perceiv'd by the eyes, it must be a colour; if by the ears, a sound; if by the palate, a taste; and so of the other senses. But I believe none will assert, that substance is either a colour, or sound, or a taste. The idea of substance must therefore be deriv'd from an impression or reflection, if it really exist. But the impressions of reflection resolve themselves into our passions and emotions; none of which can possibly represent a substance. We have therefore no idea of substance, distinct from that of a collection of particular qualities, nor have we any other meaning when we either talk or reason concerning it.[1]

The idea of a substance as well as that of a mode, is nothing but a collection of simple ideas, *that are united by the imagination*, and have a particular name assigned them, by which we are able to recall, either to ourselves or others, that collection. But the difference betwixt these ideas consists in this, that the particular qualities, which form a substance, are commonly refer'd to an unknown *something*, in which they are supposed to inhere; or granting this fiction should not take place, are at least supposed to be closely and inseparably connected by the relations of contiguity and causation. The effect of this is, that whatever new simple quality we discover to have the same connexion with the rest, we immediately comprehend it among them, even tho' it did not enter into the first conception of the substance. Thus our idea of gold may at first be a yellow colour, weight, malleableness, fusibility; but upon the discovery of its dissolubility in *aqua regia*, we join that to the other qualities, and suppose it to belong to the substance as much as if its idea had from the beginning made a part of the compound one. The principle of union being regarded as the chief part of the complex idea, gives entrance to whatever quality afterwards occurs, and is equally comprehended by it, as are the others, which first presented themselves.[2]

That this cannot take place in modes, is evident from considering their nature. The simple ideas of which modes are formed, either represent qualities, which are not united by contiguity and causation, but are dispers'd in different subjects; or if they be all united together, the uniting principle is not regarded as the foundation of the complex idea. The idea of a dance is an instance of the first kind of modes; that of beauty of the second. The reason is obvious, why such complex ideas cannot receive any new idea, without changing the name, which distinguishes the mode.

[1] Cf. Green and Grose's *Introduction*, §208.
[2] *Ibid.* §214.

PART III.   OF KNOWLEDGE AND PROBABILITY

SECTION I.   OF KNOWLEDGE

THERE are [1] seven different kinds of philosophical relation, *viz. resemblance, identity, relations of time and place, proportion in quantity or number, degrees in any quality, contrariety, and causation.* These relations may be divided into two classes; into such as depend entirely on the ideas, which we compare together, and such as may be chang'd without any change in the ideas. 'T is from the idea of a triangle, that we discover the relation of equality, which its three angles bear to two right ones; and this relation is invariable, as long as our idea remains the same. On the contrary, the relations of *contiguity* and *distance* betwixt two objects may be chang'd merely by an alteration of their place, without any change on the objects themselves or on their ideas; and the place depends on a hundred different accidents, which cannot be foreseen by the mind. 'T is the same case with *identity* and *causation.* Two objects, tho' perfectly resembling each other, and even appearing in the same place at different times, may be numerically different; And as the power, by which one object produces another, is never discoverable merely from their idea, 't is evident *cause* and *effect* are relations, of which we receive information from experience, and not from any abstract reasoning or reflection. There is no single phænomenon, even the most simple, which can be accounted for from the qualities of the objects, as they appear to us; or which we cou'd foresee without the help of our memory and experience.

It appears, therefore, that of these seven philosophical relations, there remain only four, which depending solely upon ideas, can be the objects of knowledge and certainty. These four are *resemblance, contrariety, degrees in quality, and proportions in quantity or number.* Three of these relations are discoverable at first sight, and fall more properly under the province of intuition than demonstration. When any objects

---

[1] Part I. sect. 5.

resemble each other, the resemblance will at first strike the eye, or rather the mind; and seldom requires a second examination. The case is the same with *contrariety*, and with the *degrees* of any *quality*. No one can once doubt but existence and non-existence destroy each other, and are perfectly incompatible and contrary. And tho' it be impossible to judge exactly of the degrees of any quality, such as colour, taste, heat, cold, when the difference betwixt them is very small; yet 't is easy to decide, that any of them is superior or inferior to another, when the difference is considerable. And this decision we always pronounce at first sight, without any enquiry or reasoning.

We might proceed, after the same manner, in fixing the *proportions* of *quantity* or *number*, and might at one view observe a superiority or inferiority betwixt any numbers, or figures; especially where the difference is very great and remarkable. As to equality or any exact proportion, we can only guess at it from a single consideration; except in very short numbers, or very limited portions of extension; which are comprehended in an instant, and where we perceive an impossibility of falling into any considerable error. In all other cases we must settle the proportions with some liberty, or proceed in a more *artificial* manner.

I have already observ'd, that geometry, or the *art*, by which we fix the proportions of figures, tho' it much excels, both in universality and exactness, the loose judgments of the senses and imagination, yet never attains a perfect precision and exactness. Its first principles are still drawn from the general appearance of the objects; and that appearance can never afford us any security, when we examine the prodigious minuteness of which nature is susceptible. Our ideas seem to give a perfect assurance, that no two right lines can have a common segment; but if we consider these ideas, we shall find, that they always suppose a sensible inclination of the two lines, and that where the angle they form is extremely small, we have no standard of a right line so precise as to assure us of the truth of this proposition. 'T is the same case with most of the primary decisions of the mathematics.

There remain, therefore, algebra and arithmetic as the only sciences, in which we can carry on a chain of reasoning to any degree of intricacy, and yet preserve a perfect exactness and certainty. We are possest of a precise standard, by which we can judge of the equality and proportion of numbers; and according as they correspond or not to that standard, we determine their relations, without any possibility of error. When two numbers are so combin'd, as that the one has always an unite answering to every unite of the other, we pronounce them equal; and 't is for want of such a standard of equality in extension, that geometry can scarce be esteem'd a perfect and infallible science.

But here it may not be amiss to obviate a difficulty, which may arise from my asserting, that tho' geometry falls short of that perfect precision and certainty, which are peculiar to arithmetic and algebra, yet it excels the imperfect judgments of our senses and imagination. The reason why I impute any defect to geometry, is, because its original and fundamental principles are deriv'd merely from appearances; and it may perhaps be imagin'd, that this defect must always attend it, and keep it from ever reaching a greater exactness in the comparison of objects or ideas, than what our eye or imagination alone is able to attain. I own that this defect so far attends it, as to keep it from ever aspiring to a full certainty: But since these fundamental principles depend on the easiest and least deceitful appearances, they bestow on their consequences a degree of exactness, of which these consequences are singly incapable. 'T is impossible for the eye to determine the angles of a chiliagon to be equal to 1996 right angles, or make any conjecture, that approaches this proportion; but when it determines, that right lines cannot concur; that we cannot draw more than one right line between two given points; its mistakes can never be of any consequence. And this is the nature and use of geometry, to run us up to such appearances, as, by reason of their simplicity, cannot lead us into any considerable error.

I shall here take occasion to propose a second observation

concerning our demonstrative reasonings, which is suggested by the same subject of the mathematics. 'T is usual with mathematicians, to pretend, that those ideas, which are their objects, are of so refin'd and spiritual a nature, that they fall not under the conception of the fancy, but must be comprehended by a pure and intellectual view, of which the superior faculties of the soul are alone capable. The same notion runs thro' most parts of philosophy, and is principally made use of to explain our abstract ideas, and to shew how we can form an idea of a triangle, for instance, which shall neither be an isoceles nor scalenum, nor be confin'd to any particular length and proportion of sides. 'T is easy to see, why philosophers are so fond of this notion of some spiritual and refin'd perceptions; since by that means they cover many of their absurdities, and may refuse to submit to the decisions of clear ideas, by appealing to such as are obscure and uncertain. But to destroy this artifice, we need but reflect on that principle so oft insisted on, *that all our ideas are copy'd from our impressions.* For from thence we may immediately conclude, that since all impressions are clear and precise, the ideas, which are copy'd from them, must be of the same nature, and can never, but from our fault, contain any thing so dark and intricate. An idea is by its very nature weaker and fainter than an impression; but being in every other respect the same, cannot imply any very great mystery. If its weakness render it obscure, 't is our business to remedy that defect, as much as possible, by keeping the idea steady and precise; and till we have done so, 't is in vain to pretend to reasoning and philosophy.

SECTION II. OF PROBABILITY; AND OF THE IDEA OF CAUSE AND EFFECT

THIS is all I think necessary to observe concerning those four relations, which are the foundation of science; but as to the other three, which depend not upon the idea, and may be absent or present even while *that* remains the same, 't will be proper to explain them more particularly. These three relations are *identity, the situations in time and place, and causation.*

All kinds of reasoning consist in nothing but a *comparison*, and a discovery of those relations, either constant or inconstant, which two or more objects bear to each other. This comparison we may make, either when both the objects are present to the senses, or when neither of them is present, or when only one. When both the objects are present to the senses along with the relation, we call *this* perception rather than reasoning; nor is there in this case any exercise of the thought, or any action, properly speaking, but a mere passive admission of the impressions thro' the organs of sensation.[1] According to this way of thinking, we ought not to receive as reasoning any of the observations we may make concerning *identity*, and the *relations* of *time* and *place;* since in none of them the mind can go beyond what is immediately present to the senses, either to discover the real existence or the relations of objects. 'T is only *causation*, which produces such a connexion, as to give us assurance from the existence or action of one object, that 't was follow'd or preceded by any other existence or action; nor can the other two relations be ever made use of in reasoning, except so far as they either affect or are affected by it. There is nothing in any objects to perswade us, that they are either always *remote* or always *contiguous;* and when from experience and observation we discover, that their relation in this particular is invariable, we always conclude there is some secret *cause*, which separates or unites them. The same reasoning extends to *identity*. We readily suppose an object may continue individually the same, tho' several times absent from and present to the senses; and ascribe to it an identity, notwithstanding the interruption of the perception, whenever we conclude, that if we had kept our eye or hand constantly upon it, it wou'd have convey'd an invariable and uninterrupted perception. But this conclusion beyond the impressions of our senses can be founded only on the connexion of *cause and effect;* nor can we otherwise have any security, that the

[1] Cf. Green and Grose's *Introduction*, § 327.

object is not chang'd upon us, however much the new object may resemble that which was formerly present to the senses. Whenever we discover such a perfect resemblance, we consider whether it be common in that species of objects; whether possibly or probably any cause cou'd operate in producing the change and resemblance; and according as we determine concerning these causes and effects, we form our judgment concerning the identity of the object.[1]

Here then it appears, that of those three relations, which depend not upon the mere ideas, the only one, that can be trac'd beyond our senses, and informs us of existences and objects, which we do not see or feel, is *causation*. This relation, therefore, we shall endeavour to explain fully before we leave the subject of the understanding.

To begin regularly, we must consider the idea of *causation* and see from what origin it is deriv'd. 'T is impossible to reason justly, without understanding perfectly the idea concerning which we reason; and 't is impossible perfectly to understand any idea, without tracing it up to its origin, and examining that primary impression, from which it arises. The examination of the impression bestows a clearness on the idea; and the examination of the idea bestows a like clearness on all our reasoning.

Let us therefore cast our eye on any two subjects, which we call cause and effect, and turn them on all sides, in order to find that impression, which produces an idea of such prodigious consequence. At first sight I perceive, that I must not search for it in any of the particular *qualities* of the objects; since, which-ever of these qualities I pitch on, I find some object, that is not possest of it, and yet falls under the denomination of cause or effect. And indeed there is nothing existent, either externally or internally, which is not to be consider'd either as a cause or an effect; tho' 't is plain there is no one quality, which universally belongs to all beings, and gives them a title to that denomination.

The idea, then, of causation must be deriv'd from some *relation* among objects; and that relation we must now en-

[1] Cf. Green and Grose's *Introduction*, § 313.

deavour to discover. I find in the first place, that whatever objects are consider'd as causes or effects, are *contiguous;* and that nothing can operate in a time or place, which is ever so little remov'd from those of its existence. Tho' distant objects may sometimes seem productive of each other, they are commonly found upon examination to be link'd by a chain of causes, which are contiguous among themselves, and to the distant objects; and when in any particular instance we cannot discover this connexion, we still presume it to exist. We may therefore consider the relation of CONTIGUITY as essential to that of causation; at least may suppose it such, according to the general opinion, till we can find a more [1] proper occasion to clear up this matter, by examining what objects are or are not susceptible of juxtaposition and conjunction.

The second relation I shall observe as essential to causes and effects, is not so universally acknowledg'd, but is liable to some controversy. 'T is that of PRIORITY of time in the cause before the effect. Some pretend that 't is not absolutely necessary a cause shou'd precede its effect; but that any object or action, in the very first moment of its existence, may exert its productive quality, and give rise to another object or action, perfectly co-temporary with itself. But beside that experience in most instances seems to contradict this opinion, we may establish the relation of priority by a kind of inference or reasoning. 'T is an establish'd maxim both in natural and moral philosophy, that an object, which exists for any time in its full perfection without producing another, is not its sole cause; but is assisted by some other principle, which pushes it from its state of inactivity, and makes it exert that energy, of which it was secretly possest. Now if any cause may be perfectly co-temporary with its effect, 't is certain, according to this maxim, that they must all of them be so; since any one of them, which retards its operation for a single moment, exerts not itself at that very individual time, in which it might have operated, and therefore is no proper cause. The consequence of this wou'd be no less than the destruction of that succession of

[1] Part IV, sect. 5.

causes, which we observe in the world; and indeed, the utter annihilation of time. For if one cause were co-temporary with its effect, and this effect with *its* effect, and so on, 't is plain there wou'd be no such thing as succession, and all objects must be co-existent.

If this argument appear satisfactory, 't is well. If not, I beg the reader to allow me the same liberty, which I have us'd in the preceding case, of supposing it such. For he shall find, that the affair is of no great importance.

Having thus discover'd or suppos'd the two relations of *contiguity* and *succession* to be essential to causes and effects, I find I am stopt short, and can proceed no farther in considering any single instance of cause and effect. Motion in one body is regarded upon impulse as the cause of motion in another. When we consider these objects with the utmost attention, we find only that the one body approaches the other; and that the motion of it precedes that of the other, but without any sensible interval. 'T is in vain to rack ourselves with *farther* thought and reflection upon this subject. We can go no *farther* in considering this particular instance.

Shou'd any one leave this instance, and pretend to define a cause, by saying it is something productive of another, 't is evident he wou'd say nothing. For what does he mean by *production?* Can he give any definition of it, that will not be the same with that of causation? If he can; I desire it may be produc'd. If he cannot; he here runs in a circle, and gives a synonymous term instead of a definition.

Shall we then rest contented with these two relations of contiguity and succession, as affording a complete idea of causation? By no means. An object may be contiguous and prior to another, without being consider'd as its cause. There is a NECESSARY CONNEXION to be taken into consideration; and that relation is of much greater importance, than any of the other two above-mention'd. [1]

. . . .

[1] Cf. Green and Grose's *Introduction*, § 286.

SECTION XIV. OF THE IDEA OF NECESSARY CONNEXION

. . . .

It has been establish'd as a certain principle, that general or abstract ideas are nothing but individual ones taken in a certain light, and that, in reflecting on any object, 't is as impossible to exclude from our thought all particular degrees of quantity and quality as from the real nature of things. If we be possest, therefore, of any idea of power in general, we must also be able to conceive some particular species of it; and as power cannot subsist alone, but is always regarded as an attribute of some being or existence, we must be able to place this power in some particular being, and conceive that being as endow'd with a real force and energy, by which such a particular effect necessarily results from its operation. We must distinctly and particularly conceive the connexion betwixt the cause and effect, and be able to pronounce, from a simple view of the one, that it must be follow'd or preceded by the other. This is the true manner of conceiving a particular power in a particular body: and a general idea being impossible without an individual; where the latter is impossible, 't is certain the former can never exist. Now nothing is more evident, than that the human mind cannot form such an idea of two objects, as to conceive any connexion betwixt them, or comprehend distinctly that power or efficacy, by which they are united. Such a connexion wou'd amount to a demonstration, and wou'd imply the absolute impossibility for the one object not to follow, or to be conceived not to follow upon the other: Which kind of connexion has already been rejected in all cases. If any one is of a contrary opinion, and thinks he has attain'd a notion of power in any particular object, I desire he may point out to me that object. But till I meet with such-a-one, which I despair of, I cannot forbear concluding, that since we can never distinctly conceive how any particular power can possibly reside in any particular object, we deceive ourselves in imagining we can form any such general idea.

Thus upon the whole we may infer, that when we talk of any

being, whether of a superior or inferior nature, as endow'd with a power or force, proportion'd to any effect; when we speak of a necessary connexion betwixt objects, and suppose, that this connexion depends upon an efficacy or energy, with which any of these objects are endow'd; in all these expressions, *so apply'd* we have really no distinct meaning, and make use only of common words, without any clear and determinate ideas. But as 't is more probable, that these expressions do here lose their true meaning by being *wrong apply'd*, than that they never have any meaning; 't will be proper to bestow another consideration on this subject, to see if possibly we can discover the nature and origin of those ideas, we annex to them.

Suppose two objects to be presented to us, of which the one is the cause and the other the effect; 't is plain, that from the simple consideration of one, or both these objects we never shall perceive the tie, by which they are united, or be able certainly to pronounce, that there is a connexion betwixt them. 'T is not, therefore, from any one instance, that we arrive at the idea of cause and effect, of a necessary connexion of power, of force, of energy, and of efficacy. Did we ever see any but particular conjunctions of objects, entirely different from each other, we shou'd never be able to form any such ideas.

But again; suppose we observe several instances, in which the same objects are always conjoin'd together, we immediately conceive a connexion betwixt them, and begin to draw an inference from one to another. This multiplicity of resembling instances, therefore, constitutes the very essence of power or connexion, and is the source, from which the idea of it arises. In order, then, to understand the idea of power, we must consider that multiplicity; nor do I ask more to give a solution of that difficulty, which has so long perplex'd us. For thus I reason. The repetition of perfectly similar instances can never *alone* give rise to an original idea, different from what is to be found in any particular instance, as has been observ'd, and as evidently follows from our fundamental principle, *that all ideas are copy'd from impressions*. Since therefore the idea of power is a new original idea, not to be found in any one instance, and which yet arises from the repetition of several instances, it follows, that the repetition *alone* has not that effect, but must either *discover* or *produce* something new, which is the source of that idea. Did the repetition neither discover nor produce any thing new, our ideas might be multiply'd by it, but wou'd not be enlarg'd above what they are upon the observation of one single instance. Every enlargement, therefore, (such as the idea of power or connexion) which arises from the multiplicity of similar instances, is copy'd from some effects of the multiplicity, and will be perfectly understood by understanding these effects. Wherever we find any thing new to be discover'd or produc'd by the repetition, there we must place the power, and must never look for it in any other object.

But 't is evident, in the first place, that the repetition of like objects in like relations of succession and contiguity *discovers* nothing new in any one of them; since we can draw no inference from it, nor make it a subject either of our demonstrative or probable reasonings; as has been already prov'd. Nay suppose we cou'd draw an inference, 't wou'd be of no consequence in the present case; since no kind of reasoning can give rise to a new idea, such as this of power is; but wherever we reason, we must antecedently be possest of clear ideas, which may be the objects of our reasoning. The conception always precedes the understanding; and where the one is obscure, the other is uncertain; where the one fails, the other must fail also.

Secondly, 'T is certain that this repetition of similar objects in similar situations *produces* nothing new either in these objects, or in any external body. For' t will readily be allow'd, that the several instances we have of the conjunction of resembling causes and effects are in themselves entirely independent, and that the communication of motion, which I see result at present from the shock of two billiard-balls, is totally distinct from that which I saw result from such an impulse a twelve-month ago. These impulses have no influence on each other. They are entirely divided by time and place; and the one might have existed and communicated motion, tho' the other never had been in being.

There is, then, nothing new either discover'd or produc'd in any objects by their constant conjunction, and by the uninterrupted resemblance of their relations of succession and contiguity. But 't is from this resemblance, that the ideas of necessity, of power, and of efficacy, are deriv'd. These ideas, therefore, represent not any thing, that does or can belong to the objects, which are constantly conjoin'd. This is an argument, which, in every view we can examine it, will be found perfectly unanswerable. Similar instances are still the first source of our idea of power or necessity; at the same time that they have no influence by their similarity either on each other, or on any external object. We must therefore, turn ourselves to some other quarter to seek the origin of that idea.

Tho' the several resembling instances, which give rise to the idea of power, have no influence on each other, and can never produce any new quality *in the object*, which can be the model of that idea, yet the *observation* of this resemblance produces a new impression *in the mind*, which is its real model. For after we have observ'd the resemblance in a sufficient number of instances, we immediately feel a determination of the mind to pass from one object to its usual attendant, and to conceive it in a stronger light upon account of that relation. This determination is the only effect of the resemblance; and therefore must be the same with power or efficacy, whose idea is deriv'd from the resemblance. The several instances of resembling conjunctions leads us into the notion of power and necessity. These instances are in themselves totally distinct from each other, and have no union but in the mind, which observes them, and collects their ideas. Necessity, then, is the effect of this observation, and is nothing but an internal impression of the mind, or a determination to carry our thoughts from one object to another. Without considering it in this view, we can never arrive at the most distant notion of it, or be able to attribute it either to external or internal objects, to spirit or body, to causes or effects.

The necessary connexion betwixt causes and effects is the foundation of our inference from one to the other. The foundation of our inference is the transition arising from the accustom'd union. These are, therefore, the same.

The idea of necessity arises from some impression. There is no impression convey'd by our senses, which can give rise to that idea. It must, therefore, be deriv'd from some internal impression, or impression of reflection. There is no internal impression, which has any relation to the present business, but that propensity, which custom produces, to pass from an object to the idea of its usual attendant. This therefore is the essence of necessity. Upon the whole, necessity is something, that exists in the mind, not in objects; nor is it possible for us ever to form the most distant idea of it, consider'd as a quality in bodies. Either we have no idea of necessity, or necessity is nothing but that determination of the thought to pass from causes to effects and from effects to causes, according to their experienc'd union.

Thus as the necessity, which makes two times two equal to four, or three angles of a triangle equal to two right ones, lies only in the act of the understanding, by which we consider and compare these ideas; in like manner the necessity or power, which unites causes and effects, lies in the determination of the mind to pass from the one to the other. The efficacy or energy of causes is neither plac'd in the causes themselves, nor in the deity, nor in the concurrence of these two principles; but belongs entirely to the soul, which considers the union of two or more objects in all past instances. 'T is here that the real power of causes is plac'd, along with their connexion and necessity.

I am sensible, that of all the paradoxes, which I have had, or shall hereafter have occasion to advance in the course of this treatise, the present one is the most violent, and that 't is merely by dint of solid proof and reasoning I can ever hope it will have admission, and overcome the inveterate prejudices of mankind. Before we are reconcil'd to this doctrine, how often must we repeat to ourselves, *that* the simple view of any two objects or actions, however related, can never give us any idea of power, or of a connexion betwixt them: *that* this idea arises from the repetition of their union: *that* the repetition neither discovers nor causes any thing in the objects, but has an influence only on the mind, by that customary transition it produces: *that* this customary transition is, therefore, the same with the power and necessity; which are consequently qualities of perceptions, not of objects, and are internally felt by the soul, and not perceiv'd externally in bodies? There is commonly an astonishment attending every thing extraordinary; and this astonishment changes immediately into the highest degree of esteem or contempt, according as we approve or disapprove of the subject. I am much afraid, that tho' the foregoing reasoning appears to me the shortest and most decisive imaginable; yet with the generality of readers the biass of the mind will prevail, and give them a prejudice against the present doctrine.

This contrary biass is easily accounted for. 'T is a common observation, that the mind has a great propensity to spread itself on external objects, and to conjoin with them any internal impressions, which they occasion, and which always make their appearance at the same time that these objects discover themselves to the senses. Thus as certain sounds and smells are always found to attend certain visible objects, we naturally imagine a conjunction, even in place, betwixt the objects and qualities, tho' the qualities be of such a nature as to admit of no such conjunction, and really exist no where. But of this more fully [1] hereafter. Mean while 't is sufficient to observe, that the same propensity is the reason, why we suppose necessity and power to lie in the objects we consider, not in our mind, that considers them; notwithstanding it is not possible for us to form the most distant idea of that quality, when it is not taken for the determination of the mind, to pass from the idea of an object to that of its usual attendant.

But tho' this be the only reasonable account we can give of necessity, the contrary notion is so riveted in the mind from the principles above-mention'd, that I doubt not but my sentiments will be treated by many as extravagant and ridiculous.

[1] Part IV, sect. 5.

What! the efficacy of causes lie in the determination of the mind! As if causes did not operate entirely independent of the mind, and wou'd not continue their operation, even tho' there was no mind existent to contemplate them, or reason concerning them. Thought may well depend on causes for its operation, but not causes on thought. This is to reverse the order of nature, and make that secondary, which is really primary. To every operation there is a power proportion'd; and this power must be plac'd on the body, that operates. If we remove the power from one cause, we must ascribe it to another: But to remove it from all causes, and bestow it on a being, that is no ways related to the cause or effect, but by perceiving them, is a gross absurdity, and contrary to the most certain principles of human reason.

I can only reply to all these arguments, that the case is here much the same, as if a blind man shou'd pretend to find a great many absurdities in the supposition, that the colour of scarlet is not the same with the sound of a trumpet, nor light the same with solidity. If we have really no idea of a power or efficacy in any object, or of any real connexion betwixt causes and effects, 't will be to little purpose to prove, that an efficacy is necessary in all operations. We do not understand our own meaning in talking so, but ignorantly confound ideas, which are entirely distinct from each other. I am, indeed, ready to allow, that there may be several qualities both in material and immaterial objects, with which we are utterly unacquainted; and if we please to call these *power* or *efficacy*, 't will be of little consequence to the world. But when, instead of meaning these unknown qualities, we make the terms of power and efficacy signify something, of which we have a clear idea, and which is incompatible with those objects, to which we apply it, obscurity and error begin then to take place, and we are led astray by a false philosophy. This is the case, when we transfer the determination of the thought to external objects, and suppose any real intelligible connexion betwixt them; that being a quality, which can only belong to the mind that considers them.

As to what may be said, that the operations of nature are

independent of our thought and reasoning, I allow it; and accordingly have observ'd, that objects bear to each other the relations of contiguity and succession; that like objects may be observ'd in several instances to have like relations; and that all this is independent of, and antecedent to the operations of the understanding. But if we go any farther, and ascribe a power or necessary connexion to these objects; this is what we can never observe in them, but must draw the idea of it from what we feel internally in contemplating them. And this I carry so far, that I am ready to convert my present reasoning into an instance of it, by a subtility, which it will not be difficult to comprehend.

When any object is presented to us, it immediately conveys to the mind a lively idea of that object, which is usually found to attend it; and this determination of the mind forms the necessary connexion of these objects. But when we change the point of view, from the objects to the perceptions; in that case the impression is to be considered as the cause, and the lively idea as the effect; and their necessary connexion is that new determination, which we feel to pass from the idea of the one to that of the other. The uniting principle among our internal perceptions is as unintelligible as that among external objects, and is not known to us any other way than by experience. Now the nature and effects of experience have been already sufficiently examin'd and explain'd. It never gives us any insight into the internal structure or operating principle of objects, but only accustoms the mind to pass from one to another.

'T is now time to collect all the different parts of this reasoning, and by joining them together form an exact definition of the relation of cause and effect, which makes the subject of the present enquiry. This order wou'd not have been excusable, of first examining our inference from the relation before we had explain'd the relation itself, had it been possible to proceed in a different method. But as the nature of the relation depends so much on that of the inference, we have been oblig'd to advance in this seemingly preposterous manner, and make use of terms before we were able exactly to define them, or fix their meaning.

We shall now correct this fault by giving a precise definition of cause and effect.

There may two definitions be given of this relation, which are only different, by their presenting a different view of the same object, and making us consider it either as a *philosophical* or as a *natural* relation; either as a comparison of two ideas, or as an association betwixt them. We may define a CAUSE to be 'An object precedent and contiguous to another, and where all the objects resembling the former are plac'd in like relations of precedency and contiguity to those objects, that resemble the latter.' If this definition be esteem'd defective, because drawn from objects foreign to the cause, we may substitute this other definition in its place, *viz.* 'A CAUSE is an object precedent and contiguous to another, and so united with it, that the idea of the one determines the mind to form the idea of the other, and the impression of the one to form a more lively idea of the other.' Shou'd this definition also be rejected for the same reason, I know no other remedy, than that the persons, who express this delicacy, should substitute a juster definition in its place. But for my part I must own my incapacity for such an undertaking. When I examine with the utmost accuracy those objects, which are commonly denominated causes and effects, I find, in considering a single instance, that the one object is precedent and contiguous to the other; and in inlarging my view to consider several instances, I find only, that like objects are constantly plac'd in like relations of succession and contiguity. Again, when I consider the influence of this constant conjunction, I perceive, that such a relation can never be an object of reasoning, and can never operate upon the mind, but by means of custom, which determines the imagination to make a transition from the idea of one object to that of its usual attendant, and from the impression of one to a more lively idea of the other. However extraordinary these sentiments may appear, I think it fruitless to trouble myself with any farther enquiry or reasoning upon the subject, but shall repose myself on them as on establish'd maxims.

'T will only be proper, before we leave this subject, to draw some corrollaries from it, by which we may remove several prejudices and popular errors, that have very much prevail'd in philosophy. First, We may learn from the foregoing doctrine, that all causes are of the same kind, and that in particular there is no foundation for that distinction, which we sometimes make betwixt efficient causes, and causes *sine qua non;* or betwixt efficient causes, and formal, and material, and exemplary, and final causes. For as our idea of efficiency is deriv'd from the constant conjunction of two objects, wherever this is observ'd, the cause is efficient and where it is not, there can never be a cause of any kind. For the same reason we must reject the distinction betwixt *cause* and *occasion,* when suppos'd to signify any thing essentially different from each other. If constant conjunction be imply'd in what we call occasion, 't is a real cause. If not, 't is no relation at all, and cannot give rise to any argument or reasoning.

Secondly, The same course of reasoning will make us conclude, that there is but one kind of *necessity,* as there is but one kind of cause, and that the common distinction betwixt *moral* and *physical* necessity is without any foundation in nature. This clearly appears from the precedent explication of necessity. 'T is the constant conjunction of objects, along with the determination of the mind, which constitutes a physical necessity: And the removal of these is the same thing with *chance.* As objects must either be conjoin'd or not, and as the mind must either be determin'd or not to pass from one object to another, 't is impossible to admit of any medium betwixt chance and an absolute necessity. In weakening this conjunction and determination you do not change the nature of the necessity; since even in the operation of bodies, these have different degrees of constancy and force, without producing a different species of that relation.

The distinction, which we often make betwixt *power* and the *exercise* of it, is equally without foundation.

Thirdly, We may now be able fully to overcome all that repugnance, which 't is so natural for us to entertain against the foregoing reasoning, by which we endeavour'd to prove, that the necessity of a cause to every beginning of existence is not founded on any arguments either demonstrative or intuitive. Such an opinion will not appear strange after the foregoing definitions. If we define a cause to be *an object precedent and contiguous to another, and where all the objects resembling the former are plac'd in a like relation of priority and contiguity to those objects, that resemble the latter;* we may easily conceive, that there is no absolute nor metaphysical necessity, that every beginning of existence shou'd be attended with such an object. If we define a cause to be, *An object precedent and contiguous to another, and so united with it in the imagination, that the idea of the one determines the mind to form the idea of the other, and the impression of the one to form a more lively idea of the other;* we shall make still less difficulty of assenting to this opinion. Such an influence on the mind is in itself perfectly extraordinary and incomprehensible; nor can we be certain of its reality, but from experience and observation.

I shall add as a fourth corollary, that we can never have reason to believe that any object exists, of which we cannot form an idea. For as all our reasonings concerning existence are deriv'd from causation, and as all our reasonings concerning causation are deriv'd from the experienc'd conjunction of objects, not from any reasoning or reflection, the same experience must give us a notion of these objects, and must remove all mystery from our conclusions. This is so evident, that 't wou'd scarce have merited our attention, were it not to obviate certain objections of this kind, which might arise against the following reasonings concerning *matter* and *substance.* I need not observe, that a full knowledge of the object is not requisite, but only of those qualities of it, which we believe to exist.

DAVID HARTLEY

(1705–1757)

OBSERVATIONS ON MAN, HIS FRAME, HIS DUTY, AND HIS EXPECTATIONS*

PART I. INTRODUCTION †

MAN consists of two parts, body and mind.

The first is subjected to our senses and inquiries, in the same manner as the other parts of the external material world.

The last is that substance, agent, principle, &c. to which we refer the sensations, ideas, pleasures, pains, and voluntary motions.

Sensations are those internal feelings of the mind, which arise from the impressions made by external objects upon the several parts of our bodies.

All our other internal feelings may be called *ideas*. Some of these appear to spring up in the mind of themselves, some are suggested by words, others arise in other ways. Many writers comprehend *sensations* under *ideas;* but I every where use these words in the senses here ascribed to them.

* London, 1749; 2d ed. (with Life), 1791; 6th rev. ed. 1834.

† Hartley describes the origin of the *Observations on Man*, in its Preface, as follows: — "About eighteen years ago [1731] I was informed, that the Rev. Mr. Gay, then living, asserted the possibility of deducing all our intellectual pleasures and pains from association. This put me upon considering the power of association. Mr. Gay published his sentiments on this matter, about the same time, in a *Dissertation on the Fundamental Principle of Virtue*, prefixed to Mr. Archdeacon Law's translation of Archbishop King's *Origin of Evil*."

The internal evidence, moreover, tends to prove that the anonymous tract entitled, *An Enquiry into the Origin of the Human Appetite and Affections, shewing how each arises from Association*, Lincoln 1747, which is the fourth of Rev. Samuel Parr's *Metaphysical Tracts*, Lond. 1837, was also written by the 'modest' Gay, whose priority as regards the doctrine of association is thereby more firmly secured.

The ideas which resemble sensations, are called *ideas of sensation:* all the rest may therefore be called *intellectual ideas.*

It will appear in the course of these observations, that the *ideas of sensation* are the elements of which all the rest are compounded. Hence *ideas of sensation* may be termed *simple, intellectual* ones *complex.*

The *pleasures* and *pains* are comprehended under the sensations and ideas, as these are explained above. For all our pleasures and pains are internal feelings, and conversely, all our internal feelings seem to be attended with some degree either of *pleasure* or *pain.* However, I shall, for the most part, give the names of *pleasure* and *pain* only to such degrees as are considerable; referring all low evanescent ones to the head of *mere sensations* and *ideas.*

The pleasures and pains may be ranged under seven general classes; viz.

1. Sensation;
2. Imagination;
3. Ambition;
4. Self-Interest;
5. Sympathy;
6. Theopathy; and,
7. The Moral Sense; according as they arise from,
1. The impressions made on the external senses;
2. Natural or artificial beauty or deformity;
3. The opinions of others concerning us;
4. Our possession or want of the means of happiness, and security from, or subjection to, the hazards of misery;
5. The pleasures and pains of our fellow-creatures;
6. The affections excited in us by the contemplation of the Deity; or
7. Moral beauty and deformity.

The human mind may also be considered as endued with the faculties of *memory, imagination,* or *fancy, understanding, affection,* and *will.*

CHAPTER I. THE DOCTRINES OF VIBRATIONS AND ASSOCIATION IN GENERAL

My chief design in the following chapter is briefly to explain, establish, and apply the doctrines of *vibrations* and *association*. The first of these doctrines is taken from the hints concerning the performance of sensation and motion, which Sir Isaac Newton has given at the end of his Principia,[1] and in the Questions annexed to his Optics[2]; the last, from what Mr. Locke,[3] and other ingenious persons since his time, have delivered concerning the influence of *association* over our opinions and affections, and its use in explaining those things in an accurate and precise way, which are commonly referred to the power of habit and custom, is a general and indeterminate one.

The doctrine of *vibrations* may appear at first sight to have no connexion with that of *association;* however, if these doctrines be found in fact to contain the laws of the bodily and mental powers respectively, they must be related to each other, since the body and mind are. One may expect, that *vibrations* should infer *association* as their effect, and *association* point to *vibrations* as its cause. I will endeavour, in the present chapter, to trace out this mutual relation.

The proper method of philosophizing seems to be, to discover and establish the general laws of action, affecting the subject under consideration, from certain select, well-defined, and well-attested phænomena, and then to explain and predict the other phænomena by these laws. This is the method of analysis and synthesis recommended and followed by Sir Isaac Newton.

I shall not be able to execute, with any accuracy, what the reader might expect of this kind, in respect of the doctrines of *vibrations* and *association*, and their general laws, on account of the great intricacy, extensiveness, and novelty of the subject. However, I will attempt a sketch in the best manner I can, for the service of future inquirers.

[1] Newton's *Philosophiae naturalis principia mathematicoa*, Lond. 1687.
[2] Newton's *Treatise of Optics*, Lond. 1784.
[3] Locke's *An Essay Concerning Human Understanding*, Lond. 1690.

SECTION I. THE DOCTRINE OF VIBRATIONS, AND ITS USE FOR
EXPLAINING THE SENSATIONS

PROP. I. — *The white medullary Substance of the Brain, spinal
Marrow, and the Nerves proceeding from them, is the immediate Instrument of Sensation and Motion.*

UNDER the word *brain*, in these observations, I comprehend
all that lies within the cavity of the skull, *i.e.* the *cerebrum*, or
brain properly so called, the *cerebellum*, and the *medulla
oblongata*.

This proposition seems to be sufficiently proved in the writings of physicians and anatomists; from the structure and functions of the several organs of the human body; from experiments on living animals; from the symptoms of diseases, and
from dissections of morbid bodies. Sensibility, and the power
of motion, seem to be conveyed to all the parts, in their natural
state, from the brain and spinal marrow, along the nerves.
These arise from the medullary, not the cortical part, every
where, and are themselves of a white medullary substance.
When the nerves of any part are cut, tied, or compressed in any
considerable degree, the functions of that part are either
entirely destroyed, or much impaired. When the spinal marrow is compressed by a dislocation of the *vertebræ* of the back,
all the parts, whose nerves arise below the place of dislocation,
become paralytic. When any considerable injury is done to the
medullary substance of the brain, sensation, voluntary motion,
memory, and intellect, are either entirely lost, or much impaired; and if the injury be very great, this extends immediately to the vital motions also, *viz.* to those of the heart, and
organs of respiration, so as to occasion death. But this does not
hold equally in respect of the cortical substance of the brain;
perhaps not at all, unless as far as injuries done to it extend
themselves to the medullary substance. In dissections after
apoplexies, palsies, epilepsies, and other distempers affecting
the sensations and motions, it is usual to find some great disorder in the brain, from preternatural tumours, from blood,
matter, or serum, lying upon the brain, or in its ventricles, &c.

This may suffice as general evidence for the present. The particular reasons of some of these phænomena, with more definite evidences, will offer themselves in the course of these observations.

PROP. II. — *The white medullary Substance of the Brain is also the immediate Instrument, by which Ideas are presented to the Mind: or, in other words, whatever Changes are made in this Substance, corresponding Changes are made in our Ideas; and vice versa.*

THE evidence for this proposition is also to be taken from the writings of physicians and anatomists; but especially from those parts of these writings which treat of the faculties of memory, attention, imagination, &c. and of mental disorders. It is sufficiently manifest from hence, that the perfection of our mental faculties depends upon the perfection of this substance; that all injuries done to it affect the trains of ideas proportionably; and that these cannot be restored to their natural course till such injuries be repaired. Poisons, spirituous liquors, opiates, fevers, blows upon the head, &c. all plainly affect the mind, by first disordering the medullary substance. And evacuations, rest, medicines, time, &c. as plainly restore the mind to its former state, by reversing the foregoing steps. But there will be more and more definite evidence offered in the course of these observations.

PROP. III. — *The Sensations remain in the Mind for a short time after the sensible Objects are removed.*

THIS is very evident in the sensations impressed on the eye. Thus, to use Sir Isaac Newton's words, "If a burning coal be nimbly moved round in a circle, with gyrations continually repeated, the whole circle will appear like fire; the reason of which is, that the sensation of the coal, in the several places of that circle, remains impressed on the *sensorium* until the coal return again to the same place. And so in a quick consecution of the colours," (*viz.* red, yellow, green, blue, and purple, mentioned in the experiment, whence this passage is taken,) "the impression of every colour remains on the *sensorium* until a revolution of all the colours be completed, and that first colour return again. The impressions therefore of all the successive colours are at once in the *sensorium* — and beget a sensation of white." *Opt.* b. I. p. 2. Experiment 10.

Thus also, when a person has had a candle, a window, or any other lucid and well-defined object, before his eyes for a considerable time, he may perceive a very clear and precise image thereof to be left in the *sensorium*, fancy, or mind (for these I consider as equivalent expressions in our entrance upon these disquisitions,) for some time after he has closed his eyes. At least this will happen frequently to persons who are attentive to these things in a gentle way; for, as this appearance escapes the notice of those who are entirely inattentive, so too earnest a desire and attention prevents it, by introducing another state of mind or fancy.

To these may be referred the appearance mentioned by Sir Isaac Newton, *Opt.* Qu. 16. *viz.* "When a man in the dark presses either corner of his eye with his finger, and turns his eye away from his finger, he will see a circle of colours like those in the feather of a peacock's tail. And this appearance continues about a second of time after the eye and finger have remained quiet." The sensation continues therefore in the mind about a second of time after its cause ceases to act.

The same continuance of the sensations is also evident in the ear. For the sounds which we hear are reflected by the neighbouring bodies, and therefore consist of a variety of sounds, succeeding each other at different distances of time, according to the distances of the several reflecting bodies; which yet causes no confusion or apparent complexity of sound, unless the distance of the reflecting bodies be very considerable, as in spacious buildings. Much less are we able to distinguish the successive pulses of the air, even in the gravest sounds.

As to the senses of taste and smell, there seems to be no clear direct evidence for the continuance of their sensations after the proper objects are removed. But analogy would incline one to believe, that they must resemble the senses of sight and hearing in this particular, though the continuance cannot be perceived distinctly, on account of the shortness of it, or other circumstances. For the sensations must be supposed to bear such an analogy to each other, and so to depend in common upon the brain, that all evidences for the continuance of sensations in any one sense, will extend themselves to the rest. Thus all the senses may be considered as so many kinds of feeling; the taste is nearly allied to the feeling, the smell to the taste, and the sight and hearing to each other. All which analogies will offer themselves to view when we come to examine each of these senses in particular.

In the sense of feeling, the continuance of heat, after the heating body is removed, and that of the smart of a wound, after the instant of infliction, seem to be of the same kind with the appearances taken notice of in the eye and ear.

But the greatest part of the sensations of this sense resemble those of taste and smell, and vanish to appearance as soon as the objects are removed.

Prop. IV. — *External Objects impressed upon the Senses occasion, first in the Nerves on which they are impressed, and then in the Brain, Vibrations of the small, and as one may say, infinitesimal, medullary Particles.*

These vibrations are motions backwards and forwards of the small particles; of the same kind with the oscillations of pendulums, and the tremblings of the particles of sounding bodies. They must be conceived to be exceedingly short and small, so as not to have the least efficacy to disturb or move the whole bodies of the nerves or brain. For that the nerves themselves should vibrate like musical strings, is highly absurd; nor was it ever asserted by Sir Isaac Newton, or any of those who have embraced his notion of the performance of sensation and motion, by means of *vibrations*.

In like manner we are to suppose the particles which vibrate, to be of the inferior orders, and not those biggest particles, on which the operations in chemistry, and the colours of natural bodies, depend, according to the opinion of Sir Isaac Newton.

Hence, in the *proposition*, I term the medullary particles, which vibrate, *infinitesimal*.

Now that external objects impress vibratory motions upon the medullary substance of the nerves and brain (which is the immediate instrument of sensation, according to the first proposition) appears from the continuance of the sensations mentioned in the third; since no motion, besides a vibratory one, can reside in any part for the least moment of time. External objects, being corporeal, can act upon the nerves and brain, which are also corporeal, by nothing but impressing motion on them. A vibrating motion may continue for a short time in the small medullary particles of the nerves and brain, without disturbing them, and after a short time would cease; and so would correspond to the above-mentioned short continuance of the sensations; and there seems to be no other species of motion that can correspond thereto.

Cor. As this proposition is deduced from the foregoing, so if it could be established upon independent principles, (of which I shall treat under the next,) the foregoing might be deduced from it. And on this supposition there would be an argument for the continuance of the sensations, after the removal of their objects; which would extend to the senses of feeling, taste, and smell, in the same manner as to those of sight and hearing.

Section II. — Of Ideas, their Generation and Associations; and of the Agreement of the Doctrine of Vibrations with the Phænomena of Ideas.

Prop. VIII. — *Sensations, by being often repeated, leave certain Vestiges, Types, or Images, of themselves, which may be called, Simple Ideas of Sensation.*

I took notice in the Introduction, that those ideas which resemble sensations were called ideas of sensation; and also that they might be called *simple* ideas, in respect of the intellectual ones which are formed from them, and of whose very essence it is to be *complex*. But the ideas of sensation are not entirely simple, since they must consist of parts both co-existent and successive, as the generating sensations themselves do.

Now, that the simple ideas of sensation are thus generated, agreeably to the proposition, appears, because the most vivid of these ideas are those where the corresponding sensations are most vigorously impressed, or most frequently renewed; whereas if the sensation be faint, or uncommon, the generated idea is also faint in proportion, and, in extreme cases, evanescent and imperceptible. The exact observance of the order of place in visible ideas, and of the order of time in audible ones, may likewise serve to shew, that these ideas are copies and offsprings of the impressions made on the eye and ear, in which the same orders were observed respectively. And though it happens, that trains of visible and audible ideas are presented in sallies of the fancy, and in dreams, in which the order of time and place is different from that of any former impressions, yet the small component parts of these trains are copies of former impressions; and reasons may be given for the varieties of their compositions.

It is also to be observed, that this proposition bears a great resemblance to the third; and that, by this resemblance, they somewhat confirm and illustrate one another. According to the third proposition, sensations remain for a short time after the impression is removed; and these remaining sensations grow feebler and feebler, till they vanish. They are therefore, in some part of their declension, of about the same strength with ideas, and in their first state, are intermediate between sensations and ideas. And it seems reasonable to expect, that, if a single sensation can leave a perceptible effect, trace, or vestige, for a short time, a sufficient repetition of a sensation may leave a perceptible effect of the same kind, but of a more permanent nature, *i.e.* an idea, which shall recur occasionally, at long distances of time, from the impression of the corresponding sensation, and *vice versa*. As to the occasions and causes, which make ideas recur, they will be considered in the next proposition but one.

The method of reasoning used in the last paragraph is farther confirmed by the following circumstance; *viz.* that both the diminutive declining sensations, which remain for a short space after the impressions of the objects cease, and the ideas, which are the copies of such impressions, are far more distinct and vivid in respect of visible and audible impressions, than of any others. To which it may be added, that, after travelling, hearing music, &c. trains of vivid ideas are very apt to recur, which correspond very exactly to the late impressions, and which are of an intermediate nature between the remaining sensations of the third proposition, in their greatest vigour, and the ideas mentioned in this.

The sensations of feeling, taste and smell, can scarce be said to leave ideas, unless very indistinct and obscure ones. However, an analogy leads one to suppose that these sensations may leave traces of the same kind, though not in the same degree, as those of sight and hearing; so the readiness with which we reconnoitre sensations of feeling, taste, and smell, that have been often impressed, is an evidence that they do so; and these generated traces or dispositions of mind may be called the ideas of feeling, taste, and smell. In sleep, when all our ideas are magnified, those of feeling, taste, and smell, are often sufficiently vivid and distinct; and the same thing happens in some few cases of vigilance.

PROP. IX. — *Sensory Vibrations, by being often repeated, beget, in the medullary Substance of the Brain, a Disposition to diminutive Vibrations, which may also be called Vibratiuncles, and Miniatures, corresponding to themselves respectively.*

THIS correspondence of the diminutive vibrations to the original sensory ones, consists in this, that they agree in kind, place, and line of direction; and differ only in being more feeble, *i.e.* in degree.

This proposition follows from the foregoing. For since sensations, by being often repeated, beget ideas, it cannot but be that those vibrations, which accompany sensations, should beget something which may accompany ideas in like manner; and this can be nothing but feebler vibrations, agreeing with the sensory generating vibrations in kind, place, and line of direction.

Or thus: By the first proposition it appears, that some motion must be excited in the medullary substance, during each sensation; by the fourth, this motion is determined to be a vibratory one: since therefore some motion must also, by the second, be excited in the medullary substance during the presence of each idea, this motion cannot be any other than a vibratory one: else how should it proceed from the original vibration attending the sensation, in the same manner as the idea does from the sensation itself? It must also agree in kind, place, and line of direction, with the generating vibration. A vibratory motion, which recurs t times in a second, cannot beget a diminutive one that recurs $\frac{1}{2}$ t, or 2 t times; nor one originally impressed on the region of the brain corresponding to the auditory nerves, beget diminutive vibrations in the region corresponding to the optic nerves; and so of the rest. The line of direction must likewise be the same in the original and derivative vibrations. It remains therefore, that each simple idea of sensation be attended by diminutive vibrations of the same kind, place, and line of direction, with the original vibrations attending the sensation itself: or, in the words of the proposition, that sensory vibrations, by being frequently repeated, beget a disposition to diminutive vibrations corresponding to themselves respectively. We may add, that the vibratory nature of the motion which attends ideas, may be inferred from the continuance of some ideas, visible ones for instance, in the fancy for a few moments.

. . . .

PROP. X. — *Any Sensations* A, B, C, &c. *by being associated with one another a sufficient Number of Times, get such a Power over the corresponding Ideas* a, b, c, &c. *that any one of the Sensations* A, *when impressed alone, shall be able to excite in the Mind,* b, c, &c. *the Ideas of the rest.*

SENSATIONS may be said to be associated together, when their impressions are either made precisely at the same instant of time, or in the contiguous successive instants. We may therefore distinguish association into two sorts, the synchronous, and the successive.

The influence of association over our ideas, opinions, and affections, is so great and obvious, as scarcely to have escaped the notice of any writer who has treated of these, though the word *association*, in the particular sense here affixed to it, was first brought into use by Mr. Locke. But all that has been delivered by the ancients and moderns, concerning the power of habit, custom, example, education, authority, party-prejudice, the manner of learning the manual and liberal arts, &c. goes upon this doctrine as its foundation, and may be considered as the detail of it, in various circumstances. I here begin with the simplest case, and shall proceed to more and more complex ones continually, till I have exhausted what has occurred to me upon this subject.

This proposition, or first and simplest case of association, is manifest from innumerable common observations. Thus, the names, smells, tastes, and tangible qualities of natural bodies, suggest their visible appearances to the fancy, *i.e.* excite their visible ideas; and, *vice versâ*, their visible appearances impressed on the eye raise up those powers of reconnoitring their names, smells, tastes, and tangible qualities, which may not improperly be called their ideas, as above noted; and in some cases raise up ideas, which may be compared with visible ones, in respect of vividness. All which is plainly owing to the association of the several sensible qualities of bodies with their names, and with each other. It is remarkable, however, as being agreeable to the superior vividness of visible and audible ideas, before taken notice of, that the suggestion of the visible appearance from the name is the most ready of any other; and, next to this, that of the name from the visible appearance; in which last case, the reality of the audible idea, when not evident to the fancy, may be inferred from the ready pronunciation of the name. For it will be shewn hereafter, that the audible idea is most commonly a previous requisite to pronunciation. Other instances of the power of association may be taken from compound visible and audible impressions. Thus the sight of part of a large building suggests the idea of the rest instantaneously; and the sound of the words which begin a familiar sentence, brings the remaining part to our memories in order, the association of the parts being synchronous in the first case, and successive in the last.

It is to be observed, that, in successive associations, the power of raising the ideas is only exerted according to the order in which the association is made. Thus, if the impressions A, B, C, be always made in the order of the alphabet, B impressed alone will not raise a, but c only. Agreeably to which it is easy to repeat familiar sentences in the order in which they always occur, but impossible to do it readily in an inverted one. The reason of this is, that the compound idea, c, b, a, corresponds to the compound sensation C, B, A; and therefore requires the impression of C, B, A, in the same manner as a, b, c, does that of A, B, C. This will, however, be more evident, when we come to consider the associations of vibratory motions, in the next proposition.

It is also to be observed, that the power of association grows feebler, as the number either of synchronous or successive impressions is increased, and does not extend, with due force, to more than a small one, in the first and simplest cases. But, in complex cases, or the associations of associations, of which the memory, in its full extent, consists, the powers of the mind, deducible from this source, will be found much greater than any person, upon his first entrance on these inquiries, could well imagine.

PROP. XI. — *Any Vibrations, A, B, C, &c. by being associated together a sufficient Number of Times, get such a Power over a, b, c, &c. the corresponding Miniature Vibrations, that any of the Vibrations A, when impressed alone, shall be able to excite b, c, &c. the Miniatures of the rest.*

THIS proposition may be deduced from the foregoing, in the same manner as the ninth has been from the eighth.

But it seems also deducible from the nature of vibrations, and of an animal body. Let A and B be two vibrations, associated synchronically. Now, it is evident, that the vibration A (for I will, in this propcsition, speak of A and B in the singular number, for the sake of greater clearness) will, by endeavouring to diffuse itself into those parts of the medullary substance which are affected primarily by the vibration B, in some measure modify and change B, so as to make B a little different from what it would be, if impressed alone. For the same reasons the vibration A will be a little affected, even in its primary seat, by the endeavour of B to diffuse itself all over the medullary substance. Suppose now the vibrations A and B to be impressed at the same instant, for a thousand times; it follows, from the ninth proposition, that they will first overcome the disposition to the natural vibrations N, and then leave a tendency to themselves, which will now occupy the place of the original natural tendency to vibrations. When therefore the vibration A is impressed alone, it cannot be entirely such as the object would excite of itself, but must lean, even in its primary seat, to the modifications and changes induced by B, during their thousand joint impressions; and therefore much more, in receding from this primary seat, will it lean that way; and when it comes to the seat of B, it will excite B's miniature a little modified and changed by itself.

Or thus: When A is impressed alone, some vibration must take place in the primary seat of B, both on account of the heat and pulsation of the arteries, and because A will endeavour to diffuse itself over the whole medullary substance. This cannot be that part of the natural vibrations N, which belongs to this region, because it is supposed to be overruled already. It cannot be that which A impressed alone would have propagated this region, because that has always hitherto been overruled, and converted into B; and therefore cannot have begotten a tendency to itself. It cannot be any full vivid vibration, such as B, C, D, &c. belonging to this region, because all full vibrations require the actual impression of an object upon the corresponding external organ. And of miniature vibrations belonging to this region, such as b, c, d, &c. it is evident, that b has the preference, since A leans to it a little, even in its own primary seat, more and more, in receding from this, and almost entirely, when it comes to the primary seat of *B*. For the same reasons *B* impressed alone will excite *a;* and, in general, if *A, B, C,* &c. be vibrations synchronically impressed on different regions of the medullary substance, *A* impressed alone will at last excite *b, c,* &c. according to the proposition.

If *A* and *B* be vibrations impressed successively, then will the latter part of *A, viz.* that part which, according to the third and fourth propositions, remains, after the impression of the object ceases, be modified and altered by *B*, at the same time that it will a little modify and alter it, till at last it be quite over-powered by it, and end in it. It follows therefore, by a like method of reasoning, that the successive impression of *A* and *B*, sufficiently repeated, will so alter the medullary substance, as that when *A* is impressed alone, its latter part shall be not such as the sole impression of *A* requires, but lean towards *B*, and end in *b* at last. But *B* will not excite *a* in a retrograde order; since, by supposition, the latter part of *B* was not modified and altered by *A*, but by some other vibration, such as *C* or *D*. And as *B*, by being followed by *C*, may at last raise *c;* so *b*, when raised by *A*, in the method here proposed, may be also suffi-cient to raise *c;* inasmuch as the miniature *c* being a feeble mo-tion, not stronger, perhaps, than the natural vibrations *N*, requires only to have its kind, place, and line of direction, de-termined by association, the heat and arterial pulsation con-veying to it the requisite degree of strength. And thus *A* im-pressed alone will raise *b, c,* &c. in successive associations, as well as in synchronous ones, according to the proposi-tion.

It seems also, that the influence of *A* may, in some degree, reach through *B* to *C;* so that *A* of itself may have some effect to raise *c*, as well as by means of *b*. However, it is evident, that this chain must break off, at last, in long successions; and that sooner or later, according to the number and vigour of the repeated impressions. The power of miniature vibrations to raise other miniatures may, perhaps, be made clearer to mathe-maticians, by hinting, that the efficacy of any vibration to raise any other, is not in the simple ratio of its vividness, but as some power thereof less than unity; for thus b may raise c, a weaker vibration than b, c may raise d, &c. with more facility than if the efficacy was in the simple ratio of the vividness, and yet so that the series shall break off at last.

If the ninth proposition be allowed, we may prove this in somewhat a shorter and easier manner, as follows. Since the vibrations A and B are impressed together, they must, from the diffusion necessary to vibratory motions, run into one vibration; and consequently, after a number of impressions sufficiently repeated, will leave a trace, or miniature, of themselves, as one vibration, which will recur every now and them, from slight causes. Much rather, therefore, may the part b of the compound miniature $a+b$ recur, when the part A of the compound original vibration $A+B$ is impressed.

And as the ninth proposition may be thus made to prove the present, so it ought to be acknowledged and remarked here, that unless the ninth be allowed, the present cannot be proved, or that the power of association is founded upon, and necessarily requires, the previous power of forming ideas, and miniature vibrations. For ideas, the miniature vibrations, must first be generated, according to the eighth and ninth propositions, before they can be associated, according to the tenth and this eleventh. But then (which is very remarkable) this power of forming ideas, and their corresponding miniature vibrations, does equally presuppose the power of association. For since all sensations and vibrations are infinitely divisible, in respect of time and place, they could not leave any traces or images of themselves, $i.e.$ any ideas, or miniature vibrations, unless their infinitesimal parts did cohere together through joint impression, $i.e.$ association. Thus, to mention a gross instance, we could have no proper idea of a horse, unless the particular ideas of the head, neck, body, legs, and tail, peculiar to this animal, stuck to each other in the fancy, from frequent joint impression. And, therefore, in dreams, where complex associations are much weakened, and various parcels of visible ideas, not joined in nature, start up together in the fancy, contiguous to each other, we often see monsters, chimeras, and combinations, which have never been actually presented.

. . . .

PROP. XII. — *Simple Ideas will run into complex ones, by Means of Association.*

IN order to explain and prove this proposition, it will be requisite to give some previous account of the manner in which simple ideas of sensation may be associated together.

Case 1. Let the sensation *A* be often associated with each of the sensations *B, C, D,* &c. *i.e.* at certain times with *B,* at certain other times with *C,* &c. it is evident, from the tenth proposition, that *A,* impressed alone, will, at last, raise *b, c, d,* &c. all together, *i.e.* associate them with one another, provided they belong to different regions of the medullary substance; for if any two, or more, belong to the same region, since they cannot exist together in their distinct forms, *A* will raise something intermediate between them.

Case 2. If the sensations *A, B, C, D,* &c. be associated together, according to various combinations of twos, or even threes, fours, &c. then will *A* raise *b, c, d,* &c. also *B* raise *a, c, d,* &c. as in case the first.

It may happen, indeed, in both cases, that *A* may raise a particular miniature, as *b,* preferably to any of the rest, from its being more associated with *B,* from the novelty of the impression of *B,* from a tendency in the medullary substance to favour *b,* &c. and in like manner, that *b* may raise *c* or *d* preferably to the rest. However, all this will be overruled, at last, by the recurrency of the associations; so that any one of the sensations will excite the ideas of the rest at the same instant, *i.e.* associate them together.

Case 3. Let *A, B, C, D,* &c. represent successive impressions, it follows from the tenth and eleventh propositions, that *A* will raise *b, c, d,* &c. *B* raise *c, d,* &c. And though the ideas do not, in this case, rise precisely at the same instant, yet they come nearer together than the sensations themselves did in their original impression; so that these ideas are associated almost synchronically at last, and successively from the first. The ideas come nearer to one another than the sensations, on account of their diminutive nature, by which all that appertains to them is contracted. And this seems to be as agreeable to observation as to theory.

Case 4. All compound impressions $A+B+C+D$, &c. after sufficient repetition leave compound miniatures $a+b+c+d$, &c. which recur every now and then from slight causes, as well such as depend on association, as some which are different from it. Now, in these recurrences of compound miniatures, the parts are farther associated, and approach perpetually nearer to each other, agreeably to what was just now observed; *i.e.* the association becomes perpetually more close and intimate.

Case 5. When the ideas a, b, c, d, &c. have been sufficiently associated in any one or more of the foregoing ways, if we suppose any single idea of these, a for instance, to be raised by the tendency of the medullary substance that way, by the association of A with a foreign sensation or idea X or x, &c. this idea a, thus raised, will frequently bring in all the rest, b, c, d, &c. and so associate all of them together still farther.

And upon the whole, it may appear to the reader, that the simple ideas of sensation must run into clusters and combinations, by associations; and that each of these will, at last, coalesce into one complex idea, by the approach and commixture of the several compounding parts.

It appears also from observation, that many of our intellectual ideas, such as those that belong to the heads of beauty, honour, moral qualities, &c. are, in fact, thus composed of parts, which, by degrees, coalesce into one complex idea.

CHARLES BONNET
(1720-1793)

ABSTRACT OF THE ANALYTICAL ESSAY UPON THE FACULTIES OF THE SOUL

Translated from the French* by
BENJAMIN RAND

I. *The senses the first source of our ideas*

I HAVE set out from a well known and indubitable fact, and one which no person will venture to deny. It is that one born blind can never acquire our ideas of light and colors.[1] His soul has however the same faculties as ours. What then does he lack in order to have these visual sensations ? — the organ suitable to these sensations.

Suppose the person born blind were at the same time born deaf, and had also from his birth been deprived of the senses of touch, taste, and smell. I ask what ideas his soul would be able to acquire?

The reply will possibly be made to me as it already has been, that it would have at least the consciousness of its existence. But how do we acquire the consciousness of our own existence? Is it not by reflecting upon our own sensations? Or at least are not our first sensations united to that consciousness, which our soul always has that it is itself which experiences them? And is this consciousness anything else than that of its existence? But how could a soul which has never had a sensation know that it exists?

It would not be well to admit here a certain confused consciousness of existence of which we could not form any idea. It

* Ch. Bonnet's *Essai Analytique sur les facultés de l'âme.* Copenh. 1760. Translated here from Bonnet's *Analyse abrégée de l'essai analytique* (1769), in his *Oeuvres d'histoire naturelle et de philosophie.* Neufchatel, 1779-83, tom. xv.

[1] Bonnet's *Essai analytique sur les facultés de l'âme,* § 17.

is better doubtless to receive only clear things and those about which one can reason. The present thought cannot constitute the essence of the soul. What would constitute it, at least partly, would be rather the capacity for thoughts (cogitabilité).

II. *Reflection, the second source of our ideas*

I HAVE thus supposed as a principle that all our ideas are derived originally from the senses. I have not said that our ideas are purely sensory. I have shown very clearly and in great detail, how reflection aided by the different kinds of signs rises by degrees from sensations to the most abstract conceptions.[1] I have sufficiently investigated the theory of abstractions, and have traced in general that of ideas.[2]

III. *The union of soul and body and its law*

THE objects themselves or the corpuscles which emanate from them act upon the senses only by impulsion. They communicate to them a certain shock, which is transmitted to the brain, and the soul experiences sensations.

The philosopher does not investigate how the movement of a nerve causes an idea to arise in the soul. He simply admits the fact and readily renounces the attempt of discovering the cause. He knows that it springs from the mystery of the union of two substances, and that this mystery is for him inscrutable.

It suffices for him to know that to the disturbance of this or that nerve there always corresponds in the soul this or that sensation. He does not regard the sensation as the physical and immediate effect of the movement of the nerve, but as the inseparable sequence of that movement. He regards this movement as in some sort a natural sign of the sensation by divine establishment.

IV. *Man a composite being*

I HAVE not affirmed that it is impossible for the soul to think without a body. There perhaps exist pure spirits which have ideas; but I am profoundly ignorant how they have them.

[1] Chaps. XVI, XIX, § 28.　　　　[2] Chaps. XIV, XV, XVI.

I know only that the feeling that I have of my ego is always one, simple, indivisible; from which I infer that I am not wholly material. I have very much amplified this excellent proof. I admit then the existence of my soul as that of an immaterial substance, which it has pleased the Creator to unite to an organised body. I learn from the contemplation of my being, that I result from the union of two very different substances.

In this order of things I perceive that I have ideas only by the intervention of my body, and the more I reflect upon myself, the more I am compelled to recognise the great influence of the machine[1] upon all the operations of my soul.

I learn also from revelation that my soul will be eternally joined to a portion of matter. I shall therefore be eternally a composite being.

The purpose of the author of my being has therefore not been that I should be a pure spirit. He has consequently willed that my soul should use its faculties only by means of a body. If he had willed otherwise I should have philosophized differently, because I should have had another way of perceiving and judging.

I have thus followed in my researches upon the economy of our being the course which has appeared to me most to conform to that of nature. My soul has no hold upon itself; it cannot see itself, and it cannot feel itself; but it sees, and it feels bodies, by the aid of the body to which it is united.

Its senses place it in relation with everything about it; through them it is related to all parts of the universe; by them it appropriates in some fashion all of nature, and even reascends to its divine author.

V. *The objects of our sensations real*

I studied then the constitution of my senses, which are the universal instruments of the operations of my soul. I gave attentive heed to everything that takes place in them when objects happen to strike them. I meditated upon the effects of

---

[1] The group of organs which constitute the body of man.

those shocks, and upon the relationship that the fibres, which are the seat of them, sustain with one another, and on the most immediate consequences of these relationships.

As I was assured that my soul experiences no modification, except upon occasion of something which happens to and through its senses to that part of the brain which is the immediate seat of feeling and of thought, I considered the play and modifications of the sensory fibres as a sort of representation of the corresponding modifications of my soul.

It is of very little importance for my purpose that I do not err about the existence of bodies. Although the whole material system should be only a phenomenon, a pure appearance, relative to my manner of perceiving and of judging, I should none the less distinguish my sensations from one another. I would not be the less assured that some are in my power, and that others are not at all. I would also be none the less certain that there exists apart from my soul something which excites in it sensations independent of its will. That thing, whatever it may be, is what I term *matter*.

I do not affirm that matter is in effect what it seems to me to be; but I can reasonably affirm, that what seems to be results essentially, both from that which it is itself, as well as from what I am by reference to it. Beings which observe it under other relationships than mine are of a different nature from mine. I would see myself under other relationships, if my nature happened to change.

It would also be wholly indifferent to the purpose of my researches to discuss the different hypotheses which have been made in order to explain the union of the soul and of the body, since all such hypotheses equally suppose a constant relationship between the modifications of the soul and the movements of the body.

It was necessary then always to devote one's attention to the play of the organs. It is fully permitted afterward to translate every reasoning into the special language of the hypothesis that has been adopted. I have confined myself to *physical influence*, not as a fact, but as that which seems to be.

VI. *Specific differences of the sensory fibres*

EACH sense has its mechanics, its manner of action, its end. Each sense transmits to the soul a multitude of different impressions to which correspond a like number of different sensations.

It was not possible for me to conceive of fibres perfectly similar being capable of receiving and transmitting without confusion so many diverse impressions. It has seemed to me, that each sensory fibre would in such a case be like a body impelled at the same time by several forces acting in different directions. This body would thereby receive a composite movement which would be the product of those forces, and which would represent none of those forces in particular.

In assuming this point of view I have not been able to render an account to myself of the difference in my sensations. I have, therefore, been compelled to suppose that there is in each sense certain fibres appropriate to each kind of sensation.

I believe that I have discerned in the organisation of the senses peculiarities which justify my supposition, and I have indicated them.[1] The observations upon the difference of refrangability of colored rays, and upon those of the vibrations of strings of musical instruments, have appeared to me to add an additional degree of probability to that conjecture.

VII. *The physics of reminiscence*

BUT my soul is not limited to feeling through the agency of my senses. It has likewise recollection of that which it has felt. It has the consciousness of the newness of a sensation. A sensation which has been presented to it many times does not affect it precisely as at the first time.

It is always through the senses that objects come to the soul. Those fibres which have been shocked many times cannot be precisely in the state in which they were before they had been disturbed. The repeated action of the object must change them in some respect.

If a particular kind of sensation has been associated with a

[1] Chap. VIII.

special kind of fibre, the recollection of the sensation, or the reminiscence, may have been associated with the present state of the fibre. I have thus conjectured that the *virgin* fibres do not affect the soul precisely as those do which are not so, and I have attributed the feeling of novelty to that state of *virginity* of the sensory fibres.[1]

By virtue of the union of the two substances nothing can take place in the soul without something in the body corresponding to it. It is this something which I have always sought, though I do not flatter myself to have always encountered, and that very often I have only caught a glimpse of it.

VIII. *The action of the soul upon the Senses indicated by the nature and effects of the attention*

My soul has a will, and exerts it. It has certain desires, and is active. This activity, whatever may be its nature, must have a subject on which it displays itself. It has not been possible for me to discover for it any other than the sensory fibres. I have therefore thought that as the senses act upon the soul, so the soul may act in its turn upon the senses.

I have not said that the soul acts after the manner of the body, as it is not body; but I have said that the effect of its action corresponds to that of a body. In one word I have admitted, that the soul causes the sensory fibres to vibrate at its pleasure, and I have not undertaken to investigate the manner of it.

Divers facts have appeared to me to establish that motive power of the soul, and in particular the exercise of attention. When it is too long continued, it gives rise in the soul to that uncomfortable feeling, which we express by the term *fatigue.*

Strictly speaking can fatigue have its seat anywhere else than in the organs? And is it not the soul itself, which occasions fatigue, by an act of its will? If it did not will to be attentive, it would not experience any fatigue. It acts, therefore, upon the fibres which are the seat of this fatigue.

If the fatigue ceases when the soul changes its object, that is

[1] Chap. IX.

because it is acting upon other fibres. For we have seen, that it is probable, that every object has in the brain certain fibres which are adapted to it.

It is by the aid of these principles that I, perhaps the first, have attempted to analyze the nature, and the effects of attention, and to prove that it is this valuable faculty which establishes the most difference between one man and another.[1]

Excellent rules have been given us for directing and fixing the attention; but sufficient investigation has not been made of the physical foundation of these rules. You will never succeed better in guiding man, than when you set out from the physical constitution. It is always through the physical that you must pass to reach the soul.

IX. *The physics of the imagination and of the memory*

THE ideas that objects excite in the soul can be recalled by it without the intervention of objects. This reproduction of ideas is due to imagination, and to memory. I have sought to investigate how they operate, or what is the same thing, wherein consists the physics of the imagination, and of the memory.[2]

The method, that I have followed to succeed, has seemed to me very simple and sufficiently luminous. It is the same that I have pursued in all my psychological researches. I have at first directed my attention to what has immediately preceded. Before investigating how an idea is reproduced, I have investigated how it was produced.

I have clearly seen that the soul never has a new sensation, except through the medium of the senses. It is to the shock of certain fibres that such sensation has been originally associated. Its reproduction or its recall by imagination will still be related to the shock of these same fibres.

Accidents, which can effect only the body, enfeeble and even destroy the imagination and the memory. They have therefore their seat in the body. And how could this seat be anything else than the organs which transmit to the soul all outer impressions.

---

[1] Chaps. XI, XIX, § 628, 530, 533.

[2] Chap. XIV, § 212, 213, 214; chap. XX, § 546; chap. XXII, § 623, 624.

It is therefore my belief that the sensory fibres are constituted in such a manner, that the action more or less continued of the objects produces on them determinations more or less durable, which constitute the physics of memory.

I have never been able to say what these determinations are, because the structure of the sensory fibres is to me unknown. But if sense has its mechanics, I have thought that every kind of sensory fibre can also have its own.

X. *Important remarks upon the sensory fibres*

I HAVE thus regarded each sensory fibre as a very small organ, which has its own functions, or as a very small machine, which the action of the objects keys to the tone which is adapted to it. I have judged that the play or the conduct of the fibre must result essentially from its primordial structure, and this latter from the nature and arrangement of the elements.

It is impossible for me to represent these elements as of the nature of simple bodies. I have regarded them as constituent parts of a small organ, or as the different parts of a small machine, designed to receive, to transmit, and to reproduce the impression of the object to which it has been adapted.

I have therefore supposed that every kind of sensory fibre has been originally patterned upon relationships that are adapted to the manner of acting of its object.

This supposition has not appeared to me gratuitous. If the eye does not act as the ear, it is because its structure is essentially different, because light does not act like sound. The fibres appropriate to different visual sensations have therefore probably another structure than that of fibres adapted to perceptions of hearing.

Nay more: each perception has its peculiar character which makes us distinguish it from every other. For example, every colored ray has an essence which is unchangeable. A red ray for instance does not act precisely as a blue ray. There are consequently still among the fibres of vision certain differences corresponding to those which exist among the rays.

I have not simply admitted that the fibres of sight are finer than those of hearing; that the vibrations of one are more prompt than those of the other; and that among the fibres of sight those which are adapted to the action of red rays are less fine than those which are suited to the action of blue rays. This does not appear to me sufficient to render an account of the phenomena of memory.

I have indeed surmised that oscillations more or less rapid, or other analogous movements, might perhaps suffice to characterize the kind of *sensation*. I have not, however, understood that they can at the same time serve to recall to the soul the memory of the sensation. It has seemed to me that since this memory is connected with the body, it must depend upon some change which happened to the primitive state of the sensory fibres through the action of objects.[1]

I have, therefore, admitted as probable that the state of the fibres upon which an object has acted, is not precisely the same after that action, as it was before. I have conjectured that the sensory fibres thus experience modifications more or less durable, which constitutes the physics of recollection, and of memory.

I have not undertaken to determine in what these modifications consist. I know no fact which could throw light upon this obscure point. But having regarded the sensory fibres as very small organs, it has not been difficult for me to conceive that the constituent parts of these organs may assume with reference to one another new positions, or new relationships, to which was attached the physics of memory.

This is the result of habit, of which so much is said, which has so great an influence in human life, and of which I am not aware that anyone has well developed the principle. I have endeavored to explain how it is formed, rooted, weakened, and obliterated.[2]

I have said on that occasion, " not only does the fibre transmit to the soul the impression of the object, but it recalls to it furthermore the recollection of this impression. This remem-

[1] Chap. VII, § 57, 58, 59.
[2] Chap. IX, p. 96, 97, etc.; chap. XXII, p. 641, 642, etc.

brance differs from the sensation itself only in the degree of its intensity. It has therefore the same origin. It depends then as the sensation itself upon a movement which is aroused in the fibre; but on a weaker movement.

The carrying out of this movement requires a certain disposition in the integral parts of the fibre. The elements, therefore, retain during a period of more or less length, the determinations which they have received from the action of the object. It keys up, so to speak, the fibre to its own tone, and while the fibre remains keyed up in this way, it preserves the power of recalling to the soul the memory of the sensation of the object."

I added finally: "It is necessary therefore to regard the fibre as a very small machine designed to produce a certain movement. The capacity of this small machine to carry out that movement depends originally upon its construction; and that construction differentiates it from every other machine of the same sort. The action of the object makes this capacity active. It is that action which keys up the machine. As soon as it is keyed up it plays at the moment that some impulse occurs."

For the rest, the reader ought not to have much difficulty in understanding, how nature has been able to vary sufficiently the structure of sensory fibres to provide for that prodigious diversity of perceptions which we experience. How much human art, so crude, so imperfect, so limited, varies its productions of the same kind! How many different forms has it not been able to give to a chain! What variety has it not put among the links of different chains! Of how many combinations are not the same elements susceptible! And how will it be when we suppose the elements have been themselves diversified!

ÉTIENNE BONNOT DE CONDILLAC
(1715–1780)

TREATISE ON SENSATIONS

*Translated from the French * by*
FREDERICK C. DE SUMICHRAST

CHAPTER I. THE FIRST NOTIONS OF A MAN POSSESSING THE SENSE OF SMELL ONLY

1. THE notions of our statue being limited to the sense of smell, can include odours only. It cannot have any conception of extent, of form, of anything external to itself, or to its sensations, any more than it can have of colour, sound or taste.

2. If we offer the statue a rose, it will be, in its relation to us, a statue which smells a rose; but in relation to itself, it will be merely the scent itself of the flower.

Therefore, according to the objects which act upon its organ, it will be scent of rose, of carnation, of jasmine, of violet. In a word, odours are, in this respect, merely modifications of the statue itself or modes of being; and it is not capable of believing itself aught else, since these are the only sensations it can feel.

3. Let those philosophers to whom it is so evident that everything is material, put themselves for a moment in the place of the statue, and let them reflect how they could suspect that there exists anything resembling what we call *matter.*

4. We may then already be convinced that it is sufficient to increase or to diminish the number of the senses to cause us to come to conclusions wholly different from those which are at present so natural to us, and our statue, limited to the sense of smell, may thus enable us to comprehend somewhat the class of beings whose notions are the most restricted.

* From *Traité des Sensations*, Paris and London, 1754.

CHAPTER II. OF THE OPERATIONS OF THE MIND IN A MAN LIMITED TO THE SENSE OF SMELL, AND OF THE FACT THAT THE DIFFERENT DEGREES OF PLEASURE AND OF PAIN CONSTITUTE THE PRINCIPLE OF THESE OPERATIONS.

1. With the first odour the capacity for feeling of our statue is wholly taken up by the impression made upon its organ. I call this attention.

2. From that moment it begins to enjoy or to suffer: for if the power of feeling is wholly devoted to a pleasant odour, enjoyment is the result; and if it be wholly devoted to an unpleasant odour, suffering results.

3. But our statue has yet no idea of the different changes it may experience. Therefore it is well; or it is not well, without the desire to be better. Suffering is no more capable of exciting in the statue a longing for an enjoyment of which it has no knowledge, than enjoyment is capable of making it fear an ill of which it is equally ignorant. Consequently, no matter how disagreeable the first sensation may be, even to the point of wounding the organ and of being a violent pain, it cannot cause desire.

While suffering with us is always accompanied by the desire not to suffer, it cannot be so with the statue. Pain creates that desire in us only because the condition of non-suffering is already known to us. The habit we have contracted of looking upon pain as a thing we have been without and of which we may be freed, is the cause that the moment we suffer we immediately desire not to suffer, and this condition is inseparable from a state of suffering.

But the statue which, at the first moment, is conscious of its feeling only through the very pain it experiences, does not know whether it can cease to be a statue and become something else, or cease to exist. It has, as yet, no conception of change, of succession or of duration. Therefore it exists without having the power to form a desire.

4. Once it has observed that it is capable of ceasing to be what it is, in order to become once more what it was before, we shall see its desires spring from a condition of pain, which it will compare with a condition of pleasure recalled to it by memory. Thus it is that pleasure and pain are the sole principle which, determining all the operations of its soul, will gradually raise it to all the knowledge of which it is capable; and in order to determine the progress of which it is susceptible, it will suffice to observe the pleasure it will have to desire, the pains it will have to fear, and the influence of either according to circumstances.

5. Supposing the statue to have no remembrance of the changes it has undergone, then on every occasion of a change it would believe itself to be conscious of sensation for the first time: whole years would be swallowed up in each present moment. Therefore by ever confining its attention to a single mode of being, it would never reckon two together, and would never note their relations to each other: it would enjoy or suffer, without yet knowing desire or fear.

6. But the odour it smells does not, so soon as the odoriferous object ceases to act upon its organ, become wholly lost to the statue. The attention it bestowed upon it still retains the odour, and there remains a more or less strong impression of that odour in proportion as the attention itself has been more or less active. That is memory.

7. When, therefore, our statue is a new odour, there is still present to it the odour that it was the moment before. Its power of feeling is divided between memory and the sense of smell, the former of these faculties being attentive to the past sensation, while the latter is attentive to the present sensation.

8. Thus there are in the statue two modes of feeling, differing only in this, that the one is concerned with a present sensation and the other with a sensation no longer existent, but the impression of which still remains. Unaware of the fact that there are objects which act upon it, unaware even of the fact that it possesses an organ, the statue ordinarily distinguishes between the remembrance of a sensation and a present sensation merely

by dimly feeling what it has been and feeling strongly what it is at the moment.

9. I say *ordinarily*, because remembrance will not always be a faint sentiment, nor sensation a lively one. For every time that memory recalls very strongly these states of being, while, on the contrary, the organ itself receives but slight impressions, the consciousness of a present sensation will be much less vivid than the remembrance of a sensation which has ceased to be.

10. As, therefore, one odour is present to the sense of smell through the impression made by an odoriferous body upon the organ itself, so is another odour present in the memory, because the impression made by another odoriferous body continues in the brain, to which the organ of smell has transmitted it. Passing thus through two states of being, the statue feels that it is no longer what it has been: the knowledge of this change causes it to refer the first state to a different moment from that in which it experiences the second state, and this it is which causes the statue to make a distinction between existing in one way and having existed in another way.

11. The statue is active in relation to one of its two modes of feeling, and passive in relation to the other. It is active when it remembers a sensation, because it has within itself the cause which brings about that recollection, that is memory. It is passive at the moment when it experiences a sensation, because the cause which produces it is external to the statue itself, that is, it lies in the odoriferous bodies which act upon its sense of smell.

12. But, unable even to suspect the action upon itself of objects external to it, it cannot distinguish between a cause within itself and a cause outside of itself. As far as the statue is concerned all the modifications of its state of being appear to it due to itself, and whether it experiences a sensation or merely recalls one, it is never aware of aught save that it is or has been in such and such a state of being. It cannot, therefore, observe any difference between the condition in which it is itself active or that in which it is wholly passive.

13. Nevertheless the more numerous the occasions for the

exercise of the memory the more readily will the memory act. And it is in this way that the statue will acquire the habit of recalling without an effort the changes through which it has passed, and of dividing its attention between what it has been and what it is. For habit is merely the facility of repeating what one has done, and that facility is acquired by the reiteration of the actions.

14. If, after having repeatedly smelled a rose and a carnation, the statue once more smells a rose, the passive attention, acting by the sense of smell, will be wholly given up to the present odour of the rose, and the active attention, which acts through the memory, will be divided between the remains of the scents of the rose and of the carnation. Now these two states of being cannot share the capacity for feeling without comparing themselves one with the other, for comparing is nothing else than bestowing one's attention upon two ideas at the same time.

15. From the moment that comparison exists, judgment exists. Our statue cannot at one and the same time be attentive to the scent of the rose and that of the carnation, without perceiving that the one is not the same as the other, and it cannot be attentive to the odour of a rose which it smells and to that of a rose which it has previously smelled without perceiving that they are a similar modification. Judgment, therefore, is simply the perception of the relation between two ideas which are being compared.

16. As the comparisons and conclusions become more frequent the statue acquires greater facility in making them. It contracts therefore the habit of comparing and judging. Consequently it will be sufficient to make it smell other odours in order to cause it to make additional comparisons, come to additional conclusions and contract new habits.

17. The first sensation it experiences causes no surprise to the statue, for it is as yet unaccustomed to form any kind of judgment, nor is it surprised when, on smelling successively different odours, it perceives each but for a moment. Under these conditions it does not abide by any conclusion it has formed, and the more the statue changes the more it feels itself naturally inclined to change.

Nor will it feel any more surprise if we lead it, by unnoticeable gradations, from the habit of believing itself one odour to the conclusion that it is another odour, for the statue changes without having the power of noticing the change.

But it cannot fail to be surprised if it passes suddenly from a condition to which it was accustomed to a totally different state of which it had no previous conception.

18. This amazement causes it to feel more distinctly the differences between its modes of being. The more abrupt the change from one to the other the greater the astonishment of the statue, and the more is it struck by the contrast between the pleasures and the pains which mark these changes. Its attention, excited by pains which are more keenly felt, applies itself with greater acuteness to the sensations which succeed each other. It therefore compares them more carefully; it judges more accurately their relations to each other. Amazement consequently increases the activity of the operations of its mind. But, because it is by bringing out a more marked opposition between feelings of pleasure and feelings of pain that amazement thus increases activity of mind, it follows that it is always pleasure and pain which are the primary motive cause of its faculties.

19. If each successive odour acts with equal force upon the statue's attention, the memory will remember them in the order in which they followed each other, and they will by this means become connected one with another.

If the series is numerous, the impression made by the most recent odours, being the most recent, will be the strongest; the impression made by the first in order will be imperceptibly weakened, then disappear altogether, and these sensations will be as if they had never been.

But if there be any which have acted but slightly upon the attention, they will leave no impression behind them and will be forgotten as soon as they have been perceived.

Finally the impressions which will have more vividly struck the attention, will be more vividly recalled, and will so strongly engage it that they will be capable of making it forget the others.

20. Memory therefore is a series of ideas forming a sort of

chain. It is this connection which enables us to pass from one idea to another, and to recall the most distant. Therefore we remember an idea that we had some time since only because we recall, more or less rapidly, the intermediary ideas.

21. In the case of the second sensation our statue experiences, it has not to make any selection: it can remember but the first sensation. It will merely act more or less vigorously, according as it is inclined thereto by the intensity of the pleasure or the pain.

But when there has been a succession of changes, the statue, having a great number in remembrance, will be inclined to recall preferably those which can best contribute to its happiness, passing rapidly over the others or dwelling on them only in spite of itself.

To make this truth fully plain it is necessary to know the different degrees of pain and of pleasure of which we are susceptible, and the comparisons which may be drawn between them.

22. Pleasures and pains are of two kinds. Some pertain more especially to the body: they are of the senses; others are within the memory and all the faculties of the soul: these are intellectual or spiritual. But this is a difference which the statue is incapable of observing.

This inability preserves it from an error which we find it difficult to avoid, seeing that these sentiments do not differ one from another as greatly as we imagine. In truth, they are all intellectual and spiritual, since it is the soul only which is capable of feeling. It may be said also that they are all likewise in a certain sense sensible or corporeal, since the body is their sole occasioning cause. It is only with reference to their relation to the faculties of the body or those of the soul that we divide them into two kinds.

23. Pleasure may diminish or increase by degrees; when it diminishes, it tends to disappear, and it vanishes with the sensation. On the contrary, when it increases, it may attain to pain, because the impression becomes too strong for the organ. Thus there are two extreme points in pleasure: the weaker is that in which sensation begins with the least power; it is the first step

from nothingness to feeling; the strongest is that when the sensation cannot augment without ceasing to be agreeable; it is the condition nearest to pain.

The impression of a faint pleasure seems to become concentrated in the organ which transmits it to the soul. But when it has a certain amount of intensity, it is accompanied by an emotion which spreads throughout the whole body. This emotion is a fact which our experience places beyond the shadow of a doubt.

Pain, likewise, may increase or diminish. When it increases it tends to the total destruction of the animal; but, when it diminishes, it does not, like pleasure, tend to the privation of all sense of feeling; on the contrary, the moment which puts an end to it is always pleasant.

24. It is impossible to discover among these various degrees a state of indifference; with the first sensation, no matter how weak it may be, the statue is necessarily ill or well. But once it shall have experienced successively the sharpest pains and the liveliest pleasures, it will consider indifferent, or will cease to regard as agreeable or disagreeable, the weaker sensations which it will have compared with the stronger.

We may therefore suppose that there are for it divers degrees, agreeable or disagreeable, in the modes of being, and others which it regards as indifferent.

25. Whenever it is ill or less well, it recalls its past sensations, compares them with its actual condition, and feels that it is important that it should become once more what it was formerly. Hence springs the need or knowledge of a state of well-being, which it concludes that it needs to enjoy.

Therefore it knows that it has wants only because it compares the pain from which it is suffering with the pleasures it has enjoyed. Destroy in it the remembrance of these pleasures, and the statue will be ill, without suspecting that it has any want, for, in order to feel the need of anything, one must be acquainted with it. Now, in the above supposititious case, the statue is not acquainted with any other state of being than that in which it finds itself. But once it recalls a happier state, its existing condition at once causes it to feel the want of that state. Thus it is that pleasure and pain will always determine the action of its faculties.

26. The want experienced by the statue may be caused by a genuine pain, by a disagreeable sensation, by a sensation less agreeable than those which have preceded it, or, finally, by a state of languor, in which it is reduced to one of those states of being which it has become accustomed to consider indifferent.

If its need is caused by an odour which gives it lively pain, the need appropriates the power of feeling almost wholly, and leaves only strength enough to the memory to remind the statue that it has not always been so ill. Then it becomes incapable of comparing the various states of being through which it has passed; it is unable to judge which is the most agreeable. All that it desires is to emerge from that condition in order to enjoy another, no matter what it may be; and if it were acquainted with a means of escaping from its suffering, it would apply all its faculties to the making use of that means. It is thus that in serious sickness we cease to desire the pleasures we formerly ardently sought, and think only of regaining our health.

When it is a less agreeable sensation which gives rise to the want, there are two cases to be distinguished: either the pleasures with which the statue compares that sensation have been lively, and accompanied by the strongest emotions, or else they have been less powerful and have scarcely moved it.

In the former case, the past happiness is recalled with the greater force the more it differs from the immediate sensation. The emotion which accompanied it is partly reproduced, and drawing to itself almost the totality of the power of feeling, does not permit the agreeable feelings which have preceded or followed it to be noticed. The statue, then, experiencing no distraction, compares more accurately that happiness with its present state; it judges more truly how greatly that state differs from the former, and, as it endeavours to depict it to itself in the most vivid manner, the privation of that happiness gives rise to a more insistent need, and the possession of it becomes a much more necessary welfare.

In the second case, on the contrary, that state of happiness is recalled with much less intensity: other pleasures divide the attention; the advantages it offers are less felt; it reproduces but little emotion or none at all. Therefore the statue is less interested in its return, and does not apply its faculties to it so earnestly.

Finally, if the need springs from one of those sensations which it has got into the habit of considering indifferent, it lives at first without feeling either pain or pleasure. But this state, compared with the happy situations in which it has found itself, soon becomes disagreeable to the statue, and the pain it then experiences is what we term *ennui*. Meanwhile the ennui lasts, increases, becomes unbearable, and determines powerfully all the faculties towards that happiness of which the statue feels the loss.

This ennui may be as crushing as pain, in which case the statue has no other thought than to get rid of it, and turns, without selecting, to all the conditions of being which are fitted to cause it to disappear. But if we diminish the burden of ennui the condition of the statue will be less unhappy, it will feel less imperiously the need of being rid of it, it will be in a condition to devote its attention to all the agreeable sentiments of which it has any recollection, and it is the pleasure, the remembrance of which it recalls in the liveliest manner, which will draw all the faculties to itself.

27. There are then two principles which determine the degree of action of its faculties: on the one hand, the lively remembrance of a well-being it has lost; on the other, the small amount of pleasure in the sensation actually felt, or else the pain by which it is accompanied.

When these two principles unite, the statue makes a greater effort to recall what it has ceased to be, and it feels less what it actually is. For its power of feeling being necessarily limited, memory cannot attract a part of this power to itself without leaving less to the sense of smell. Even if the action of this faculty should be so strong as to appropriate to itself the whole power of feeling, the statue will not observe any more the impression made upon its organ, and it will recall its former condition in so lively a manner that it will believe itself to be still in that condition.

28. But if its actual condition is the happiest it knows, then pleasure induces it to enjoy it by preference. There no longer exists any cause capable of inducing the mind to act strongly enough to overbear the sense of smell to the extent of destroying the feeling in it. Pleasure, on the contrary, concentrates at least the greater part of the attention or of the capacity for feeling upon the present sensation; and if the statue even yet recalls what it has been, it is because the comparison with its present state causes it to enjoy its happiness still more.

29. Here then are two of the effects of memory: the one is a sensation which is recalled as strongly as if it were acting upon the organ itself; the other is a sensation of which naught remains but a faint recollection.

There are thus in the action of this faculty of memory two degrees which we can establish: the weaker is that in which it causes pleasure in the past to but a slight extent; the other that in which it causes enjoyment of that past just as if the past were the present.

It is called *memory* when it recalls things as past only, and it is called *imagination* when it recalls them so strongly that they appear to be present. Imagination, therefore, is found in our statue, as well as memory, and these two faculties differ in degree only. Memory is the beginning of an imagination which is yet still weak; imagination is memory itself, which has attained the fullest power of which it is susceptible.

Having distinguished two forms of attention in the statue, the one acting through the sense of smell, the other through the memory, we may now note a third, which acts through the imagination, and the peculiarity of which is to stay the impressions of the senses in order to substitute in their place a feeling independent of external objects.

30. Nevertheless when the statue imagines a sensation which it no longer is experiencing, and when it recalls it in as lively a manner as if it were still experiencing it, it is not aware that there exists in itself a cause which produces the same effect as would

be produced by an odoriferous body acting upon its organ of smell. It cannot therefore distinguish, as we do, between imagination and feeling.

31. But we may presume that the imagination of the statue will be more active than is our own. Its power of feeling is wholly concentrated on a single kind of sensation; the whole force of its faculties is devoted solely to odours; nothing can distract it. But we are divided between a multitude of sensations and ideas, which are constantly assailing us, and, devoting to our imagination but a part of our powers, we imagine but feebly. Besides, our senses, continually on their guard against our imagination, warn us constantly of the objects we seek to imagine, while, on the contrary, the imagination of our statue is entirely free to act. Therefore it recalls trustingly an odour which it has enjoyed, and it does actually enjoy it, just as if its sense of smell were affected by it. Finally the ease with which we can put aside things offensive to us, and seek those the enjoyment of which we prize, further contributes to render our imagination lazy. But since our statue can escape from a disagreeable feeling only by imagining strongly a condition of being in which it takes pleasure, its imagination is more exercised by it, and must produce effects out of the power of our own to attain.

32. Yet there is one case in which the action of the statue's imagination is wholly suspended, and even also that of memory. It is when a sensation is so vivid as to fulfil completely the power of feeling. Then the statue is wholly passive. Pleasure becomes for it a species of intoxication, in which there is scarcely any enjoyment, and pain a crushing in which it scarcely suffers.

33. But the moment the sensation loses some degrees of its intensity, forthwith the faculties of the soul become active once more, and need becomes once again the cause which determines their action.

34. The modifications which must give the greatest pleasure to the statue are not always those it has most recently experienced. They may occur in the beginning or in the middle of the chain of its knowledge, or at the end. Imagination, therefore, is frequently compelled to pass rapidly over intermediate

ideas. It brings nearer the more distant, changes the order they were in in the memory, and out of them forms an entirely new chain.

The connection of ideas does not then follow the same order in its faculties. The more that order it derives from the imagination becomes familiar to the statue, the less will it preserve that order which memory has furnished it with. Thus ideas are connected in innumerable different ways, and often the statue will recall less the order in which it experienced its sensations than the order in which it has imagined them to be.

35. All these series, however, are formed only through the comparisons which have been made between each preceding and each succeeding link in the chain, and through the conclusions which have been drawn concerning their relation to each other. This connection becomes stronger in proportion as the use of the faculties strengthens the habits of recollection and imagination; and this is the reason why we possess the surprising advantage of recognizing sensations we have already experienced.

36. For, indeed, if we cause our statue to smell an odour with which it is familiar, it is a state of being which it has compared, which it has drawn a conclusion from, and which it has linked to some of the parts of the series which its memory is in the habit of reviewing. That is why it concludes that the state in which it finds itself is the same as that in which it formerly found itself. But an odour which it has not yet smelled does not come within this case, and therefore must strike it as quite new.

37. It is needless to point out that when it recognizes a state of being it does so without being able to account for the fact. The cause of a phenomenon of this sort is so difficult to make out that all men who do not know how to observe and analyze what is going on within them, are unable to perceive it.

38. But when the statue goes on a long time without thinking of a state of being, what becomes, during that period, of the idea it has formed of that state? When, later, that idea is recalled by the memory, whence does it spring? Is it in the soul or in the body that it has been preserved? In neither.

It is not in the soul, since an alteration in the brain is sufficient to destroy the power of recalling the idea.

It is not in the body. The physical cause alone could be preserved there, and for that it would be necessary to suppose that the brain would remain precisely in the condition into which it was brought by the sensation which the statue remembers. But how can that supposition be maintained in view of the continual movements of the mind? How can it be maintained, especially when one considers the innumerable ideas stored in the memory? The phenomenon may be explained in a much simpler way.

I experience a given sensation when there occurs in one of my organs a movement which is transmitted to the brain. If the same movement originates in the brain and is transmitted to the organ, I believe I experience a sensation which I do not really experience: it is an illusion. But if the movement begins and ends in the brain, I remember the sensation I have experienced.

When the statue recalls an idea, then, it is not because the idea has been preserved in the body or in the soul; it is because the movement, which is the physical and occasioning cause of it, is reproduced in the brain. This, however, is not the place to venture on conjectures concerning the mechanism of memory. We preserve the remembrance of our sensations, we recall them, although we have been a long time without thinking of them. To bring this about it is sufficient that they should have strongly impressed themselves upon us, or that we should have experienced them repeatedly. These facts authorize me to suppose that our statue, organized as we are, is, like ourselves, able to remember.

39. We conclude then that it has contracted several habits: the habit of bestowing its attention; the habit of remembering; a third habit of comparing; a fourth of judging; a fifth of imagining; and finally one of recognizing.

40. The same causes which have produced habits are alone capable of maintaining them. I mean that habits will become lost unless they are renewed by actions reiterated from time to time. In that case our statue will recall neither the comparisons

between states of being which it has made, nor the conclusions it has drawn from them, and it will experience a state of being for the third or fourth time without being able to recognize it.

41. But we may ourselves help to maintain the practice of its memory and of all its faculties. It is sufficient to induce it, by different degrees of pleasure or of pain, to cling to its state of being or to escape from it. The skill with which we make use of its sensations will enable us to fortify and extend more and more its habits. There is even ground for conjecturing that the statue will distinguish, in a succession of odours, differences which we fail to note. Compelled to apply all its faculties to a single sort of sensation, may not the statue exhibit more discernment therein than we do?

42. Yet the relations which its judgment can discover are very few in number. It merely is aware that one state of being is the same as a state in which it has already been, or else that it is different; that the one is agreeable, the other disagreeable, and both in a greater or less degree.

But will it distinguish between several odours smelled together? That is a power of discernment which we ourselves acquire only by long practice, and even then within very narrow limits, for there is no one who can recognize by the sense of smell all the components of a sachet. Now it seems to me that any mingling of odours must be a sachet to our statue.

It is the knowledge of odoriferous bodies, as we shall see later, which has taught us to recognize two odours within a third. After having smelled in turn a rose and a jonquil, we smelled them together, and thus learned that the sensation caused in us by these two flowers together is composed of two other sensations. But if the odours be multiplied we can distinguish those only which are strongest, and even then we shall not distinguish these if the mingling has been made so skilfully that no one odour shall prevail over the others. In such a case they appear to pass one into another, like colours ground up together; they unite and mingle so thoroughly that not one of them remains what it originally was, and of many odours one alone remains.

So if our statue, at the first moment of its existence, smells two odours, it will not conclude that it is at one and the same time in two states of being. But let us suppose that having learned to know them separately, it smells them together: will it recognize them? That does not appear probable to me. For, unaware that they come from two different bodies, nothing can lead it to suspect that the sensation it experiences is the sum of two other sensations. Indeed, if neither prevail, it would be the same with us, and if one of the two is fainter, it will merely alter the stronger and they will together seem to be a simple state of being. To convince ourselves of this we need only smell odours which we are not accustomed to refer to separate bodies; I am persuaded that we would not venture to affirm whether they are one odour or several odours. And this is precisely the case of the statue.

Therefore the statue acquires discernment only through the attention it gives at one and the same time to a state of being which it is actually experiencing and to another state which it has previously experienced. Thus its judgments do not bear upon two odours smelled at one and the same time, but upon successive sensations.

CHAPTER III. OF THE DESIRES, THE PASSIONS, LOVE, HATE, HOPE, FEAR AND WILL IN A MAN LIMITED TO THE SENSE OF SMELL

1. We have just seen the character of the various kinds of wants, and that they are the causes of the degrees of intensity with which the faculties of the soul attach themselves to a state of well-being, the enjoyment of which becomes a necessity. Now desire is nothing else than the action of these faculties, when these are directed towards the thing of which we feel the need.

2. Therefore every desire presupposes that the statue conceives of a condition better than the one wherein it finds itself at the time, and that it compares the difference between two states of being succeeding each other. If they differ but little, its suffering is less, in consequence of the deprivation of the mode of being

that it desires; and I give the name of *discomfort* or *slight discontent*, to the feeling it experiences. In such a case both the action of its faculties is less energetic and its desires are less strong. On the contrary, it suffers more if the difference be great, and I give the name of *anxiety*, or even of *torment*, to the impression it then experiences. Therefore the difference between these two states is the measure of the desire, and it is sufficient to remember by how much the action of the faculties gains or loses in intensity in order to know all the degrees of desires.

3. For instance, they are never so violent as when the faculties of the statue tend to a state of well-being the loss of which causes an anxiety the greater in proportion to the difference of that wished-for state from the existing state. In such cases, nothing can distract the statue's attention from that condition: it recalls it, it imagines it; all its faculties are concentrated upon it. Consequently the more it desires it, the more it accustoms itself to desire. In a word, it feels for it what we call a *passion*, that is, a desire which prevents our feeling any other, or at least is the most powerful one.

4. This passion persists so long as the state which is the object of it continues to appear the most agreeable, and so long as the absence of that state is accompanied by the same anxieties. But it is replaced by another passion, if the statue has occasion to become accustomed to another condition to which it will give the preference.

5. From the moment that enjoyment, suffering, need, desire, passion exist in the statue, love and hate exist likewise. For the statue loves a pleasant odour, which it enjoys or desires. It hates a disagreeable odour, which causes it to suffer; finally, it likes less a less agreeable odour, which it would fain exchange for another. In proof of this, it is sufficient to note that to love is always synonymous with to enjoy or to desire, and that to hate is similarly synonymous with suffering from discomfort, from discontent, in the presence of some object.

6. As there may be several gradations in the amount of anxiety caused by the loss of a pleasant object, and in the discontent caused by the sight of an odious one, so may similar gradations

be noted in love and in hate. Indeed we even have words to denote them: such as taste, inclination, tendency, aloofness, repugnance, disgust. Although these words cannot be substituted for the words love, hate, none the less the feelings they express are but the beginnings of these passions; they differ from these merely in being weaker.

7. For the rest, the love of which our statue is capable, is but love of self, or that which bears the name of self-love. For, in truth, it loves but itself, seeing that the things it loves are but its own states of being.

8. Hope and fear spring from the same principle as love and hate.

Our statue, being in the habit of experiencing agreeable or disagreeable sensations, is led to conclude that it can experience further sensations of the same sort. If this conclusion combines with a sensation which pleases, it produces hope; and if it combines with a sensation that displeases, it causes fear. For, in fact, to hope is to flatter one's self that one shall possess a certain good; to fear, is to be threatened by an evil. It may be noted that hope and fear contribute to increase desire. It is from the conflict of these two feelings that the most violent passions arise.

9. The remembrance that it has satisfied some of its desires causes our statue to hope all the more to be able to satisfy other desires, that, unaware of the obstacles which stand in the way, it does not see why what it desires should not be within its power, like what it has desired on other occasions. It is true that the statue cannot make sure of this, but, on the other hand, it has no proof of the contrary. If it more particularly remembers that the same desire which it feels has formerly been followed by enjoyment, it will believe itself capable of realizing it in proportion as its want of it becomes greater. Thus two causes will contribute to inspire it with confidence: the knowledge that it has satisfied such a desire before, and its interest in satisfying it once again. Henceforth the statue will not be satisfied with desiring; it will *will;* for by *will* is meant an absolute desire, such that we consider that a thing we desire is in our power.

CHAPTER VI. OF THE EGO, OR PERSONALITY OF A MAN LIMITED TO THE SENSE OF SMELL

1. Our statue being capable of remembering, it is no sooner one odour than it remembers that it has been another. That is its personality, for if it could say *I*, it would say it at every instant of its own duration, and each time its *I* would comprise all the moments it remembered.

2. True, it would not say it at the first odour. What is meant by that term seems to me to suit only a being which notes in the present moment, that it is no longer what it has been. So long as it does not change, it exists without thought of itself; but as soon as it changes, it concludes that it is the selfsame which was formerly in such another state, and it says *I*.

This observation confirms the fact that in the first instant of its existence the statue cannot form desires, for before being able to say *I wish*, one must have said *I*.

3. The odours which the statue does not remember do not therefore enter into the notion it has of its own person. Being as foreign to its *Ego* as are colours and sounds, of which it has no knowledge, they are, in respect of the statue, as if the statue had never smelled them. Its *Ego* is but the sum of the sensations it experiences and of those which memory recalls to it. In a word, it is at once the consciousness of what it is and the remembrance of what it has been.

CHAPTER VII. CONCLUSIONS FROM THE PRECEDING CHAPTERS

1. Having proved that the statue is capable of being attentive, of remembering, of comparing, of judging, of discerning, of imagining; that it possesses abstract notions, notions of number and duration; that it is acquainted with general and particular truths; that desires are formed by it, that it has the power of passions, loves, hates, wills; and finally that it contracts habits, we must conclude that the mind is endowed with as many facul-

ties when it has but a single organ as when it has five. We shall see that the faculties which appear to be peculiar to us are nothing else than the same faculties which, applied to a greater number of objects, develop more fully.

2. If we consider that to remember, compare, judge, discern, imagine, be astonished, have abstract notions, have notions of duration and number, know general and particular truths, are but different modes of attention; that to have passions, to love, to hate, to hope, to fear and to will are but different modes of desire, and that, finally, attention and desire are in their essence but sensation, we shall conclude that sensation calls out all the faculties of the soul.

3. Lastly, if we consider that there are no absolutely indifferent sensations, we shall further conclude that the different degrees of pleasure and of pain constitute the law according to which the germ of all that we are has developed in order to produce all our faculties.

This principle may be called want, astonishment, or otherwise, but it remains ever the same, for we are always moved by pleasure or by pain in whatever we are led to do by need or astonishment.

The fact is that our earliest notions are pain or pleasure only. Many others soon follow these, and give rise to comparisons, whence spring our earliest needs and our earliest desires. Our researches, undertaken for the purpose of satisfying these needs and desires, cause us to acquire additional notions which in their turn produce new desires. The surprise which makes us feel intensely any extraordinary thing happening to us, increases from time to time the activity of our faculties, and there is formed a chain the links of which are alternately notions and desires, and it is sufficient to follow up this chain to discover the progress of the enlightening of man.

4. Nearly all that I have said about the faculties of the soul, while treating of the sense of smell, I might have said if I had taken any other sense; it is easy to apply all to each of the senses. I have now only to examine what is peculiar to each of them.

•   •   •   •   •   •   •   •   •   •   •   •

THOMAS REID

(1710–1796)

ESSAYS ON THE INTELLECTUAL POWERS OF MAN*

ESSAY II. OF THE POWERS WE HAVE BY MEANS OF OUR EXTERNAL SENSES

CHAPTER V. — OF PERCEPTION

In speaking of the impressions made on our organs in perception, we build upon facts borrowed from anatomy and physiology, for which we have the testimony of our senses. But, being now to speak of perception itself, which is solely an act of the mind, we must appeal to another authority. The operations of our minds are known, not by sense, but by consciousness, the authority of which is as certain and as irresistible as that of sense.

In order, however, to our having a distinct notion of any of the operations of our own minds, it is not enough that we be conscious of them; for all men have this consciousness. It is farther necessary that we attend to them while they are exerted, and reflect upon them with care, while they are recent and fresh in our memory. It is necessary that, by employing ourselves frequently in this way, we get the habit of this attention and reflection; and, therefore, for the proof of facts which I shall have occasion to mention upon this subject, I can only appeal to the reader's own thoughts, whether such facts are not agreeable to what he is conscious of in his own mind.

If, therefore, we attend to that act of our mind which we call the perception of an external object of sense, we shall find in it these three things: — *First*, Some conception or notion of the

* Edinburgh, 1785.

object perceived; *Secondly*, A strong and irresistible conviction and belief of its present existence; and, *Thirdly*, That this conviction and belief are immediate, and not the effect of reasoning.

First, It is impossible to perceive an object without having some notion or conception of that which we perceive. We may, indeed, conceive an object which we do not perceive; but, when we perceive the object, we must have some conception of it at the same time; and we have commonly a more clear and steady notion of the object while we perceive it, than we have from memory or imagination when it is not perceived. Yet, even in perception, the notion which our senses give of the object may be more or less clear, more or less distinct, in all possible degrees.

Thus we see more distinctly an object at a small than at a great distance. An object at a great distance is seen more distinctly in a clear than in a foggy day. An object seen indistinctly with the naked eye, on account of its smallness, may be seen distinctly with a microscope. The objects in this room will be seen by a person in the room less and less distinctly as the light of the day fails; they pass through all the various degrees of distinctness according to the degrees of the light, and, at last, in total darkness they are not seen at all. What has been said of the objects of sight is so easily applied to the objects of the other senses, that the application may be left to the reader.

In a matter so obvious to every person capable of reflection, it is necessary only farther to observe, that the notion which we get of an object, merely by our external sense, ought not to be confounded with that more scientific notion which a man, come to the years of understanding, may have of the same object, by attending to its various attributes, or to its various parts, and their relation to each other, and to the whole. Thus, the notion which a child has of a jack for roasting meat, will be acknowledged to be very different from that of a man who understands its construction, and perceives the relation of the parts to one another, and to the whole. The child sees the jack and every part of it as well as the man. The child, therefore, has all the notion of it which sight gives; whatever there is more in the notion which the man forms of it, must be derived from other powers of the mind, which may afterwards be explained. This observation is made here only that we may not confound the operations of different powers of the mind, which by being always conjoined after we grow up to understanding, are apt to pass for one and the same.

Secondly, In perception we not only have a notion more or less distinct of the object perceived, but also an irresistible conviction and belief of its existence. This is always the case when we are certain that we perceive it. There may be a perception so faint and indistinct as to leave us in doubt whether we perceive the object or not. Thus, when a star begins to twinkle as the light of the sun withdraws, one may, for a short time, think he sees it without being certain, until the perception acquire some strength and steadiness. When a ship just begins to appear in the utmost verge of the horizon, we may at first be dubious whether we perceive it or not; but when the perception is in any degree clear and steady, there remains no doubt of its reality; and when the reality of the perception is ascertained, the existence of the object perceived can no longer be doubted.

By the laws of all nations, in the most solemn judicial trials, wherein men's fortunes and lives are at stake, the sentence passes according to the testimony of eye or ear witnesses of good credit. An upright judge will give a fair hearing to every objection that can be made to the integrity of a witness, and allow it to be possible that he may be corrupted; but no judge will ever suppose that witnesses may be imposed upon by trusting to their eyes and ears. And if a sceptical counsel should plead against the testimony of the witnesses, that they had no other evidence for what they declared but the testimony of their eyes and ears, and that we ought not to put so much faith in our senses as to deprive men of life or fortune upon their testimony, surely no upright judge would admit a plea of this kind. I believe no counsel, however sceptical, ever dared to offer such an argument; and, if it was offered, it would be rejected with disdain.

Can any stronger proof be given that it is the universal judgment of mankind that the evidence of sense is a kind of evidence which we may securely rest upon in the most momentous concerns of mankind; that it is a kind of evidence against which we ought not to admit any reasoning; and, therefore that to reason either for or against it is an insult to common sense?

The whole conduct of mankind in the daily occurrences of life, as well as the solemn procedure of judicatories in the trial of causes civil and criminal, demonstrates this. I know only of two exceptions that may be offered against this being the universal belief of mankind.

The first exception is that of some lunatics who have been persuaded of things that seem to contradict the clear testimony of their senses. It is said there have been lunatics and hypochondriacal persons, who seriously believed themselves to be made of glass; and, in consequence of this, lived in continual terror of having their brittle frame shivered into pieces.

All I have to say to this is, that our minds, in our present state, are, as well as our bodies, liable to strange disorders; and, as we do not judge of the natural constitution of the body from the disorders or diseases to which it is subject from accidents, so neither ought we to judge of the natural powers of the mind from its disorders, but from its sound state. It is natural to man, and common to the species, to have two hands and two feet; yet I have seen a man, and a very ingenious one, who was born without either hands or feet. It is natural to man to have faculties superior to those of brutes; yet we see some individuals whose faculties are not equal to those of many brutes; and the wisest man may, by various accidents, be reduced to this state. General rules that regard those whose intellects are sound are not overthrown by instances of men whose intellects are hurt by any constitutional or accidental disorder.

The other exception that may be made to the principle we have laid down is that of some philosophers who have maintained that the testimony of sense is fallacious, and therefore ought never to be trusted. Perhaps it might be a sufficient answer to this to say, that there is nothing so absurd which some philosophers have not maintained. It is one thing to profess a doctrine of this kind, another seriously to believe it, and to be governed by it in the conduct of life. It is evident that a man who did not believe his senses could not keep out of harm's way an hour of his life; yet, in all the history of philosophy, we never read of any sceptic that ever stepped into fire or water because he did not believe his senses, or that shewed in the conduct of life less trust in his senses than other men have. This gives us just ground to apprehend that philosophy was never able to conquer that natural belief which men have in their senses; and that all their subtile reasonings against this belief were never able to persuade themselves.

It appears, therefore, that the clear and distinct testimony of our senses carries irresistible conviction along with it to every man in his right judgment.

I observed, *Thirdly*, That this conviction is not only irresistible, but it is immediate; that is, it is not by a train of reasoning and argumentation that we come to be convinced of the existence of what we perceive; we ask no argument for the existence of the object, but that we perceive it; perception commands our belief upon its own authority, and disdains to rest its authority upon any reasoning whatsoever.

The conviction of a truth may be irresistible, and yet not immediate. Thus, my conviction that the three angles of every plain triangle are equal to two right angles, is irresistible, but it is not immediate; I am convinced of it by demonstrative reasoning. There are other truths in mathematics of which we have not only an irresistible but an immediate conviction. Such are the axioms. Our belief of the axioms in mathematics is not grounded upon argument — arguments are grounded upon them; but their evidence is discerned immediately by the human understanding.

It is, no doubt, one thing to have an immediate conviction of a self-evident axiom; it is another thing to have an immediate conviction of the existence of what we see; but the conviction is equally immediate and equally irresistible in both cases. No man thinks of seeking a reason to believe what he sees; and, before we are capable of reasoning, we put no less confidence in our senses than after. The rudest savage is as fully convinced of what he sees, and hears, and feels, as the most expert logician. The constitution of our understanding determines us to hold the truth of a mathematical axiom as a first principle, from which other truths may be deduced, but it is deduced from none; and the constitution of our power of perception determines us to hold the existence of what we distinctly perceive as a first principle, from which other truths may be deduced; but it is deduced from none. What has been said of the irresistible and immediate belief of the existence of objects distinctly perceived, I mean only to affirm with regard to persons so far advanced in understanding as to distinguish objects of mere imagination from things which have a real existence. Every man knows that he may have a notion of Don Quixote, or of Garagantua, without any belief that such persons ever existed; and that of Julius Cæsar and Oliver Cromwell, he has not only a notion, but a belief that they did really exist. But whether children, from the time that they begin to use their senses, make a distinction between things which are only conceived or imagined, and things which really exist, may be doubted. Until we are able to make this distinction, we cannot properly be said to believe or to disbelieve the existence of anything. The belief of the existence of anything seems to suppose a notion of existence — a notion too abstract, perhaps, to enter into the mind of an infant. I speak of the power of perception in those that are adult and of a sound mind, who believe that there are some things which do really exist; and that there are many things conceived by themselves, and by others, which have no existence. That such persons do invariably ascribe existence to everything which they distinctly perceive, without seeking reasons or arguments for doing so, is perfectly evident from the whole tenor of human life.

The account I have given of our perception of external objects, is intended as a faithful delineation of what every man, come to years of understanding, and capable of giving attention to what passes in his own mind, may feel in himself. In what manner the notion of external objects, and the immediate belief of their existence, is produced by means of our senses, I am not able to shew, and I do not pretend to shew. If the power of perceiving external objects in certain circumstances, be a part of the original constitution of the human mind, all attempts to account for it will be vain. No other account can be given of the constitution of things, but the will of Him that made them. As we can give no reason why matter is extended and inert, why the mind thinks and is conscious of its thoughts, but the will of Him who made both; so I suspect we can give no other reason why, in certain circumstances, we perceive external objects, and in others do not.

The Supreme Being intended that we should have such knowledge of the material objects that surround us, as is necessary in order to our supplying the wants of nature, and avoiding the dangers to which we are constantly exposed; and he has admirably fitted our powers of perception to this purpose. If the intelligence we have of external objects were to be got by reasoning only, the greatest part of men would be destitute of it; for the greatest part of men hardly ever learn to reason; and in infancy and childhood no man can reason: Therefore, as this intelligence of the objects that surround us, and from which we may receive so much benefit or harm, is equally necessary to children and to men, to the ignorant and to the learned, God in his wisdom conveys it to us in a way that puts all upon a level. The information of the senses is as perfect, and gives as full conviction to the most ignorant as to the most learned.

CHAPTER XVI. OF SENSATION

HAVING finished what I intend, with regard to that act of mind which we call the preception of an external object, I proceed to consider another, which, by our constitution, is conjoined with perception, and not with perception only, but with many other acts of our minds; and that is sensation.

Almost all our perceptions have corresponding sensations which constantly accompany them, and, on that account, are very apt to be confounded with them. Neither ought we to expect that the sensation, and its corresponding perception, should be distinguished in common language, because the purposes of common life do not require it. Language is made to serve the purposes of ordinary conversation; and we have no reason to expect that it should make distinctions that are not of common use. Hence it happens, that a quality perceived, and the sensation corresponding to that perception, often go under the same name.

This makes the names of most of our sensations ambiguous, and this ambiguity hath very much perplexed philosophers. It will be necessary to give some instances, to illustrate the distinction between our sensations and the objects of perception.

When I smell a rose, there is in this operation both sensation and perception. The agreeable odour I feel, considered by itself, without relation to any external object, is merely a sensation. It affects the mind in a certain way; and this affection of the mind may be conceived, without a thought of the rose, or any other object. This sensation can be nothing else than it is felt to be. Its very essence consists in being felt; and, when it is not felt, it is not. There is no difference between the sensation and the feeling of it — they are one and the same thing. It is for this reason that we before observed that, in sensation, there is no object distinct from that act of the mind by which it is felt — and this holds true with regard to all sensations.

Let us next attend to the perception which we have in smelling a rose. Perception has always an external object; and the object of my perception, in this case, is that quality in the rose which I discern by the sense of smell. Observing that the agreeable sensation is raised when the rose is near, and ceases when it is removed, I am led, by my nature, to conclude some quality to be in the rose, which is the cause of this sensation. This quality in the rose is the object perceived; and that act of my mind by which I have the conviction and belief of this quality, is what in this case I call perception.

But it is here to be observed, that the sensation I feel, and the quality in the rose which I perceive, are both called by the same name. The smell of a rose is the name given to both: so that this name hath two meanings; and the distinguishing its different meanings removes all perplexity, and enables us to give clear and distinct answers to questions about which philosophers have held much dispute.

Thus, if it is asked, whether the smell be in the rose, or in the mind that feels it, the answer is obvious: That there are two different things signified by the smell of a rose; one of which is in the mind, and can be in nothing but in a sentient being; the other is truly and properly in the rose. The sensation which I feel is in my mind. The mind is the sentient being; and, as the rose is insentient, there can be no sensation, nor anything resembling sensation in it. But this sensation in my mind is occasioned by a certain quality in the rose, which is called by the same name with the sensation, not on account of any similitude, but because of their constant concomitancy.

All the names we have for smells, tastes, sounds, and for the various degrees of heat and cold, have a like ambiguity; and what has been said of the smell of a rose may be applied to them. They signify both a sensation, and a quality perceived by means of that sensation. The first is the sign, the last the thing signified. As both are conjoined by nature, and as the purposes of common life do not require them to be disjoined in our thoughts, they are both expressed by the same name: and this ambiguity is to be found in all languages, because the reason of it extends to all.

The same ambiguity is found in the names of such diseases as are indicated by a particular painful sensation: such as the toothache, the headache. The toothache signifies a painful sensation, which can only be in a sentient being; but it signifies also a disorder in the body, which has no similitude to a sensation, but is naturally connected with it.

Pressing my hand with force against the table, I feel pain, and I feel the table to be hard. The pain is a sensation of the mind, and there is nothing that resembles it in the table. The hardness is in the table, nor is there anything resembling it in the mind. Feeling is applied to both; but in a different sense; being a word common to the act of sensation, and to that of perceiving by the sense of touch.

I touch the table gently with my hand, and I feel it to be smooth, hard, and cold. These are qualities of the table perceived by touch; but I perceive them by means of a sensation which indicates them. This sensation not being painful, I commonly give no attention to it. It carries my thought immediately to the thing signified by it, and is itself forgot, as if it had never been. But, by repeating it, and turning my attention to it, and abstracting my thought from the thing signified by it, I find it to be merely a sensation, and that it has no similitude to the hardness, smoothness, or coldness of the table, which are signified by it.

It is indeed difficult, at first, to disjoin things in our attention which have always been conjoined, and to make that an object of reflection which never was so before; but some pains and practice will overcome this difficulty in those who have got the habit of reflecting on the operations of their own minds.

Although the present subject leads us only to consider the sensations which we have by means of our external senses, yet it will serve to illustrate what has been said, and, I apprehend, is of importance in itself, to observe, that many operations of mind, to which we give one name, and which we always consider as one thing, are complex in their nature, and made up of several more simple ingredients; and of these ingredients sensation very often makes one. Of this we shall give some instances.

The appetite of hunger includes an uneasy sensation, and a desire of food. Sensation and desire are different acts of mind. The last, from its nature, must have an object; the first has no object. These two ingredients may always be separated in thought — perhaps they sometimes are, in reality; but hunger includes both.

Benevolence towards our fellow-creatures includes an agreeable feeling; but it includes also a desire of the happiness of others. The ancients commonly called it desire. Many moderns choose rather to call it a feeling. Both are right: and they only err who exclude either of the ingredients. Whether these two ingredients are necessarily connected, is, perhaps, difficult for us to determine, there being many necessary connections which we do not perceive to be necessary; but we can disjoin them in thought. They are different acts of the mind.

An uneasy feeling, and a desire, are, in like manner, the ingredients of malevolent affections; such as malice, envy, revenge. The passion of fear includes an uneasy sensation or feeling, and an opinion of danger; and hope is made up of the contrary ingredients. When we hear of a heroic action, the sentiment which it raises in our mind, is made up of various ingredients. There is in it an agreeable feeling, a benevolent affection to the person, and a judgment or opinion of his merit.

If we thus analyse the various operations of our minds, we shall find that many of them which we consider as perfectly simple, because we have been accustomed to call them by one name, are compounded of more simple ingredients; and that sensation, or feeling, which is only a more refined kind of sensation, makes one ingredient, not only in the perception of external objects, but in most operations of the mind.

A small degree of reflection may satisfy us that the number and variety of our sensations and feelings is prodigious; for, to omit all those which accompany our appetites, passions, and affections, our moral sentiments and sentiments of taste, even our external senses, furnish a great variety of sensations, differing in kind, and almost in every kind an endless variety of degrees. Every variety we discern, with regard to taste, smell, sound, colour, heat, and cold, and in the tangible qualities of bodies, is indicated by a sensation corresponding to it.

The most general and the most important division of our sensations and feelings, is into the agreeable, the disagreeable, and the indifferent. Everything we call pleasure, happiness, or enjoyment, on the one hand; and, on the other, everything we call misery, pain, or uneasiness, is sensation or feeling; for no man can for the present be more happy or more miserable than he feels himself to be. He cannot be deceived with regard to the enjoyment or suffering of the present moment.

But I apprehend that, besides the sensations that are either agreeable or disagreeable, there is still a greater number that are indifferent. To these we give so little attention, that they have no name, and are immediately forgot, as if they had never been; and it requires attention to the operations of our minds to be convinced of their existence.

For this end we may observe, that, to a good ear, every human voice is distinguishable from all others. Some voices are pleasant, some disagreeable; but the far greater part can neither be said to be one nor the other. The same thing may be said of other sounds, that no less of tastes, smells, and colours; and, if we consider that our senses are in continual exercise while we are awake, and some sensation attends every object they present to us, and that familiar objects seldom raise any emotion, pleasant or painful, we shall see reason, besides the agreeable and disagreeable, to admit a third class of sensations that may be called indifferent.

The sensations that are indifferent, are far from being useless. They serve as signs to distinguish things that differ; and the information we have concerning things external, comes by their means. Thus, if a man had no ear to receive pleasure from the harmony or melody of sounds, he would still find the sense of hearing of great utility. Though sounds give him neither pleasure nor pain of themselves, they would give him much useful information; and the like may be said of the sensations we have by all the other senses.

As to the sensations and feelings that are agreeable or disagreeable, they differ much not only in degree, but in kind and in dignity. Some belong to the animal part of our nature, and are common to us with the brutes; others belong to the rational and moral part. The first are more properly called *sensations;* the last, *feelings.* The French word *sentiment* is common to both.

I shall conclude this chapter by observing that, as the confounding our sensations with that perception of external objects which is constantly conjoined with them, has been the occasion of most of the errors and false theories of philosophers with regard to the senses; so the distinguishing these operations seems to me to be the key that leads to a right understanding of both.

Sensation, taken by itself, implies neither the conception nor belief of any external object. It supposes a sentient being, and a certain manner in which that being is affected; but it supposes no more. Perception implies an immediate conviction and belief of something external — something different both from the mind that perceives, and from the act of perception. Things so different in their nature ought to be distinguished; but, by our constitution, they are always united. Every different perception is conjoined with a sensation that is proper to it. The one is the sign, the other the thing signified. They coalesce in our imagination. They are signified by one name, and are considered as one simple operation. The purposes of life do not require them to be distinguished.

It is the philosopher alone who has occasion to distinguish them, when he would analyse the operation compounded of them. But he has no suspicion that there is any composition in it; and to discover this requires a degree of reflection which has been too little practised by philosophers.

THOMAS BROWN
(1778–1820)

LECTURES ON THE PHILOSOPHY OF
THE HUMAN MIND *

PART II

CHAPTER V. SECTION I. THE MUSCULAR
SENSATIONS

. . . .

In defining *sensation*, when we began our inquiry into its
nature, to be that affection of the mind, which is immediately
subsequent to the affection of certain organs, induced by the
action of external bodies; two assumptions were made, — the
existence of foreign changeable external bodies, as separate
from the mind, — and the existence of organs, also separate
from the mind, and in relation to it truly external, like other
bodies, but forming a permanent part of our corporeal frame,
and capable of being affected, in a certain manner, by the other
bodies, of which the existence was assumed. As far as our
analytical inquiry has yet proceeded, these assumptions are
assumptions still. We have not been able to detect, in the sensations considered more than in any of our internal pleasures
or pains, any circumstances that seem to be indicative of a
material world without.

Our analytical inquiry itself, however, even in attempting to
trace the circumstances in which the belief originates, must proceed on that very belief. Accordingly, in examining our senses
of smell, taste, and hearing, I uniformly took for granted the
existence of odoriferous, sapid, and vibrating bodies, and con-

* Edinburgh, 1820. Reprinted from T. Brown's *A Treatise on the Philosophy
of the Human Mind*, abridged by Levi Hedge, Cambridge, 1827, vol. 1.

sidered merely, whether the sensations excited by these, were, of themselves, capable of communicating to us any knowledge of the external and independent existence of the bodies which excited them.

In the present stage of our inquiry, I must, in like manner, take for granted the existence of bodies, which act, by their contiguity or pressure, on our organs of *touch*, as the odoriferous or sapid particles act on our nerves of smell and taste. All our language is at present adapted to a system of external things. There is no direct vocabulary of skepticism; and even the most cautious and philosophic inquirer, therefore, must often be obliged to express his doubt, or his dissent, in language that implies affirmation. In the present case, when we attempt to analyze our sensations, it is impossible to speak of the circumstances in which the infant is placed, or even to speak of the infant himself, without that assumption which we have been obliged to make. The real existence of an external universe, and the belief of that existence, are, however, in themselves, perfectly separate and distinct; and it is not the existence of an external world which we are now endeavouring to establish as an object of belief. We are only endeavouring, in our analysis of the sensations afforded by our different organs, to ascertain in what circumstance the belief arises. There might be a world of suns and planets, though there were no human being, whose mind could be affected with belief of it; and even the most zealous defenders of the reality of external nature must admit, that, though no created thing but ourselves were in existence, our mind might still have been so constituted, as to have the very series of feelings, which form at present its successive phenomena, and which are ascribed in no small number to the action of external things.

Are the *primary* sensations derived from the organ of touch, then, of such a kind as to afford us that knowledge, which they are supposed to give of things without?

Let us imagine a being, endowed with the sense of *touch*, and with every other sense and faculty of our mind, but not with any previous knowledge of his own corporeal frame, or of other things external, — and let us suppose a small body, of any shape, to be pressed, for the first time, on his open hand. Whatever feeling mere touch can give, directly of itself, would of course be the same in this case, as now, when our knowledge is increased and complicated, from many other sources.

Let the body, thus impressed, be supposed to be a small cube, of the same temperature with the hand itself, that all considerations of heat or cold may be excluded, and the feeling produced be as simple as possible.

What, then, may we suppose the consequent feeling to be?

It will, I conceive, be a simple feeling of the kind already spoken of, as capable of arising from the affection of a single point of our organ of touch, — a feeling that varies indeed with the quantity of pressure as the sensation of fragrance varies with the number of the odorous particles, but involves as little the notion of extension, as that notion is involved in the mere fragrance of a violet or a rose. The connexion of this original tactual feeling, however, with that of extension, is now so indissoluble, as, indeed, it could not fail to become, in the circumstance in which it has uniformly arisen, that it is almost impossible to conceive it as separate. We may perhaps, however, make a near approach to the conception of it, by using the gentle gradual pressure of a small pointed body, which, in the various slight feelings, excited by it, — before it penetrate the cuticle, or cause any considerable pain, — may represent, in some measure, the simple and immediate effect, which pressure in any case produces, — exclusively of the associate feelings which it indirectly suggests.

Those who have the curiosity to try the experiment, with any small bodies, not absolutely pointed, — such as the head of a pin, or any body of similar dimensions, — will be astonished to feel, how very slightly, if at all, the notion of extension, or figure, is involved in the feeling, even after all the intimate associations of our experience; — certainly far less than the notion of longitudinal distance seems to us to be involved in the immediate affections of our sense of sight.

But the pressure of such a large body as the cube, which we

have supposed to be pressed against our organ of touch, now awakens very different feelings. We perceive, as it were immediately, *form* and *hardness*. May not, then, the knowledge of resistance and extension, and consequently the belief of the essential qualities of matter, be originally communicated by the affections of this organ?

The feeling of *resistance*, — to begin with this, — is, I conceive, to be ascribed, not to our organ of touch, but to our muscular frame, as forming a distinct organ of sense; the affections of which, particularly as existing in combination with other feelings, and modifying our judgments concerning these, (as in the case of distant vision, for example,) are not less important than those of our other sensitive organs. The sensations of this class, are, indeed, in common circumstances, so obscure, as to be scarcely heeded or remembered; but there is probably no contraction, even of a single muscle, which is not attended with some faint degree of sensation, that distinguishes it from the contraction of other muscles, or from other degrees of contraction of the same muscle. Each motion of the visible limb, whether produced by one or more of the invisible muscles, is accompanied with a certain feeling, that may be complex, indeed, as arising from various muscles, but which is considered by the mind as one; and it is this particular feeling, accompanying the particular visible motion, — whether the feeling and the invisible parts contracted be truly simple or compound, — which we distinguish from every other feeling accompanying every other quantity of contraction. It is as if a man, born blind, were to walk, for the first time, in a flower garden. He would distinguish the fragrance of one parterre from the fragrance of another, though he might be altogether ignorant of the separate odours united in each; and might even consider as one simple perfume, what was, in truth, the mingled product of a thousand.

Obscure as our muscular sensations are in common circumstances, there are other circumstances in which they make themselves abundantly manifest. It is sufficient to refer to phenomena of which every one must have been conscious in-

numerable times, and which imply no disease nor lasting difference of state. What is the feeling of fatigue, for example, but a
muscular feeling? that is to say, a feeling of which our muscles
are as truly the organ, as our eye or ear is the organ of sight or
hearing. When a limb has been long exercised, without sufficient intervals of rest, the repetition of the contraction of its
muscles is accompanied, not with a slight and obscure sensation, but with one which amounts, if it be gradually increased,
to severe pain, and which, before it arrives at this, has passed
progressively through various stages of uneasiness. Even when
there has been no previous fatigue, we cannot make a single
powerful effort at any time, without being sensible of the muscular feeling connected with this effort. Of the pleasure which
attends more moderate exercise, every one must have been conscious in himself, even in his years of maturity, when he seldom
has recourse to it for the pleasure alone; and must remember,
still more, the happiness which it afforded him in other years,
when happiness was of less costly and laborious production
than at present. By that admirable provision, with which Nature accommodates the blessings which she gives, to the wants
that stand in need of them, she has, in that early period, —
when the pleasure of mental freedom, and the ambitions of
busy life, are necessarily excluded, — made ample amends to
the little slave of affections, in that disposition to spontaneous
pleasure, which renders it almost an effort to be sad, as if existence itself were delight; giving him a fund of independent happiness in the very air which she has poured around him, and the
ready limbs which move through it almost without his bidding.
In that beautiful passage, in which Goldsmith describes the
sounds that come in one mingled murmur from the village, who
does not feel the force of the happiness which is comprised in
the single line, that speaks of

" The playful children just let loose from school ? " [1]

It is not the mere freedom from the intellectual task, of which
we think; it is much more that burst of animal pleasure, which

[1] Deserted Village, v. 120.

is felt in every limb, when the long constraint that has repressed it is removed, and the whole frame is given once more to all the freedom of nature.

With the same happy provision with which she has considered the young of our own species, Nature has, in the other animals, whose sources of general pleasure are still more limited than in the child, converted their muscular frame into an organ of delight. It is not in search of richer pasture, that the horse gallops over his field, or the goat leaps from rock to rock; it is for the luxury of the exercise itself. It is this appearance of happy life which spreads a charm over every little group with which Nature animates her scenery; and he who can look without interest on the young lamb, as it frolics around the bush, may gaze, indeed, on the magnificent landscape as it opens before him, — but it will be with an eye which looks languidly, and in vain, for pleasure which it cannot find.

Our muscular frame is not merely a part of the living machinery of motion, but is also truly an *organ of sense.* When I move my arm, without resistance, I am conscious of a certain feeling; when the motion is impeded by the presence of an external body, I am conscious of a different feeling, arising partly, indeed, from the mere sense of touch, in the moving limb compressed, but not consisting merely in this compression, since, when the same pressure is made by a foreign force, without any muscular effort on my part, my general feeling is very different. It is the feeling of this resistance to our progressive effort, (combined, perhaps, with the mere tactual feeling) which forms what we term our feeling of *solidity,* or *hardness;* and without it the tactual feeling would be nothing more than a sensation indifferent or agreeable, or disagreeable or severely painful, according to the force of the pressure, in the particular case; in the same way as the matter of heat, acting in different degrees on this very organ of touch, and on different portions of its surface at different times, produces all the intermediate sensations, agreeable, disagreeable, or indifferent, from the pain of excessive cold, to the pain of burning; and produces them in like manner, without suggesting the presence of any solid body external to ourselves.

Were the cue, therefore, in the case supposed, pressed for the first time on the hand, it would excite a certain sensation, indeed, but not that of resistance, which always implies a muscular effort that is resisted, and consequently not that of hardness which is a mode of resistance. It would be very different, however, if we fairly made the attempt to press against it; for then our effort would be impeded, and the consequent feeling of resistance would arise; which, as co-existing in this case, and in every case of effort, with the particular sensation of touch, might afterwards be suggested by it, on the simple recurrence of the same sensation of touch, so as to excite the notion of hardness in the body touched, without the renewal of any muscular effort on our part, in the same manner as the angular surfaces of the cube, if we chance to turn our eye upon it, are suggested by the mere plane of colour, which it presents to our immediate vision, and which is all that our immediate vision would, of itself, have made known to us. The feeling of resistance, then, it will be admitted, and consequently of hardness, and all the other modes of resistance, is a muscular, not a tactual feeling.

.   .   .   .

SECTION II.   SPACE PERCEPTION

.   .   .   .

The proof, that our perception of extension by touch, is not an original and immediate perception of that sense, is altogether independent of the success of any endeavour which may be made, to discover the elements of the compound perception. It would not be less true, that touch does not afford it, though we should be incapable of pointing out any source, from which it can be supposed to be derived.

To those who are wholly unacquainted with the theory of vision, nothing certainly can seem more absurd than the assertion, that we see, not with our eyes merely, but chiefly by the medium of another organ, which the blind possess in as great perfection as ourselves, and which at the moment of vision, may perhaps be absolutely at rest. It will not be surprising, therefore, though the element which seems to me to form the most important constituent of our notion of extension should in the same manner seem a very unlikely one.

This element is our feeling of *succession*, or *time*, — a feeling, which necessarily involves the notion of divisibility or series of parts, that is so essential a constituent of our more complex notion of matter, — and to which notion of continuous divisibility, if the notion of resistance be added, it is scarcely possible for us to imagine, that we should not have acquired, by this union, the very notion of physical extension, — that which has parts, and that which resists our effort to grasp it.

That *memory* is a part of our mental constitution, and that we are thus capable of thinking of a series of feelings, as successive to each other, the experience of every moment teaches us sufficiently. This succession frequently repeated, suggests immediately, or implies the notion of length, not metaphorically, as is commonly said, but as absolutely as extension itself; and, the greater the number of the successive feelings may have been, the greater does this length appear. It is not possible for us to look back on the years of our life, since they form truly a progressive series, without regarding them as a sort of length, which is more distinct indeed, the nearer the succession of feelings, may be to the moment at which we consider them, but which, however remote, is still felt by us as *one continued length*, in the same manner, as when, after a journey of many hundred miles, we look back, in our memory, on the distance over which we have passed, we see, as it were, a long track of which some parts, particularly the nearer parts, are sufficiently distinct, but of which the rest seems lost in a sort of distant obscurity. The line of our long journeying, — or, in other words, that almost immeasurable line of plains, hills, declivities, marshes, bridges, woods, — to endeavour to comprehend which in our thought, seems an effort as fatiguing as the very journey itself, — we know well, can be divided, into those various parts; and, in like manner, the progressive line of time — or, in other words, the continued succession, of which the joy, the hope, the fragrance, the regret, the melody, the fear, and innumerable other affections of the mind, were parts, we feel that we can mentally divide into those separate portions of the train. Continuous *length* and *divisibility*, those great elementary notions of space, and of all that space contains, are thus found in every succession of our feelings. There is no language in which time is not described as long or short, — not from any metaphor — for no mere arbitrary metaphor can be thus universal and inevitable, as a form of human thought — but because it is truly impossible for us to consider succession, without this notion of progressive divisibility attached to it; and it appears to us as absurd to suppose, that by adding, to our retrospect of a week, the events of the month preceding, we do not truly lengthen the succession, as it would be to suppose, that we do not lengthen the line of actual distance, by adding, to the few last stages of a long journey, the many stages that preceded it.

That which is progressive must have *parts*. Time, or succession, then involves the very notions of longitudinal extension and divisibility, and involves these, without the notion of any thing external to the mind itself; — for though the mind of man had been susceptible only of joy, grief, fear, hope, and the other varieties of internal feeling, without the possibility of being affected by external things, he would still have been capable of considering these feelings, as successive to each other, in a long continued progression, divisible into separate parts. The notions of length, then, and of divisibility, are not confined to external things, but are involved in that very memory, by which we consider the series of the past, — not in the memory of distant events only, but in those first successions of feeling, by which the mind originally became conscious of its own permanence and identity. The notion of time, then, is precisely coeval with that of the mind itself; since it is implied in the knowledge of succession, by which alone the mind acquires the knowledge of its own reality, as something more than the mere sensation of the present moment.

Conceiving the notion of *time*, therefore, that is to say, of feelings past and present, to be thus one of the earliest notions which the infant mind can form, so as to precede its notions of external things, and to involve the notions of length and divisibility, I am inclined to reverse exactly the process commonly supposed; and, instead of deriving the measure of time from extension, to derive the knowledge and original measure of extension from time. That one notion or feeling of the mind may be united indissolubly with other feelings, with which it has frequently co-existed, and to which, but for this co-existence, it would seem to have no common relation, is sufficiently shown by the phenomena of vision.

In what manner, however, is the notion of time peculiarly associated with the simple sensation of touch, so as to form, with it, the perception of extension? We are able, in the theory of vision, to point out the co-existence of sensations which produce the subsequent union, that renders the perception of distance apparently immediate. If a similar co-existence of the original sensations of touch, with the notion of continued and divisible succession, cannot be pointed out in the present case, the opinion which asserts it, must be considered merely as a wild and extravagant conjecture.

The source of such a co-existence is not merely to be found, but is at least as obvious, as that which is universally admitted in the case of vision.

To proceed, then, — The hand is the great organ of touch. It is composed of various articulations, that are easily moveable, so as to adapt it readily to changes of shape, in accommodation to the shape of the bodies which it grasps. If we shut our hand gradually, or open it gradually, we find a certain series of feelings, varying with each degree of the opening or closing, and giving the notion of succession of a certain length. In like manner, if we gradually extend our arms, in various directions, or bring them nearer to us again, we find that each degree of the motion is accompanied with a feeling that is distinct, so as to render us completely conscious of the progression. The gradual closing of the hand, therefore, must necessarily give a succession of feelings, — a succession, which, of itself, might, or rather must, furnish the notion of length in the manner before stated, the length being different, according to the degree of the closing; and the gradual stretching out of the arm gives a succession of feelings, which, in like manner, must furnish the notion of length, — the length being different according to the degree of the stretching of the arm. To those who have had opportunities of observing infants, I need not say, how much use, or rather what constant use, the future inquirer makes of his little fingers and arms; by the frequent contraction of which, and the consequent renewal of the series of feelings involved in each gradual contraction, he cannot fail to become so well acquainted with the progress, as to distinguish each degree of contraction, and, at last, after innumerable repetitions, to associate with each degree the notion of a certain length of succession. The particular contraction, therefore, when thus often repeated, becomes the representative of a certain length, in the same manner as shades of colour in vision become ultimately representative of distance, — the same principle of association, which forms the combination in the one case, operating equally in the other.

In these circumstances of acquired knowledge, — after the series of muscular feelings, in the voluntary closing of the hand, has become so familiar, that the whole series is anticipated and expected, as soon as the motion has begun, — when a ball, or any other substance, is placed for the first time in the infant's hand, he feels that he can no longer perform the usual contraction, — or, in other words, since he does not fancy that he has muscles which are contracted, he feels that the usual series of sensations does not follow his will to renew it, — he knows how much of the accustomed succession is still remaining; and the notion of this particular length, which was expected, and interrupted by a new sensation, is thus associated with the particular tactual feeling excited by the pressure of the ball, — the greater or less magnitude of the ball preventing a greater or less portion of the series of feelings in the accustomed contraction. By the frequent repetition of this tactual feeling, as associated with that feeling which attends a certain progress of contraction, the two feelings at last flow together, as in the acquired perceptions of vision; and when the process has been repeated with various bodies innumerable times, it becomes, at last, as impossible to separate the mere tactual feeling from the feeling of length, as to separate the whiteness of a sphere, in vision, from that convexity of the sphere, which the eye, of itself, would have been for ever incapable of perceiving.

As yet, however, the only dimension of the knowledge of which we have traced the origin, is mere length; and it must still be explained, how we acquire the knowledge of the other dimensions. If we had had but one muscle, it seems to me very doubtful whether it would have been possible for us to have associated with touch any other notion than that of mere length. But nature has made provision for giving us a wider knowledge, in the various muscles, which she has distributed over different parts, so as to enable us to perform motions in various directions at the same instant, and thus to have co-existing series of feelings, each of which series was before considered as involving the notion of length. The infant bends one finger gradually on the palm of his hand; the finger, thus brought down, touches one part of the surface of the palm, producing a certain affection of the organ of touch, and a consequent sensation; and he acquires the notion of a certain length, in the remembered succession of muscular feelings during the contraction; — he bends another finger; it, too, touches a certain part of the surface of the palm, producing a certain feeling of touch, that co-exists and combines, in like manner, with the remembrance of a certain succession of muscular feelings. When both fingers move together, the co-existence of the two series of successive feelings, with each of which the mind is familiar, gives the notion of co-existing lengths, which receive a sort of unity, from the proximity in succession of the tactual feelings in the contiguous parts of the palm which they touch, — feelings, which have before been found to be proximate, when the palm has been repeatedly pressed along a surface, and the tactual feelings of these parts, which the closing fingers touch at the same moment, were always immediately successive, — as immediately successive, as any of the muscular feelings in the series of contraction. When a body is placed in the infant's hand, and its little fingers are bent by it as before, sometimes one finger only is impeded in its progress, sometimes two, sometimes three, — and he thus adds to the notion of mere length, which would have been the same, whatever number of fingers had been impeded, the notion of a certain number of proximate and co-existing lengths, which is the very notion of breadth; and with these, according as the body is larger or smaller, is combined always the tactual affection produced by the pressure of the body, on more, or fewer, of the interior parts of the palm, and fingers, which had before become, of themselves, representative of certain lengths, in the manner described; and the concurrence of these three varieties of length, in the single feeling of resistance, in which they all seem to meet, when an incompressible body is placed within the sphere of the closing fingers, — however rude the notions of concurring dimensions may be, or rather must be, as at first formed, — seems at least to afford the rude elements, from which, by the frequent repetition of the feeling of resistance, together with the proximate lengths, of which it has become representative, clearer notions of the kind may gradually arise.

The progressive contractions of the various muscles which move the arms as affording similar successions of feelings, may be considered in precisely the same light, as sources of the knowledge of extension; and, by their motion in various directions, at the same time with the motion of the fingers, they concur powerfully, in modifying, and correcting, the information received from these. The whole hand is brought, by the motion of the arm, to touch one part of the face or body; it is then moved, so as to touch another part, and with the frequent succession of the simple feelings of touch, in these parts, is associated the feeling of the intervening *length*, derived from the sensations that accompanied the progressive contraction of the arm. But the motion is not always the same; and, as the same feeling of touch, in one part, is thus followed by various feelings of touch in different parts, with various series of muscular feelings between, the notion of length in various directions, that is to say, of length in various series commencing from one power, is obtained in another way. That the knowledge of extension, or in other words, the association of the notion of succession with the simple feelings of touch, will be rude and indistinct at first, I have already admitted; but it will gradually become more and more distinct and precise; as we can have no doubt, that the perception of distance by the eye is, in the first stages of visual association, very indistinct, and becomes clearer after each repeated trial. For many weeks or months, all is confusion in the visual perceptions, as much as in the tactual and muscular. Indeed, we have abundant evidence of this continued progress of vision, even in mature life, when, in certain professions that require nice perceptions of distance, the power of perception itself, by the gradual acquisitions which it obtains from experience, seems to unfold itself more and more, in proportion to the wants that require it.

It may be thought that the notion of *time*, or *succession*, is, in this instance, a superfluous incumbrance of the theory, and that the same advantage might be obtained, by supposing the muscular feelings themselves, independently of the notion of their succession, to be connected with the notion of particular lengths. But this opinion, it must be remarked, would leave the difficulty precisely as before; and sufficient evidence in confutation of it, may be found in a very simple experiment, which it is in the power of any one to make. The experiment I cannot but consider as of the more value, since it seems to me strongly corroborative of the theory which I have ventured to propose; for it shows, that, even after all the acquisitions which our sense of touch has made, the notion of extension is still modified, in a manner the most striking and irresistible, by the mere change of accustomed *time*. Let any one, with his eyes shut, move his hand, with moderate velocity, along a part of a table, or any other hard smooth surface; the portion over which he presses, will appear of a certain length; let him move his hand more rapidly, the portion of the surface pressed will appear less; let him move his hand very slowly, and the length, according to the degree of the slowness, will appear increased, in a most wonderful proportion. In this case, there is precisely the same quantity of muscular contraction, and the same quantity of the organ of touch compressed, whether the motion be rapid, moderate, or slow. The only circumstance of difference is the time occupied in the succession of the feelings; and this difference is sufficient to give complete diversity to the notion of length.

If any one, with his eyes shut, suffer his hand to be guided by another, very slowly along any surface unknown to him, he will find it impossible to form any accurate guess as to its length. But it is not necessary, that we should be previously unacquainted with the extent of surface, along which the motion is performed; for the illusion will be nearly the same, and the experiment, of course, be still more striking, when the motion is along a surface with which we are perfectly familiar, as a book which we hold in our hand, or a desk at which we are accustomed to sit.

This experiment is well fitted to show the influence of mere difference of time, in our estimation of longitudinal extent. It is an experiment, tried, unquestionably, in most unfavourable circumstances, when our tactual feelings, representative of extension, are so strongly fixed, by the long experience of our life; and yet, even now, it will be found, on moving the hand, slowly and rapidly, along the same extent of surface, though with precisely the same degree of pressure in both cases, that it is as difficult to conceive the extent, thus slowly and rapidly traversed, to be the same, as it is difficult to conceive the extent of visual distance to be exactly the same when we look alternately through the different ends of an inverted telescope. If, when all other circumstances are the same, the different visual feelings, arising from difference of the mere direction of light, be representative of length in the one case, — the longer or shorter succession of time, when all other circumstances are the same, has surely as much reason to be considered a representative of it, in the other case.

Are we, then, to believe, that feeling of extension, or in other words, of the definite figure of bodies, is a *simple* feeling of touch, immediate, original, and independent of time; or is there not rather reason to think, that it is a *compound* feeling, of which *time*, that is to say, our notion of succession, is an *original element* ?

PART III

CHAPTER I. SECTION II. SIMPLE AND RELATIVE SUGGESTION

.   .   .   .

OUR various states or affections of the mind, I have already divided into two classes, according to the nature of the circumstances which precede them, — the *External* and the *Internal*, — and this latter class into two orders, — our *Intellectual States of Mind*, and our *Emotions*. It is with the intellectual phenomena that we are at present concerned; and this order I would arrange under two generic capacities, that appear to me to comprehend or exhaust the phenomena of the order. The whole order, as composed of feelings which arise immediately, in consequence of certain former feelings of the mind may be technically termed, in reference to these feelings which have induced them, Suggestions; but, in the suggested feelings themselves, there is one striking difference. If we analyze out trains of intellectual thought exclusively of the *Emotions* which may co-exist or mingle with them, and of sensations that may be accidentally excited by external objects, we shall find them to be composed of two very distinct sets of feelings, — one set of which are mere *conceptions* or images of the past, that rise, image after image in regular sequence, but simply in succession, without any feeling of relation necessarily involved, — while the perceptions of *relation*, in the various objects of our thought, form another set of feelings, of course as various as the relations perceived. Conceptions and relations, — it is with these, and with these alone, that we are intellectually conversant. There is thus an evident ground for the arrangement of the internal suggestions, that form our trains of thought, under two heads, according as the feeling excited directly by some former feeling, may be either a simple conception, in its turn, perhaps, giving place to some other conception as transient; or may be, the feeling of a relation which two or more objects of our thought are considered by us as bearing to each other. There is, in short, in the mind, a capacity of *association;* or, as for reasons afterwards to be stated, I would rather term it, — the capacity of *Simple Suggestion,* — by which feelings formerly existing, are revived, in consequence of the mere existence of other feelings, as there is also a capacity of feeling resemblance, difference, proportion, or relation in general, when two or more external objects, or two or more feelings of the mind itself, are considered by us, — which mental capacity, in distinction from the former, I would term the capacity of *Relative Suggestion;* and of these simple and relative suggestions, the whole of our intellectual trains of thought are composed. As I am no lover of new phrases, when the old can be used without danger of mistake, I would very willingly substitute for the phrase, *relative suggestion,* the term *comparison,* which is more familiar, and expresses very nearly the same meaning. But comparison, though it involve the feeling of relation, seems also to imply a voluntary seeking for some relation, which is far from necessary to the mere internal suggestion or feeling of the relation itself. The resemblance of two objects strikes me, indeed, when I am studiously comparing them; but it strikes me also, with not less force, on many other occasions, when I had not previously been forming the slightest intentional comparison. I prefer, therefore, a term which is applicable alike to both cases, when a relation is sought, and when it occurs, without any search or desire of finding it.

The term *judgment,* in its strict philosophic sense, as the mere perception of relation, is more exactly synonymous with the phrase which I have employed, and might have been substituted with safety, if the vulgar use of the term, in many vague significations, had not given some degree of indistinctness even to the philosophical use of it. I may remark, too, that in our works of logic and intellectual physiology, *judgment* and *reason-*

ing are usually discussed separately, as if there were some essential difference of their nature; and, therefore, since I include them both, in the relative suggestions of which I shall afterwards have to treat, it seems advisable, not to employ for the whole, a name which is already appropriated, and very generally limited, to a part. As the rise in the mind of the feeling of relation, from the mere perception or conception of objects, is however, what I mean to denote by the phrase *Relative Suggestion;* and as *judgment,* in its strictest sense, is nothing more than this feeling of relation, — or any two or more objects, considered by us together, — I shall make no scruple to use the shorter and more familiar term, as synonymous when there can be no danger of its being misunderstood.

The intellectual states of the mind, then, to give a brief illustration of my division, I consider as all referable to two generic susceptibilities, — those of *Simple Suggestion* and *Relative Suggestion.* Our perception or conception of one object excites, of itself, and without any known cause, external to the mind, the conception of some other object, as when the mere sound of our friend's name, suggests to us the conception of our friend himself, — in which case, the conception of our friend, which follows the perception of the sound, involves no feeling of any common property with the sound which excites it, but is precisely the same state of mind, which might have been induced, by various other previous circumstances, by the sight of the chair on which he sat, — of the book which he read to us, — of the landscape which he painted. This is *Simple Suggestion.*

But, together with this capacity of Simple Suggestion, by which conception after conception arises in the mind, — precisely in the same manner, and in the same state, as each might have formed a part of other trains, and in which the particular state of mind that arises by suggestion does not necessarily involve any consideration of the state of mind which preceded it, — there is a suggestion of a very different sort, which in every case involves the consideration, not of one phenomenon of mind, but of two or more phenomena, and which constitutes the feeling of agreement, disagreement, or relation of some sort. I perceive, for example, a horse and a sheep at the same moment. The perception of the two is followed by that different state of mind which constitutes the feeling of their agreement in certain respects, or of their disagreement in certain other respects. I think of the square of the hypotenuse of a right-angled triangle, and of the squares of the two other sides; — I feel the relation of equality. I see a dramatic representation; I listen to the cold conceits which the author of the tragedy, in his omnipotent command over warriors and lovers of his own creation, gives to his hero, in his most impassioned situations; — I am instantly struck with their unsuitableness to the character and the circumstances. All the intellectual successions of feeling, in these cases, which constitute the perception of relation, differ from the results of simple suggestion in necessarily involving the consideration of two or more objects or affections of mind, that immediately preceded them. I may think of my friend, in the case of simple suggestion, — that is to say, my mind may exist in the state which constitutes the conception of my friend, without that previous state which constitutes the perception of the sound of his name; for the conception of him may be suggested by various objects and remembrances. But I cannot in the cases of relative suggestion, think of the resemblance of a horse and a sheep; of the proportion of the squares of the sides of a right-angled triangle; or of the want of the truth of nature in the expressions of a dramatic hero, without those previous states of mind, which constitute the conceptions of a horse and a sheep — of the sides of the triangle, — or of the language of the warrior or lover, and the circumstances of triumph, or hope, or despair, in which he is exhibited to us by the creative artist.

With these two capacities of suggested feelings, simple and relative, which are all that truly belong to the class of intellectual states of the mind, — various *emotions* may concur, particularly that most general of all emotions, the emotion of desire, in some one or other of its various forms. According as this desire does or does not concur with them, the intellectual states themselves appear to be different; and, by those who do not make the necessary analysis, are supposed, therefore, to be indicative of different powers. By simple suggestion, the images of things, persons, events, pass in strange and rapid succession; and a variety of names, expressive of different powers, — conception, association, memory, — have been given to this one simple law of our intellectual nature. But, when we *wish* to remember some object; that is to say, when we wish our mind to be affected in that particular manner, which constitutes the conception of a particular thing, or person, or event, — or when we wish to combine new images, in some picture of fancy, this co-existence of desire, with the simple course of suggestion, which continues still to follow its own laws, as much as when no desire existed with it, — seems to render the suggestion itself different; and recollection, and imagination, or fancy, which are truly, as we shall afterwards find, nothing more than the union of the suggested conceptions with certain specific permanent desires, are to us, as it were, distinct additional powers of our mind, and are so arranged in the systems of philosophers, who have not made the very simple analysis, which alone seems to be necessary for a more precise arrangement.

In like manner, those suggestions of another class, which constitute our notions of proportion, resemblance, difference, and all the variety of relations, may arise, when we have had no previous desire of tracing the relations, or may arise after that previous desire. But, when the feelings of relation seem to us to arise spontaneously, they are not in themselves different from the feelings of relation, that arise, in our intentional comparisons or judgments, in the longest series of ratiocination. Of such ratiocination, they are truly the most important elements. The permanent desire of discovering something unknown, or of establishing, or confuting, or illustrating, some point of belief or conjecture, may co-exist, indeed, with the continued series of relations that are felt, but does not alter the nature of that law, by which these judgments, or relative suggestions, succeed each other.

There is no power to be found, but only the union of certain intellectual states of the mind, with certain desires, — a species of combination not more wonderful in itself, than any other complex mental state, as when we, at the same moment, see and smell a rose, — or listen to the voice of a friend, who has been long absent from us, and see, at the same moment, that face of affection, which is again giving confidence to our heart, and gladness to our very eyes.

Our intellectual states of mind, then, are either those resemblances of past affections of the mind, which arise by *simple* suggestion, or those feelings of relation, which arise by what I have termed *relative* suggestions, — the one set resulting, indeed, from some prior states of the mind, but not involving, necessarily, any consideration of these previous states of mind, which suggested them, — the other set, necessarily involving the consideration of two or more objects, or two or more affections of mind, as subjects of the relation which is felt.

JOHANN FRIEDRICH HERBART
(1776–1841)

A TEXT BOOK IN PSYCHOLOGY

Translated from the German * *by*
MARGARET K. SMITH

PART FIRST. FUNDAMENTAL PRINCIPLES

CHAPTER I. THE CONDITION OF CONCEPTS, WHEN THEY ACT AS FORCES

10. CONCEPTS become forces when they resist one another. This resistance occurs when two or more opposed concepts encounter one another.

At first let us take this proposition as simply as possible. In this connection, therefore, we shall not think of complex nor of compound concepts of any kind whatever; nor of such as indicate an object with several characteristics, neither of anything in time nor space, but of entirely simple concepts or sensations — e.g., red, blue, sour, sweet, etc. It is not our purpose to consider the general notions of the above-mentioned sensations, but to consider such representations as may result from an instantaneous act of sense-perception.

Again, the question concerning the origin of the sensations mentioned does not belong here, much less has the discussion to do with the consideration of anything else that might have previously existed or occurred in the soul.

The proposition as it stands is that opposed concepts resist one another. Concepts that are not opposed — e.g., a tone and a color — may exist, in which case it will be assumed that such

* From *Lehrbuch zer Psychologie*, Lpg., 1816; 3 Aufl. 1882. Reprinted here from J. F. Herbart's *A Text-Book in Psychology*, translated by M. K. Smith, New York, D. Appleton & Co., 1891.

concepts offer no resistance to one another. (Exceptions to this latter proposition may occur, of which more hereafter.)

Resistance is an expression of force. To the resisting concept, however, its action is quite accidental; it adjusts itself to the attack which is mutual among concepts, and which is determined by the degree of opposition existing between them. This opposition may be regarded as that by which they are affected collectively. In themselves, however, concepts are not forces.

11. Now, what is the result of the resistance mentioned?

Do concepts partially or wholly destroy one another, or, notwithstanding the resistance, do they remain unchanged?

Destroyed concepts are the same as none at all. However, if, notwithstanding the mutual attack, concepts remain unchanged, then one could not be removed or suppressed by another (as we see every moment that they are). Finally, if all that is conceived of each concept were changed by the contest, then this would signify nothing more than, at the beginning, quite another concept had been present in consciousness.

The presentation (concept), then, must yield without being destroyed — i.e., the real concept is changed into an effort to present itself.

Here it is in effect stated that, as soon as the hindrance yields, the concept by its own effort will again make its appearance in consciousness. In this lies the possibility (although not for all cases the only ground) of reproduction.

12. When a concept becomes not entirely, but only in part, transformed into an effort, we must guard against considering this part as a severed portion of the whole concept. It has certainly a definite magnitude (upon the knowledge of which much depends), but this magnitude indicates only a degree of the obscuration of the whole concept. If the question be in regard to several parts of one and the same concept, these parts must not be regarded as different, severed portions, but the smaller divisions may be regarded as being contained in the larger. The same is true of the remainders after the collisions — i.e., of those parts of a concept which remain unobscured, for those parts are also degrees of the real concept.

CHAPTER II. EQUILIBRIUM AND MOVEMENT OF CONCEPTS

13. WHEN a sufficiency of opposition exists between concepts, the latter are in equilibrium. They come only gradually to this point. The continuous change of their degree of obscuration may be called their movement.

The statics and mechanics of the mind have to do with the calculation of the equilibrium and movement of the concepts.

14. All investigations into the statics of the mind begin with two different quantitative factors, viz., the sum (or the aggregate amount) of the resistances and the ratio of their limitation. The former is the quantity which rises from their encounter, to be divided between the opposing concepts. If one knows how to state it, and knows also the ratio in which the different concepts yield in the encounter, then, by a simple calculation in proportion, the statical point of each concept — i.e., the degree of its obscuration in equilibrium — may be found.

15. The sum as well as the ratio of the mutual limitation depends upon the strength of each individual concept which is affected in inverse ratio to its strength, and upon the degree of opposition between the two concepts. For their influence upon each other stands in direct ratio to the strength of each.

The principle determining the sum of the mutual limitation is, that it shall be considered as small as possible, because all concepts strive against suppression, and certainly submit to no more of it than is absolutely necessary.

16. By actual calculation, the remarkable result is obtained that, in the case of the two concepts, the one never entirely obscures the other, but, in the case of three or more, one is very easily obscured, and can be made as ineffective — notwithstanding its continuous struggle — as if it were not present at all. Indeed, this obscuration may happen to a large number of concepts as well as to one, and may be effected through the agency of two, and even through the combined influence of concepts less strong than those which are suppressed.

Here the expression "threshold of consciousness" must be

explained, as we shall have occasion to use it. A concept is in consciousness in so far as it is not suppressed, but is an actual representation. When it rises out of a condition of complete suppression, it enters into consciousness. Here, then, it is on the threshold of consciousness. It is very important to determine by calculation the degree of strength which a concept must attain in order to be able to stand beside two or more stronger ones exactly on the threshold of consciousness, so that, at the slightest yielding of the hindrance, it would begin to rise into consciousness.

NOTE. — The expression "A concept is in consciousness" must be distinguished from that, "I am conscious of my concept." To the latter belongs inner perception; to the former not. In psychology, we need a word that will indicate the totality of all simultaneous actual presentations. No word except consciousness can be found for this purpose.

Here we are obliged to be content with a circumlocution — and this all the more, because the inner perception which is usually attributed to consciousness has no fixed limit where it begins or ceases, and, moreover, the act of perceiving is not itself perceived; so that, since we are not conscious of it in ourselves, we must exclude it from consciousness, although it is an active knowing, and in no way a restricted or suppressed concept.

17. Among the many, and, for the most part, very complicated laws underlying the movement of concepts, the following is the simplest:

While the arrested portion (*Hemmungssumme*) of the concept sinks, the sinking part is at every moment proportional to the part unsuppressed.

By this it is possible to calculate the whole course of the sinking even to the statical point.

NOTE. — Mathematically, the above law may be expressed: $\sigma = S \left(1 - e^{-t} \right)$ in which S = the aggregate amount suppressed, t = the time elapsed during the encounter, σ = the suppressed portion of all the concepts in the time indicated by t.

As the latter quantity is apportioned among the individual concepts, it is found that those which fall directly beneath the statical threshold (16) are very quickly driven thence, while the rest do not reach exactly their statical point in any given finite time. On account of this latter circumstance, the concepts in the mind of a man of most equable temperament are, while he is awake, always in a state of gentle motion. This is also the primary reason why the inner perception never meets an object which holds it quite motionless.

18. When to several concepts already near equilibrium a new one comes, a movement arises which causes them to sink for a short time beneath their statical point, after which they quickly and entirely of themselves rise again — something as a liquid, when an object is thrown into it, first sinks and then rises. In this connection several remarkable circumstances occur:

19. First, upon an occasion of this kind, one of the older concepts may be removed entirely out of consciousness even by a new concept that is much weaker than itself. In this case, however, the striving of the suppressed concept is not to be considered wholly ineffective, as shown above (see 16); it works with all its force against the concepts in consciousness. Although its object is not conceived, it produces a certain condition of consciousness. The way in which these concepts are removed out of consciousness and yet are effective therein may be indicated by the expression, "They are on the mechanical threshold." The threshold mentioned above (16) is called for the sake of distinction the statical threshold.

NOTE. — If the concepts on the statical threshold acted in the same way as on the mechanical threshold we should find ourselves in a state of the most intolerable uneasiness, or rather the body would be subjected to a condition of tension that must in a few moments prove fatal, even as under present conditions sudden fright will sometimes cause death; for all the concepts which, as we are accustomed to say, the memory preserves, and which we well know can upon the slightest occasion be reproduced, are in a state of incessant striving to rise, although the condition of consciousness is not at all affected by them.

20. Second, the time during which one or more concepts linger upon the mechanical threshold can be extended if a series of new, although weaker, concepts come in succession to them.

Every employment to which we are unaccustomed puts us in this condition. The earlier concepts are pressed back of the later ones. The former, however, because they are the stronger, remain tense, affect the physical organism more and more, and finally make it necessary that the employment cease, when the old concepts immediately rise, and we experience what is called a feeling of relief which depends in part upon the physical organism, although the first cause is purely psychological.

21. Third, when several concepts are driven in succession to the mechanical threshold, several sudden successive changes in the laws of reciprocal movements arise.

In this way is to be explained the fact that the course of our thoughts is so often inconsequent, abrupt, and apparently irregular. This appearance deceives in the same way as the wandering of the planets. The conformity to law in the human mind resembles exactly that in the firmament.

NOTE. — As a counterpart to the concepts which sink simultaneously are to be observed those which rise simultaneously, especially when they rise free — i.e., when a restricting environment or a general pressure suddenly disappears. With the rising the amount of suppression increases. Hence, in the case of three, one may be, as it were, bent back, and under certain conditions may sink quite to the threshold. Their elevation is greater than the depression to which, sinking together, they would have pressed one another, because in sinking the sum of their mutual limitation depends upon the total strength, which in the gradual rising is not the case.

CHAPTER III. COMPLICATIONS AND BLENDINGS

22. THE easily conceivable metaphysical reason why opposed concepts resist one another is the *unity of the soul, of which they are the self-preservations*. This reason explains without difficulty the combination of our concepts (which combina-

tion is known to exist). If, on account of their opposition, they did not suppress one another, all concepts would compose but one act of one soul; and, indeed, in so far as they are not divided into a manifold by any kind of arrests whatever, they really constitute but one act. Concepts that are on the threshold of consciousness can not enter into combination with others, as they are completely transformed into effort directed against other definite concepts, and are thereby, as it were, isolated. In consciousness, however, concepts combine in two ways: First, concepts which are not opposed or contrasted with one another (as a tone and a color) so *far as they meet unhindered, form a complex;* second, *contrasted concepts* [e.g., red and yellow], in so far as they are effected neither by accidental foreign concepts nor by unavoidable opposition, become blended (*fused*).

Complexes may be complete; blendings (fusions) from their nature must always be (more or less) incomplete.

NOTE. — Of such complexes as are partially or almost complete, we have remarkable instances in the concepts of things with several characteristics and of words used as signs of thoughts. In the mother-tongue the latter, words and thoughts, are so closely connected that it would appear that we think by means of words. (Concerning both examples more hereafter.) Among the blendings are especially remarkable, partly those which include in themselves an æsthetic relation (which, taken psychologically, is created at the same time with the blending), partly those which involve succession, in which serial forms have their origin.

23. That which is complicated or blended out of several concepts furnishes an aggregate of force, and for this reason works according to quite other statical and mechanical laws than those according to which the individual concepts would have acted. Also the thresholds of consciousness change according to the complex or blending (fusion), so that on account of a combination a concept of the very weakest kind may be able to remain and exert an influence in consciousness.

NOTE 1. — The computation for complexes and blendings depends upon the same principles as that for simple concepts; it is, however, much more intricate, especially for the reason that in the case of incomplete combinations the forces as well as their arrests are only partially interwoven with one another (and do not fully enter as factors into the product).

NOTE 2. — Combinations of concepts consist not only of two or three members, but they often contain many members in very unequal degrees of complication, or blending, in which case no calculation can estimate the multiplicity. Nevertheless, from the latter, the simplest cases may be chosen and the more intricate ones estimated according to them. For every science the simplest laws are the most important.

24. *Problem:* After an encounter between two concepts, P and Π, the remainders, r and ρ, are blended (or incompletely united). The problem is to indicate what help one of the two concepts, in case it should be still more suppressed, would receive from the other.

NOTE. — *Solution :* Let P be the helping concept; it helps with a force equal to r, but Π can only appropriate this force in the ratio of $\rho : \Pi$. Hence through P, Π receives the help $\frac{r\rho}{\Pi}$, and in the same way P receives from Π the help $\frac{r\rho}{P}$.

The proof lies immediately in the analysis of the ideas. It is plain that the two remainders, r and ρ, taken together, determine the degree of union between the two concepts. One of them is the helping force; the other, compared with the concept to which it belongs, is to be considered as a fraction of the whole; and, of the totality of help which could be rendered by the first remainder, it yields that portion which here attains efficient activity.

25. The following principles may be observed here:

a. Beyond the point of union no help extends its influence.

If the concept Π has more clearness in consciousness than the remainder ρ indicates, then by striving of the concept P, which might come to the help of the former, already more than enough has been done; hence for the present it exerts no more influence.

b. The farther the one of the concepts is below the point of union, so much the more effectively does the other help.

NOTE. — This gives the following differential equation:

$$\frac{r\rho}{\Pi}\frac{\rho-\omega}{\rho}\,dt \equiv d\omega,$$

whence by integration $\omega = \rho\left(1 - e^{\frac{-rt}{\Pi}}\right).$

This equation contains the germ of manifold investigations which penetrate the whole of psychology. It is indeed so simple that it can never really occur in the human soul, but all investigations into applied mathematics begin with such simple presuppositions as only exist in abstraction — e.g., the mathematical lever, or the laws of bodies falling in a vacuum. Here merely the influence of the help is considered, which, if everything depended upon it alone, would bring into consciousness during the time *t* a quantity ω from Π. Besides, if we take into consideration the single circumstance that Π meets with an unavoidable arrest from other concepts, then the calculation becomes so complicated that it can be only approximately solved by an integration of the following form:

$$d^3\omega = ad^2\omega dt + bd\omega dt^2 + c\omega dt^3.$$

It is self-evident that it much more nearly expresses the facts which are to be observed experimentally.

26. The foregoing contains the foundation of the theory of mediate reproduction, which, according to ordinary language, is derived from the association of ideas or concepts. Before pursuing this further we must mention immediate reproduction — i.e., that reproduction which by its own force follows upon the yielding of the hindrances. The ordinary case is that a concept gained by a new act of perception causes the old concept of the same or of a similar object to rise into consciousness. This occurs when the concept furnished by the new act of perception presses back everything present in consciousness opposed to the old concept, which is similar to the new one. Then, without further difficulty, the old concept rises of itself. From this are to be observed the following conditions, which are to be found by calculation, of which, however, no idea can be given here:

a. In the beginning the rising is in proportion to the square of the time, if the new act of perception occurs suddenly; but to the cube of the time, if the latter (as is usual) is formed by a gradual and lingering act of apprehension.

b. The course of the rising is adjusted principally to the strength of the concept furnished by the new act of perception in proportion to the opposing one which it has pressed back; but the individual strength of the rising concept only has influence under special conditions. It can, as it were, only use this strength in the free space which is given to it.

c. The rising concept blends as such with the concept, similar to it, furnished by the new act of perception. Since it does not rise entirely, however, the blending is incomplete.

d. The fact that immediate reproduction is not limited entirely to the old concept of exactly the same kind, but extends to the more or less similar so far as to receive partial freedom from the new act of perception, is of special importance. The whole reproduction may be indicated by the name of vaulting (or arching). In the case of a long duration, or of a frequent repetition of a new act of perception, a second important process, which we call tapering (or pointing), follows. The peculiarity of this latter consists in the fact that the concepts which are less similar are again arrested by the concepts received through the new act of perception, as the old concepts bring with them into consciousness others which are opposed to the new, so that finally the concept that is entirely homogeneous finds itself alone favored, and forms, as it were, a tapering summit where the highest point of the vault (or arch) was heretofore.

27. Where the circumstances allow, with this immediate reproduction is united that mediate reproduction mentioned in 25. The concept P, mentioned above, is reproduced immediately (i.e., without the mediation of others), then the free space allowed it may be regarded as that r (spoken of in 25) or as a force which strives to raise the Π blended with it to its point of blending ρ.

Note. — As the free space gradually increasing (and again decreasing) is given, we must for the present observation regard r in the formula $\omega = \rho \left(1 - e^{\frac{-rt}{\Pi}}\right)$ as a variable quantity, and indeed as a function of that quantity upon which the propositions in 26 depend.

28. The most important applications of the previous theories are, if with different remainders r, r', r'', etc., of one and the same concept P several Π, Π', Π'', etc., are united, by which, for the sake of brevity, we may assume the remainders of the latter, viz., ρ, ρ', ρ'', to be equal; also, Π, Π', etc., may be equal.

A concept acts upon several united with it in the same series according to the time in which its remainders (by which it is united with those others according to quantity) stand.

Note. — In order to avoid diffuseness, this most important law is here only very incompletely expressed in words. We recognize it better and more clearly in the formula given: $\omega = \rho \left(1 - e^{\frac{-rt}{\Pi}}\right)$, if instead of one r we substitute different smaller and greater, r, r', r'', etc. But the more exact calculation mentioned in 25 shows that the Π, Π', Π'', etc., blended with them, not only rise, but sink again, as it were, to make place for each other, in and the order of r, r', r'', etc.

29. Here is discovered the ground of the genuine reproduction or of memory so far as it brings to us a series of concepts in the same order in which they were first received. In order to comprehend this, we must consider what union arises among several concepts that are successively given.

Let a series, a, b, c, d, be given by perception; then, from the first movement of the perception and during its continuance, a is exposed to an arrest from other concepts already in consciousness. In the mean time, a, already partially sunken in consciousness, became more and more obscured when b came to it. This b at first, unobscured, blended with the sinking a; then followed c, which itself unobscured, united with b, which was becoming obscured, and also with a, which was still more obscured. Similarly followed d, to become united in different degrees with a, b, c. From this arises a law for each of these concepts that states how, after the whole series has been, for a time, removed out of consciousness, upon the re-emergence of one of the concepts of such a series into consciousness, every other concept of the same series is called up. Let it be assumed that a rises first, then it is united more with b, less with c, and still less with d; backward, however, b, c, and d are blended collectively in an unobscured condition with the remainders of a; hence a seeks to bring them all again into an unobscured condition [i.e., into full consciousness]. But a acts the most quickly and strongly upon b, more slowly upon c, still more slowly upon d, etc., by which close investigation shows that b sinks again, while c rises, even as c sinks when d rises; in short, the series follows in the same order as first given. On the contrary, let us assume that c is originally reproduced, then c acts upon d and the following members of the series exactly in the same way as was indicated in the case of a — i.e., the series c, d, etc., unfolds gradually in the order of its succession. On the contrary, b and a experience quite another influence. The unobscured c was blended with their different remainders. Then c acts upon them with its whole strength, and without delay, but only to call back the remainders of a and b united with it, to bring a part of b and a smaller part of a into consciousness. Thus it happens that when we remember something in the middle of a known series, the preceding part of the series presents itself all at once in a lessened degree of clearness, while the portion following comes before the mind in the same order as the series it brings with it. But the series never runs backward; an anagram from a well-comprehended word never originates without intentional effort.

30. Several series may cross one another, e.g., a, b, c, d, e, and a, β, c, δ, ϵ, in which c is common to the two series. If c were reproduced alone, it would strive to call up d and e as well as δ and ϵ. If, however, b comes into consciousness first, then the first series comes decidedly forward on account of the united help of b and c, yet the oppositions among the members of both series, in this case, have each their own influence.

We may remark that, to the simple type or model here given, a variety of complicated psychological occurrences may be adjusted. The same c can be held as the common point of intersection for many hundred series. On account of the manifold oppositions in these series, the common c may cause none of the members to rise perceptibly, but so soon as b and a come forward, determining c more closely, the indecision will disappear, and the uppermost series will really come before the mind.

31. The foregoing depends upon the difference presupposed in the remainders r, r', r'', etc. (28). But in order that this difference may have its influence, the concept to which these remainders belong must come forward sufficiently into consciousness. Let it be granted that it is arrested to such a degree that its active representation amounts to no more than that of the smallest among the remainders r, r', r'', etc., then it works equally on the whole series of concepts blended with it so that a vague total impression of all comes into consciousness. The reason for this is explained in sections 27 and 12. The remainders are not different parts severed from one and the same concept; hence if a little of the latter is in consciousness, we must not first question whether this little may be one and perhaps quite the smallest among those remainders, but we must assume that it really is so, although at the same time it may be a part of every other greater remainder. If the active concept gradually rises into consciousness, then the remainders, from the smaller to the greater, one after the other, gain a special law of action. By this the above vague impression of the whole rises, in which lies a whole series of concepts, and these are gradually developed out of one another.

NOTE. — Here, among others, must be compared the phenomena resulting from exercise and skill; that, moreover, not every course of thought repeats faithfully the series constructed; and upon that is based, in part, the ground of the inequalities in the quantities Π and ρ (25), with whose possible difference we can not deal further here. Additional facts may be deduced from the following.

32. If free-rising concepts (of which mention was made in the closing remarks of the last chapter) should blend in regular

gradation, they would be subject to other laws of reproduction which originate out of the blending, and are distinguished and determined according to their differences. Upon occasion, likewise arises a process of construction and formation of series which differ from the form of analogous concepts in case the latter are given and then sink out of consciousness. From this may be explained the conflict between things as we perceive them and as we think them, as well as the tendency to regard them otherwise than as they first present themselves; consequently the modifying action of the self-activity upon that which lies before the perception. This may be observed especially in the case of children who can have no set purpose in the matter.

CHAPTER IV. CONCEPTS AS THE SOURCE OF MENTAL STATES

33. ONE of the objections against mathematical psychology is that mathematics defines only quantity, while psychology must especially consider quality. It is now time to meet this objection, and to collect the explanations of those mental states which the foregoing presents.

Here we must first remark that the peculiar striving of concepts for representation (11) never appears immediately in consciousness, for, just so far as concepts change into striving, they are removed out of consciousness. Also, the gradual sinking of concepts can not be perceived. A special instance of this is, that no one is able to observe his own falling asleep.

So far as it represents or conceives, the soul is called *mind;* so far as it feels and desires, it is called the heart or disposition (*Gemüth.*) *The disposition of the heart, however, has its source in the mind* — in other words, feeling and desiring are conditions, and, for the most part, changeable conditions of concepts. The emotions indicate this, while experience, upon the whole, confirms it: the man feels little of the joys and sorrows of his youth; but what the boy learns correctly, the graybeard still knows. The extent, however, to which a *steadfast disposition* and, above all, *character* can be given, will be shown later in the explanations of the principles above presented.

34. First, there is a blending of concepts not only after the arrest (22), but quite a different one before it, provided the degree of opposition (15) be sufficiently small. A principle of æsthetic judgment lies in this. Pleasant feelings in their narrowest sense, together with their opposites, must be regarded as analogous to these æsthetic judgments — i.e., as springing from the relation of many concepts which do not assert themselves individually, but rather which perhaps, for psychological reasons, can not be perceived when separated.

NOTE. — In carrying out this investigation, the series of tone relations upon which music depends may be presented as a subject of experiment. Among simple tones, the degree of arrest (the interval of tones), entirely alone and without means, determines the æsthetic character of its relation. It is also certain that the psychological explanation (widely different from the acoustical) of all harmony is to be sought in the difference between the degrees of arrest, and that it must be found there. The necessary calculations for this are, for the most part, to be found in the second volume of the Königsberg Archives for Philosophy. Of the somewhat extensive investigations, only the principal ones which experience decidedly confirms can be given here:

When the forces, into which concepts, through their similarity and their contrasts, separate one another, are equally strong, there arises disharmony. If, however, one of these forces be opposed to the others in such a relation that it is driven to the statical threshold (16) by them, then a harmonious relation will prevail.

35. Second, a principle of contrast is to be found in the complexes (22), which we here consider complete. The complexes $a+\alpha$ and $b+\beta$ are similar, provided $a:\alpha = b:\beta$; if not, they are dissimilar. Let the degree of arrest between a and b equal p, and that between α and β equal π. Now, if in similar complexes, $p = \pi$, then, and then only, will the individual concepts be arrested, exactly as if they had not been in any combination; also no feeling of contrast arises, inasmuch as the arrest is successful only when the opposing forces bring the feeling of

contrast with them; but, in every variation from the case presented, the less opposed concepts are affected by their combination with the other two, but in this very way a part of the arrest will be withheld from the latter; consequently, notwithstanding the opposition, something remains in consciousness that resists, and in this lies the feeling of contrast. If $\pi < p$, then the contrast between a and b will be felt, not that between a and β. If $\pi > p$, the case is reversed. When $\pi = 0$, the contrast between a and b is the greatest.

36. Third, a complex $a + a$ is reproduced by a concept furnished by a new act of perception similar to a (26). Now, when a, on account of its combination with a, comes forward, it meets in consciousness a concept opposed to it, β. *Then a will be at the same time, driven forward and held back.* In this situation, it is the source of an unpleasant feeling which may give rise to *desire*, viz., for the object represented by a provided the opposition offered by β is weaker than the force which a brings with it.

This is ordinarily the case; desires are excited by a remembrance of their object. When the remembrance is strengthened by several incidental concepts, the impulses of desire are renewed. As often as the opposing concepts (i.e., concepts of the hindrances which stand in the way of the longing) attain preponderance, they produce a painful feeling of privation.

37. Fourth, a concept comes forward into consciousness by its own strength (perhaps reproduced according to the method described in 26), at the same time being called forward by several helping concepts (24). Since each of these helps has its own measure of time in which it acts (according to the formula in 25), then the helps may strengthen one another against a possible resistance, but they can not increase their own velocity. The movement in advancing takes place only with that velocity which is the greatest among several concepts meeting together, *but it is favored by all the rest.* This favoring is part of the process which takes place in consciousness, but in no way is it anything represented or conceived. Hence it can only be called a feeling — without doubt a feeling of pleasure.

Here is the source of the cheerful disposition, especially of joy in successful activity. Here belong various movements, instigated from without, which do not accelerate but favor one another as in the case of dancing and music. Of the same character is the action according to several centering motives, and such too is the insight based on understanding several reasons which confirm one another.

38. In general, it may be observed that feelings and desires have not their source in the process or act of conception in general, but always in certain particular concepts. Hence there may be at the same time many different feelings and desires, and these may either agree or entirely disagree one with the other.

CHAPTER V.   THE CO-OPERATION OF SEVERAL MASSES OF CONCEPTS OF UNEQUAL STRENGTH

39. FROM the foregoing, it may, in a way, be perceived that after a considerable number of concepts in all kinds of combinations is present, every new act of perception must work as an excitant by which some will be arrested, others called forward and strengthened, progressing series interrupted or set again in motion, and this or that mental state occasioned. These manifestations must become more complex if, as is usual, the concept received by the new act of perception contains in itself a multiplicity or variety, that at the same time enables it to hold its place in several combinations and series, and gives them a fresh impulse which brings them into new relations of opposition or blending with one another. By this, the concepts brought by the new act of perception are assimilated to the older concepts in such a way as to suffer somewhat after the first excitation has worked to the extent of its power, because the old concepts — on account of their combinations with one another — are much stronger than the new individuals which are added.

40. If, however, already very strong complexes and blendings with many members have been formed, then the same rela-

tion which existed between the old and the new concepts may be repeated within between the old concepts. Weaker concepts, which, according to any kind of law, enter into consciousness, act as excitants upon those masses before mentioned, and are received and appropriated by them (apperceived) just as in the case of a new sense-impression; hence *the inner perception* is analogous to the outer. Self-consciousness is not the subject of discussion here, although it is very often combined with the above.

41. In what has been said, lies that which experience confirms, viz., that the inner perception is never a passive apprehension, but always (even against the will) active. The apperceived concepts do not continue rising or sinking according to their own laws, but they are interrupted in their movements by the more powerful masses which drive back whatever is opposed to them although it is inclined to rise; and in the case of that which is similar to them although it is on the point of sinking, they take hold of it and blend it with themselves.

42. It is worth the trouble to indicate how far this difference among concepts — which we might be inclined to divide into dead and living — may be carried.

Let us recall the concepts on the statical threshold (16). These are, indeed, in effect nothing less than dead; for, in the condition of arrest in which they stand, they are not able by their own effort to effect anything whatever [toward rising into consciousness]. Nevertheless, through the combination in which they stand, they may be reproduced, and, besides, they will often be driven back in whole heaps and series by those more powerful masses, as when the leaves of a book are turned hurriedly.

43. If the apperceived concepts — or at least some of them — are not on the statical threshold, then the apperceiving concepts suffer some violence from them; also the latter may be subject to arrest from another side, in which case the inner perception is interrupted; through this, uncertainty and irresolution may be explained.

The apperceiving mass may be, in its turn apperceived by

another mass; but for this to occur, there must be present several concept masses of distinctly different degrees of strength. Hence it is somewhat seldom that the inner perception rises to this second power [the apperception of apperception], and only in the case of philosophical ideas is this series considered as one which might be prolonged into infinity.

CHAPTER VI. A GLANCE OVER THE CONNECTION BETWEEN BODY AND SOUL

44. Up to the present chapter, concepts have been considered as present in the soul without any question concerning their origin or concerning foreign influences. This has been done for simplicity. Now, sense-perception in part and physiological influences in part, together with concepts already present, must be considered.

45. Even from experience it may be assumed that each act of perception of any considerable strength requires a short space of time for its creation; but experience and metaphysics at the same time teach that by delaying longer, the strength of the perception in no way increases in proportion to the time, but, *the stronger the perception already is, so much the less does it increase*, and from this it follows, by an easy calculation, that there is a final limit to its strength which the attained concept very soon reaches, and above which even by an infinite delay the same perception will not be able to rise. This is the law of *diminishing susceptibility*, and the strength of the sense-impression is quite indifferent in regard to this limit. The weakest sense-perception may give the concept quite as much strength as the strongest, only it requires for this a somewhat longer time.

46. Every human concept really consists of infinitely small elementary apprehensions very unlike one another, which in the different moments of time during the continuance of the act of perception were created little by little. However, if during the continuance of the perception an arrest caused by old opposed concepts did not occur, these apprehensions would be

all necessarily blended into a single, undivided total force. For this reason the total force will be perceptibly less than the sum of all the elementary apprehensions.

47. In early childhood a much larger supply of simple sense-concepts is generated than in all the following years. Indeed, the work of the after-years consists in making the greatest possible number of combinations from this supply. Although this susceptibility is never entirely extinguished, yet, if there were not a kind of renewal of it, the age of manhood would be more indifferent and more unfruitful in sense-impressions than it really is.

Though concepts on the statical threshold are quite without influence for that which goes on in consciousness (16), they can not weaken the susceptibility to new perceptions similar to themselves. Hence this receptivity would be completely re-established if the earlier ratio of arrest were not quite changed by the new acts of perception, and a certain freedom to repro-duce themselves directly given to the older concepts (26). When this happens, the receptivity decreases. The greater the number of old concepts of the same kind present in conscious-ness — this means usually the longer one has lived — so much greater is the number of concepts which upon a given occasion enter at the same time into consciousness; and thus with years the renewal of receptivity diminishes.

48. The above statements refer not only to concepts of exactly the same kind, but to all whose degree of opposition is a fraction. This can not be developed here, since in the foregoing nothing exact could be said of the difference between the degrees of opposition.

49. It is to be especially observed that the influence of the body upon psychical manifestations is shown in three ways — its repression (*Druck*), its excitation (*Resonanz*), and its co-operation in action. Upon this are the following preliminary remarks:

50. Physiological repression arises when the accompanying conditions, which should correspond to the changes in the soul, can not follow without hindrance: hence the hindrance will also

be felt as such in the soul because the conditions of each affect both. This repression is often merely a retarding force, to suit which the mental movements must proceed more slowly, as is the case with slow minds that consume time and are stupefied by quick changes. Often, however, repression is similar to an arresting force, and as such it can be mathematically calculated, as when it increases the number of opposed concepts by one or more. By it all active concepts may be driven to the statical threshold; and here we have the explanation of sleep. In this case it would be a deep and complete sleep.

51. Physiological excitation (*Resonanz*) arises when the accompanying bodily conditions change, more quickly or become stronger than would be necessary to merely cause no hindrance to the mental movements. Then the soul, again in response to the body, will act more quickly and more vigorously. The soul must also share the resulting relaxations of the body, as in intoxication and passion.

52. The co-operation of the soul and body in external action can not originally proceed from the soul, for the will does not know in the least what influence it really exerts upon the nerves and muscles. But in the child exists an organic necessity for movement. At first the soul accompanies this and the active movements arising from it, with its feelings. The feelings, however, become connected with perceptions of the members moved. If, in the result, the concept arising from such a perception acts as a means of arousing desire (16), then the feeling connected with it arises, and to this latter as accompanying bodily condition belong all those phenomena in the nerves and muscles by which organic movement is actually determined or defined. Thus it happens that concepts come to appear as a source of mechanical forces in the outer world.

FRIEDRICH EDUARD BENEKE
(1798–1854)

A TEXTBOOK OF PSYCHOLOGY
AS NATURAL SCIENCE

Translated from the German * *by*
BENJAMIN RAND

CHAPTER I. FUNDAMENTAL PROCESSES OF
PSYCHICAL DEVELOPMENT

§ 22. *First fundamental process.* Sensations and perceptions are formed in the human soul in consequence of impressions or excitations which come to it from without. The usual view is that we receive the external impressions primarily through the bodily organs, and only thereafter do they proceed to the soul by means of the nerves and of the brain. But of this our self-consciousness, which we have designated (§ 1) as the only fundamental source for psychological knowledge, gives no hint whatever. The excitation of the bodily organs presents itself to us as an effect concomitant with the formation of the sensory impressions, or as running parallel with it; and we must regard as a false inference if one endeavors in the manner indicated to place the same in causal connection therewith. There is no scientific justification (§ 47 ff.) for this assumption as it is ordinarily made. Furthermore nothing is in the least gained thereby for the doing away with the offensive dissimilarity between external objects and the soul. For we are still even as little able to conceive how a psychical seeing, hearing, etc., can arise from a material vibration of the nerves, or of the brain, as how the soul itself can be immediately excited by external impressions into the formations of sensations. Let anatomy and

* From F. E. Beneke's *Lehrbuch der Psychologie als Naturwissenschaft.* Berlin, 1833; bearb. von J. G. Dressler, 4 Aufl. *ib.*, 1877.

physiology, therefore, explain and establish the results of observation in their domain. In psychology we hold firmly to the fact that our self-consciousness says nothing about any such mediation.

§ 23. The creation of sensations and perceptions necessarily presupposes: (1) certain external elements (excitations, impressions) which are received and appropriated by our soul; and (2) certain inner forces, or faculties, by which it receives and appropriates these elements. These forces, which, like the excitations aforesaid, show themselves at the first glance to be manifold, or to form several characteristic systems, we style sensory faculties, just because they respond to external excitations; and, furthermore, we call them original faculties (Urvermögen) of the soul, in so far as we are unable to derive them from anything else. It is to be observed, however, that the sensory excitations so soon as they are received and appropriated are transformed likewise into psychical elements. We attribute to the sensory faculties in respect to this process a higher or lesser degree of sensitiveness to excitation. By means of this variable degree the extent of the excitation received, or the vividness of the sensation, is shown to be conditioned from within.

§ 24. *Second fundamental process.* The human soul is constantly acquiring original faculties. Of this innermost life-process, by which alone the soul is able to continue its life, we obtain knowledge only from the fact, that from time to time the original faculties become exhausted. There is in other words an inability to form sensory perceptions, or to carry on activities, which demand new and original faculties, and these remain for a subsequent more or less extended use. As an explanation of this phenomenon the effect indicated proves to be the most plausible hypothesis. We cannot, indeed, determine more exactly the nature of this process, not merely because it wholly escapes consciousness, but also because among all other processes of which we are conscious there is none analogous to it. An indication of the circumstances under which this process occurs, and occurs more perfectly, we reserve for later consideration (§ 335) on account of this very obscurity, and in order to make use in fuller measure of the results of observation.

§ 25. The original faculties are essentially volitions so long and so far as they have not as yet adopted excitation for their completion; that is to say, they strive for this fulfilment as for a complement intended for them by their nature. We also term this striving "tension." This character appears especially in the uneasiness which develops if they have accumulated unused in rather a large number. This is an uneasiness which as experience shows can mount to any conceivable degree, and can lead even to despair of life and to suicide. Moreover, the use of the original faculties is by no means restricted to the formation of sensations and perceptions. On the contrary, attaching themselves to inner formations they become effective for the same excitations and for achievements of the most varied sort. Especially do they form in this way the fundamental active principle in all action as well as in all psychical products.

§ 26. *Third fundamental process.* The combination of faculties and excitations, such as are originally grounded in sensations and perceptions, and maintained in their reproductions, reveals sometimes a firmer and sometimes a less firm interpenetration of these two classes of elements. A more accurate observation now teaches us, that when elements are less firmly united and therefore mobile, they can be transferred in the greatest variety of combinations from one psychical formation to another. In all psychical developments at every moment of our lives there is an active striving towards a balancing or equalizing of the mobile elements in them. In a preliminary way we may give as examples of this fact the increase of intensity, which all the operations of our mind experience through the emotions of joy, of enthusiasm, of love, of anger, etc.; as well as upon the other hand, the depressions of the same, through sorrow, fear, etc.

§ 27. Our self-consciousness constantly exhibits a change, which sometimes mounts to an appalling variety and rapidity. But this change does not extend so far as at first glance it appears to do, and moreover chiefly effects only the excited state. For every psychical product that thus became formed in the human soul with any degree of perfection persists, even after it has disappeared from consciousness or from the sphere of excited psychical development, in the unconscious or inner being of the soul, out of which it can later enter into the conscious psychical development or be reproduced. We term that which persists in an unconscious state, with reference to the psychical development which continues unconsciously to exist, "a trace"; and in reference to those developments which are either constructed upon this basis, or which proceed therefrom, "a rudiment." (There is prefigured or predisposed in the same a presentation of imagination, a sensation, etc.) Every such trace consists therefore of two elements: faculty and excitation.

§ 28. We know indeed these traces or rudiments only by means of the reproductions thereof. We are, nevertheless, perfectly certain of them, because of the fact that these reproductions, where no hindrance occurs, always take place not only qualitatively, but also quantitatively, in the strictest agreement with the earlier psychical formations. The kind of the excitation and the strength of the faculty (the two elements out of which every trace was formed) return to consciousness in the same way, as at their coalescence they conditioned the development of the trace. In fact, strictly speaking, even this persistence of the trace needs no explanation, since there is represented in it only the universally evident fact, that what has once come into existence continues until it is destroyed through the agency of special causes. What, therefore, is here subject to explanation is not the continued subsistence, but only the transition into unconsciousness of what previously had been conscious; and this is easily comprehended from the aforesaid process of balancing. Inasmuch as the conscious developments balance or transfer in every direction, so far as an immediate combination takes place, those elements which are not firmly appropriated by them and are mobile, it follows, that such a depression must take place in them that they become unconscious forms or mere traces (§ 30).

§ 29. In reference to the presentation of these traces, which, as they are essentially unconscious cannot be made immediately by means of these themselves, we must hold absolutely to the effects which have led to their assumption. These traces hence have no actual place of existence. As is the soul in general, so also all its parts are nowhere; for self consciousness, which is our single source of knowledge, contains with itself immediately, and by itself, (without the addition of perceptions of the external senses), nothing whatever of spatial relations. The traces are also united to no bodily organ. For the intuitive notions of space, and the transformations thereof, which run parallel to the psychical developments, are in the strictest sense merely parallel to them, that is to say, synchronous, or at best always synchronous. They can thus in no wise be made essential to them, to say nothing of being postulated as their substantial basis (§ 43 ff.). The trace is what comes between the production of a psychical activity, (e.g., a sensory perception), and its reproduction, (e.g., as recollection). Since both of these acts are psychical we may also conceive of the trace only in psychical form. We are, nevertheless, in general able to acquire very definite ideas of it, since the fundamental conditions for this conception are given us in any case on two sides, and not infrequently, (when there traces are manifoldly reproduced), on several sides.

§ 30. Faculties and excitations exist in the traces in the relatively constant combination, which they have entered into with one another (§ 26). Since nothing can escape from the faculties, the loss by which the previously conscious or aroused developments become mere traces, must effect the received excitations; and so far as this loss occurs, to that extent is the faculty filled by them again emptied or free. In so far all traces are as such volitions (Strebungen); that is to say, the original faculties given in them strive for the recovery of that which they have lost, or for the renewed attainment of consciousness.

§ 31. The certainty, which we receive by a strict comparison of facts concerning this inner persistence, is, likewise, in two respects, invaluable for the perfecting of general psychological knowledge. First, because we apply them in a progressive direction. Since all previous developments of the soul, so far as they have not again been destroyed, continue to exist in the inner being of the soul, it follows, that this must, or (what is the same thing) the forces or faculties of the soul must, consist of traces of the earlier aroused developments. We can, therefore, perceive these faculties not merely from their effects, (which lead only to a summary or rough determination), but likewise from their causes too, or from the conscious developments preceding them. Since now these latter separate in far greater extension and far more decidedly, (in hundreds of cases and more), we thus derive by this means for the perception of their nature and organisation the same advantages as those which magnifying glasses afford when applied to external nature. Secondly, we can furthermore turn to account the doctrine of inner persistence in a retrogressive construction. This matter has been provisionally discussed (§ 21). If we have clearly recognised in a certain series of developments the manner in which the traces are formed, we can thus disregard that which is added to these in our thoughts, and, since we continually repeat this, can at last attain to a knowledge of the original nature of the soul.

§ 32. How far this persistence extends in reference to the quality of the developments, and the length of time, can scarcely be established with perfect certitude from the foregoing experiences. We know of the inner persistence only through the reproductions (§ 28). But from the fact that something has not heretofore been reproduced, and even now cannot be reproduced, it does not immediately follow that the same is not yet present, nor even that it is not capable of reproduction. Experiments which have been made in this matter in violent fevers and injuries, etc., have shown, that what one has believed to have long disappeared, because it has never been reproduced under the ordinary conditions of reproduction, was raised into consciousness and psychical activity under unusual conditions of production. The presumption, therefore, is great, that in general whatever has once formed a part with any degree of completeness of our soul is never again lost.

§ 33. Since the persistence of the traces consists in nothing except the continuance of whatever has once attained existence, the perfection in general of the traces must also be dependent upon the perfection with which the developments have originally been formed. In the sensations and perceptions, therefore, it would depend upon the perfection with which the excitations have been appropriated. We ascribe to the sensory original faculties in this connection a higher or lower degree of strength.

§ 34. In the innermost soul traces remain of this transference of mobile elements from one psychical form to another, and thereby are established, in the same manner as all permanent combinations, even the combinations of incompatible formations into groups and series: the combinations between the qualities of a thing, between the spatial and temporal coincidence, and the connection between causes and effects. These are, therefore, by no means to be regarded merely as ideal relations, but to be viewed, just as much as the single presentation, as some real abiding existence in the inner being of the soul.

§ 35. *Fourth fundamental process.* Identical formations of the human soul, and similar ones according to the measure of their likeness, attract one another, or strive to enter into closer relations with each other. This presents itself to our observation so frequently, not merely in its products but also in its occurrence, that it needs no further explanation. Familiar examples are such as, the witty combination of ideas, the formation of similies and judgments, the fusion of similar feelings and endeavors, etc. If now in these examples the coalescing formations are only partly similar to one another, this attraction, as is confirmed in the most evident manner by a stricter analysis of the facts in various cases, must take place between formations which are totally similar with still greater strength, and decisiveness. Nevertheless, the more critical observation shows that in all these attractions only a coalition of similar formations, but still no permanent combination or fusion of them is affected. Rather the process of balancing must enter in a complementary way for these latter, just as it must enter in permanent combinations between dissimilar formations. This balancing process reveals itself as active here with most remarkable strength, so that the blending gains a higher degree of intimacy, since a specially favorable basis is prepared for it by the indicated attraction (§ 91).

§ 36. The process of formation is of exceptional importance, especially for the judgment of quantitative development. If we suppose one and the same sensation, presentation, desire, etc., to be frequently produced, the traces remaining therefrom enter not only into relation with one another, but they also coalesce owing to their complete similarity into one total formation. And such formation appears to us as one to that degree in which we cannot become at all aware immediately of its complexity (qualitative), but only by means of its augmentation (quantitative). The strict conception and application of this will lead us to a number of highly significant conclusions, which have heretofore escaped the notice of science, because it has only very inaccurately taken these results into account.

§ 37. All the processes explained in the preceding paragraphs are of such an elementary character, and of so great universality, that scarcely one even of the simplest developments of our matured soul could be pointed out, in which they do not altogether, and even repeatedly, collaborate. But they show themselves active in very different relations of combinations and degree; and thus there is indeed nothing that prevents one from indicating this or that single fundamental process as the conditioning cause for this or that effect, when its agency is particularly conspicuous above the others. A more exact observation teaches, that these processes can occur with very various degrees of rapidity and vivacity. And since these processes, (at least so far as there is no external condition), manifest themselves uniformly in all developments, which take place in a human being within the range of a certain fundamental system, we are justified in deriving them in so far from the original faculties, and in attributing to the latter in respect thereof a higher or lower degree of animation as a primordial quality.

CHAPTER II. THE FUNDAMENTAL NATURE OF THE HUMAN SOUL

§ 38. If we summarize first of all the most general character-istics concerning the nature of the human soul which result from our preceding exposition, it presents itself to us: (1) as a perfectly immaterial being (§§ 22 and 29), consisting of certain fundamental systems, which not only in themselves, but also in combination with each other, are most intimately one, or constitute one being (§ 26); (2) as a sensory being, i.e., the ele-mentary forces of the soul are capable of certain stimulations from without by excitations, which are assimilated and retained by these forces (§ 22 f.). To these must still be added: (3) the forces of the soul gain by this assimilation a more positive organisation, and in this they enter upon manifold closer com-binations with one another, partly by means of the fusion of similar forms into one total form (§ 35 f.), and partly by means of the combination of dissimilar forms into groups and series (§ 34). (4) But the forces and faculties of the soul have also an original determinateness, which is twofold: the original de-terminateness of the fundamental systems to which they be-long, and the original determinateness of certain degrees of strength (§ 33), and vivacity (§ 37), and sensitiveness of stimulus (§ 23). Observation teaches us that every degree of any one of these fundamental conditions can occur together with any degree of the others.

§ 39. For a more exact determinateness we must compare human souls with the souls of lower animals. If we compare that which appears in the latter as the effect of the psychical, with that immediately perceived in us and the effects thereof, the most striking characteristic of human souls appears to be, that they are spiritual, (that is to say, if for the present we formulate this superiority in its greatest universality and as it immediately appears), — souls, which are capable of a clearer, more definite, and more comprehensive consciousness, and which necessarily develop such consciousness up to a certain point of time, although some in greater, others in lesser perfection. The question now arises, what we have to regard as that which fundamentally conditions this superiority.

§ 40. We here first encounter a view which was especially in the last century, and even in our time has been again, propounded. According to it, the original forces of human souls are said to be in and of themselves entirely similar to those of the lower animals, and the spiritual character of the human soul is derived solely from the more excellent bodily organisation with which this is united. In support of this view three things have been especially emphasized: first, the possession of hands by which man is enabled to change the position and form of objects, and thus become acquainted with an incomparably greater number of these qualities; secondly, the possession of speech, which makes possible a manifold expression of acquired ideas, etc., as well as a more extended and more perfect retention of them; and, thirdly, the slower growth owing to a longer period of childhood, in consequence of which there is a more varied accumulation and elaboration of ideas.

§ 41. The reasons specified in the preceding paragraph concerning the spiritual character of the human soul in no wise give a perfectly satisfactory explanation. From the greater mass of heterogeneous ideas which are acquired through the medium of the hands and speech, there would result in and for itself only a greater throng of them, and as a consequence rather a more rapid and more complete obliteration of the single idea. It is just as difficult to perceive from the slower growth of the body how it should transform the unspiritual into something spiritual without the addition of another positive factor. We have on the contrary to regard the slower formations of the body not as a cause, but as a consequence of spiritual development, which constantly exerts a certain modification upon the bodily development. The higher perfection of the human soul, therefore, cannot be in such wise merely externally conditioned, but must be a perfection that is internally and qualitatively conditioned, and which affects the innermost nature of the psychical original faculties themselves.

§ 42. Of the three fundamental characteristics of the original faculties as designated (§ 38), the susceptibility of excitation occurs not merely in many of the lower animals in like perfection with man, but also in case of some of them in greater perfection than in man. Vivacity occurs with men as with the lower animals in very many degrees. But what is peculiar and essential to human souls is a higher power of susceptibility and of appropriation of the excitation, as well as a greater force of inner persistence of the developments founded thereupon. By means of this more perfect inner persistence, there is made possible in the psychical developments of men an infinite increase of strength, of clearness, and of capacity of coalescence. In combination therewith, but also only in combination therewith, the hands, the speech, and the longer period of childhood are, to be sure, of no little significance for the development of the human soul. We can best designate this superiority of man over the lower animals by ascribing to the former a spiritual sensuousness. Besides the superiority of the higher energy of the original faculties there is another in which the possession of speech and hands are ranked only as single constituents. This is the more individual and more definite determinateness, and in consequence of that, the more definite separation of the different elementary systems, both as to the qualities of the several susceptibilities and activities, and as to the combinations and interweavings.

CHAPTER III. THE RELATION OF THE SOUL AND THE BODY

§ 43. THERE is still need of a more exact determination concerning the relation of the soul to the body. We have already remarked (§ 1), that these are very definitely separated in the perception (Auffassung), and the knowledge based thereupon; since to the knowledge of the soul everything belongs that we perceive by means of self-consciousness, and to the knowledge of the body everything by means of the external senses. We must leave to metaphysics the deeper determination of their real relation. We have here only to do with the question, how they must stand to one another for the purposes of psychology.

§ 44. Transferring the contrary kinds of knowledge mentioned in the foregoing paragraphs to the real, without due consideration those who have set as their task a strictly philosophical knowledge, in most cases have represented the soul and the body as being in their innermost nature opposed to one another. And from this the most remarkable hypotheses have been evolved; since upon the other hand the experience of every moment presents their immediate union in one and the same being, and also their immediate interaction and co-operation.

§ 45. When on the contrary there was set as a task no deeper philosophical knowledge, but there was in mind only the practical application, which a synthesis of both rendered desirable for a common knowledge, it has been attempted in most cases to refer the psychical developments to the bodily; indeed, some have gone so far as quite generally to designate the former as mere products of the bodily organization peculiar to man. This is the fundamental view of materialism. But the history of psychology shows, that never at any time has it been possible, either to explain or to construct from the material the very least of the developments of the soul. And not only so, but it can also admit of no doubt, that this will be just as little possible in the entire future. Both kind of ideas are much too dissimilar for this. In whatever way we may determine and combine the material forms and processes, we never attain to anything that has even the remotest resemblance to a thought, or to any other psychical product.

§ 46. What has given rise to the materialistic view indicated in the preceding paragraph is only the greater distinctness and definiteness, which the presentations of the bodily have over those of the psychical for those unused to self-examination. But this advantage is nevertheless purely subjectively grounded (in the nature of the presentation); and the transference of it to the objective, or real, can be in no wise justified. And as a subjective advantage it is to be regarded not even as essentially necessary, but only as accidental and temporary;

since in a practice continued for some time and intelligently conducted, an equally great, indeed a still greater, clearness and definiteness can be gained for the perception of psychical products and results.

§ 47. To this must be added, that we are able to observe (§ 13) the developments of our soul far more immediately and more intimately. This, in connection with what has been remarked in the preceding paragraph, enables us to develop the knowledge of the psychical forms and processes to such great definiteness, exactness, and acuteness, that the knowledge of the bodily stands far in the background. Indeed, we can foresee with the highest probability, that a completeness of understanding and construction for the bodily, such as we already have for the psychical, can never be gained (granted the highest possible perfection of magnifying glasses, etc.) even approximately. Even regardless of reasons of inner truth, it appears from the standpoint of the products of knowledge itself as far more desirable, that, in direct opposition to the materialistic view, we should be able to conceive and to construct the bodily according to the forms and the laws of the psychical.

§ 48. The problem which presents itself (§ 44) in the apparently opposed fundamental natures of the soul and body can be solved after deeper reflection (Aufassung) very simply, in that, we also perceive our own body, as everything else corporeal, only by means of the impressions upon our senses, and, therefore, not immediately as in the case of the soul, where the powers and developments are apprehended as they are in themselves. But there correspond certain forces to the perceptions of our own body as its being (in itself), which as they effect those sensory perceptions, permit still many other results to proceed from themselves. And the opposition in our observations of the two kinds of developments can arise just as well from the difference in the faculties of perception, as from the difference of the perceived objects and events. That this difference is not so great as it appears is already in the highest degree probable, even (we can truly say) certain, from the fact, that there exists no kind of bodily developments which cannot become conscious under certain circumstances, and which as conscious cannot be immediately perceived by us. But in that event it becomes psychical (§§ 1 and 43); as it stands also in fact in this case to the positively psychical developments entirely in the same relations of reciprocal aid, of combination, and of opposition, as the psychical developments stand to one another. Such a transformation of a thing most ordinarily to be conceived as non-psychical into one to be conceived as psychical, would be unthinkable, if in their fundamental nature they were opposed.

On the contrary we are led to conclude that both kinds of forces must stand very close to one another in their innermost nature; and no artificial hypotheses (§ 44) are necessary for the explanation of their intimate relationship and reciprocal action. What through the senses we learn of the human body, or what we commonly term the body, we have to view only as external signs or representatives of the innermost nature of the body, which, like the soul, consists of certain forces and their developments, that are indeed distinct from those of the soul, but are nevertheless essentially of the same kind.

§ 49. On the other hand, it must be added, that the different fundamental systems of the soul also do not develop consciousness in equal perfection, but rather in very significant gradations. And they show the gradations in all relations parallel, as we observe between the positively psychical developments and the bodily developments raised to the psychical. Thus the difference between the soul and the body stands forth still more definitely than a mere difference of degree. They even approach so near to one another that no real line of separation can be drawn between them in the living man, and in general they are not farther separated than the different psychical fundamental systems from one another. A real separation between soul and body takes place first only at death.

§ 50. In any event we are justified according to the conclusions reached, to include the bodily, so far as it develops

consciousness, in our science, and to make the attempt to discover whether its developments, and especially its action upon
the soul, may not be construed according to the laws, which
have come to light for the positive psychical developments from
the facts observed by our self-consciousness. It furthermore
immediately appears from this, that we have throughout to
suppose no other bond for the connection of soul and body, than
that by which the psychical systems themselves are united.

§ 51. Even the most general survey of the bodily developments permits no doubt concerning the fact, that the four fundamental laws which have been established for the psychical,
likewise have their application as determining and regulating
the bodily, though to be sure with some modifications. The
bodily forces also need support from without, and they strive
after and appropriate it; and in them, too, life is propagated
from within by means of continual acquisition of new homogeneous faculties or forces. In them also, received stimuli are
balanced with reference to the formations which stand in relation therewith; and the developments deprived in this way of
excitation continue to exist in the forms of traces or forces,
which thereafter enter as rudiments into future developments.
Finally, in them too, a reciprocal attraction between homogeneous developments manifests itself. They enter into closer
relation, or even totally fuse with each other. As a result of all
this there is formed that which one terms (favorably or unfav-
orably etc.) the bodily constitution. What is lacking to the
bodily developments in all these relations, is only a more independent development of elementary acts and forces, which
distinguish psychical development (§ 42). They coalesce too
with less regard to distinctions; and the forms of organisation
have therefore no such definite determination (§ 47).

§ 52. It is thus obvious, that the recognised fundamental
laws prove effective for the interaction between soul and body,
and the rudiments remaining from these. Here only the adjustment of the mobile elements and the attraction of the homogeneous formations come into consideration. By means of the
former all transferences and influences which proceed from the

soul to the body, or from the body to the soul, are determined: especially in the first direction every bodily doing or action produced by the soul, as well as the involuntary manifestations of the emotions, etc.; and in the second direction the manifold aids which the psychical development experiences from the bodily, and by means of which the soul as it were constantly feeds upon the bodily. The attraction in relation to those things homogeneous, shows itself operative especially in the distribution of the tones from the one to the other, and in the associations between similarly toned psychical and bodily developments. Moreover, these are operative in various forms, e.g., in passions and other emotions, for the production of balancings among the corresponding bodily developments, when psychical developments meet, which by their firmer forms of organization, or otherwise, are prevented from balancing. Thus blushing accompanies shame and anger, etc.; tears of emotion accompany the unexpected proofs of love, and deserved but long withheld marks of distinction, etc. From all this it follows, that we have to conceive the bodily life as subordinated to the psychical; whereas materialism affirms that the life of the soul is only an intensified bodily; and that as an independent existence in man there is no soul.

MORITZ WILHELM DROBISCH
(1802–1896)

EMPIRICAL PSYCHOLOGY ACCORDING TO THE METHODS OF NATURAL SCIENCE

Translated from the German* by
BENJAMIN RAND

FIFTH SECTION: THE FUNDAMENTAL EXPLANATION OF THE PSYCHICAL LIFE

III. THE DYNAMICS OF IDEAS AS A PRINCIPLE OF EXPLANATION OF PSYCHICAL PHENOMENA

§ 138. *THE INTERDEPENDENCE OF PSYCHICAL PHENOMENA*

In the explanation of psychical phenomena it is most necessary, that their connection and interdependence be not neglected in the consideration of their diversity, because otherwise we should set up unavoidable hindrances to any theory seeking for unity. Of this character is particularly the assumption of an original two- or threefold division of the activity of the mind, which is supposed to rest upon the qualitative difference of inner phenomena. After the detailed examination of the latter we should still find impossible to place in one and the same category as regards their origin, ideas, feelings, and desires; on the contrary, we must rather regard the lack of independence, and even actual dependence of the forms of the latter two kinds of phenomena upon the ideas, as an indication that these in some way lie at their foundation, and that they are capable of being made comprehensible as derived states. In-

* From M. W. Drobisch's *Empirische Psychologie nach naturwissenschaftlicher Methode*, Hamburg und Leipzig, 1842; 2te Aufl. 1898.

deed, so many earlier psychologists have sought to prove this, that we may say the atomistic trichotomy of the soul was first introduced by Kant and his school.

If now the uselessness of abstract powers of the mind has been made clear in what has preceded, no one can desire to revert, either to a general faculty of ideas, or to any specific kinds of it, under the names of sense, imagination, understanding, etc. On the contrary, the ever increasing specialisation of these faculties, which becomes necessary if one somewhat more than superficially considers inner experience, shows that we cannot pursue this method with success, but have to take one directly opposed. This consists in supposing each single idea itself as an independent state of the mind, and accordingly an indefinitely large number of such states. If now to each one of these a power is ascribed as cause, we thus acquire, to be sure, instead of a moderate number of faculties of the mind, an almost unlimited number of individual powers of the mind. We do not fail to perceive that we are thereby still further, and in a far more hazardous way, removed from the unity of the soul,than is the case with the theory of faculties. But if we do not succeed in comprehending the unity of ten or twenty faculties, the failure consequently is essentially not greater if a thousand or ten thousand powers of forming ideas appear hard to combine. Nevertheless this would only be a lamentable consolation, which we are far from claiming. Therefore, either we must seek so to justify that hypothesis, that it no longer controverts the unity of the soul, or this principle is not adequately established, and must be given up. Let us then first test somewhat more closely this demand for the unity of the soul, as the possessor of the powers of the mind.

§ 139. *THE UNITY OF THE SOUL*

If it must be conceded that the powers of the mind, as causes of its states, are not objects of inner observation, it holds still more true of the mind itself, as the possessor of those powers. For self-consciousness by no means reveals to us the mind, on the contrary, shows only the empirical I, from which through abstraction of its changing content the pure I is first attained; but which, for that very reason, is an empty and really formal idea. The identity of our psychical being is, therefore, by no means immediately guaranteed as a fact by the identity of our self-consciousness, and it is merely upon inferences that this conviction is based. Without deeper metaphysical argumentation the following observations can be made upon this subject.

All our ideas have a tendency to become united, to exchange their multiplicity for unity, and they actually coalesce, so far as the contradictions of their contents do not prevent. Our sensuous perception, as well as our intellectual conception, is a constant process of unification, either through the percept, or the concept; therefore, every theoretical science involves the effort to reduce the principles of explanation to the lowest possible number. The fact, that only a few ideas can enter our consciousness at once, shows to be sure at first glance, that they displace, suppress, therefore, as it were, expel one another; but also on the other hand, that they are not able to avoid one another, but are held together by an attractive force. The same thing likewise appears in associations, these quite involuntary and artless combinations of simultaneous ideas. It is, therefore, possible to attribute similar attractive and repellant forces to ideas, after the analogy of the physical-chemical hypothesis of attractions and repulsions of elements. But leaving out of consideration the fact, that here attraction and repulsion must be ascribed simultaneously to the same elements of psychical life, which beyond controversy is inconceivable (the physicist attributes attraction to the molecules, and transfers repulsion to the surrounding sphere of heat), there is furthermore this difference, that the elements of bodies have an independent existence, so that the existence of the body depends upon that of its elements, which become thereby the constituents out of which it is composed.

Nevertheless, it will not occur to anyone to affirm that the mind is composed of its ideas, and that these have also existence apart from the mind. The mind, in which they are, and because they are in it, which has no constituents (for what apart from ideas, could otherwise be its constituents?), and is consequently simple, must moreover itself be assumed to be the principle of unity. This also leads to the same conclusion, that the body is external to the mind, but ideas, feelings, and desires, are within it. The mind is, therefore, in a middle ground between outer and inner experience, as the unit of measure — belonging to no experience — of things and states of the external and internal world. With a measure one can indeed measure; but one cannot wish to measure it itself, or it ceases to be a measure. One can indeed distinguish the parts in it; but these are only accidental parts, and not essential constituents.

§ 140. *THE REFUTATION OF THE FACULTY CONCEPT*

If accordingly the hypothesis of the unity of the soul appear to us reasonably established, so that we have to think of it as having strict simplicity of being because otherwise a new principle of unification would be needed, the question is all the more seriously renewed, how the other hypothesis of an unlimited number of states of the mind is supposed to be compatible with it. There corresponds to every individual sensation a simple idea as a state of the mind, and combined ideas originate from these as their elements. Shall we endow the mind with as many faculties as it has simple ideas? And if not, what else shall we do? In order to decide this question, it is necessary first to determine, what must be understood by faculties. If we oppose activity to it, as reality to possibility, the entire concept of faculty is at bottom an empty thought, which can signify nothing other, than that after an activity has originated we can then add in thought, that nevertheless the possibility must have been present for it beforehand. But this possibilty is also only a mode of forming ideas in the mind of the thinker, and is nothing in the things themselves; for we should thereby conceive an actual possibility, which is a gross absurdity.

In this merely logical sense we will not want to have the concept of possibility taken, but we seek to express thereby, that an activity is existent in the germ (potentia), and only awaits the opportunity to develop into actuality (actu). We cannot, indeed, strictly mean thereby, that the activity is retained wholly as it afterwards manifests itself, only in a concentrated undeveloped condition in the mind, so that, therefore, e.g., the sensuous ideas before they appear in consciousness through stimulation of the senses, dwell in the mind in the same way as they abide in the recesses of the memory, after they have become forgotten. This would make every excitation of ideas from without a mere appearance, and would therefore be a view compatible only with the most thoroughgoing idealism. This is rather what we mean, that, just as the seed-corn, in order to germinate and develop, requires earth, air, moisture, and warmth, but nevertheless these potencies can still bring into development only a seed-corn, but by no means a stone, or even a blossom; so likewise a diversified capacity for forming ideas, is to be understood as belonging to the mind, by virtue of which, if certain external conditions are associated therewith, an actual formation of ideas take place in it.

If we would discuss this concept metaphysically we should put the question, whether the multiplicity of capacities harmonises better with the demanded unity of the soul, than a multiplicity of actual powers; or whether the soul, if it originally carries in itself as the mode of its existence such a multiplicity of capacities, would be strictly regarded anything more than a system of the same, therefore, a compound, and what then must be deemed the significance of these capacities apart from this compound? But this may be left out of the present discussion.

Possibly one might think of seeking aid through the analogy of physics, by saying that the activity is still united to the capacity, *latent*, and becomes *free* through development under the coöperation of external conditions. To this suggestion we should oppose the observation, that latent heat or electricity presupposes the free; that this latter is the first and original, the former only the secondary and derived condition. Latent activities of the mind may therefore indeed be termed ideas stored in memory beyond consciousness; but the ideas originating according to common conviction through sensory impressions if, as becoming free, they are to be viewed as previously bound, would have to be taken as platonic remembrances out of a previous existence, and their sensuous origin would have to be a vain delusion. To prove this latter has up to now been impossible for any scepticism, or any idealism.

§ 141. *IDEAS AS STATES AND NOT POWERS OF THE MIND*

According to the foregoing every return to faculties, or power of forming ideas, in whatever way we may conceive these, appears to lead to no acceptable result. We must, therefore, attempt to obtain another point of view of ideas, which without being content to regard them as mere inner phenomena, explains both their existence, and promises to make conceivable, as coming from them, feelings and desires. In this attempt the comparison with physical science affords us the safest guidance. If the physicist says that this body possesses the capacity to become more heated, luminous, electrical, magnetic, to resound, to enter into many chemical combinations, etc., he does not mean by that, that the body possesses certain faculties or dormant powers, which under certain conditions can awaken and produce those phenomena, but he signifies thereby only certain dispositions or qualities of the body, whether these may have their location in the bulk of its matter, in its mechanical composition, or in the relation of the quality of its matter to that of some other body. If we here speak of a force as the cause of such a physical condition of a body, it is not transferred to this, but is established outside of it, and the body appears only as a thing which is placed in a certain condition, to which we do not on that account ascribe peculiar powers; or would we attribute to a heavy body a power to fall, to the resonant a power to sound? How far even the older physics was from any such theory as this, its hypothesis of a force of inertia shows. It did not attribute to a mobile body a power of movement, but a power to resist movement. The new physics, on the other hand, discards both, and views rest and motion as states which are alike accidental to the bodies, but if they are placed in them, they continue unchanged until a removal or modification of the same ensues. The thought of the capacity of bodies for these states drops entirely as idle and unfruitful.

To heed this example of physics might now be by far the most profitable method for psychology. It has been already remarked above, that in our immediate consciousness the forming of ideas appears neither as an actuality, nor a capacity of the mind, but only as a happening in it. Accordingly, in harmony with experience, we will designate the ideas as states of the mind, and can affirm at least of the sensuous ideas, which form the basis of all others, that the mind is placed in these states by means of external causes through the agency of the organs of sense, which, like the produced motion of a body, continues unchanged so long as they are not removed or modified by additional inner or outer causes. We consequently lay claim to the principle of permanence (the law of inertia) for these states, and regard the mind as existence in itself, barren of ideas, and accordingly also of feelings and desires, which, on account of its simplicity, can attain to those states only through the manifold relations of its quality to the qualities of the things with which it stands in relation, — comparable to chemical affinity.

The nature and mode in which external things affect the mind, the conditions of the production of any idea, remain partly physiological and partly metaphysical problems. But since it is assumed, that the manifoldness of the relations of the individual mind to the external causes of its simple ideas creates likewise a manifold constitution in the latter, the question how the unity of the mind is consistent with the multiplicity of its inner happenings has at least in general no more difficulties. One and the same number can enter into infinitely numerous relations, and the exponent of the relations is in every case a different one. With such exponents the ideas may be compared; and with the common fundamental unit (the first member) of them, the mind itself may be compared. But if one desires more than comparisons, one has then to do with metaphysics, which has to discuss this question in the systematic relation of concepts. For the immediate purpose it suffices to observe that the formation of ideas must be conceived not from the point of view of a manifestation of power of the mind, but as a state of the same, or as a happening befalling it. The ideas must not be compared with powers, but with movements of the mind; and if a sensuous image is desired, they can best be compared with the oscillations of a body, otherwise externally at rest.

§ 142. *THE FREEDOM AND INHIBITION OF IDEAS*

The facts of the changing attention and of the disappearance of ideas from consciousness, as well as their reappearance in it, reveal clearly, that ideas although themselves only states of the mind, nevertheless are capable of having in their turn different states of their own. These are the states of freedom and of inhibition of ideas. An idea will then be free, if simultaneously there be represented no others of opposite quality, but only of a like or dissimilar constitution. But if opposed ideas occur simultaneously, a diminution of that freedom takes place, which can be termed inhibition. For as experience adequately shows, ideas do not mutually suppress one another, not even when some of them become forgotten — for they can be again aroused under certain conditions — but they are merely brought into a state in which they cease wholly or in a certain degree to be ideas; but for all that are neither destroyed, nor suffer a diminution of their being, which rather assumes only another form. This is the form of *striving*.

In the same degree namely, in which vividness or the conscious clearness of an idea diminishes, in that degree a resistance to this violent state and a striving to free itself therefrom arises in it. Under such circumstances the idea certainly becomes a force, but one which is directed against a definite hindrance obstructing its freedom. It ceases at once to be a force so soon as that hindrance disappears, and it has attained again its natural uninhibited state. In this striving is found the principle for the explanation of desire; it would, however, be rash if one were to affirm this striving to be in general the desire itself. For manifestly no idea could disappear from consciousness, unless its return were desired; and all ideas, which we any time have had and have long since forgotten, would have to be desired, and consequently press for return into consciousness. Of this, however, we do not observe the least, and we are not even aware of any such pressure on the part of the ideas, from which our attention is momentarily diverted. A conscious and an unconscious striving must therefore be distinguished, and the conditions of this distinction must be investigated.

§ 143. *THE INHIBITION OF OPPOSING IDEAS*

In fact our inhibited striving is to be conceived as at one time united with the feeling of pressure, and as at another time without any such feeling. This indicates an essential difference in the inhibition, according as this occurs before or after the complete balancing of the opposing striving of ideas. The former is combined with a feeling of obstruction, the latter is free therefrom, and can be termed an equilibrium of ideas, which takes place within or without consciousness, according as the balanced ideas are in part only, or wholly inhibited. Ideas which are not yet in equilibrium will possess a striving after it; for only the balanced condition can have a point of rest, and the inhibition connected with it will be that which under the given circumstances imposes upon the ideas the least proportionate pressure. More precise determinations of this state, the conditions of equilibrium of ideas, cannot be developed without the aid of mathematics. Ideas in equilibrium are united in general neither with feelings nor with desires; but both accompany the still unbalanced ideas. Feelings and desires as distinct from ideas are inconceivable. They lack a definite representable *what*, a *quale;* nevertheless they are actually in consciousness. They must, therefore, be found in it as the manifold changeable *how* of presentation. Wherein now does this consist, and how do they differ from one another? By what means do I know of my desires? Do I perceive an act of desire immediately? Not at all, I certainly feel only the state of desire, but still distinguish therefrom the feeling which accompanies it. The desire destroys the calm, the equilibrium of the mind, or to speak more correctly, the equilibrium of its ideas. If I have a feeling of this equilibrium, a change in it will be a feeling of disturbance. The feeling of psychical equilibrium is precisely similar to that of bodily health. Of both there exists no positive feeling. The body as well as the mind is in a state of equilibrium when one has no feeling of its activities, just as a machine in which there is the least possible friction makes but little noise. Desires and feelings are, therefore, the indices of the deviation from the state of equilibrium of ideas.

It is to be remembered if we wish to comprehend their difference, that desires are the activity, feelings the passivity of the mind. Now desire is the striving of that idea, whose content is desired, against obstructions, which have their ground it is true outside of the mind, but nevertheless must be felt by it, since otherwise the striving idea, which always abides in the mind, would find no obstruction. Obstructions are, therefore, at least in the broadest sense of the term, themselves ideas. But whilst the hindrances obstruct, they react against the striving idea, and thereby become unpleasant. This latter idea presses and is pressed; in it is the seat of desire; in its obstructions is the seat of the unpleasant feeling of resistance united therewith. The overcoming striving of an idea against such obstructions is therefore the desire of its content; and the succumbing resistance of what is opposed is therefore the painful feeling, which is constantly united with the postponement of the attainment of what is desired. The former is the striving, the latter is the suffering of the one desiring. The desire is, therefore, not felt only in the idea of the desired thing, also not alone in that which resists it. but in both at the same time, and in their relation, which is none other than the disturbance of the preceding equilibrium. But the striving idea, however, does not itself alone possess the power for this disturbance, but gains it only through union with an internal or external perception related to it, which reproduces and lifts above the point of equilibrium, and which therefore appears as the external cause of the origin, or the reawakening of desire. The desire appears herewith as a progressing or retrogressing movement of ideas; if we regard the maximum of their clearness as the goal or culminating point. But the mind itself is thereby immediately neither active, nor passive. It is both, only mediately, in so far, that is to say as its ideas are found in these states.

§ 144. *THE ORIGIN OF FEELINGS AND DESIRES*

This is the first, and, to be sure, only a very meagre outline of the origin of feelings and desires, of which a further and more exhaustive explanation would demand a more exact and more varied development of the explanatory principle postulated as its basis, than is here possible and consistent with the desired aim. Nevertheless, it is at least possible to add the following corollaries.

(1) Just as the idea striving against abstractions causes desire, the idea retreating reluctantly from consciousness causes repugnance. For manifestly the content represented in it is the object of repugnance, but the energy of the repugnance is contained in the ideas opposed to this idea, which repel and gradually suppress it; the stronger the resistance of the receding idea, so much the stronger is the emotion of abhorrence.

(2) Feelings of oppression can also arise without desire and abhorrence, that is to say, without a progressive or retrogressive movement of ideas. For granted an idea is in itself too weak to continue in consciousness when opposed by many stronger ones, and thus to be in equilibrium with them, it can nevertheless happen by the following means, that it is associated with an idea of a dissimilar content, which affords the support demanded for equilibrium with the others. The

memory-image of the room which I occupied many years ago as a schoolboy is itself not capable of continuing beside the intuitions of the present; but if by a related perception the damp, musty smell is reproduced, which at that time made its occupancy not the most agreeable, then the image emerges with full vividness and continues in my consciousness. But nevertheless, any such recollection always demands a certain effort, and this consists in the fact that the retained idea is in a pressed position between the opposed ideas seeking to supplant it, and those dissimilar which afford to it the necessary support. Hence arises a feeling of oppression.

(3) An idea, finally, can also arise notwithstanding opposing hindrances, that is to say, when this rising occurs under the protection of a stronger idea entirely homogeneous with it, which removes the obstacles in its way, and thereby makes for it a free path. Then the obstacles disappear as if dispelled by magic, like the impotent spectres of the night before the light of day. Under such circumstances the rising idea possesses more elasticity than it can expend, and the character of its movement creates a feeling of pleasure.

With these corollaries we must here be content, for the conditions under which the feelings of the good and the beautiful arise, lie too deep to permit of being here developed with any clearness.

§ 145. *THE EQUILIBRIUM AND MOVEMENT OF IDEAS*

The concepts of freedom and inhibition, of equilibrium and movements, of striving and resistance of ideas, developed with the sharpest lines of differentiation, must henceforth, solely and alone, take the place of the theory of the abstract faculties of ideas, feeling, and desire, as explanatory principles. But they serve, moreover, to supplant the more special faculties subordinated to these in a manner more conformable to experience. Our entire analysis of psychical phenomena must have demonstrated, that association and reproduction are the keys which open the portals of the inner life of the soul. But the principles themselves henceforth can be proved to be derived from others lying deeper. For association is the result of the unity of the soul, by means of which all the states of the latter, so far as their contrasts admit it, unite and enter combinations under all circumstances. But reproduction rests in part immediately upon associations, and in part upon the concepts of freedom and inhibition of ideas.

In general the apparent manifestation of the faculties of the mind rests upon combinations, aggregations of ideas in the large, which we can style with Herbart masses of ideas (*Vorstellungsmassen*), which developed with more or less regularity are interwoven out of series, and series of series; and movements and transformations of these masses of ideas appear in place of the activity of the faculties. The individual faculties are distinguished in part formally by the different kind of the formation of the masses in which they have their location; and in part materially by the kind of ideas which make up the material of the mass. By means of the latter we can understand the so frequently occurring partiality of memory, of imagination, and of the understanding.

Memory, therefore, we may ascribe to our mind in so far as it possesses ideas, which still bear the characteristics of their first origin, and which return to consciousness, out of which they have been crowded by others, according to the same temporal order as that in which they originated, in that train of recollected thought which is conformable to the laws of memory.

Imagination we can ascribe to our mind in so far as it possesses ideas, in which the characteristics of their first sensuous origin are obliterated, which therefore no longer occupy a definite place among other after images of former perceptions, and are no longer reproduced in the temporal sequence of the same. But the most manifold combinations are entered upon, according to all the laws of association, which enable it to perform even as manifold reproductions, and to give them that easy mobility, by which the making of more and more numerous combinations of surpassing novelty is rendered possible.

Understanding belongs to our mind in so far as there exists in it masses of ideas whose combinations, independent of all accidental circumstances of their encounter, are completely adapted to the nature of their content, and therefore correspond to the relations of things; it may be, that, as in theoretical understanding, this content is sharply separated in conceptual definitions, or, as in the practical understanding, is rightly recognised only in relation to the content of another idea.

Our mind possesses *will*, in so far as it has masses of ideas, whose content represent what is willed, and whose striving exercises a decisive control over other ideas and combinations of ideas.

The mind is *rational*, if the moral insight has become the kernel and centre of the mass-of-ideas ruling all others. But man as a natural creature is called rational in so far as adaptations have been made in his physical organisation, which makes possible the development of moral insight, and the attainment of it to power, but do not prevent it as in the case of the lower animals.

Finally with momentary perceptions the mind possesses *sensibility*.

§ 146. THE STAGES IN THE FORMATION OF THE SPIRIT

With this explanation and limitation of the apparent faculties of the mind the view can now be united, which discerns the different stages in the formation of the spirit. Indeed it is obvious, that thereby the transformations must at the same time be considered, which affect the body in its different periods of life, and which without doubt favor and support the psychical processes. But after the subtraction of these bodily conditions there remain nevertheless always a series of purely psychical transformations residual, resting chiefly upon the changes which take place in the combinations of ideas.

Ideas are barren of connection and therefore purely sensuous in their first origin in the newborn child, but after a short time those associations have already been formed which are necessary to memory, and a little later that desire appears, which not always the need of food, but often only the sight of the nurse calls forth. In the boy, it is true, highly manifold combinations of ideas have been formed, and we must concede to him memory and imagination, understanding and will, in very many spheres of his capacity for forming ideas. But nevertheless, sensibility, memory, and imagination still dominate in him, to which his fondness for sweetmeats, his love of sightseeing and curiosity, his ability for learning by heart, his joy in narratives of adventure, his desire for sport, sufficiently testify. The youth begins to feel: the scattered ideas concentrate in him to form a more abiding and more powerful empirical self, by which he not only acquires power over his actions and thereby becomes responsible, but also learns to guide his imagination in poetic composition, and to formulate his thought in reflection. With higher self-consciousness the inner world opens before him, and with it the finer feeling for the beautiful in nature, art, poetry, and the other sex. — Still experience is lacking, which gives maturity to the understanding. This manhood gives with increasing needs and cares, for the supplying of which understanding must serve; but the execution of its decisions demands energy of the will, and the duties to society and to the family, a moral content of the will. Self-control must, therefore, now be present in constant increase, and a constant, true, and reasonable activity towards the outer world must take the place of youthful vacillation. With self-control reason is finally acquired, the strength of which must increase in the same measure as that in which sensuous impressionability, the power of desires and passions, decrease.

Thus the combinations among ideas become greater in number, and more perfected in the course of life, and as a result of it restrain and control its movements. The stress of emotions and passions give place to more mature considerations; absentmindedness and the flightiness of imagination yield to the sharp attention and many sided circumspectness of reflection; knowledge tempers the disquietude of doubt; and when this knowledge can go no further, faith succeeds to its function. The entire development of the mind progresses always towards a more and more harmonious form, and its activity towards a more and more peaceful movement. But there are not newly awakening faculties of the mind which produce this change of phenomena; but there are always only the ideas, their combinations and movements, ideation and its states, by means of which they become intelligible.

FRANÇOIS PIERRE GONTHIER MAINE DE BIRAN
(1766–1824)

ESSAY UPON THE FOUNDATIONS OF PSYCHOLOGY

Translated from the French * *by*
BENJAMIN RAND

CHAPTER I. FACTS OF THE INNER SENSE

. . . .

I SHALL characterise from the present this inner sense (*sens intime*) in a more explicit manner under the name of *sense of effort*, of which the cause or productive force becomes *self*, by the single fact of the distinction which is established between the subject of that free effort, and the object which resists immediately through its own inertia. I say immediately, in order to announce here in advance another very essential distinction, that I believe myself authorized to set up between the resistance or relative inertia of one's own body, which yields to or obeys voluntary effort, and the absolute resistance of the foreign body, which may be invincible.

The sense of effort has not been designated until now by its specific name, precisely because it is the innermost, or the nearest to ourselves, or rather because it is ourselves. If one should demand at this stage to be made acquainted with it by a more detailed exposition, I should reply, that each of our senses defines itself by its exercise. If there were, for example, one born paralytic who had never acted voluntarily to move

* From Maine de Biran's *Essai sur les fondements de la psychologie* (1812), in his *Œuvres inédites*, publiées par Ernest Naville, Paris, 1859, tom. 1.

his limbs or to set in motion foreign bodies, — supposing that such a person, which appears impossible to me, could have had the least degree of intelligence, — there would be no more possibility to make him understand by language what effort is, than there is to explain to one born blind what color and the sense of sight are. Nevertheless, as one explains not the sense or the phenomenon of vision, but rather the conditions, instruments, and physical or organic means, which serve to effect it, it will perhaps not be useless to analyse also physically the instruments and means of exercise of the internal sense of effort, in order to learn the better to circumscribe its domain by distinguishing it from that of an external sense with which it might be confused. I shall therefore enter upon some considerations which appear to me important.

This study, foreign as it is to the proper analysis of the phenomena of the inner sense, which excludes everything that belongs to the province of external observation, will be included more expressly in the object of another portion of this work, where we shall be occupied more particularly with the relation of the phenomena of physical or organic nature than with those of psychology; but I cannot proceed without giving the following physiological hints as indispensable to my actual purpose.

1. The organs of sensation with which the physiologists have heretofore been exclusively occupied, appear confined to the cerebral nervous system, distinguished by a well known observer [1] under the title of the *Nervous system of animal life*. The sense of effort, here in question, is limited by that part of the muscular system, which the action of the will expressly sets in play, and which physiology distinguishes also under the title of a *System of the voluntary muscles of the animal life*.

2. In the natural and original state of the sentient being there is no affection felt in any part whatsoever of its organism, nor any object perceived externally, except in so far as the nervous extremities are at first excited by some cause foreign to the self, and as this first impression is uninterruptedly transmitted by the sensory nerves which receive it as far as the

[1] Cf. Bichat's works: *De la vie et la mort* and *Anatomie Physiologique*.

centre of the brain, where perception is supposed to occur, although we are profoundly ignorant of what takes place in the nerves and the brain whenever an impression is felt or perceived. Nevertheless, daily experience proves that such perception is always preceded or accompanied by the organic conditions which we have just mentioned. But in the exercise of the sense of effort something more takes place.

Let us first suppose that the muscular organ be excited by an external cause, or by a *stimulus* adapted to set in play that vital property that the physiologists name irritability or sensory organic contractility; or again, let us suppose that a movable part may be aroused or strongly agitated by an external force, there will indeed clearly result from it a particular impression, which one may call muscular sensation or sensation of movement, but which could not be confused with that mode of our activity which we designate by the term of willed effort. In fact, this muscular sensation is subject to the same laws or organic conditions which determine the general sensory functions; it is always an impression received and transmitted to the brain, where it is felt as a passive mode foreign to the will or to the *self*. But in effort such as we perceive and reproduce at each instant, there is no excitation, no foreign stimulus, and nevertheless the muscular organ is set in play, the contraction effected, the movement produced, without any cause other than this inner force which is felt or immediately perceived in its exercise, and also without any sign being capable of representing it to the imagination or to some sense other than its own.

Let us however represent this force in exercise by an image, and, by placing ourselves for a moment at the physiological point of view, let us suppose that it be localised in the centre of the brain. When the effort is made, this central spring to the release of which there is referred by a sort of imaginary fiction the feeling of our activity, *will be said to enter into action of itself*.[1] I adopt this last expression, as a material sign of voluntary effort, or of an action which is neither actually compelled nor

[1] An expression of M. Cabanis in his great work upon the *Rapports du physique et du moral de l'homme*.

provoked by any sensory impression coming from without, nor even produced in any part of the nervous system outside the centre. The first motor determination being thus begotten in the centre, is immediately transmitted by the nerves to the muscular organ. This is contracted, or extended; its specific irritability is set in action, as it could be by a foreign stimulus. But, whereas, in this last case, the simple passive muscular sensation commences at the external organ in order to terminate at the centre which receives it; here the active motor stimulus commences in the centre where the cause resides, which, after having performed the contraction or movement, perceives as effect by means of the nervous transmission the muscular impression which it originates in the beginning. I here discover the symbol of complete action, the physiological signs of which I must endeavor to analyse more expressly; because, it is upon these signs alone that the analysis can here be based, since every action of the will is truly indivisible and instantaneous as known through the inner sense.

In considering, therefore, this action from the point of view of physiology, I distinguish two elements, or two moments, in which it is accomplished. To the first corresponds the simple motor determination or the release of the central spring affecting the nerves. However, that part of the action, thus limited to the nervous system, does not appear to be accompanied by a particular internal perception; but supposing there were such perception, and that it were not such as to be necessarily confused with that of resistance or inertia of the contracted muscle, which accompanies or immediately follows it, one still could not regard it as the symbolical sign of individuality or of the *self*, which can begin to know itself, or to exist for itself, only so far as it can distinguish itself as subject of effort from an object which resists. Thus the kind of obscure perception which would correspond to this incomplete action which is performed from a single centre upon a homogeneous nervous system, would be still only a vague and confused feeling of existence, to which perhaps some species of animals are limited. To the second moment corresponds that which takes place in the motor system, from the instant when the muscle contracts, until the effect of the contraction is transmitted or carried to the centre, where the muscular sensation then takes on this characteristic of reduplication which constitutes the inner consciousness of effort, inseparable from a resistance, or the inner consciousness of the *self* which knows itself by distinguishing itself from the resisting object.

Let us now pass from the symbol or the sign to the thing signified, and compare the internal facts with the hypotheses or the physiological facts.

We know, from a very constant experience, that the sentient being can never give to itself by any exercise of its activity, those agreeable or disagreeable impressions which affects it in spite of itself; that it is not the artisan nor the creator of those sensations or of those images which come into existence, succeed one another or disappear, without any concurrence of its will, or even against its desire. We know, moreover, from the observation of sentient nature, and from the various experiments of physiologists, that there exist sure and constant means to set in play the animal sensitivity by appropriate excitations, and to draw from the sentient being all the signs of the affections, of pain, or of physical pleasure, that one makes it undergo. The internal sense of effort on the other hand can be set in play only by this force, which is interior and *sui generis*, that we call will, and with which what we call our *self* is completely identified.

The power of effort, or the ability to commence and to continue any series of movements or of actions, is a fact of inner sense as evident as that of our existence itself. There is no foreign force to which that power is necessarily subordinated. Observe thus, how powerless all the external or artificial means may be which would tend to imitate the results of that acting force, or to reproduce and to provoke the signs of its manifestation. If you apply a *stimulus*, either directly upon a muscle, or upon the trunk, or the nervous centre which send ramifications to it, you of a certainty bring about contractions, sensed in the living, and purely organic in the dead. In regard to the will of man, or the power of effort, it dwells in independence in the *innermost being*, beyond all reach of any excitation from without. Neither the inducements of pleasure, nor the goads of pain, are capable of irresistibly compelling it. When it exercises itself, all physiological laws are disturbed; all the external signs of sensitivity or of contractility are uncertain, and can be quiescent or deceptive. How powerless, for example, the most excruciating pain over the will of a Mucius Scevola? Before it yields, the arm which it holds motionless upon the burning coals will be reduced to ashes. Is not then the force which thus dominates sensibility and rules it by its own laws, which compels the body to stop or to rush forward, even when its instinct urges it to flight, a force that is specific and *sui juris*.

But still we cannot speak of that moral force guided by motives which can render effort sublime. Before motives to act exist, there is surely a power of movement or of action; before this movement has become means, it has first been itself the aim or proper end of the willing. Finally it is necessary that the *self* shall have begun to exist for itself, or to circumscribe itself in its own domain, before extending over nature its constitutive force. Thereby are justified those considerations which might appear to us somewhat too minute, and to others too closely allied to this materialism which they are calculated to attack in its first foundation.

For us, therefore, who are here occupied only with a primitive fact of the inner sense, the will is as yet only the power of effort. We have just characterised this force through the signs, or the first conditions, or the instruments of its exercise. We now need to seek by analysis, what may be the origin of this exercise, and that of the individual personality which cannot be separated from it. But before entering upon this analysis, let us summarise the consequences of what precedes.

1. The primitive fact of the inner sense is none other than that of a voluntary effort, inseparable from some organic resistance, or from some muscular sensation of which the *self* is cause. This fact is thus a relation of which the two terms are distinct with-

out being separated. In order that they should be separated, it would be necessary, under the physiological hypothesis taken as a symbol, that the immediate action exerted from the centre upon the motor nerves be accompanied by a particular internal perception, distinct and separate from the muscular sensation; but therefore, the same internal perception would consist in another relation still more inner, between the hyperorganic force exerted from the centre and the nerves upon which it immediately acts. It would be, therefore, the nervous inertia which would replace in that case the muscular inertia, and the character of the primitive fact would not be changed.

2. The essential character of the primitive fact consists in that, that neither one nor the other of the terms of the fundamental relation is constituted in necessary dependence upon the impressions from without. Hence the knowledge of the *self* can be separated in its principle from that of the external universe.

3. The effort-cause, or the *self* has the internal consciousness of its existence as soon as it can distinguish this cause, which is itself, from the effect or from the contraction referred to the organic object, which is no longer itself, and which it places outside.[1]

4. The primitive fact which necessarily serves as the point of departure to science, therefore resolves itself into a primary effort, where analysis is still able to distinguish two elements: a hyperorganic force naturally in relation with a living resistance.

5. The idea or reflexive abstract notion of force is later deduced from the fact, or from the primitive feeling of effort. In following an inverse course and starting from the idea of absolute force, all the metaphysicians, up to and inclusive of Locke, have displaced the origin of science. They have desired to deduce the actual and the real from the possible: that was to begin in darkness.

We do not fear to lose ourselves in darkness by seeking at present how effort can begin to be willed, what the origin is of this primary action, of this free will, which is the primary condi-

[1] We shall see that this *outside* is not external extensity, nor even the form of space, such as the Kantians conceive it, as inherent to sensibility.

tion of the consciousness of one's self, and, consequently, of all other consciousness. We have a thread which guides us in these researches, and which, if it does not lead to the absolute truth which we seek, enables us at least not to lose ourselves in ideal regions, whence there would be no outlet or means to retrace our steps.

CHAPTER II. THE ORIGIN OF EFFORT, AND OF PERSONALITY

IF it were true, as philosophers who have attempted to derive everything from desire think, that will were nothing other than desire, which itself is confused with a first need of the organised living being; if it were true, or conformed to the facts of the inner sense, that instinctive determinations, regarded as completed sensations, embraced judgment, desire, or will; if finally it were true, that the very first movement made by each of us had been accompanied by will, it would be very useless to seek, I do not say, the origin of that absolute force identical with the soul, or of that which stands for it in all systems, but the origin of the feeling of its exercise, or of the effort with which the *ego* identifies itself. This origin indeed would be confused with the first rudiments of life, and would be traced back to the organic germ which possibly exists before fecundation. If this system were that of nature, it would turn out I have pursued up to the present only a chimera, and all the precise distinctions I have sought to establish would disappear like vain shadows. The obligation is thus imposed upon me to make it evident that my present researches have a real object, or that there may be an origin of voluntary effort or of the *self*, posterior in order of time to the birth of the sentient being, to the first instinctive determinations, to the needs, and even to the desire, which differ from the will, properly so called, as passion differs from action.

I am going at the outset to place myself anew at the physiological point of view, and upon the very ground of the philosophers who have assimilated or confounded in the origin, everything that I believe should be distinguished or even separated, in order to have a science of principles. If the distinctions that I establish turn out to be confirmed by physiology itself they are doubtless likely to receive in consequence more weight and value in the eyes of those to whom I take the liberty of opposing them.

According to the principles of a physiologist,[1] who was gifted with the genius of experiment rather than with the talent for classification, one is justified in the recognition of three modes, or three kinds of muscular contractility, which are distinguished among themselves in the same manner as the causes which produce or determine the contractions. The first kind is a simple organic property inherent to the muscular fibre, and which has been known since Haller by the term *irritability*. We have no need to know up to what point the nervous influence contributes to set it in action, because this property, simply vital, happens to be outside of the object of our researches. What is of importance to us, is to recognise the truly distinguishing characteristics in the sentient contractility, which may also be called *animal*, and a contractility properly *voluntary*. Let us seek, therefore, to specify clearly the physiological characteristics of these two kinds. Both of them expressly relate to cerebral influence, but under very different conditions, and it is not permissible to confuse them even physiologically.

Affective impressions excited in the nervous system by foreign or inner causes, being transmitted to the brain or to some other of the partial centres, determine those powerful reactions which tend to set in play the locomotor organs: hence the animal contractions and all the instinctive movements. I have just spoken of partial centres as of points of reaction, because it is not proved that it is the direct influence of a single centre which determines always the instinctive locomotion of animals as of the foetus, and several analogies tend to prove the opposite. Supposing, what appears to be contradicted by many physiological observations, that a single centre determines solely by its reaction the kind of movement which is in question here, at

[1] Cf. Bichat's *Recherches physiologiques sur la vie et la mort*.

least it is true that this centre plays in that case a passive or merely sympathetic rôle influenced, as it is, by the impressions of the internal or external nervous organs which are the true determining causes of these animal contractions.

But in the contraction that is strictly *voluntary*, it is clearly in a single centre that the action commences which, without being provoked or compelled by any foreign impression, is transmitted directly to the organs of movement by the intermediary of the nerves. We find here the only true sign of voluntary effort, such as we have characterised it.

As the voluntary contraction thus differs from the animal contraction, so likewise the will, the individual and free power of effort and movement, differ from appetite, need, and all feelings of discomfort, of disquietude, etc. which have been arbitrarily united under the general term of *will*. Here both the psychological and physiological points of view perfectly correspond. The sympathetic reaction of the centre, which occasions the animal contractions or the instinctive movements, is the sign of *affective desire* very improperly called will. The action, commencing in a single centre, which occasions the voluntary movement that is in the power of the individual to make or not to make, is the proper sign of an impelling *will*. The general faculty in question from the first physiological point of view, is not only subordinated to, but identical with the sensibility considered as the principle or the cause which determines animal movement. It is, therefore, not necessary to seek any other origin for it than that of life itself of the organised being, which feels only so far as it is moved, and which moves only as far as it feels. In this case, it is conditionally true to say that the first of all movements has been accompanied by desire or by will, and that the instinctive determinations, being sensations as the others, include judgment, desire, etc. The individual faculty which is in question in the second point of view, far from being subordinate to the sensibility, is most often in opposition to it; and we have already seen that it has its peculiar and primordial laws, outside the circle of all *affective* impressions.

The experience of the inner sense suffices to assure us in fact that, in the cases in which movements of any kind are compelled and abruptly incited by violent appetites, passions, or too emotional excitations of the sensibility, we ourselves move, or rather our body moves without our leave, without, or even against the explicit orders of the will, which is oppressed and as it were nullified, by the very fact that sensibility predominates or rules exclusively. How could it therefore be possible that the same affective impressions, which destroy the control of the will, and absorb or hamper that power, even when it is already fully established, would originally serve to develop it and to set it in exercise? How is it possible to suppose that the being, which begins to live, can perceive or feel its own movements, and begin to derive therefrom some knowledge, when we ourselves are completely ignorant alike of the cause and of the effect of those movements, in the midst of the disturbance of the affections which provoke or even prevail over them? How finally could the very principle, which obscures and so often extinguishes in us the light of consciousness, have been the first source of it?

We are, therefore, justified in saying from our present standpoint, that the first movements, which are determined by appetite or organic need, or even accompanied by desire, differ as much from will properly so-called, as the peculiar and direct action exerted from a single centre differs from all sympathetic reactions. Thus, the first acts of this nascent will, explained in its principles, differ from the blind determinations of instinct, which precedes them in the order of time, but without serving them in their origin. There is then occasion to seek by an explicit analysis of primitive facts, what is the order of progress or of conditions which may have produced the first exercise of the individual power of effort, and with it the first feeling of the *self*; that which is equivalent to asking what is the law, either physiological or psychological, of the transition from instinctive movements, to voluntary and free movements, accompanied by effort.

As long as the organic centre, to which physiologists refer motor determination, only reacts in consequence of the impressions which it receives from diverse sensitive organs with which it is in relation, the movements thus produced, not being capable of being perceived or felt as distinct from their producing causes, cannot even begin to be voluntary. For if distinct perception is not anterior, as I believe, to any exercise whatever of the will, neither can this latter in its turn precede any degree whatsoever of perception; and although it may be true to say, that the thinking being cannot begin to know save in so far as he begins to act and to will, it is none the less true, in the ordinary phrase, that one cannot expressly will that of which one has no knowledge.

If one appears to revolve here in a vicious circle, the reason is, that as a result of having failed to recognize the truly primitive fact, one wishes to distinguish or separate two acts which are reduced to one in this fact, and that one already applies the law of succession, or like the Kantians, the complete form of time, to the first term of every succession, at the origin of all time.

Through the indeterminate order of the progress of being, simple in the vital stage, but destined to become double in the human stage,[1] a period arrives when the exclusive rule of instinct tends to end or to be united to another order of faculties. Already the impressions begin to become less vivid, less general, less tumultuous; habit has blunted their edge which was at first strongly affective; the appetites are less pressing, the movements less brusque, less automatic; the organs of locomotion begin to harden, their special irritability diminishes; they yield less promptly to every external cause of contraction. Thus, on the one side, these organs have contracted habits in repeated instinctive locomotion, and they are disposed in such way to comply with more facility to the new contractions that the will is to impose upon them; on the other hand, the motor centre has also acquired in reacting such determinations that it is capable of entering spontaneously into action, by virtue of that general law of habit, in consequence of which a living organ

---

[1] *Homo simplex in vitalitate, duplex in humanitate,* says Boerhaave energetically, and with profound truth.

tends to renew of itself the impressions or the movements that a foreign cause has a number of times aroused in it, or in consequence of which makes it own the dispositions of another organ with which it has sympathetically shared.

When the centre thus accomplishes movements by its own and initial action, the latter take a wholly different character, and become *spontaneous*, instead of being *instinctive* as they were at the outset. Now this spontaneity is still not the will, or the power of effort, but it immediately precedes it. By virtue of the spontaneity of action of the centre, which is the immediate term or proper instrument of the hyperorganic force of the soul, that force, which could neither perceive nor distinctly feel the instructive movements, begins to feel the spontaneous movements which no emotion troubles or disturbs. But it cannot begin to feel them thus as produced by its immediate instrument, without appropriating to itself their power. As soon as it feels that power, it exerts it by accomplishing that movement itself. As soon as it effects it, it perceives its effort with the resistance, it is a cause for itself, and in relation to the effect that it produces, with freedom, it is the *self*.

Thus personality begins with the first complete action of a hyperorganic force which is for itself, or as *self*, only in so far as it knows itself, and which begins to know itself only in so far as it begins to act with freedom. The problem is not to know what that force is in itself, how it exists, or when it begins absolutely to exist, but when it begins to exist as an identical person, as *self*. Now it exists for itself only in so far as it knows itself, and it knows itself only in so far as it acts.

Although the primitive fact, of which we seek to determine the source, seems to escape, in that source itself, from every kind of experiment, and presents itself only as an hypothesis, we can nevertheless discover some examples adapted to explain, up to a certain point, the origin of personality, such as we have just established it.

1. In sleep of the mind or of the *self*, it occurs sometimes that one is awakened with a start in consequence of movements, of words or of voices, produced by a spontaneity resembling that

which serves originally as intermediary between instinct and will. At the very instant of this sudden awakening, the individual feels these movements, not accompanied with effort as they are in the state of waking, but with a feeling of power to make them, which is, in this case, the memory of that effort. It is in this way that he appropriates to himself in their result those spontaneous movements that he has not determined in their principle, and that conscious appropriation characterises solely the perfect awakening. Therefore, in the origin of personality, spontaneous movement awakens the soul, causes to arise in it, as it were, the presentiment of a power which determines the first voluntary effort, and with it the first knowledge.

2. In the newborn infant, and even during a certain period after birth, the locomotion and voice are set in action only by instinct. The infant frets and cries because it suffers, and in so far as it is affected by simple needs or appetites. As long as this purely sensitive state continues, will and apperception cannot exist; for how can you suppose that the first cries of pain, the first automatic movements, are acts of a faculty of will and of judgment already in exercise, unless you admit these faculties as innate or unconditioned? Without doubt the cries of an infant have a significance or a natural sense, but that is for an intelligent being capable of understanding or of interpreting it, and not for the infant reduced to sensations and to animal contractions. But apart from the exclusive domain of the affections, of the needs or appetites of instinct, the infant still cries and frets by virtue of the determinations or of the habits contracted by the motor centre and by the organs of movement or of the voice. These movements then spontaneous are veritable sensations. Soon they will be perceived, willed and transformed by the infant itself, into *involuntary signs* of which it will make use in order to call for aid. Behold the first stage of man, *duplex in humanitate*, the first sign of nascent personality. The transition sought for is then accomplished. But how could it have been possible, if the movements had always been the products of an instinctive and sympathetic reaction, carried away and repelled by vivid emotions, and finally if there had not

been an intermediary mode of motility such, that sensation, distinct from the movement performed, be accompanied by a feeling of power, and gives rise consequently to the exercise of the will? Such is the order or the series of progress; such is the transition from instinct to spontaneity, and from that to the will, which constitutes the person, the *self*. The animal rapidly passes beyond the first two degrees; man alone can attain to the third, but he attains it only progressively, according to certain laws or conditions, that philosophy should seek to know in order to find the principles and origin of science. If we have not been able to dispel all the clouds which conceal that origin, we have at least shown how, and in what sense, it is necessary to admit an assignable origin of personality; how or by what procedure of analysis, one can hope to find it identified, not with the first sensation of a passive substance, but with the first action of a hyperorganic force.

JAMES MILL

(1773–1836)

ANALYSIS OF THE PHENOMENA OF THE HUMAN MIND*

CHAPTER III. THE ASSOCIATION OF IDEAS

"To have a clear view of the phenomena of the mind, as mere affections or states of it, existing successively, and in a certain series, which we are able, therefore, to predict, in consequence of our knowledge of the past, is, I conceive, to have made the most important acquisition which the intellectual inquirer can make."

Brown, Lectures, i. 544.

THOUGHT succeeds thought; idea follows idea, incessantly. If our senses are awake, we are continually receiving sensations, of the eye, the ear, the touch, and so forth; but not sensations alone. After sensations, ideas are perpetually excited of sensations formerly received; after those ideas, other ideas: and during the whole of our lives, a series of those two states of consciousness, called sensations, and ideas, is constantly going on. I see a horse: that is a sensation. Immediately I think of his master: that is an idea. The idea of his master makes me think of his office; he is a minister of state: that is another idea. The idea of a minister of state makes me think of public affairs; and I am led into a train of political ideas; when I am summoned to dinner. This is a new sensation, followed by the idea of dinner, and of the company with whom I am to partake it. The sight of the company and of the food are other sensations; these suggest ideas without end; other sensations perpetually intervene, suggesting other ideas: and so the process goes on.

In contemplating this train of feelings, of which our lives consist, it first of all strikes the contemplator, as of importance

* London, 1829; new ed., with notes illustrative and critical by Alexander Bain, Andrew Findlater, and George Grote, edited with additional notes by John Stuart Mill, *ib.* 1869, vol. i.

to ascertain, whether they occur casually and irregularly, or according to a certain order.

With respect to the SENSATIONS, it is obvious enough that they occur, according to the order established among what we call the objects of nature, whatever those objects are; to ascertain more and more of which order is the business of physical philosophy in all its branches.

Of the order established among the objects of nature, by which we mean the objects of our senses, two remarkable cases are all which here we are called upon to notice; the SYNCHRONOUS ORDER and the SUCCESSIVE ORDER. The synchronous order, or order of simultaneous existence, is the order in space; the successive order, or order of antecedent and consequent existence, is the order in time. Thus the various objects in my room, the chairs, the tables, the books, have the synchronous order, or order in space. The falling of the spark, and the explosion of the gunpowder, have the successive order, or order in time.

According to this order, in the objects of sense, there is a synchronous, and a successive, order of our sensations. I have SYNCHRONICALLY, or at the same instant, the sight of a great variety of objects; touch of all the objects with which my body is in contact; hearing of all the sounds which are reaching my ears; smelling of all the smells which are reaching my nostrils; taste of the apple which I am eating; the sensation of resistance both from the apple which is in my mouth, and the ground on which I stand; with the sensation of motion from the act of walking. I have SUCCESSIVELY the sight of the flash from the mortar fired at a distance, the hearing of the report, the sight of the bomb, and of its motion in the air, the sight of its fall, the sight and hearing of its explosion, and lastly, the sight of all the effects of that explosion.

Among the objects which I have thus observed synchronically, or successively; that is, from which I have had synchronical or successive sensations; there are some which I have so observed frequently; others which I have so observed not frequently: in other words, of my sensations some have been frequently synchronical, others not frequently; some frequently successive, others not frequently. Thus, my sight of roast beef, and my taste of roast beef, have been frequently SYNCHRONICAL; my smell of a rose, and my sight and touch of a rose, have been frequently synchronical; my sight of a stone, and my sensations of its hardness, and weight, have been frequently synchronical. Others of my sensations have not been frequently synchronical: my sight of a lion, and the hearing of his roar; my sight of a knife, and its stabbing a man. My sight of the flash of lightning, and my hearing of the thunder, have been often SUCCESSIVE; the pain of cold, and the pleasure of heat, have been often successive; the sight of a trumpet, and the sound of a trumpet, have been often successive. On the other hand, my sight of hemlock, and my taste of hemlock, have not been often successive: and so on.

It so happens, that, of the objects from which we derive the greatest part of our sensations, most of those which are observed synchronically, are frequently observed synchronically; most of those which are observed successively, are frequently observed successively. In other words, most of our synchronical sensations, have been frequently synchronical; most of our successive sensations, have been frequently successive. Thus, most of our synchronical sensations are derived from the objects around us, the objects which we have the most frequent occasion to hear and see; the members of our family; the furniture of our houses; our food; the instruments of our occupations or amusements. In like manner, of those sensations which we have had in succession, we have had the greatest number repeatedly in succession; the sight of fire, and its warmth; the touch of snow, and its cold; the sight of food, and its taste.

Thus much with regard to the order of SENSATIONS; next with regard to the order of IDEAS.

As ideas are not derived from objects, we should not expect their order to be derived from the order of objects; but as they are derived from sensations, we might by analogy expect, that they would derive their order from that of the sensations; and this to a great extent is the case.

Our ideas spring up, or exist, in the order in which the sensations existed, of which they are the copies.

This is the general law of the "Association of Ideas"; by which term, let it be remembered, nothing is here meant to be expressed, but the order of occurrence.

In this law, the following things are to be carefully observed.

1. Of those sensations which occurred synchronically, the ideas also spring up synchronically. I have seen a violin, and heard the tones of the violin, synchronically. If I think of the tones of the violin, the visible appearance of the violin at the same time occurs to me. I have seen the sun, and the sky in which it is placed, synchronically. If I think of the one, I think of the other at the same time.

One of the cases of synchronical sensation, which deserves the most particular attention, is, that of the several sensations derived from one and the same object; a stone, for example, a flower, a table, a chair, a horse, a man.

From a stone I have had, synchronically, the sensation of colour, the sensation of hardness, the sensations of shape, and size, the sensation of weight. When the idea of one of these sensations occurs, the ideas of all of them occur. They exist in my mind synchronically; and their synchronical existence is called the idea of the stone; which, it is thus plain, is not a single idea, but a number of ideas in a particular state of combination.

Thus, again, I have smelt a rose, and looked at, and handled a rose, synchronically; accordingly the name rose suggests to me all those ideas synchronically; and this combination of those simple ideas is called my idea of the rose.

My idea of an animal is still more complex. The word thrush, for example, not only suggests an idea of a particular colour and shape, and size, but of song, and flight, and nestling, and eggs, and callow young, and others.

My idea of a man is the most complex of all; including not only colour, and shape, and voice, but the whole class of events in which I have observed him either the agent or the patient.

2. As the ideas of the sensations which occurred synchron-

ically, rise synchronically, so the ideas of the sensations which occurred successively, rise successively.

Of this important case of association, or of the successive order of our ideas, many remarkable instances might be adduced. Of these none seems better adapted to the learner than the repetition of any passage, or words; the Lord's Prayer, for example, committed to memory. In learning the passage, we repeat it; that is, we pronounce the words, in successive order, from the beginning to the end. The order of the sensations is successive. When we proceed to repeat the passage, the ideas of the words also rise in succession, the preceding always suggesting the succeeding, and no other. *Our* suggests *Father*, *Father* suggests *which*, *which* suggests *art;* and so on, to the end. How remarkably this is the case, any one may convince himself, by trying to repeat backwards, even a passage with which he is as familiar as the Lord's Prayer. The case is the same with numbers. A man can go on with the numbers in the progressive order, one, two, three, &c. scarcely thinking of his act; and though it is possible for him to repeat them backward, because he is accustomed to subtraction of numbers, he cannot do so without an effort.

Of witnesses in courts of justice it has been remarked, that eye-witnesses, and ear-witnesses, always tell their story in the chronological order; in other words, the ideas occur to them in the order in which the sensations occurred; on the other hand, that witnesses, who are inventing, rarely adhere to the chronological order.

3. A far greater number of our sensations are received in the successive, than in the synchronical order. Of our ideas, also, the number is infinitely greater that rise in the successive than the synchronical order.

4. In the successive order of ideas, that which precedes, is sometimes called the suggesting, that which succeeds, the suggested idea; not that any power is supposed to reside in the antecedent over the consequent; suggesting, and suggested, mean only antecedent and consequent, with the additional idea, that such order is not casual, but, to a certain degree, permanent.

5. Of the antecedent and consequent feelings, or the suggesting, and suggested; the antecedent may be either sensations or ideas; the consequent are always ideas. An idea may be excited either by a sensation or an idea. The sight of the dog of my friend is a sensation, and it excites the idea of my friend. The idea of Professor Dugald Stewart delivering a lecture, recalls the idea of the delight with which I heard him; that, the idea of the studies in which it engaged me; that, the trains of thought which succeeded; and each epoch of my mental history, the succeeding one, till the present moment; in which I am endeavouring to present to others what appears to me valuable among the innumerable ideas of which this lengthened train has been composed.

6. As there are degrees in sensations, and degrees in ideas; for one sensation is more vivid than another sensation, one idea more vivid than another idea; so there are degrees in association. One association, we say, is stronger than another: First, when it is more permanent than another: Secondly, when it is performed with more certainty: Thirdly, when it is performed with more facility.

It is well known, that some associations are very transient, others very permanent. The case which we formerly mentioned, that of repeating words committed to memory, affords an apt illustration. In some cases, we can perform the repetition, when a few hours, or a few days have elapsed; but not after a longer period. In others, we can perform it after the lapse of many years. There are few children in whose minds some association has not been formed between darkness and ghosts. In some this association is soon dissolved; in some it continues for life.

In some cases the association takes place with less, in some with greater certainty. Thus, in repeating words, I am not sure that I shall not commit mistakes, if they are imperfectly got; and I may at one trial repeat them right, at another wrong: I am sure of always repeating those correctly, which I have got perfectly. Thus, in my native language, the association between the name and the thing is certain; in a language with which I am imperfectly acquainted, not certain. In expressing myself in my own language, the idea of the thing suggests the idea of the name with certainty. In speaking a language with which I am imperfectly acquainted, the idea of the thing does not with certainty suggest the idea of the name; at one time it may, at another not.

That ideas are associated in some cases with more, in some with less facility, is strikingly illustrated by the same instance, of a language with which we are well, and a language with which we are imperfectly, acquainted. In speaking our own language, we are not conscious of any effort; the associations between the words and the ideas appear spontaneous. In endeavouring to speak a language with which we are imperfectly acquainted, we are sensible of a painful effort: the associations between the words and ideas being not ready, or immediate.

7. The causes of strength in association seem all to be resolvable into two; the vividness of the associated feelings; and the frequency of the association.

In general, we convey not a very precise meaning, when we speak of the vividness of sensations and ideas. We may be understood when we say that, generally speaking, the sensation is more vivid than the idea; or the primary, than the secondary feeling; though in dreams, and in delirium, ideas are mistaken for sensations. But when we say that one sensation is more vivid than another, there is much more uncertainty. We can distinguish those sensations which are pleasurable, and those which are painful, from such as are not so; and when we call the pleasurable and painful more vivid, than those which are not so, we speak intelligibly. We can also distinguish degrees of pleasure, and of pain; and when we call the sensation of the higher degree more vivid than the sensation of the lower degree, we may again be considered as expressing a meaning tolerably precise.

In calling one IDEA more vivid than another, if we confine the appellation to the ideas of such SENSATIONS as may with precision be called more or less vivid; the sensations of pleasure and pain, in their various degrees, compared with sensations which we do not call either pleasurable or painful; our language will still have a certain degree of precision. But what is the meaning which I annex to my words, when I say, that my idea of the taste of the pine-apple which I tasted yesterday is vivid; my idea of the taste of the foreign fruit which I never tasted but once in early life, is not vivid? If I mean that I can more certainly distinguish the more recent, than the more distant sensation, there is still some precision in my language; because it seems true of all my senses, that if I compare a distant sensation with the present, I am less sure of its being or not being a repetition of the same, than if I compare a recent sensation with a present one. Thus, if I yesterday had a smell of a very peculiar kind, and compare it with a present smell, I can judge more accurately of the agreement or disagreement of the two sensations, than if I compared the present with one much more remote. The same is the case with colours, with sounds, with feelings of touch, and of resistance. It is therefore sufficiently certain, that the idea of the more recent sensation affords the means of a more accurate comparison, generally, than the idea of the more remote sensation. And thus we have three cases of vividness, of which we can speak with some precision: the case of sensations, as compared with ideas; the case of pleasurable and painful sensations, and their ideas as compared with those which are not pleasurable or painful; and the case of the more recent, compared with the more remote.

That the association of two ideas, but for once, does, in some cases, give them a very strong connection, is within the sphere of every man's experience. The most remarkable cases are probably those of pain and pleasure. Some persons who have experienced a very painful surgical operation, can never afterwards bear the sight of the operator, however strong the gratitude which they may actually feel towards him. The meaning is, that the sight of the operator, by a strong association, calls up so vividly the idea of the pain of the operation, that it is itself a pain. The spot on which a tender maiden parted with her lover, when he embarked on the voyage from which he never returned, cannot afterwards be seen by her without an agony of grief.

These cases, also, furnish an apt illustration of the superiority which the sensation possesses over the idea, as an associating cause. Though the sight of the surgeon, the sight of the place, would awaken the ideas which we have described, the mere thought of them might be attended with no peculiar effect. Those persons who have the association of frightful objects with darkness, and who are transported with terrors when placed in the dark, can still think of darkness without any emotion.

The same cases furnish an illustration of the effect of recency on the strength of association. The sight, of the affecting spot by the maiden, of the surgeon by the patient, would certainly produce a more intense emotion, after a short, than after a long interval. With most persons, time would weaken, and at last dissolve, the association.

So much with regard to vividness, as a cause of strong associations. Next, we have to consider frequency or repetition; which is the most remarkable and important cause of the strength of our associations.

Of any two sensations, frequently perceived together, the ideas are associated. Thus, at least, in the minds of Englishmen, the idea of a soldier, and the idea of a red coat are associated; the idea of a clergyman, and the idea of a black coat; the idea of a quaker, and of a broad-brimmed hat; the idea of a woman and the idea of petticoats. A peculiar taste suggests the idea of an apple; a peculiar smell the idea of a rose. If I have heard a particular air frequently sung by a particular person, the hearing of the air suggests the idea of the person.

The most remarkable exemplification of the effect of degrees of frequency, in producing degrees of strength in the associations, is to be found in the cases in which the association is purposely and studiously contracted; the cases in which we learn something; the use of words, for example.

Every child learns the language which is spoken by those around him. He also learns it by degrees. He learns first the names of the most familiar objects; and among familiar objects, the names of those which he most frequently has occasion to name; himself, his nurse, his food, his playthings.

A sound heard once in conjunction with another sensation; the word mamma, for example, with the sight of a woman, would produce no greater effect on the child, than the conjunction of any other sensation, which once exists and is gone forever. But if the word mamma is frequently pronounced, in conjunction with the sight of a particular woman, the sound will by degrees become associated with the sight; and as the pronouncing of the name will call up the idea of the woman, so the sight of the woman will call up the idea of the name.

The process becomes very perceptible to us, when, at years of reflection, we proceed to learn a dead or foreign language. At the first lesson, we are told, or we see in the dictionary, the meaning of perhaps twenty words. But it is not joining the word and its meaning once, that will make the word suggest its meaning to us another time. We repeat the two in conjunction, till we think the meaning so well associated with the word, that whenever the word occurs to us, the meaning will occur along with it. We are often deceived in this anticipation; and finding that the meaning is not suggested by the word, we have to renew the process of repetition, and this, perhaps, again, and again. By force of repetition the meaning is associated, at last, with every word of the language, and so perfectly, that the one never occurs to us without the other.

Learning to play on a musical instrument is another remarkable illustration of the effect of repetition in strengthening associations, in rendering those sequences, which, at first, are slow, and difficult, afterwards, rapid, and easy. At first, the learner, after thinking of each successive note, as it stands in his book, has each time to look out with care for the key or the string which he is to touch, and the finger he is to touch it with, and is every moment committing mistakes. Repetition is well known to be the only means of overcoming these difficulties. As the repetition goes on, the sight of the note, or even the idea of the note, becomes associated with the place of the key or the string; and that of the key or the string with the proper finger.

The association for a time is imperfect, but at last becomes so strong, that it is performed with the greatest rapidity, without an effort, and almost without consciousness.

In few cases is the strength of association, derived from repetition, more worthy of attention, than in performing arithmetic. All men, whose practice is not great, find the addition of a long column of numbers, tedious, and the accuracy of the operation, by no means certain. Till a man has had considerable practice, there are few acts of the mind more toilsome. The reason is, that the names of the numbers, which correspond to the different steps, do not readily occur; that is, are not strongly associated with the names which precede them. Thus, 7 added to 5, make 12; but the antecedent, 7 added to 5, is not strongly associated with the consequent 12, in the mind of the learner, and he has to wait and search till the name occurs. Thus, again, 12 and 7 make 19; 19 and 8 make 27, and so on to any amount; but if the practice of the performer has been small, the association in each instance is imperfect, and the process irksome and slow. Practice, however; that is, frequency of repetition; makes the association between each of these antecedents and its proper consequent so perfect, that no sooner is the one conceived than the other is conceived, and an expert arithmetician can tell the amount of a long column of figures, with a rapidity, which seems almost miraculous to the man whose faculty of numeration is of the ordinary standard.

8. Where two or more ideas have been often repeated together, and the association has become very strong, they sometimes spring up in such close combination as not to be distinguishable. Some cases of sensation are analogous. For example; when a wheel, on the seven parts of which the seven prismatic colours are respectively painted, is made to revolve rapidly, it appears not of seven colours, but of one uniform colour, white. By the rapidity of the succession, the several sensations cease to be distinguishable; they run, as it were, together, and a new sensation, compounded of all the seven, but apparently a simple one, is the result. Ideas, also, which have been so often conjoined, that whenever one exists in the

mind, the others immediately exist along with it, seem to run into one another, to coalesce, as it were, and out of many to form one idea; which idea, however in reality complex, appears to be no less simple, than any one of those of which it is compounded.

The word gold, for example, or the word iron, appears to express as simple an idea, as the word colour, or the word sound. Yet it is immediately seen, that the idea of each of those metals is made up of the separate ideas of several sensations; colour, hardness, extension, weight. Those ideas, however, present themselves in such intimate union, that they are constantly spoken of as one, not many. We say, our idea of iron, our idea of gold; and it is only with an effort that reflecting men perform the decomposition.

The idea expressed by the term weight, appears so perfectly simple, that he is a good metaphysician, who can trace its composition. Yet it involves, of course, the idea of resistance, which we have shewn above to be compounded, and to involve the feeling attendant upon the contraction of muscles; and the feeling, or feelings, denominated Will; it involves the idea, not of resistance simply, but of resistance in a particular direction; the idea of direction, therefore, is included in it, and in that are involved the ideas of extension, and of place and motion, some of the most complicated phenomena of the human mind.

The ideas of hardness and extension have been so uniformly regarded as simple, that the greatest metaphysicians have set them down as the copies of simple sensations of touch. Hartley and Darwin, were, I believe, the first who thought of assigning to them a different origin.

We call a thing hard, because it resists compression, or separation of parts; that is, because to compress it, or separate it into parts, what we call muscular force is required. The idea, then, of muscular action, and of all the feelings which go to it, are involved in the idea of hardness.

The idea of extension is derived from the muscular feelings in what we call the motion of parts of our own bodies; as for example, the hands. I move my hand along a line; I have certain sensations; on account of these sensations, I call the line long, or extended. The idea of lines in the direction of length, breadth, and thickness, constitutes the general idea of extension. In the idea of extension, there are included three of the most complex of our ideas; motion; time, which is included in motion; and space, which is included in direction. We are not yet prepared to explain the simple ideas which compose the very complex ideas, of motion, space, and time; it is enough at present to have shewn, that in the idea of extension, which appears so very simple, a great number of ideas are nevertheless included; and that this is a case of that combination of ideas in the higher degrees of association, in which the simple ideas are so intimately blended, as to have the appearance, not of a complex, but of a simple idea.

It is to this great law of association, that we trace the formation of our ideas of what we call external objects; that is, the ideas of a certain number of sensations, received together so frequently that they coalesce as it were, and are spoken of under the idea of unity. Hence, what we call the idea of a tree, the idea of a stone, the idea of a horse, the idea of a man.

In using the names, tree, horse, man, the names of what I call objects, I am referring, and can be referring, only to my own sensations; in fact, therefore, only naming a certain number of sensations, regarded as in a particular state of combination; that is, concomitance. Particular sensations of sight, of touch, of the muscles, are the sensations, to the ideas of which, colour, extension, roughness, hardness, smoothness, taste, smell, so coalescing as to appear one idea, I give the name, idea of a tree.

To this case of high association, this blending together of many ideas, in so close a combination that they appear not many ideas, but one idea, we owe, as I shall afterwards more fully explain, the power of classification, and all the advantages of language. It is obviously, therefore, of the greatest moment, that this important phenomenon should be well understood.

9. Some ideas are by frequency and strength of association

so closely combined, that they cannot be separated. If one exists, the others exist along with it, in spite of whatever effort we make to disjoin them.

For example; it is not in our power to think of colour, without thinking of extension; or of solidity, without figure. We have seen colour constantly in combination with extension, spread as it were, upon a surface. We have never seen it except in this connection. Colour and extension have been invariably conjoined. The idea of colour, therefore, uniformly comes into the mind, bringing that of extension along with it; and so close is the association, that it is not in our power to dissolve it. We cannot, if we will, think of colour, but in combination with extension. The one idea calls up the other, and retains it, so long as the other is retained.

This great law of our nature is illustrated in a manner equally striking, by the connection between the ideas of solidity and figure. We never have the sensations from which the idea of solidity is derived, but in conjunction with the sensations whence the idea of figure is derived. If we handle anything solid, it is always either round, square, or of some other form. The ideas correspond with the sensations. If the idea of solidity rises, that of figure rises along with it. The idea of figure which rises, is, of course, more obscure than that of extension; because, figures being innumerable, the general idea is exceedingly complex, and hence, of necessity, obscure. But, such as it is, the idea of figure is always present when that of solidity is present; nor can we, by any effort, think of the one without thinking of the other at the same time.

Of all the cases of this important law of association, there is none more extraordinary than what some philosophers have called, the acquired perceptions of sight.

When I lift my eyes from the paper on which I am writing, I see the chairs, and tables, and walls of my room, each of its proper shape, and at its proper distance. I see, from my window, trees, and meadows, and horses, and oxen, and distant hills. I see each of its proper size, of its proper form, and at its proper distance; and these particulars appear as immediate informations of the eye, as the colours which I see by means of it.

Yet, philosophy has ascertained, that we derive nothing from the eye whatever, but sensations of colour; that the idea of extension, in which size, and form, and distance are included, is derived from sensations, not in the eye, but in the muscular part of our frame. How, then, is it, that we receive accurate information, by the eye, of size, and shape, and distance? By association merely.

The colours upon a body are different, according to its figure, its distance, and its size. But the sensations of colour, and what we may here, for brevity, call the sensations of extension, of figure, of distance, have been so often united, felt in conjunction, that the sensation of the colour is never experienced without raising the ideas of the extension, the figure, the distance, in such intimate union with it, that they not only cannot be separated, but are actually supposed to be seen. The sight, as it is called, of figure, or distance, appearing, as it does, a simple sensation, is in reality a complex state of consciousness; a sequence, in which the antecedent, a sensation of colour, and the consequent, a number of ideas, are so closely combined by association, that they appear not one idea, but one sensation.

Some persons, by the folly of those about them, in early life, have formed associations between the sound of thunder, and danger to their lives. They are accordingly in a state of agitation during a thunder storm. The sound of the thunder calls up the idea of danger, and no effort they can make, no reasoning they can use with themselves, to show how small the chance that they will be harmed, empowers them to dissolve the spell, to break the association, and deliver themselves from the tormenting idea, while the sensation or the expectation of it remains.

Another very familiar illustration may be adduced. Some persons have what is called an antipathy to a spider, a toad, or a rat. These feelings generally originate in some early fright. The idea of danger has been on some occasion so intensely excited along with the touch or sight of the animal, and hence the association so strongly formed, that it cannot be dissolved. The sensation, in spite of them, excites the idea, and produces the uneasiness which the idea imports.

The following of one idea after another idea, or after a sensation, so certainly that we cannot prevent the combination, nor avoid having the *consequent* feeling as often as we have the *antecedent*, is a law of association, the operation of which we shall afterwards find to be extensive, and bearing a principal part in some of the most important phenomena of the human mind.

As there are some ideas so intimately blended by association, that it is not in our power to separate them; there seem to be others, which it is not in our power to combine. Dr. Brown, in exposing some errors of his predecessors, with respect to the acquired perceptions of sight, observes: "I cannot blend my notions of the two surfaces, a plane, and a convex, as one surface, both plane and convex, more than I can think of a whole which is less than a fraction of itself, or a square of which the sides are not equal." The case, here, appears to be, that a strong association excludes whatever is opposite to it. I cannot associate the two ideas of assafœtida, and the taste of sugar. Why? Because the idea of assafœtida is so strongly associated with the idea of another taste, that the idea of that other taste rises in combination with the idea of assafœtida, and of course the idea of sugar does not rise. I have one idea associated with the word pain. Why can I not associate pleasure with the word pain? Because another indissoluble association springs up, and excludes it. This is, therefore, only a case of indissoluble association; but one of much importance, as we shall find when we come to the exposition of some of the more complicated of our mental phenomena.

10. It not unfrequently happens in our associated feelings, that the antecedent is of no importance farther than it introduces the consequent. In these cases, the consequent absorbs all the attention, and the antecedent is instantly forgotten. Of this a very intelligible illustration is afforded by what happens in ordinary discourse. A friend arrives from a distant country,

and brings me the first intelligence of the last illness, the last words, the last acts, and death of my son. The sound of the voice, the articulation of every word, makes its sensation in my ear; but it is to the ideas that my attention flies. It is my son that is before me, suffering, acting, speaking, dying. The words which have introduced the ideas, and kindled the affections, have been as little heeded, as the respiration which has been accelerated, while the ideas were received.

It is important in respect to this case of association to remark, that there are large classes of our sensations, such as many of those in the alimentary duct, and many in the nervous and vascular systems, which serve, as antecedents, to introduce ideas, as consequents; but as the consequents are far more interesting than themselves, and immediately absorb the attention, the antecedents are habitually overlooked; and though they exercise, by the trains which they introduce, a great influence on our happiness or misery, they themselves are generally wholly unknown.

That there are connections between our ideas and certain states of the internal organs, is proved by many familiar instances. Thus, anxiety, in most people, disorders the digestion. It is no wonder, then, that the internal feelings which accompany indigestion, should excite the ideas which prevail in a state of anxiety. Fear, in most people, accelerates, in a remarkable manner, the vermicular motion of the intestines. There is an association, therefore, between certain states of the intestines, and terrible ideas; and this is sufficiently confirmed by the horrible dreams to which men are subject from indigestion; and the hypochondria, more or less afflicting, which almost always accompanies certain morbid states of the digestive organs. The grateful food which excites pleasurable sensations in the mouth, continues them in the stomach; and, as pleasures excite ideas of their causes, and these of similar causes, and causes excite ideas of their effects, and so on, trains of pleasurable ideas take their origin from pleasurable sensations in the stomach. Uneasy sensations in the stomach, produce analogous effects. Disagreeable sensations are associated with disagreeable circumstances; a train is introduced, in which, one painful idea following another, combinations, to the last degree afflictive, are sometimes introduced, and the sufferer is altogether overwhelmed by dismal associations.

In illustration of the fact, that sensations and ideas, which are essential to some of the most important operations of our minds, serve only as antecedents to more important consequents, and are themselves so habitually overlooked, that their existence is unknown, we may recur to the remarkable case which we have just explained, of the ideas introduced by the sensations of sight. The minute gradations of colour, which accompany varieties of extension, figure, and distance, are insignificant. The figure, the size, the distance, themselves, on the other hand, are matters of the greatest importance. The first having introduced the last, their work is done. The consequents remain the sole objects of attention, the antecedents are forgotten; in the present instance, not completely; in other instances, so completely, that they cannot be recognized.

11. Mr. Hume, and after him other philosophers, have said that our ideas are associated according to three principles; Contiguity in time and place, Causation, and Resemblance. The Contiguity in time and place, must mean, that of the sensations; and so far it is affirmed, that the order of the ideas follows that of the sensations. Contiguity of two sensations in time, means the successive order. Contiguity of two sensations in place, means the synchronous order. We have explained the mode in which ideas are associated, in the synchronous, as well as the successive order, and have traced the principle of contiguity to its proper source.

Causation, the second of Mr. Hume's principles, is the same with contiguity in time, or the order of succession. Causation is only a name for the order established between an antecedent and a consequent; that is, the established or constant antecedence of the one, and consequence of the other. Resemblance only remains, as an alleged principle of association, and it is necessary to inquire whether it is included in the laws which have been above expounded. I believe it will be found that we are accustomed to see like things together. When we see a tree, we generally see more trees than one; when we see an ox, we generally see more oxen than one; a sheep, more sheep than one; a man, more men than one. From this observation, I think, we may refer resemblance to the law of frequency, of which it seems to form only a particular case.

Mr. Hume makes contrast a principle of association, but not a separate one, as he thinks it is compounded of Resemblance and Causation. It is not necessary for us to show that this is an unsatisfactory account of contrast. It is only necessary to observe, that, as a case of association, it is not distinct from those which we have above explained.

A dwarf suggests the idea of a giant. How? We call a dwarf a dwarf, because he departs from a certain standard. We call a giant a giant, because he departs from the same standard. This is a case, therefore, of resemblance, that is, of frequency.

Pain is said to make us think of pleasure; and this is considered a case of association by contrast. There is no doubt that pain makes us think of relief from it; because they have been conjoined, and the great vividness of the sensations makes the association strong. Relief from pain is a species of pleasure; and one pleasure leads to think of another, from the resemblance. This is a compound case, therefore, of vividness and frequency. All other cases of contrast, I believe, may be expounded in a similar manner.

I have not thought it necessary to be tedious in expounding the observations which I have thus stated; for whether the reader supposes that resemblance is, or is not, an original principle of association, will not affect our future investigations.

12. Not only do simple ideas, by strong association, run together, and form complex ideas: but a complex idea, when the simple ideas which compose it have become so consolidated that it always appears as one, is capable of entering into combinations with other ideas, both simple and complex. Thus two complex ideas may be united together, by a strong association, and coalesce into one, in the same manner as two or more simple ideas coalesce into one. This union of two complex ideas

into one, Dr. Hartley has called a duplex idea. Two also of
these duplex, or doubly compounded ideas, may unite into
one; and these again into other compounds, without end. It is
hardly necessary to mention, that as two complex ideas unite to
form a duplex one, not only two, but more than two may so
unite; and what he calls a duplex idea may be compounded of
two, three, four, or any number of complex ideas.

Some of the most familiar objects with which we are acquainted furnish instances of these unions of complex and
duplex ideas.

Brick is one complex idea, mortar is another complex idea;
these ideas, with ideas of position and quantity, compose my
idea of a wall. My idea of a plank is a complex idea, my idea of
a rafter is a complex idea, my idea of a nail is a complex idea.

These, united with the same ideas of position and quantity,
compose my duplex idea of a floor. In the same manner my
complex idea of glass, and wood, and others, compose my
duplex idea of a window; and these duplex ideas, united together, compose my idea of a house, which is made up of various duplex ideas. How many complex, or duplex ideas, are all
united in the idea of furniture? How many more in the idea of
merchandise? Now many more in the idea called Every
Thing?

ALEXANDER BAIN
(1818–1903)

THE SENSES AND THE INTELLECT*

THE INTELLECT

WE now proceed to view the Intellect, or the thinking function of the mind. The various faculties known as Memory, Judgment, Abstraction, Reason, Imagination, — are modes or varieties of Intellect. Although we can hardly ever exert this portion of our mental system in separation from the other elements of mind — Feeling and Volition, yet scientific method requires it to be described apart.

The primary, or fundamental attributes of Thought, or Intelligence, have been already stated to be, Consciousness of *Difference*, Consciousness of *Agreement*, and *Retentiveness*. The exposition of the Intellect will consist in tracing out the workings of these several attributes; the previous book containing the enumeration of all that we at first have to discriminate, identify, and retain.

(1.) The first and most fundamental property is the Consciousness of Difference, or DISCRIMINATION. To be distinctively affected by two or more successive impressions is the most general fact of consciousness. We are never conscious at all without experiencing transition or change. (This has been called the Law of Relativity.) When the mental outburst is characterized mainly by pleasure or pain, we are said to be under a state of *feeling*. When the prominent circumstance is discrimination of the two distinct modes of the transition, we are occupied *intellectually*. There are many transitions that give little or no feeling in the sense of pleasure or pain, and that are attended to *as* transitions, in other words, as Differences.

* London, 1855; 4th ed., 1894.

In states of enjoyment or suffering, we cannot be strictly devoid of the consciousness of difference; but we abstain from the exercise of the discriminating (and the identifying) function, and follow out the consequences of a state of feeling as such, these being to husband the pleasure and abate the pain, by voluntary actions.

. . . .

(2.) The fundamental property of Intellect, named RETEN-TIVENESS, has two aspects, or degrees.

First. The persistence or continuance of mental impressions, after the withdrawal of the external agent. When the ear is struck by a sonorous wave, we have a sensation of sound, but the mental excitement does not die away because the sound ceases; there is a certain continuing effect, generally much feebler, but varying greatly according to circumstances, and on some occasions quite equal to the effect of the actual sensation. In consequence of this property, our mental excitement, due to external causes, may greatly outlast the causes themselves; we are enabled to go on living a life in ideas, in addition to the life in actualities.

But this is not all. We have, secondly, the power of recovering, or reviving, under the form of ideas, past or extinct sensations and feeling of all kinds, without the originals, and by mental agencies alone.

After the impression of a sound has ceased entirely, and the mind has been occupied with other things, there is a possibility of recovering from temporary oblivion the idea, or mental effect, without reproducing the actual sound. We remember, or bring back to mind, sights, and sounds, and thoughts, that have not been experienced for months or years. This implies a still higher mode of retentiveness than the previous fact; it supposes that something has been engrained in the mental structure; that an effect has been produced of a kind that succeeding impressions have not been able to blot out.   Now, one medium of the restoration to consciousness of a particular past state, is the actual presence of some impression that had often occurred *in company* with that state. Thus we are reminded of a *name* — as ship, star, tree — by seeing the *thing;* the previous concurrence of name and thing has led to a mental companionship between the two. Impressions that have frequently accompanied one another in the mind grow together, so as to become at last almost inseparable: we cannot have one without a disposition or prompting to renew all the rest. This is the highest form of the Retentive, or plastic, property of the mind. It will be exemplified at length under the title of *Association* by *Contiguity*.

(3.) The remaining property of Intellect is consciousness of AGREEMENT. Besides the consciousness of difference, the mind is also affected by agreement rising out of partial difference. The continuance of the same impression produces no effect, but after experiencing a certain impression and passing away from it to something else, the recurrence of the first causes a certain shock or start, — the shock of recognition; which is all the greater according as the circumstances of the present and of the past occurrence are different. Change produces one effect, the effect called discrimination; Similarity in the midst of change produces a new and distinct effect; and these are the two modes of intellectual stimulation, the two constituents of knowledge. When we see in the child the features of the man, we are struck by agreement in the midst of difference.

This power of recognition, identification, or discovery of likeness in unlikeness, is another means of bringing to mind past ideas; and is spoken of as the *Associating*, or *Reproductive* principle of SIMILARITY. We are as often reminded of things by their *resemblance* to something present, as by their previous *proximity* to what is now in the view. Contiguity and Similarity express two great principles or forces of mental *reproduction;* they are distinct powers of the mind, varying in degree among individuals — the one sometimes preponderating, and sometimes the other. The first governs Acquisition, the second Invention.

The commonly recognized intellectual faculties, enumerated by Psychologists with much discrepancy, in so far as they do not involve Feeling and Volition, are resolvable into these three primitive properties of Intellect — Discrimination, Retention, Similarity. The faculty called Memory is almost exclusively founded in the Retentive power, although sometimes aided by Similarity. The processes of Reason and Abstraction involve Similarity chiefly; there being in both the identification of resembling things. What is termed Judgment may consist in Discrimination on the one hand, or in the Sense of Agreement on the other: we determine two or more things either to differ or to agree. It is impossible to find any case of Judging that does not, in the last resort, mean one or other of these two essential activities of the intellect. Lastly, Imagination is a product of all the three fundamentals of our intelligence, with the addition of an element of Emotion.

．　．　．　．　．　．　．　．　．　．　．　．

CHAPTER I. RETENTIVENESS — LAW OF CONTIGUITY

1. THIS principle is the basis of Memory, Habit, and the Acquired Powers in general. Writers on Mental Science have described it under various names. Sir William Hamilton terms it the law of "Redintegration," regarding it as the principle whereby one part of a whole brings up the other parts, as when the first words of a quotation recall the remainder, or one house in a street suggests the succeeding ones. The associating links called Order in Time, Order in Place, and Cause and Effect, are all included under it. We might also name it the law of Association proper, of Adhesion, Mental Adhesiveness, or Acquisition.

The following is a general statement of this mode of mental reproduction.

Actions, Sensations, and States of Feeling, occurring together or in close succession, tend to grow together, or cohere, in such a way that, when any one of them is afterwards presented to the mind, the others are apt to be brought up in idea.

There are various circumstances or conditions that regulate and modify the operation of this principle, so as to render the adhesive growth more or less rapid and secure. These will be best brought out by degrees in the course of the exposition. As a general rule, Repetition is necessary in order to render coherent in the mind a train or aggregate of images, as, for example, the successive aspects of a panorama, with a sufficient degree of force to make one suggest the others at an after period. The precise degree of repetition needed depends on a variety of causes, the quality of the individual mind being one.

4. In regard to the conditions that regulate the pace of our various acquisitions, some are general, others are special to individual kinds.

The general conditions are these: —

I. A certain amount of Continuance, or Repetition of the matter to be learned, is requisite: and the greater the continuance, or the more frequent the repetition, the greater the progress of the learner. Deficiency in the other conditions has to be made up by a protracted iteration.

II. The Concentration of the mind is an important condition. This means physically that the forces of the nevous system are strongly engaged upon the particular act, which is possible only by keeping the attention from wandering to other things. It is well known that distraction of mind is a bar to acquirement.

There are various modes of attaining the desired concentration. It is a voluntary act, prompted by present and by future pleasures and pains.

The greatest of all motives to concentration is a present enjoyment of the work in hand. Any exercise possessing a special charm detains us by immediate attraction; everything else is neglected so long as the fascination lasts. This is the inherent power of the will in its immediate and most efficient manifestation — a present pleasure furthering a present action. It explains the great influence of what is called the Taste for a special pursuit. The taste or fascination for music, for science, for business, — keeps the mind of the learner exclusively bent upon the subject; and the pace of acquisition is proportionally rapid.

Next to present enjoyment, is associated, or future, enjoyment; as when we devote ourselves to something uninteresting or painful in itself, but calculated to bring future gratification. This is, generally speaking, a less urgent stimulation, as being the influence of pleasure existing only in idea. There may, however, be all degrees of intensity of the motive, according to the strength of the ideal representation of the pleasure to come. It is on this stimulation, that we go through the dry studies necessary to a lucrative profession or a favourite object of pursuit. The young are insufficiently actuated by prospective pleasure, owing to their inferior ideal hold of it; and are therefore not powerfully moved in this way.

A third form of concentration is when present pain is made use of to deter and withdraw the mind from causes of distraction, or matters having an intrinsically superior charm. This is the final resort in securing the attention of the volatile learner. It is an inferior motive, on the score of economy, but cannot be dispensed with in early training. By an artificial appliance, the subject is made *comparatively* the most attractive. So with the use of future pains; the same allowance being made for the difference in their character, as for pleasures existing only in prospect.

Mere Excitement, whether as pleasure or as pain, or as neither, is a power of intellectual concentration. An idea that excites us very much persists in the mind, even if painful; and the remembrance of it will be stamped in consequence. This influence will be especially noticed, a few pages hence.

It is not uncommon, in stating the general conditions of Retentiveness, or memory, to specify the *vividness* or *intensity* of an impression; thus, we readily remember such effects as an intense odour, a speech uttered with vehemence, a conflagration. This, however, resolves itself into the concentration of mental and nervous force, due to the emotional excitement. Apart from the feelings, an idea may be more or less distinct and clear, but is not properly more or less intense. If an inscription is legible with ease, it is everything that the intellect demands; the adventitious aid of glaring characters, as when, at a public illumination, a sentiment is written in gas jets, is a species of excitement, securing an inordinate amount of attention or concentration of mind.

If we compare an object sharply defined with another whose lineaments are faded and obscure, there is a wide difference in the hold that the two would severally take on the memory; but such impressions differ in kind, and not simply in degree. The names 'vivid' and 'intense' are scarcely applicable except by a figure. Without a decisive difference or contrast, the mind is not impressed at all; everything that favours the contrast favours discrimination, and also depth of impression. All this, however, is pre-supposed, as a fact or property of the *Discriminating* function of intellect; and is not to be repeated as appertaining to the *Retentive* function.

III. There appears to be *specific to each individual* a certain degree of General Retentiveness, or a certain aptitude for acquirement generally. We find a great inequality in the progress of learners placed almost exactly in the same circumstances. Sometimes the difference refers only to single departments, as mechanical art, music, or language; it is then referable to special and local endowments, as muscular sensibility, the musical ear, and so forth. Often, however, the superiority of individuals is seen in acquirement as a whole, in which form it is better regarded as a General power of Retentiveness.

5. We shall advert, as we proceed, to the modifying circumstances of a local kind peculiar to each class of acquisitions. As respects the present class, Movements, the special conditions seem to be as follows: —

(1.) Bodily Strength, or mere muscular vigour, must be regarded as favouring acquisition. Not only is it an indication of a large share of vitality in the muscles, which is likely to attend their acquired aptitudes; it also qualifies for enduring, without fatigue, a great amount of continuance or practice of the operations required.

(2.) Distinct from mere muscular power is Spontaneity, or the active temperament; meaning the natural proneness to copious muscular activity. This must be regarded as a property, not of the muscular tissue, but of the nerve-centres on the active side of the brain. Hence there is a likelihood, if not a certainty, that the endowment is accompanied with a greater facility in the association of movements. Observation accords with the view. It is usually men of abounding natural activity that make adroit mechanics, good sportsmen, and able combatants.

(3.) Of still greater importance is Muscular Delicacy, or Discrimination, which is not necessarily involved in either of the foregoing heads, although more allied to the second. The power of discriminating nice shades of muscular movement is at the foundation of muscular expertness in every mode. We have abundant proof that, wherever delicacy of discrimination exists, there exists also a special retentiveness of that class of impressions. The physical groundwork of the property is the abundance of the nerve elements — fibres and corpuscles — out of which also must spring the capacity for varied groupings and fixed associations.

Physical vigour in general, and those modes of it that are the counterparts of mental vigour in particular, must be reckoned among the conditions of Retentiveness. Other things being the same, acquisition is most rapid in health, and in the nourished and fresh condition of all the organs. When the forces of the system run strongly to the nervous system in general, there is a natural exuberance of all the mental manifestations; and energy of mind is then compatible with much bodily feebleness, yet not with any circumstances that restrict the nourishment of the brain.

CHAPTER II. AGREEMENT — LAW OF SIMILARITY

> *Present* Actions, Sensations, Thoughts, or Emotions tend to revive their LIKE among *previous* Impressions, or States.

1. CONTIGUITY joins together things that occur together, or that are, by any circumstance, presented to the mind at *the same time;* as when we associate heat with light, a falling body

with a concussion. But, in addition to this link of reproductive connexion, we find that one thing will, by virtue of Similarity, recall another *separated from it in time,* as when a portrait recalls the original.

The second fundamental property of Intellect, termed Consciousness of Agreement, or Similarity, is a great power of mental reproduction, or a means of recovering past mental states. It was noticed by Aristotle as one of the links in the succession of our thoughts.

As regards our *knowledge,* or perception, of things, the consciousness of Agreement is second only to Discrimination, or the consciousness of Difference. When we know a thing, we do so by its differences and its agreements. Our full knowledge of red, is our having contrasted it with all other colours, and our having compared it with itself and with its various shades. Our knowledge of a chair is made up of our experiences of the distinction between it and other articles of furniture, &c., and of the agreement between it and other chairs. Both modes are involved in a complete act of cognition, and nothing else (except, of course, the Retentiveness implied in the one and the other) is necessary. Our knowledge of man is the sum of the points of contrast between a man and all other things, and the sum of the points of identity on comparing men with one another. Our increase in knowledge is constantly proceeding in both directions: we note new differences, and also new agreements, among our experiences, object and subject. We do not begin to be conscious till we have the shock of difference; and we cannot make that analysis of our conscious states, called the recognition of plurality, combination, or complication, till we discover agreements, and refer each part of the impression to its like among our previous impressions. To perceive is, properly, to recognize, or identify.

2. Some preliminary explanation of the kind of relationship subsisting between the two principles of Contiguity and Similarity, is requisite in order to guard against mistakes, and especially to prevent misapprehension, as to the separate existence of the two modes of action in the mental framework. When the cohesive link between any two contiguous actions, or images, is confirmed by a new occurrence or repetition,

obviously the present impression must revive the sum total of the past impressions, or reinstate the whole mental condition left on the occasion immediately preceding. Thus, if I am disciplining myself in the act of drawing a round figure with my hand any one present effort must recall the state of the muscular and nervous action, or the precise bent acquired at the end of the previous effort, while that effort had to reinstate the condition at the end of the one preceding, and so on. It is only in this way that repetition can be of any avail in confirming a physical habit, or in forming an intellectual aggregate. But this reinstatement of a former condition by a present act of the same kind, is really and truly a case of the operation of the associating principle of similarity, or of like recalling like; and we here plainly see, that without such recall, the adhesion of contiguous things would be impossible. Hence it would appear, that all through the exposition of Contiguity, the principle of Similarity has been tacitly assumed; we have everywhere taken for granted, that a present occurrence of any object to the view recalls the total impression made by all the previous occurrences, and adds its own effect to that total.

But, by thus tacitly assuming the power of anything present to reinstate the past impressions of the same thing, we restrict ourselves to those cases where the reinstatement is sure and certain, in fact to cases of absolute identity of the present and past. Such is the nature of the instances dwelt upon in the previous chapter: in all of them, the new movement, or the new image, was supposed precisely *identical* with the old, and went simply to reinstate and to deepen an impression already made. We must, however, now pass beyond this field of examples, and enter upon a new class where the identity is only partial, and is on that account liable to be missed; where the restoration, instead of being sure, is doubtful; and where, moreover, the reinstatement serves higher purposes than the mere iteration and deepening of the impression already made. In all mental restorations whatsoever, both Contiguity and Similarity are at work; in one class, the question is as to the sufficiency of the contiguous bond, the similarity being sure; in another class, the question is as to the sufficiency of the attractive force of the likeness, the contiguous adhesiveness being believed certain. If I chance to meet with a person I have formerly seen, and endeavour to remember his name, it will depend upon the goodness of a cohesive link whether or not I succeed; there will be no difficulty in my recalling the past impression of his personal appearance through the force of the present impression; but having recalled the full total of the past impressions, I may not be able to recover the *accompaniment* of the name; the contiguity may be at fault, although the similarity works its perfect work of restoring to me my previous conception of the personal aspect. If, on the other hand, I see a man on the street, and if I have formerly seen a portrait of that man, it is a question whether the living reality shall recall the portrait; the doubt hangs not upon the contiguity, or coherence of the parts and surroundings of the picture, if it could be recovered, but upon the chance of its being recovered. Where things are identical, the operation of similarity, in making the present case revive the former ones, is so certain that it is not even mentioned; we talk of the goodness of the cohesive bond between the revived part and its accompaniments, as if contiguity expressed the whole fact of the restoration. To make up for this partiality of view, which was indispensable to a clear exposition, we now embrace, with the like partial and prominent consideration, the element that was left in a latent condition; and allow to sink, into the latent state, the one that has hitherto been made exclusively prominent.

3. In the perfect identity between a present and a past impression, the past is recovered and fused with the present, instantaneously and surely. So quick and unfaltering is the process that we lose sight of it altogether; we are scarcely made aware of the existence of an associating link of similarity in the chain of sequence. When I look at the full moon, I am instantly impressed with the state arising from all my former impressions of her disc added together; so natural and necessary does this restoration seem, that we rarely reflect on the principle implied in it, namely, the power of the new stimulus

to set on the nervous currents, with all the energy acquired in the course of many hundred repetitions of the same visual impetus. But when we pass from perfect to imperfect or partial identity, we are more readily made aware of the existence of this link of attraction between similars, for we find that sometimes the restoration does not take place; cases occur where we fail to be struck with a similitude; the spark does not pass between the new currents and the old dormant ones. The failure in reinstating the old condition by virtue of the present stimulus, is, in the main, ascribable to *imperfect identity*. When, in some new impression of a thing, the original form is muffled, obscured, distorted, disguised, or in any way altered, it is a chance whether or not we identify it; the amount of likeness that remains will have a reviving power, or a certain amount of reinstating energy, but the points of difference or unlikeness will operate to resist the supervention of the old state, and will tend to revive objects like *themselves*. If I hear a musical air that I have been accustomed to, the new impression revives the old as a matter of course; but if the air is played with complex harmonies and accompaniments, it is possible that the effect of these additions may be to check my recognition of the piece; the unlike circumstances may repel the reinstatement of the old experience more powerfully than the remaining likeness attracts it; and I may find in it no identity whatever with an air previously known, or even identify it with something altogether different. If my hold of the essential character of the melody is but feeble, and if I am stunned and confounded with the new accompaniments, there is every likelihood that I shall not experience the restoration of my past hearing of the air intended, and consequently I shall not identify the performance.

4. The obstructives to the revival of the past through similitude, may be classed under the two heads — Faintness and Diversity. There are instances where a new impression is too *feeble* to strike into the old-established track of the same impression, and to make it alive again; as when we are unable to identify the taste of a very weak solution, or to discern an object in

twilight dimness. The most numerous and interesting cases come, however, under the other head — Diversity, or mingled likeness and unlikeness; as when we meet an old acquaintance in a new dress, or in circumstances where we have never seen the same person before. The modes of diversity are countless, and incapable of being classified. We might, indeed, include under diversity the other of the two heads, seeing that faintness implies diversity of *degree*, if not of any other circumstance; but I prefer considering the obstruction arising from faintness by itself, after which we shall proceed to the larger field of examples marked by unlikeness in other respects.

5. The difficulty or facility in resuming a past mental condition, at the suggestion of a present similitude, will plainly depend upon the *hold* that the past impression has acquired; it is much easier to revive a familiar image than an unfamiliar, by the force of a new presentation. We shall, therefore, have to keep this circumstance in view, among others, in the course of our illustration of the law of Similarity.

It has to be considered how far natural character — that is, a primitive endowment of the intellect, enters into the power of reviving similars, or of bringing together like things in spite of the repulsion of unlike accompaniments. There is much to be explained in the preferences shown by different minds, in the objects that they most readily recall to the present view; which preferences determine varieties of character, such as the scientific and the artistic minds. The explanation of these differences was carried up to a certain point under the Law of Contiguity; but, if I am not mistaken, there is still a portion referable to the existence of various modes and degrees of susceptibility to the force of Similarity. From all that I have been able to observe, the two energies of contiguous adhesion, and of attraction of similars, do not rise and fall together in the character; we may have one feeble and the other strong, in all proportions and degrees of adjustment. I believe, moreover, that there is such a thing as an energetic power of recognizing *similarity in general*, and that this is productive of remarkable consequences. Whether I shall be able to impress these convictions upon my readers, will depend upon the success of the detailed exposition of this noted peculiarity of our intellectual nature.

CHAPTER III. COMPOUND ASSOCIATION

1. HITHERTO we have restricted our attention to single threads or indivisible links of association, whether of Contiguity or Similarity. It remains for us to consider the case where several threads, or a Plurality of links or bonds of connexion, unite in reviving some previous thought or mental state. No new principle is introduced here; we have merely to note, what seems an almost unavoidable effect of the combined action, that the reinstatement is thereby made more easy and certain. Associations that are individually too weak, to operate the revival of a past idea, may succeed by acting together; and there is thus opened up to our view a means of aiding our recollection, or invention, when the one thread in hand is too feeble to effect a desired recall. It happens in fact, that, in a very large number of our mental transitions, there is present a multiple bond of association.

The combinations may be made up of Contiguities alone, of Similarities alone, or of Contiguity and Similarity mixed. Moreover, we shall find that in Emotion and in Volition there are influences either assisting or obstructing the proper intellectual forces. In the reviving of a past image or idea, it is never unimportant, that the revival gratifies a favourite emotion, or is strongly willed in the pursuit of an end. We must endeavour to appreciate, as far as we are able, the influence of these extra-intellectual energies within the sphere of intellect; but, as they would rarely suffice for the reproduction of thought, if acting apart and alone, we are led to look at them chiefly as modifying the effects of the strictly intellectual forces, or as combining elements in the composition of associations.

The general law may be stated as follows: —

Past actions, sensations, thoughts, or emotions, are recalled more easily, when associated either through contiguity or through similarity, with *more than one* present object or impression.

COMPOSITION OF CONTIGUITIES

2. We begin with the composition of contiguities. Instances might be cited under all the heads of the first chapter; but a less profuse selection will suffice. There will, however, be a gain in clearness by taking Conjunctions and Successions separately.

Conjunctions. — For a simple example of a compound conjunction, we may suppose a person smelling a liquid and identifying the smell as something felt before, but unable to recall to mind the material causing it. Here the bond between an odour and the odorous substance is too feeble for reproducing the idea or the name of the substance. Suppose farther that the person could taste the liquid without feeling the odour, and that in the taste he could recognize a former taste, but could not remember the thing. If, in these circumstances, the concurrence of the two present sensations of taste and smell brought the substance to the recollection, we should have a true instance of composite association. If one of the two links is fully equal to the restoring effect, there is no case under the present law; in order to constitute a proper example, each should be insufficient when acting singly. Although there can be no doubt as to the fact of such revivals, we might easily suppose it otherwise. Combination is not strength under all circumstances. A gallon of water at 40°, cannot yield a spoonful at 41°. Ten thousand commonplace intellects would not make one genius, under any system of co-operation. The multiplication of unaided eyes could never equal the vision of one person with a telescope, or a microscope.

We have seen that the *complex wholes* around us in the world, are held together in the recollection by the adhesive force of Contiguity; such objects as a tree, a human figure, a scene in nature, cannot continue in the mind, or be revived as ideas, until frequent repetition has made all the parts coherent. After the requisite iteration, a complex object, such as a rural village, may be revived by the presence of a single portion of it, as some street, or building, or marked locality. But, if the village is one not very well known, that is, if the notion of it is not very firmly aggregated in the mind, the traveller just entering may be not ready to identify it by the first thing that strikes him; he may require to go on till several other objects come in view, when probably their joint impression will be able to bring up the whole, in other words, will remind him what village he is now entering.

So in regarding objects as *concretes*, or combinations of many distinct qualities, — an orange, for example, which affects all the senses, — a fixing process makes the different sensations hold together in one complex idea. Here, too, there is room for the joint action of associating links in recalling an image to the mind. I have already imagined a case of this description, where the united action of smell and of taste was supposed to revive the idea of the concrete object causing them, either being of itself insufficient for the purpose.

5. *Successions.* — I have dwelt at length, in a previous chapter, on the contiguous association of successions of various kinds. Here, too, in the circumstance of imperfect adhesion, the recovery may be due to a composite action. I have witnessed a series of events, and these are, in consequence, associated in my mind. In endeavouring to recall the series from the commencement, a link fails, until some other association, such as place, or person, contributes an assisting thread.

There is one succession that contains the whole of our experience, that is, the Order of Time, or the sequence of events in each one's own history. If all the minutiæ of this succession were to cohere perfectly in the mind, everything that we have ever done, seen, or been cognizant of, could be recovered by means of it. But although all the larger transactions, and the more impressive scenes, of our personal history, are linked in this order with a sufficient firmness, yet for smaller incidents the bond is too weak. I cannot remember fully my yesterday's train of thoughts; nor repeat verbatim an address of five minutes' length, whether spoken or heard. Things related in the order of time are, strictly speaking, experienced only once, and we usually require repetition to fix any mental train. It constantly happens, therefore, that we are in search of some reinforcing connexion to help us in recovering the stream of events, as they occurred in the order of time. We seek for other conjunctions and successions to enable us to recommence after every break.

Experience teaches us, that the only way of making up a defective adhesion is to compass in our minds some other connexion, or to get at the missing object through a new door. The inability to recollect the next occurring particular of a train that we are in want of, stimulates a great effort of volition, and the true course for the mind to take is to get upon some chain or current that is likely to cross the line of the first near the break.

At every moment of life, each person stands immersed in a complicated scene, and each object of this scene may become a starting point for a train of recollections. All the internal feelings of the body; everything that surrounds us and strikes the eye, ear, touch, taste, or smell; all the ideas, emotions, and purposes occupying the mind; — these form so many beginnings of trains of association passing far away into the remotest regions of recollection and thought; and we have it in our power to stop and change the direction as often as we please. From some one of these present things, we must commence our outgoings towards the absent and the distant, whether treading in single routes, or introducing composite action.

6. *Language.* — The recall of names by things, and of things by names, gives special occasion for bringing in additional links to aid a feeble tie. When we have forgotten the name of a person, or of an object, we are under the necessity of referring back to the situation and circumstances where we have heard the name, to see if any other bond of connexion will spring up. Often we are unable, at the moment, to recover the lost sound by any means; but, afterwards, an auxiliary circumstance crosses the view, and the revival is effected.

Many of our recollections, thoughts, conceptions, and imaginings, are an inextricable mixture of language and ideas of things. The notions that we acquire through oral instruction, or from books, are made up in part by the subject matter purely, and in part by the phraseology that conveyed it. Thus, my recollection of a portion of history is made up of the train of words, with the train of historical facts and scenes, as I might have seen them with my own eyes. So in many sciences, there is a combination of visual or tactual notions with language. Geometry is a compound of visible diagrams with the language of definitions, axioms, and demonstrations. Now, in all these cases, recollection may depend, either on the associations of words, or on those of visual and other conceptions, or on a compound of both. If I listen to a geographical description, there is, in the first place, a train of words dropping on my ear; and, by virtue of a perfect verbal cohesion, I might recall the whole description and recite it to another party. In the second place, there is a series of views of objects — of mountain, river, plain, and forest — which I picture in my mind and retain independently of the language used to suggest them. Were my pictorial adhesion strong enough, I could recall the whole of the features in the order that I was made to conceive them, and leave aside the language. The common case, however, is that the recollection is effected by a union of both the threads of cohesion; the pictorial train is assisted by the verbal, and the verbal by the pictorial, as may happen.

Composition of Similarities

7. The influence of the multiplication of points of likeness, in securing the revival of a past object, is liable to no uncertainty. It is only an extension of the principle maintained all through the discussion of the law of similarity, that the greater the similitude, and the more numerous the points of resemblance, the surer is the stroke of recall. If I meet a person very like some one else I have formerly known, the probability of my recalling this last person to view is increased, if the likeness in face and feature is combined with similarity of dress, of speech, of gait, or of any still more extraneous points, such as occupation, or history. Increase of resemblance *extensively,*

that is by outward connexions, has the same power as increase of resemblance *intensively*, in rendering the restoration of the past more certain. It might admit of a doubt whether four faint links of contiguous adhesion would be equal to one strong link, but it would be against our whole experience of the workings of similarity, to doubt the utility of multiplying faint resemblances, when there was no one sufficiently powerful to effect the revival. At the same time, we must admit that much more is contributed to the chances of reinstatement by intensifying one point of likeness, than by adding new ones of a faint character. By raising some single feature almost up to the point of identity, we should do more good than could be done by scattering faint and detached likenesses over the picture. This, however, is not always in our power; and we are glad to find, that, when the similarity, in any one particular, is too feeble to suggest the resembling past, the existence of a plurality of weak resemblances will be the equivalent of a single stronger one.

On this view, I might set forth the workings of composite similarities, from the various classes of examples gone over in the preceding chapter. In all very complicated conjunctions, as, for example, a landscape, there may be a multiplication of likenesses, unable to strike singly, but, by their concurrence suggesting a parallel scene. Hence, in endeavouring to recall resembling things, we may proceed, as in Contiguity, by hunting out new collaterals, on the chance of increasing the amount of similitude. and, with that, the attractive power of the present for the absent. If I am endeavouring to recall to mind some historic parallel to a present political situation, supposing one to exist and to have been at some former time impressed on my mind, there may be a want of any single salient likeness, such as we admit to be the most effective medium of reinstatement; and I must, therefore, go over in my mind all the minute features of the present, to enhance, in this way, the force of the attraction of similitude for the forgotten parallel.

8. The case noticed at the conclusion of the preceding head,

namely, the combination of language with subject-matter in a mixed recollection, is favourable to the occurrence of compound similarity. If an orator has to deal with a special point, the conduct of an individual, for example, which he wishes to denounce by a cutting simile, his invention may be aided by some similarity in the phrases descriptive of the case, as well as in the features of the case itself. If one who has at a former time read the play of Œdipus, now commences to read Lear, the similarity is not at first apparent, but long before the conclusion there will be a sufficient accumulation of features of similitude, in dramatic situation and in language, to bring Œdipus to mind without any very powerful stretch of intellectual force. So, in scientific invention; a fact described in language has a double power of suggestion; and if, by good luck, the fact has a likeness to some other fact, and the description resembles the language that accompanied that other when formerly present to the mind, there is so much the more chance of the revival taking place.

Mixed Contiguity and Similarity

9. Under this head, there are several interesting examples.

If any one, in describing a storm, employ the phrase 'a war of elements,' the metaphor has been brought to mind partly by similitude, but partly also by contiguity, seeing that the comparison has already been made. The person that first used the phrase came upon it by similarity; he that used it next had contiguity to assist him; and, after frequent repetition, the bond of contiguity may be so well confirmed, that the force of similarity is entirely superseded. In this way, many things that were originally strokes of genius, end in being efforts of mere adhesive recollection; while, for a time previous to this final consummation, there is a mixed effort of the two suggesting forces. Hence Johnson's remark on the poet Ogilvie, that his poem contained what was once imagination, but in him had come to be memory.

In all regions of intellectual exertion — industry, science, art, literature — there is a kind of ability displayed in taking up great and original ideas and combinations, before they have been made easy by iteration. Minds unable for the highest efforts of origination may yet be equal to this second degree of genius, wherein a considerable force of similarity is assisted by a small thread of contiguity. To master a large multitude of the discoveries of identification, a power of similarity short of the original force that gave birth to them, is aided by the contiguous bond that has grown up, during a certain number of repetitions of each.

10. A second case is, when a similarity is struck out in circumstances such as to bring the absent object into near *proximity* in some contiguous train. Thus, a poet falls upon a beautiful metaphor, while dwelling in the region where the material of the simile occurs. In the country, rural comparisons are most easily made; on ship-board, nautical metaphors are naturally abundant.

If we chance to be studying by turns two different sciences that throw much light on each other, we are in the best position for deriving the benefit of the comparison. When we know the most likely source of fertile similitudes for some difficult problem, we naturally keep near that source, in order that we may be struck with the faintest gleam of likeness, through the help of proximity. A historian of the ancient republics cultivates a familiarity with all the living instances of the republican system. Now that physical science is largely indebted to mathematical handling, the physicist has to maintain his freshness in mathematics. It is not safe to trust to an acquisition of old date, however pertinacious the mind be in retaining the subject in question. The great discoveries of identification that astonish the world and open up new vistas of knowledge, have doubtless often been helped by the accidental proximity of the things made to flash together. For illustration's sake, we might suppose Newton in the act of meditating upon the planetary attraction, at the time that the celebrated apple fell to the ground before his eyes; a proximity so very close would powerfully aid in bringing on the stroke of identification.

CHAPTER IV. CONSTRUCTIVE ASSOCIATION

By means of Association, the mind has the power to form *new* combinations, or aggregates, *different* from any that have been presented to it in the course of experience.

1. THROUGHOUT the whole of the preceding exposition, we have had in view the literal resuscitation, revival, or reinstatement of former actions, images, emotions, and trains of thought. No special reference has been made to the operations known by such names as Imagination, Creation, Constructiveness, Origination; through which we are supposed to put together new forms, or to construct images, conceptions, pictures, and modes of working, such as we have never before had any experience of. Yet the genius of the Painter, the Poet, the Musician, and the Inventor in the arts and sciences, evidently implies a process of this nature.

Under the head of Similarity, we have had to recognize a power tending to originality and invention, as when — in virtue of the identifying of two things lying far apart in nature — whatever is known of the one is instantly transferred to the other, thereby constituting a new and instructive combination of ideas. Such was the case when Franklin's identification of electricity and thunder, led to the application of the Leyden jar to explain a thunderstorm. The power of recalling like by like, in spite of remoteness, disguise, and false lures, enters into a very large number of inventive efforts, both in the sciences and in the arts. But we have now to deal with constructions of a higher order of complexity. There are discoveries that seem nothing short of absolute creations, as the whole science of Mathematics; while, in the Fine Arts, a frieze of the Parthenon, a Gothic cathedral, a Paradise Lost, are very far beyond the highest stretches of the identifying faculty taken by itself.

Nevertheless, the intellectual forces operating in those creations, are no other than the associating forces already discussed. The new combinations grow out of elements already possessed by the mind, and brought to view according to the laws above laid down.

HERBERT SPENCER

(1820–1903)

THE PRINCIPLES OF PSYCHOLOGY *

PART II. THE INDUCTIONS OF PSYCHOLOGY

CHAPTER II. THE COMPOSITION OF MIND

§ 64. IN the last chapter we incidentally encroached on the topic to which this chapter is to be devoted. Certain apparently-simple feelings were shown to be compounded of units of feeling; whence it was inferred that possibly, if not probably, feelings of other classes are similarly compounded. And 'n thus treating of the composition of feelings, we, by implication, treated of the composition of Mind, of which feelings are themselves components.

Here, however, leaving speculations about the ultimate composition of Mind, we pass to observations on its proximate composition. Accepting as really simple those constituents of Mind which are not decomposable by introspection, we have to consider what are their fundamental distinctive characters, and what are the essential principles of arrangement among them.

§ 65. The proximate components of Mind are of two broadly-contrasted kinds — Feelings and the Relations between feelings. Among the members of each group there exist multitudinous unlikenesses, many of which are extremely strong; but such unlikenesses are small compared with those which distinguish members of the one group from members of the other. Let us, in the first place, consider what are the characters which all Feelings have in common, and what are the characters which Relations between feelings have in common.

* London, 1855; 2d ed. *ib.* 1870; 3d ed. *ib.* 1881; 5th ed. 1890.

Each feeling, as we here define it, is any portion of consciousness which occupies a place sufficiently large to give it a perceivable individuality; which has its individuality marked off from adjacent portions of consciousness by qualitative contrasts; and which, when introspectively contemplated, appears to be homogeneous. These are the essentials. Obviously if under introspection, a state of consciousness is decomposable, into unlike parts that exist either simultaneously or successively, it is not one feeling but two or more. Obviously if it is indistinguishable from an adjacent portion of consciousness, it forms one with that portion — is not an individual feeling but part of one. And obviously if it does not occupy in consciousness an appreciable area, or an appreciable duration, it cannot be known as a feeling.

A relation between feelings is, on the contrary, characterized by occupying no appreciable part of consciousness. Take away the terms it unites, and it disappears along with them; having no independent place — no individuality of its own. It is true, that, under an ultimate analysis, what we call a relation proves to be itself a kind of feeling — the momentary feeling accompanying the transition from one conspicuous feeling to an adjacent conspicuous feeling. And it is true that, notwithstanding its extreme brevity, its qualitative character is appreciable; for relations are (as we shall hereafter see) distinguishable from one another only by the unlikenesses of the feelings which accompany the momentary transitions. Each relational feeling may, in fact, be regarded as one of those nervous shocks which we suspect to be the units of composition of feelings; and, though instantaneous, it is known as of greater or less strength and as taking place with greater or less facility. But the contrast between these relational feelings and what we ordinarily call feelings, is so strong that we must class them apart. Their extreme brevity, their small variety, and their dependence on the terms they unite, differentiate them in an unmistakeable way.[1]

---

[1] It will perhaps be objected that some relations, as those between things which are distant in Space or in Time, occupy distinguishable portions of con-

Perhaps it will be well to recognize more fully the truth that this distinction cannot be absolute. Besides admitting that, as an element of consciousness, a relation is a momentary feeling, we must also admit that just as a relation can have no existence apart from the feelings which form its terms, so a feeling can exist only by relations to other feelings which limit it in space or time or both. Strictly speaking, neither a feeling nor a relation is an independent element of consciousness: there is throughout a dependence such that the appreciable areas of consciousness occupied by feelings, can no more possess individualities apart from the relations which link them, than these relations can possess individualities apart from the feelings they link. The essential distinction between the two, then, appears to be that whereas a relational feeling is a portion of consciousness inseparable into parts, a feeling ordinarily so-called, is a portion of consciousness that admits imaginary division into like parts which are related to one another in sequence or co-existence. A feeling proper is either made up of like parts that occupy time, or it is made up of like parts that occupy space, or both. In any case, a feeling proper is an aggregate of related like parts, while a relational feeling is undecomposable. And this is exactly the contrast between the two which must result if, as we have inferred, feelings are composed of units of feeling, or shocks.

§ 66. Simple feelings as above defined, are of various kinds. To say anything here about the classification of them, involves some forestalling of a future chapter. This breach of order, however, is unavoidable; for until certain provisional groupings have been made, further exposition is scarcely practicable.

Limiting our attention to seemingly-homogeneous feelings as primarily experienced, they may be divided into the feelings which are centrally initiated and the feelings which are peri-

sciousness. These, however, are not the simple relations between adjacent feelings which we are here dealing with. They are relations that bridge over great numbers of intervening feelings and relations; and come into existence only by quick transitions through these intervening states, ending in the consolidation of them.

pherally initiated — emotions and sensations. These have widely unlike characters. Towards the close of this volume evidence will be found that while the sensations are relatively simple, the emotions, though seeming to be simple are extremely compound; and that a marked contrast of character between them hence results. But without referring to any essential unlikeness of composition, we shall shortly see that between the centrally-initiated feelings and the peripherally-initiated feelings, fundamental distinctions may be established by introspective comparison.

A subdivision has to be made. The peripherally-initiated feelings, or sensations, may be grouped into those which, caused by disturbances at the ends of nerves distributed on the outer surface, are taken to imply outer agencies, and those which, caused by disturbances at the ends of nerves distributed within the body, are not taken to imply outer agencies; which last, though not peripherally initiated in the ordinary sense, are so in the physiological sense. But as between the exterior of the body and its interior, there are all gradations of depth, it results that this distinction is a broadly marked one, rather than a sharply marked one. We shall, however, find that certain differential characters among the sensations accompany this difference of distribution of the nerves in which they arise; and that they are decided in proportion to the relative superficiality or centrality of these nerves.

In contrast with this class of primary or real feelings, thus divided and subdivided, has to be set the complementary class of secondary or ideal feelings, similarly divided and subdivided. Speaking generally, the two classes differ greatly in intensity. While the primary or originally-produced feelings are relatively vivid, the secondary or reproduced feelings are relatively faint. It should be added that the vivid feelings are taken to imply objective exciting agents then and there acting on the periphery of the nervous system; while the faint feelings, though taken to imply objective exciting agents which thus acted at a past time, are not taken to imply their present action.

We are thus obliged to carry with us a classification based

on structure and a classification based on function. The division into centrally-initiated feelings, called emotions, and peripherally-initiated feelings, called sensations; and the subdivision of these last into sensations that arise on the exterior of the body and sensations that arise in its interior; respectively refer to differences among the parts in action. Whereas the division into vivid or real feelings and faint or ideal feelings, cutting across the other divisions at right angles as we may say, refers to difference of amount in the actions of these parts. The first classification has in view unlikenesses of kind among the feelings; and the second, a marked unlikeness of degree, common to all the kinds.

§ 67. From the classes of simple feelings we pass to the classes of simple relations between feelings, respecting which also, something must be said before we can proceed. In default of an ultimate analysis, which cannot be made at present, certain brief general statements must suffice.

As already said, the requisite to the existence of a relation is the existence of two feelings between which it is the link. The requisite to the existence of two feelings is some difference. And therefore the requisite to the existence of a relation is the occurrence of a change — the passage from one apparently-uniform state to another apparently-uniform state, implying the momentary shock produced by the commencement of a new state.

It follows that the degree of the change or shock, constituting in other words the consciousness of the degree of difference between the adjacent states, is the ultimate basis of the distinctions among relations. Hence the fundamental division of them into relations between feelings that are equal, or those of likeness (which however must be divided by some portion of consciousness that is unlike them), and relations between feelings that are unequal, or those of unlikeness. These last fall into what we may distinguish as relations of descending intensity and relations of ascending intensity, according as the transition is to a greater or to a less amount of feeling. And they

are further distinguishable into relations of quantitative unlikeness, or those occurring between feelings of the same nature
but different in degree, and relations of qualitative unlikeness,
or those occurring between feelings not of the same nature.

Relations thus contemplated simply as changes, and grouped
according to the degree of change or the kind of change, severally belong to one or other of two great categories which take
no account of the terms as like or unlike in nature or amount,
but which take account only of their order of occurrence, as
either simultaneous or successive. This fundamental division
of relations into those of co-existence and those of sequence, is,
however, itself dependent on the preceding division into relations of equality between feelings and relations of inequality
between them. For relations themselves have to be classed as of
like or unlike kinds by comparing the momentary feelings that
attend the establishment of them, and observing whether these
are like or unlike, and, as we shall hereafter see, the relations of
co-existence and sequence are distinguished from one another
only by process of this kind.

§ 68. Having defined simple feelings and simple relations,
and having provisionally classified the leading kinds of each,
we may now go on to observe how Mind is made up of these
elements, and how different portions of it are characterized by
different modes of combination of them.

Tracts of consciousness formed of feelings that are centrally
initiated, are widely unlike tracts of consciousness formed of
feelings that are peripherally initiated; and of the tracts of consciousness formed of peripherally-initiated feelings, those parts
occupied by feelings that take their rise in the interior of the
body are widely unlike those parts occupied by feelings that
take their rise on the exterior of the body. The marked unlikenesses are in both cases due to the greater or smaller proportions of the relational elements that are present. Whereas
among centrally-initiated feelings, the mutual limitations, both
simultaneous and successive, are vague and far between; and
whereas among peripherally-initiated feelings caused by inter-

nal disturbances, some are extremely indefinite, and few or none definite in a high degree; feelings caused by external disturbances are mostly related quite clearly, alike by co-existence and sequence, and among the highest of them the mutual limitations in space or time or both, are extremely sharp. These broad contrasts, dependent on the extent to which the elements of feeling are compounded with the elements of relation, cannot be understood, and their importance perceived, without illustrations. We will begin with those parts of Mind distinguished by predominance of the relational elements.

Remembering that the lenses of the eye form a nonsentient optical apparatus that casts images on the retina, we may fairly say that the retina is brought more directly into contact with the external agent acting on it than is any other peripheral expansion of the nervous system. And it is in the tracts of consciousness produced by the various lights reflected from objects around and concentrated on the retina, that we find the elements of feeling most intimately woven up with the elements of relation. The multitudinous states of consciousness yielded by vision, are above all others sharp in their mutual limitations; the differences that occur between adjacent ones are extremely definite. It is further to be noted that the relational element is here dominant under both of its fundamental forms. Some of the feelings simultaneously limit one another with great distinctness, and some of them with equal distinctness successively limit one another. The feelings caused by actions on the general surface of the body are marked off clearly, though by no means so clearly as those which arise in the retina. Sensations of touch initiated at points on the skin very near one another, form parts of consciousness that are separate though adjacent; and these are distinguishable not only as co-existing in close proximity, but also as distinct from kindred sensations immediately preceding or immediately succeeding them. Moreover the definiteness of their mutual limitations, in space if not in time, is greatest among the sensations of touch proceeding from parts of the surface which have, in a sense, the greatest externality — the parts which, like the tips of the fingers and the tip of the tongue, have the most frequent and varied converse with outer objects.[1]   Next in the definiteness of their mutual limitations come the auditory feelings. Among such of these as occur together, the relations are marked with imperfect clearness. Received through uncultivated ears, only a few simultaneous sounds are vaguely separable in consciousness; though received through the ears of a musician, many such sounds may be distinguished and identified. But among successive sounds the relational components of mind are conspicuous. Differences between tones that follow one another, even very rapidly, are clearly perceived. But the demarcations are less decided than those between contrasted sensations in the field of vision.   Passing to the sensations of taste, we see that these, less external in their origin (for it is not in the tip of the tongue, but over its hinder part and the back of the palate, that the gustatory nerves are distributed), are comparatively indefinite in their relations. Such distinctions as may be perceived between tastes that co-exist are comparatively vague, and can be extended to but two or three. Similarly, the beginnings and ends of successive tastes are far less sharp than the beginnings and ends of the visual impressions we receive at every glance; nor can successive tastes be distinguished with anything like the same rapidity as successive tones.   Even more undecided are the mutual limitations among sensations of smell, which, like the last, originate at a considerable distance from the surface (for the nose is not the seat of smell: the olfactory chamber, with which the nostrils communicate, is seated high up between the eyes). Of simultaneous smells the discrimination is very vague; and probably not more than three can be separately identified. Of smells that follow one another, it is manifest that they begin and end indefinitely, and that they cannot be experienced in rapid succession.

---

[1] The tongue is a much more active tactual organ than at first appears. The mechanical impressions it receives are not limited to those given by the food which it manages during mastication; but at other times it is perpetually exploring the inner surfaces of the teeth, which are to it external bodies.

We come now to the peripherally-initiated feelings set up by internal disturbances. Among these the most superficial in origin and most relational as they exist in consciousness, are the sensations of muscular tension. Though, except when making vigorous efforts, these are but feeble; though such as are present together mutually limit one another in a very vague way; and though their beginnings and ends are so blurred that a series of them is but indistinctly separable into parts; yet they are juxta-posed and contrasted to the extent implied by discriminations and recognitions of them — discriminations and recognitions so partial, however, as frequently to require indirect verifications. It should be added that the relations among muscular feelings are variable in abundance and distinctness. They are most con-spicuous when the feelings come from muscles that are small, and in perpetual action, as those which move the eyes, the fin-gers, and the vocal organs; and least conspicuous when the feelings come from muscles that are large or centrally seated, or both, as those of the legs and of the trunk. Pass-ing over abnormal feelings of pain and discomfort due to dis-turbances of nerves distributed within the limbs and body, among which the small proportion of the relational element is manifest, it will suffice if we come at once to the feelings origin-ating in parts that are remotest from the external world, and which, at least relational, are most distinguished from those we set out with. Hunger is extremely vague in its beginning and end. Commencing unobtrusively and ceasing gradually, it is utterly unlike those feelings which, closely contiguous in time, make one another distinct by mutual limitation. Neither is it appreciably marked out by co-existing feelings; its position among simultaneous states of consciousness is indeterminate. And this indefiniteness of relation, both in space and time, characterizes other visceral feelings, both normal and ab-normal.

Of the centrally-initiated feelings, or emotions, much the same has to be said as of the last. Their beginnings and endings in time are comparatively indefinite, and they have no definite localizations in space. That is to say, they are not limited by

preceding and succeeding states of consciousness with any precision; and no identifiable bounds are put to them by states of
consciousness that co-exist. Here, then, the relational element
of mind is extremely inconspicuous. The sequences among
emotions that can occur in a given period, are comparatively
few and indeterminate; and between such two or three emotions as can co-exist it is impossible to distinguish in more than
a vague way.

§ 69. Further and equally important distinctions obtain
between the tracts of consciousness thus broadly contrasted,
and they are similarly caused. Presence of the relational elements, seen in the mutual limitations of feelings, simultaneous
and successive, is accompanied by the mutual cohesion of
feelings; and absence of the relational elements, seen in the
indeterminate boundaries of feelings in space and time, is
accompanied by their incoherence. Let us re-observe the tracts
of consciousness above compared.

The sharply-defined patches of colour that occur together
in a visual impression, are indissolubly united — held rigidly
in juxtaposition. And successive visual feelings, such as are
produced by transferring the gaze from one object to another,
have a strength of connection that gives a fixed consciousness
of their order. Thus the visual feelings, above all others distinguished by the sharpness of their mutual limitations, are
absolutely coherent in space and very coherent in time.
Between sensations of touch given by an object grasped, the
cohesion is not so great. Though the two feelings produced by
two points felt simultaneously by a finger, hold together so
that they cannot be removed far from one another in consciousness; yet the bond uniting them has much less rigidity
than the bond uniting the visual feelings produced by the
two points; and when the feelings are more than two, their
connections in consciousness are loose enough to permit of
much variation in the conception of their relative positions.
Still the strength of links between co-existing feelings of touch
is considerable; as is also that between successive feelings of the

same kind.   Among the simultaneous feelings caused by simultaneous sounds, especially if they are not in harmony, the defect of cohesion is as marked as the defect of mutual limitation. But among the successive feelings produced by successive sounds, we find that along with distinct mutual limitations there go decided mutual cohesions. Sequent notes, or articulations, cling together with tenacity.   Much less clearly bounded by one another as are tastes, simultaneous and successive, they are also comparatively incoherent. Among co-existent tastes there are no connections like those between co-existent visual feelings, or even like those between the sounds produced at the same instant by a band; and tastes do not hold together in sequence as do the tones of cadence. Of smells the like is true. Along with vagueness in the bounding of one by another there goes but a feeble linking together.

The feelings accompanying muscular actions have cohesions that are hidden in much the same way as are their limitations. The difficulty of observing the mutual limitations of muscular feelings, is due to the fact that each muscle, or set of muscles, passes from a state of rest to a state of action or from a state of action to a state of rest, through gradations that occupy an appreciable time; and that, consequently, the accompanying feeling, instead of beginning and ending strongly, shades off at both extremes. Being thus weak at the places where they are contiguous, these feelings are incapable of strong cohesions. Indeed, if we except those which accompany great efforts, we may say that they are altogether so faint compared with most others that their relations, both in kind and order, are necessarily inconspicuous. Their cohesions are in a great degree those of automatic nervous acts; and are by so much the less the cohesions of conscious states.   Those very vague feelings which have their seats in the viscera, may, as before, be exemplified by hunger. Here where we reach such extreme indefiniteness of limitation, both in space and time, we reach an extreme want of cohesion. Hunger does not suddenly follow some other into consciousness; nor is it suddenly followed by some other. Neither is there any simultaneous feeling to which

it clings. The relational element of Mind is almost absent;
holding only in a feeble degree with some tastes and smells.

Lastly, among the centrally-initiated feelings, or emotions,
the same connection of characters occurs. When emotions
co-exist, they can scarcely be said to hold together: the bond
between them is so feeble, that each may disappear without
affecting the others. Between sequent emotions the links have
no appreciable strength: no one is attached to another in such
way as to produce constancy of succession. And though between emotions and certain more definite feelings which precede them, there are strong connections, yet these connections
are not between emotions and single antecedent feelings, but
between emotions and large groups of antecedent feelings; and
even this cohesion, very variable in its strength, may entirely
fail.

§ 70. A further trait in the composition of Mind, dependent
on these correlated traits, may next be set down. We have seen
that tracts of consciousness formed of feelings produced by
external disturbances, are mostly distinguished by predominance of the relational element, involving clearness of mutual
limitation and strength of cohesion among the component
feelings; and we have seen that, contrariwise, the feelings produced by internal disturbances, peripheral and central are
mostly distnguished by comparative want of the relational
element, involving proportionate defect of mutual limitation
and cohesion. We have now to observe that the tracts of consciousness thus broadly contrasted, are, by consequence, broadly
contrasted in the respect that, in the one case, the component
feelings can unite into coherent and well-defined clusters, while,
in the other case, they cannot so unite.

The state of consciousness produced by an object seen is
composed of sharply-outlined lights, shades, and colours, and
the co-existent feelings and relations entering into one of these
groups form an indissoluble whole. To a considerable degree,
successive visual feelings cling together in defined groups. As
most of them are caused by moving objects more or less com-

plex, it is difficult to trace this clustering of them in sequence apart from their clustering in co-existence. But if we take the case of a bird that suddenly flies past close to a window out of which we are looking, it is manifest that the successive feelings form a consciousness of its line of movement so defined and coherent that we know, without having moved the eyes, what was its exact course. The clustering of auditory feelings, comparatively feeble among those occurring simultaneously, is comparatively strong among those occurring successively. Hence the consolidated groups of sounds which we know in consciousness as words. Hence the chains of notes which we remember as musical phrases. The clustering of tactual feelings in relations of co-existence, though by no means so decided as the clustering of co-existent visual feelings, either in the extent or complexity of the clusters or the firmness with which their components are united, is nevertheless considerable. When the hand is laid on some small object, as a key, a number of impressions may be distinguished as separate though near one another; but while their mutual relations are so far fixed that approximate limits within which they exist are known, they do not constitute anything like such a fixed and defined group as those given by vision of the key. This imperfect clustering in co-existence is accompanied by imperfect clustering in sequence. The successive feelings produced by a fly creeping over the hand, hold together strongly enough and definitely enough to constitute a consciousness of its general movement as being towards the wrist or from the wrist, across from right to left or from left to right; but they do not form a consciousness of its exact course. Tastes unite only into very simple and incoherent clusters in co-existence; while in sequence they scarcely unite at all. And the like is true of smells.

Such capability of clustering as is displayed by the peripherally-initiated feelings caused by internal disturbances, occurs among those accompanying the movements of muscles. But, along with the comparative vagueness of limitation and want of strong cohesion which characterize these feelings, there goes a comparative indistinctness of the clusters. Though the nervous acts of which muscular motions are results, combine into groups with much precision, yet the combination of them, at first feeble, becomes strong only by repetition. And as the repetition which makes the combination strong, makes it to the same extent automatic, the concomitant feelings become less and less distinct, and fade from consciousness as fast as they unite. How, in muscular acts, complete clustering and unconsciousness go together, is seen in the fact that consciousness impedes clustered muscular acts. After having many times gone through the series of compound movements required, it is possible to walk across the room in the dark and lay hold of the handle of the door — so long, that is, as the movements are gone through unthinkingly. If they are consciously made, failure is almost certain.   Of the further class of feelings initiated within the body, including appetites, pains, &c., it is scarcely needful to say that there is among them no formation of coherent groups. Their great indefiniteness of limitation and accompanying want of cohesion, forbid unions of them, either simultaneous or successive.

Obviously the emotions are characterized by a like want of combining power. A confused and changing chaos is produced by any of them which co-exist. In fact, the absence among them of capacity for uniting, is as marked as its presence among those visual feelings with which we set out.

§ 71. We come now to more complex manifestations of these general contrasts. In tracts of consciousness where the relational element predominates, and where the clustering of feelings is consequently decided, the clusters themselves enter into relations one with another. Grouped feelings, together with the relations uniting them, are fused into wholes which, comporting themselves as single feelings do, combine with other such consolidated groups in definite relations; and even groups of groups, similarly fused, become in like manner limited by, and coherent with, other groups of groups. Conversely, in tracts of consciousness where the relations are few and vague, nothing of the kind takes place.

It is among the visual feelings, above all others multitudinous, definite, and coherent in their relations, that this compound clustering is carried to the greatest extent. Along with
the ability to form that complex consciousness of lights, shades,
and colours, joined in relative positions, which constitute a
man as present to sight, there goes the ability to form a consciousness of two men in a definite and coherent relation of
position — there goes the ability to form a consciousness
of a crowd of such men; nay, two or more such crowds
may be mentally combined. The aggregate of definitely-
related visual feelings known as a house, itself aggregates
with others such to form the consciousness of a street, and the
streets to form the consciousness of a town. Though the compound clustering of visual feelings in sequence is not so distinct
or so strong, it is still very marked. Numerous complicated
images produced by objects seen in succession, hang together
in consciousness with considerable tenacity.   There is
little, if any, clustering of clusters among the simultaneous
auditory feelings. But among the successive auditory feelings
there are definite and coherent combinations of groups with
groups. The fused set of sounds we call a word, unites with
many others such into a sentence. In some minds these clusters of clusters of successive sounds again cluster very definitely and coherently: many successive sentences are, as we say,
accurately remembered. And similarly, musical phrases will
cling together into a long and elaborate melody.   Among
the tactual feelings this compound clustering is scarcely traceable, either in space or time; and there is not the remotest
approach to it in the olfactory and gustatory feelings.

For form's sake it is needful to say that these higher degrees
of mental composition are entirely wanting among the inter-
nally-initiated feelings. Only among those which accompany
muscular motion is there any approach to it; and here the
compound clustering, like the simple clustering, entails progressing unconsciousness.

§ 72. One more kindred trait of composition must be set

down. Thus far we have observed only the degrees of mutual
limitation, of cohesion, and of complex combining power,
among feelings within each order. It remains to observe the
extent to which feelings of one order enter into relations with
those of another, and the consequent amounts of their mutual
limitations and of their combining powers. To trace out these
at all fully would carry us into unmanageable detail. We must
confine ourselves to leading facts.

Feelings of different orders do not limit one another as clearly
as feelings of the same order do. The clustered colours produced by an object at which we look are but little interfered
with by a sound: the sound does not put any appreciable
boundary to them in consciousness, but serves merely to diminish their dominance in consciousness. Neither the combined
noises which make up a conversation at table, nor the impressions received through the eyes from the dishes on the table,
are excluded from the mind by the accompanying tactual feelings and tastes and smells, as much as colours are excluded by
colours, sounds by sounds, tastes by tastes, or one tactual feeling
by another. Of sensations arising within the body, and still
more of emotions, it may be said that, unless intense, they disturb but slightly the sensations otherwise arising. It would
almost seem as though a sensation of colour, a sensation of
sound, and a pleasurable emotion produced by the sound,
admit of being superposed in consciousness with but little mutual obscuration. Doubtless in most cases two simple feelings,
or two clustered feelings of different orders, put bounds to one
another in time if not in space: there is an extremely rapid
extrusion of each by the other rather than a continuous presence of either. But it is manifest that these alternating ex-
trusions, partial or complete, by feelings of different orders, are
less distinct than the extrusion of one another by feelings of the
same order.

It is a correlative truth that feelings of different orders cohere
with one another less strongly than do feelings of the same
order. The impressions which make up the visual consciousness of an object, hang together more firmly than the group of

them does with the group of sounds making up the name of the object. The notes composing a melody have a stronger tendency to drag one another into consciousness than any one, or all of them, have to drag into consciousness the sights along with which they occurred: these last may or may not cohere with them; but the following of one note by the next is often difficult to prevent. Similarly, though there is considerable cohesion between the visual sensations produced by an orange and the taste or smell of the orange, yet it is quite usual to have a visual consciousness of an orange without its taste or its smell arising in consciousness; while it is scarcely possible to have before the mind one of its apparent characters unaccompanied by other apparent characters.

A further fact of moment must be added. The feelings of different orders which enter into definite relations and cohere most strongly, are those among which there is a predominance of the relational elements; and there is an especial facility of combination between those feelings of different orders which are respectively held together by relations of the same order. Thus the co-existent visual feelings, most relational of all, enter into very definite and coherent relations with co-existent tactful feelings. To the group of lights and shades an object yields to the eyes, there attaches itself very strongly the group of impressions produced by touching and grasping the object. Next in order of strength are the connections between sensations received through the eyes and those received through the ears; or rather — between clusters of the one and clusters of the other. But though the feelings clustered in co-existence that form the visual consciousness of anything, are linked with much strength to the feelings clustered in sequence that form the consciousness of its name; yet, probably because the feelings forming the one cluster not only differ in kind from those forming the other but are held together by relations of a different order, the cohesion of the two clusters is not so strong. As we descend towards the unrelational feelings we find that this combining power of class with class decreases. Between tastes and smells and certain visceral sensations, such as hunger and nausea, there is, indeed, a considerable aptitude to cohere. But after admitting exceptions, it remains true on the average that the extremely un-relational states of consciousness of different orders, connect but feebly with one another and with the extremely-relational states of consciousness.

§ 73. Thus far we have proceeded as though Mind were composed entirely of the primary or vivid feelings, and the relations among them; ignoring the secondary or faint feelings. Or if, as must be admitted, there has been a tacit recognition of these secondary feelings in parts of the foregoing sections which deal with the relations and cohesions of feelings in sequence (since in a sequence of feelings those which have passed have become faint, and only the one present is vivid); yet there has been no avowed recognition of them as components of Mind different from, though closely allied with, the primary feelings. We must now specially consider them and the part they play.

The cardinal fact to be noted as of co-ordinate importance with the facts above noted, is that while each vivid feeling is joined to, but distinguished from, other vivid feelings, simultaneous or successive, it is joined to, and identified with, faint feelings that have resulted from foregoing similar vivid feelings. Each particular colour, each special sound, each sensation of touch, taste, or smell, is at once known as unlike other sensations that limit it in space or time, and known as like the faint forms of certain sensations that have preceded it in time — unites itself with foregoing sensations from which it does not differ in quality but only in intensity.

On this law of composition depends the orderly structure of Mind. In its absence there could be nothing but a perpetual kaleidoscopic change of feelings — an ever-transforming present without past or future. It is because of this tendency which vivid feelings have severally to cohere with the faint forms of all preceding feelings like themselves, that there arise what we call *ideas*. A vivid feeling does not by itself constitute a unit of that aggregate of ideas entitled knowledge. Nor does a single faint feeling constitute such a unit. But an idea, or unit of knowledge, results when a vivid feeling is assimilated to, or coheres with, one or more of the faint feelings left by such vivid feelings previously experienced. From moment to moment the feelings that constitute consciousness segregate — each becoming fused with the whole series of others like itself that have gone before it; and what we call knowing each feeling as such or such, is our name for this act of segregation.

The process so carried on does not stop with the union of each feeling, as it occurs, with the faint forms of all preceding like feelings. Clusters of feelings are simultaneously joined with the faint forms preceding like clusters. An idea of an object or act is composed of groups of similar and similarly-related feelings that have arisen in consciousness from time to time, and have formed a consolidated series of which the members have partially or completely lost their individualities.

This union of present clustered feelings with past clustered feelings is carried to a much greater degree of complexity. Groups of groups coalesce with kindred groups of groups that preceded them; and in the higher types of Mind, tracts of consciousness of an excessively composite character are produced after the same manner.

To complete this general conception it is needful to say that as with feelings, so with the relations between feelings. Parted so far as may be from the particular pairs of feelings and pairs of groups of feelings they severally unite, relations themselves are perpetually segregated. From moment to moment relations are distinguished from one another in respect of the degrees of contrast between their terms and the kinds of contrast between their terms; and each relation, while distinguished from various concurrent relations, is assimilated to previously-experienced relations like itself. Thus result *ideas* of relations as those of strong contrast or weak contrast, of descending intensity or ascending intensity, of homogeneity of kind or heterogeneity of kind. Simultaneously occurs a segregation of a different species. Each relation of co-existence is classed with other like relations of co-existence and separated from relations of co-existence that are unlike it; and a kindred classing goes on among relations of sequence. Finally, by a further segregation, are formed that consolidated abstract of relations of co-existence which we know as Space, and that consolidated abstract of relations of sequence which we know as Time. This process, here briefly indicated merely to show its congruity with the general process of composition, cannot be explained at length: the elucidation must come hereafter.

§ 74. And now having roughly sketched the composition of Mind — having, to preserve clearness of outline, omitted details and passed over minor qualifications; let me go on to indicate the essential truth which it is a chief purpose of this chapter to bring into view — the truth that the method of composition remains the same throughout the entire fabric of Mind from the formation of its simplest feelings up to the formation of those immense and complex aggregates of feelings which characterize its highest developments.

In the last chapter we saw that what is objectively a wave of molecular change propagated through a nerve-centre, is subjectively a unit of feeling, akin in nature to what we call a nervous shock. In one case we found conclusive proof that when a rapid succession of such waves yield a rapid succession of such units of feeling, there results the continuous feeling known as a sensation; and that the quality of the feeling changes when these waves and corresponding units of feeling recur with a different rapidity. Further, it was shown that by unions among simultaneous series of such units recurring at unlike rates, countless other seemingly-simple sensations are produced. And we inferred that what unquestionably holds among these primary feelings of one order, probably holds among primary feelings of all orders. To what does this conclusion amount, expressed in another way? It amounts to the conclusion that one of these feelings which, as introspectively contemplated, appears uniform, is really generated by the perpetual assimilation of a new pulse of feeling to pulses of feeling immediately preceding it: the sensation is constituted by the linking of each vivid pulse as it occurs, with the series of past pulses that were severally vivid but have severally become faint. And what, otherwise stated, is the conclusion that compound sensations result from unions among different concurrent series of such pulses? It is that while the component pulses of each series are, as they occur, severally assimilated to, or linked with, preceding pulses of their own kind, they are also severally combined in some relation with the pulses of concurrent series; and the compound sensation so generated is known as different from other compound sensations of the same order, by virtue of some speciality in the relations among the concurrent series.

Consider now, under its most general form, the process of composition of Mind described in foregoing sections. It is no other than this same process carried out on higher and higher platforms, with increasing extent and complication. As we have lately seen, the feelings called sensations cannot of themselves constitute Mind, even when great numbers of various kinds are present together. Mind is constituted only when each sensation is assimilated to the faint forms of antecedent-like sensations. The consolidation of successive units of feeling to form a sensation, is paralleled in a larger way by the consolidation of successive sensations to form what we call a knowledge of the sensation as such or such — to form the smallest separable portion of what we call thought, as distinguished from mere confused sentiency. So too is it with the relations among those feelings that occur together and limit one another in space or time. Each of these relations, so long as it stands alone in experience with no antecedent like relations, is not fully cognizable as a relation: it assumes its character as a component of intelligence only when, by recurrence of it, there is produced a serial aggregate of such relations. Observe further that while each special sensation is raised into a proixmate constituent of simple thought only by being fused with like predecessors, it becomes a proximate constituent of compound thought by simultaneously entering into relations of unlikeness with other sensations which limit it in space or time; just as we saw that the units or pulses that form simple sensations by serial union

with their kind, may simultaneously help to form complex sensations by entering into relations of difference with units of
other kinds. The same thing obviously holds of the relations
themselves, that exist between these unlike sensations. And
thus it becomes manifest that the method by which simple sensations, and the relations among them, are compounded into
states of definite consciousness, is essentially analogous to the
method by which primitive units of feeling are compounded into
sensations.

The next higher stage of mental composition shows us this
process repeating itself. The vivid cluster of related sensations
produced in us by a special object, has to be united with the
faint forms of clusters like it that have been before produced
by such objects. What we call knowing the object, is the assimilation of this combined group of real feelings it excites,
with one or more preceding ideal groups which objects of the
same kind once excited; and the knowledge is clear only when
the series of ideal groups is long.   Equally does this
principle hold of the connexions, static and dynamic, between
each such special cluster and the special clusters generated by
other objects. Knowledge of the powers and habits of things,
dead and living, is constituted by assimilating the more or less
complex relations exhibited by their actions in space and time
with other such complex relations. If we cannot so assimilate
them, or parts of them, we have no knowledge of their actions.

That the same law of composition continues without definite
limit through tracts of higher consciousness, formed of clusters
of clusters of feelings held together by relations of an extremely
involved kind, scarcely needs adding.

§ 75. How clearly the evolution of Mind, as thus traced
through ascending stages of composition, conforms to the laws
of Evolution in general, will be seen as soon as it is said. We
will glance at the correspondence under each of its leading
aspects.

Evolution is primarily a progressing integration; and
throughout this chapter, as well as the last, progressing inte-

gration has thrust itself upon us as the fundamental fact in mental evolution. We came upon it quite unexpectedly in the conclusion that a sensation is an integrated series of nervous shocks or units of feeling; and in the further conclusion that by integration of two or more such series, compound sensations are formed. We have lately seen that by an integration of successive like sensations, there arises the knowledge of a sensation as such or such; and that each sensation as it occurs, while thus integrated with its like, also unites into an aggregate with other sensations that limit it in space or time. And we have similarly seen that the integrated clusters resulting, enter into higher integrations of both these kinds; and so on to the end. The significance of these facts will be appreciated when it is remembered that the tracts of consciousness in which integration is undecided, are tracts of consciousness hardly included in what we commonly think of as Mind; and that the tracts of consciousness presenting the attributes of Mind in the highest degree, are those in which the integration is carried furthest. Hunger, thirst, nausea, and visceral feelings in general, as well as feelings of love, hatred, anger, &c., which cohere little with one another and with other feelings, and thus integrate but feebly into groups, are portions of consciousness that play but subordinate parts in the actions we chiefly class as mental. Mental actions, ordinarily so called, are nearly all carried on in terms of those tactual, auditory, and visual feelings, which exhibit cohesion, and consequent ability to integrate, in so conspicuous a manner. Our intellectual operations are indeed mostly confined to the auditory feelings (as integrated into words) and the visual feelings (as integrated into impressions and ideas of objects, their relations, and their motions). After closing the eyes and observing how relatively-immense is the part of intellectual consciousness that is suddenly shorn away, it will be manifest that the most developed portion of perceptive Mind is formed of these visual feelings which cohere so rigidly, which integrate into such large and numerous aggregates, and which re-integrate into aggregates immensely exceeding in their degree of composition all aggregates formed by other feelings. And then, on rising to what we for convenience distinguish as rational Mind, we find the integration taking a still wider reach.

The ascending phases of Mind show us no less conspicuously, the increasing heterogeneity of these integrated aggregates of feelings. In the last chapter, we saw how sensations that are all composed of units of one kind, are rendered heterogeneous by the combination and re-combination of such units in multitudinous ways. We have lately seen that the portions of consciousness occupied by the internal bodily feelings and by the emotions, are, as judged by introspection, relatively very simple or homogeneous: thirst is not made up of contrasted parts, nor can we separate a gust of passion into many distinguishable components. But on passing upwards to intellectual consciousness, there meets us an increasing variety of kinds of feelings present together. When we come to the auditory feelings, which play so important a part in processes of thought, we find that the groups of them are formed of many components, and that those groups of groups used as symbols of propositions are very heterogeneous. As before however with integration, so where with heterogeneity, a far higher degree is reached in that consciousness formed of visual feelings, which is the most developed part of perceptive Mind. And much more heterogeneous still are those tracts of consciousness distinguished as ratiocinative tracts, in which the multiform feelings given us by objects through eyes, ears, and tactual organs, nose, and palate, are formed into conceptions that answer to the objects in all their attributes, and all their activities.

With equal clearness does Mind display the further trait of Evolution — increase of definiteness. Both the centrally-initiated feelings and the internal peripherally-initiated feelings, which play so secondary a part in what we understand as Mind, we found to be very vague — very imperfectly limited by one another. Contrariwise, it was shown that the mutual limitations are decided among those peripherally-initiated feelings which, arising on the outer surface, enter largely into our intellectual operations; and that the visual feelings, which enter by far the most largely into our intellectual operations, are not only by far the sharpest in their mutual limitations, but form aggregates that are much more definitely circumscribed than any others, and aggregates between which there exist relations much more definite than those entered into by other aggregates.

Thus the conformity is complete. Mind rises to what are universally recognized as its higher developments, in proportion as it manifests the traits characterizing Evolution in general (*First Principles*, §§ 98–145). A confused sentiency, formed of recurrent pulses of feeling having but little variety of kind and but little combination, we may conceive as the nascent Mind possessed by those low types in which nerves and nerve-centres are not yet clearly differentiated from one another, or from the tissues in which they lie. At a stage above this, while yet the organs of the higher senses are rudimentary and such nerves as exist are incompletely insulated, Mind is present probably under the form of a few sensations, which, like those yielded by our own viscera, are simple, vague, and incoherent. And from this upwards, the mental evolution exhibits a differentiation of these simple feelings into the more numerous kinds which the special senses yield; an ever-increasing integration of such more varied feelings with one another and with feelings of other kinds; an ever-increasing multiformity in the aggregates of feelings produced; and an ever-increasing distinctness of structure in such aggregates. That is to say, there goes on subjectively a change "from an indefinite, incoherent homogeneity to a definite, coherent heterogeneity;" parallel to that redistribution of matter and motion which constitutes Evolution as objectively displayed.

JOHANNES MUELLER

(1801–1858)

ELEMENTS OF PHYSIOLOGY

Translated from the German * *by*

WILLIAM BALY

BOOK V. OF THE SENSES

THE GENERAL LAWS OF SENSATION

THE senses, by virtue of the peculiar properties of their several nerves, make us acquainted with the states of our own body, and they also inform us of the qualities and changes of external nature, as far as these give rise to changes in the condition of the nerves. Sensation is a property common to all the senses; but the kind (*"modus,"*) of sensation is different in each: thus we have the sensations of light, of sound, of taste, of smell, and of feeling, or touch. By feeling, or touch, we understand the peculiar kind of sensation of which the ordinary sensitive nerves generally — as, the nervus trigeminus, vagus, glosso-pharyngeus, and the spinal nerves, — are susceptible; the sensations of itching, of pleasure and pain, of heat and cold, and those excited by the act of touch in its more limited sense, are varieties of this mode of sensation. That which through the medium of our senses is actually perceived by the sensorium, is indeed merely a property or change of condition of our nerves; but the imagination and reason are ready to interpret the modifications in the state of the nerves produced by external influences as properties of the external bodies themselves. This

---

* From J. Müller's *Handbuch der Physiologie des Menschen für Vorlesungen,* 2 Bde Coblenz, 1834-40. Reprinted from J. Müller's *Elements of Physiology,* translated by William Baly. London, 1837-42, vol. II.

mode of regarding sensations has become so habitual in the case of the senses which are more rarely affected by internal causes, that it is only on reflection that we perceive it to be erroneous. In the case of the sense of feeling or touch, on the contrary, where the peculiar sensations of the nerves perceived by the sensorium are excited as frequently by internal as by external causes, it is easily conceived that the feeling of pain or pleasure, for example, is a condition of the nerves, and not a property of the things which excite it. This leads us to the consideration of some general laws, a knowledge of which is necessary before entering on the physiology of the separate senses.

I. In the first place, it must be kept in mind that *external agencies can give rise to no kind of sensation which cannot also be produced by internal causes, exciting changes in the condition of our nerves.*

In the case of the sense of touch, this is at once evident. The sensations of the nerves of touch (or common sensibility) are those of cold and heat, pain and pleasure, and innumerable modifications of these, which are neither painful nor pleasurable, but yet have the same kind of sensation as their element, though not in an extreme degree. All these sensations are constantly being produced by internal causes in all parts of our body endowed with sensitive nerves; they may also be excited by causes acting from without, but external agencies are not capable of adding any new element to their nature. The sensations of the nerves of touch are therefore states or qualities proper to themselves, and merely rendered manifest by exciting causes external or internal. The sensation of smell also may be perceived independently of the application of any odorous substance from without, the nerve of smell being thrown by an internal cause into the condition requisite for the production of the sensation. This perception of the sensation of odours without an external exciting cause, though not of frequent occurrence, has been many times observed in persons of an irritable nervous system; and the sense of taste is probably subject to the same affection, although it would be always difficult to determine whether the taste might not be owing to a change in the qualities of the saliva or mucus of the mouth; the sensation of nausea, however, which belongs to the sensations of taste, is certainly very often perceived as the result of a merely internal affection of the nerves. The sensations of the sense of vision, namely, colour, light, and darkness, are also perceived independently of all external exciting cause. In the state of the most perfect freedom from excitement, the optic nerve has no other sensation than that of darkness. The excited condition of the nerve is manifested, even while the eyes are closed, by the appearance of light, or luminous flashes, which are mere sensations of the nerve, and not owing to the presence of any matter of light, and consequently are not capable of illuminating any surrounding objects. Every one is aware how common it is to see bright colours while the eyes are closed, particularly in the morning when the irritability of the nerves is still considerable. These phenomena are very frequent in children after waking from sleep. Through the sense of vision, therefore, we receive from external nature no impressions which we may not also experience from internal excitement of our nerves; and it is evident that a person blind from infancy in consequence of opacity of the transparent media of the eye, must have a perfect internal conception of light and colours, provided the retina and optic nerve be free from lesion. The prevalent notions with regard to the wonderful sensations supposed to be experienced by persons blind from birth when their sight is restored by operation, are exaggerated and incorrect. The elements of the sensation of vision, namely, the sensations of light, colour, and darkness, must have been previously as well known to such persons as to those of whom the sight has always been perfect. If, moreover, we imagine a man to be from his birth surrounded merely by external objects destitute of all variety of colours, so that he could never receive the impressions of colours from without, it is evident that the sense of vision might nevertheless have been no less perfect in him than in other men; for light and colours are innate endowments of his nature, and require merely a stimulus to render them manifest.

The sensations of hearing also are excited as well by internal as by external causes; for, whenever the auditory nerve is in a state of excitement, the sensations peculiar to it, as the sounds of ringing, humming, &c. are perceived. It is by such sensations that the diseases of the auditory nerve manifest themselves; and, even in less grave, transient affections of the nervous system, the sensations of humming and ringing in the ears afford evidence that the sense of hearing participates in the disturbance.

No further proof is wanting to show, that external influences give rise in our senses to no other sensations, than those which may be excited in the corresponding nerves by internal causes.

II. *The same internal cause excites in the different senses different sensations; — in each sense the sensations peculiar to it.*

One uniform internal cause acting on all the nerves of the senses in the same manner, is the accumulation of blood in the capillary vessels of the nerve, as in congestion and inflammation. This uniform cause excites in the retina, while the eyes are closed, the sensation of light and luminous flashes; in the auditory nerve, humming and ringing sounds; and in the nerves of feeling, the sensation of pain. In the same way, also, a narcotic substance introduced into the blood excites in the nerves of each sense peculiar symptoms; in the optic nerves the appearance of luminous sparks before the eyes; in the auditory nerves, "tinnitus aurium;" and in the common sensitive nerves the sensation of ants creeping over the surface.

III. *The same external cause also gives rise to different sensations in each sense, according to the special endowments of its nerve.*

The mechanical influence of a blow, concussion, or pressure excites, for example, in the eye the sensation of light and colours. It is well known that by exerting pressure upon the eye, when the eyelids are closed, we can give rise to the appearance of a luminous circle; by more gentle pressure the appearance of colours may be produced, and one colour may be made to change to another. Children, waking from sleep before daylight, frequently amuse themselves with these phenomena. The light thus produced has no existence external to the optic nerve, it is merely a sensation excited in it. However strongly we press upon the eye in the dark, so as to give rise to the appearance of luminous flashes, these flashes, being merely sensations, are incapable of illuminating external objects. Of this any one may easily convince himself by experiment. I have in repeated trials never been able, by means of these luminous flashes in the eye, to recognise in the dark the nearest objects, or to see them better than before; nor could another person, while I produced by pressure on my eye the appearance of brilliant flashes, perceive in it the slightest trace of real light.

.　.　.　.　.　.　.　.　.　.　.　.

A mechanical influence excites also peculiar sensations of the auditory nerve; at all events, it has become a common saying, "to give a person what will make his ears ring," or "what will make his eyes flash fire," or "what will make him feel "; so that the same cause, a blow, produces in the nerves of hearing, sight, and feeling, the different sensations proper to these senses. It has not become a part of common language that a blow shall be given which will excite the sense of smell, or of taste; nor would such sayings be correct; yet mechanical irritation of the soft palate, of the epiglottis and root of the tongue, excites the sensation of nausea. The actions of sonorous bodies on the organ of hearing is entirely mechanical. A sudden mechanical impulse of the air upon the organ of hearing produces the sensation of a report of different degrees of intensity according to the violence of the impulse, just as an impulse upon the organ of vision gives rise to the sensation of light. If the action of the mechanical cause on the organ of hearing be of continued duration, the sound is also continued; and when caused by a rapid succession of uniform impulses, or vibrations, it has a musical character. If we admit that the matter of light acts on bodies by mechanical oscillation (the undulation theory), we shall have another example of a mechanical influence, producing different effects on different senses. These undulations, which produce in the eye the sensation of light, have no such effects on other senses; but in the nerves of feeling they produce the sensation of warmth.

The stimulus of electricity may serve as a second example, of a uniform cause giving rise in different nerves of sense to different sensations. A single pair of plates of different metals applied so as to include the eye within the circle, excites the sensation of a bright flash of light when the person experimented upon is in a dark room; and, even though the eye do not lie within the circle, if it be not distant from it, — as, for example, when one of the plates is applied to one of the eyelids, and the other to the interior of the mouth, — the same effect will be produced, owing to a part of the current of electricity being diverted to the eye. A more intense electric stimulus gives rise to more intense sensations of light. In the organ of hearing, electricity excites the sensation of sound. Volta states that, while his ears were included between the poles of a battery of forty pairs of plates, he heard a hissing and pulsatory sound, which continued as long as the circle was closed.* Ritter perceived a sound like that of the fiddle G at the moment of the closure of the galvanic circle.

The electricity of friction, developed by the electrical machine, excites in the olfactory nerves the odour of phosphorus. The application of plates of different metals to the tongue, gives rise to an acid or a saline taste, according to the length of the plates which are applied one above, and the other beneath the tongue. The facts detailed with regard to the other senses are sufficient to show that these latter phenomena cannot be attributed to decomposition of the salts of the saliva.

The effects of the action of electricity on the nerves of common sensation or feeling, are neither the sensation of light, of sound, of smell, nor of taste, but those proper to the nerves of feeling, namely, the sensations of pricking, of a blow, &c.

Chemical influences also probably produce different effects on different nerves of sense. We have, of course, but few facts illustrating their action on these nerves; but we know that in the sensitive nerves of the skin they excite the different kinds of common sensation, — as the sensations of burning, pain, and heat; in the organ of taste, sensations of taste; and, when volatile, in the nerves of smell, the sensations of odours. Without

* Philos. Transact. 1800, p. 427.

the infliction of great injury on the textures, it is impossible to apply chemical agents to the nerves of the higher senses, sight and hearing, except through the medium of the blood. Chemical substances introduced into the blood act on every nerve of sense, and excite in each a manifestation of its properties. Hence the internal sensations of light and sound, which are well known to result from the action of narcotics.

IV. *The peculiar sensations of each nerve of sense can be excited by several distinct causes internal and external.*

The facts on which this statement is founded have been already mentioned; for we have seen that the sensation of light in the eye is excited:

1. By the undulations or emanations which from their action on the eye are called light, although they have many other actions than this; for instance, they effect chemical changes, and are the means of maintaining the organic processes in plants.

2. By mechanical influences; as concussion, or a blow.

3. By electricity.

4. By chemical agents, such as narcotics, digitalis, &c. which, being absorbed into the blood, give rise to the appearance of luminous sparks, &c. before the eyes independently of any external cause.

5. By the stimulus of the blood in the state of congestion.

The sensation of sound may be excited in the auditory nerve:

1. By mechanical influences, namely, by the vibrations of sonorous bodies imparted to the organ of hearing through the intervention of media capable of propagating them.

2. By electricity.

3. By chemical influences taken into the circulation; such as the narcotics, or alterantia nervina.

4. By the stimulus of the blood.

The sensation of odours may be excited in the olfactory nerves:

1. By chemical influences of a volatile nature, — odorous substances.

2. By electricity.

The sensation of taste may be produced:

1. By chemical influences acting on the gustatory nerves either from without or through the medium of the blood; for, according to Magendie, dogs taste milk injected into their blood-vessels, and begin to lap with their tongue.

2. By electricity.

3. By mechanical influences; for we must refer to taste the sensation of nausea produced by mechanically irritating the velum palati, epiglottis, and root of the tongue.

The sensations of the nerves of touch or feeling are excited:

1. By mechanical influences; as sonorous vibrations, and contact of any kind.

2. By chemical influences.

3. By heat.

4. By electricity.

5. By the stimulus of the blood.

V. *Sensation consists in the sensorium receiving through the medium of the nerves, and as the result of the action of an external cause, a knowledge of certain qualities or conditions, not of external bodies, but of the nerves of sense themselves; and these qualities of the nerves of sense are in all different, the nerve of each sense having its own peculiar quality or energy.*

The special susceptibility of the different nerves of sense for certain influences, — as of the optic nerve for light, of the auditory nerve for vibrations, and so on, — was formerly attributed to these nerves having each a specific irritability. But this hypothesis is evidently insufficient to explain all the facts. The nerves of the senses have assuredly a specific irritability for certain influences; for many stimuli, which exert a violent action upon one organ of sense, have little or no effect upon another: for example, light, or vibrations so infinitely rapid as those of light, act only on the nerves of vision and common sensation; slower vibrations, on the nerves of hearing and common sensation, but not upon those of vision; odorous substances only upon the olfactory nerves. The external stimuli must therefore be adapted to the organ of sense — must be "homogeneous:" thus light is the stimulus adapted to the

nerve of vision; while vibrations of less rapidity, which act upon
the auditory nerve, are not adapted to the optic nerve, or are
indifferent to it; for if the eye be touched with a tuning-fork
while vibrating, a sensation of tremours is excited in the conjunctiva, but no sensation of light. We have seen, however,
that one and the same stimulus, as electricity, will produce different sensations in the different nerves of the senses; all the
nerves are susceptible of its action, but the sensations in all are
different. The same is the case with other stimuli, as chemical
and mechanical influences. The hypothesis of a specific irritability of the nerves of the senses for certain stimuli, is therefore
insufficient; and we are compelled to ascribe, with Aristotle, peculiar energies to each nerve, — energies which are vital qualities of the nerve, just as contractility is the vital property of
muscle. The truth of this has been rendered more and more
evident in recent times by the investigation of the so-called
"subjective" phenomena of the senses by Elliot, Darwin, Ritter, Goethe, Purkinje, and Hjort. Those phenomena of the
senses, namely, are now styled "subjective," which are produced, not by the usual stimulus adapted to the particular
nerve of sense, but by others which do not usually act upon it.
These important phenomena were long spoken of as "illusions
of the senses," and have been regarded in an erroneous point of
view; while they are really true actions of the senses, and must
be studied as fundamental phenomena in investigations into
their nature.

The sensation of sound, therefore, is the peculiar "energy"
or "quality" of the auditory nerve; the sensation of light and
colours that of the optic nerve; and so of the other nerves of
sense. An exact analysis of what takes place in the production
of a sensation would of itself have led to this conclusion. The
sensations of heat and cold, for example, make us acquainted
with the existence of the imponderable matter of caloric, or of
peculiar vibrations in the vicinity of our nerves of feeling. But
the nature of this caloric cannot be elucidated by sensation,
which is in reality merely a particular state of our nerves; it
must be learnt by the study of the physical properties of this

agent, namely, of the laws of its radiation, its development from the latent state, its property of combining with and producing expansion of other bodies, &c. All this again, however, does not explain the peculiarity of the sensation of warmth as a condition of the nerves. The simple fact devoid of all theory is this, that warmth, as a sensation, is produced whenever the matter of caloric acts upon the nerves of feeling; and that cold as a sensation, results from this matter of caloric being abstracted from a nerve of feeling.

So, also, the sensation of sound is produced when a certain number of impulses or vibrations are imparted, within a certain time, to the auditory nerve: but sound, as we perceive it, is a very different thing from a succession of vibrations. The vibrations of a tuning-fork, which to the ear give the impression of sound, produce in a nerve of feeling or touch the sensation of tickling; something besides the vibrations must consequently be necessary for the production of the sensation of sound, and that something is possessed by the auditory nerve alone. Vision is to be regarded in the same manner. A difference in the intensity of the action of the imponderable agent, light, causes an inequality of sensation at different parts of the retina: whether this action consists in impulses or undulations, (the undulation theory,) or in an infinitely rapid current of imponderable matter, (the emanation theory,) is a question here of no importance. The sensation of moderate light is produced where the action of the imponderable agent on the retina is not intense; of bright light where its action is stronger, and of darkness or shade where the imponderable agent does not fall; and thus results a luminous image of determinate form according to the distribution of the parts of the retina differently acted on. Colour is also a property of the optic nerve; and when excited by external light, arises from the peculiarity of the so-called coloured rays, or of the oscillations necessary for the production of the impression of colour, — a peculiarity, the nature of which is not at present known. The nerves of taste and smell are capable of being excited to an infinite variety of sensations by external causes: but each taste is due to a determinate condition of the nerve excited by the external cause; and it is ridiculous to say that the property of acidity is communicated to the sensorium by the nerve of taste, while the acid acts equally upon the nerves of feeling, though it excites there no sensation of taste.

The essential nature of these conditions of the nerves, by virtue of which they see light and hear sound, — the essential nature of sound as a property of the auditory nerve, and of light as a property of the optic nerve, of taste, of smell, and of feeling, — remains, like the ultimate causes of natural phenomena generally, a problem incapable of solution. Respecting the nature of the sensation of the colour "blue," for example, we can reason no farther; it is one of the many facts which mark the limits of our powers of mind. It would not advance the question to suppose the peculiar sensations of the different senses excited by one and the same cause, to result from the propagation of vibrations of the nervous principle of different rapidity to the sensorium. Such an hypothesis, if at all tenable, would find its first application in accounting for the different sensations of which a single sense is susceptible; for example, in explaining how the sensorium receives the different impressions of blue, red, and yellow, or of an acute and a grave tone, or of painful and pleasurable sensations, or of the sensations of heat and cold, or of the tastes of bitter, sweet, and acid. It is only with this application that the hypothesis is worthy of regard: tones of different degrees of acuteness are certainly produced by vibrations of sonorous bodies of different degrees of rapidity; and a slight contact of a solid body, which singly excites in a nerve of common sensation merely the simple sensation of touch, produces in the same nerve when repeated rapidly, as the vibrations of a sonorous body, the feeling of tickling; so that possibly a pleasurable sensation, even when it arises from internal causes independently of external influences, is due to the rapidity of the vibrations of the nervous principle in the nerves of feeling.

.   .   .   .

The accuracy of our discrimination by means of the senses depends on the different manner in which the conditions of our nerves are affected by different bodies; but the preceding considerations show us the impossibility that our senses can ever reveal to us the true nature and essence of the material world. In our intercourse with external nature it is always our own sensations that we become acquainted with, and from them we form conceptions of the properties of external objects, which may be relatively correct; but we can never submit the nature of the objects themselves to that immediate perception to which the states of the different parts of our own body are subjected in the sensorium.

VI. *The nerve of each sense seems to be capable of one determinate kind of sensation only, and not of those proper to the other organs of sense; hence one nerve of sense cannot take the place and perform the function of the nerve of another sense.*

The sensation of each organ of sense may be increased in intensity till it become pleasurable, or till it becomes disagreeable, without the specific nature of the sensation being altered, or converted into that of another organ of sense. The sensation of dazzling light is an unpleasant sensation of the organ of vision; harmony of colours, an agreeable one. Harmonious and discordant sounds are agreeable and disagreeable sensations of the organ of hearing. The organs of taste and smell have their pleasant and unpleasant tastes and odours; the organ of touch its pleasurable and painful feelings. It appears, therefore, that, even in the most excited condition of an organ of sense, the sensation preserves its specific character. It is an admitted fact that the sensations of light, sound, taste, and odours, can be experienced only in their respective nerves; but in the case of common sensation this is not so evidently the case, for it is a question whether the sensation of pain may not be felt in the nerves of the higher senses, — whether, for example, violent irritation of the optic nerve may not give rise to the sensation of pain. This question is difficult of solution. There are filaments of the nerves of common sensation distributed in the nerves of the other organs of sense: the nostrils are supplied with nerves of common sensation from the second division of the nervus trigeminus in addition to the olfactory nerves; the tongue has common sensibility as well as taste, and may retain the one while it loses the other; the eye and organ of hearing likewise are similarly endowed.

To determine this question, it is necessary to institute experiments on the isolated nerves of special sense themselves. As far as such experiments have hitherto gone, they favour the view that the nerves of sense are susceptible of no other kind of sensation than that peculiar to each, and are not endowed with the faculty of common sensibility.

.   .   .   .

Among the well-attested facts of physiology, again, there is not one to support the belief that one nerve of sense can assume the functions of another. The exaggeration of the sense of touch in the blind will not in these days be called seeing with the fingers; the accounts of the power of vision by the fingers and epigastrium, said to be possessed in the so-called magnetic state, appear to be mere fables, and the instances in which it has been pretended to practise it, cases of deception. The nerves of touch are capable of no other sensation than that of touch or feeling. Hence, also, no sounds can be heard except by the auditory nerve; the vibrations of bodies are perceived by the nerves of touch as mere tremours wholly different in its nature from sound; though it is indeed even now not rare for the different modes of action of the vibrations of bodies upon the sense of hearing, and upon that of feeling, to be confounded. Without the organ of hearing with its vital endowments, there would be no such a thing as sound in the world, but merely vibrations; without the organ of sight, there would be no light, colour, nor darkness, but merely a corresponding presence or absence of the oscillations of the imponderable matter of light.

VII. *It is not known whether the essential cause of the peculiar "energy" of each nerve of sense is seated in the nerve itself, or in the parts of the brain and spinal cord with which it is connected; but it is certain that the central portions of the nerves included in the encephalon are susceptible of their peculiar sensations, independently of the more peripheral portion of the nervous cords which form the means of communication with the external organs of sense.*

The specific sensibility of the individual senses to particular stimuli, — owing to which vibrations of such rapidity or length as to produce sound are perceived, only by the senses of hearing and touch, and mere mechanical influences, scarcely at all by the sense of taste, — must be a property of the nerves themselves; but the peculiar mode of reaction of each sense, after the excitement of its nerve, may be due to either of two conditions. Either the nerves themselves may communicate impressions different in quality to the sensorium, which in every instance remains the same; or the vibrations of the nervous principle may in every nerve be the same and yet give rise to the perception of different sensations in the sensorium, owing to the parts of the latter with which the nerves are connected having different properties.

The proof of either of these propositions I regard as at present impossible. . . .

VIII. *The immediate objects of the perception of our senses are merely particular states induced in the nerves, and felt as sensations either by the nerves themselves or by the sensorium; but inasmuch as the nerves of the senses are material bodies, and therefore participate in the properties of matter generally occupying space, being susceptible of vibratory motion, and capable of being changed chemically as well as by the action of heat and electricity, they make known to the sensorium, by virtue of the changes thus produced in them by external causes, not merely their own condition, but also properties and changes of condition of external bodies. The information thus obtained by the senses concerning external nature, varies in each sense, having a relation to the qualities or energies of the nerve.*

Qualities which are to be regarded rather as sensations or modes of reaction of the nerves of sense, are light, colour, the bitter and sweet tastes, pleasant and unpleasant odours, painful and pleasant impressions on the nerves of touch, cold and warmth: properties which may belong wholly to external nature are "extension," progressive and tremulous motion, and chemical change.

All the senses are not equally adapted to impart the idea of "extension" to the sensorium. The nerve of vision and the nerve of touch, being capable of an exact perception of this property in themselves, make us acquainted with it in external bodies. In the nerves of taste, the sensation of extension is less distinct, but is not altogether deficient; thus we are capable of distinguishing whether the seat of a bitter or sweet taste be the tongue, the palate, or the fauces. In the sense of touch and sight, however, the perception of space is most acute. The retina of the optic nerve has a structure especially adapted for this perception; for the ends of the nervous fibres in the retina are, as Treviranus discovered, so arranged as to be at last perpendicular to its inner surface, and by their papillar extremities form a pavement-like composite membrane. On the great number of these terminal fibrils depends the delicate power of discriminating the position of bodies in space possessed by the sense of vision; for each fibre represents a greater or less field of the visible world, and imparts the impression of it to the sensorium.

The sense of touch has a much more extended sphere of action for the perception of space than has the sense of vision; but its perception of this quality of external bodies is much less accurate; and considerable portions of the surface of the body or skin are in many instances represented in the sensorium by very few nervous fibres; hence, in many parts of the surface, impressions on two points considerably removed from each other are, as E. H. Weber has shown, felt as one impression. Although the senses of vision, touch, and taste are all capable of perceiving the property of extension in space, yet the quality of the sensations which give the conception of extension is different in each of these senses; the sensation in one is an image of which the essential quality is light; in another, a perception of extension with any of the modifications of the quality of touch, between pain, cold, heat, and pleasure; in the third, a perception of extension with the quality of taste.

RUDOLF HERMANN LOTZE

(1817–1881)

OUTLINES OF PSYCHOLOGY

Translated from the German * *by*
GEORGE TRUMBULL LADD

CHAPTER IV. THE THEORY OF LOCAL SIGNS

§ 27. Metaphysic raises the doubt, whether space is actually extended and we, together with 'Things,' are contained in it; whether — just the reverse — the whole spatial world is not rather only a form of intuition in us.

This question we for the present leave one side, and in the meantime take our point of departure from the assumption, previously alluded to, with which we are all conversant. But since Things in space can never become the object of our perception by virtue of their bare existence, and, on the contrary, become such solely through the effects which they exercise upon us, the question arises: How do the Things by their influence upon us bring it to pass, that we are compelled mentally to represent them in the same reciprocal position in space, in which they actually exist outside of us?

§ 28. In the case of the eye, nature has devised a painstaking structure, such that the rays of light which come from a luminous point are collected again at one point on the retina, and that the different points of the image, which originate here, assume the same reciprocal relation toward one another as the

---

* From H. Lotze's *Grundzüge der Psychologie : Dictate aus den Vorlesungen.* Lpz. 1881; 3 Aufl. 1884. Reprinted from H. Lotze's *Outlines of Psychology : Dictated Portions of the Lectures.* Translated and edited by George T. Ladd. Boston: Ginn & Co. 1886.

points of the object outside of us, to which they correspond. Without doubt, this so-called 'image of the object,' so carefully prepared, is an indispensable condition of our being able mentally to present the object in its true form and position. But it is the source of all the errors in this matter to believe that the bare existence of this image, without anything else, explains our idea of the position of its parts. The entire image is essentially nothing but a representative of the external object, transposed into the interior of the organ of sense; and how we know and experience aught of it, is now just as much the question as the question previously was, — How can we perceive the external object?

§ 29. If one wished to conceive of the soul itself as an extended being, then the impressions on the retina would, of course, be able to transplant themselves, with all their geometrical regularity, to the soul. One point of the soul would be excited as green, the other red, a third yellow; and these three would lie at the corners of a triangle precisely in the same way as the three corresponding excitations on the retina.

It is also obvious, however, that there is no real gain in all this. The bare fact that three different points of the soul are excited is, primarily, a disconnected three-fold fact. A knowledge thereof, however, and therefore a knowledge of this three-foldness, and of the reciprocal positions of the three points, is, nevertheless, by no means given in this way: but such knowledge could be brought about only by means of a uniting and relating activity; and this itself, like every activity, would be perfectly foreign to all predicates of extension and magnitudes in space.

§ 30. The same thought is more immediately obvious if we surrender this useless notion of the soul being extended, and consider it as a supersensible essence, which, in case we wish to bring it at all into connection with spatial determinations, could be represented only as an indivisible point.

On making the transition into this indivisible point, the

manifold impressions must obviously lose all the geometrical relations which they might still have upon the extended retina, — just in the same way as the rays of light, which converge at the single focus of a lens, are not side by side with one another, but only all together, in this point. Beyond the focus, the rays diverge in the same order as that in which they entered it. Nothing analogous to this, however, happens in our consciousness; that is to say, the many impressions, which were previously side by side with one another, do not actually again separate from each other; but, instead of this, the aforesaid activity of mental presentation simply occurs, and it transposes their images to different places in the space that is only 'intuited' by it.

Here, too, the previous observation holds good: The mental presentation *is* not that which it presents; and the idea of a point on the left does not lie on the left of the idea of a point on the right; but of one mental presentation, which in itself has no spatial properties whatever, both points are merely themselves so presented before the mind, as though one lay to the left, the other to the right.

§ 31. The following result now stands before us: Many impressions exist conjointly in the soul, although not spatially side by side with one another; but they are merely together in the same way as the synchronous tones of a chord; that is to say, qualitatively different, but not side by side with, above or below, one another. Notwithstanding, the mental presentation of a spatial order must be produced again from these impressions. The question is, therefore, in the first place, to be raised: How in general does the soul come to apprehend these impressions, not in the form in which they actually are, — to wit, non-spatial, — but as they are not, in a spatial juxtaposition?

The satisfactory reason obviously cannot lie in the impressions themselves, but must lie solely in the nature of the soul in which they appear, and upon which they themselves act simply as stimuli.

On this account, it is customary to ascribe to the soul this tendency to form an intuition of space, as an originally inborn capacity. And indeed we are compelled to rest satisfied with this. All the 'deductions' of space, hitherto attempted, which have tried to show on what ground it is necessary to the nature of the soul to develop this intuition of space, have utterly failed of success. Nor is there any reason to complain over this matter; for the simplest modes of the experience of the soul must always merely be recognized as given facts, — just as, for example, no one seriously asks why we only hear, and do not rather taste, the waves of air.

§ 32. The second question is much more important. Let it be assumed that the soul once for all lies under the necessity of mentally presenting a certain manifold as in juxtaposition in space; How does it come to localize every individual impression at a definite place in the space intuited by it, in such manner that the entire image thus intuited is similar to the external object which acted on the eye?

Obviously, such a clue must lie in the impressions themselves. The simple quality of the sensation 'green' or 'red' does not, however, contain it; for every such color can in turn appear at every point in space, and on this account does not, of itself, require always to be referred to the one definite point.

We now remind ourselves, however, that the carefulness with which the regular position on the retina of the particular excitations is secured, cannot be without a purpose. To be sure, an impression is not *seen* at a definite point on account of its *being situated* at such point; but it may perhaps by means of this definite situation *act* on the soul otherwise than if it were elsewhere situated.

Accordingly we conceive of this in the following way: Every impression of color r — for example, red — produces on all places of the retina, which it reaches, the same sensation of redness. In addition to this, however, it produces on each of these different places, a, b, c, a certain accessory impression, a, β, γ, which is independent of the nature of the color seen, and dependent merely on the nature of the place excited. This second local impression would therefore be associated with every impression of color r, in such manner that ra signifies a red that acts on the point a, $r\beta$ signifies the same red in case it acts on the point b. These associated accessory impressions would, accordingly, render for the soul the clue, by following which it transposes the same red, now to one, now to another spot, or simultaneously to different spots in the space intuited by it.

In order, however, that this may take place in a methodical way, these accessory impressions must be completely different from the main impressions, the colors, and must not disturb the latter. They must be, however, not merely of the same kind among themselves, but wholly definite members of a series or a system of series; so that for every impression r there may be assigned, by the aid of this adjoined 'local sign,' not merely a particular, but a quite definite spot among all the rest of the impressions.

§ 33. The foregoing is the theory of '*Local Signs.*' Their fundamental thought consists in this, that all spatial differences and relations among the impressions on the retina must be compensated for by corresponding non-spatial and merely intensive relations among the impressions which exist together without space-form in the soul; and that from them in reverse order there must arise, not a new actual arrangement of these impressions in extension, but only the mental presentation of such an arrangement in us. To such an extent do we hold this principle to be a necessary one.

On the contrary, only hypotheses are possible in order to answer the question, In what do those accessory impressions requisite consist, so far as the sense of sight is concerned? We propose the following conjecture: —

In case a bright light falls upon a lateral part of the retina, on which — as is well known — the sensitiveness to impressions is more obtuse than in the middle of the retina, then there follows a rotation of the eye until the most sensitive middle part of the retina, as the receptive organ, is brought beneath this light: we are accustomed to style this the "fixation of vision" upon the aforesaid light. Such motion happens involuntarily, without any original cognition of its purpose, and uniformly without cognition of the means by which it is brought about. We may therefore reckon it among the so-called reflex motions, which originate by means of an excitation of one nerve, that serves at other times for sensation, being transplanted to motor nerves without any further assistance from the soul and in accordance with the pre-existing anatomical connections; and these latter nerves being therefore stimulated to execute a definite motion in a perfectly mechanical way. Now in order to execute such a rotation of the eye as serves the purpose previously alluded to, every single spot in the retina, in case it is stimulated, must occasion a magnitude and direction of the aforesaid rotation peculiar to it alone. But at the same time all these rotations of the eye would be perfectly comparable motions, and, of course, members of a system of series that are graded according to magnitude and direction.

§ 34. The application of the foregoing hypothesis (many more minute particular questions being disregarded) we conceive of as follows: — In case a bright light falls upon a lateral point P of a retina, which has not yet had any sensation of light whatever, then there arises, in consequence of the connection in the excitation of the nerves, such a rotation of the eye as that, instead of the place P, the place E of clearest vision is brought beneath the approaching stimulus of the light. Now while the eye is passing through the arc PE, the soul receives at each instant a feeling of its momentary position, — a feeling of the same kind as that by which we are, when in the dark, informed of the position of our limbs. To the arc PE there corresponds then a series of constantly changing feelings of position, the first member of which we call π, and the last of which we call ϵ.

If now, in a second instance, the place P is again stimulated by the light, then there originates not simply the rotation PE for a second time, but the initial member of the series of feeling of position π, reproduces in memory the entire series associated with it, $\pi\epsilon$; and this series of mental presentations is independent of the fact that at the same time also the rotation of the eye PE actually follows.

Exactly the same thing would hold good of another point R; only the arc RE, the series of feelings $\rho\epsilon$, and also the initial member of the series, ρ, would have other values.

Now finally, in case it came about that both places, P and R, were simultaneously stimulated with an equal intensity, and that the arcs PE and RE were equal but in opposite directions to each other, then the actual rotation of the eye PE and RE could not take place; on the other hand, the excitation upon the places P and R is nevertheless not without effect; each produces the series of feelings of position belonging to it, — respectively, $\pi\epsilon$ and $\rho\epsilon$. Although therefore the eye does not now move, yet there is connected with every excitation of the places P and R the mental presentation of the magnitude and of the qualitative peculiarity of a series of changes, which consciousness or the common feeling would have to experience, in order that these excitations may fall upon the place of clearest vision, or, according to the customary expression, in the line of vision.

And now we assert that to see anything 'to the right' or 'to the left' of this line of vision means nothing more than this, to be conscious of the magnitude of the achievement which would be necessary to bring the object into this line.

§ 35. By the foregoing considerations nothing further would be established than the relative position of the single colored points in the field of vision. The entire image, on the contrary, would still have no place at all in a yet larger space; indeed, even the mental presentation of such a place would as yet have no existence.

Now this image first attains a place with reference to the eye, the repeated opening and closing of which, since it can become known to us in another way, is the condition of its existence or non-existence. That is to say, the visible world is *in front* before our eyes. What is behind us not merely has no existence whatever for us, but we do not once know that there is anything which should be called 'behind.'

The motions of the body lead us further. If the field of vision in a position of rest contains from left to right the images *a b c,* and we then turn ourselves to the right upon our axis, *a* vanishes, but *d* appears on the right, and therefore the image *bcd, cde, def,* . . . *xyz, yza, zab, abc,* succeed in order. As a result of such recurrence of the images with which we began, the two following thoughts originate; namely, that the visible world of objects exists in a closed circuit of extension about us, and that the alteration of our own position, which we perceive by means of the changing feelings of position while turning, depends upon an alteration of our relation to this immovable world of objects, — that is to say, upon a *motion.*

It is easily understood that the mental picture of a spherical extension originates from the aforesaid mental picture of a closed horizon by means of repeatedly turning in a similar way in various other directions.

§ 36. But, nevertheless, this spherical surface also would always have only a superficial extension no intimation would as yet exist of a *depth* to space.

Now the mental presentation, to the effect that something like a third dimension of space in general exists, cannot originate of itself, but only through the experience which we have in case we move about among the visible objects. From the manifold displacements which the particular visual images experience, in a manner that is tedious to describe but very easy to imagine, we gain the impression, that each line in an image originally seen is the beginning of new surfaces which do not coincide with that previously seen, but which lead out into this space, now extended on all sides, to greater or less distances from the line.

Another question to be treated subsequently is this: By what means do we estimate the different magnitudes of the distance into this depth of space?

§ 37. The crossing of the rays of light in the narrow opening of the pupil is the cause of the image of the upper points of the object being formed beneath, that of the lower points above on the retina; and of the whole picture having therefore a position the reverse of the object. But it is a prejudice on this account to consider seeing in inverse position to be natural, and seeing in upright position to be mysterious. Like every geometrical property of the image, so this one of its position, too, on passing into consciousness, is completely lost; and the position in which we see things is in no way prejudiced by the aforesaid position of the image on the retina.

Now, however, in order that we may be able to ascribe to objects a position at all, in order therefore that the expressions 'above,' 'below,' 'upright,' and 'inverted,' may have a meaning, we must have, independent of all sensation by sight, a mental picture of a space in which the entire content of the field of vision shall be arranged, and in which 'above' and 'below' are two qualitatively opposite and, on this account, not exchangeable directions.

The muscular feeling affords us such a mental presentation. 'Below' is the place toward which the direction of gravity moves; 'above,' the opposite. Both directions are distinguished perfectly for us by means of an immediate feeling; and, on this account, we are never deceived even in the dark about the position and situation of our body.

Accordingly we see objects 'upright' in case the lower points of the object are reached by one and the same movement of the eyes simultaneously with those points of our own body which are 'below' according to the testimony of the aforesaid muscular feeling; and the upper points by a movement which, according to the same testimony, renders visible simultaneously the upper parts of our own selves.

Now it is exactly such agreement that is secured in *our* eye, in which the axis lies in front of the sensitive retina, by means of the inverted position of the retinal image. In an other eye in which the sensitive surface should be placed in front of the axis, and yet the greatest sensitiveness also should appear in the middle portion of that surface, the retinal image would have to stand upright to serve the same purpose.

§ 38. The final and valid answer to the question, why we have single vision with two eyes, is not to be given. As is well known, it does not always happen. The rather must two impressions fall on two quite definite points of the retina in order to coalesce. We see double, on the contrary, if they fall on other points. Naturally, we shall say: The two places which belong together would have to impart like local signs to their impressions, and thereby render them indistinguishable; but we are not able to demonstrate in what manner this postulate is fulfilled. Physiology, too, in the last analysis, satisfies itself with a mere term for the fact; it calls 'identical' those places in both retinas which give one simple impression, and 'nonidentical' those which give a double impression.

§ 39. Irritations of the skin we naturally refer at once to the place of the skin on which we see them acting. But in case of their repetition, when we are not able to see them, we have no assistance from remembering them; for the most ordinary stimuli have already in the course of our life touched all possible places of the skin, and could therefore now as well be referred to one place as to another. In order that they may be correctly localized, they would have at every instant to tell us anew where they belong; that is to say, there must be attached to the main impression (impact, pressure, heat or cold) an auxiliary impression which is independent of the latter and, on the contrary, dependent on the place of the skin that is irritated.

The skin can supply such local signs; for since it is connected without interruption, a single point of it cannot be irritated at all, without the surrounding portion experiencing a displacement, pulling, stretching, or concussion of some kind. But, further, since the skin possesses at different places a different thickness, different tension or liability to displacement, — extends sometimes above the firm surfaces of the bones, sometimes over the flesh of the muscles, sometimes over cavities; since, moreover, the members being manifold, these relations change from one stretch of skin to another; therefore the aforesaid sum of secondary effects around the point irritated will be different for each one from the remainder; and such effects, if they are taken up by the nerve-endings and act on consciousness, may occasion the feelings so difficult to describe, according to which we distinguish a contact at one place from the same contact at another.

It cannot be said, however, that each point of the skin has its special local sign. It is known from the investigations of E. H. Weber, that on the margin of the lips, the tip of the tongue, the tips of the fingers, being touched in two places (by the points of a pair of compasses) can be distinguished as two at an interval of only $\frac{1}{2}$ line; while there are places on the arms, legs, and on the back, which require for making the distinction a distance between them of as much as 20 lines. We interpret this in the following way. Where the structure of the skin changes little for long stretches, the local signs also alter only a little from point to point. And if two stimuli act simultaneously, and accordingly a reciprocal disturbance of these secondary effects occurs, they will be undistinguishable; on the contrary, in cases where both stimuli act successively, and therefore the aforesaid disturbance ceases, both are still frequently distinguishable. On the other hand, we know nothing further to allege as to how the extraordinary sensitiveness — for example — of the lips is occasioned.

§ 40. The preceding statement merely explains the possibility of distinguishing impressions made at different places; but each impression must also be referred to the definite place at which it acts.

This is easy for one who sees, since he already possesses a picture of the surface of his own body; and, on this account, he now by means of the unchanging local sign, even in the dark, translates each stimulus which he has once seen act on a definite place, to the same place in this picture of the body that is mentally presented before him. One born blind would be compelled to construct such a picture first by means of the sense of touch; and this naturally is accomplished through motions of the tactual members and by estimating the distances which they would have to travel in order to reach from contact at the point *a* to contact at the other point *b*. It is to be considered, however that these motions — which in this case are not seen — are perceivable only by so-called muscular feelings; — that is to say by feelings which in themselves are merely certain species of the way *we feel*, and do not of themselves at all indicate the motions which are in fact the causes of them.

Now it cannot be described, how it is that this interpretation of the muscular feelings actually originates in the case of those born blind; but the helps which lead to it are very probably found in the fact, that the sense of touch as well as the eye can receive many impressions simultaneously, and that, in case of a movement, the previous impression does not vanish without trace and have its place taken by a wholly new one; but that, in the manner previously alleged, the combinations *abc*, *bcd*, etc., follow one another, and therefore some part in common is always left over for the next two impressions. By this alone does it seem possible to awaken the idea that the same occurrence, from which the series of changeable muscular feelings originates for us, consists in an alteration of our relation to a series of objects previously existent side by side and to be found arranged in a definite order; it consists, therefore, in a *motion*.

§ 41. It is questionable whether the mental picture of space which one born blind attains solely by the sense of touch will be altogether like that of one who sees; it is rather to be assumed that a much less intuitable system of mental presentations of time, of the magnitude of motion, and of the exertion which is needed in order to reach from contact at one point to that at another, takes the place of the clear, easy, and at once all-comprehending intuition, with which he who sees is endowed.

ERNST HEINRICH WEBER
(1795–1878)

THE SENSE OF TOUCH AND THE COMMON FEELING

Translated from the German* by

BENJAMIN RAND

WEBER'S LAW †

CONCERNING THE SMALLEST PERCEPTIBLE DIFFERENCES OF
WEIGHTS WHICH WE CAN DISTINGUISH BY THE SENSE OF
TOUCH, OF THE LENGTH OF LINES WHICH WE CAN DISTIN-
GUISH BY SIGHT, AND OF TONES WHICH WE CAN DISTINGUISH
BY HEARING

THE smallest perceptible difference between two weights,
which we can distinguish by the feeling of muscular exertion,
appears according to my experiments to be that between
weights which stand approximately in the relation of 39 to 40:
that is to say, of which one is about 1-40 heavier than the
other. By means of the feeling of pressure, which two weights
make upon our skin, all we are able to distinguish is a difference of weight that amounts to only 1-30, so that the weights
accordingly stand in the relation of 29 to 30.

* From *Der Tastsinn und das Gemeingefühl* in R. Wagner's *Handwörterbuch
der Physiologie*, Braunschweig, 1846, iii, 2; [separately,] Leipzig, 1849; *ib.*, 1851;
ib., 1905.

† The first formulation of what is known as Weber's Law was made by Weber
in 1834 in a monograph entitled De tactu. It reads as follows:
" In comparing objects and observing the distinction between them, we perceive not the difference between the objects, but the ratio of this difference to the
magnitude of the objects compared. If we are comparing by touch two weights,
the one of 30 and the other of 29 half-ounces, the difference is not more easily
perceived than that between weights of 30 and 29 drachms. . . . Since the dis-

If we look at one line after another, any one who possesses a very exceptional visual discrimination can according to my experiments discover a difference between two lines whose lengths are related as 50 : 51, or even as 100 : 101. Those who have a less delicate visual discrimination distinguish lines, which are separated from one another by 1-25 of their length. The smallest perceptible difference of the pitch of two tones, (which are really in unison), that a musician perceives, if he hears two tones successively, is according to Delezenne[1] 1-4 *Komma* (81-80) 1-4. A lover of music according to him distinguishes only about 1-2 *Komma* (81-80) 1-2. If the tones are heard simultaneously we cannot, according to Delezenne's experiments, perceive such small tonal differences. 1-4 *Komma* is nearly the relation of 321 : 322, but 1-2 *Komma* is nearly the relation of 160 : 161.

tinction is not perceived more easily in the former case than in the latter, it is clear that not the weights of the differences but their ratios are perceived. . . . Experience has taught us that apt and practised o's sense the difference between weights, if it is not less than the thirtieth part of the heavier weight, and that the same o's perceive the difference not less easily, if drachms are put in the place of half-ounces.

" That which I have set forth with regard to weights compared by touch holds also of lines to be compared by sight. For, whether you compare longer or shorter lines, you will find that the difference is not sensed by most o's if the second line is less by a hundredth part. . . . The length in which the distinction resides, therefore, although [in the case of lines of 50 and 50.5 mm.] it is twice as small [as it is in the case of lines of 100 and 101 mm.], is nevertheless no less easily apprehended, for the reason that in both cases the difference of the compared lines is one hundredth of the longer line.

" I have made no experiments upon comparison of tones by the ear. [Delezenne, however, determined the j. n. d. of the b of 240 vs.] As this author does not say that this difference is discriminated less easily in deeper, more easily in higher tones, and as I have never heard that a difference is more easily perceived in higher tones, . . . I imagine that in audition also not the absolute difference between the vibrations of two tones, but the relative compared with the number of vibrations of the tones is discriminated.

" The observation, confirmed in several departments of sense, that in observing the distinction between objects we perceive not the absolute but the relative differences, has again and again impelled me to investigate the cause of this phenomenon; and I hope that when this cause is sufficiently understood, we shall be able to judge more correctly regarding the nature of the senses " (172 ff.). Translation in E. B. Titchener's *Experimental Psychology*, ii, part ii, p. xvi.

[1] Delezenne in *Recueil des Travaux de la soc. des sci. de Lille*, 1827.

I have shown that the result in the determinations of weight is the same, whether one takes ounces or half ounces; for it does not depend upon the number of grains that form the increment of weight, but depends on the fact that this increment makes up the thirtieth or fiftieth [should be fortieth] part of the weight which we are comparing with the second weight. This likewise holds true of the comparison of the length of two lines and of the pitch of two tones. It makes no difference whether we compare lines that are, say, two inches or one inch long, if we examine them successively, and can see them lying parallel to each other; and yet the extent by which the one line exceeds the other is in the former case twice as great as in the latter. To be sure, if both lines lie close together and parallel, we compare only the ends of the lines to discover how much the one line exceeds the other; and in this test the question is only how great that length of line which overlaps the other really is, and how near the two lines lie to one another.

So too in the comparison of the pitch of two tones, it does not matter whether the two tones are seven tonal stops [i.e. an octave] higher or lower, provided only they do not lie at the end of the tonal series, where the exact discrimination of small tonal differences becomes more difficult. Here again, therefore, it is not a question of the number of vibrations, by which the one tone exceeds the other, but of the relation of the numbers of the vibrations of the two tones which we are comparing. If we counted the vibrations of the two tones it would be conceivable, that we should pay attention only to the number of vibrations by which one tone exceeds the other. If we fix the eyes first upon one line and afterwards upon a second, and thus permit both to be pictured successively upon the most sensitive parts of the retina, we should be inclined to suppose, that we compared the traces of the impression which the first image left, with the impression which the second image made upon the same parts of the retina, and that we thereby perceived how much the second image exceeds the first, and conversely. For this is the way we compare two scale-units: we place one upon the other, so that they coincide, and thus perceive how much the one exceeds the other. From the fact, that we do not employ this method which is so very advantageous, it seems to follow, that we are unable to employ it, and that therefore the preceding impression left behind no such trace upon the retina, or in the brain, as would permit of comparison in the manner mentioned with succeeding impressions. That it is possible for us to proceed otherwise in the comparison of the length of two lines appears from the fact, that we can compare two lines, which are longer than we can picture at once in their entirety on the most sensitive part of the retina. In this case we must move the eye and thereby cause the different parts of the same line to be pictured successively upon the same parts of the retina. Under these circumstances we must take account of the movement of the eye, and only thus do we form an idea of the length of the lines. Were the impressions of visible things, which we preserve in memory, traces, which the sensuous impressions left behind in the brain, and whose spatial relations corresponded to the spatial relations of the sensuous impressions, and were thus so to speak photographs of the same, it would be difficult to remember a figure, which is larger than could be pictured at once wholly upon the sensitive part of the retina. It appears to me, indeed, as if a figure, which we can survey at a single glance, impressed itself better upon our memory and our imagination, than a figure, which we can survey only successively by moving the eyes; but we can nevertheless represent also the former by means of the imagination. But in this case the representation of the whole figure seems to be composed by us of the parts which we perceive all at once.

If we compare two lines, which are 20 and 21 *Linien* [i.e. 1–10 of an inch] long, the latter is 1-20 longer, but the absolute difference of length amounts to 1 *Linie*. If, on the other hand, we compare two lines, which are 1 *Linie* and 1.05 *Linie* long, the difference amounts also to 1–20, but the line is only 1–20 longer than the other. Consequently in the latter case the absolute difference is 20 times smaller. But 1–20 *Linie* is a size like a fine pinhole which lies at the very threshold of vision. The smallest possible point that we are able to see, is one whose diameter amounts to 1–20 *Linie*, and yet one who has a very good visual discrimination can distinguish in respect to their length two lines of which one is 1–20 *Linie* longer than the other. Two observers, before whom I placed such lines, both distinguished the longer from the shorter, and their visual discrimination extended even farther. I myself distinguished two lines, whose relative difference of length amounted to 1–20, and of which the one was between 1–17 and 1–18 longer than the other. The apprehension of the relations of whole magnitudes, without our having measured the magnitudes by a smaller scale-unit, and without our having ascertained the absolute difference between them, is a most interesting psychological phenomenon. In music we apprehend the relations of tone, without knowing their rate of vibration [i.e., their absolute pitch]; in architecture, the relation of spatial magnitudes, without having determined them by inches; and in the same way we apprehend the magnitudes of sensation or of force in the comparison of weights.

GUSTAV THEODOR FECHNER
(1801–1887)

ELEMENTS OF PSYCHOPHYSICS

Translated from the German * by
HERBERT SIDNEY LANGFELD

VII. THE MEASUREMENT OF SENSATION

· · · · · · · · · · · ·

WEBER'S law, that equal relative increments of stimuli are proportional to equal increments of sensation, is, in consideration of its generality and the wide limits within which it is absolutely or approximately valid, to be considered fundamental for psychic measurement. There are, however, limits to its validity as well as complications, which we shall have carefully to examine later. Yet even where this law ceases to be valid or absolute, the principle of psychic measurement continues to hold, inasmuch as any other relation between constant increments of sensation and variable increments of stimulus, even though it is arrived at empirically and expressed by an empirical formula, may serve equally well as the fundamental basis for psychic measurement, and indeed must serve as such in those parts of the stimulus scale where Weber's law loses its validity. In fact such a law, as well as Weber's law, will furnish a differential formula from which may be derived an integral formula containing an expression for the measurement of sensation.

This is a fundamental point of view, *in which Weber's law, with its limitations, appears, not as limiting the application of psychic measurement, but as restricted in its own application toward that end and beyond which application the general*

* From G. F. Fechner's *Elemente der Psychophysik*, Leipzig, 1860; unverand. Aufl. 1889.

principle of psychic measurement nevertheless continues to hold.
It is not that the principle depends for its validity upon
Weber's law, but merely that the application of the law is
involved in the principle.

Accordingly investigation in the interest of the greatest
possible generalization of psychic measurement has not essentially to commence with the greatest possible generalization of
Weber's law, which might easily produce the questionable inclination to generalize the law beyond its natural limitation, or
which might call forth the objection that the law was general-
ized beyond these limits solely in the interest of psychic measurement; but rather it may quite freely be asked how far
Weber's law is applicable, and how far not; for the three
methods which are used in psychic measurement are applicable
even when Weber's law is not, and where these methods are
applicable psychic measurement is possible.

In short, Weber's law forms merely the basis for the most
numerous and important applications of psychic measurement,
but not the universal and essential one. The most general
and more fundamental basis for psychic measurement is rather
those methods by which the relation between stimulus increments and sensation increment in general is determined,
within, as well as without, the limits of Weber's law; and the
development of these methods towards ever greater precision
and perfection is the most important consideration in regard
to psychic measurement.

And yet a great advantage would be lost, if so simple a law as
Weber's law could not be used as an exact or at least sufficiently approximate basis for psychic measurement; just such
an advantage as would be lost if we could not use the Kepler
law in astronomy, or the laws of simple refraction in the theory
of the dioptric instruments. Now there is just the same difficulty with these laws as with Weber's law. In the case of
Kepler's law we abstract from deviations. In the case of simple
lens refraction we abstract from optical aberration. In fact
they may become invalid as soon as the simple hypotheses for
which they are true no longer exist. Yet they will always re-

main decisive for the principle relation with which astronomy and dioptrics are concerned. Weber's law may in like manner, entirely lose its validity, as soon as the average or normal conditions under which the stimulus produces the sensation are unrealized. It will always, however, be decisive for these particular conditions.

Further, just as in physics and astronomy, so can we also in psychic measurement, neglect at first the irregularities and small departures from the law in order to discover and examine the principle relations with which the science has to do. The existence of these exceptions must not, however, be forgotten, inasmuch as the finer development and further progress of the science depends upon the determination and calculation of them, as soon as the possibility of doing so is given.

The determination of psychic measurement is a matter for outer psychophysics and its first applications lie within its boundary; its further applications and consequences, however, extend necessarily into the domain of inner psychophysics and its deeper meaning lies there. It must be remembered that the stimulus does not cause sensation directly, but rather through the assistance of bodily processes with which it stands in more direct connection. The dependence, quantitatively considered of sensation on stimulus, must finally be translated into one of sensation on the bodily processes which directly underlie the sensation — in short the psycho-physical processes; and the sensation, instead of being measured by the amount of the stimulus, will be measured by the intensity of these processes. In order to do this, the relation of the inner process to the stimulus must be known. Inasmuch as this is not a matter of direct experience it must be deduced by some exact method. Indeed it is possible for this entire investigation to proceed along exact lines, and it cannot fail at some time or other to obtain the success of a critical study, if one has not already reached that goal.

Although Weber's law, as applied to the relation of stimulus to sensation, shows only a limited validity in the domain of outer psychophysics, it has, as applied to the relation of sensation to kinetic energy, or as referred to some other function of the psycho-physical process, in all probability an unlimited validity in the domain of inner psychophysics, in that all exceptions to the law which we find in the arousal of sensation by external stimulus, are probably due to the fact that the stimulus only under normal or average conditions engenders a kinetic energy in those inner processes proportional to its own amount. From this it may be foreseen, that this law, after it has been restated as a relation between sensation and the psychophysical processes, will be as important, general, and fundamental for the relations of mind to body, as is the law of gravity for the field of planetary motion. And it also has that simplicity which we are accustomed to find in fundamental laws of nature.

Although, then, psychic measurement depends upon Weber's law only within certain limitations in the domain of outer psycho-physics, it may well get its unconditional support from this law in the field of inner psychophysics. These are nevertheless for the present merely opinions and expectations, the verification of which lies in the future.

XIV. THE FUNDAMENTAL FORMULA AND THE MEASUREMENT FORMULA

Although not as yet having a measurement for sensation, still one can combine in an exact formula the relation expressed in Weber's law, — that the sensation difference remains constant when the relative stimulus difference remains constant, — with the law, established by the mathematical auxiliary principle, that small sensation increments are proportional to stimulus increments. Let us suppose, as has generally been done in the attempts to preserve Weber's law, that the difference between two stimuli, or, what is the same, the increase in one stimulus, is very small in proportion to the stimulus itself. Let the stimulus which is increased be called β, the small increase $d\beta$, where the letter d is to be considered not as a special magnitude, but simply as a sign that $d\beta$ is the small increment of

β. This already suggests the differential sign. The relative stimulus increase therefore is $\frac{d\beta}{\beta}$. On the other hand, let the sensation which is dependent upon the stimulus β be called γ, and let the small increment of the sensation which results from the increase of the stimulus by $d\beta$ be called $d\gamma$, where d again simply expresses the small increment. The terms $d\beta$ and $d\gamma$ are each to be considered as referring to an arbitrary unit of their own nature.

According to the empirical Weber's law, $d\gamma$ remains constant when $\frac{d\beta}{\beta}$ remains constant, no matter what absolute values $d\beta$ and β take; and according to the *a priori* mathematical auxiliary principle the changes $d\gamma$ and $d\beta$ remain proportional to one another so long as they remain very small. The two relations may be expressed together in the following equation:

$$d\gamma = \frac{K d\beta}{\beta} \qquad (^1)$$

where κ is a constant (dependent upon the units selected for γ and β). In fact, if one multiplies βd and β by any number, so long as it is the same number for both, the proportion remains constant, and with it also the sensation difference $d\gamma$. This is Weber's law. If one doubles or triples the value of the variation $d\beta$ without changing the initial value β, then the value of the change $d\gamma$ is also doubled or tripled. This is the mathematical principle. The equation $d\gamma = \frac{K d\beta}{\beta}$ therefore entirely satisfies both Weber's law and this principle; and no other equation satisfies both together. This is to be called the *fundamental formula*, in that the deduction of all consequent formulas will be based upon it.

The fundamental formula does not presuppose the measurement of sensation, nor does it establish any; it simply expresses the relation holding between small relative stimulus increments and sensation increments. In short, it is nothing more than Weber's law and the mathematical auxiliary principle united and expressed in mathematical symbols.

There is, however, another formula connected with this formula by infinitesimal calculus, which expresses a general quantitative relation between the stimulus magnitude as a summation of stimulus increments, and the sensation magnitude as a summation of sensation increments, in such a way, that with the validity of the first formula, together with the assumption of the fact of limen, the validity of this latter formula is also given.

Reserving for the future a more exact deduction, I shall attempt first to make clear in a general way the connection of the two formulas.

One can readily see, that the relation between the increments $d\gamma$ and $d\beta$ in the fundamental formula corresponds to the relation between the increments of a logarithm and the increments of the corresponding number. For as one can easily convince oneself, either from theory or from the table, the logarithm does not increase by equal increments when the corresponding number increases by equal increments, but rather when the latter increases by equal relative amounts; in other words, the increases in the logarithms remain equal, when the relative increases of the numbers remain equal. Thus, for example, the following numbers and logarithms belong together:

Number.	Logarithm.
10	1.000000
11	1.0413927
100	2.000000
110	2.0413927
1000	3.000000
1100	3.0413927

where an increase of the number 10 by 1 brings with it just as great an increase in the corresponding logarithm, as the increase of the number 100 by 10 or 1000 by 100. In each instance the increase in the logarithm is 0.0413927. Further, as was already shown in explaining the mathematical auxiliary principle, the increases in the logarithms are proportional to the increases of the numbers, so long as they remain very small. Therefore one can say, that Weber's law and the mathematical auxiliary principle are just as valid for the increases of logarithms and numbers in their relation to one another, as they are for the increases of sensation and stimulus.

The fact of the threshold appears just as much in the relation of a logarithm to its number as in the relation of sensation to stimulus. The sensation begins with values above zero, not with zero, but with a finite value of the stimulus — the threshold; and so does the logarithm begin with values above zero, not with a zero value of the number, but with a finite value of the number, the value 1, inasmuch as the logarithm of 1 is equal to zero.

If now, as was shown above, the increase of sensation and stimulus stands in a relation similar to that of the increase of logarithm and number, and, the point at which the sensation begins to assume a noticeable value stands in a relation to the stimulus similar to that which the point at which the logarithm attains positive value stands to the number, then one may also expect that sensation and stimulus themselves stand in a relation to one another similar to that of logarithm to number, which, just as the former (sensation and stimulus) may be regarded as made up of a sum of successive increments.

Accordingly the simplest relation between the two that we can write is $\gamma = \log \beta$.

In fact it will soon be shown that, provided suitable units of sensation and stimulus are chosen, the functional relation between both reduces to this very simple formula. Meanwhile it is not the most general formula that can be derived, but one which is only valid under the supposition of particular units of sensation and stimulus, and we still need a direct and absolute deduction instead of the indirect and approximate one.

The specialist sees at once how this may be attained, namely, by treating the fundamental formula as a differential formula and integrating it. In the following chapter one will find this done. Here it must be supposed already carried out, and those who are not able to follow the simple infinitesimal deduction, must be asked to consider the result as a mathematical fact. This result is the following functional formula between stimulus and sensation, which goes by the name of the measurement formula and which will now be further discussed:

$$\gamma = \kappa \ (\log \beta - \log b) \qquad (^2)$$

In this formula κ again stands for a constant, dependent upon the unit selected and also the logarithmic system, and b a second constant which stands for the threshold value of the stimulus, at which the sensation γ begins and disappears.

According to the rule, that the logarithm of a quotient of two numbers may be substituted for the difference of their logarithms, . . . one can substitute for the above form of the measurement formula the following, which is more convenient for making deductions.

$$\gamma = \kappa \ \log \frac{\beta}{b} \qquad (^3)$$

From this equation it follows that the sensation magnitude γ is not to be considered as a simple function of the stimulus value β, but of its relation to the threshold value b, where the sensation begins and disappears. This relative stimulus value, $\frac{\beta}{b}$ is for the future to be called the fundamental stimulus value, or the fundamental value of the stimulus.

Translated in words, the measurement formula reads:

The magnitude of the sensation (γ) is not proportional to the absolute value of the stimulus (β), but rather to the logarithm of the magnitude of the stimulus, when this last is expressed in terms of its threshold value(b), i. e. that magnitude considered as unit at which the sensation begins and disappears. In short, it is proportional to the logarithm of the fundamental stimulus value.

Before we proceed further, let us hasten to show that that relation between stimulus and sensation, from which the measurement formula is derived, may be correctly deduced in turn from it, and that this latter thus finds its verification in so far as these relations are found empirically. We have here at the same time the simplest examples of the application of the measurement formula.

The measurement formula is founded upon Weber's law and the fact of the stimulus threshold; and both must follow in turn from it.

Now as to Weber's law. In the form that equal increments of sensation are proportional to relative stimulus increments, it may be obtained by differentiating the measurement formula, inasmuch as in this way one returns to the fundamental formula, which contains the expression of the law in this form.

In the form, that equal sensation differences correspond to equal relations of stimulus, the law may be deduced in quite an elementary manner as follows.

Let two sensations, whose difference is to be considered, be called γ and γ', and the corresponding stimuli β and β'. Then according to the measurement formula

$$\gamma = \kappa \ (\log \beta - \log b)$$
$$\gamma' = \kappa \ (\log \beta' - \log b)$$

and likewise for the sensation difference

$$\gamma - \gamma' = \kappa \ (\log \beta - \log \beta')$$

or, since $\log \beta - \log \beta' = \log \dfrac{\beta}{\beta'}$

$$\gamma - \gamma' = \kappa \ \log \frac{\beta}{\beta'}.$$

From this formula it follows, that the sensation difference $\gamma - \gamma'$ is a function of the stimulus relation $\dfrac{\beta}{\beta'}$, and remains the same no matter what values β, β' may take, so long as the relation remains unchanged, which is the statement of Weber's law.

In a later chapter we shall return to the above formula under the name of the difference formula, as one of the simplest consequences of the measurement formula.

As for the fact of the threshold, which is caused by the sensation having zero value not at zero but at a finite value of the stimulus, from which point it first begins to obtain noticeable values with increasing values of stimulus, it is so far contained in the measurement formula as γ does not, according to this formula, have the value zero when $\beta = o$, but when β is equal to a finite value b. This follows as well from equation

(2) as (3) of the measurement formula, directly from (2), and from (3) with the additional consideration of the fact, that when β equals b, $\log \dfrac{\beta}{b}$ equals log 1, and log 1 = 0.

Naturally all deduction from Weber's law and the fact of the threshold will also be deductions from our measurement formula.

It follows from the former law, that every given increment of stimulus causes an ever decreasing increment in sensation in proportion as the stimulus grows larger, and that at high values of the stimulus it is no longer sensed, while on the other hand, at low values it may appear exceptionally strong.

In fact the increase of a large number β by a given amount is accompanied by a considerably smaller increase in the corresponding logarithm γ, than the increase of a small number β by the same amount. When the number 10 is increased by 10, (that is, reaches 20), the logarithm corresponding to 10, which is 1, is increased to 1.3010. When, however, the number 1000 is increased by 10, the logarithm corresponding to 1000, namely 3, is only increased to 3.0043. In the first case the logarithm is increased by 1-3 of its amount, in the latter case by about 1-700.

In connection with the fact of the threshold belongs the deduction, that a sensation is further from the perception threshold the more the stimulus sinks under its threshold value. This distance of a sensation from the threshold, is represented in the same manner by the negative values of γ, according to our measurement formula, as the increase above the threshold is represented by the positive values.

In fact one sees directly from equation (2), that when β is smaller than b and with it log β smaller than log b, the sensation takes on negative values, and the same deduction follows in equation (3), in that $\dfrac{\beta}{b}$ becomes a proper fraction when $\beta < b$, and the logarithm of a proper fraction is negative.

In so far as sensations, which are caused by a stimulus which is not sufficient to raise them to consciousness, are called unconscious, and those which affect consciousness are called conscious, we may say that the unconscious sensations are represented in our formula by negative, the conscious by positive values. We will return to this statement in a special chapter (chapter 18) since it is of great importance, and perhaps not directly evident to everyone. For the present I shall not let it detain me longer.

According to the foregoing our measurement formula corresponds to experience:

1. In the cases of equality, where a sensation difference remains the same when the absolute intensity of the stimulus is altered (Weber's law).

2. In the cases of the thresholds, where the sensation itself ceases, and where its change becomes either imperceptible or barely perceptible. In the former case, when the sensation reaches its lower threshold; in the latter case, when it becomes so great that a given stimulus increase is barely noticed.

3. In the contrasting cases, between sensations which rise above the threshold of consciousness and those that do not reach it, — in short, conscious and unconscious sensations. From the above the measurement formula may be considered well founded.

In the measurement formula one has a general dependent relation between the size of the fundamental stimulus and the size of the corresponding sensation and not one which is valid only for the cases of equal sensations. This permits the amount of sensation to be calculated from the relative amounts of the fundamental stimulus and thus we have a measurement of sensation.

HERMANN VON HELMHOLTZ

(1821–1894)

A MANUAL OF PHYSIOLOGICAL OPTICS

Translated from the German * *by*

BENJAMIN RAND

THEORY OF COLOR VISION

HYPOTHESES. The facts to be deduced from the laws of color-mixture, that three constituents of sensation which proceed independently of one another are produced by external stimulation, have received their more definite and more significant expression in the hypotheses, which assume, that these different constituents are excited and transmitted in different portions of the optic nerve; but that they simultaneously attain to consciousness, and thereby, so far as they have become excited from the same place of the retina, they are also localized in the same place of the field of vision.

Such a theory was first proposed by Thomas Young.[1] The more detailed development of it is essentially conditioned by

---

* From H. von Helmholtz's *Handbuch der Physiologischen Optik*. Leipzig, 1856–66; 2te. umgearb. Aufl. Hamb. u. Lpz. 1896.

[1] Thomas Young's theory of color vision is as follows: "From three simple sensations, with their combinations, we obtain seven primitive distinctions of colours; but the different proportions, in which they may be combined, afford a variety of traits beyond all calculation. The three simple sensations being red, green, and violet, the three binary combinations are yellow, consisting of red and green; crimson, of red and violet; and blue, of green and violet; and the seventh in order is white light, composed by all three united. But the blue thus produced, by combining the whole of the green and violet rays, is not the blue of the spectrum, for four parts of green and one of violet make a blue differing very little from green; while the blue of the spectrum appears to contain as much violet as green: and it is for this reason that red and blue usually make a purple, deriving its hue from the predominance of the violet." Thomas Young's *A Course of Lectures on Natural Philosophy*. Lond. 1807, vol. I, p. 440.

the fact, that its author would ascribe to the sensitive nerves of the eye only the properties and capacities, which we positively know as belonging to the motor nerves of men and of animals. We have a much more favorable opportunity to discover these latter by experiment than is the case with the nerves of sensation, since we are able comparatively easily and definitely both to discern and to measure the finest changes of their excitation and excitability by means of the contractions occurring in the muscles, and their changes. What we furthermore have been able to ascertain concerning the structure, the chemical constitution, the excitability, the conductivity, and the electrical behavior of the sensitive nerves, harmonises so perfectly with the corresponding behavior of the motor nerves, that fundamental differences in the nature of their activity are extremely improbable, at least so far as these do not depend upon the other organic apparatus connected with them, upon which they exert their influence.

Now we know in regard to motor nerves only the contrast between the state of rest and of activity. In the former state the nerve can remain unaltered a long time without important chemical change or development of heat; and at the same time the muscle dependent upon the nerve remains lax. If we stimulate the nerve, heat develops in it material changes, electrical oscillations are shown, and the muscle is contracted. In a cut nerve-preparation the sensitiveness is quickly lost, probably on account of the expansion of the chemical constituents necessary for activity. Under the action of atmospheric oxygen, or better still of the arterial blood containing oxygen, the sensitiveness is wholly or partially slowly restored, save that these processes of restoration excite contractions of the muscle, or changes of electrical relation in nerve and muscle coincident with the activity. We are acquainted also with no external means which can produce this process of restoration so quickly and intensively, and which can permit it at the same time so suddenly to appear and again to cease, as would be necessary, if this process were to serve as the physiological basis of a powerful sensation occurring with precision.

If we confine our assumptions concerning the development of a theory of color vision to the properties belonging with certainty to the nerves, there is presented in fairly secure outline the theory of Thomas Young.

The sensation of dark corresponds to the state of rest of the optic nerve, that of colored or white light to an excitement of it. The three simple sensations which correspond to the excitement only of a single one of the three nerve systems, and from which all the others can be composed, must correspond in the table of colors to the three angles of the color triangle.

In order to assume the finest possible color sensations not demonstrable by objective stimulus, it appears appropriate so to select the angles of the color triangle that its sides include in the closest possibie way the curves of the colors of the spectrum.

Thomas Young has therefore assumed:

1. There are in the eye three kinds of nerve fibres. The excitation of the first produces the sensation of red; the excitation of the second, the sensation of green; the excitation of the third, the sensation of violet.

2. Objective homogeneous light excites these three kinds of fibres with an intensity which varies according to the length of the wave. The fibres sensitive to red are excited most strongly by light of the greatest wave-length; and those sensitive to violet by light of the smallest wave-length. Nevertheless, it is not precluded, but rather to be assumed, for the explanation of a series of phenomena, that each color of the spectrum excites all the kinds of fibres, but with different intensity. If we suppose in *Fig. 1* the spectrum colors placed horizontally and in their natural order, beginning from red R up to violet V, the three curves may represent more or less exactly the strength of the excitation of the three kinds of fibres: no. 1 those sensitive to red; no. 2 those sensitive to green; and no. 3 those sensitive to violet.

The simple red excites strongly the fibres sensitive to red, and weakly the two other kinds of fibres; sensation: red.

The simple yellow excites moderately the fibres sensitive to red and green, weakly the violet; sensation: red.

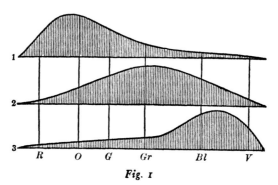

Fig. 1

The simple green excites strongly the fibres sensitive to green, much more weakly the two other kinds; sensation: green.

The simple blue excites moderately the fibres sensitive to green and violet, weakly the red; sensation: blue.

The simple violet excites strongly the fibres which belong to it, and weakly the others; sensation: violet.

The excitation of all the fibres of nearly equal strength gives the sensation of white, or of whitish colors.

Perhaps it may be objected at first view to this hypothesis, that three times the number of nerve fibres and nerve endings must be presumed than in the older assumption, according to which each separate nerve fibre was thought capable of transmitting all kinds of chromatic excitations. But I do not believe, that in this connection the supposition of Young is in contradiction with the anatomical facts. An hypothesis was previously discussed,[1] which explains the accuracy of sight by the aid of a much smaller number of visual nerve fibres, than the number of distinguishable places in the field of vision.

The choice of the three fundamental colors seems at first, as we have observed, somewhat arbitrary. Any other three colors might be chosen from which white can be composed. Young was guided probably by the consideration that the colors at the end of the spectrum appear to claim a privileged position. If we were not to select these it would be necessary to take for one of the fundamental colors a purple shade, and the curve which cor-

---

[1] Helmholtz's *Hdb. d. Physiol. Optik.* 2 Aufl., S. 264.

responds to it in the foregoing figure (*Fig. 1*), would have two maxima: one in red, and the other in violet.

The single circumstance, which is of direct importance in the mode of sensation and appears to give a clue for the determination of the fundamental colors, is the apparent greater color-saturation of the red and violet; a thing which also manifests itself, although indeed less markedly, for green. Since we style colors the more saturated the farther they are removed from white, we must expect that great saturation must belong particularly to those colors of the spectrum which produce most purely the simplest sensations of color. In fact, these colors, if they are very pure, have even with inferior brilliancy, something of an intensively glowing, almost dazzling quality. There are especially red, violet, or blue violet flowers, e.g. of the cameraria, whose colors display this characteristic blending of darkness and brilliancy. Young's hypothesis affords for this a simple explanation. A dark color can cause an intensive excitation of one of the three nerve systems, while the corresponding bright white causes a much weaker excitation of the same. The difference appears analogous to that between the sensation of very hot water upon a small portion of the skin and lukewarm water striking a greater surface.

In particular violet makes upon me this impression of a deeply saturated color. But inasmuch as the strictly violet rays, even when they occur in sunlight, are of slight intensity and are modified by fluorescence, ultramarine blue, which has far the advantage of greater intensity of light, produces an effect approximately equal to it. The strictly pure violet of the spectrum is very little known among the laity, since the violet pigments give nearly always the effect of a slight admixture of red, or appear very dark. For that very reason, the shades of the ultramarine blue coming near to the violet excite the general attention much more, are much better known, and are designated by a much older name, — that of blue, — than the violet strictly so called. In addition one has in the deep ultramarine blue of the cloudless sky a highly imposing, well known, and constant example of this color.

In this fact I seek the reason why in former times blue has always been regarded as the one fundamental color. And the more recent observers, like Maxwell and A. König, who have sought to determine the composition of color, have also in part returned to it. For both of these had, to be sure, a more definite reason in the above mentioned elevation of the curve of the colors of the spectrum in violet.

It should still be mentioned that the Venetian school of painters, which creates effects chiefly by the intense richness of its color, is especially fond of putting in juxtaposition the three colors, red, green, and violet.

Furthermore, I decidedly question the opinion expressed by various investigators, that the need of designating primary sensations has manifested itself in the names of the colors, and that these might therefore give a clue for the determination of colors. Our forefathers had before them in colors a domain of vague distinctions. If they wanted to determine sharp degrees of difference they had first of all to look for good old examples of striking shade, which were everywhere known, and any-where observable. The names for red led back to the Sanscrit *rudhira* = blood, and also "red." From this ἐρυθρός, rufus, ruber, roth, red, etc. For "blue" the Greeks have πορφύρεος and κυάνεος, which appear to refer to the sea; the Latins cœruleus, from cœlum, the sky; the Germans "blau"; the English, blue; the Dutch, blau; the old German, blaw; which appear to lead to the English "blow," that is, the color of the air. The names for green may be traced back to vegetation, πράσῖνος (leek-green), ποώδες (grass-green), viridis from vis, virescere (to grow strong); German: green, English: green, refer to "grow."

The oldest designations of color were very vague: ξανθός appears to have extended from golden yellow to blue green. It was clearly a difficult task to fix in sharp degrees of difference this vague domain. To-day even it is difficult for gifted children to learn the names of colors. One should not infer from these facts that the ancients were color blind.

That from the series of colors which may be stimulated by

objective light, it is impossible to select three which can be regarded as fundamental sensations, has already been discussed. For this very reason A. König and C. Dieterici have distinguished a middle section of the spectrum, the colors of which we can no longer obtain by the mixture of the end-colors and one of the spectrum colors lying within it. The table of colors drawn according to the measurements of the same observers reveals the same fact in graphic representation. Just on this account the supposition is necessary for Thomas Young's theory, that every color of the spectrum excites simultaneously, even though in different intensity, not merely one, but two or all three, of the three nerve systems which are sensitive to color. At best the hypothesis of simplicity would be permissible for the end-colors of the spectrum, red and violet. But precisely in the case of violet we know, that the fluorescence of the retina produced by the violet rays must vitiate the sensation, and it appears to me not improbable, that the height of the curve between F and Y, found even by Maxwell, is conditioned by the fluorescence of the retina.

It further follows, that it must appear theoretically possible to produce sensations of more saturated colors through other conditions of excitation. That this is also practically possible, and that this demand can be actually fulfilled by Young's theory, I shall have to explain in the description of after-images.

The color theory of Thomas Young, above outlined, is, as compared with the general theory of nervous activity as it was worked out by Johannes Müller, a more special application of the law of specific sensations. Corresponding to its hypotheses the sensations of red, green, and violet would be regarded as determined by the specific energy of sensation of the corresponding three nerve systems. Any sort of excitation whatever, which can in any degree excite the nerve system aforesaid, would always be able to produce in it only its specific sensation. As for the cause of the particular quality of these sensations we hardly need look for it in the retina or the constitution of its fibres, but in the activity of the central parts of the brain associated with them.

I have up to the present kept the analysis of this theory relatively abstract in order to keep it as free as possible from farther hypothetical additions. Nevertheless, there are as great advantages for the certain understanding of such abstractions, if one tries to imagine for oneself pictures as concrete as possible, even though these occasion many a presupposition that is not directly necessary for the nature of the case. In this sense I permit myself to set forth Young's theory in the following somewhat more manifest form. That objections to these additions do not contradict the essence of Young's hypothesis, I have no need to explain.

1. Three kinds of photochemically decomposible substances are deposited in the end organs of the visual nerve fibres, which have different sensitiveness for the different parts of the spectrum. The three color values of the colors of the spectrum depend essentially upon the photochemical reaction of these three substances to the light. In the eyes of birds and reptiles besides colorless cones there occur in fact rods with red, and rods with yellow-green, drops of oil, which might produce a favoring of some simple light in their action upon the back element of these formations. In the case of human beings and other mammals nothing similar has up to the present time been found.

2. By the disintegration of all the substances sensitive to light, the nerve fibre laden therewith, is set into a state of excitation. There is only one kind of activity capable of exciting sensation in every nerve fibre which accompanies the disintegration of the organic substance and the development of heat, as we know from our study of the nerves of muscles. These phenomena in the three systems of fibres are probably also thoroughly similar one to the other. They act differently in the brain only for the reason that they are united to different functioning parts of the brain. The nerve fibres need here as everywhere to play only the part of conducting wires, by which entirely similar electric currents which pass through them can precipitate or call forth the most various activities in the apparatus connected with the ends. These excitations of the three systems of fibre form the above separated three elementary excitations, provided always that the intensity of excitation, for which we still have no universally valid measure, is thereby made proportional to the strength of light. This does not prevent the intensity of the elementary excitation being any involved function whatever of the use of material or of the negative variation of the current in

the nerves, which latter phenomena might occasionally be employed as a measure of excitation.

3. In the brain the three systems of fibres stand in alliance with the three different functioning systems of ganglionic cells, which are perhaps spatially so close to one another, that those corresponding to the same parts of the retina lie close together. This appears to follow from recent investigations concerning the influence of lesions of the brain upon the field of vision.

EWALD HERING

(1834–   )

THEORY OF LIGHT SENSATION

*Translated from the German * by*

BENJAMIN RAND

FUNDAMENTAL PRINCIPLES OF A THEORY OF LIGHT SENSATION

§ 25. *PREFATORY REMARKS*

ALTHOUGH strictly speaking a theory of light sensation has to consider all visual sensations, I mean here chiefly to consider only the sensations of white, black, and the transitions from one to the other, that is to say, only the colorless, or, as I have termed them (§ 21), white-black sensations. Later, I shall enter upon a special discussion of color-sensations in the stricter sense of that term.

Colors, to be sure, are everywhere intermingled, and especially in the after-images of the closed eye; but I shall wholly disregard color in all such more or less colored sensations, and confine myself only to that which can be designated as the whitishness or blackishness of sensation. Later it will appear, that this special consideration of the sensations of colorless light even has its complete theoretical justification.

The sensation of white or colorless light has been regarded as a mixed sensation, because it is produced by a simultaneous effect of so called complementary kinds of light upon the retina. Nevertheless we see simultaneously in white, neither yellow and blue, nor red and green, nor any other two complementary

* From E. Hering's *Zur Lehre vom Lichtsinne*, (*Sitzber. Akad. Wiss. Wien, math.-naturw. Cl.*, LXVI–LXX.) Wien. 1872-74; ib. 1878.

colors, but at most the white shades off into yellow or blue, red or green, never, however, into two complementary colors. The designation of white, therefore, as a sensation of red and green, or yellow and blue, or of all colors simultaneously mixed, appears inadmissible, and has indeed arisen only from the abstract confusion of sensations with their causes. Not everyone, who has termed white a mixed sensation, meant to say that the sensations were actually mixed, but only, that in order to excite the sensation of white we must mix light of different wave lengths. This sensation aroused by the simultaneous reaction of divers kinds of rays can very well be regarded as a simple resultant of mingled physical causes.

The Young-Helmholtz hypothesis can only in this sense be acceptable to a certain extent. For if we were to say to a disinterested person, even though he had a highly developed sense of color such as a painter has, that white is a compound sensation in which one perceives not only simultaneously, but also with equal intensity, red, green, and violet, he would reply with an incredulous shake of the head, or, if he felt no special respect for the trustworthiness of science, with a smile. That three tones of different pitch are contained in a triad, everyone hears who is skilled in music, though only in a slight degree; but no one is able, try as he may, to extract the sensations of red, green, and violet, from one and the same white.

To one, who enters upon the investigation of his visual sensations without physical or physiological presuppositions, white is a sensation of its own kind, just as black, red, green, yellow, and blue. Something can be combined with the white from one or the other, or even from several of the last mentioned sensations so that it more or less clearly reminds us of them. If, however, we imagine these intermingled traces of other sensations to be absent, a sensation is left of an entirely specific and pure quality, which decidedly gives the impression of something simple, and which the unprejudiced sees no occasion whatever to regard as compound. The same, moreover, is quite true of the sensation of black.

Since the physiologist must deem all sensations as conditioned and supported by physical processes of the nervous system, because otherwise every further physiological investigation would be useless, he must also accept the so-called psycho-physical processes or movements, which correspond to the sensations of black, of white, and of all transitions from one to the other. It is not possible to say as yet in what part of the nervous system these psychophysical processes are to be conceived as localized. Suffice it to say, that somewhere in the nervous apparatus of the eye and the parts of the brain standing in functional connection therewith, the substance must be sought with whose change or movement sensation is connected. This substance we might designate as the psychophysical substance of the organ of sight relative to the brain. It will be shorter to designate it as the visual substance, because the visual sensations are connected with it and immediately dependent upon it. Whether this visual substance is to be sought only in the brain, or likewise in the nerves of sight, and in the retina, and in what histological constituents of the same, — all this remains outside the present discussion.

It is manifest, that we can draw conclusions at first only from the nature and course of our visual sensations in regard to the course of the psychophysical processes, which occur in the visual substance; for with these the sensations are to be regarded as immediately and legitimately connected. If we can determine in this way to a certain extent the laws of psychophysical reactions in the visual substance, not until we do is it in order for us to seek the laws of functional relation between those psychophysical processes and the vibrations of aether. The reverse method which proceeds from the vibrations of aether has led heretofore to no result, so far as it has dealt not merely with the vicissitudes of the rays of light in the optical media, that is to say exclusively with an application of physical optics to the eye. We know nothing at all of what takes place after the light waves have penetrated the retina. On the other hand we certainly obtain through numerous physical investigations the most valuable conclusions concerning the relations between the vibrations of aether and visual sensations. But all physiological links and especially their psychophysical processes have been simply ignored in these investigations, as was quite appropriate under the circumstances of a preliminary research.

Only the psychophysical investigations, especially Fechner's, have a closer regard to the physiological intermediaries, especially in so far as Fechner proposed a law of functional connection between the psychophysical movement and the so called intensity of sensations. I refer to that psychophysical law called by Fechner's name,* the validity of which I must challenge not merely for the sense of sight, but for the domain of all the senses.

§ 26. *THE NATURE OF THE PSYCHOPHYSICAL PROCESSES*

If we desire to form an idea of the nature of the psychophysical processes, we have from the outset a choice between such inner movements of the psychophysical, or (briefly) psychical substance, as occur without change of chemical composition, and such movements as appear to be at the same time changes of chemical composition. The physiologist of the present can nevertheless no longer be in doubt about his decision. For the general physiology of the nerves has sufficiently proven, that every movement or activity of the nervous substance changes it at once chemically; and upon the hypothesis of chemical changes all our ideas of changes of sensitiveness, fatigue, and recuperation after activity are based.

How Du Bois-Reymond † could propose a purely physical hypothesis concerning processes in the nerve-fibres becomes conceivable, when you consider that he aimed in reality only at the explanation of what the multiplicator testified to him about the processes in the nerves. If he had had for the changes of the nerve as fine a chemical reagent, as he possessed in the

* *Supra*, p. 570.
† Cf. Emil du Bois-Reymond's *Untersuchungen über thierische Electricität*, Berlin, 1848-49.

multiplicator an electrical one, he would then of course have proposed a chemical hypothesis. At all events, the hypothesis of Du Bois-Reymond does not form a conclusive objection against my affirmation, that according to our present knowledge the activity of the psychophysical substance is not easily conceivable without simultaneous chemical changes.

The hypothesis developed in Fechner's psychophysics, according to which all psychophysical processes are regarded as oscillatory movements of a substance not more exactly to be designated as ponderable or imponderable, also cannot be cited against the above affirmation. For first, the hypothesis according to the whole nature of the case rests upon only an empirical basis which up to the present is very narrow; and secondly, although it is purely mechanical, it still permits to the chemical processes their significance in psychical happening, and, so to speak, includes them.

In whatever way one may regard these questions this much is certain, that the continuous existence of chemical process is in every living and consequently sensitive substance a fact, and transformation is for us the most universal known characteristic of living things.

So much in the way of proof for the justification by principle of the following theory, which is related primarily to the chemical action in the nerve substance. A definite view as to whether we actually apprehend in this chemical action the real psychophysical movement, or whether an intermediate link intervenes, as it were, between this and the sensation, I do not for the present mean to have said. Furthermore, it was by no means my intention in this brief discussion to enter upon a real investigation of the difficult question concerning the nature of psychophysical movement. On the contrary, it was intended only to show that the physiologist is perfectly right in conceiving the life of the nerve-substance primarily as chemical, and likewise that of the psychophysical substance, which even, if one does not insert a new and completely unknown link, must be wholly or partially identified with the nerve-substance.

§ 27. *VISUAL SENSATION AS PSYCHICAL CORRELATE OF CHEMICAL PROCESSES IN THE VISUAL SUBSTANCE*

That light occasions chemical changes in the nervous apparatus of the visual organ will probably not be disputed after what has been said. What we term fatigue and in general change of sensitivity of this process rest according to the universal view, here as everywhere, upon chemical change of a sensitive substance. Fechner himself, who sought to develop farther the theory of resonance proposed by the physicists Herschell, Melloni, and Seebeck, for the excitation of the retina by light, saw occasion to take account of the chemical influences of light upon the nerve substance and to include them in his reckoning.[1]

The chemical processes occasioned by light in the visual organ were first regarded as localised in the retina. But if certain parts of the brain participate in the production of visual sensations and representations, those chemical processes of the retina must on their part also occasion chemical changes in the substance of the visual nerve, and these in turn in the substance of the brain. Since, however, as already stated, we do not know whether we have to consider the entire substance of the visual organ, or only a part of it, and in the latter instance which part, as the true psychophysical visual substance, we must for the present be content with the current hypothesis, that the vibrations of aether set free in general chemical changes in the nervous visual apparatus. And those changes, whether the series of these chemical processes be long or short, whether it be composed of similar or dissimilar members, lead finally to sensation.

Furthermore, whatever ideas of the nature and place of the processes occurring in the visual organ investigators entertained, one thing was lacking to all: viz., they merely conceived the sensations of bright or white — color here too I entirely disregard — as conditioned by and based upon certain changes of the visual substance; the sensation of dark or black in reference

[1] *Psychophysik*, ii. Theil, § 283.

to its physiological or psychophysical correlate was entirely neglected. How this came about, and to what contradictions this onesided consideration of the sensation of brightness led, I have more fully set forth in my foregoing chapter (§ 21–23). The facts there developed compel us henceforth to abandon this onesided attitude in the investigation of the visual sensations, and to give an equal consideration to the two chief variables in visual sensation, the dark or black, just as much as the bright or white.

I have explained in § 21, how all sensations of the black-white series of sensations appear related to one another in a twofold manner, and have in common two different kinds of factors, namely, the sensation of brightness and of darkness, the black and the white. I have also set forth how each member of this sensation series can be characterised by the relation in which both these factors are contained in the given sensation. If now we ask concerning the psychical correlates of those sensations, and concerning the psychophysical or psychochemical processes lying at their basis; not only does the hypothesis, that the physical correlate of the blackest sensation is nothing further than the lowest degree of intensity of the same process which conditions in its highest intensity the clearest or purest white sensation, have nothing in its favor, but even appears to be extravagant and contradictory. For this hypothesis demands one and the same kind of psychophysical process for two clearly fundamentally different qualities of sensation. But our entire psychophysics is based upon the hypothesis, that there exists a certain parallelism between physical and psychical events, and especially that to different qualities of sensation there correspond different qualities or forms of psychophysical phenomena.[1]

---

[1] Although this ought to be self evident to everyone who accepts a legitimate functional relation between psychical and physical, between sensation and nerve process, it still has often been forgotten, and even Fechner, although he is guided by the same presupposition, nevertheless makes, as I deem, too little application of it. Mach styles this fundamental presupposition of the entire psychophysics merely as "a heuristic principle of psychophysical research"; but it is more, it is the conditio sine qua non of all such research, if it is to bear any fruit. Mach

If we do not desire, therefore, at the outset to introduce in like manner into this difficult domain an hypothesis which stands in a yet unsolved contradiction to the fundamental presupposition of the entire science of psychophysics, and probably furnishes a bad precedent for other wholly capricious and theoretically improbable hypotheses, we must abandon the present current view. And we can do this the more readily as another hypothesis presents itself which is thoroughly in accord with the aforementioned presupposition of psychophysics, and at the same time satisfies far better than the present theory the demands which must be taken into consideration from the point of view of the general physiology of the nerves. This hypothesis is the following:

To the two qualities of sensation, which we designate as white or bright and as black or dark, correspond two different qualities of chemical activity in the visual substance; and to the different relations of brightness or intensity, with which these two sensations appear in single transitions between pure white and pure black, or to the relations in which they appear mixed, correspond the same relations of intensities of those two psychophysical processes.

It will be readily acknowledged after reflection, that this hypothesis is the simplest there is, because it states the simplest formula that can be conceived for the functional connection between physical and psychical phenomena.

But it also satisfies every demand that the general physio-

remarks (*Uber d. Wirk, d. rauml, Vertheil. d. Lichtreizes auf die Netzhaut.* Sitzungsber. d. Akad. 52 Bd., 1868). "To every psychical there corresponds a physical, and the reverse. To like psychical processes there correspond like physical, to unlike, unlike. If a psychical process can be resolved in a purely psychological way into a number of qualities a, b, c, there will correspond to these likewise an equal number of different physical processes a, β, γ. To all details of the psychical there correspond details of the physical." Barring the omission from the statement, of all reference to the fact that psychophysical processes of very different size can produce the same sensation, because it depends everywhere not upon the absolute size of this process, but solely upon their reciprocal relation (cf. § 29), I can entirely accept these words of Mach.

My theory of the spatial sense of the retina was founded upon the same principle. Mach is the only one who has concurred in its fundamental thought.

logy of the nerves can make. We must suppose a substance in the nervous visual apparatus, which suffers change under the influence of the light that falls upon it, and this change, even though it may be characterised as physical, is nevertheless, as the physiology of the nerves must assume, at the same time a chemical process. If the action of the light ceases, the changed (more or less exhausted) substance reverts sooner or later to its original condition. This reversion can in turn be nothing but a chemical change in the opposite direction. If the occurring change of the excitable substance under the direct influence of light is conceived as a partial consumption, the reversion to the former condition must be conceived as a restitution; and if the former is viewed as an analytic process, the latter must be viewed as a synthetic process.

It has also been customary to designate the latter process, by means of which the living organic substance again restores the loss suffered by excitation or activity as *assimilation*, and I will retain this expression. Now every living and excitable organic substance forms in the excitation or activity according to general assumption certain chemical products. The formation of these products I will designate analogously as the process of *dissimilation*.

The propositions concerning assimilation (A) and dissimilation (D) just set forth are derived from the experiences of general physiology, and particularly of the physiology of the nerves. They have, therefore, been developed wholly independently of our hypothesis. Granted their correctness, it is by no means plausible, that merely the one kind of chemical activity in the visual substance, namely dissimilation, should have a psychophysical significance, but the other, the process of assimilation, none. The common view, that the chemical process taking place under the direct influence of light, namely dissimilation, is alone perceived, is clearly onesided and unjustified. On the contrary, it appears from the outset proper to ascribe an equal value for sensation to both kinds of chemical process. But this leads to none other than the hypothesis above formulated. For we need only to make this hypothesis still more precise, by saying, *that the dissimilation of the visual substance corresponds to the sensation of white or bright, and the assimilation of the visual substance to the sensation of black or dark;* and then the hypothesis, as I shall show, satisfies not only the facts of sensation, but also the demands of the general physiology of the nerves.

If my hypothesis is correct we have the means, through the visual sensations, of observing closely the "building up" process of the visual substance, and its two principal factors, assimilation and dissimilation. We do not, therefore, deal hereafter only with the fact, that a complex of sensations is transmitted from the eye to the human soul, which afterwards moulds it into presentations by the aid of correct or false judgments or inferences; but what comes to consciousness as visual sensation is the physical expression or the conscious correlate of the chemical change of the visual substance.

We have, therefore, a test of great sensitiveness for this chemical change, namely our consciousness. It tells us, indeed, nothing directly concerning the nature of the chemical compounds or disintegrations, but it reveals to us the whole temporal process of assimilation and dissimilation, the law of their dependence upon one another and upon the vibrations of aether, the elevation and depression of excitability of the visual substance, and the dependence of these changes of excitability upon assimilation and dissimilation. In this way the chapter on visual sensations first becomes a truly integral section of physiology, whereas heretofore it necessarily contained more physical and philosophical, than strictly physiological discussions.

From the above hypothesis we derive, as is shown in what follows, a complete series of propositions concerning fatigue, excitability, chemical change of the visual substance, which are in harmony with certain propositions of the general physiology of the nerves; but we are able also in addition to give to those propositions in part a more precise expression, as well as to test certain new propositions, which follow as the result of our hypothesis, in regard to other excitable substances. In brief, a way opens up for the further development of the general physiology of the nerves, also of the physiology of the " excitable " substances, and finally of the doctrine of the whole organic life. That this way is not improbable, I hope to demonstrate in later chapters on several subjects in physiology.

We have employed our sense-perceptions so abundantly in order to comprehend our external world, and they make it serviceable to us; let us now employ them also in order to investigate the material activity of our own body, examining first by their aid what we feel, not as the external objects only mediately, but immediately, that is to say, the chemical change of our nervous system.

§ 28. THE DEDUCTION OF VARIOUS COROLLARIES

In my fourth chapter I derived by means of an analysis of visual sensations, independent of every physical or physiological presupposition, the proposition, that every sensation of colorless light is determined by the relation of the perceptible black to the simultaneous perceptible white in it, and that this relation determines the quality — brightness or darkness — of every white-black sensation.

If we now apply to this problem the hypothesis advanced in the preceding section, we come to the further proposition that the quality — brightness or darkness — of a sensation of colorless light, is conditioned by the relation in which the intensity or extent of dissimilation of the visual substance stands to the intensity or degree of its simultaneous assimilation.

From this it follows further, that to the gray, which I have designated as the middle or neutral, corresponds that condition of the visual substance in which dissimilation and assimilation are in equilibrium, so that the quantity of the excitable substance remains constant.

Further it follows, that in every rather bright sensation the dissimilation is greater than the assimilation, so that the excitable substance decreases; and the more rapidly, the greater the relation $\frac{w}{s}$, or the brighter the sensation is, and so much the more, the longer it continues.

On the contrary it follows, that in every sensation, which is darker than the middle gray, the dissimilation is smaller than the simultaneous assimilation, so that the excitable substance increases; and, indeed, the more rapidly, the darker the sensation is, and so much the more, the longer it continues.

What now does the increase or decrease of the excitable substance signify?

If we style all stimuli which favor the dissimilation of the visual substance, stimuli of dissimilation or D stimuli, and if we borrow from general physiology the proposition, that the degree of the reaction with which an organ responds to a stimulus depends among other things upon the quantity of excitable substance contained in it and affected by the stimulus, we arrive at the farther proposition, that the degree of the dissimilation conditioned by a D stimulus (e.g., light) depends not merely upon the degree of the stimulus, but also upon the quantity of the excitable substance contained at any time in the stimulated portions and affected by the stimulus.

The capacity of an excitable substance to become excited by stimuli, that is, to respond to these stimuli by a definite chemical process, we term its excitability. Accordingly, we can designate the capacity of the visual substance to react upon the D stimuli with dissimilation as its D excitability, and can now also express the foregoing proposition as follows:

Every increase of the excitable substance conditions an enhancement, and every decrease a depression, of the D excitability in the corresponding part of the visual organ.

It follows further, that the sensation of medium gray conditions an equilibrium, every rather bright sensation a decrease, every rather dark sensation an increase, of the D excitability of the affected part.

If sensations of different degrees of brightness or darkness are simultaneously produced in two places of nearest equal D excitability, the place of the brighter (less dark) sensation has always a smaller D excitability at the conclusion of the excitation, than the place of the less bright (darker) sensation; and it makes no difference whether one or both sensations were brighter or darker than the neutral gray. Furthermore, the remaining difference of D excitability is so much the greater, as the difference was greater between the brightness of both sensations, or between the values of the two corresponding relations $\frac{w}{s+w}$ and $\frac{w'}{s'+w'}$.

Since according to what has been said the degree of dissimilation is always dependent on the one hand upon the degree of the stimulus, and upon the other hand upon the quantity of the excitable substance present in the stimulated part, we have the right from the outset to affirm, that the assimilation also does not always occur with constant intensity, but that it has likewise a variable degree dependent upon definite conditions.

For the process of dissimilation clearly presupposes, that on the one hand the necessary chemical conditions, that is to say, certain substances, are present; and on the other hand certain physical conditions, (such as a certain temperature). According as whatever assimilation is present in greater or less degree, it takes place more quickly and more abundantly, or more slowly and less abundantly. The A material necessary to assimilation, present in the visual organ, which is constantly used in assimilation and constantly renewed by the blood, can become more or less exhausted as soon as its consumption is greater than the simultaneous restoration from the blood. For the degree of the assimilation probably also depends upon the quantity of the assimilative excitable substance present at the time. From what precedes it is already possible quite theoretically to deduce a series of propositions concerning the enhancement or depression of the capacity for assimilation or of the A excitability, and concerning the A stimuli in contrast with the D stimuli, etc. Nevertheless, I shall refer for the present only to such propositions from the general nerve physiology as are already accepted, and shall postpone a full discussion of them until later.

THE WEIGHT OF VISUAL SENSATIONS

If the brightness or darkness of a sensation of colorless light depends solely upon the relation of dissimilation to the simultaneous assimilation, and is therefore independent of the absolute magnitude of the corresponding psychophysical processes, the question arises, what is the significance of this absolute magnitude. Without entering here more closely into this question, which belongs to general psychophysics, I shall endeavor to give briefly a preliminary answer.

The absolute extent of a given psychophysical process determines the *weight* — to introduce here a new expression — of the corresponding sensation. If two simultaneous psychophysical processes of different quality lie at the basis of a sensation, as for instance the gray, then the sum of the magnitudes of both processes gives the weight of the resulting or mixed sensation. The clearness, with which every single relatively simple sensation appears in such a compound sensation, depends upon the relation in which its individual weight stands to the total weight of the resulting or compound sensation. Thus, as we saw, the brightness or whitishness of a gray sensation is determined by the relation of the weight of the white sensation (or the degree of dissimilation) to the total weight of the gray sensation, that is, to the sum of the weights of the white and of the black sensation, (or of the degree of dissimilation and assimilation).

If a compound sensation, e.g., gray, is in itself a component of a still more complicated compound, e.g., of gray-blue, the clearness, with which the gray emerges in this sensation, depends in turn upon the relation in which the weight of the gray sensation stands to the total-weight of the gray-blue. If, for example, in such a sensation the blue, white, and black appear with equal clearness, this depends upon the fact, that the blue, the white, and the black sensation have equal weight. We can also conceive such a sensation as composed of two parts of neutral gray and one part of blue. The character or quality of a sensation is therefore independent of its total weight, but is determined by the relation of the individual weights of the simple or relatively simple sensations composing it; and the weight of a black-white sensation does not gain significance until it appears with other visual sensations, or in general only so far as its relations to the other simultaneous processes come into consideration.

The well informed reader must have recognised, from what has already been said, the general psychophysical law, from which I proceed in opposition to Fechner. This law says, *that the purity or clearness of any sensation or presentation depends upon the relation, in which its weight, that is, the degree of the corresponding psychophysical process, stands to the total weight of all simultaneously present sensations and representations,* (or however else one may denominate the psychical states), *namely, to the sum of the degrees of all corresponding psychophysical processes.*

Most of the sensations, which we accept as simple, are highly complex; that partial sensation, which has the greatest weight, gives the total sensation its character and name. If the fragment of the total weight of a sensation, belonging to one of its components, sinks below a certain value, we are no longer in a position to feel these components as such. Nevertheless, a weak component also affects a sensation and determines by its character the quality thereof. Fechner would say the partial sensation remains "below the threshold." Thus every visual sensation, as I shall later seek to prove, is composed of various simple sensations, and if I have here presented the sensations of the black-white series as only binary sensations, it has been done provisionally in the interest of simplicity of treatment. In black and white even the colors simultaneously perceived are " below the threshold " because their relative weight is too small.

ERNST MACH

(1838–   )

CONTRIBUTIONS TO THE ANALYSIS OF SENSATIONS

Translated from the German* by

C. M. WILLIAMS

THE SENSATIONS AS ELEMENTS

ANTIMETAPHYSICAL

1. THE splendid success achieved by physical science in modern times, a success which is not restricted to its own sphere but embraces that of other sciences which employ its help, has brought it about that physical ways of thinking and physical modes of procedure enjoy on all hands unwonted prominence, and that the greatest expectations are associated with their employment. In keeping with this drift of modern inquiry, the physiology of the senses, gradually leaving the paths which were opened by men like Goethe, Schopenhauer, and others, but with particular success by Johannes Müller, has also assumed an almost exclusively physical character. This tendency must appear to us as not exactly the proper one, when we reflect that physics despite its considerable development nevertheless constitutes but a portion of a *larger* collective body of knowledge, and that it is unable, with its limited intellectual implements, created for limited and special purposes, to exhaust all the subject-matter of science. Without renouncing the support of physics, it is possible for the physiology of the senses, not only to pursue its own course of development, but also to afford to physical science itself powerful assistance;

* From *Beiträge zur Analyse der Empfindungen.* Jena, 1886: 4 verm. Aufl. 1903. Reprinted from E. Mach's *Contributions to the Analysis of Sensations,* translated by C. M. Williams, Chicago, The Open Court Publishing Co., 1897.

a point which the following simple considerations will serve to illustrate.

2. Colors, sounds, temperatures, pressures, spaces, times, and so forth, are connected with one another in manifold ways; and with them are associated moods of mind, feelings, and volitions. Out of this fabric, that which is relatively more fixed and permanent stands prominently forth, engraves itself in the memory, and expresses itself in language. Relatively greater permanency exhibit, first, certain *complexes* of colors, sounds, pressures, and so forth, connected in time and space, which therefore receive special names, and are designated *bodies*. Absolutely permanent such complexes are not.

My table is now brightly, now dimly lighted. Its temperature varies. It may receive an ink stain. One of its legs may be broken. It may be repaired, polished, and replaced part for part. But for me, amid all its changes, it remains the table at which I daily write.

My friend may put on a different coat. His countenance may assume a serious or a cheerful expression. His complexion, under the effects of light or emotion, may change. His shape may be altered by motion, or be definitely changed. Yet the number of the permanent features presented, compared with the number of the gradual alterations, is always so great, that the latter may be overlooked. It is the same friend with whom I take my daily walk.

My coat may receive a stain, a tear. My very manner of expression shows that we are concerned here with a sum-total of permanency, to which the new element is added and from which that which is lacking is subsequently taken away.

Our greater intimacy with this sum-total of permanency, and its preponderance as contrasted with the changeable, impel us to the partly instinctive, partly voluntary and conscious economy of mental representation and designation, as expressed in ordinary thought and speech. That which is perceptually represented in a single image receives *a single* designation, *a single* name.

As relatively permanent, there is exhibited, further, that complex of memories, moods, and feelings, joined to a particular body (the human body), which is denominated the "I" or "Ego." I may be engaged upon this or that subject, I may be quiet or animated, excited or ill-humored. Yet, pathological cases apart, enough durable features remain to identify the ego. Of course, the ego also is only of relative permanency.

After a first survey has been obtained, by the formation of the substance-concepts " body " and " ego " (matter and soul), the will is impelled to a more exact examination of the *changes* that take place in these relatively permanent existences. The changeable features of bodies and of the ego, in fact, are exactly what moves the will to this examination. Here the component parts of the complex are first exhibited as its properties. A fruit is sweet; but it can also be bitter. Also, other fruits may be sweet. The red color we are seeking is found in many bodies. The neighborhood of some bodies is pleasant; that of others, unpleasant. Thus, gradually, different complexes are found to be made up of common elements. The visible, the audible, the tangible, are separated from bodies. The visible is analysed into colors and into form. In the manifoldness of the colors, again, though here fewer in number, other component parts are discerned — such as the primary colors, and so forth. The complexes are disintegrated into *elements*.

3. The useful habit of designating such relatively permanent compounds by *single* names, and of apprehending them by *single* thoughts, without going to the trouble each time of an analysis of their component parts, is apt to come into strange conflict with the tendency to isolate the component parts. The vague image which we have of a given permanent complex, being an image which does not perceptibly change when one or another of the component parts is taken away, gradually establishes itself as something which exists *by itself*. Inasmuch as it is possible to take away *singly* every constituent part without destroying the capacity of the image to *stand for* the totality and of being recognised again, it is imagined that it is possible

to subtract *all* the parts and to have something still remaining. Thus arises the monstrous notion of a *thing in itself*, unknowable and different from its "phenomenal" existence.

Thing, body, matter, are nothing apart from their complexes of colors, sounds and so forth — nothing apart from their so-called attributes. That Protean, supposititious problem, which springs up so much in philosophy, of a single thing with *many* attributes, arises wholly from a mistaking of the fact, that summary comprehension and precise analysis, although both are provisionally justifiable and for many purposes profitable, cannot and must not be carried on *simultaneously*. A body is one and unchangeable only so long as it is unnecessary to consider its details. Thus both the earth and a billiard-ball are spheres, if the purpose in hand permits our neglecting deviations from the spherical form, and great precision is not necessary. But when we are obliged to carry on investigations in orography or microscopy, both bodies cease to be spheres.

4. Man possesses, in its highest form, the power of consciously and arbitrarily determining his point of view. He can at one time disregard the most salient features of an object, and immediately thereafter give attention to its smallest details; now consider a stationary current, without a thought of its contents, and then measure the width of a Fraunhofer line in the spectrum; he can rise at will to the most general abstractions or bury himself in the minutest particulars. The animal possesses this capacity in a far less degree. It does not assume a point of view, but is usually forced to it. The babe who does not know its father with his hat on, the dog that is perplexed at the new coat of its master, have both succumbed in this conflict of points of view. Who has not been worsted in similar plights? Even the man of philosophy at times succumbs, as the grotesque problem, above referred to, shows.

In this last case, the circumstances appear to furnish a real ground for justification. Colors, sounds, and the odors of bodies are evanescent. But the tangible part, as a sort of constant durable nucleus, not readily susceptible of annihilation, remains behind; appearing as the vehicle of the more fugitive properties annexed to it. Habit, thus, keeps our thought firmly attached to this central nucleus, even where the knowledge exists that seeing, hearing, smelling, and *touching* are intimately akin in character. A further consideration is, that owing to the singularly extensive development of mechanical physics a kind of *higher reality* is ascribed to space and time than to colors, sounds, and odors; agreeably to which, the temporal and spatial *links* of colors, sounds, and odors appear to be *more real* than the colors, sounds, and odors themselves. The physiology of the senses, however, demonstrates, that spaces and times may just as appropriately be called sensations as colors and sounds.

5. The ego, and the relation of bodies to the ego, give rise to similar pseudo-problems, the character of which may be briefly indicated as follows:

Let those complexes of colors, sounds, and so forth, commonly called bodies, be designated, for the sake of simplicity, by $A \ B \ C \ . \ . \ .$; the complex, known as our own body, which constitutes a part of the former, may be called $K \ L \ M \ . \ . \ .$; the complex composed of volitions, memory-images, and the rest, we shall represent by $\alpha \beta \gamma \ . \ . \ .$ Usually, now, the complex $\alpha \beta \gamma \ . \ . \ . K \ L \ M \ . \ . \ .$, as making up the ego, is opposed to the complex $A \ B \ C \ . \ . \ .$, as making up the world of substance; sometimes, also, $\alpha \beta \gamma \ . \ . \ .$ is viewed as ego, and $K \ L \ M \ . \ . \ . A \ B C \ . \ . \ .$ as world of substance. Now, at first blush, $A \ B \ C \ . \ . \ .$ appears independent of the ego, and opposed to it as a separate existence. But this independence is only relative, and gives way upon closer inspection. Much, it is true, may change in the complex $\alpha \beta \gamma \ . \ . \ .$ without a perceptible change being induced in $A \ B \ C \ . \ . \ .$; and *vice versa*. But many changes in $\alpha \beta \gamma \ . \ . \ .$ do pass, by way of changes in $K \ L \ M \ . \ . \ .$, to $A \ B C \ . \ . \ .$; and *vice versa*. (As, for example, when powerful ideas burst forth into acts, or our environment induces noticeable changes in our body.) At the same time the group $K \ L \ M \ . \ . \ .$ appears to be more intimately connected with

$a \beta \gamma$ . . . and with $A B C$ . . ., than the latter do with one another; relations which find their expression in common thought and speech.

Precisely viewed, however, it appears that the group $A B C$ . . . is *always* codetermined by $K L M$. A cube of wood when seen close at hand, looks large; when seen at a distance, small; it looks different with the right eye from what it does with the left; sometimes it appears double; with closed eyes it is invisible. The properties of the same body, therefore, appear modified by our own body; they appear conditioned by it. But where, now, is that *same* body, which to the appearance is so *different?* All that can be said is, that with different $K L M$ different $A B C$ . . . are associated.

We see an object having a point S. If we touch S, that is, bring it into connexion with our body, we receive a prick. We can see S, without feeling the prick. But as soon as we feel the prick we find S. The visible point, therefore, is a *permanent fact or nucleus*, to which the prick is annexed, according to circumstances, as something accidental. From the frequency of such occurrences we ultimately accustom ourselves to regard *all* properties of bodies as "effects" proceeding from permanent nuclei and conveyed to the ego through the medium of the body; which effects we call *sensations*. By this operation, however, our imagined nuclei are deprived of their entire sensory contents, and converted into mere mental symbols. The assertion, then, is correct that the world consists only of our sensations. In which case we have knowledge *only* of sensations, and the assumption of the nuclei referred to, or of a reciprocal action between them, from which sensations proceed, turns out to be quite idle and superfluous. Such a view can only suit with a half-hearted realism or a half-hearted philosophical criticism.

6. Ordinarily the complex $a \beta \gamma$ . . . $K L M$ . . . is contrasted as ego with the complex $A B C$. Those elements only of $A B C$ . . . that more strongly alter $a \beta \gamma$ . . ., as a prick, a pain, are wont to be comprised in the ego. Afterwards, however, through

observations of the kind just referred to, it appears that the right to annex *A B C* . . . to the ego nowhere ceases. In conformity with this view the ego can be so extended as ultimately to embrace the entire world. The ego is not sharply marked off, its limits are very indefinite and arbitrarily displaceable. Only by failing to observe this fact, and by unconsciously narrowing those limits, while at the same time we enlarge them, arise, in the conflict of points of view, the metaphysical difficulties met with in this connection.

As soon as we have perceived that the supposed unities "body" and "ego" are only makeshifts, designed for provisional survey and for certain practical ends (so that we may take hold of bodies, protect *ourselves* against pain, and so forth), we find ourselves obliged, in many profound scientific investigations, to abandon them as insufficient and inappropriate. The antithesis of ego and world, sensation (phenomenon) and thing, then vanishes, and we have simply to deal with the *connexion* of the *elements a β γ* . . . *A B C* . . . *K L M* . . . , of which this antithesis was only a partially appropriate and imperfect expression. This connexion is nothing more nor less than the combination of the above-mentioned elements with other similar elements (time and space). Science has simply to *accept* this connexion, and to set itself aright (get its bearings) in the intellectual environment which is thereby furnished, without attempting to explain its existence.

On a superficial examination the complex *a β γ* . . . appears to be made up of much more evanescent elements than *A B C* . . . and *K L M* . . . in which last the elements seem to be connected with greater *stability* and *in a more permanent manner* (being joined to solid nuclei as it were). Although on closer inspection the elements of all complexes prove to be *homogeneous*, yet in spite of the knowledge of this fact, the early notion of an antithesis of body and spirit easily regains the ascendancy in the mind. The philosophical spiritualist is often sensible of the difficulty of imparting the needed solidity to his mind-created world of bodies; the materialist is at a loss when required to endow the world of matter with sensation. The *monistic* point of view, which artificial reflexion has evolved, is easily clouded by our older and more powerful instinctive notions.

7. The difficulty referred to is particularly felt in the following case. In the complex $A\ B\ C$ . . ., which we have called the world of matter, we find as parts, not only our own body $K\ L\ M$ . . ., but also the bodies of other persons (or animals) $K'\ L'\ M'$ . . ., $K''\ L''\ M''$ . . ., to which, by analogy, we imagine other $\alpha'\ \beta'\ \gamma'$ . . . , $\alpha''\ \beta''\ \gamma''$ . . ., annexed, similar to $\alpha\ \beta\ \gamma$ . . . So long as we deal with $K'\ L'\ M'$ . . ., we find ourselves in a thoroughly familiar province at every point sensorially accessible to us. When, however, we inquire after the sensations or feelings appurtenant to the body $K'\ L'\ M'$ . . ., we no longer find the elements we seek in the province of sense: *we add them in thought*. Not only is the domain which we now enter far less familiar to us, but the transition into it is also relatively unsafe. We have the feeling as if we were plunging into an abyss. Persons who adopt this method only, will never thoroughly rid themselves of this sense of insecurity, which is a frequent source of illusive problems.

But we are not restricted to this course. Let us consider, first, the reciprocal relations of the elements of the complex $A\ B\ C$ . . ., without regarding $K\ L\ M$ . . . (our body). All physical investigations are of this sort. A white bullet falls upon a bell; a sound is heard. The bullet turns yellow before a sodium lamp, red before a lithium lamp. Here the elements ($A\ B\ C$. . .) appear to be connected only *with one another* and to be independent of our body ($K\ L\ M$ . . .). But if we take santonine, the bullet again turns yellow. If we press one eye to the side, we see two bullets. If we close our eyes entirely, we see none at all. If we sever the auditory nerve, no sound is heard. The elements $A\ B\ C$ . . ., therefore, are not only connected among one another, but also with $K\ L\ M$. To this extent, and to this extent *only*, do we call $A\ B\ C$ . . . *sensations*, and regard $A\ B\ C$ as belonging to the ego. In this way, accordingly, we do not find the gap between bodies and sensations above described, between what is without and what is within.

between the material world and the spiritual world.[1] All elements $A B C \ldots, K L M \ldots$ constitute a single coherent mass only, in which, when any one element is disturbed, *all* is put in motion; except that a disturbance in $K L M \ldots$ has a more extensive and profound action than in $A B C$. A magnet in our neighborhood disturbs the particles of iron near it; a falling boulder shakes the earth; but the severing of a nerve sets in motion the *whole* system of elements.

8. That traditional gulf between physical and psychological research, accordingly, exists only for the habitual stereotyped method of observation. A color is a physical object so long as we consider its dependence upon its luminous source, upon other colors, upon heat, upon space, and so forth. Regarding, however, its dependence upon the retina (the elements $K L M \ldots$) it becomes a psychological object, a sensation. Not the subject, but the direction of our investigation, is different in the two domains.

Both in reasoning from the observation of the bodies of other men or animals, to the sensations which they possess, as well as in investigating the influence of our own body upon our own sensations, we must complete observed facts by analogy. This is accomplished with much greater readiness and certainty, when it relates, say, only to nervous processes, which cannot be fully observed in our own bodies — that is, when it is carried out in the more familiar physical domain — than when it is made in connexion with psychical processes. Otherwise there is no essential difference.

10. Reference has already been made to the different character of the groups of elements designated by $A B C \ldots$ and $a \beta \gamma$. As a matter of fact, when we *see* a green tree before us, or *remember* a green tree, that is, represent a green tree to ourselves, we are perfectly aware of the difference of the two cases. The represented tree has a much less determinate, a much more

---

[1] Compare my *Grundlinien der Lehre von den Bewegungsempfindungen,* Leipsic, Engelmann, 1875, p. 54.

changeable form; its green is much paler and more evanescent; and, what is of especial note, it is plainly situated in a *different* domain. A movement that we *propose* to execute is never more than a represented movement, and appears in a different sphere from that of the executed movement, which always takes place when the image is vivid enough. The statement that the elements A and a appear in different spheres, means, if we go to the bottom of it, simply this, that these elements are united with different other elements. Thus far, therefore, the fundamental constituents of $A BC. . ., a \beta \gamma . . .$ would seem to be *the same* (colors, sounds, spaces, times, motor sensations. . .), and only the character of their connexion different.

Ordinarily pleasure and pain are regarded as different from sensations. Yet not only tactile sensations, but all other kinds of sensations, may pass gradually into pleasure and pain. Pleasure and pain also may be justly termed sensations. Only they are not so well analysed and so familiar as the common sensations. In fact, sensations of pleasure and pain, however faint they may be, really, make up the contents of all so-called emotions. Thus, perceptions, ideas, volition, and emotion, in short the whole inner and outer world, are composed of a small number of homogeneous elements connected in relations of varying evanescence or permanence. Usually, these elements are called sensations. But as vestiges of a one-sided theory inhere in that term, we prefer to speak simply of *elements*, as we have already done. The aim of all research is to ascertain the mode of connexion of these elements.[1]

11. That in this complex of elements, which fundamentally is *one*, the boundaries of bodies and of the ego do not admit of being established in a manner definite and sufficient for all cases, has already been remarked. The comprehending of the elements that are most intimately connected with pleasure and pain, under one ideal mental-economical unity, the ego, is a work of the highest significance for the intellect in the functions which

[1] Compare the note at the conclusion of my treatise, *Die Geschichte und die Wurzel des Satzes der Erhaltung der Arbeit*, Prague, Calve, 1872.

it performs for the pain-avoiding, pleasure-seeking will. The delimitation of the ego, therefore, is instinctively effected, is rendered familiar, and possibly becomes fixed through heredity. Owing to their high practical value, not only for the individual, but for the entire species, the composites "ego" and "body" assert instinctively their claims, and operate with all the power of natural elements. In special cases, however, in which practical ends are not concerned, but where knowledge is an object in itself, the delimitation in question may prove to be insufficient, obstructive, and untenable.[1]

The primary fact is not the *I*, the ego, but the elements (sensations). The elements *constitute* the *I*. That *I* have the sensation green, signifies that the element green occurs in a given complex of other elements (sensations, memories). When *I* cease to have the sensation green, when *I* die, then the elements no longer occur in their ordinary, familiar way of association. That is all. Only an ideal mental-economical unity, not a real unity, has ceased to exist.

If a knowledge of the connexion of the elements (sensations) does not suffice us, and we ask, *Who* possesses this connexion of sensations, *Who* experiences the sensations? then we have succumbed to the habit of subsuming every element (every sensation) under some *unanalysed* complex, and we are falling back imperceptibly upon an older, lower and more limited point of view.

The so-called unity of consciousness is not an argument in point. Since the apparent antithesis of *real* world and *perceived* world is due entirely to our mode of view, and no actual gulf

---

[1] Similarly, *esprit de corps*, class bias, national pride, and even the narrowest minded local patriotism may have a high value, *for certain purposes*. But such attitudes will not be shared by the broad-minded inquirer, at least not in moments of research. All such egoistic views are adequate only for practical purposes. Of course, even the inquirer may succumb to habit. Trifling pedantries and nonsensical discussions, the cunning appropriation of others' thoughts, with perfidious silence as to the sources, the metaphorical dysphagia suffered when recognition must be given, and the crooked illumination of others' performances when this is done, abundantly show that the scientist and scholar have also the battle of existence to fight, that the ways of science still lead to the mouth, and that the *pure* quest of knowledge in our present social conditions is still an ideal.

exists between them, a rich and variously interconnected content of consciousness is in no respect more difficult to understand than a rich and diversified interconnexion of the world.

If we regard the ego as a *real* unity, we become involved in the following dilemma: either we must set over against the ego a world of unknowable entities (which would be quite idle and purposeless), or we must regard the whole world, the egos of other people included, as comprised in our own ego (a proposition to which it is difficult to yield serious assent).

But if we take the ego simply as a *practical* unity, put together for purposes of provisional survey, or simply as a more strongly coherent group of elements, less strongly connected with other groups of this kind, questions like those above discussed will not arise and research will have an unobstructed future.

In his philosophical notes Lichtenberg says: "We become conscious of certain percepts that are not dependent upon us; of others that we at least think are dependent upon us. Where is the border-line? We know only the existence of our sensations, percepts, and thoughts. We should say, *It thinks*, just as we say, *it lightens*. It is going too far to say *cogito*, if we translate *cogito* by *I think*. The assumption, or postulation, of the ego is a mere practical necessity." Though the method by which Lichtenberg arrived at this result is somewhat different from ours, we must nevertheless give our full assent to his conclusion.

12. Bodies do not produce sensations, but complexes of sensations (complexes of elements) make up bodies. If, to the physicist, bodies appear the real, abiding existences, whilst sensations are regarded merely as their envanescent, transitory show, the physicist forgets, in the assumption of such a view, that all bodies are but thought-symbols for complexes of sensations (complexes of elements). Here, too, the *elements* form the real, immediate, and ultimate foundation, which it is the task of physiological research to investigate. By the recognition of this fact, many points of psychology and physics as-

sume more distinct and more economical forms, and many spurious problems are disposed of.

For us, therefore, the world does not consist of mysterious entities, which by their interaction with another, equally mysterious entity, the ego, produce sensations, which alone are accessible. For us, colors, sounds, spaces, times, . . . are the ultimate elements, whose given connexion it is our business to investigate. In this investigation we must not allow ourselves to be impeded by such intellectual abridgments and delimitations, as body, ego, matter, mind, etc., which have been formed for special, practical purposes and with wholly provisional and limited ends in view. On the contrary, the fittest forms of thought must be created in and by that research *itself*, just as is done in every special science. In place of the traditional, instinctive ways of thought, a freer, fresher view, conforming to developed experience, must be substituted.

13. Science always takes its origin in the adaptation of thought to some definite field of experience. The results of the adaptation are thought-elements, which are able to represent the field. The outcome, of course, is different, according to the character and extent of the province surveyed. If the province of experience in question is enlarged, or if several provinces heretofore disconnected are united, the traditional, familiar thought-elements no longer suffice for the extended province. In the struggle of acquired habit with the effort after adaptation, *problems* arise, which disappear when the adaptation is perfected, to make room for others which have arisen in the interim.

To the physicist, *quâ* physicist, the idea of "body" is productive of a real facilitation of view, and is not the cause of disturbance. So, also, the person with purely practical aims, is materially assisted by the idea of the *I* or ego. For, unquestionably, every form of thought that has been designedly or undesignedly constructed for a given purpose, possesses for that purpose a *permanent* value. When, however, research in physics and in psychology meets, the ideas held in the one domain prove to be untenable in the other. From the attempt at mutual adaptation arise the various atomic and monadic theories — which, however, never attain their end. If we regard *sensations*, in the sense above defined, as the *elements of the world*, the problems referred to are practically disposed of, and the *first* and most important adaptation effected. This fundamental view (without any pretension to being a philosophy for all eternity) can at present be adhered to in all provinces of experience; it is consequently the one that accommodates itself with the least expenditure of energy, that is, more economically than any other, to the present *temporary collective state of knowledge*. Furthermore, in the consciousness of its purely economical office, this fundamental view is eminently tolerant. It does not obtrude itself into provinces in which the current conceptions are still adequate. It is ever ready, upon subsequent extensions of the domain of experience, to yield the field to a better conception.

The philosophical point of view of the average man — if that term may be applied to the naïve realism of the ordinary individual — has a claim to the highest consideration. It has arisen in the process of immeasurable time without the conscious assistance of man. It is a product of nature, and is preserved and sustained by nature. Everything that philosophy has accomplished — the *biological* value of every advance, nay, of every error, admitted — is, as compared with it, but an insignificant and ephemeral product of art. The fact is, every thinker, every philosopher, the moment he is forced to abandon his narrow intellectual province by practical necessity, immediately returns to the universal point of view held by all men in common.

To discredit this point of view is not then the purpose of the foregoing "introductory remarks." The task which we have set ourselves is simply to show *why* and to what *purpose* for the greatest portion of life we hold it, and *why* and for what *purpose* we are provisorily obliged to abandon it. No point of view has absolute, *permanent* validity. Each has importance only for some given end.[1]

---

[1] A kindred view will be found in Avenarius, *Kritik der reinen Erfahrung.*

THE SPACE-SENSATIONS

1. THE tree with its hard, rough grey trunk, its numberless branches swayed by the wind, its smooth soft, shining leaves, appears to us at first a single, indivisible whole. In like manner, we regard the sweet, round, yellow fruit, the warm, bright fire, with its manifold moving tongues, as a single thing. One name designates the whole, one word draws forth from the depths of cblivion all associated memories, as if they were strung upon a single thread.

The reflexion of the tree, the fruit, or the fire in a mirror is visible, but not tangible. When we turn our glance away or close our eyes, we can touch the tree, taste the fruit, feel the fire, but we cannot see them. Thus the apparently indivisible thing is separated into parts, which are not only connected with one another but are also joined to *other* conditions. The visible is separable from the tangible, from that which may be tasted,

The visible also appears at first sight to be a single thing. But we may see a round, yellow fruit together with a yellow, star-shaped blossom. A second fruit is just as round as the first, but is green or red. Two things may be alike in color but unlike in form; they may be different in colour but like in form. Thus sensations of sight are separable into *color-sensations* and *space-sensations*.

2. Color-sensation, into the details of which we shall not enter here, is essentially a sensation of favorable or unfavorable *chemical* conditions of life. In the process of adaptation to these conditions, color-sensation may have been developed and modified. Light introduces organic life. The green chlorophyll and the (complementary) red hæmoglobin play a prominent part in the chemical processes of the plant-body and in the contrary processes of the animal body. The two substances present themselves to us in the most varied modifications of tint. The discovery of the visual purple, observations in photogra-

phy and photochemistry render the conception of processes of sight as chemical processes permissible. The rôle which color plays in analytical chemistry, in spectrum-analysis, in crystallography, is well known. It suggests a new conception for the so-called vibrations of light, according to which they are regarded, not as mechanical, but as chemical vibrations, as successive union and separation, as an oscillatory process of the same sort that takes place, though only in one direction, in photo-chemical phenomena. This conception, which is substantially supported by recent investigations in abnormal dispersion, accords with the electro-magnetic theory of light. In the case of electrolysis, in fact, chemistry yields the most intelligible conception of the electric current, regarding the two components of the electrolyte as passing through each other in opposite directions. It is likely, therefore, that in a future theory of colors, many biologico-psychological and chemico-physical threads will be united.

3. Adaptation to the chemical conditions of life which manifest themselves in color, renders *locomotion* necessary to a far greater extent than adaptation to those which manifest themselves through taste and smell. At least this is so in the case of man, concerning whom alone we are able to judge with immediacy and certainty. The close association of space-sensation (a mechanical factor) with color-sensation (a chemical factor) is herewith rendered intelligible. We shall now proceed to the analysis of space-sensations.

4. In examining two figures which are alike but differently colored (for example, two letters of the same size and shape, but

Fig. 1.

of different colors), we recognise their sameness of form at the first glance, in spite of the difference of color-sensation. The sight-perceptions, therefore, must contain some like sensation-components. These are the space-sensations — which are the same in the two cases.

5. We will now investigate the character of the space-sensations that physiologically condition the recognition of a figure. First, it is clear that this recognition is not the result of geometrical considerations — which are a matter, not of sensation, but of intellect. On the contrary, the space-sensations in question serve as the starting-point and foundation of all geometry. Two figures may be geometrically congruent, but physiologically quite different. . . .

6. In what, now, does the essential nature of optical similarity, as contrasted with geometrical similarity, consist? In geometrically similar figures, all homologous distances are proportional. But this is an affair of the intellect, not of sensation. If we place beside a triangle with the sides a, b, c, a triangle with the sides $2a$, $2b$, $2c$, we do not recognise the simple relation of the two immediately, but intellectually, by measurement. If the similiarity is to become optically perceptible, the proper position must be added. That a simple intellectual relationship of two objects does not necessarily condition a similarity of sensation, may be perceived by comparing two triangles having respectively the sides a, b, c, and $a+m$, $b+m$, $c+m$. The two triangles do not look at all alike. Similarly all conic sections do not look alike, although all stand in a simple *geometric* relation to each other; still less do curves of the third order exhibit optical similiarity; etc.

7. The geometrical similarity of two figures is determined by all their homologous lines being proportional or by all their homologous angles being equal. But to appear optically similar the figures must also be *similarly situated*, that is all their homologous lines must be parallel or, as we prefer to say, have the 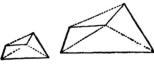 *same* direction (Fig. 2). By likeness of direction, accordingly, are determined like space-sensations, and these are characteristic of the physiologico-optical similarity of figures.

Fig. 2.

We may obtain an idea of the physiological significance of

the *direction* of a given straight line or curve-element, by the following reflexion. Let $y = f(x)$ be the equation of a plane curve. We can read at a glance the course of the values of dy/dx on the curve, for they are determined by its slope; and the eye gives us, likewise, qualitative information concerning the values of d^2y/dx^2, for they are characterised by the curvature. The question naturally presents itself why can we not arrive at as immediate conclusions concerning the values d^3y/dx^3, d^4y/dx^4, etc. The answer is easy. What we *see* are not the differential coefficients, which are an intellectual affair, but only the *direction* of the curve-elements, and the *declination* of the direction of one curve-element from that of another.

In fine, since we are immediately cognisant of the similarity of figures lying in similar positions, and are also able to distinguish without ado the special case of congruity, therefore our space-sensations yield us information concerning *likeness or unlikeness of directions and equality or inequality of spatial dimensions.*

8. It is extremely probable that sensations of space are produced by the motor apparatus of the eye. Without entering into particulars, we may observe, first, that the whole apparatus of the eye, and especially the motor apparatus, is symmetrical with respect to the median plane of the head. Hence, symmetrical movements of looking will determine like or approximately like space-sensations. Children constantly confound the letters *b* and *d*, as *p* and *q*. Adults, too, do not readily notice a change from left to right unless some special points of apprehension for sense or intellect render it perceptible. The symmetry of the motor apparatus of the eye is very perfect. The like excitation of its symmetrical organs would, by itself scarcely account for the distinction of right and left. But the whole human body, especially the brain, is affected with a slight asymmetry, — which leads, for example, to the preference of one (generally the right) hand, in motor functions. And this leads, again, to a further and better development of the motor functions of the right side, and to a modification of

the attendant sensations. After the space-sensations of the eye have become associated, through writing, with the motor functions of the right hand, a confusion of those vertically symmetrical figures with which the art and habit of writing are concerned no longer ensues. This association may, indeed, become so strong that remembrance follows only the accustomed tracks, and we read, for example, the reflexion of written or printed words in a mirror only with the greatest difficulty. The confusion of right and left still occurs, however, with regard to figures which have no motor, but only a purely optical (for example, ornamental) interest. A noticeable difference between right and left must be felt, moreover, by animals, as in many predicaments they have no other means of finding their way. The similarity of sensations connected with symmetrical motor functions is easily remarked by the attentive observer. If, for example, supposing my right hand to be employed, I grasp a micrometer-screw or a key with my left hand, I am certain (unless I reflect beforehand) to turn it in the wrong direction, — that is, I always perform the movement which is symmetrical to the usual movement, confusing the two because of the similarity of the sensation. The observations of Heidenhain regarding the reflected writing of persons hypnotised on one side should also be cited in this connexion.

With looking upwards and looking downwards, fundamentally different space-sensations are associated, as ordinary observations will show. This is, moreover, comprehensible, since the motor apparatus of the eye is asymmetrical with respect to a horizontal plane. The direction of gravity is so very decisive and important for the motor apparatus of the rest of the body that the same factor has assuredly also found its expression in the apparatus of the eye, which serves the rest. It is well known that the symmetry of a landscape and of its reflexion in water is not felt. The portrait of a familiar personage, when turned upside down, is strange and puzzling to a person who does not recognise it intellectually. If we place ourselves behind the head of a person lying upon a couch and unreflectingly give ourselves up to the impression which the face makes upon us,

we shall find that it is altogether strange, especially when the
person speaks. The letters *b* and *p*, and *d* and *q*, are not confused by children.

Our previous remarks concerning symmetry, similarity, and
the rest, naturally apply not only to plane figures, but also to
those in space. Hence, we have yet a remark to add concerning the sensation of space-depth. Looking at objects afar off
and looking at objects near at hand determine different sensations. These sensations *must* not be confused, because of the
supreme importance of the difference between near and far,
both for animals and human beings. They *cannot* be confused
because the motor apparatus is asymmetrical with respect to a
plane perpendicular to the direction from front to rear. The
observation that the bust of a familiar personage cannot be
replaced by the mould in which the bust is cast is quite
analogous to the observations consequent upon the inversion
of objects.

9. If equal distances and like directions excite like space-sensations, and directions symmetrical with respect to the median
plane of the head excite similar space-sensations, the explanation of the above-cited facts is not far to seek. The straight
line has, in all its elements, the same direction, and everywhere
excites the same space-sensations. Herein consists its æsthetic
value. Moreover, straight lines which lie in the median plane
or are perpendicular to it are brought into special relief by the
circumstance that, through this position of symmetry, they
occupy a like position to the two halves of the visual apparatus.
Every other position of the straight line is felt as awryness, or
as a deviation from the position of symmetry.

The repetition of the same space-figure in the same position
conditions a repetition of the same space-sensation. All lines
connecting prominent (noticeable) homologous points have the
same direction and excite the same sensation. Likewise when
merely geometrically similar figures are placed side by side in
the same positions, this relation holds. The sameness of the
dimensions alone is absent. But when the positions are dis-

turbed, this relation, and with it, the impression of unity —
the æsthetic impression — are also disturbed.

In a figure symmetrical with respect to the median plane,
similar space-sensations corresponding to the symmetrical directions take the place of the *identical* space-sensations. The
right half of the figure stands in the same relation to the right
half of the visual apparatus as the left half of the figure does to
the left half of the visual apparatus. If we alter the sameness
of the dimensions, the sensation of symmetrical similarity is
still felt. An oblique position of the plane of symmetry disturbs the whole effect.

If we turn a figure through 180°, contrasting it with itself in
its original position, centric symmetry is produced. That is, if
two pairs of homologous points be connected, the connecting
lines will cut each other at a point O, through which, as their
point of bisection, all lines connecting homologous points will
pass. Moreover, in the case of centric symmetry, all lines of
connexion between homologous points have the same direction,
— a fact which produces an agreeable sensation. If the sameness of the dimensions is eliminated, there still remains, for
sensation, centrically symmetrical similarity.

Regularity appears to have no special physiological value,
in distinction from symmetry. The value of regularity probably lies rather in its *manifold* symmetry, which is perceptible
in more than one *single* position.

10. The correctness of these observations will be apparent
on glancing over the work of Owen Jones — *A Grammar of
Ornament* (London, 1865). In almost every plate one finds
new and different kinds of symmetry as fresh testimony in
favor of the conceptions above advanced. The art of decoration, which, like pure instrumental music, aims at no ulterior
end, but ministers only to pleasure in form (and color), is
the best source of material for our present studies. Writing
is governed by other considerations than that of beauty.
Nevertheless, we find among the twenty-four large Latin letters
ten which are vertically symmetrical (A, H, I, M, O, T, V,

W, X, Y), five which are horizontally symmetrical (B, C, D, E, K), three which are centrically symmetrical (N, S, Z), and only six which are unsymmetrical (F, G, L, P, Q, R).

11. It is to be remarked again that the geometrical and the physiological properties of a figure in space are to be sharply distinguished. The physiological properties are determined by the geometrical properties coincidently with these, but are not determined by these solely. On the other hand, physiological properties very probably gave the first impulse to geometrical investigations. The straight line doubtless attracted attention not because of its being the shortest line between two points, but because of its physiological simplicity. The plane likewise possesses, in addition to its geometrical properties, a special physiologico-optical (æsthetic) value, which claims notice for it, as will be shown later on. The division of the plane and of space by right angles has not only the advantage of producing equal parts, but also an additional and special symmetry-value. The circumstance that congruent and similar geometrical figures can be brought into positions where their relationship is physiologically felt, led, no doubt, to an earlier investigation of these kinds of geometrical relationship than of those that are less noticeable, such as affinity, collineation, and others. Without the co-operation of sense-perception and understanding, a scientific geometry is inconceivable. . . .

CARL STUMPF
(1848–   )

THE PSYCHOLOGY OF TONE

Translated from the German* by

BENJAMIN RAND

§ 19. THE DEGREES OF TONAL FUSION

1. What tonal fusion is and what it is not.

Iт has already been mentioned in what precedes, that not
merely do simultaneous as contrasted with successive tones
enter into a special relation in sensation, which renders their
analysis difficult, but that also there are differences in this
respect among simultaneous tones, according to the numerical
ratio of their vibrations. We must now turn our attention to
this fact. I will first illustrate it by two extreme examples.

If two tones, the number of whose vibrations are related as
1:2, are simultaneously produced, they can be very imperfectly
discriminated in comparison with the case where, for example,
under otherwise precisely similar conditions, the ratio is as 40:77.
When I say, "imperfectly," I mean that the question is not as
to a difficulty, which might be overcome by increased attention
and practise, but as to an unchangeable characteristic of the material of sensation, which persists even after all other obstacles to
an analysis have been removed, and which, moreover, after the
analysis is completed and the tones clearly recognized as two,
can first likewise be perceived in itself. In 40:77 the tones in the
sensation appear so to speak farther apart than in the case of
1:2, so that in the first case even the unmusical person is less,
or not at all, in danger of taking them for one; whereas on the
contrary, the octave tones cannot be kept distinct even by the

* From C. Stumpf's *Tonpsychologie*, Leipzig, 1890, Bd. II.

most delicate and practised ear, in the same degree as those of the seventh, or of the unmusical relation 40:77. When the unpractised designate simultaneous octave tones as one tone, there is accordingly a double hindrance to analysis, namely: one an imperfect practise, and the other in the tone itself; one, which influences the judgment directly, and the other which influences the sensation and in consequence of it the judgment.

What is most essential for the general characterisation of the concept of *fusion*, as we understand it, has been fairly exhausted in what has been said,[1] and can be set forth still more clearly only in the more inclusive range of a universal theory of relations, which is one of the most urgent needs of philosophical science. We term fusion that relation of two contents, especially sensation-contents, in which they form not a mere sum, but a whole. The consequence of this relation is, that in its higher degrees the total impression under otherwise like conditions approaches more and more that of a single unified sensation, and becomes more and more difficult to analyze. These results can also be employed for a definition, and we can say: fusion is that relation of two sensations as a consequence of which, etc. But in either way, the matter would remain an empty concept for everyone to whom the phenomena in question, and especially the phenomena of tones, were foreign. The real truth of the assertion, that sensations form a whole and approximate more or less the impression of a single unified sensation, can after all be learned only by means of examples.

Nevertheless, I remark, that the inclusion of the concept of tonal fusion under that more general quality of simultaneous as opposed to successive sensations, of which we have elsewhere spoken, is not indispensable for what follows. The tonal fusion will acquire for us more and more an interest of its own, independent of the questions previously discussed (§ 16 and 17); and would also claim it even if a similar relation did not further occur in the entire domain of sensations. It is far from being an hypothesis devised for the solution of those difficulties. It is a sensuous phenomena which was observed even before those

---

[1] Cf. Stumpf's *Tonpsychologie*, p. 64 f.

theoretical difficulties appeared within the intellectual horizon. It suffices perfectly for the attainment of the concept here necessary, to perceive and in perceiving to contrast, the differences of the cases which exist already within the tonal domain, and which will be more accurately described in what follows. We must hear and compare tonal fusions, just as we must hear and contrast tones, in order to know what a tone is.

Perhaps, however, it is expedient to preclude expressly some misconceptions which the term *fusion* might occasion. It is precisely one of those psychological expressions which have been most misused, and to which the most impossible conceptions and entirely fictitious theories have become attached. For this reason I have chosen it with reluctance, owing to the lack of a safer and at the same time more specific word.

It is above all, therefore, not meant by fusion, that two simultaneous tones coalesce in a certain unity in consciousness only by degrees, however quickly. Fusion signifies to us here not a process, but a present relation. I would, therefore, rather use "blend" (Schmelz), or "coalescence" (Schmalz), if this had also not its objections. Such expressions also as "to separate" (auseinandertreten) etc., are to be understood in this sense of an already existent being; just as they are likewise used in the sense of rest in the description of architectonic forms.

That fusion is not to be viewed as originating a third tonal quality in addition to or instead of the other two, needs no farther amplification after what has preceded (§ 16 and 17).

Henceforth we must reject especially the metaphorical use of spatial concepts. The naturalist is accustomed to think of everything by the aid of spatial analogies; and psychologists also, like Herbart and Beneke, who desire to approach the exactness of natural science, employ them most extensively for their psychological descriptions (such as, falling and rising, overflowing, etc.). We are to disregard all such analogies as might erroneously suggest them. Everything extended in space is either outside, or identical with everything else. But simultaneous tones afford us an example of interpenetration; and, indeed, an interpenetration of a lower and higher degree. The lack of all spatial perceptibility is wholly immaterial. It is, however, wanting in the relation of quality and intensity. Spatial perceptivity ceases moreover with psychical states as such (cf. § 100-104). The concepts here too must be adapted to the observations. Only a contradiction is *a priori* an impossibility. But that the two tones are at the same time one, is not affirmed.

In general the difficulties, which one still could, and will find, in the concept of tonal fusion, as it is here understood, are bound to be of a similar kind and origin to those raised from time immemorial against the concept of motion. And as the physicist gets rid of these after the example of Diogenes, who stepping from his tub walked about with a "solvitur ambulando," so here in a similar manner the first thing we have to do is to oppose to all reasoning a "solvitur audiendo." But then here as there, it becomes evident that the difficulties are avoided, the moment that the mixture of heterogeneous concepts is avoided.

Finally it is to be remarked, that the expression and concept of fusion stands here in no relation, either essentially or historically, with the general psychological doctrine of Herbart, in which "fusion" plays such a prominent part; and which for the sake of clearness everyone, who has knowledge of it, is asked for the present to banish from his mind. In a subsequent chapter, where the cause and origin of fusion are treated, we will attempt to show how far Herbart's theory of fusion in general, and of tonal fusion in particular, is from being correct.

Our conception of fusion has also not many points of contact with the ideas which have been brought forward under the same name oftentimes in the most recent psychology, and in my judgment on every occasion is in contradiction with the truth.

· · · · · · · · · ·

2. *The Degrees of Fusion*

If in the first place we confine ourselves to a tonal domain, which is limited by the ratio of vibrations 1:2, I remark the following degrees of different tones, from the highest to the lowest.

First the fusion of the octave $(1:2)$.

Secondly that of the fifth $(2:3)$.

Thirdly that of the fourth $(3:4)$.

Fourthly that of the so-called natural thirds and sixths $(4:5, 5:6, 3:5, 5:8)$, between which I find in this respect no clear distinctions.

Fifthly that of all the remaining musical and unmusical tonal combinations, which, for my hearing at least, offer no discernible differences of fusion, but on the contrary all the least degree of it. At most the so-called natural seventh $(4:7)$ could indeed fuse somewhat more than the others.

If we employ here the modern names of the intervals, and the general expression *interval* itself, we do so not in any musical sense at all, but only to have a known and short term for the numerical relations of vibrations with which we are here concerned.

When we speak of *degrees* of fusion, we mean that we are dealing with the degrees of differences, which, as is well known, constantly pass over into one another, from the highest to the lowest degree. Further we make use also of the general expression *degrees of fusion*.

3. *The Laws of Fusion*

The dependence of the degrees of fusion upon the so-called ratio of vibrations is the principal law of tonal fusion. In addition to it stand the following:

(a) The degree of fusion is independent of the tonal region. In the lowest pitch, where analysis meets with difficulties, the recognition and comparison of degrees of fusion become naturally difficult and impossible. But where it is possible, we find the fusion unchanged with the change of pitch, so long only as the ratio of vibrations of the two tones remain the same.

Only in the very highest pitch, approximating about 4000 vibrations, that is, from the octave five tones above the staff upward, do the differences of fusion appear to me, so far as I have yet been able to observe, to vanish. With tuning-forks 2000: 3000 I still discern with full clearness the fusion of the fifth, whereas with 3000:5000, 5000:10000, etc., I can discern only the slightest degree of fusion at all.

(b) The degree of fusion is also independent of the strength, whether indeed it be the absolute or the relative strength. That it is not changed by the mere change of the absolute strength of the two tones is at once clear. With the change of relative strength it is again noteworthy, that ultimately analysis becomes impossible with great difference of strength, since the softer is suppressed by the stronger tone, so far as perception or even sensation is concerned. But so long as they remain distinguishable, I cannot notice any change of the degree of fusion. For example, if I make c and g at first of equal strength, then c noticeably stronger than g, or the reverse.

(c) The degree of fusion of two given tones is in no way influenced by the addition at pleasure of a third and fourth tone. Indeed, a consonance is so much the less easily analyzed, the more tones it contains, and becomes at last wholly confused and not analysable. But so long as two tones are at all distinguishable in a composite sound, their fusion also is recognised as the same as if the two alone were sounded.

In this proposition together with (b), there is also expressed the fact, that the overtones especially, and thereby the timbre, make no change in the ratio of two fundamental tones of musical sounds, as is also confirmed by direct observation.

(d) As in general the changes of stimulus below a certain degree effect no perceptible changes of sensation, so likewise very minute deviations of the number of vibrations from the abovementioned ratios create no perceptible change of the degree of fusion. If the deviation is increased, the fusion in all pairs of tones which do not belong to the very lowest degree of fusion, passes into this degree without running through the intermediate degrees, if any. And this transition occurs the more rapidly, (with the smaller relative differences of vibrations), the greater was the initial fusion.

We say, as is known in the case of small but perceptible deviations, that the interval is "out of tune" or "impure." This saying possesses, as we may remark by anticipation, not merely a reference to the disagreeable feeling which is only a consequence of perception, but above all to an actual and perceived behavior of sensations.

With regard to the size of the deviation in which the change of the degree of fusion is discernible, practise besides other circumstances (e.g., pitch) makes a difference. But this forms no objection to the definition of the degree of fusion as a fact of sensation. As a sensation itself can change, so also can the ratio of two sensations, without the change being remarked; and this can be imperceptible to another through the equality of sensations, (not merely of stimuli).

(e) The fusion remains and retains its degree when both tones do not affect the same ear, but one is presented exclusively to the right, the other exclusively to the left. A tuning-fork of medium pitch, that is not sounded too loud, held before one ear is not perceived by the other, as we discover from the fact, that if the first is stopped up nothing is heard. If now we apply two forks which for example form a fifth, one to each ear, no difference is observable between this fusion, and the perception by one and the same ear. On the contrary, the analysis can be facilitated by this process (cf § 23, 1 and 24, a).

(f) Fusion remains also in the mere representation of the imagination. If I merely represent c and g as sounding at the same time, I can conceive them only as fusing, and indeed with the definite degree of fusion which they possess in the actual hearing. The same is true of any other two tones. A priori this is not necessarily to be expected, even if we recognise sensations and representations of the imagination in general as similar. Not all properties of simultaneous sensations pass over of necessity to the representation of the imagination: c and c sharp in actual hearing (upon the same ear) necessarily make vibrations, but in the imagination I can represent them perfectly without vibrations. Moreover, if I represent them as vibrating, I can represent them with slow or quick, strong or weak vibrations; whilst the choice of the degree of fusion is not free to me.

In regard to the representation of the imagination we must accordingly complete the fundamental law as follows: Tones represented as simultaneous fuse in the degree which corresponds to the ratio of vibration of tones of the same pitch created objectively.

(g) If we proceed above an octave, the same degrees of fusion recur with the rates of vibration increased one or more octaves. The ninths have the same fusion as the seconds, the tenths as the thirds, the double and triple octave as the octave; and in general $m:n.2^x$, the same as $m:n$, if $m < n$ and x a small whole number.

We must not be misled here by the greater ease of the analysis. C and c^4 sounding together are more easily and certainly analyzed by the unmusical than C and c, even than C and G; although these two tones fuse less with one another than the former. The analysis depends upon very different conditions; it is peculiarly difficult especially in the lowest register; it is further facilitated by increase in the difference of pitch of the two tones. But if analysis takes place in both cases, we shall also further find, that C and c^4 are nevertheless in sensuous impression less perfectly sundered than C and G, and not more perfectly than C and c.

If I compare the sounds of the tuning-fork CG with Cg, CA with Ca, etc., it is evident to me, that detection of difference between every second combination is always easier, but the fusion is the same as in the first.

If I play upon the d^1 string of the violin the octave d^1, and then the double octave d^2 (on the a^1 string), I have in both cases the same impression of homogeneity and of approximation to a real tonal unity. We can always for sake of contrast play the d in question with the free e^2 string; the difference of the fusion is always the same, that of the highest and of the lowest degree.

If an orchestra plays the entire 7 octave tones from C up to c^5, we still designate the impression as *unison*. The seven tones are more homogeneous than the two tones c and a, to say nothing of c and b. We cannot here assume as true, that only the two neighboring members of the series always fuse with one another, C with c, c with c^1, etc., and that the farther removed do so only by means of the intermediate; for if C and c^5 fuse by themselves less than C and c, or even c and g, this could not be changed by means of the intervening octaves, according to (c).

Moreover, the special laws enunciated in the preceding principles can be directly observed in the enlarged intervals themselves. For example, this is true of that presented under (b), the recognition of which with many possibly meets with difficulties. Play upon the piano first c alone and observe the overtone g^1 (the twelfth), which we clearly hear sound at the same time, in respect to its fusion with the fundamental tone. Now add g^1, by means of which this tone, too, becomes noticeably strengthened: the fusion with c remains unchanged. The fusion, therefore, in the intervals beyond the octave is independent also of the relation of strength.

4. Rules of observation

Those who are skilled in the judgment of tones can test, whether what precedes corresponds to their own perceptions. Where it is a question of relations which are based on the material of sensation itself, there is, indeed, no fear that very great individual differences will appear in those hearing normally. It is rather to be expected, that those capable of judgment will find among themselves more and more harmony, the longer and more carefully they examine. But I will not by any means claim to have found the correct solution in each of the mentioned points, and to have expressed it in an entirely correct manner.

It is necessary in these observations above everything to direct the attention exclusively upon the point in question, especially, therefore, to disregard theoretical knowledge of relationship, etc., as well as of the musical significance and position; and also to disregard the impression of feeling of an interval, whether it be harmonious or unharmonious, agreeable or disagreeable, and furthermore in a different way agreeable or disagreeable. The character and value of the feeling of an interval depends, indeed, as we shall show later, upon its degree of fusion; but yet not solely upon this. The most agreeable interval is not one of strongest fusion. The great seventh is in isolated state more disagreeable than the small; and this cannot be mistaken for a lesser fusion, or explained by that. It has other grounds. The same is true of the great and small third, etc.

In general it will also be well first to take tones of the same sensation-strength, because then the danger is best avoided that any one of them should remain totally imperceptible or obscure. In order to produce similar strength of sensation in large intervals of tone, one must frequently — according to the instrument — give the higher tone with less physical strength. Further the greatest possible similarity in the initial utterance and duration of tone is naturally preferable, since inequalities of every kind divert the attention. Likewise, similar tone color is desirable, although this is of no influence in the fusion of the keynotes. Purity of interval, that is, exact harmony with the respective numbers of vibrations, is so much the more necessary, the more acute the hearing; although minimal variations, which can never be avoided, do no important injury to the fusion particularly in the lower grades. The piano with its tempered pitch permits the differences of the higher degrees still to appear (the octave is even here pure); but not between the last two degrees. It is even here $c:d$ sharp $= c:e$ flat, and $c:g$ sharp $= c:a$ flat.

But all these are measures of the kind that are matters of course for every observation. Nobody affirms that the phenomenon would be perceptible under only especially chosen circumstances. It is on the contrary in itself one of the most obvious, and so to speak most unavoidable, in the whole subject of unison. The entire task consists only in not confounding it with others which are based upon it, particularly with facts of judgment and of feeling (possibility and impossibility of analysis, pleasurableness and impleasureableness of an interval).

5. *Confirmation through unmusical persons*

For the guidance of my own judgment I have pursued still another method. As the question is here put, it can only be addressed to those who are sufficiently endowed with power of tonal observations to analyze the fifths and octaves easily and directly. With such there exists only the difficulty last mentioned, and many times previously touched upon, as to the dominating consciousness of the harmonious character and sensation-value of the interval. But we can obtain information also in an indirect way through unmusical persons, and those unpractised in the judgment of tones: by means of the use of the aforementioned difficulty of analysis. The different degrees of fusion must reveal themselves in the different degrees of difficulty of analysis, if all the remaining circumstances upon which the latter depend are taken precisely equal. We shall recognise them in the results. In this way we can even obtain figures, by the enumeration of correct and false judgments, upon the question, whether one or more tones are present in each interval. The combinations of more strongly fusing tones under otherwise similar conditions will more rarely be judged to be two tones than those fusing less strongly.

. . . .

§ 20. THE CAUSE OF TONAL FUSION

6. *The cause of fusion is physiological*

All the attempts at the explanation of tonal fusion previously considered have been psychological. Their failure signifies, that we can by no means seek the source of tonal fusion in the psychological domain. In favor of this view from the outset appeared to be the circumstance, that such tonal fusion is a fact of sensation, a relation immanent in simultaneous tonal qualities, and independent of practice in the individual life. But relations of sensation, like the sensations themselves, are not referable to more remote causes, but only to physical.

The physically objective characteristics of successive waves do not help us at all. To be sure, the total wave formed by two waves in the ratio 1:2 is most similar to the simple sine-wave; then follows 2:3, 3:4, etc. more and more complicated forms. But these objective relations are, as was previously remarked, neither themselves the content of any sensation, nor the immediate cause of one; but on the contrary, they lie far back in the chain of causes. Moreover, if we consider it more closely from that standpoint, we find, that the so-called characteristic of the vibrations of the air disappear in the organ, if it is true here that every compound vibration is resolved into simple vibrations. Also as was previously mentioned, the circumstance that colors in which objectively the selfsame relations of vibrations occur, (1:2 in the extreme outer colors of the spectrum, 2:3 in blue and red, orange and indigo-violet, greenish-blue, and extreme red), reveal no phenomenon analogous to the tonal fusion, must prevent the objective forms of the waves from being made in any way responsible for the fusion.

That also within the organ, especially of the labyrinth in the ear, the physical processes do not yet possess that characteristic which corresponds to the fusion of the tones in sensation, appears not merely from the just-mentioned isolated transmission but also from the fact, that the fusion is perceptible in the same way when the two tones are divided between the two ears, as well as when they are merely imagined. At least it would be a violent and improbable assumption, that the process creating fusion in the case of simultaneous hearing occurs in the ear itself, but in the division of the tones occurs first in the brain.

Certain differences in the last processes of the centre of hearing must therefore correspond to the differences in the degrees of fusion as a physical correlate, or as a cause, (according as one thinks in a monistic or a dualistic way). But we know nothing of what nature these differences are, for this reason, if for no other, that in general we know nothing concerning the nature of the last processes. Indeed I must say, that although up to a certain point we can express in physical or chemical terms the occurrence of vibrations, competition, contrast, and other phenomena, in respect to the processes of the brain, which might lie at the basis of the phenomena of fusion, such a hypothetical image does not even occur to me. Perhaps the practised fancy of certain mind readers will succeed better. But who knows, whether we shall not find ourselves gradually induced to recast or to extend our fundamental physical conceptions. Is it then *a priori* certain that the world beyond consciousness, (to which the brain indeed belongs), is spatial, and only spatial, or may be so conceived? Spatial properties are nothing but a small part of those which we abstract from our sense perceptions. We have found them serviceable for the rational construction of the external world, and for the derivation of its laws. But all other qualitative and remaining moments and relations of sensations have of themselves the same right to be transferred to the external world. And possibly fusion is itself destined sometime to participate in this dignity; perchance in application to chemical processes. But this is a mere play with the possibilities of thought, and we will not in place of physiological indulge in metaphysiological fancies.

If we are willing in the lack of adequate apprehension to content ourselves with an abstract notion (which after all is nothing but a word), we might once more speak of specific energies. The specific energies, which lie at the foundation of fusion, have only this peculiarity, that they are not aroused by means of isolated stimuli, but by the concurrence of two stimuli. For this reason, we can call them specific energies of a higher rank, or still better, *specific synergies.* By such specific synergy we should therefore understand a determinate mode of coöperation of two nervous formations, having its ground in the structure of the brain, of such a kind that whenever these two formations produce their corresponding sensations, there arises at the same time a determinate degree of fusion of these sensations. As adequate and inadequate stimuli are distinguished in the production of sensations, by means of both of which nevertheless one and the same quality of sensation is produced; so likewise a determinate degree of fusion is here not united as such exclusively and unconditionally to the "adequate" stimulus-relation, (e.g., $1:2$), but the same specific synergy can also, by way of exception, be aroused by another objective relation of vibration, and the octave relation, etc., be established in the sensation. On the other hand, these specific energies of higher rank are, to be sure, inseparably united with those of the first rank: for the fusion reveals itself constantly as the same between two determinate qualities of tone.

That fusion remains preserved in imagination, is not opposed to what has been said, but is only a new example in proof of the fact, that the mere ideas of the imagination have themselves a physical basis, and indeed in general the same as the sensations.

In contrast to the theories of fusion already summarized, which give a very exact explanation concerning the process, our formulation must appear slight. But we would prefer honorable poverty to suspicious wealth, and remain mindful of the fact, that everywhere no other formulation than one in such general and abstract terms, is as yet certainly possible for the immediate and ultimate bases of our entire sensational life.

WILLIAM JAMES
(1842–1910)

PSYCHOLOGY *

CHAPTER XI.† THE STREAM OF CONSCIOUS-
NESS

The order of our study must be analytic. We are now prepared to begin the introspective study of the adult consciousness itself. Most books adopt the so-called synthetic method.
Starting with ' simple ideas of sensation,' and regarding these
as so many atoms, they proceed to build up the higher states of
mind out of their ' association,' ' integration,' or ' fusion,' as
houses are built by the agglutination of bricks. This has the
didactic advantages which the synthetic method usually has.
But it commits one beforehand to the very questionable theory
that our higher states of consciousness are compounds of units;
and instead of starting with what the reader directly knows,
namely his total concrete states of mind, it starts with a set of
supposed ' simple ideas ' with which he has no immediate
acquaintance at all, and concerning whose alleged interactions
he is much at the mercy of any plausible phrase. On every
ground, then, the method of advancing from the simple to the
compound exposes us to illusion. All pedants and abstrac-
tionists will naturally hate to abandon it. But a student who
loves the fulness of human nature will prefer to follow the
' analytic' method, and to begin with the most concrete facts,
those with which he has a daily acquaintance in his own inner
life. The analytic method will discover in due time the ele-

* New York, Henry Holt and Company, 1892.
† This chapter first appeared in substance as an article *On Some Omissions
of Introspective Psychology* in *Mind* for January, 1884; and again as a chapter
on *The Stream of Thought* in the author's *Principles of Psychology* in 1890.

mentary parts, if such exist, without danger of precipitate assumption. The reader will bear in mind that our own chapters on sensation have dealt mainly with the physiological conditions thereof. They were put first as a mere matter of convenience, because incoming currents come first. *Psychologically* they might better have come last. Pure sensations were described [*Psychology*, page 12] as processes which in adult life are well-nigh unknown, and nothing was said which could for a moment lead the reader to suppose that they were the *elements of composition* of the higher states of mind.

The Fundamental Fact. — The first and foremost concrete fact which every one will affirm to belong to his inner experience is the fact that *consciousness of some sort goes on.* ' *States of mind* ' *succeed each other in him.* If we could say in English ' it thinks,' as we say ' it rains ' or ' it blows,' we should be stating the fact most simply and with the minimum of assumption. As we cannot, we must simply say that *thought goes on.*

Four Characters in Consciousness. — How does it go on? We notice immediately four important characters in the process, of which it shall be the duty of the present chapter to treat in a general way:

(1) Every ' state ' tends to be part of a personal consciousness.

(2) Within each personal consciousness states are always changing.

(3) Each personal consciousness is sensibly continuous.

(4) It is interested in some parts of its object to the exclusion of others, and welcomes or rejects — *chooses* from among them, in a word — all the while.

In considering these four points successively, we shall have to plunge *in medias res* as regards our nomenclature and use psychological terms which can only be adequately defined in later chapters of the book. But every one knows what the terms mean in a rough way; and it is only in a rough way that we are now to take them. This chapter is like a painter's first charcoal sketch upon his canvas, in which no niceties appear.

When I say *every* ' *state* ' *or* ' *thought* ' *is part of a personal consciousness,* ' personal consciousness ' is one of the terms in question. Its meaning we know so long as no one asks us to define it, but to give an accurate account of it is the most difficult of philosophic tasks. This task we must confront in the next chapter; here a preliminary word will suffice.

In this room — this lecture-room, say — there are a multitude of thoughts, yours and mine, some of which cohere mutually, and some not. They are as little each-for-itself and reciprocally independent as they are all-belonging-together. They are neither: no one of them is separate, but each belongs with certain others and with none beside. My thought belongs with *my* other thoughts, and your thought with *your* other thoughts. Whether anywhere in the room there be a *mere* thought, which is nobody's thought, we have no means of ascertaining, for we have no experience of its like. The only states of consciousness that we naturally deal with are found in personal consciousnesses, minds, selves, concrete particular I's and you's.

Each of these minds keeps its own thoughts to itself. There is no giving or bartering between them. No thought even comes into direct *sight* of a thought in another personal consciousness than its own. Absolute insulation, irreducible pluralism, is the law. It seems as if the elementary psychic fact were not *thought* or *this thought* or *that thought,* but *my thought,* every thought being *owned.* Neither contemporaneity, nor proximity in space, nor similarity of quality and content are able to fuse thoughts together which are sundered by this barrier of belonging to different personal minds. The breaches between such thoughts are the most absolute breaches in nature. Every one will recognize this to be true, so long as the existence of *something* corresponding to the term ' personal mind ' is all that is insisted on, without any particular view of its nature being implied. On these terms the personal self rather than the thought might be treated as the immediate datum in psychology. The universal conscious fact is not ' feelings and thoughts exist,' but ' I think ' and ' I feel.' No psychology, at any rate, can question the *existence* of personal selves. Thoughts connected as we feel them to be connected are *what we mean* by

personal selves. The worst a psychology can do is so to interpret the nature of these selves as to rob them of their *worth*.

Consciousness is inconstant change. — I do not mean by this
to say that no one state of mind has any duration — even if
true, that would be hard to establish. What I wish to lay stress
on is this, that *no state once gone can recur and be identical with
what it was before*. Now we are seeing, now hearing; now reasoning, now willing; now recollecting, now expecting; now loving, now hating; and in a hundred other ways we know our
minds to be alternately engaged. But all these are complex
states, it may be said, produced by combination of simpler
ones; — do not the simpler ones follow a different law? Are not
the *sensations* which we get from the same object, for example,
always the same? Does not the same piano-key, struck with
the same force, make us hear in the same way? Does not the
same grass give us the same feeling of green, the same sky the
same feeling of blue, and do we not get the same olfactory sensation no matter how many times we put our nose to the same
flask of cologne? It seems a piece of metaphysical sophistry to
suggest that we do not; and yet a close attention to the matter
shows that *there is no proof that an incoming current ever gives us
just the same bodily sensation twice*.

What is got twice is the same OBJECT. We hear the same *note*
over and over again; we see the same *quality* of green, or smell
the same objective perfume, or experience the same *species* of
pain. The realities, concrete and abstract, physical and ideal,
whose permanent existence we believe in, seem to be constantly
coming up again before our thought, and lead us, in our care-
lessness, to suppose that our 'ideas' of them are the same
ideas. When we come, some time later, to the chapter on Perception, we shall see how inveterate is our habit of simply using
our sensible impressions as stepping-stones to pass over to the
recognition of the realities whose presence they reveal. The
grass out of the window now looks to me of the same green in
the sun as in the shade, and yet a painter would have to paint
one part of it dark brown, another part bright yellow, to give
its real sensational effect. We take no heed, as a rule, of the dif-

ferent way in which the same things look and sound and smell at different distances and under different circumstances. The sameness of the *things* is what we are concerned to ascertain; and any sensations that assure us of that will probably be considered in a rough way to be the same with each other. This is what makes off-hand testimony about the subjective identity of different sensations well-nigh worthless as a proof of the fact. The entire history of what is called Sensation is a commentary on our inability to tell whether two sensible qualities received apart are exactly alike. What appeals to our attention far more than the absolute quality of an impression is its *ratio* to whatever other impressions we may have at the same time. When everything is dark a somewhat less dark sensation makes us see an object white. Helmholtz calculates that the white marble painted in a picture representing an architectural view by moonlight is, when seen by daylight, from ten to twenty thousand times brighter than the real moonlit marble would be.

Such a difference as this could never have been *sensibly* learned; it had to be inferred from a series of indirect considerations. These make us believe that our sensibility is altering all the time, so that the same object cannot easily give us the same sensation over again. We feel things differently accordingly as we are sleepy or awake, hungry or full, fresh or tired; differently at night and in the morning, differently in summer and in winter; and above all, differently in childhood, manhood, and old age. And yet we never doubt that our feelings reveal the same world, with the same sensible qualities and the same sensible things occupying it. The difference of the sensibility is shown best by the difference of our emotion about the things from one age to another, or when we are in different organic moods. What was bright and exciting becomes weary, flat, and unprofitable. The bird's song is tedious, the breeze is mournful, the sky is sad.

To these indirect presumptions that our sensations, following the mutations of our capacity for feeling, are always undergoing an essential change, must be added another presumption, based on what must happen in the grain. Every sensation corresponds to some cerebral action. For an identical sensation to recur it would have to occur the second time *in an unmodified brain*. But as this, strictly speaking, is a physiological impossibility, so is an unmodified feeling an impossibility; for to every brain-modification, however small, we suppose that there must correspond a change of equal amount in the consciousness which the brain subserves.

But if the assumption of ' simple sensations ' recurring in immutable shape is so easily shown to be baseless, how much more baseless is the assumption of immutability in the larger masses of our thought!

For there it is obvious and palpable that our state of mind is never precisely the same. Every thought we have of a given fact is, strictly speaking, unique, and only bears a resemblance of kind with our other thoughts of the same fact. When the identical fact recurs, we *must* think of it in a fresh manner, see it under a somewhat different angle, apprehend it in different relations from those in which it last appeared. And the thought by which we cognize it is the thought of it-in-those-relations, a thought suffused with the consciousness of all that dim context. Often we are ourselves struck at the strange differences in our successive views of the same thing. We wonder how we ever could have opined as we did last month about a certain matter. We have outgrown the possibility of that state of mind, we know not how. From one year to another we see things in new lights. What was unreal has grown real, and what was exciting is insipid. The friends we used to care the world for are shrunken to shadows; the women once so divine, the stars, the woods, and the waters, how now so dull and common! — the young girls that brought an aura of infinity, at present hardly distinguishable existences; the pictures so empty; and as for the books, what *was* there to find so mysteriously significant in Goethe, or in John Mill so full of weight? Instead of all this, more zestful than ever is the work, the work; and fuller and deeper the import of common duties and of common goods.

I am sure that this concrete and total manner of regarding the mind's changes is the only true manner, difficult as it may be to carry it out in detail. If anything seems obscure about it, it will grow clearer as we advance. Meanwhile, if it be true, it is certainly also true that no two ' ideas ' are ever exactly the same, which is the proposition we started to prove. The proposition is more important theoretically than it at first sight seems. For it makes it already impossible for us to follow obediently in the footprints of either the Lockian or the Herbartian school, schools which have had almost unlimited influence in Germany and among ourselves. No doubt it is often *convenient* to formulate the mental facts in an atomistic sort of way, and to treat the higher states of consciousness as if they were all built out of unchanging simple ideas which ' pass and turn again.' It is convenient often to treat curves as if they were composed of small straight lines, and electricity and nerve-force as if they were fluids. But in the one case as in the other we must never forget that we are talking symbolically, and that there is nothing in nature to answer to our words. *A permanently existing ' Idea ' which makes its appearance before the footlights of consciousness at periodical intervals is as mythological an entity as the Jack of Spades.*

Within each personal consciousness, thought is sensibly continuous. — I can only define ' continuous ' as that which is without breach, crack, or division. The only breaches that can well be conceived to occur within the limits of a single mind would either be *interruptions, time*-gaps during which the consciousness went out; or they would be breaks in the content of the thought, so abrupt that what followed had no connection whatever with what went before. The proposition that consciousness feels continuous, means two things:

a. That even where there is a time-gap the consciousness after it feels as if it belonged together with the consciousness before it, as another part of the same self;

b. That the changes from one moment to another in the quality of the consciousness are never absolutely abrupt.

The case of the time-gaps, as the simplest, shall be taken first.

a. When Paul and Peter wake up in the same bed, and recognize that they have been asleep, each one of them mentally reaches back and makes connection with but *one* of the two streams of thought which were broken by the sleeping hours. As the current of an electrode buried in the ground unerringly finds its way to its own similarly buried mate, across no matter how much intervening earth; so Peter's present instantly finds out Peter's past, and never by mistake knits itself on to that of Paul. Paul's thought in turn is as little liable to go astray. The past thought of Peter is appropriated by the present Peter alone. He may have a *knowledge*, and a correct one too, of what Paul's last drowsy states of mind were as he sank into sleep, but it is an entirely different sort of knowledge from that which he has of his own last states. He *remembers* his own states, whilst he only *conceives* Paul's. Remembrance is like direct feeling; its object is suffused with a warmth and intimacy to which no object of mere conception ever attains. This quality of warmth and intimacy and immediacy is what Peter's *present* thought also possesses for itself. So sure as this present is me, is mine, it says, so sure is anything else that comes with the same warmth and intimacy and immediacy, me and mine. What the qualities called warmth and intimacy may in themselves be will have to be matter for future consideration. But whatever past states appear with those qualities must be admitted to receive the greeting of the present mental state, to be owned by it, and accepted as belonging together with it in a common self. This community of self is what the time-gap cannot break in twain, and is why a present thought, although not ignorant of the time-gap, can still regard itself as continuous with certain chosen portions of the past.

Consciousness, then, does not appear to itself chopped up in bits. Such words as 'chain' or 'train' do not describe it fitly —as it presents itself in the first instance. It is nothing jointed; it flows. A 'river' or a 'stream' are the metaphors by which it is most naturally described. *In talking of it hereafter, let us call it the stream of thought, of consciousness, or of subjective life.*

b. But now there appears, even within the limits of the same self, and between thoughts all of which alike have this same sense of belonging together, a kind of jointing and separateness among the parts, of which this statement seems to take no account. I refer to the breaks that are produced by sudden *contrasts in the quality* of the successive segments of the stream of thought. If the words ' chain ' and ' train ' had no natural fitness in them, how came such words to be used at all? Does not a loud explosion rend the consciousness upon which it abruptly breaks, in twain? No; for even into our awareness of the thunder the awareness of the previous silence creeps and continues; for what we hear when the thunder crashes is not thunder *pure*, but thunder-breaking-upon-silence-and-contrasting-with-it. Our feeling of the same objective thunder, coming in this way, is quite different from what it would be were the thunder a continuation of previous thunder. The thunder itself we believe to abolish and exclude the silence; but the *feeling* of the thunder is also a feeling of the silence as just gone; and it would be difficult to find in the actual concrete consciousness of man a feeling so limited to the present as not to have an inkling of anything that went before.

' Substantive ' and ' Transitive ' States of Mind. — When we take a general view of the wonderful stream of our consciousness, what strikes us first is the different pace of its parts. Like a bird's life, it seems to be an alternation of flights and perchings. The rhythm of language expresses this, where every thought is expressed in a sentence, and every sentence closed by a period. The resting-places are usually occupied by sensorial imaginations of some sort, whose peculiarity is that they can be held before the mind for an indefinite time, and contemplated without changing; the places of flight are filled with thoughts of relations, static or dynamic, that for the most part obtain between the matters contemplated in the periods of comparative rest.

Let us call the resting-places the ' substantive parts,' and the places of flight the ' transitive parts,' of the stream of thought. It then appears that our thinking tends at all times towards some other substantive part than the one from which it has just been dislodged. And we may say that the main use of the transitive parts is to lead us from one substantive conclusion to another.

Now it is very difficult, introspectively, to see the transitive parts for what they really are. If they are but flights to a conclusion, stopping them to look at them before the conclusion is reached is really annihilating them. Whilst if we wait till the conclusion *be* reached, it so exceeds them in vigor and stability that it quite eclipses and swallows them up in its glare. Let anyone try to cut a thought across in the middle and get a look at its section, and he will see how difficult the introspective observation of the transitive tracts is. The rush of the thought is so headlong that it almost always brings us up at the conclusion before we can arrest it. Or if our purpose is nimble enough and we do arrest it, it ceases forthwith to be itself. As a snowflake crystal caught in the warm hand is no longer a crystal but a drop, so, instead of catching the feeling of relation moving to its term, we find we have caught some substantive thing, usually the last word we were pronouncing, statically taken, and with its function, tendency, and particular meaning in the sentence quite evaporated. The attempt at introspective analysis in these cases is in fact like seizing a spinning top to catch its motion, or trying to turn up the gas quickly enough to see how the darkness looks. And the challenge to *produce* these transitive states of consciousness, which is sure to be thrown by doubting psychologists at anyone who contends for their existence, is as unfair as Zeno's treatment of the advocates of motion, when, asking them to point out in what place an arrow *is* when it moves, he argues the falsity of their thesis from their inability to make to so preposterous a question an immediate reply.

The results of this introspective difficulty are baleful. If to hold fast and observe the transitive parts of thought's stream be so hard, then the great blunder to which all schools are liable must be the failure to register them, and the undue emphasizing of the more substantive parts of the stream. Now the blunder has historically worked in two ways. One set of thinkers have been led by it to *Sensationalism*. Unable to lay their hands on any substantive feelings corresponding to the innumerable relations and forms of connection between the sensible things of the world, finding no *named* mental states mirroring such relations, they have for the most part denied that any such states exist; and many of them, like Hume, have gone on to deny the reality of most relations *out* of the mind as well as in it. Simple substantive ' ideas,' sensations and their copies, juxtaposed like dominoes in a game, but really separate, everything else verbal illusion, — such is the upshot of this view. The *Intellectualists*, on the other hand, unable to give up the reality of relations *extra mentem*, but equally unable to point to any distinct substantive feelings in which they were known, have made the same admission that such feelings do not exist. But they have drawn an opposite conclusion. The relations must be known, they say, in something that is no feeling, no mental ' state,' continuous and consubstantial with the subjective tissue out of which sensations and other substantive conditions of consciousness are made. They must be known by something that lies on an entirely different plane, by an *actus purus* of Thought, Intellect, or Reason, all written with capitals and considered to mean something unutterably superior to any passing perishing fact of sensibility whatever.

But from our point of view both Intellectualists and Sensationalists are wrong. If there be such things as feelings at all, *then so surely as relations between objects exist* in rerum naturâ, *so surely, and more surely, do feelings exist to which these relations are known*. There is not a conjunction or a preposition, and hardly an adverbial phrase, syntactic form, or inflection of voice, in human speech, that does not express some shading or other of relation which we at some moment actually feel to exist between the larger objects of our thought. If we speak objectively, it is the real relations that appear revealed; if we speak subjectively, it is the stream of consciousness that matches each of them by an inward coloring of its own. In either case the relations are numberless, and no existing language is capable of doing justice to all their shades.

We ought to say a feeling of *and*, a feeling of *if*, a feeling of *but*, and a feeling of *by*, quite as readily as we say a feeling of *blue* or a feeling of *cold*. Yet we do not: so inveterate has our habit become of recognizing the existence of the substantive parts alone, that language almost refuses to lend itself to any other use. Consider once again the analogy of the brain. We believe the brain to be an organ whose internal equilibrium is always in a state of change — the change affecting every part. The pulses of change are doubtless more violent in one place than in another, their rhythm more rapid at this time than at that. As in a kaleidoscope revolving at a uniform rate, although the figures are always rearranging themselves, there are instants during which the transformation seems minute and interstitial and almost absent, followed by others when it shoots with magical rapidity, relatively stable forms thus alternating with forms we should not distinguish if seen again; so in the brain the perpetual rearrangement must result in some forms of tension lingering relatively long, whilst others simply come and pass. But if consciousness corresponds to the fact of rearrangement itself, why, if the rearrangement stop not, should the consciousness ever cease? And if a lingering rearrangement brings with it one kind of consciousness, why should not a swift rearrangement bring another kind of consciousness as peculiar as the rearrangement itself?

The object before the mind always has a 'Fringe.' — There are other unnamed modifications of consciousness just as important as the transitive states, and just as cognitive as they. Examples will show what I mean.

Suppose three successive persons say to us: 'Wait!' 'Hark!' 'Look!' Our consciousness is thrown into three quite different attitudes of expectancy, although no definite object is before it in any one of the three cases. Probably no one will deny here the existence of a real conscious affection, a sense of the direction from which an impression is about to come, although no positive impression is yet there. Meanwhile we have no names for the psychoses in question but the names hark, look, and wait.

Suppose we try to recall a forgotten name. The state of our consciousness is peculiar. There is a gap therein; but no mere gap. It is a gap that is intensely active. A sort of wraith of the name is in it, beckoning us in a given direction, making us at moments tingle with the sense of our closeness, and then letting us sink back without the longed-for term. If wrong names are proposed to us, this singularly definite gap acts immediately so as to negate them. They do not fit into its mould. And the gap of one word does not feel like the gap of another, all empty of content as both might seem necessarily to be when described as gaps. When I vainly try to recall the name of Spalding, my consciousness is far removed from what it is when I vainly try to recall the name of Bowles. There are innumerable consciousnesses of *want*, no one of which taken in itself has a name, but all different from each other. Such a feeling of want is *toto cœlo* other than a want of feeling: it is an intense feeling. The rhythm of a lost word may be there without a sound to clothe it; or the evanescent sense of something which is the initial vowel or consonant may mock us fitfully, without growing more distinct. Every one must know the tantalizing effect of the blank rhythm of some forgotten verse, restlessly dancing in one's mind, striving to be filled out with words.

What is that first instantaneous glimpse of some one's meaning which we have, when in vulgar phrase we say we 'twig' it? Surely an altogether specific affection of our mind. And has the reader never asked himself what kind of a mental fact is his *intention of saying a thing* before he has said it? It is an entirely definite intention, distinct from all other intentions, an absolutely distinct state of consciousness, therefore; and yet how much of it consists of definite sensorial images, either of words or of things? Hardly anything! Linger, and the words and things come into the mind; the anticipatory intention, the divination is there no more. But as the words that replace it arrive, it welcomes them successively and calls them right if they agree with it, it rejects them and calls them wrong if they do not. The intention *to-say-so-and-so* is the only name it can receive. One may admit that a good third of our psychic life consists in these rapid premonitory perspective views of schemes of thought not yet articulate. How comes it about that

a man reading something aloud for the first time is able immediately to emphasize all his words aright, unless from the very
first he have a sense of at least the form of the sentence yet to
come, which sense is fused with his consciousness of the present
word, and modifies its emphasis in his mind so as to make him
give it the proper accent as he utters it? Emphasis of this kind
almost altogether depends on grammatical construction. If we
read 'no more,' we expect presently a 'than'; if we read 'however,' it is a 'yet,' a 'still,' or a 'nevertheless,' that we expect.
And this foreboding of the coming verbal and grammatical
scheme is so practically accurate that a reader incapable of
understanding four ideas of the book he is reading aloud
can nevertheless read it with the most delicately modulated
expression of intelligence.

It is, the reader will see, the reinstatement of the vague and
inarticulate to its proper place in our mental life which I am so
anxious to press on the attention. Mr. Galton and Prof. Huxley
have, as we shall see in the chapter on Imagination, made one
step in advance in exploding the ridiculous theory of Hume and
Berkeley that we can have no images but of perfectly definite
things. Another is made if we overthrow the equally ridiculous
notion that, whilst simple objective qualities are revealed to
our knowledge in 'states of consciousness,' relations are not.
But these reforms are not half sweeping and radical enough.
What must be admitted is that the definite images of traditional psychology form but the very smallest part of our minds
as they actually live. The traditional psychology talks like one
who should say a river consists of nothing but pailsful, spoons-
ful, quartpotsful, barrelsful, and other moulded forms of water.
Even were the pails and the pots all actually standing in the
stream, still between them the free water would continue to
flow. It is just this free water of consciousness that psychologists resolutely overlook. Every definite image in the mind is
steeped and dyed in the free water that flows round it. With it
goes the sense of its relations, near and remote, the dying echo
of whence it came to us, the dawning sense of whither it is to
lead. The significance, the value, of the image is all in this halo

or penumbra that surrounds and escorts it, — or rather that is fused into one with it and has become bone of its bone and flesh of its flesh; leaving it, it is true, an image of the same *thing* it was before, but making it an image of that thing newly taken and freshly understood.

Let us call the consciousness of this halo of relations around the image by the name of 'psychic overtone' or ' fringe.'

Cerebral Conditions of the 'Fringe.'—Nothing is easier than to symbolize these facts in terms of brain-action. Just as the echo of the *whence*, the sense of the starting point of our thought, is probably due to the dying excitement of processes but a moment since vividly aroused; so the sense of the whither, the foretaste of the terminus, must be due to the waxing excitement of tracts or processes whose psychical correlative will a moment hence be the vividly present feature of our thought. Represented by a curve, the neurosis underlying consciousness must at any moment be like this:

Let the horizontal in Fig. 1 be the line of time, and let the

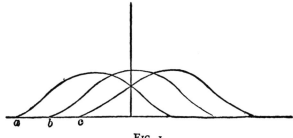

FIG. 1.

three curves beginning at *a*, *b*, and *c* respectively stand for the neural processes correlated with the thoughts of those three letters. Each process occupies a certain time during which its intensity waxes, culminates, and wanes. The process for *a* has not yet died out, the process for *c* has already begun, when that for *b* is culminating. At the time-instant represented by the vertical line all three processes are *present*, in the intensities shown by the curve. Those before *c*'s apex *were* more intense a moment ago; those after it *will be* more intense a moment hence. If I recite *a*, *b*, *c*, then, at the moment of uttering *b*, neither *a* nor *c* is out of my consciousness altogether, but both, after their respective fashions, ' mix their dim lights ' with the stronger *b*, because their processes are both awake in some degree.

It is just like ' overtones ' in music: they are not separately heard by the ear; they blend with the fundamental note, and suffuse it, and alter it; and even so do the waxing and waning brain-processes at every moment blend with and suffuse and alter the psychic effect of the processes which are at their culminating point.

The ' Topic ' of the Thought. — If we then consider the *cognitive function* of different states of mind, we may feel assured that the difference between those that are mere ' acquaintance ' and those that are ' knowledges-*about* ' is reducible almost entirely to the absence or presence of psychic fringes or overtones. Knowledge *about* a thing is knowledge of its relations. Acquaintance with it is limitation to the bare impression which it makes. Of most of its relations we are only aware in the penumbral nascent way of a ' fringe ' of unarticulated affinities about it. And, before passing to the next topic in order, I must say a little of this sense of affinity, as itself one of the most interesting features of the subjective stream.

Thought may be equally rational in any sort of terms.—*In all our voluntary thinking there is some* TOPIC or SUBJECT about which all the members of the thought revolve. Relation to this topic or interest is constantly felt in the fringe, and particularly the relation of harmony and discord, of furtherance or hindrance of the topic. Any thought the quality of whose fringe lets us feel ourselves ' all right,' may be considered a thought that furthers the topic. Provided we only feel its object to have a place in the scheme of relations in which the topic also lies, that is sufficient to make it of a relevant and appropriate portion of our train of ideas.

Now we may think about our topic mainly in words, or we may think about it mainly in visual or other images, but this need make no difference as regards the furtherance of our knowledge of the topic. If we only feel in the terms, whatever they be, a fringe of affinity with each other and with the topic, and if we are conscious of approaching a conclusion, we feel that our thought is rational and right. The words in every language have contracted by long association fringes of mutual repugnance or affinity with each other and with the conclusion, which run exactly parallel with like fringes in the visual, tactile, and other ideas. The most important element of these fringes is, I repeat, the mere feeling of harmony or discord, of a right or wrong direction in the thought.

If we know English and French and begin a sentence in French, all the later words that come are French; we hardly ever drop into English. And this affinity of the French words for each other is not something merely operating mechanically as a brain-law, it is something we feel at the time. Our understanding of a French sentence heard never falls to so low an ebb that we are not aware that the words linguistically belong together. Our attention can hardly so wander that if an English word be suddenly introduced we shall not start at the change. Such a vague sense as this of the words belonging together is the very minimum of fringe that can accompany them, if ' thought ' at all. Usually the vague perception that all the words we hear belong to the same language and to the same special vocabulary in that language, and that the grammatical sequence is familiar, is practically equivalent to an admission that what we hear is sense. But if an unusual foreign word be introduced, if the grammar trip, or if a term from an incongruous vocabulary suddenly appear, such as ' rat-trap ' or ' plumber's bill ' in a philosophical discourse, the sentence detonates as it were, we receive a shock from the incongruity, and the drowsy assent is gone. The feeling of rationality in these cases seems rather a negative than a positive thing, being the mere absence of shock, or sense of discord, between the terms of thought.

Conversely, if words do belong to the same vocabulary, and if the grammatical structure is correct, sentences with absolutely no meaning may be uttered in good faith and pass unchallenged. Discourses at prayer-meetings, reshuffling the same collection of cant phrases and the whole genus of penny-a-line-isms and newspaper-reporter's flourishes give illustrations of this. " The birds filled the tree-tops with their morning song, making the air moist, cool, and pleasant," is a sentence I remember reading once in a report of some athletic exercises in Jerome Park. It was probably written unconsciously by the hurried reporter, and read uncritically by many readers.

We see, then, that it makes little or no difference in what sort of mind-stuff, in what quality of imagery, our thinking goes on. The only images *intrinsically* important are the halting-places, the substantive conclusions, provisional or final, of the thought. Throughout all the rest of the stream, the feelings of relation are everything, and the terms related almost naught. These feelings of relation, these psychic overtones, halos, suffusions, or fringes about the terms, may be. the same in very different

systems of imagery. A diagram may help to accentuate this indifference of the mental means where the end is the same. Let *A* be some experience from which a number of thinkers start. Let *Z* be the practical conclusion rationally inferrable

FIG. 2.

from it. One gets to this conclusion by one line, another by another ; one follows a course of English, another of German, verbal imagery. With one, visual images predominate; with another, tactile. Some trains are tinged with emotions, others not; some are very abridged, synthetic and rapid; others, hesitating and broken into many steps. But when the penultimate terms of all the trains, however differing *inter se*, finally shoot into the same conclusion, we say, and rightly say, that all the thinkers have had substantially the same thought. It would probably astound each of them beyond measure to be let into his neighbor's mind and to find how different the scenery there was from that in his own.

The last peculiarity to which attention is to be drawn in this first rough description of thoughts' stream is that —

Consciousness is always interested more in one part of its object than in another, and welcomes and rejects, or chooses, all the while it thinks.

The phenomena of selective attention and of deliberative will are of course patent examples of this choosing activity. But few of us are aware how incessantly it is at work in operations not ordinarily called by these names. Accentuation and Emphasis are present in every perception we have. We find it quite impossible to disperse our attention impartially over a number of impressions. A monotonous succession of sonorous strokes is broken up into rhythms, now of one sort, now of another, by the different accent which we place on different strokes. The simplest of these rhythms is the double one, tick-tŏck, tick-tŏck, tick-tŏck. Dots dispersed on a surface are perceived in rows and groups. Lines separate into diverse figures. The ubiquity of the distinctions, *this* and *that, here* and *there, now* and *then*, in our minds is the result of our laying the same selective emphasis on parts of place and time.

But we do far more than emphasize things, and unite some, and keep others apart. We actually *ignore* most of the things before us. Let me briefly show how this goes on.

To begin at the bottom, what are our very senses themselves, but organs of selection? Out of the infinite chaos of movements, of which physics teaches us that the outer world consists, each sense-organ picks out those which fall within certain limits of velocity. To these it responds, but ignores the rest as completely as if they did not exist. Out of what is in itself an undistinguishable, swarming *continuum*, devoid of distinction or emphasis, our senses make for us, by attending to this motion and ignoring that, a world full of contrasts, of sharp accents, of abrupt changes, of picturesque light and shade.

If the sensations we receive from a given organ have their causes thus picked out for us by the conformation of the organ's termination, Attention, on the other hand, out of all the sensations yielded, picks out certain ones as worthy of its notice and suppresses all the rest. We notice only those sensations which are signs to us of *things* which happen practically or æsthetically to interest us, to which we therefore give substantive names, and which we exalt to this exclusive status of independence and dignity. But in itself, apart from my interest, a particular dust-wreath on a windy day is just as much of an individual *thing*, and just as much or as little deserves an individual name, as my own body does.

And then, among the sensations we get from each separate thing, what happens? The mind selects again. It chooses certain of the sensations to represent the thing most *truly*, and considers the rest as its appearances, modified by the conditions of the moment. Thus my table-top is named *square*, after but one of an infinite number of retinal sensations which it yields, the rest of them being sensations of two acute and two obtuse angles; but I call the latter *perspective* views, and the four right angles the *true* form of the table, and erect the attribute squareness into the table's essence, for æsthetic reasons of my own. In like manner, the real form of the circle is deemed to be the sensation it gives when the line of vision is perpendicular to its centre — all its other sensations are *signs* of this sensation. The real sound of the cannon is the sensation it makes when the ear is close by. The real color of the brick is the sensation it gives when the eye looks squarely at it from a near point, out of the sunshine and yet not in the gloom; under other circumstances it gives us other color-sensations which are but signs of this — we then see it look pinker or bluer than it really is. The reader knows no object which he does not represent to himself by preference as in some typical attitude, of some normal size, at some characteristic distance, of some standard tint, etc., etc. But all these essential characteristics, which together form for us the genuine objectivity of the thing and are contrasted with what we call the subjective sensations it may yield us at a given moment, are mere sensations like the latter. The mind chooses to suit itself, and decides what particular sensation shall be held more real and valid than all the rest.

Next, in a world of objects thus individualized by our mind's selective industry, what is called our ' experience ' is almost entirely determined by our habits of attention. A thing may be present to a man a hundred times, but if he presistently fails to notice it, it cannot be said to enter into his experience. We are all seeing flies, moths, and beetles by the thousand, but to whom, save an entomologist, do they say anything distinct? On the other hand, a thing met only once in a lifetime may leave an indelible experience in the memory. Let four men make a tour in Europe. One will bring home only picturesque impressions — costumes and colors, parks and views and works of architecture, pictures and statues. To another all this will be non-existent; and distances and prices, populations and drainage-arrangements, door- and window-fastenings, and other useful statistics will take their place. A third will give a rich account of the theatres, restaurants, and public halls, and naught beside; whilst the fourth will perhaps have been so wrapped in his own subjective broodings as to be able to tell little more than a few names of places through which he passed. Each has selected, out of the same mass of presented objects, those which suited his private interest and has made his experience thereby.

If now, leaving the empirical combination of objects, we ask how the mind proceeds *rationally* to connect them, we find selection again to be omnipotent. In a future chapter we shall see that all Reasoning depends on the ability of the mind to break up the totality of the phenomenon reasoned about, into parts, and to pick out from among these the particular one which, in the given emergency, may lead to the proper conclusion. The man of genius is he who will always stick in his bill at the right point, and bring it out with the right element — ' reason ' if the emergency be theoretical, ' means ' if it be practical — transfixed upon it.

If now we pass to the æsthetic department, our law is still more obvious. The artist notoriously selects his items, rejecting all tones, colors, shapes, which do not harmonize with each other and with the main purpose of his work. That unity, harmony, ' convergence of characters,' as M. Taine calls it, which gives to works of art their superiority over works of nature, is wholly due to *elimination*. Any natural subject will do, if the artist has wit enough to pounce upon some one feature of it as characteristic, and suppress all merely accidental items which do not harmonize with this.

Ascending still higher, we reach the plane of Ethics, where choice reigns notoriously supreme. An act has no ethical quality whatever unless it be chosen out of several all equally possible. To sustain the arguments for the good course and keep them ever before us, to stifle our longing for more flowery ways, to keep the foot unflinchingly on the arduous path, these are characteristic ethical energies. But more than these; for these but deal with the means of compassing interests already felt by the man to be supreme. The ethical energy *par excellence* has to go farther and choose which *interest* out of several, equally coercive, shall become supreme. The issue here is of the utmost pregnancy, for it decides a man's entire career. When he debates, Shall I commit this crime? choose that profession? accept that office, or marry this fortune? — his choice really lies between one of several equally possible future Characters. What he shall *become* is fixed by the conduct of this moment. Schopenhauer, who enforces his determinism by the argument that with a given fixed character only one reaction is possible under given circumstances, forgets that, in these critical ethical moments, what consciously *seems* to be in question is the complexion of the character itself. The problem with the man is less what act he shall now resolve to do than what being he shall now choose to become.

Taking human experience in a general way, the choosings of different men are to a great extent the same. The race as a whole largely agrees as to what it shall notice and name; and among the noticed parts we select in much the same way for accentuation and preference, or subordination and dislike. There is, however, one entirely extraordinary case in which no two men ever are known to choose alike. One great splitting of the whole universe into two halves is made by each of us;

and for each of us almost all of the interest attaches to one of the halves; but we all draw the line of division between them in a different place. When I say that we all call the two halves by the same names, and that those names are ' me ' and ' not-me ' respectively, it will at once be seen what I mean. The altogether unique kind of interest which each human mind feels in those parts of creation which it can call *me* or *mine* may be a moral riddle, but it is a fundamental psychological fact. No mind can take the same interest in his neighbor's *me* as in his own. The neighbor's me falls together with all the rest of things in one foreign mass against which his own *me* stands out in startling relief. Even the trodden worm, as Lotze somewhere says, contrasts his own suffering self with the whole remaining universe, though he have no clear conception either of himself or of what the universe may be. He is for me a mere part of the world; for him it is I who am the mere part. Each of us dichotomizes the Kosmos in a different place.

CHAPTER XXIV. EMOTION [1]

Emotions compared with Instincts. — An emotion is a tendency to feel, and an instinct is a tendency to act, characteristically, when in presence of a certain object in the environment. But the emotions also have their bodily ' expression,' which may involve strong muscular activity (as in fear or anger, for example); and it becomes a little hard in many cases to separate the description of the ' emotional' condition from that of the ' instinctive ' reaction which one and the same object may provoke. Shall *fear* be described in the chapter on Instincts or in that on Emotions? Where shall one describe *curiosity, emulation*, and the like? The answer is quite arbitrary from the scientific point of view, and practical convenience may decide. As inner mental conditions, emotions are quite indescribable. Description, moreover, would be superfluous, for the reader

---

[1] The substance of this chapter first appeared in an article published in *Mind* in 1884, and again as a chapter in the author's *Principles of Psychology*, in 1890.

knows already how they feel. Their relations to the objects which prompt them and to the reactions which they provoke are all that one can put down in a book.

Every object that excites an instinct excites an emotion as well. The only distinction one may draw is that the reaction called emotional terminates in the subject's own body, whilst the reaction called instinctive is apt to go farther and enter into practical relations with the exciting object. In both instinct and emotion the mere memory or imagination of the object may suffice to liberate the excitement. One may even get angrier in thinking over one's insult than one was in receiving it; and melt more over a mother who is dead than one ever did when she was living. In the rest of the chapter I shall use the word *object* of emotion indifferently to mean one which is physically present or one which is merely thought of.

The varieties of emotion are innumerable. — *Anger, fear, love, hate, joy, grief, shame, pride*, and their varieties, may be called the *coarser* emotions, being coupled as they are with relatively strong bodily reverberations. The *subtler* emotions are the moral, intellectual, and æsthetic feelings, and their bodily reaction is usually much less strong. The mere description of the objects, circumstances, and varieties of the different species of emotion may go to any length. Their internal shadings merge endlessly into each other, and have been partly commemorated in language, as, for example, by such synonyms as hatred, antipathy, animosity, resentment, dislike, aversion, malice, spite, revenge, abhorrence, etc., etc. Dictionaries of synonyms have discriminated them, as well as text-books of psychology — in fact, many German psychological text-books *are* nothing but dictionaries of synonyms when it comes to the chapter on Emotion. But there are limits to the profitable elaboration of the obvious, and the result of all this flux is that the merely descriptive literature of the subject, from Descartes downwards is one of the most tedious parts of psychology. And not only is it tedious, but you feel that its subdivisions are to a great extent either fictitious or unimportant, and that its pretences to accuracy are a sham. But unfortunately there is little psychological writing about the emotions which is not merely descriptive. As emotions are described in novels, they interest us, for we are made to share them. We have grown acquainted with the concrete objects and emergencies which call them forth, and any knowing touch of introspection which may grace the page meets with a quick and feeling response. Confessedly literary works of aphoristic philosophy also flash lights into our emotional life, and give us a fitful delight. But as far as the ' scientific psychology ' of the emotions goes, I may have been surfeited by too much reading of classic works on the subject, but I would as lief read verbal descriptions of the shapes of the rocks on a New Hampshire farm as toil through them again. They give one nowhere a central point of view, or a deductive or generative principle. They distinguish and refine and specify *in infinitum* without ever getting on to another logical level. Whereas the beauty of all truly scientific work is to get to ever deeper levels. Is there no way out from this level of individual description in the case of the emotions? I believe there is a way out, if one will only take it.

The Cause of their Varieties. — The trouble with the emotions in psychology is that they are regarded too much as absolutely individual things. So long as they are set down as so many eternal and sacred psychic entities, like the old immutable species in natural history, so long all that *can* be done with them is reverently to catalogue their separate characters, points, and effects. But if we regard them as products of more general causes (as ' species ' are now regarded as products of heredity and variation), the mere distinguishing and cataloguing becomes of subsidiary importance. Having the goose which lays the golden eggs, the description of each egg already laid is a minor matter. I will devote the next few pages to setting forth one very general cause of our emotional feeling, limiting myself in the first instance to what may be called the *coarser* emotions.

The feeling, in the coarser emotions, results from the bodily expression. — Our natural way of thinking about these coarser emotions is that the mental perception of some fact excites the mental affection called the emotion, and that this latter state of mind gives rise to the bodily expression. My theory, on the contrary, is that *the bodily changes follow directly the perception of the exciting fact, and that our feeling of the same changes as they occur* IS *the emotion*. Common-sense says, we lose our fortune, are sorry and weep; we meet a bear, are frightened and run; we are insulted by a rival, are angry and strike. The hypothesis here to be defended says that this order of sequence is incorrect, and the one mental state is not immediately induced by the other, that the bodily manifestations must first be interposed between, and that the more rational statement is that we feel sorry because we cry, angry because we strike, afraid because we tremble, and not that we cry, strike, or tremble because we are sorry, angry, or fearful, as the case may be. Without the bodily states following on the perception, the latter would be purely cognitive in form, pale, colorless, destitute of emotional warmth. We might then see the bear and judge it best to run, receive the insult and deem it right to strike, but we should not actually *feel* afraid or angry.

Stated in this crude way, the hypothesis is pretty sure to meet with immediate disbelief. And yet neither many nor far-fetched considerations are required to mitigate its paradoxical character, and possibly to produce conviction of its truth.

To begin with, *particular perceptions certainly do produce wide-spread bodily effects by a sort of immediate physical influence, antecedent to the arousal of an emotion or emotional idea.* In listening to poetry, drama, or heroic narrative we are often surprised at the cutaneous shiver which like a sudden wave flows over us, and at the heart-swelling and the lachrymal effusion that unexpectedly catch us at intervals. In hearing music the same is even more strikingly true. If we abruptly see a dark moving form in the woods, our heart stops beating, and we catch our breath instantly and before any articulate idea of danger can arise. If our friend goes near to the edge of a precipice, we get the well-known feeling of ' all-overishness,' and we shrink back, although we positively *know* him to be safe, and have no distinct imagination of his fall. The writer well remembers his astonishment, when a boy of seven or eight, at fainting when he saw a horse bled. The blood was in a bucket, with a stick in it, and, if memory does not deceive him, he stirred it round and saw it drip from the stick with no feeling save that of childish curiosity. Suddenly the world grew black before his eyes, his ears began to buzz, and he knew no more. He had never heard of the sight of blood producing faintness or sickness, and he had so little repugnance to it, and so little apprehension of any other sort of danger from it, that even at that tender age, as he well remembers, he could not help wondering how the mere physical presence of a pailful of crimson fluid could occasion in him such formidable bodily effects.

The best proof that the immediate cause of emotion is a physical effect on the nerves is furnished by *those pathological cases in which the emotion is objectless.* One of the chief merits, in fact, of the view which I propose seems to be that we can so easily formulate by its means pathological cases and normal cases under a common scheme. In every asylum we find examples of absolutely unmotived fear, anger, melancholy, or conceit; and others of an equally unmotived apathy which persists in spite of the best of outward reasons why it should give way. In the former cases we must suppose the nervous machinery to be so ' labile ' in some one emotional direction that almost every stimulus (however inappropriate) causes it to upset in that way, and to engender the particular complex of feelings of which the psychic body of the emotion consists. Thus, to take one special instance, if inability to draw deep breath, fluttering of the heart, and that peculiar epigastric change felt as ' precordial anxiety,' with an irresistible tendency to take a somewhat crouching attitude and to sit still, and with perhaps other visceral processes not now known, all spontaneously occur together in a certain person, his feeling of their combination *is* the emotion of dread, and he is the victim of what is known as morbid fear. A friend who has had occasional attacks of this most distressing of all maladies tells me that in his case the whole drama seems to centre about the region of the heart and respiratory apparatus, that his main effort during the attacks is to get control of his inspirations and to slow his heart, and that the moment he attains to breathing deeply and to holding himself erect, the dread, *ipso facto*, seems to depart.

The emotion here is nothing but the feeling of a bodily state, and it has a purely bodily cause.

The next thing to be noticed is this, that *every one of the bodily changes, whatsoever it be, is* FELT, *acutely or obscurely, the moment it occurs.* If the reader has never paid attention to this matter, he will be both interested and astonished to learn how many different local bodily feelings he can detect in himself as characteristic of his various emotional moods. It would be perhaps too much to expect him to arrest the tide of any strong gust of passion for the sake of any such curious analysis as this; but he can observe more tranquil states, and that may be assumed here to be true of the greater which is shown to be true of the less. Our whole cubic capacity is sensibly alive; and each morsel of it contributes its pulsations of feeling, dim or sharp, pleasant, painful, or dubious, to that sense of personality that every one of us unfailingly carries with him. It is surprising what little items give accent to these complexes of sensibility. When worried by any slight trouble, one may find that the focus of one's bodily consciousness is the contraction often quite inconsiderable, of the eyes and brows. When momentarily embarrassed, it is something in the pharynx that compels either a swallow, a clearing of the throat, or a slight cough; and so on for as many more instances as might be named. The various permutations of which these organic changes are susceptible make it abstractly possible that no shade of emotion should be without a bodily reverberation as unique, when taken in its totality, as is the mental mood itself. The immense number of parts modified is what makes it so difficult for us to reproduce in cold blood the total and integral expression of any one emotion. We may catch the trick with the voluntary muscles, but fail with the skin, glands, heart, and other viscera. Just as an artificially imitated sneeze lacks something of the reality, so the attempt to imitate grief or enthusiasm in the absence of its normal instigating cause is apt to be rather ' hollow.'

I now proceed to urge the vital point of my whole theory, which is this: *If we fancy some strong emotion, and then try to abstract from our consciousness of it all the feelings of its bodily symptoms, we find we have nothing left behind*, no ' mind-stuff ' out of which the emotion can be constituted, and that a cold and neutral state of intellectual perception is all that remains. It is true that, although most people, when asked, say that their introspection verifies this statement, some persist in saying theirs does not. Many cannot be made to understand the question. When you beg them to imagine away every feeling of laughter and of tendency to laugh from their consciousness of the ludicrousness of an object, and then to tell you what the feeling of its ludicrousness would be like, whether it be anything more than the perception that the object belongs to the class '.funny,' they persist in replying that the thing proposed is a physical impossibility, and that they always *must* laugh if they see a funny object. Of course the task proposed is not the practical one of seeing a ludicrous object and annihilating one's tendency to laugh. It is the purely speculative one of subtracting certain elements of feeling from an emotional state supposed to exist in its fulness, and saying what the residual elements are. I cannot help thinking that all who rightly apprehend this problem will agree with the proposition above laid down. What kind of an emotion of fear would be left if the feeling neither of quickened heart-beats nor of shallow breathing, neither of trembling lips nor of weakened limbs, neither of goose-flesh nor of visceral stirrings, were present, it is quite impossible for me to think. Can one fancy the state of rage and picture no ebullition in the chest, no flushing of the face, no dilatation of the nostrils, no clenching of the teeth, no impulse to vigorous action, but in their stead limp muscles, calm breathing, and a placid face? The present writer, for one, certainly cannot. The rage is as completely evaporated as the sensation of its so-called manifestations, and the only thing that can possibly be supposed to take its place is some cold-blooded and dispassionate judicial sentence, confined entirely to the intellectual realm, to the effect that a certain person or persons merit chastisement for their sins. In like manner of grief: what would it be without its tears, its sobs, its suffocation of the heart, its pang in the breast-bone? A feelingless cognition that certain circumstances are deplorable, and nothing more. Every passion in turn tells the same story. A disembodied human emotion is a sheer nonentity. I do not say that it is a contradiction in the nature of things, or that pure spirits are necessarily condemned to cold intellectual lives; but I say that for *us* emotion dissociated from all bodily feeling is inconceivable. The more closely I scrutinize my states, the more persuaded I become that whatever 'coarse' affections and passions I have are in very truth constituted by, and made up of, those bodily changes which we ordinarily call their expression or consequence; and the more it seems to me that, if I were to become corporeally anæsthetic, I should be excluded from the life of the affections, harsh and tender alike, and drag out an existence of merely cognitive or intellectual form. Such an existence, although it seems to have been the ideal of ancient sages, is too apathetic to be keenly sought after by those born after the revival of the worship of sensibility, a few generations ago.

Let not this view be called materialistic. — It is neither more nor less materialistic than any other view which says that our emotions are conditioned by nervous processes. No reader of this book is likely to rebel against such a saying so long as it is expressed in general terms; and if any one still finds materialism in the thesis now defended, that must be because of the special processes invoked. They are *sensational* processes, processes due to inward currents set up by physical happenings. Such processes have, it is true, always been regarded by the platonizers in psychology as having something peculiarly base about them. But our emotions must always be *inwardly* what they are, whatever be the physiological ground of their apparition. If they are deep, pure, worthy, spiritual facts on any conceivable theory of their physiological source, they remain no less deep, pure, spiritual, and worthy of regard on this present sensational theory. They carry their own inner measure of worth with them; and it is just as logical to use the present theory of the emotions for proving that sensational processes need not be vile and material, as to use their vileness and materiality as a proof that such a theory cannot be true.

This view explains the great variability of emotion. — If such a theory is true, then each emotion is the resultant of a sum of elements, and each element is caused by a physiological process of a sort already well known. The elements are all organic changes, and each of them is the reflex effect of the exciting object. Definite questions now immediately arise — questions very different from those which were the only possible ones without this view. Those questions were of classification: " Which are the proper genera of emotion, and which the species under each? " — or of description: " By what expression is each emotion characterized? " The questions now are *causal:* "Just what changes does this object and what changes does that object excite? " and " How come they to excite these particular changes and not others? " We step from a superficial to a deep order of inquiry. Classification and description are the lowest stage of science. They sink into the background the moment questions of causation are formulated, and remain important only so far as they facilitate our answering these. Now the moment an emotion is causally accounted for, as the arousal by an object of a lot of reflex acts which are forthwith felt, *we immediately see why there is no limit to the number of possible different emotions which may exist, and why the emotions of different individuals may vary indefinitely*, both as to their constitution and as to the objects which call them forth. For there is nothing sacramental or eternally fixed in reflex action. Any sort of reflex effect is possible, and reflexes actually vary indefinitely, as we know.

In short, *any classification of the emotions is seen to be as true and as ' natural ' as any other*, if it only serves some purpose; and such a question as " What is the ' real ' or ' typical ' expression of anger, or fear? " is seen to have no objective meaning at all. Instead of it we now have the question as to how any given ' expression ' of anger or fear may have come to exist; and that is a real question of physiological mechanics on the one hand, and of history on the other, which (like all real questions) is in essence answerable, although the answer may be hard to find. On a later page I shall mention the attempts to answer it which have been made.

A Corollary verified. — If our theory be true, a necessary corollary of it ought to be this: that any voluntary and cold-blooded arousal of the so-called manifestations of a special emotion should give us the emotion itself. Now within the limits in which it can be verified, experience corroborates rather than disproves this inference. Everyone knows how panic is increased by flight, and how the giving way to the symptoms of grief or anger increases those passions themselves. Each fit of sobbing makes the sorrow more acute, and calls forth another fit stronger still, until at last repose only ensues with lassitude and with the apparent exhaustion of the machinery. In rage, it is notorious how we ' work ourselves up ' to a climax by repeated outbreaks of expression. Refuse to express a passion, and it dies. Count ten before venting your anger, and its occasion seems ridiculous. Whistling to keep up courage is no mere figure of speech. On the other hand, sit all day in a moping posture, sigh, and reply to everything with a dismal voice, and your melancholy lingers. There is no more valuable precept in moral education than this, as all who have experience know if we wish to conquer undesirable emotional tendencies in ourselves, we must assiduously, and in the first instance cold-bloodedly, go through the *outward movements* of those contrary dispositions which we prefer to cultivate. The reward of persistency will infallibly come, in the fading out of the sullenness or depression, and the advent of real cheerfulness and kindliness in their stead. Smooth the brow, brighten the eye, contract the dorsal rather than the ventral aspect of the frame, and speak in a major key, pass the genial compliment, and your heart must be frigid indeed if it do not gradually thaw!

Against this it is to be said that many actors who perfectly mimic the outward appearances of emotion in face, gait, and voice declare that they feel no emotion at all. Others, however, according to Mr. Wm. Archer, who has made a very instructive statistical inquiry among them, say that the emotion of the part masters them whenever they play it well. The explanation for the discrepancy amongst actors is probably simple. The *visceral and organic* part of the expression can be suppressed in some men, but not in others, and on this it must be that the chief part of the felt emotion depends. Those actors who feel the emotion are probably unable, those who are inwardly cold are probably able, to affect the dissociation in a complete way.

An Objection replied to. — It may be objected to the general theory which I maintain that stopping the expression of an emotion often makes it worse. The funniness becomes quite excruciating when we are forbidden by the situation to laugh, and anger pent in by fear turns into tenfold hate. Expressing either emotion freely, however, gives relief.

This objection is more specious than real. *During* the expression the emotion is always felt. *After* it, the centres having normally discharged themselves, we feel it no more. But where the facial part of the discharge is suppressed the thoracic and visceral may be all the more violent and persistent, as in suppressed laughter; or the original emotion may be changed, by the combination of the provoking object with the restraining pressure, into *another emotion altogether*, in which different and possibly profounder organic disturbance occurs. If I would kill my enemy but dare not, my emotion is surely altogether other than that which would possess me if I let my anger explode. — On the whole, therefore, this objection has no weight.

The Subtler Emotions. — In the æsthetic emotions the bodily reverberation and the feeling may both be faint. A connoisseur is apt to judge a work of art dryly and intellectually, and with no bodily thrill. On the other hand, works of art may arouse intense emotion; and whenever they do so, the experience is completely covered by the terms of our theory. Our theory requires that *incoming currents* be the basis of emotion. But, whether secondary organic reverberations be or be not aroused by it, the perception of a work of art (music, decoration, etc.) is always in the first instance at any rate an affair of in-coming currents. The work is an object of sensation; and, the perception of an object of sensation being a ' coarse ' or vivid experience, what pleasure goes with it will partake of the ' coarse ' or vivid form.

That there may be subtle pleasure too, I do not deny. In other words, there may be purely cerebral emotion, independent of all currents from outside. Such feelings as moral satisfaction, thankfulness, curiosity, relief at getting a problem solved, may be of this sort. But the thinness and paleness of these feelings, when unmixed with bodily effects, is in very striking contrast to the coarser emotions. In all sentimental and impressionable people the bodily effects mix in: the voice breaks and the eyes moisten when the moral truth is felt, etc. Wherever there is anything like *rapture*, however intellectual its ground, we find these secondary processes ensue. Unless we actually laugh at the neatness of the demonstration or witticism; unless we thrill at the case of justice, or tingle at the act of magnanimity, our state of mind can hardly be called emotional at all. It is in fact a mere intellectual perception of how certain things are to be called — neat, right, witty, generous, and the like. Such a judicial state of mind as this is to be classed among cognitive rather than among emotional acts.

Description of Fear. — For the reasons given on p. 656, I will append no inventory or classification of emotions or description of their symptoms. The reader has practically almost all the facts in his own hand. As an example, however, of the best sort of descriptive work on the symptoms, I will quote Darwin's account of them in fear.

" Fear is often preceded by astonishment, and is so far akin to it that both lead to the senses of sight and hearing being instantly aroused. In both cases the eyes and mouth are widely opened and the eyebrows raised. The frightened man at first stands like a statue, motionless and breathless, or crouches down as if instinctively to escape observation. The heart beats quickly and violently, so that it palpitates or knocks against the ribs; but it is very doubtful if it then works more efficiently

than usual, so as to send a greater supply of blood to all parts of
the body; for the skin instantly becomes pale as during incipient faintness. This paleness of the surface, however, is probably in large part, or is exclusively, due to the vaso-motor
centre being affected in such manner as to cause the contraction of the small arteries of the skin. That the skin is much
affected under the sense of great fear, we see in the marvellous
manner in which perspiration immediately exudes from it.
This exudation is all the more remarkable, as the surface is
then cold, and hence the term, a cold sweat; whereas the
sudorific glands are properly excited into action when the surface is heated. The hairs also on the skin stand erect, and the
superficial muscles shiver. In connection with the disturbed
action of the heart the breathing is hurried. The salivary
glands act imperfectly; the mouth becomes dry and is often
opened and shut. I have also noticed that under slight fear
there is strong tendency to yawn. One of the best marked symptoms is the trembling of all the muscles of the body; and this is
often first seen in the lips. From this cause, and from the dryness of the mouth, the voice becomes husky or indistinct or
may altogether fail. '*Obstupui steteruntque comæ, et vox fauci-
bus hæsit.*' . . . As fear increases into an agony of terror, we
behold, as under all violent emotions, diversified results. The
heart beats wildly or must fail to act and faintness ensue; there
is a death-like pallor; the breathing is labored; the wings of the
nostrils are widely dilated; there is a gasping and convulsive
motion of the lips, a tremor on the hollow cheek, a gulping and
catching of the throat; the uncovered and protruding eyeballs
are fixed on the object of terror; or they may roll restlessly from
side to side, *huc illuc volens oculos totumque pererrat.* The pupils
are said to be enormously dilated. All the muscles of the body
may become rigid or may be thrown into convulsive movements. The hands are alternately clenched and opened, often
with a twitching movement. The arms may be protruded as if
to avert some dreadful danger, or may be thrown wildly over
the head. The Rev. Mr. Hagenauer has seen this latter action
in a terrified Australian. In other cases there is a sudden and

uncontrollable tendency to headlong flight; and so strong is this that the boldest soldiers may be seized with a sudden panic." [1]

Genesis of the Emotional Reactions. — How come the various objects which excite emotion to produce such special and different bodily effects? This question was not asked till quite recently, but already some interesting suggestions towards answering it have been made.

Some movements of expression can be accounted for as *weakened repetitions of movements which formerly* (when they were stronger) *were of utility to the subject.* Others are similarly weakened repetitions of movements which under other conditions were *physiologically necessary concomitants of the useful movements.* Of the latter reactions the respiratory disturbances in anger and fear might be taken as examples — organic reminiscences, as it were, reverberations in imagination of the blowings of the man making a series of combative efforts, of the pantings of one in precipitate flight. Such at least is a suggestion made by Mr. Spencer which has found approval. And he also was the first, so far as I know, to suggest that other movements in anger and fear could be explained by the nascent excitation of formerly useful acts.

"To have in a slight degree," he says, " such psychical states as accompany the reception of wounds, and are experienced during flight, is to be in a state of what we call fear. And to have in a slight degree such psychical states as the processes of catching, killing, and eating imply, is to have the desires to catch, kill, and eat. That the propensities to the acts are nothing else than nascent excitations of the psychical state involved in the acts, is proved by the natural language of the propensities. Fear, when strong, expresses itself in cries, in efforts to escape, in palpitations, in tremblings; and these are just the manifestations that go along with an actual suffering of the evil feared. The destructive passion is shown in a general tension of the muscular system, in gnashing of teeth and protrusion of the claws, in dilated eyes and nostrils in growls; and these are weaker forms of the actions that accompany the

[1] Origin of the Emotions (N. Y. ed.), p. 292.

killing of prey. To such objective evidences every one can add subjective evidences. Every one can testify that the psychical state called fear consists of mental representations of certain painful results; and that the one called anger consists of mental representations of the actions and impressions which would occur while inflicting some kind of pain."

The principle of *revival, in weakened form, of reactions useful in more violent dealings with the object inspiring the emotion,* has found many applications. So slight a symptom as the snarl or sneer, the one-sided uncovering of the upper teeth, is accounted for by Darwin as a survival from the time when our ancestors had large canines, and unfleshed them (as dogs now do) for attack. Similarly the raising of the eyebrows in outward attention, the opening of the mouth in astonishment, come, according to the same author, from the utility of these movements in extreme cases. The raising of the eyebrows goes with the opening of the eye for better vision; the opening of the mouth with the intensest listening, and with the rapid catching of the breath which precedes muscular effort. The distention of the nostrils in anger is interpreted by Spencer as an echo of the way in which our ancestors had to breathe when, during combat, their " mouth was filled up by a part of an antagonist's body that had been seized " (!). The trembling of fear is supposed by Mantegazza to be for the sake of warming the blood (!) The reddening of the face and neck is called by Wundt a compensatory arrangement for relieving the brain of the blood-pressure which the simultaneous excitement of the heart brings with it. The effusion of tears is explained both by this author and by Darwin to be a blood-withdrawing agency of a similar sort. The contraction of the muscles around the eyes, of which the primitive use is to protect those organs from being too much gorged with blood during the screaming fits of infancy, survives in adult life in the shape of the frown, which instantly comes over the brow when anything difficult or displeasing presents itself either to thought or action.

" As the habit of contracting the brows has been followed by infants during innumerable generations, at the commencement of every crying or screaming fit," says Darwin, " it has become firmly associated with the incipient sense of something distressing or disagreeable. Hence, under similar circumstances, it would be apt to be continued during maturity, although never then developed, into a crying fit. Screaming or weeping begins to be voluntarily restrained at an early period of life, whereas frowning is hardly ever restrained at any age."

Another principle, to which Darwin perhaps hardly does sufficient justice, may be called the principle of *reacting similarly to analogous-feeling stimuli.* There is a whole vocabulary of descriptive adjectives common to impressions belonging to different sensible spheres — experiences of all classes are *sweet*, impressions of all classes *rich* or *solid*, sensations of all classes *sharp*. Wundt and Piderit accordingly explain many of our most expressive reactions upon moral causes as symbolic gustatory movements. As soon as any experience arises which has an affinity with the feeling of sweet, or bitter, or sour, the same movements are executed which would result from the taste in point. " All the states of mind which language designates by the metaphors bitter, harsh, sweet, combine themselves, therefore, with the corresponding mimetic movements of the mouth." Certainly the emotions of disgust and satisfaction do express themselves in this mimetic way. Disgust is an incipent regurgitation or retching, limiting its expression often to the grimace of the lips and nose; satisfaction goes with a sucking smile, or tasting motion of the lips. The ordinary gesture of negation — among us, moving the head about its axis from side to side — is a reaction originally used by babies to keep disagreeables from getting into their mouth, and may be observed in perfection in any nursery. It is now evoked where the stimulus is only an unwelcome idea. Similarly the nod forward in affirmation is after the analogy of taking food into the mouth. The connection of the expression of moral or social disdain or dislike, especially in women, with movements having a perfectly definite original olfactory function, is too obvious for comment. Winking is the effect of any threatening surprise, not only of what puts the eyes in danger; and a momentary aversion of the eyes is very apt to be one's first symptom of response to an unexpectedly unwelcome proposition. — These may suffice as examples of movements expressive from analogy.

But if certain of our emotional reactions can be explained by the two principles invoked — and the reader will himself have felt how conjectural and fallible in some of the instances the explanation is — there remain many reactions which cannot so be explained at all, and these we must write down for the present as purely idiopathic effects of the stimulus. Amongst them are the effects on the viscera and internal glands, the dryness of the mouth and diarrhœa and nausea of fear, the liver-disturbances which sometimes produce jaundice after excessive rage, the urinary secretion of sanguine excitement, and the bladder-contraction of apprehension, the gaping of expectancy, the ' lump in the throat ' of grief, the tickling there and the swallowing of embarrassment, the ' precordial anxiety ' of dread, the changes in the pupil, the various sweatings of the skin, cold or hot, local or general, and its flushings, together with other symptoms which probably exist but are too hidden to have been noticed or named. Trembling, which is found in many excitements besides that of terror, is, *pace* Mr. Spencer and Sig. Mantegazza, quite pathological. So are terror's other strong symptoms: they are harmful to the creature who presents them. In an organism as complex as the nervous system there must be many *incidental* reactions which would never themselves have been evolved independently, for any utility they might possess. Sea-sickness, ticklishness, shyness, the love of music, of the various intoxicants, nay, the entire æsthetic life of man, must be traced to this accidental origin. It would be foolish to suppose that none of the reactions called emotional could have arisen in this *quasi*-accidental way.

CARL GEORG LANGE

(1834–1900)

THE EMOTIONS

Translated from the German* of H. Kurella by

BENJAMIN RAND

THE MECHANISM OF THE EMOTIONS

WE approach now the question which possesses a vital interest from the psycho-physiological standpoint, and for that reason forms the centre of this investigation. The question concerns the nature of the relation between the emotions and their accompanying bodily expressions.

Heretofore I have constantly used phrases, though under protest, such as "the physiological phenomena occasioned by the emotions," or "the physiological phenomena which accompany emotion," etc. I have employed provisionally these customary expressions for the relation in question in order to be understood. Strangely enough up to the present time this relation never has been in any way accurately defined. I know of no attempt to determine its exact nature. The matter is very simple in the popular conception. Here emotions are entities, substances, forces, daemons, which seize man and produce in him bodily as well as mental manifestations: "grief seized me," "a joy came to me," "anger controlled me," "fear overwhelmed me," etc.

As often happens in popular and sometimes even in scientific psychology, this conception has rather a metaphorical than an explicative value. Modern psychology would scarcely adopt it,

* C. Lange *Om Sindsbevaegelser.* Kjöbenhavn, 1885. Translated here from C. Lange's *Ueber Gemuthsbewegungen. Eine psycho-physiologische Studie.* Uebersetzt von H. Kurella, Leipzig, 1887.

if it could offer in its place any more comprehensible or exact explanation. Most modern authors in the domain of scientific psychology do not enter[1] at all into this question. They appear almost deliberately to pass it over in silence, in order probably from the lack of a physiological explanation not to have recourse to the mysterious language of speculative psychology. Indeed one can say that scientific psychology also shares the theory, that the emotions induce and determine the accompanying bodily expressions. But as to what emotions strictly are, that they can have such power over the body, one seeks, I think, in vain for any explanation in the whole of modern psychology.

If we desire a clear understanding of the relation here discussed, we must, as it appears to me, formulate the problem approximately in the following way. We have in every emotion as certain and manifest factors: (1) a cause, — a sense impression, which acts as a rule by the aid of memory, or of an associated idea; — and thereafter (2) an effect, namely, the previously discussed vasomotor changes, and further, issuing from them, the changes in the bodily and mental functions.

The question now arises:

What lies between these two factors? Is there anything at all? If I begin to tremble because I am threatened with a loaded pistol, does first a psychical process occur in me, does terror arise, and is that what causes my trembling, palpitation of the heart, and confusion of thought; or are these bodily phenomena produced directly by the terrifying cause, so that the emotion consists exclusively of the functional disturbances in my body?

The answer to this question is, as one easily perceives, not merely of decisive significance for the psychology of the emotions; but also of the greatest practical significance for any physician, who has to do with the pathological results of violent emotions.

The current opinion, as already remarked, amounts to the

[1] The external movement springs always from the inner, the emotion. Wundt's *Ueber den Ausdruck der Gemuthsbewegungen*. Deutsche Rundschau, April, 1877.

statement, that the immediate effect of a process followed by an emotion is of a purely psychical nature, (therefore, either the creation of a new mental force, or the modification of a previous mental state). Furthermore, it affirms, that this event in the soul is the actual emotion, the true joy, sorrow, etc.; whereas the bodily phenomena are only subsidiary phenomena, which indeed are never lacking, but are nevertheless in and of themselves wholly unessential.

The purely psychical emotion is an hypothesis, and like every hypothesis, has its justification only if it fulfils two conditions: namely, (1) to explain the phenomena for which it is propounded, and (2) that it be necessary for the explanation of these phenomena.

Respecting the first of these conditions, the hypothesis in question has just as easy a task as all the metaphysical hypotheses in general have. Without being restricted by objections of experience, one can elaborate them at pleasure, attributing to them any quality or power, and without further difficulty they perform every service that is required of them. But can psychical terror explain why one grows pale, or why one trembles? Although we do not understand the explanation, we are still free to assume it, and we are accustomed to be therewith content.

If the hypothesis of the psychical nature of the emotions is accordingly unassailable at this point, (indeed more because it escapes, than because it stands criticism,) the question arises, whether it fulfils the second condition? Is it indispensable for the explanation of the group of phenomena which we call emotions? Can these phenomena be understood without its aid?

Whoever would make clear to some one who has grown up with the common idea upon this subject, that if he is frightened his terror is only a perception of change in his body, would probably encounter the following objection: "Any such assumption of this relation is decisively contradicted by personal experience, since we have in terror, as in every emotion, a perfectly distinct sensation of a peculiar change, or of a definite, psychical state, wholly independent of anything bodily."

I can readily understand, that this objection has very great significance for the majority, and is difficult to overcome. Nevertheless it has of course in and of itself not the least value.

We have in fact no absolute and immediate means of determining whether a sensation is of a psychical or bodily character. Furthermore, no one is able to indicate the difference between psychical and somatic feelings. Whoever speaks of a psychical impression does so indeed solely upon the basis of a theory, and not upon an immediate perception. Without doubt, the mother who sorrows over her dead child would resist, probably even become indignant, if anyone were to say to her, that what she feels, is the exhaustion and inertness of her muscles, the numbness in her bloodless skin, the lack of mental power for clear and rapid thought [1]— all of which is made clear by the idea of the cause of these phenomena. There is no reason, however, for her to be indignant, for her feeling is just as strong, as deep and pure, whether it springs from the one, or the other source. But it cannot exist without its bodily attributes.

If from one terrified the accompanying bodily symptoms are removed, the pulse permitted to beat quietly, the glance to become firm, the color natural, the movements rapid and secure, the speech strong, the thoughts clear, — what is there left of his terror?

If we cannot rely, therefore, in this question upon the testimony of personal experience, because it is here incompetent, the matter is thereby naturally not yet explained. If the hypothesis of psychical emotions be not made necessary by subjective experience, it may nevertheless be requisite if without it one cannot perhaps understand how the bodily manifestations of the emotions come into existence.

We have consequently first to investigate, whether the bodily manifestations of the emotions can come into existence in

---

[1] I will not be deterred by the fact that it will probably be objected that one can feel pure psychical grief, joy, etc. if the emotion is not strong enough to lead to bodily symptoms. Such a supposition naturally rests only upon insufficient observation, or because one regards purely subjective sensations — those of lightness or pressure, of strength or weakness — as psychical.

purely bodily ways. If that is the case, the necessity of the psychical hypothesis is thereby removed.

In fact, it is not difficult to show from every day experience, which establishes and constantly verifies the truth, that emotions can be produced by many causes, which have nothing to do with movements of the mind; as on the other hand, that they can equally as well be checked and subdued by purely bodily means. It is known, though without clear consciousness of the true relation of things, that our entire mode of existence, our daily dietetics, has been formed during the course of generations essentially with the aim to promote the agreeable emotions, and to lessen or entirely to remove the painful. I will merely cite a single example, and that will serve to recall others. It is one of the oldest experiences of mankind "that wine maketh glad the heart of man;" and the power of spirituous beverages to combat the closely related states of grief and fear, and to replace them with joy and courage, has found an application, which is in and for itself natural enough, and would be unconditionally beneficial if the means did not possess in addition still other effects.

We all understand why Jeppe [1] drinks. It is because he will escape thereby from his conjugal troubles, and his fear of the master Erich. He will sing again, and recall the happy time when he was "in the militia." The glass makes him jovial and courageous, without the addition of a single pleasing or enlivening impression which could have any direct effect upon his mind, and without in the least forgetting his troubles or his enemies. All he wants is the influence of wine to view them in a manner different from the customary. He desires to impress his importance upon the sexton, and for once to chastise his wife. The alcohol has excited his vasomotor apparatus, has caused his heart to beat more rapidly and strongly, has enlarged his capillary ducts and thereby heightened his voluntary innervations, and as a consequence, he talks loudly, sings, and blusters, instead of lingering about, whimpering, and whining on the public way. He has the feeling of warmth, airiness, and

[1] Jeppe am Berge, a character in the classical comedy of Holberg.

strength, in place of his customary limpness and incapacity. His dull brain awakes again to new life by the quick circulation of blood, the thoughts come in a rush, old memories revive and displace the wonted feeling of his daily misery. And all this is due merely to a "peg" of spirits, the effect of which upon the circulation we can understand, and which has no need of the intervention of the mind to act upon the vasomotor centre.

All those who drink spirits have an experience of a similar nature to Jeppe's, and thus we have it in general among the means of enjoyment, in addition to the many arrangements that we make to procure for ourselves comfort and well being. So long as we remain within the easy and customary routine of daily life, the connection between our emotional states and material influences, (e.g., nutrition), naturally comes only rarely into the foreground. The relation is otherwise in the enjoyment of certain substances, which act upon the body so powerfully that they are employed like drugs, or are ranked under the category of poisons. Thus it is known that the eating of certain fungi, especially the fly agaric, can produce the most violent paroxysms of fury, and of violence. It has been conjectured that our warlike ancestors used such means to create the right mood for martial enterprises; therefore entirely similar to the way, in which one to-day drinks spirits to "revive courage." Fits of temper also often follow the partaking of hashish (indian hemp), which, ordinarily however like alcohol and opium, evokes a vivacious disposition, even outbursts of unbounded merriment.

Certain emetics, as ipecacuanha and tartar emetic, produce a feeling of depression, which oftentimes resembles fear, sometimes also grief, and like these emotions is accompanied by symptoms of collapse.

If emotional states can be precipitated by the enjoyment of certain substances, or in other purely bodily ways, it follows that one can combat and abate painful emotions in the same way. If spirits or opium produce joy, they are an antidote for sorrow.

The power of cold water to subdue temper and outbreaks of

passion finds occasionally a practical use, and can, when applied to the body, scarcely act directly upon the mind; but so much the more does it act upon the vasomotor functions. By the agency of a medicine, the well-known bromide of potassium, which causes paralysis of the vasomotor apparatus, we have it in our power not only to allay fear and anxiety, and similar uncomfortable emotions, but also, if we wish, to cause a perfectly apathetic condition, in which the individual is even as little able to become festive or sad, as anxious and angry, simply because the vasomotor functions are suspended.

If the theory of the nature of the emotions here advocated, is well founded, we may in a general way expect that every action connected with functional changes of the vasomotor system must also have an emotional expression. Naturally we should not expect that emotions originated in this way would conform in every way with the phenomenon for which we commonly reserve this designation; the differences in the causes naturally must find expression in this domain through differences in the effects. The different psychical causes have also in reality effects which are not at all congruous. The fear of ghosts is not imagined in the same form as fear of the bullets of an enemy. Nevertheless, the similarity in many cases between the bodily and the psychically conditioned emotions has been sufficiently striking to force itself upon immediate apprehension, as the many linguistic designations clearly prove. Thus in all languages there is one and the same expression for mental and bodily pain. We have recognized their great physiological similarity, although the marked phenomenon of bodily pain, namely the subjective sensation in consequence of the transmission of the peripheral stimulus to the sensorium, is lacking in the case of mental pain. The cause of similarity of the physical to the emotional pain is the reflex innervation of the vascular nerves, a normal effect of every rather strong stimulation of the sensitive nerves.

The term *shudder*, in this way, is the common designation in speech for the phenomena arising from the sudden effects of cold upon the skin, and also from terrifying impressions. That the naïve intelligence recognizes no distinction between the shuddering due to emotional, and that due to purely bodily causes, we perceive in the fairy tale of the youth, who went forth in order to find out what shuddering was, and who after seeking in vain to discover it in the company of the dead and of ghosts, had his wish fulfilled when he was thrown from his bed into a tub of ice cold water, which produced a more painful effect upon his vasomotor apparatus than the sight of corpses, and of ghosts.

The designation *feverish* for the man who is very impatient, likewise shows, that we have been impressed by the similarity which exists between the light symptoms of fever with their vasomotor disturbances, and those bodily conditions which are produced by disquieting expectations.

As already remarked, I shall not enter in this small treatise more minutely into the large question concerning the relation of the emotions with the corresponding pathological states, or with mental and bodily diseases.

But there exists in this connection a relation which I cannot pass entirely by, because it throws much light upon the question with which we are here occupied, that is, the necessity of the hypothesis of purely psychical emotions. If there is anything that in a striking way can prove the superfluous nature of this hypothesis, it is certainly the circumstance that the emotions arise without being evoked by any external impression, or by any occurrence which acts upon our mental life, or by any memory or association of ideas; and that they originate in optima forma solely upon the basis of the pathological conditions, which are developed in our bodies, or are inherited from parents.

If we set out from the theory here advocated this cannot be astonishing; for the vasomotor apparatus can of course upon occasion become diseased as readily as any other portion of the nervous system, so that it functions in an abnormal manner, or cannot function at all. We may even regard it as especially exposed to the danger of functioning in a pathological manner, because it is that part of the nervous system which has least rest and is most frequently liable to functional disturbances.

Where this happens in an individual, he becomes according to circumstances, depressed or distracted, anxious or unrestrainedly merry, embarrassed, etc. Everything is without apparent motive, and even though he is conscious of having no reason whatever for his anger, his fear, or his joy. Where is there any support here for the hypothesis of psychical emotion?

Such cases are extraordinarily frequent. Every alienist knows the sharply developed forms which appear as melancholia or mania; every physician who occupies himself at all thoroughly with nervous diseases has ample opportunity to observe the even more instructive light forms on the borderland between the real diseases of the mind and mere depressions, such as are included under the ordinary names of irritability, oddity, and dejection. Very frequently we find the dejection, the imaginary grief, or even despair, which often results in suicide, combined with clear consciousness of the entire absence of a single psychical motive for grief. Not much less frequent is the pathological anxiety, which often accompanies that related emotion of grief, but often enough is found alone. It goes without saying, that joy appears more rarely in actual pathological manifestations. The mere circumstance that a joy appears without motive will naturally, at least among the laity, seldom suffice to cause it to be regarded as pathological, and still less to cause medical treatment to be sought for the cure of this state. For such action it will be commonly necessary, that either the joy manifest itself in an entirely unrestrained and immoderate manner in the form of a more or less pronounced mania, or that it alternate in a striking fashion with periods of dejection, and thus attract attention as something unnatural. The same holds true of anger. We are in fact accustomed, as regards this emotion, to put up with a good deal without surmising it to be anything pathological, and as a rule we are not exacting as to its cause. But everything indeed has its limits, and there are outbreaks of anger often enough so groundless and unrestrained, that all will agree in recognizing them as manifestations of a pathological state.

There exists probably for those who have no medical training scarcely anything that can be more clarifying with reference to the diseased states of the mind here discussed, than the observation of such a pathological paroxysm of temper. Especially is this true, if it appears wholly uncomplicated by other psychical disturbances, as is the case in the form of illness which goes by the name of "transitory mania," and is indeed of rare occurrence. The attack comes often without the least apparent cause to an otherwise entirely sane person, if disposed thereto; and throws him — to use the language of a recent writer[1] upon this disease — into a state of wild paroxysm of rage, accompanied by a terrible and blindly furious impulse to injure and to destroy. The patient suddenly assails everything, strikes, kicks, and strangles whomsoever he can seize, throws everything about him that he can lay hands upon, breaks to pieces whatever comes near him, rends his clothes, screams, howls and roars with glaring rolling eyes, and thereby exhibits all the symptoms of vasomotor congestion which we have come to recognize as the accompaniment of madness. The face is flushed and swollen, the cheeks are hot, the eyes are bulging, their conjunctiva are filled with blood, the beating of the heart is increased, and the pulse reaches 100–120 strokes a minute. The neck arteries swell and throb, the veins are distended, the saliva flows. The fit lasts only a few hours, ends suddenly in a sleep of eight to ten hours duration, and upon waking the patient has entirely forgotten what has happened.

The pathological emotions here mentioned, which originate as stated from abnormal bodily conditions, can appear also as the results of other diseases, or proceed from digestive derangements. They are on that account influenced also by therapeutic methods, and can be alleviated or cured. The transitory mania above described, which has so evidently its cause in a sudden congestion of the brain, can, according to the author cited, be checked oftentimes by a bandage of ice upon the head.

I foresee here an objection which I shall not pass unnoticed in spite of its logical weakness. Undoubtedly many will say, in harmony with common usage, that the states which are occa-

[1] O. Schwartz. *Die transitorische Tobsucht.* Wien. 1880.

sioned by purely bodily influences or by diseased bodily conditions, can indeed be similar to the emotions, but they are not emotions. For example, the delirium that the fly agaric occasions, or that appears in mania, presents indeed the picture of rage, but is not "actual" rage, any more than the happiness which comes from drinking wine is "real" happiness. One cannot for that reason conclude from the absence of moral wrath in the person poisoned by fly agaric or possessed of a mania, that there does not exist at all any such purely psychical state, provided the wrath is brought about in the ordinary way by a moral impression.

It is easy to see that any such division of emotions into real and apparent, or any such limitation of the domain of real emotions is entirely arbitrary, and based upon a petitio principii. The reason of the claim to an exceptional position for the emotions of intellectual origin, as if they were the only real ones, is purely and solely the belief, that they are due to the activity of the mind. But that is precisely the question under discussion.

In reality the difference between the passion of the warrior frenzied by the fly agaric, or of the maniac, and of one who has suffered a mortal offence, exists only in the difference and in the consciousness of the respective causes, or in the absence of the consciousness of any cause. If one desires upon this basis to establish a distinction, there is naturally no objection to be made, provided only one is clear wherein the difference consists.

Moreover it is not so easy, as it probably appears, to draw a sharp line of distinction between material and psychical causes of emotion; if we seek to analyse their physiological difference, it resolves itself into something physiologically quite irrelevant, and slips from our grasp.

No one has ever thought of distinguishing a true emotion from one produced by an uncommonly loud noise. No one hesitates to regard it as a sort of fright; and in fact it shows all the usual characteristics of fright. And yet it is by no means united with the idea of danger, or in any way occasioned by an association of ideas, a memory, or any intellectual process whatever. The phenomena of fright follow the noise immediately without a trace of "mental" fear. Merely because of the noise of the report, many persons can never become accustomed to stand beside a cannon when it is discharged, although they know perfectly well there is no danger, either for themselves or for others. The case, moreover, of the infant can be cited, which exhibits all the symptoms of fear whenever it hears a loud noise, and yet we cannot reasonably assume that the sound excited in the child any idea of danger. In this case, we must assume that if the vasomotor reflexes are not directly caused by the acoustic nerves, they are at least by the direct action of the acoustic centres, and we have therefore an emotion of purely material origin.[1] We must therefore either exclude this fear from the true emotions, or we cannot strictly maintain the distinction between the mentally and the bodily conditioned emotions.

We are placed in the same dilemma by the emotions, as a rule certainly less intensive but nevertheless sufficiently distinct, which are produced by the simple impressions of the other sense organs, and are not united with any kind of association. Such are, for example, the pleasure from a charming color or combination of colors, the repugnance towards a disagreeable taste or odor, or the discomfort from a pain.

If one has only once begun to feel uncertain about the establishment of a line of demarcation between the mental and bodily causes of emotions, there arises a strong impulse to investigate what physiological significance can be attributed to their difference. One seeks then what difference exists in the cerebral mechanism of the emotions, according as they are determined by a so-called mental cause, or by one purely material.

To-day with our still very imperfect knowledge of cerebral physiology, it is certainly not very tempting to make an attempt at an explanation of what takes place in the brain as the result of mental work. Naturally, we can only sketch some fundamental outlines very roughly, and, in truth, with every

---

[1] That we here deal with a simple reflex, immediately produced in the motor nerves, as Preyer appears to suppose (*Die Seele des Kindes*, 2te Aufl. p. 51) is not probable; partly because these motor phenomena have not in general the character of reflex movement excited by a sudden impression, and partly because the effects in question are not confined to motor phenomena.

possible reserve with reference to the accuracy of the results. Nevertheless, in psychological investigations it is not only justifiable, but is also correct and useful to examine how closely we can approach a solution with our present physiological knowledge. At all events we can take courage from the fact, that we know the relations here discussed — in their chief characteristics at least — are of their kind almost the simplest, and the easiest to fathom.*

---

* "The only point," says Th. Ribot in his *The Psychology of the Emotions,* "in which I differ from these authors [James and Lange] relates to their way of putting the proposition, not to its substance.

" It is evident that our two authors, whether consciously or not, share the dualist point of view with the common opinion which they are combating; the only difference being in the interversion of cause and effect. Emotion is a cause of which the physical manifestations are the effect, says one party; the physical manifestations are the cause of which emotion is the effect, says the other. In my view, there would be a great advantage in eliminating from the question every notion of cause and effect, every relation of causality, and in substituting for the dualistic position a unitary or monistic one. The Aristotelian formula of matter and form seems to me to meet the case better, if we understand by 'matter' the corporeal facts, and by 'form' the corresponding psychical state: the two terms, by-the-bye, only existing in connection with each other and being inseparable except as abstract conceptions. It was traditional in ancient psychology to study the relations of 'the soul and the body' — the new psychology does not speak of them. In fact, if the question takes a metaphysical form, it is no longer psychology; if it takes an experimental form, there is no reason to treat it separately, because it is treated in connection with everything. No state of consciousness can be dissociated from its physical conditions: they constitute a natural whole, which must be studied as such. Every kind of emotion ought to be considered in this way: all that is objectively expressed by the movements of the face and body, by vasomotor, respiratory, and secretory disturbances, is expressed subjectively by correlative states of consciousness, classed by external observation according to their qualities. It is a single occurrence expressed in two languages. We have previously assimilated the emotions to psycho-physiological organisms; this unitary point of view, being more conformable to the nature of things and to the present tendencies of psychology, seems to me, in practice, to eliminate many objections and difficulties. Whether we adopt this theory or not, we have in any case acquired the certainty that the organic and motor manifestations are not accessories, that the study of them is part of the study of emotion." Pp. 111–112.

WILHELM WUNDT
(1832–   )

PRINCIPLES OF PHYSIOLOGICAL PSYCHOLOGY

Translated from the German * by
EDWARD BRADFORD TITCHENER

INTRODUCTION

§ 1. The Problem of Physiological Psychology

THE title of the present work is in itself a sufficiently clear indication of the contents. In it, the attempt is made to show the connexion between two sciences whose subject-matters are closely interrelated, but which have, for the most part, followed wholly divergent paths. Physiology and psychology cover, between them, the field of vital phenomena; they deal with the facts of life at large, and in particular with the facts of human life. Physiology is concerned with all those phenomena of life that present themselves to us in sense perception as bodily processes, and accordingly, form part of that total environment which we name the external world. Psychology, on the other hand, seeks to give account of the interconnexion of processes which are evinced by our own consciousness, or which we infer from such manifestations of the bodily life in other creatures as indicate the presence of a consciousness similar to our own.

This division of vital processes into physical and psychical is useful and even necessary for the solution of scientific problems. We must, however, remember that the life of an organ-

---

* From *Grundzüge der physiologischen Psychologie*, 2 Bde. Leipzig, 1873–74; 5 umgearb. Aufl. 3 Bde. 1902. Reprinted here from W. Wundt's *Principles of Physiological Psychology*, translated by E. B. Titchener, New York, The Macmillan Co. 1904.

ism is really one; complex, it is true, but still unitary. We can, therefore, no more separate the processes of bodily life from conscious processes than we can mark off an outer experience, mediated by sense perceptions, and oppose it, as something wholly separate and apart, to what we call 'inner' experience, the events of our own consciousness. On the contrary: just as one and the same thing, e.g., a tree that I perceive before me, falls as external object within the scope of natural science, and as conscious contents within that of psychology, so there are many phenomena of the physical life that are uniformly connected with conscious processes, while these in turn are always bound up with processes in the living body. It is a matter of every-day experience that we refer certain bodily movements directly to volitions, which we can observe as such only in our consciousness. Conversely, we refer the ideas of external objects that arise in consciousness either to direct affection of the organs of sense, or, in the case of memory images, to physiological excitations within the sensory centres, which we interpret as after-effects of foregone sense impressions.

It follows then, that physiology and psychology have many points of contact. In general, there can of course be no doubt that their problems are distinct. But psychology is called upon to trace out the relations that obtain between conscious processes and certain phenomena of the physical life; and physiology, on its side, cannot afford to neglect the conscious contents in which certain phenomena of this bodily life manifest themselves to us. Indeed, as regards physiology, the interdependence of the two sciences is plainly in evidence. Practically everything that the physiologists tell us, by way of fact or of hypothesis, concerning the processes in the organs of sense and in the brain, is based upon determinate mental symptoms: so that psychology has long been recognised, explicitly or implicitly, as an indispensable auxiliary of physiological investigation. Psychologists, it is true, have been apt to take a different attitude towards physiology. They have tended to regard as superfluous any reference to the physical organism; they have supposed that nothing more is required for a science of mind than the direct apprehension of conscious processes themselves. It is in token of dissent from any such standpoint that the present work is entitled a "physiological psychology." We take issue, upon this matter, with every treatment of psychology that is based on simple self-observation or on philosophical presuppositions. We shall, whenever the occasion seems to demand, employ physiology in the service of psychology. We are thus, as was indicated above, following the example of physiology itself, which has never been in a position to disregard facts that properly belong to psychology, — although it has often been hampered in its use of them by the defects of the empirical or metaphysical psychology which it has found current.

Physiological psychology is, therefore, first of all *psychology*. It has in view the same principal object upon which all other forms of psychological exposition are directed: *the investigation of conscious processes in the modes of connexion peculiar to them.* It is not a province of physiology; nor does it attempt, as has been mistakenly asserted, to derive or explain the phenomena of the psychical from those of the physical life. We may read this meaning into the phrase 'physiological psychology,' just as we might interpret the title 'microscopical anatomy' to mean a discussion, with illustrations from anatomy, of what has been accomplished by the microscope; but the words should be no more misleading in the one case than they are in the other. As employed in the present work, the adjective 'physiological' implies simply that our psychology will avail itself to the full of the means that modern physiology puts at its disposal for the analysis of conscious processes. It will do this in two ways.

(1) Psychological inquiries have, up to the most recent times, been undertaken solely in the interest of philosophy; physiology was enabled, by the character of its problems, to advance more quickly towards the application of exact experimental methods. Since, however, the experimental modification of the processes of life, as practised by physiology, oftentimes effects a concomitant change, direct or indirect, in the processes of consciousness, — which, as we have seen, form part of vital processes at large,

— it is clear that physiology is, in the very nature of the case, qualified to assist psychology on the side of *method;* thus rendering the same help to psychology that it itself received from physics. In so far as physiological psychology receives assistance from physiology in the elaboration of experimental methods, it may be termed *experimental psychology.* This name suggests, what should not be forgotten that psychology, in adopting the experimental methods of physiology, does not by any means take them over as they are, and apply them without change to a new material. The methods of experimental psychology have been transformed — in some instances, actually remodelled — by psychology itself, to meet the specific requirements of psychological investigation. Psychology has adapted physiological, as physiology adapted psychical methods, to its own ends.

(2) An adequate definition of life, taken in the wider sense, must (as we said just now) cover both the vital processes of the physical organism and the processes of consciousness. Hence, wherever we meet with vital phenomena that present the two aspects, physical and psychical, there naturally arises a question as to the relations in which these aspects stand to each other. So we come face to face with a whole series of special problems, which may be occasionally touched upon by physiology or psychology, but which cannot receive their final solution at the hands of either, just by reason of that division of labour to which both sciences alike stand committed. Experimental psychology is no better able to cope with them than is any other form of psychology, seeing that it differs from its rivals only in method, and not in aim or purpose. Physiological psychology, on the other hand, is competent to investigate the relations that hold between the processes of the physical and those of the mental life. And in so far as it accepts this second problem, we may name it a *psychophysics.* If we free this term from any sort of metaphysical implication as to the relation of mind and body, and understand by it nothing more than an investigation of the relations that may be shown empirically to obtain between the psychical and the physical aspects of vital processes, it is clear at once that psychophysics becomes

for us not, what it is sometimes taken to be, a science intermediate between physiology and psychology, but rather a science that is auxiliary to both. It must, however, render service more especially to psychology, since the relations existing between determinate conditions of the physical organisation, on the one hand, and the processes of consciousness, on the other, are primarily of interest to the psychologist. In its final purpose, therefore, this psychophysical problem that we have assigned to physiological psychology proves to be itself psychological. In execution, it will be predominantly physiological, since psychophysics is concerned to follow up the anatomical and physiological investigation of the bodily substrates of conscious processes, and to subject its results to critical examination with a view to their bearing upon our psychical life.

There are thus two problems which are suggested by the title " physiological psychology ": the problem of *method*, which involves the application of experiment, and the problem of a psychophysical *supplement*, which involves a knowledge of the bodily substrates of the mental life. For psychology itself, the former is the more essential; the second is of importance mainly for the philosophical question of the unitariness of vital processes at large.   As an experimental science, physiological psychology seeks to accomplish a reform in psychological investigation comparable with the revolution brought about in the natural sciences by the introduction of the experimental method. From one point of view, indeed, the change wrought is still more radical: for while in natural science it is possible, under favorable conditions, to make an accurate observation without recourse to experiment, there is no such possibility in psychology. It is only with grave reservations that what is called 'pure self-observation' can properly be termed observation at all, and under no circumstances can it lay claim to accuracy. On the other hand, it is of the essence of experiment that we can vary the conditions of an occurrence at will and, if we are aiming at exact results, in a quantitatively determinable way. Hence, even in the domain of natural science, the aid of the experimental method becomes indispensable whenever the problem set is the analysis of transient and impermanent phenomena, and not merely the observation of persistent and relatively constant objects. But conscious contents are at the opposite pole from permanent objects; they are processes, fleeting occurrences, in continual flux and change. In their case, therefore, the experimental method is of cardinal importance; it and it alone makes a scientific introspection possible. For all accurate observation implies that the object of observation (in this case the psychical process) can be held fast by the attention, and any changes that it undergoes attentively followed. And this fixation by the attention implies, in its turn, that the observed object is independent of the observer. Now it is obvious that the required independence does not obtain in any attempt at a direct self-observation, undertaken without the help of experiment. The endeavour to observe oneself must inevitably introduce changes into the course of mental events, — changes which could not have occurred without it, and whose usual consequence is that the very process which was to have been observed disappears from consciousness. The psychological experiment proceeds very differently. In the first place, it creates external conditions that look towards the production of a determinate mental process at a given moment. In the second place, it makes the observer so far master of the general situation, that the state of consciousness accompanying this process remains approximately unchanged. The great importance of the experimental method, therefore, lies not simply in the fact that, here as in the physical realm, it enables us arbitrarily to vary the conditions of our observations, but also and essentially in the further fact that it makes observation itself possible for us. The results of this observation may then be fruitfully employed in the examination of other mental phenomena, whose nature prevents their own direct experimental modification.

We may add that, fortunately for the science, there are other sources of objective psychological knowledge, which become accessible at the very point where the experimental method fails us. These are certain products of the common mental life, in which we may trace the operation of determinate psychical motives: chief among them are language, myth and custom. In part determined by historical conditions, they are also, in part, dependent upon universal psychological laws; and the phenomena that are referable to these laws form the subject-matter of a special psychological discipline, *ethnic* psychology. The results of ethnic psychology constitute, at the same time, our chief source of information regarding the general psychology of the complex mental processes. In this way, experimental psychology and ethnic psychology form the two principal departments of scientific psychology at large. They are supplemented by *child* and *animal* psychology, which in conjunction with ethnic psychology attempt to resolve the problems of psychogenesis. Workers in both these fields may, of course, avail themselves within certain limits of the advantages of the experimental method. But the results of experiment are here matters of objective observation only, and the experimental method accordingly loses the peculiar significance which it possesses as an instrument of introspection. Finally, child psychology and experimental psychology in the narrower sense may be bracketed together as *individual* psychology, while animal psychology and ethnic psychology form the two halves of a *generic* or *comparative* psychology. These distinctions within psychology are, however, by no means to be put on a level with the analogous divisions of the province of physiology. Child psychology and animal psychology are of relatively slight importance, as compared with the sciences which deal with the corresponding physiological problems of ontogeny and phylogeny. On the other hand, ethnic psychology must always come to the assistance of individual psychology, when the developmental forms of the complex mental processes are in question.

§ 3. PREPSYCHOLOGICAL CONCEPTS

The human mind is so constituted, that it cannot gather experiences without at the same time supplying an admixture of its own speculation. The first result of this naïve reflection is the system of concepts which language embodies. Hence, in all departments of human experience, there are certain concepts that science finds ready made, before it proceeds upon its own proper business, — results of that primitive reflection which has left its permanent record in the concept-system of language. 'Heat' and 'light,' e.g., are concepts from the world of external experience, which had their immediate origin in sense perception. Modern physics subsumes them both under the general concept of motion. But it would not be able to do this, if the physicist had not been willing provisionally to accept the concepts of the common consciousness, and to begin his inquiries with their investigation. 'Mind,' 'intellect,' 'reason,' 'understanding,' etc., are concepts of just the same kind, concepts that existed before the advent of any scientific psychology. The fact that the naïve consciousness always and everywhere points to internal experience as a special source of knowledge, may, therefore, be accepted for the moment as sufficient testimony to the rights of psychology as science. And this acceptance implies the adoption of the concept of 'mind,' to cover the whole field of internal experience. 'Mind,' will accordingly be the subject, to which we attribute all the separate facts of internal observation as predicates. The subject itself is determined wholly and exclusively by its predicates; and the reference of these to a common substrate must be taken as nothing more than an expression of their reciprocal connexion. In saying this, we are declining once and for all to read into the concept of 'mind' a meaning that the naïve linguistic consciousness always attaches to it. Mind, in popular thought, is not simply a subject in the logical sense, but a substance, a real being; and the various 'activities of mind,' as they are termed, are its modes of expression or action. But there is here involved a metaphysical presupposition, which psychology may possibly be led to honour at the conclusion of her work, but which she cannot on any account accept, untested, before she has entered upon it. Moreover, it is not true of this assumption as it was of the discrimination of internal experience at large, that it is necessary for the starting of the investigation. The words coined by language to symbolise certain groups of experiences still bear upon them marks which show that, in their primitive meanings, they stood not merely for separate modes of existence, for 'substances,' in general, but actually for personal beings. This personification of substances has left its most indelible trace in the concept of genus. Now the word-symbols of conceptual ideas have passed so long from hand to hand in the service of the understanding, that they have gradually lost all such fanciful reference. There are many cases in which we have seen the end, not only of the personification of substances, but even of the substantialising of concepts. But we are not called upon, on that account, to dispense with the use whether of the concepts themselves or of the words that designate them. We speak of virtue, honour, reason; but our thought does not translate any one of these concepts into a substance. They have ceased to be metaphysical substances, and have become logical subjects. In the same way, then, we shall consider mind, for the time being, simply as the logical subject of internal experience. Such a view follows directly from the mode of concept-formation employed by language, except that it is freed of all those accretions of crude metaphysics which invariably attach to concepts in their making by the naïve consciousness.

We must take up a precisely similar attitude to other ready-made concepts that denote special departments or special relations of the internal experience. Thus our language makes a distinction between 'mind' and 'spirit.' The two concepts carry the same meaning, but carry it in different contexts: their correlates in the domain of external experience are 'body' and 'matter.' The name 'matter' is applied to any object of external experience as it presents itself directly to our senses, without reference to an inner existence of its own. 'Body' is matter thought of with reference to such an inner existence. 'Spirit,' in the same way, denotes the internal existence as considered out of all connexion with an external existence; whereas 'mind,' especially where it is explicitly opposed to spirit, presupposes this connexion with a corporeal existence, given in external experience.

While the terms 'mind' and 'spirit' cover the whole field of internal experience, the various 'mental faculties,' as they are called, designate the special provinces of mind as distinguished by a direct introspection. Language brings against us an array of concepts like 'sensibility,' 'feeling,' 'reason,' 'understanding,' — a classification of the processes given in internal perception against which, bound down as we are to the use of these words, we are practically powerless. What we can do, however, and what science is obliged to do, is to reach an exact definition of the concepts, and to arrange them upon a systematic plan. It is probable that the mental faculties stood originally not merely for different parts of the field of internal experience, but for as many different beings; though the relation of these to the total being, the mind or spirit, was not conceived of in any very definite way. But the hypostatisation of these concepts lies so far back in the remote past, and the mythological interpretation of nature is so alien to our modes of thought, that there is no need here to warn the reader against a too great credulity in the matter of metaphysical substances. Nevertheless, there is one legacy which has come down to modern science from the mythopœic age. All the concepts that we mentioned just now have retained a trace of the mythological concept of *force;* they are not regarded simply as — what they really are — class-designations of certain departments of the inner experience, but are oftentimes taken to be forces, by whose means the various phenomena are produced. Understanding is looked upon as the force that enables us to perceive truth; memory as the force which stores up ideas for future use; and so on. On the other hand, the effects of these different 'forces' manifest themselves so irregularly that they hardly seem to be forces in the proper sense of the word; and so the phrase 'mental faculties' came in to remove all objections. A faculty, as its derivation indicates, is not a force that must operate, necessarily and immutably, but only a force that may operate. The influence of the mythological concept of force is here as plain as it could well be; for the prototype of the operation of force as faculty is, obviously, to be found in human action. The original significance of faculty is that of a being which acts. Here, therefore, in the first formation of psychological concepts, we have the germ of that confusion of classification with explanation which is one of the besetting sins of empirical psychology. The general statement that the mental faculties are class concepts, belonging to descriptive psychology, relieves us of the necessity of discussing them and their significance at the present stage of our inquiry. As a matter of fact, one can quite well conceive of a natural science of the internal experience in which sensibility, memory, reason and understanding should be conspicuous by their absence. For the only things that we are directly cognisant of in internal perception are individual ideas, feelings, impulses, etc.; and the subsumption of these individual facts under certain general concepts contributes absolutely nothing toward their explanation.

At the present day, the uselessness of the faculty-concepts is almost universally conceded. Again, however, there is one point in which they still exercise a widespread influence. Not the general class-concepts, but the individual facts that, in the old order of things, were subsumed under them, are now regarded in many quarters as independent phenomena, existing in isolation. On this view there is, to be sure, no special faculty of ideation or feeling or volition; but the individual idea, the individual affective process, and the individual voluntary act are looked upon as independent processes, connecting with one another and separating from one another as circumstances determine. Now introspection declares that all these professedly independent processes are through and through interconnected and interdependent. It is evident, therefore, that their separation involves just the same translation of the products of abstraction into real things as we have charged to the account of the old doctrine of faculties,— only that in this case the abstractions come a little nearer to the concrete phenomena. An isolated idea, an idea that is separable from the processes of feeling and volition, no more exists than does an isolated mental force of 'understanding.' Necessary as these distinctions are, then, we must still never forget that they are based upon abstractions, — that they do not carry with them any real separation of objects. Objectively, we can regard the individual mental processes only as inseparable elements of interconnected wholes.

OUTLINES OF PSYCHOLOGY

*Translated from the German * by*
CHARLES HUBBARD JUDD

II. PSYCHICAL COMPOUNDS

§ 14. VOLITIONAL PROCESSES

1. Every emotion, made up, as it is, of a unified series of interrelated affective processes, may terminate in one of two ways. It may give place to the ordinary, variable, and relatively unemotional course of feelings. Such effective processes which fade out without any special result, constitute the *emotions in the strict sense*, such as were discussed in the last paragraph. In a second class of cases the emotional process may pass into a *sudden* change in ideational and affective content, which brings the emotion to an instantaneous close; such changes in the sensation and affective state which are prepared for by an emotion and bring about its sudden end, are called *volitional acts*. The emotion together with its result is a *volitional process*.

A volitional process is thus related to an emotion as a process of a higher stage, in the same way that an emotion is related to a feeling. Volitional act is the name of only one part of the process, that part which distinguishes a volition from an emotion. The way for the development of volitions out of emotions is prepared by those emotions in connection with which external pantomimetic expressive movements appear. These expressive movements appear chiefly at the end of the process and generally hasten its completion; this is especially true of anger, but to some extent also of joy, care, etc. Still, in these mere emotions there is an entire absence of changes

---

* From the *Grundviss der Psychologie*, Lpz. 1896; 7 verb. Aufl. 1905. Reprinted from Wundt's *Outlines of Psychology* translated by C. H. Judd, Lpz. 1897; 3 rev. ed. 1907.

in the train of ideas, which changes are the immediate causes of the momentary transformation of the emotion into volitions, and are also accompanied by characteristic feelings.

This close interconnection of volitional acts with pantomimetic expressive movements necessarily leads us to consider as the earliest stages of volitional development those volitions which end in certain bodily movements, which are in turn due to the preceding train of ideas and feelings. In other words, we come to look upon volition ending in *external* volitional acts, as the earliest stages in the development of volitions. The so-called *internal* volitional acts, on the other hand, or those which close simply with effects on ideas and feelings, appear in every case to be products of later development.

2. A volitional process which passes into an *external* act may be defined as an emotion which closes with a pantomimetic movement and has, in addition to the characteristics belonging to all such movements, the special property of *producing an external effect which removes the emotion itself*. Such an effect is not possible for all emotions, but only for those in which the very succession of component feelings produces feelings and ideas which are able to remove the preceding emotion. This is, of course, most commonly the case when the final result of the emotion is the direct opposite of the preceding feelings. The fundamental psychological condition for volitional acts is, therefore, the *contrast between feelings*, and the origin of the first volitions is most probably in all cases to be traced back to unpleasurable feelings which arouse external movements, which in turn produce contrasted pleasurable feelings. The seizing of food to remove hunger, the struggle against enemies to appease the feeling of revenge, and other similar processes are original volitional processes of this kind. The emotions coming from sense-feelings, and the most widespread social emotions such as love, hate, anger, and revenge, are thus, both in men and animals, the common origin of will. A volition is distinguished in such cases from an emotion only by the fact that the former has added to its emotional components an external act that gives rise to feelings which, through contrast

with the feelings contained in the emotion, bring the emotion itself to an end. The execution of the volitional act may then lead directly, as was originally always the case, or indirectly through an emotion of contrasted effective content, into the ordinary quiet flow of feelings.

3. The richer the ideational and affective contents of experience, the greater the variety of the emotions and the wider the sphere of volitions. There is no feeling or emotion which does not in some way prepare for a volitional act, or at least have some part in such a preparation. All feelings, even those of a relatively indifferent character, contain in some degree an effort towards or away from some end. This effort may be very general and aimed merely at the maintenance or removal of the present affective state. While volition appears as the most complex form of affective process, presupposing feelings and emotions as its components, still, we must not overlook, on the other hand, the fact that single feelings continually appear which do not unite to form emotions, and emotions appear which do not end in volitional acts. In the total interconnection of psychical processes, however, these three stages are conditions of one another and form the related parts of a single process which is complete only when it becomes a volition. In this sense a feeling may be thought of as the beginning of a volition, or a volition may be thought of as a composite affective process, and an emotion may be regarded as an intermediate stage between the two.

4. The single feelings in an emotion which closes with a volitional act are usually far from being of equal importance. Certain ones among them, together with their related ideas, are prominent as those which are *most important* in preparing for the act. Those combinations of ideas and feelings which in our subjective consciousness are the immediate antecedents of the act, are called *motives* of volition. Every motive may be divided into an ideational and an affective component. The first we may call the *moving reason*, the second the *impelling feeling* of action. When a beast of prey seizes his victim, the moving reason is the sight of the victim, the impelling feeling may be

either the unpleasurable feeling of hunger or the race-hate aroused by the sight. The reason for a criminal murder may be theft, removal of an enemy, or some such idea, the impelling feeling the feeling of want, hate, revenge, or envy.

When the emotions are of composite character, the reasons and impelling feelings are mixed, often to so great an extent that it would be difficult for the author of the act himself to decide which was the leading motive. This is due to the fact that the impelling feelings of a volitional act combine, just as the elements of composite feelings do, to form a *unitary* whole in which all other impulses are subordinated to a single predominating one; the feelings of like direction strengthening and accelerating the effect, those of opposite direction weakening it. In the combinations of ideas and feelings which we call motives, the final weight of importance in preparing for the act of will belongs to the feelings, that is, to the impelling feelings rather than to the ideas. This follows from the very fact that feelings are integral components of the volitional process itself, while the ideas are of influence only indirectly, through their connections with the feelings. The assumption that a volition may arise from pure intellectual considerations, or that a decision may appear which is opposed to the inclinations expressed in the feelings, is a psychological contradiction in itself. It rests upon the abstract concept of a will which is transcendental and absolutely distinct from actual psychical volitions. The combination of a number of motives, that is, the combination of a number of ideas and feelings which stand out from the composite train of emotions to which they belong as the ideas and feelings which determine the final discharge of the act — this combination furnished the essential condition for the *development of will*, and also for the discrimination of the *single forms of volitional action*.

5. The simplest case of volition is that in which a single feeling in an emotion of suitable constitution, together with its accompanying idea, becomes a motive and brings the process to a close through an appropriate external movement. Such volitional processes determined by a *single* motive, may be

called *simple volitions*. The movements in which they terminate are designated *impulsive acts*. In popular parlance, however, this definition of impulse by the simplicity of the motive, is not sufficiently adhered to. Another element, namely, the character of the feeling that acts as impelling force is, in popular thought, usually brought into the definition. All acts that are determined by *sense-feelings*, especially common feelings, are generally called impulsive acts without regard to whether a single motive or a plurality of motives is operative. This basis of discrimination is psychologically inappropriate and there is no justification for the complete separation to which it naturally leads between impulsive acts and volitional acts as specifically distinct kinds of psychical processes.

By impulsive act, then, we mean a *simple* volitional act, that is, one resulting from a single motive, without reference to the relative position of this motive in the series of affective and ideational processes. Impulsive action, thus defined, must necessarily be the starting point for the development of all volitional acts, even though it may continue to appear later, along with the complex volitional processes. To be sure, the earliest impulsive acts are those which come from sense-feeling. Thus, most of the acts of animals are impulsive, but such impulsive acts appear continually in the case of man, partly as the results of simple sense emotions, partly as the products of the habitual execution of certain volitional acts which were originally determined by complex motives (10).

6. When several feelings and ideas in the same emotion tend to produce external action, and when those components of an emotional train which have become motives tend at the same time toward different external ends, whether related or antagonistic, then there arises out of the simple act a *complex volitional process*. In order to distinguish this from a simple volitional act, or impulsive act, we call it a *voluntary act*.

Voluntary and impulsive acts have in common the characteristic of proceeding from *single* motives, or from complexes of motives which have fused together and operate as a single *unequivocal* impulse. They differ in the fact that in voluntary

acts the decisive motive has risen to predominance from among
a number of simultaneous and antagonistic motives. When a
clearly perceptible conflict between these antagonistic motives
precedes the act, we call the volition by the particular name
selective act, and the process preceding it we call a *choice*. The
predominance of one motive over other simultaneous motives
can be understood only when we presuppose such a conflict
in every case. But we are conscious of this conflict sometimes
clearly, sometimes only vaguely. It is only in those cases in
which we are clearly conscious of the conflict that we speak of
choice in the narrower sense of the word. The difference between a voluntary activity and a choice activity is therefore
a vanishing quantity. We may say, however, that the ordinary voluntary process is one in which the psychological condition approaches in character impulsive activity, while in
choice the difference between impulsive activity and the higher
mode of behavior is always clear. We can represent these different relations, which appear at different stages of voluntary
development, most ob-
viously through some
such schematic dia-
gram as that in Fig. 1.
In this diagram the
large circles represent
in each case the total
field of consciousness,

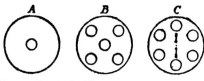

Fig. 1. Symbolical Representation of (*A*) an
Impulsive Act, (*B*) a Volitional Act, and
(*C*) a Choice.

while the small circles within the large ones indicate an idea
with a feeling tone which serves as the motive. The small
circle which lies in the middle represents the decisive motive.
Diagram *A* represents an impulsive activity, *B* a voluntary
activity, and *C* a choice activity. In *C* alone the conflict of
motives is represented. This is shown in the figure in the
arrows which extend between the circles and the central point
and represent the conflict of motives.

7. The psychical process immediately preceding the act,
in which process the final motive suddenly gains the ascend-
ency, is called in the case of voluntary acts *resolution*, in the

case of selective acts *decision*. The first word indicates merely that action is to be carried out in accordance with some consciously adopted motive; the second implies that several courses of action have been presented as possible and that a choice has finally been made.

In contrast to the *first stages* of a volition, which can not be clearly distinguished from an ordinary emotional process, the *last stages* of volition are absolutely characteristic. They are especially marked by accompanying *feelings* which never appear anywhere but in volitions, and must therefore be regarded as the specific elements peculiar to volition. These feelings are first of all *feelings of resolution and feelings of decision*. Feelings of decision differ from feelings of resolution only in the fact that the former are more intense. They are both exciting and relaxing feelings, and may be united under various circumstances with pleasurable or unpleasurable factors. The relatively greater intensity of the feeling of decision is probably due to its contrast with the preceding feeling of *doubt* which attends the wavering between different motives. The opposition between doubt and decision gives the feeling of relaxation a greater intensity. At the moment when the volitional act begins, the feelings of resolution give place to the specific *feeling* of *activity*, which has its sensation substratum, in the case of external volitional acts, in the sensations of tension accompanying the movement. This feeling of activity is clearly exciting in its character, and may, according to the special motives, of the volition, be accompanied now by pleasurable, now by unpleasurable elements, which may in turn vary in the course of the act and alternate with one another. As a total feeling, this feeling of activity is a rising and falling temporal process extending through the whole act and finally passing into the widely differing feelings, such as those of fulfilment, satisfaction, or disappointment, or into the feelings and emotions connected with the special result of the act. Taking the process as seen in voluntary and selective acts as *complete* volitional acts, the essential reason for distinguishing *impulsive* acts from complete volitional acts is to be found in the absence of the antecedent feelings of resolution, and decision. The feeling connected with the motive passes in the case of impulsive acts directly into the feeling of activity, and then into the feelings which correspond to the effect of the act.

8. The transition from simple to complex volitional acts brings with it a number of other changes which are of great importance for the development of will. The first of these changes is to be found in the fact that the *emotions* which introduce volitions lose their intensity more and more, as a result of the counteraction of different mutually inhibiting feelings, so that finally a volitional act may result from an apparently unemotional affective state. To be sure, emotion is never entirely wanting; in order that the motive which arises in an ordinary train of feelings may bring about a resolution or decision, it must always be connected with some degree of emotional excitement. The emotional excitement can, however, be so weak and transient that we overlook it. We do this the more easily the more we are inclined to unite in the *single* idea of the volition both the short emotion which merely attends the rise and action of the motive, and the resolution and execution which constitute the act itself. This weakening of the emotions results mainly from the combinations of psychical processes which we call *intellectual* development and of which we shall treat more fully in the discussion of the interconnection of psychical compounds (§ 17). Intellectual processes can, indeed, never do away with emotions; such processes are, on the contrary, in many cases the sources of new and characteristic emotions. A volition entirely without emotion, determined by a purely intellectual motive, is, as already remarked (p. 700), a psychological impossibility. Still, intellectual development exercises beyond a doubt a moderating influence on emotions. This is particularly true whenever intellectual motives enter into the emotions which prepare the way for volitional acts. This may be due partly to the counteraction of the feelings which generally takes place, or it may be due partly to the slow development of intellectual motives, for emotions usually are the stronger, the more rapidly their component feelings rise.

9. Connected with this moderation of the emotional components of volitions under the influence of intellectual motives, is still another change. It consists in the fact that the *act* which closes the volition is not an external movement. The effect which removes the exciting emotion is itself a psychical process which does not show itself directly through any external symptom whatever. Such an effect which is imperceptible for objective observation is called an *internal volitional act*. The transition from external to internal volitional acts is so bound up with intellectual development that the very character of the intellectual processes themselves is to be explained to a great extent by the influence of volitions on the train of ideas (§ 15, 9). The act which closes the volition in such a case is some change in the train of ideas, which change follows the preceding motives as the result of some resolution or decision. The feelings which accompany these acts of immediate preparation, and the feeling of activity connected with the change itself, agree entirely with the feelings observed in the case of external volitional acts. Furthermore, action is followed by more or less intense feelings of satisfaction, and a removal of preceding emotional and affective strain. The only difference, accordingly, between these special volitions connected with the intellectual development and the earlier forms of volition, is to be found in the fact that here the final effect of the volition does not show itself in an external bodily movement.

Still, we may have a bodily movement as the *secondary* result of an internal volitional act, when the resolution refers to an external act to be executed at some later time. In such a case the act itself always results from a second, later volition. The decisive motives for this second process come, to be sure, from the preceding internal volition, but the two are nevertheless distinct and different processes. Thus, for example, the formation of a resolution to execute an act in the future under certain expected conditions, is an internal volition, while the later performance of the act is an external action different from the first, even though requiring the first as a necessary antecedent. It is evident that where an external volitional act arises from a decision after a conflict among the motives, we have a transitional form in which it is impossible to distinguish clearly between the two kinds of volition, namely, that which consists in a single unitary process and that which is made up of *two* processes, that is, of an earlier and a later volition. In such a transitional form, if the decision is at all separated in time from the act itself, the decision may be regarded as an internal volitional act preparatory to the execution.

10. These two changes which take place during the development of will, namely, the moderation of emotions and the rendering independent of internal volitions, are changes of a progressive order. In contrast with these there is a *third* process which is one of *retrogradation*. When complex volitions with the same motive are often repeated, the conflict between the motives grows less intense; the opposing motives which were overcome in earlier cases grow weaker and finally disappear entirely. The complex act has then passed into a simple, or *impulsive act*. This retrogradation of complex volitional processes shows clearly the utter inappropriateness of the limitation of the concept "impulsive" to acts of will arising from sense-feelings. As a result of the gradual elimination of opposing motives, there are intellectual, moral, and æsthetic, as well as simple sensuous, impulsive acts.

This regressive development is but one step in a process which unites all the external acts of living being, whether they are volitional acts or automatic reflex movements. When the habituating practice of certain acts is carried further, the determining motives finally become, even in impulsive acts, weaker and more transient. The external stimulus originally aroused a strongly affective idea which operated as a motive, but now the stimulus causes the discharge of the act before it can arouse an idea. In this way the impulsive movement finally becomes an *automatic* movement. The more often this automatic movement is repeated, the easier it, in turn, becomes, even when the stimulus is not sensed, as for example in deep sleep or during complete diversion of the attention. The movement now appears as a pure physiological reflex, and the volitional process has become a simple *reflex process*.

This gradual *reduction of volitional to mechanical processes*, which depends essentially on the elimination of all the psychical elements between the beginning and end of the act, may take place either in the case of movements which were originally impulsive, or in the case of movements which have become impulsive through the retrogradation of voluntary acts. It is not improbable that all the reflex movements of both animals and men originate in this way. As evidence of this we have, besides the above described reduction of volitional acts through practice to pure mechanical processes, also the *purposeful character of reflexes*, which points to the presence at some time of purposive ideas as motives. Furthermore, the fact that the movements of the lowest animals are all evidently simple volitional acts, not reflexes, tells for the same view, so that here too there is no justification for the assumption frequently made that acts of will have been developed from reflex movements. Finally, we can most easily explain from this point of view the fact mentioned in § 13, namely, that *expressive movements* may belong to any one of the forms possible in the scale of external acts. Obviously the simplest movements are impulsive acts, while many complicated pantomimetic movements probably came originally from voluntary acts which passed first into impulsive and then into reflex movements. Observed phenomena make it necessary to assume that the retrogradations which begin in the individual life are gradually carried further through the transmission of acquired dispositions, so that certain acts which were originally voluntary may appear from the first in later descendants as impulsive or reflex movements.

11. The exact observation of volitional processes is, for the reasons given above, impossible in the case of volitional acts which come naturally in the course of life; the only way in which a thorough psychological investigation can be made, is, therefore, through *experimental* observation. To be sure, we can not produce volitional processes of every kind whenever we wish to do so, we must limit ourselves therefore to the ob-

¹ *Outlines of Psychology*, p. 191.

servation of such processes as can be easily influenced through external means, namely such as begin with external stimulations and terminate in external acts. The experiments which serve this purpose are called reaction experiments. They may be described in their essentials as follows. A volitional process of simple or complex character is incited by an external sense-stimulus and then after the occurrence of certain psychical processes which serve in part as motives, the volition is brought to an end by a motor reaction. Reaction experiments have a second and more general significance in addition to their significance as means for the analysis of volitional processes. They furnish means for the measurement of the *rate* of certain psychical and psycho-physical processes.

The simplest reaction experiment that can be tried is as follows. At the end of a short but always uniform interval (2—3 sec.) after a signal which serves to concentrate the attention has been given, an external stimulus is allowed to act on some sense-organ. At the moment when the stimulus is perceived, a movement which has been determined upon and prepared before, as, for example, a movement of the hand is executed. The psychological conditions in this experiment correspond essentially to those of a *simple* volition. The sense impression serves as a simple motive, and this is to be followed invariably by a particular act. If now we measure objectively by means of either graphic or other chronometric apparatus, the interval which elapses between the action of the stimulus and the execution of the movement, it will be possible, by frequently repeated experiments of the same kind, to become thoroughly acquainted with the subjective processes which make up the whole reaction, while at the same time the results of the objective measurement will furnish a check for the constancy or possible variations in these subjective processes. This check is especially useful in those cases where some condition in the experiment, and thereby the subjective course of the volition itself, is intentionally modified.

12. Such a modification may, indeed, be introduced even in the simple form of the experiment just described, by vary-

ing the way in which the reactor *prepares*, before the appearance of the stimulus, for the execution of the act. When the preparation is of such a character that expectation is directed toward the stimulus which is to serve as a motive, and the external act does not take place until the stimulus is clearly recognized, there results a *complete* or *sensorial form of reaction*. When, on the other hand, the preparatory expectation is so directed toward the act, that the movement follows the reception of the stimulus as rapidly as possible, there results a *shortened* form of reaction, or the so-called *muscular* reaction. In the first case the ideational factor of the expectation is a pale memory image of the familiar sense impression. When the period of preparation is more extended, this image oscillates between alternating clearness and obscurity. The effective element is a feeling of expectation which oscillates in a similar manner and is connected with sensations of strain from the sense-organ to be affected, as for example with tension of the tympanic membrane, or of the ocular muscles of accommodation and movement. At the moment when the impression arrives the preparatory feelings and sensations mentioned are followed by a comparatively weak relieving feeling of surprise. This surprise in turn gives place to a clearly subsequent arousing feeling of activity which accompanies the reaction movement and appears in conjunction with the inner tactual sensations. In the second case, on the other hand, where the reaction is of the shortened form, we may observe during the period of preparatory expectation a pale, wavering memory image of the *motor organ* which is to react (*e. g.*, the hand) together with strong sensations of strain in the same, and a fairly continuous feeling of expectation connected with these sensations. At the moment when the stimulus arrives the state of expectation gives place to a strong feeling of surprise. There connect with this surprise both the feeling of activity which accompanies the reaction and also the sensations which arise in the reaction. So rapid is this connection that the surprise and the subsequent state are not distinguished at all, or at most only very vaguely. The sensorial reaction-time is on the average

0.210—0.290 sec.; *muscular* reaction-time averages from 0.100—0.180 sec. (the shortest time is for sound, the longest for light).

13. By introducing special conditions we may make complete and shortened reactions the starting points for the study of the *development of volitions* in two different directions. *Complete* (sensorial) reactions furnish the means of passing from simple to complex volitions because we can in this case easily insert different psychical processes between the perception of the impression and the execution of the reaction. Thus we have a *voluntary act* of relatively simple character when we allow an act of direct sensory cognition and discrimination to follow the perception of the impression and then let the movement depend on this second process. In this case, not the immediate impression, but the idea which results from the act of cognition or discrimination is the motive for the act to be performed. This motive is only one of a greater or smaller number of equally possible motives which could have come up in place of it; as a result the reaction movement takes on the character of a voluntary act. In fact, we may observe clearly the feeling of *resolution* antecedent to the act and also the feelings preceding the feeling of resolution and connected with the perception of the impression. This is still more emphatically the case, and the succession of ideational and affective processes is at the same time more complicated, when we bring in still another psychical process, as for example memory processes, to serve as the motive for the execution of the movement. Finally, the voluntary process becomes one of *choice* when in such experiments the act is not merely influenced by a plurality of motives in such a way that several must follow one another before one determines the act, but when, in addition to that, *one* of a number of possible different acts is decided upon according to the motive presented. This kind of reaction takes place when preparations are made for different movements, for example one with the right hand another with the left hand, or one with each of the ten fingers, and the condition is prescribed for each movement that an impression of a particular quality shall serve as its motive, for example the impression blue for the right hand, red for the left.

14. *Shortened* (muscular) reactions, on the contrary, may be used to investigate the *retrogradation of volitional acts* as they become reflex movements. In this form of reaction the preparatory expectation is directed entirely toward the external act which is to be executed as rapidly as possible, so that voluntary inhibition or execution of the act in accordance with the special character of the impression can here not take place. In other words, a transition from simple to complex acts of will, is in this case impossible. On the other hand, it is easy by practice so to habituate one's self to the invariable connection of an impression and a particular movement, that the process of perception fades out more and more or takes place after the motor impulse, so that finally the movement becomes just like a reflex movement. This reduction of volition to a mechanical process, shows itself objectively most clearly in the shortening of the objective time to that observed for pure reflexes, and shows itself subjectively in the fact that for psychological observation there is a complete coincidence in point of time, of impression and reaction, while the characteristic feeling of resolution gradually disappears entirely.

III. INTERCONNECTION OF PSYCHICAL COMPOUNDS

§ 17. APPERCEPTIVE COMBINATIONS.

1. Associations in all their forms are regarded by us as *passive experiences*, because the feeling of activity, which is characteristic of all processes of volition and attention, never arises except as it is added to the already completed association process in a kind of apperception of the *resultant, given content*. Associations are, accordingly, processes which can arouse volitions but are not themselves directly influenced by volitions. This absence of any dependence on volition is, however, the criterion of a *passive* process.

The case is essentially different with the second kind of combinations which are formed between different psychical compounds and their elements, namely, the *apperceptive combinations*. Here the feeling of activity with its accompanying variable sensations of tension does not merely follow the combinations as an after-effect produced by them, but it precedes them so that the combinations themselves are *immediately recognized as formed with the aid of attention*. In this sense these experiences are called *active* experiences.

2. Apperceptive combinations include a large number of psychical processes which are distinguished in popular parlance under the general terms thinking, reflection, imagination, and understanding. These are all regarded as psychical processes of a type higher than sense perceptions or pure memory processes, while at the same time they are all looked upon as different from one another. Especially is this true of the so-called functions of imagination and understanding. In contrast with this loose view of the faculty theory, association psychology sought to find a unitary principle by subsuming also the apperceptive combinations of ideas under the general concept of association, and at the same time limiting the concept, as noted above,[1] to successive association. This reduction to successive association was effected either by neglecting the essential subjective and objective distinguishing marks of apperceptive combinations, or by attempting to avoid the difficulties of an explanation, through the introduction of certain supplementary concepts taken from popular psychology. Thus, "interest" and "intelligence" were credited with an influence on associations. Very often this view was based on the erroneous notion that the recognition of certain distinguishing features in apperceptive combinations and associations meant the assertion of a fundamental division between the former and the latter. Of course, this is not true. All psychical processes are connected with associations as much as with the original sense perceptions. Yet, just as associations always form a part of every sense perception and in spite of that appear in memory processes as relatively independent processes, so apperceptive combinations are based always on associations, but the essen-

---

[1] *Outlines of Psychology*, p. 251.

tial attributes of these apperceptive combinations are not traceable to associations.

3. In trying to account for the essential attributes of apperceptive combinations, we may divide the psychical processes which belong to this class into *simple* and *complex apperceptive functions*. The simple functions are those of *relating* and *comparing*, the complex those of *synthesis* and *analysis*.

A. Simple Apperceptive Functions (Relating and Comparing).

4. The most elementary apperceptive function is that of *relating two psychical contents to each other*. The grounds for such relating are always given in the single psychical compounds and their associations, but the actual *carrying out* of the process itself is a special apperceptive activity through which the *relation itself* becomes a special conscious content, distinct from the contents which are related, though indeed inseparably connected with them. For example, when we recognize the identity of an object with one perceived before, or when we are conscious of a definite relation between a remembered event and a present impression, there is in both cases a relating apperceptive activity connected with the associations.

So long as the recognition remains a pure association, the process of relating is limited to the feeling of familiarity which follows the assimilation of the new impression either immediately, or after a short interval. When, on the contrary, apperception is added to association, this feeling is supplied with a clearly recognized ideational substratum. The earlier perception and the new impression are separated in time and then brought into a relation of agreement on the basis of their essential attributes. The case is similar when we become conscious of the motives of a memory act. This also presupposes that a comparison of the memory image with the impression which occasioned it, is added to the merely associative process which gave rise to the image. This, it will be seen, is a process that can be brought about only through attention.

5. Thus, the *relating* function is brought into activity through associations, wherever these associations themselves or their

products are made the objects of voluntary observation. The relating function is connected, as the examples mentioned show, with the function of *comparing*, whenever the related contents of consciousness are clearly separated processes, belonging to one and the same class of psychical experiences. Relating activity is, therefore, the wider concept, comparison is the narrower. A comparison is possible only when the compared contents are brought into relation with one another.˙ On the other hand, conscious contents may be related without being compared with one another, as is the case, for example, when an attribute is related to its object, or when one process is related to another which regularly follows or precedes it. As a result of this it follows that where the fuller conditions necessary for a comparison are present, the experiences given may be merely related, or they may also be compared with each other. Thus, one calls it relating when he thinks of a present impression as the reason for remembering an earlier experience; he calls it comparing, on the other hand, when he establishes certain definite points of agreement or difference between the earlier and the present impression.

6. *The process of comparing* is, in turn, made up of *two* elementary functions which are as a rule intimately interconnected. These two elementary functions are first, the *perception of agreements*, and second, the *perception of differences*. There is a mistaken view prevalent even in present-day psychology. It originated in popular psychology and was strengthened by the discussions of logical intellectualism. It consists in the acceptance of the notion that the mere existence of psychical elements and compounds is identical with ʌtheir apperceptive comparison. Every sensation is accordingly treated as a "sensory judgment," every immediate perception of distance as a "judgment of depth," and so on through the whole series of processes. In all these cases, however, the judgment appears after the sensations and ideas; the judgment must, therefore, be recognized as a separate process. To be sure, agreements and differences arise in our psychical processes, if they did not we could not observe them. But the comparing activity

through which these likenesses and differences in sensations and ideas are made evident, is not identical with the sensations and ideas themselves. It is a function which may arise in connection with these elements, but does not necessarily so arise.

7. Even the psychical elements, that is, sensations, and simple feelings, can be compared with reference to their agreements and differences. Indeed, it is through a series of such comparison that we arrange these psychical elements into systems, each one of which contains the elements which are most closely related. Within a given system two kinds of comparison are possible, namely, comparison *in respect to quality* and comparisons *in respect to intensity*. Then, too, a comparison between grades of *clearness* is possible when attention is paid to the way in which the elements appear in consciousness. In the same way comparison is applied to intensive and extensive psychical compounds. Every psychical element and every psychical compound, in so far as it is a member of a regular system, constitutes a *psychical magnitude*. A determination of the value of such a psychical magnitude is possible only through *comparison* with some other magnitude in the same system. Psychical magnitude is, accordingly, an original attribute of every psychical element and compound. It is of various kinds, as intensity, quality, extensive (spatial and temporal) value, and when the different states of consciousness are considered, clearness. But the *determination of psychical value* can be effected only through the apperceptive function of comparison.

8. *Psychical* measurement differs from *physical* measurement in the fact that the latter may be carried out in acts of comparison separated almost indefinitely in time, because its objects are relatively constant. For example, we can determine the height of a certain mountain to-day with a barometer and then after a long time we may determine the height of another mountain, and if no sensible changes in the configuration of the land have taken place in the interval, we can compare the results of our two measurements. Psychical compounds, on the other hand, are not relatively permanent objects, but continually changing processes, so that we can compare two such

psychical magnitudes only when other conditions remain the same, and when the two factors to be compared follow each other in immediate succession. These requirements have as their immediate corollaries: first, that there is no absolute standard for the comparison of psychical magnitudes, but every such comparison stands by itself and is of merely *relative* validity; second, that finer comparisons are possible only between psychical magnitudes of the same dimension, so that a reduction, analogous to that by which the most widely separated physical quantities, such as periods of time and physical forces, are all expressed in terms of one dimension of space, is out of the question in psychical comparisons.

9. It follows that the possible relations between psychical magnitudes which can be established by direct comparison are limited in number. The establishment of such relations is possible only in certain *particularly favorable cases*. These favorable cases are (1) *the equality between two psychical magnitudes* and (2) *the just noticeable difference between two such magnitudes*, as for example two sensation intensities of like quality, or two qualities of like intensity belonging to the same dimension. As a somewhat more complex case which still lies within the limits of immediate comparison we have (3) *the equality of two differences between magnitudes*, especially when these magnitudes belong to neighboring parts of the same system. It is clear that in each of these three kinds of psychical measurements the two fundamental functions in apperceptive comparison, namely the perception of agreements and the perception of differences, are both applied together. In the first case, one of two psychical magnitudes, A and B, is gradually varied until it agrees for immediate comparison with the other; thus, for example, B is varied until it agrees with A. In the second case A and B are taken equal at first and then B is changed until it appears either just noticeably greater or just noticeably smaller than A. Finally, the *third* case is used to the greatest advantage when a whole line of psychical magnitudes, as for example of sensation intensities, extending from A as a lower limit to C as an upper limit, is so divided by a middle

quantity B, which has been found by gradual variations, and is so placed that the partial distance $4B$ is apperceived as equal to BC.

10. The most direct and most easily utilizable results derived from these methods of comparison are given by the *second* method, or the *method of minimal differences* as it is called. The difference between the physical stimuli which corresponds to the just noticeable difference between psychical magnitudes is called the *difference threshold of the stimulus*. The intensity at which the resulting psychical process, as for example a sensation, can be just apperceived, is called the *stimulus threshold*. Observation shows that the difference threshold of the stimulus increases in proportion to the distance from the stimulus threshold, in such a way that the *relation* between the difference threshold and the absolute quantity of the stimulus or the *relative difference threshold, remains constant*. If, for example, a certain sound the intensity of which is 1 must be increased 1–3 in order that the sensation may be just noticeably greater, a sound whose intensity is 2 must be increased 2–3, one with an intensity 3 must be increased 3–3, etc., to reach the difference threshold. This law is called *Weber's law*, after its discoverer E. H. WEBER. It is easily understood when we look upon it as a law of apperceptive comparison. From this point of view it must obviously be interpreted to mean that *psychical magnitudes can be compared only according to their relative values*.

This view that WEBER'S law is an expression of the *general law of the relativity of psychical magnitudes*, assumes that the psychical magnitudes which are compared, themselves increase within the limits of the validity of the law in direct proportion to their stimuli. It has not yet been possible to demonstrate the truth of this assumption on its physiological side, on account of the difficulties of measuring exactly the stimulation of nerves and sense-organs. Still, we have evidence in favor of it in the psychological fact that in certain special cases, where the conditions of observation lead very naturally to a comparison of absolute differences in magnitude, the absolute difference threshold, instead of the relative threshold, is found to be constant. We have such a case, for example, in the comparison, within wide limits, of minimal differences in pitch. Then, too, where large differences in sensations are compared according to the third method described above (p. 716), it is found in general that equal absolute stimulus differences, not relative differences, are perceived as equal. This shows that apperceptive comparison follows *two* different principles under different conditions, a principle of *relative* comparison (WEBER'S law) which is the more general, and a principle of *absolute* comparison which takes the place of the first principle under special conditions which favor such a form of apperception.

11. As special cases among the apperceptive comparisons generally falling under WEBER'S law, are the comparisons of magnitudes which are related to each other as *relatively greatest sensation differences* or, when dealing with feelings, as *opposites.* The phenomena which appear in such cases are usually grouped together under the class name *contrasts.* In the department where contrasts have been most thoroughly investigated, that is, in the case of *light sensations*, there is generally an utter lack of discrimination between two phenomena which are obviously entirely different in origin, though their results are to a certain extent related. We may distinguish these as light induction or *physiological* contrast, and true contrast or *psychological* contrast. Physiological contrasts are closely connected with the phenomena of after-images, perhaps they are the same. *Psychological* contrasts are essentially different; they are usually pushed into the background by the stronger physiological contrasts when the impressions are intense. Psychological contrasts are distinguished from physiological by two important characteristics. First, psychical contrasts do not reach their greatest intensity when the brightness and saturation are greatest, but when the sensations are at the *medium* stages, where the eye is most sensitive to changes in brightness and saturation. Second, under favorable conditions psychical contrasts can be removed by comparison with an independent object. Especially the latter characteristic shows these contrasts to be unqualifiedly the products of comparisons. Thus

for example, when a gray square is laid on a black ground and close by a similar gray square is laid on a white ground and all are covered with transparent paper, the two squares appear entirely different; the one on the black ground looks bright, nearly white, while the square on the white ground looks dark, nearly black. Now after-images and irradiations are very weak when the colors are thus seen through translucent media, so that it may be assumed that the phenomenon described is a psychical contrast. If, again, a strip of black cardboard which is also covered with the transparent paper, and is therefore exactly the same gray as the two squares, is held in such a position that it connects the two squares, the contrast will be entirely removed, or, at least, very much diminished. If in this experiment a colored ground is used instead of the achromatic ground, the gray squares will appear very clearly in the corresponding complementary color. But here, too, the contrast can be made to disappear through comparison with an independent gray object.

12. Similar contrasts appear also in other spheres of sensation when the conditions for their demonstration are favorable. They are also especially marked in the case of feelings and may arise under proper conditions in the case of spatial and temporal ideas. Sensations of pitch are relatively most free from contrast, for most persons have a well developed ability to recognize absolute pitch and this probably tends to overcome contrast. In the case of *feelings* the effect of contrast is intimately connected with the natural opposition between effective qualities. Thus, pleasurable feelings are intensified by unpleasant feelings immediately preceding, and the same holds for many feelings of relaxation following feelings of strain, as for example in the case of a feeling of fulfilment after expectation. The effect of contrast in the case of spatial and temporal ideas is most obvious when the same spatial or temporal interval is compared alternately with a longer and with a shorter interval. In such cases the interval appears different; in comparison with the shorter it appears greater, in comparison with the longer, smaller. Here, too, the contrast between spatial ideas can be

removed by bringing an object between the contrasted figures in such a way that it is possible easily to relate them.

13. We may regard the phenomena which result from the apperception of an impression the *real* character of which differs from the character *expected*, as special modifications of psychical contrast. For example, if we are prepared to lift a heavy weight, and find in the actual lifting of the weight that it proves to be light, or if we lift a heavy weight when we expected a light one, the result is in the first case an underestimation, in the second an overestimation of the real weight. If a series of exactly equal weights of different sizes are made to vary in size so that they look like a set of weights varying regularly from a lighter to a heavier they will appear to be different in weight when raised. The smallest will seem to be the heaviest and the largest to be the lightest. The familiar association that the greater volume is connected with the greater mass determines in this case the tendency of expectation. The false estimation of the weight then results from the contrast between the real and the expected sensation.

B. Complex Apperceptive Functions. (Synthesis and Analysis).

14. When the simple processes of relating and comparing are repeated and combined several times, the complex psychical functions of *synthesis* and *analysis* arise. *Synthesis* is primarily the product of the *relating* activity of apperception, *analysis* of the *comparing* activity.

As a combining function *apperceptive synthesis* is based upon fusions and associations. It differs from fusions and associations in the fact that some of the ideational and affective elements which are brought forward by the association are voluntarily emphasized and others are pushed into the background. The motives for the choice between the elements can be explained only from the whole previous development of the individual consciousness. As a result of this voluntary activity the product of this synthesis is a complex in which all the components are derived from former sense perceptions and associations, but in which the combination of these components may differ more or less from the original forms.

The ideational elements of a compound thus resulting from apperceptive synthesis may be regarded as the substratum for the rest of its contents, and so we call such a compound in general an *aggregate idea*. When the combination of the elements is peculiar, that is, markedly different from the products of associations, the aggregate idea and each of its relatively independent ideational components is called an *idea of imagination* or *image of imagination*. Since the voluntary synthesis may vary more or less from the combinations presented in sense perception and association, it follows that practically no sharp line of demarcation can be drawn between images of imagination and those of memory. But we have a more essential mark of the apperceptive process in the positive characteristic which appears in the fact that it depends on a voluntary synthesis, than we have in the negative fact that the combination does not correspond in character to any particular sense perception. This positive characteristic is also the source of a most striking difference between images of imagination and those of memory. The difference in question consists in the fact that the sensation elements of an apperceptive compound are much more like those of an immediate sense perception in clearness and distinctness, and usually also in completeness and intensity. This is easily explained by the fact that the reciprocally inhibitory influences which the uncontrolled associations exercise on one another, and which prevent the formation of fixed memory images, are diminished or removed by the voluntary emphasizing of certain particular ideational compounds. It is possible to mistake images of imagination for real experiences. In the case of memory images this is possible only when they become images of imagination, that is, when the memories are no longer allowed to arise passively, but are to some extent produced by the will. Generally, there are such voluntary modifications of memories through a mixing of real with imagined elements. All our memories are therefore made up of "fancy and truth."[1] Memory images thus change under the influence of our feelings and volition to images of imagination, and we generally deceive ourselves with their resemblance to real experiences.

[1] *Dic'tung und Wahrheit.*

15. From the aggregate ideas which thus result from apperceptive synthesis there arise *two forms of apperceptive analysis* which work themselves out in opposite directions. The one is known in popular parlance as activity of the *imagination*, the second as activity of the *understanding*. The two are by no means absolutely different, as might be surmised from these names, but are, rather, closely related and always connected with each other. Their fundamental determining motives are what distinguish them and condition all their secondary differences and also the reaction which they exercise on the synthetic function.

In the case of the activity of *"imagination"* the motive is the *reproduction of real complexes of experience or of experiences analogous to reality*. This is the earlier form of apperceptive analysis and arises directly from association. It begins with a more or less comprehensive aggregate idea made up of a variety of ideational and affective elements and embracing the general content of a complex experience in which the single components are only indefinitely distinguished. The aggregate idea is then divided in a series of successive acts into a number of more definite, connected compounds, partly spatial, partly temporal in character. The primary voluntary synthesis is thus followed by analytic acts which may in turn give rise to the motives for a new synthesis and thus to a repetition of the whole process with a partially modified, or more limited aggregate idea.

The activity of imagination shows *two* stages of development. The first is more *passive* and arises directly from the ordinary memory function. It appears continually in the train of thought especially in the form of an anticipation of the future, and plays an important part in psychical development as a preparation or antecedent of volitions. It may, however, in an analogous way, appear as a representation in thought of imaginary situations or of successions of external phenomena. The second, or *active*, form of imagination is under the influence of a fixed idea of some end, and therefore presupposes a high degree of voluntary control over the images of imagination, and a strong interference, partly inhibitory, partly selective, with the memory images that tend to push themselves into consciousness without voluntary action. Even the first synthesis of the aggregate idea is more systematic when produced by this active process. And an aggregate idea, when once formed in this way, is held more firmly and subjected to a more complete analysis than in passive imagination. Very often the components themselves are subordinate aggregate ideas to which the same process of analysis is again applied. In this way the principle of organic division according to the end in view governs all the products and processes of active imagination. The productions of *art* show this most clearly. Still, there are, in the ordinary play of imagination, the most various intermediate stages between passive imagination, or that which arises directly from memory, and active imagination, or that which is directed by fixed ends.

16. In contrast with this imagination or imaginative reproduction of real experiences, or of experiences which may be thought of as real, the function of the *"understanding"* is the *perception of agreements and differences and other derived logical relations between contents of experience.* Understanding also begins with aggregate ideas in which a number of experiences which are real or may be ideated as real, are voluntarily set in relation to one another and combined into a unitary whole. The analysis which takes place in this case, however, is turned by its fundamental motive in a different direction. Such analysis consists not merely in a clearer grasp of the single components of the aggregate idea, but it consists also in the establishment of the manifold relations which exist between the various components and which we may discover through comparison. In establishing such relations it is possible, as soon as analyses have been made several times, to introduce into any particular case the results gained through relating and comparing processes which were carried out on other occasions.

As a consequence of this stricter application of the elementary relating, and comparing functions, the activity of understanding follows definite rules even in its external form, especi-

ally when it is highly developed. The fact which showed itself
in the case of imagination and even of memory, appears here in
a developed form. The fact in question is that the apperceived
relations between the various psychical contents are presented
in imagination and memory, not merely simultaneously, but
successively, so that we proceed from one relation to the next,
and so on. In the case of understanding, this successive presentation of relations develops into the *discursive division of the
aggregate idea*. This is expiessed in the law of the *duality of the
logical forms of thought*, according to which, analysis resulting
from relating comparison divides the content of the aggregate idea into *two* parts, subject and predicate, and may then
separate each of these parts again once or several times. These
secondary divisions give rise to grammatical forms which stand
in a logical relation analogous to that of subject and predicate,
such as noun and attributive, verb and object, verb and ad-
verb. In this way the process of apperceptive analysis results
in a *judgment* which finds expression in the *sentence*.

For the psychological explanation of judgment it is of fundamental importance that judgment be regarded, not as a synthetic, but as an *analytic* function. The original aggregate ideas
which are divided by judgment into their reciprocally related
components, are exactly like ideas of imagination. The products of analysis which result from judgment are, on the other
hand, not as in the case of imagination, images of more limited
extent and greater clearness, but *conceptual ideas*, that is, ideas
which stand, with regard to other partial ideas of the same
whole, in some one of the relations which are discovered through
the general relating and comparing functions. If we call the
aggregate idea which is subjected to such a relating analysis
a *thought*, then a *judgment* is a division of this thought into its
components, and a *concept* is the product of such a division.

17. Concepts found in this way are arranged in certain
general classes according to the character of the analyses
which produced them. These classes are the *concepts of objects*,
concepts of attributes, and *concepts of states*. Judgment as a
division of the aggregate idea, sets an object in relation to its

attributes or states, or it sets various objects in relation to one another. Since a single concept can never, strictly speaking, be thought of by itself, but is always connected in the whole idea with one or more other concepts, the conceptual ideas are strikingly different from the ideas of imagination because of the indefiniteness and variableness of the former. This indefiniteness is essentially increased by the fact that as a result of the like outcome of different kinds of judgment, concepts arise which may form components of many ideas which differ in their concrete characters. A concept of this kind can therefore be used in a great variety of different applications. Such *general* concepts constitute, on account of the wide application of relating analysis to different contents of judgment, the great majority of all concepts; and they have a greater or smaller number of corresponding single ideational contents. A *single* idea is selected from this group of contents as a representative of the concept. This gives the conceptual idea of a greater definiteness. At the same time there is always connected with this idea the consciousness that it is merely a representative. This consciousness generally takes the form of a characteristic feeling, the *conceptual feeling*. This feeling may be traced to the fact that obscure ideas, which have the attributes which make them suitable to serve as representations of the concept, tend to force themselves into consciousness in the form of memory images. As evidence of this we have the fact that the feeling is very intense when any concrete image of the concept is chosen as its representative, as for example when a particular individual stands for the concept man, while it disappears almost entirely as soon as the representative idea differs entirely in content from the objects included under the concept. *Word ideas* fulfill this latter condition and that is what gives them their importance as universal aids to thought. Word ideas are furnished to the individual consciousness in a finished state, so that we must leave to social psychology the question of the psychological development of the processes of thought which are active in their formation.

18. From all that has been said it appears that the activities of imagination and understanding are not specifically different, but interrelated; that they are inseparable in their rise and manifestations, and are based at bottom on the same fundamental functions of apperceptive synthesis and analysis. What was true of the concept "*memory*"[1] holds also of the concepts "*understanding*" and "*imagination*"; they are names, not of unitary forces or faculties, but of complex phenomena made up of the usual elementary psychical processes; they are not made up of elementary processes of a specific, distinct kind. Just as memory is a general concept for certain associative processes, so imagination and understanding are general concepts for particular forms of apperceptive activity. They have a certain practical value as ready means for the classification of a variety of differences in the capacity of various persons for intellectual activity. Each class thus found may in turn contain an endless variety of gradations and shades. Thus, neglecting the general differences in grade, we have as the chief forms of individual imagination the *perceptive* and *combining* forms; as the chief forms of understanding, the *inductive* and *deductive* forms, the first being mainly concerned with the single logical relations and their combinations, the second more with general concepts and their analysis. A person's *talent* is his total capacity resulting from the special tendencies of both his imagination and understanding.

[1] *Outlines of Psychology*, p. 277.

INDEX

INDEX

Printed in the United States
22375LVS00001B/3